ON INFORMATION TECHNOLOGY

Video education courses are available on these topics through
National Education Training Group, 1751 West Diehl Road,
Naperville, IL 60563-9099 (tel: 800-526-0452 or 708-369-3000).

Database	Telecommunications	Networks and Data Communications	Society
AN END USER'S GUIDE TO DATABASE	TELECOMMUNICATIONS AND THE COMPUTER (third edition)	PRINCIPLES OF DATA COMMUNICATION	THE COMPUTERIZED SOCIETY
PRINCIPLES OF DATABASE MANAGEMENT (second edition)	COMMUNICATIONS SATELLITE SYSTEMS	TELEPROCESSING NETWORK ORGANIZATION	TELEMATIC SOCIETY: A CHALLENGE FOR TOMORROW
COMPUTER DATABASE ORGANIZATION (third edition)	**Distributed Processing**	SYSTEMS ANALYSIS FOR DATA TRANSMISSION	TECHNOLOGY'S CRUCIBLE
MANAGING THE DATABASE ENVIRONMENT (second edition)	COMPUTER NETWORKS AND DISTRIBUTED PROCESSING	DATA COMMUNICATION TECHNOLOGY	VIEWDATA AND THE INFORMATION SOCIETY
DATABASE ANALYSIS AND DESIGN	DESIGN AND STRATEGY FOR DISTRIBUTED DATA PROCESSING	DATA COMMUNICATION DESIGN TECHNIQUES	**SAA**: Systems Application Architecture
VSAM: ACCESS METHOD SERVICES AND ROGRAMMING TECHNIQUES	**Client/Server**	SNA: IBM's NETWORKING SOLUTION	SAA: COMMON USER ACCESS
DB2: CONCEPTS, DESIGN, AND PROGRAMMING	CLIENT/SERVER DATABASES: ENTERPRISE COMPUTING	LOCAL AREA NETWORKS: ARCHITECTURES AND IMPLEMENTATIONS (second edition)	SAA: COMMON COMMUNICATIONS SUPPORT: DISTRIBUTED APPLICATIONS
DMS/R: CONCEPTS, DESIGN, AND PROGRAMMING	ENTERPRISE NETWORKING: STRATEGIES AND TRANSPORT PROTOCOLS	DATA COMMUNICATION STANDARDS	SAA: COMMON COMMUNICATIONS SUPPORT: NETWORK INFRASTRUCTURE
Security	ENTERPRISE NETWORKING: DATA LINK SUBNETWORKS	COMPUTER NETWORKS AND DISTRIBUTED PROCESSING: SOFTWARE, TECHNIQUES, AND ARCHITECTURE	SAA: COMMON PROGRAMMING INTERFACE
SECURITY, ACCURACY, AND PRIVACY IN COMPUTER SYSTEMS		TCP/IP NETWORKING: ARCHITECTURE, ADMINISTRATION, AND PROGRAMMING	

LOCAL AREA NETWORKS

A *James Martin* **BOOK**

LOCAL AREA NETWORKS
Architectures and Implementations
Second Edition

JAMES MARTIN

with

Kathleen Kavanagh Chapman / Joe Leben

PRENTICE HALL P T R
Englewood Cliffs, New Jersey 07632

Library of Congress Cataloging-in-Publication Data

Martin, James (date)
   Local area networks : architectures and implementations / James
Martin, Kathleen Kavanagh Chapman, Joe Leben. — 2nd ed.
     p. cm. — (The James Martin books)
   Includes index.
   ISBN 0-13-533035-1
   1. Local area networks (Computer networks) I. Chapman, Kathleen
Kavanagh. II. Leben, Joe. III. Title. IV. Series: James Martin
book.
TK5105.7.M37 1994
004.6'8—dc20
                              93-37562
                                CIP

Editorial/production supervision: *Kathryn Gollin Marshak*
Liaison: *Colette Conboy*
Jacket design: *Wanda Lubelska*
Jacket photo: *Masterfile*
Manufacturing buyer: *Alexis Heydt*

Copyright © 1994 by James Martin

Published by Prentice Hall P T R
Prentice-Hall, Inc.
A Simon & Schuster Company
Englewood Cliffs, New Jersey 07632

The publisher offers discounts on this book when ordered
in bulk quantities. For more information, write:

        Corporate Sales Department, Prentice Hall P T R
        113 Sylvan Avenue
        Englewood CLiffs, NJ 07632
        Phone: 201-592-2863; Fax: 201-592-2249

Printed in the United States of America

10 9 8 7 6

ISBN 0-13-533035-1

Prentice-Hall International (UK) Limited, *London*
Prentice-Hall of Australia Pty. Limited, *Sydney*
Prentice-Hall Canada Inc., *Toronto*
Prentice-Hall Hispanoamericana, S.A., *Mexico*
Prentice-Hall of India Private Limited, *New Delhi*
Prentice-Hall of Japan, Inc., *Tokyo*
Simon & Schuster Asia Pte. Ltd., *Singapore*
Editora Prentice-Hall do Brasil, Ltda., *Rio de Janeiro*

TO CORINTHIA
—*JM*

TO JOHN AND MY PARENTS
—*KKC*

TO MY MOTHER
—*JL*

Contents

C   Asynchronous Transfer Mode   *523*

D   Network Management   *531*

Glossary   *545*

Index   *573*

Preface

Until early in the 1980s the mainframe was the centerpiece of computing. Terminals and various types of distributed processors were regarded as minor adjuncts to large corporate computer systems. By the end of the 1980s a radical change in perception had occurred. Individual knowledge workers began to have powerful personal computers and workstations on their desks, each with a large personal database. To them, these computers became the centerpiece of their computing world. They needed many servers to support their computing activities—central databases, departmental databases, printers, perhaps plotters or slide makers, electronic mail facilities, access to large machines for numeric-intensive computing, perhaps access to a supercomputer. The connection to these facilities needed high-bandwidth communication channels. The local area network has changed the desktop computing system from an isolated machine into a rich environment with a wealth of information and resources that the knowledge worker can access.

The need to communicate—to send messages, to share data, to access computing resources, to share expensive peripheral devices—has contributed to the development and spread of local area networks. A local area network (LAN) is a computer network that connects users in a moderately sized geographic area. Typically, a local area network connects users located in the same office, on the same floor, or in the same building. The challenge for local area networks has been to provide facilities that meet the communication needs of users at reasonable cost. Compatibility is a key issue in keeping costs reasonable. Local area networks must be able to connect a wide variety of hardware and software products in a single network, without having to build complex and costly interfaces for different products. To facilitate this compatibility, various national and international standards organizations and hardware and software vendors have cooperated to develop architectures for computer networking that allow a variety of equipment to be interconnected and to interoperate.

Since the first edition of this book was initially published, the use of local area network technology has changed dramatically. The typical local area network is no longer a small group of personal computers, wired together, that allows users to share a printer or swap files. Today, local area networks—interconnected by bridges, routers, and other devices—span entire enterprises and allow hundreds and even thousands of users to communicate and work cooperatively. Local area networks provide high-speed data transmission pipelines that support the transfer of large amounts of data, graphic images, and video signals throughout the enterprise. Local area networks are beginning to support powerful client-server applications that distribute low-cost processing power across networks. All of these new uses for data transmission facilities create challenges for those who must design, select, install, support, and use local area networks and the applications that run on them.

In order to meet the challenges created by ubiquitous high-speed networking, information systems and communications professionals must understand the technologies that underlie today's data networks. This book explains local area network technologies and describes the evolving standards that have shaped them. It also examines network interconnection technologies that allow organizations to construct complex internetworks that can span the entire enterprise and to connect the organization's information infrastructure with the information systems of other organizations to form a global internet. Finally, the book explores the capabilities, protocols, and interfaces of key networking software systems that are used to implement and exploit local area networking and wide area networking technology.

INTENDED READERS

This book is intended for a broad range of readers, including the following:

- Information systems and communications managers and technical staff members who maintain and administer local area networks and who need a thorough understanding of networking technology.

- Information systems and communcations technical staff members who select, install, and support local area network hardware and software products and who deal with the complexities of multivendor internetworking.

- Users of local area networks who desire an understanding of the technology behind the computer communication tools that are used in their work environment.

- Students who are studying computer communications technologies.

PLAN OF THE BOOK

The book's prolog consists of a single chapter that introduces local area network technology. Chapter 1 describes various purposes for LAN technology and introduces a typical LAN's component parts.

Part I explores some of the fundamental concepts and terminology associated with the various forms of LAN technology. Intelligent devices communicate in a local area network by exchanging signals over a physical medium. The data transmission techniques used in LANs are the topic of Chapter 2. Various LAN technologies use networks of communication links that have different shapes, or topologies, and the devices attached to a LAN use different methods for controlling access to the transmission facilities. Topologies and medium access management are the subjects of Chapter 3. Chapter 4 introduces information technology standardization, discusses architectures for computer networking, and describes the functional layers of the international standard *Reference Model for Open Systems Interconnection* (OSI model) on which standards for local area network data links are based. End users who employ local area networks to do useful work are more interested in what the LAN can do for them than in the underlying technologies that are used to construct the network. Chapter 5 introduces the general functions of the networking software that end users employ for accessing the facilities of computer networks.

The chapters in Part II describe the IEEE/ISO Logical Link Control standard. The LLC standard defines a common interface to the services that a local area network data link provides to a user of the LAN data link. Chapter 6 introduces OSI concepts and describes the overall architecture behind IEEE, ISO, and ANSI standards for local area networks. International standards for computer networking document both service definitions and protocol specifications. Chapter 7 describes the LLC service definition and describes the services that a LAN data link user can request; Chapter 8 examines the LLC protocol specification and describes the procedures a LAN data link follows to provide its services. Chapter 9 describes how some actual software subsystems have implemented the Logical Link Control standard to provide LAN data link services.

Part III describes the different methods for medium access control that have been standardized for LAN data link technology. Chapter 10 describes the carrier sense multiple access with collision detection (CSMA/CD), or Ethernet, form of medium access control that uses contention techniques to implement a bus- or tree-structured LAN. Chapter 11 describes the *Ethernet Version 2 Specification*, jointly developed by Digital Equipment Corporation, Intel, and Xerox, on which the CSMA/CD standard is based. Chapter 12 describes the token-bus form of medium access control that uses a token-passing technique to implement a bus- or tree-structured LAN. Chapter 13 discusses the token-ring form of medium access control that uses a token-passing technique to implement a bus- or tree-structured LAN. Chapter 14 examines the Fiber Distributed Data Interface (FDDI) form of medium access control that uses a timed token-passing technique to implement a ring-structured LAN. Chapter 15 describes the Apple LocalTalk form of LAN data link that uses carrier sense multiple access with collision avoidance (CSMA/CA) to implement a bus- or tree-structured LAN.

LAN data links can be used in conjunction with network interconnection devices and wide area network (WAN) data links to form internets. Issues surrounding the construction of enterprise internetworks are the subject of Part IV. Chapter 16 introduces the internetworking environment and describes the functions of the different types of network interconnection devices that can be used to combine data links to form internets. An internet can carry the data traffic generated by end systems that implement different communication protocols. Chapter 17 introduces the most commonly used Network layer and Transport layer protocols employed in computer networks. The construction of heterogeneous internets is discussed in Chapter 18. Chapter 19 examines the operation of bridges in an extended LAN and discusses the differences between transparent bridges and source routing bridges. Chapter 20 describes the operation of routers in an internet.

A wide variety of networking software can be used in various computing environments for making use of LAN data links in computer networks. Part V describes four widely-used, representative approaches to network software. Chapter 21 examines the protocols and mechanisms that IBM and Microsoft have implemented in networking software for the personal computer environment. Chapter 22 introduces the Novell NetWare family of networking software that is also used in the personal computer networking environment. Chapter 23 describes the TCP/IP approach to computer networking that is used in a wide variety of computing environments. Chapter 24 describes AppleTalk, Apple's approach to computer networking.

The book concludes with four appendices that describe topics related to local area network technology.

ACKNOWLEDGMENTS

The authors would like to thank the many representatives of the companies whose local area network products we describe in this book for providing us with information about their products.

James Martin
Kathleen Kavanagh Chapman
Joe Leben

List of Acronyms

AARP. AppleTalk Address Resolution Protocol.

AEP. AppleTalk Echo Protocol.

ANSI. American National Standards Institute.

API. Application Programming Interface.

APPN. Advanced Peer-to-Peer Networking.

ARP. Address Resolution Protocol.

ASC. Accredited Standards Committee.

ASN.1. Abstract Syntax Notation One.

ATM. Asynchronous Transfer Mode.

ATP. AppleTalk Transaction Protocol.

BGP. Border Gateway Protocol.

B-ISDN. Broadband ISDN.

CCB. Command control block.

CCITT. International Telegraph and Telephone Consultative Committee.

CDDI. Copper Distributed Data Interface.

CMIP. Common Management Information Protocol.

CMOT. CMIP over TCP/IP.

CSMA/CA. Carrier sense multiple access with collision avoidance.

CSMA/CD. Carrier sense multiple access with collision detection.

DAC. Dual-attachment concentrator.

DARPA. Defense Advanced Research Projects Agency.

DCE. Distributed Computing Environment.

DDP. Datagram Delivery Protocol.

DNA. Digital Network Architecture.

DNS. Domain Name System.

DQDB. Distributed Queue Dual Bus.

DRP. Digital Routing Protocol.

EGP. Exterior Gateway Protocol.

ELAP. EtherTalk Link Access Protocol.

FCS. Frame check sequence.

FDDI. Fiber Distributed Data Interface.

FOIRL. Fiber-Optic Inter-Repeater Link.

FTP. File Transfer Protocol.

HDLC. High-level Data Link Control.

ICMP. Internet Control Message Protocol.

IDP. Internetwork Datagram Protocol.

IEEE. Institute of Electrical and Electronics Engineers.

IP. Internet Protocol.

IPX. Internet Packet Exchange protocol.

ISDN. Integrated Services Digital Network.

ISO. International Organization for Standardization.

LAN. Local area network.

LLAP. LocalTalk Link Access Protocol.

LLC. Logical Link Control.

LLC-PDU. Logical-link-control-protocol-data-unit.

LLC-SDU. Logical-link-control-service-data-unit.

MAC. Medium Access Control.

MAC-PDU. Medium-access-control-protocol-data-unit.

MAC-SDU. Medium-access-control-service-data-unit.

MAN. Metropolitan Area Network.

MAP. Manufacturing Automation Protocol.

MAPI. Mail Application Programming Interface.

MIB. Management Information Base.

MIC. Medium interface connector.

NAC. Null-attachment concentrator.

NBP. Name Binding Protocol.

NCB. Network Control Block.

NCP. NetWare Core Protocol.

NFS. Network File System.

NIC. Network interface card or, in the Worldwide Internet, the Network Information Center.

NLM. NetWare Loadable Module.

NPDU. Network-protocol-data-unit.

NSP. Network Services Protocol.

OSI. Open systems interconnection.

OSF. Open Software Foundation.

OSPF. Open Shortest Path First.

PCI. Protocol-control-information.

PCMCIA. Personal Computer Memory Card International Association.

PDU. Protocol-data-unit.

PEP. Packet Exchange Protocol (Xerox Network System).

PPP. Point-to-Point Protocol.

PTT. Postal, Telegraph, and Telephone Administration.

PXP. Packet Exchange Protocol (Novell NetWare).

RARP. Reverse Address Resolution Protocol.

RFC. Request for Comments.

RIP. Routing Information Protocol.

RPC. Remote procedure call.

RTMP. Routing Table Maintenance Protocol.

SAC. Single-attachment concentrator.

SAP. Service-access-point and Service Advertising Protocol.

SAS. Single-attachment station.

SDU. Service-data-unit.

SMB. Server Message Block.

SMDS. Switched Multimegabit Data Service.

SMTP. Simple Mail Transfer Protocol.

SNA. Systems Network Architecture.

SNAP. Subnetwork Access Protocol.

SNMP. Simple Network Management Protocol.

SPP. Sequenced Packet Protocol.

SPX. Sequenced Packet Exchange Protocol.

TCP. Transmission Control Protocol.

TCP/IP. Transmission Control Protocol/Internet Protocol.

TFTP. Trivial File Transfer Protocol.

TLAP. TokenTalk Link Access Protocol.

TLI. Transport Layer Interface.

TOP. Technical and Office Protocols.

UDP. User Datagram Protocol.

VAP. Value-Added Process.

VIM. Vendor Independent Messaging.

WAN. Wide area network.

XNS. Xerox Network System.

LOCAL AREA NETWORKS

PROLOG

Chapter 1   Local Area Networks

Local Area Networks

The design, installation, and operation of computer networks is vital to the functioning of modern computerized organizations. Over the last decade, organizations have installed complex and diverse networks, tying together mainframes, minicomputers, personal computers, workstations, terminals, and other devices. This chapter introduces the types of networks that organizations use and discusses how local area network technology forms the basis of much of today's computer networking.

NETWORKING TECHNOLOGY

Computer networking technology can be classified by the distance the networking technology is designed to span. With this form of classification, we can identify wide area networks, local area networks, and metropolitan area networks.

Wide Area Networks

Many of the networks that are in use today employ public telecommunications facilities to provide users with access to the resources of centrally-located computer complexes and to permit fast interchange of information among users. As the cost of microelectronic devices has dropped, the intelligence in the various devices attached to the network has increased. Intelligent terminals, personal computers, workstations, minicomputers, and other diverse forms of programmable devices are all part of these large networks. Networks such as these that tie together users who are widely separated geographically are called *wide area networks* (WANs).

Local Area Networks

In parallel with the growth of wide area networks, there has been another area of expansion in the use of computing facilities. Personal computers and workstations have spread rapidly and widely throughout organizations. Various types of small computers are routinely used for word processing, financial analysis, sales reporting, engineering, order processing, and many other business functions. As the use of small computers has grown, so has a need for these computer systems to communicate—with each other and with the larger, centralized data processing facilities of the organization.

Small computers may initially be used for applications that are local in nature and that can be processed in a stand-alone manner. But, typically, additional requirements soon arise, for example

- Accessing data that is stored in some other area.
- Allowing a group of computer systems to share devices that are too expensive to be used by a single person only.
- Giving users a way of communicating electronically, using the small computers that are already in place.

A type of networking technology has been developed to create *local area networks* (LANs) to provide a means for meeting the requirements for relatively short-distance communication among intelligent devices. The range of distances supported by typical local area networks range from a few feet to a few miles.

The majority of local area networks that are in use today connect personal computers and workstations to one another and to larger systems, often called *servers*. However, as we will see, LAN technology is used for a number of other purposes as well.

It is interesting to note that the development of local area networking technology actually predated the personal computer revolution that has had such a large impact on business in recent years. The development of Ethernet technology, the most widely used form of LAN technology, actually began in the early 1970s, before today's personal computers were developed.

Metropolitan Area Networks

In some cases, it is desirable to identify a form of networking that falls between wide area networking and local area networking. A form of networking technology that is related to LAN technology has been identified for building *metropolitan area networks* (MANs). Metropolitan area networks operate in a similar manner to LANs but over longer distances, up to about 20 or 30 miles. Metropolitan area networks can be used to bridge the gap between wide area networks and local area networks.

LOCAL AREA NETWORK DEFINITIONS

Many definitions for the term *local area network* have been proposed. Instead of inventing a new one, we will examine the definition that has been published by the Institute of Electrical and Electronics Engineers (IEEE). The IEEE is an organization in the United

States that has developed an important set of standards for local area networks, which we describe in the chapters in Parts II and III. The IEEE definition states that a local area network is

> . . . a datacomm system allowing a number of independent devices to communicate directly with each other, within a moderately sized geographic area over a physical communications channel of moderate data rates.

Let us look at each element in this definition and examine its significance.

First, a local area network *allows a number of independent devices to communicate directly with each other*. The important point in the first part of the IEEE definition is that a LAN typically supports *many-to-many communication*, where any device attached to the LAN is able to communicate directly with any other device on the LAN. This is in contrast with *hierarchical* or *centrally-controlled* communication, where one communicating entity is assumed to be more intelligent than the others and has the primary responsibility for controlling communication.

Second, the communication *takes place within a moderately sized geographic area*. As we have already introduced, this is an important distinction between wide area networks and local area networks. Local area networks are typically confined to a single building or to a group of buildings that are relatively close together. A local area network does not ordinarily span a distance greater than a few miles. However, we will see later in this book that a number of network interconnection technologies are available that allow individual LANs that are widely separated geographically to be interconnected to form an integrated network.

Third, communication *takes place over a physical communications channel*. In a local area network, devices are typically hooked together directly via private, dedicated cables or other physical communications media. This is in contrast to wide area networks that often use public, switched telecommunications facilities or packet-switching technologies for communication.

Last, the communication channel of a local area network *supports a moderate data rate*. This distinguishes most local area networks from the very high-speed connections used within the computer room to connect peripheral devices to processors, and also from the slower speeds typically supported by the public telecommunications facilities often used to construct wide area networks. Direct computer room connections typically operate at speeds of 20 million bits per second (Mbps) and greater. Many wide area networks use dial-up or leased telephone lines, where maximum data rates are in the area of 9600, 19,200 bps, or 56,000 bps. The moderate data rates supported by typical local area networks typically fall in the 1 Mbps to 16 Mbps range.

The term "moderate data rate" in the IEEE LAN definition is beginning to have less relevance today than when the definition was first formulated. Today, technology is coming into use for local area networks that support very high bit rates—such as 100 Mbps and more—that are faster than traditional machine-room channels. Also, the lower bit rates that were typical in the past for public telecommunications facilities are also giving way to much higher bit rates, sometimes in the hundreds of Mbps. So the distinctions between machine-room cable connections, local area networks, and wide area network transmission facilities are beginning to blur, at least with respect to the bit rates supported.

Box 1.1 lists the requirements for a local area network as they were articulated many years ago by the developers of Ethernet. Many of the requirements still reflect the characteristics of most local area network technology that is in use today.

USES FOR HIGH TRANSMISSION SPEEDS

The high transmission speeds that local area networks make available to the networked computers make it possible to build new types of applications. We can place all the various uses of local area networks into two general categories:

- LANs can be used for transmission that *could* take place at low speeds, just as if local area network technology did not exist and telephone lines were used for data communication as they have been for many years.

BOX 1.1   Local area network requirements as originally stated by the developers of Ethernet.

(The comments in parentheses are our own and not those of the Ethernet developers.)

- Data rates of 1-to-10 megabits per second. (Today the requirements extend up to speeds of 100 megabits per second or higher.)
- Geographic distances spanning at most 1 kilometer. (Today longer distances are often spanned by a single LAN, and much longer distances are sometimes spanned using inter-LAN connections.)
- Ability to support several hundred independent devices. (Many thousands of devices are often networked using LAN technology.)
- Simplicity or use of the simplest possible mechanisms that have the required functionality and performance.
- Reliability and good error characteristics.
- Minimal dependence upon any centralized components or control.
- Efficient use of shared resources, particularly the communication network itself.
- Stability under high load.
- Fair access to the system by all devices.
- Easy installation of a small system, with graceful growth as the system evolves.
- Ease of reconfiguration and maintenance.
- Low cost.

- More interestingly, LANs can be used for applications that would not be possible without the high bandwidth provided by LANs.

Examples of the first category of applications include exchanging simple electronic mail messages and implementing conventional character-based transaction processing systems. Such applications operate in much the same manner over a LAN as they would over conventional telecommunications facilities.

Examples of the second type of applications include loading a large segment of an entire database into a desktop machine at reasonable speed, transferring a spreadsheet from one user to another while the two users are talking on the phone, sending bit-mapped graphics displays across a network while still maintaining short response times, and transferring large amounts of data back and forth between networked processors that may be cooperating to solve a single problem. Applications such as these would not be feasible without the very high transmission speeds provided by LANs.

Within the span of a decade or two, the transmission speed available to the typical computer user has increased from a maximum of 9600 bps to 10 Mbps and now to 100 Mbps or more in many cases. Nowhere else in computing have performance numbers changed so dramatically as in computer networking.

For years, telecommunications transmission speeds have represented a constraining bottleneck in the way we use computers. User interfaces have been designed with the assumption that transmission is no faster than 9600 bps and response times are several seconds. Unfortunately, much software is still being designed that fails to take advantage of the high transmission speeds that are now routinely available. Designers need to think in terms of megabits per second not kilobits per second. To adopt this way of thinking is a major paradigm shift for designers who have grown up with the speeds of voice-grade lines.

APPLICATIONS FOR LOCAL AREA NETWORKS

By far the largest number of local area networks that are installed today are used for interconnecting the desktop personal computers and workstations that are used by individuals and allowing them to access the facilities of more powerful server systems. However, local area networking data links are also used in other ways as well.

The following sections describe a few of the many ways in which LANs have been used.

Resource Sharing

Local area networks that interconnect desktop systems are commonly used for providing computer users with shared access to data. A local area network may allow a person using one computer on the network to access a file that is stored on another computer. Depending on how the local area network is implemented, it may be possible for several users to access the same file at the same time.

Local area networks also allow many network users to share the same printer. Print jobs created on a desktop computer can be sent to a networked printer. A computer controlling a printer may maintain print queues so that multiple print jobs from different desktop systems can be queued up until it is their turn to be printed.

Local area networks can also allow desktop computer users to send electronic mail messages to each other. Electronic mail software may provide editing and formatting aids, group addressing capabilities, and message notification and storage.

Specialized Device Interconnection

Local area network data links are used in a variety of ways to provide high-speed interconnection of specialized types of computing devices.

LAN data links are used to interconnect individual processors to form processor complexes. The VAX clusters that are marketed by Digital Equipment Corporation provide an example of such a use of a LAN data link. In a VAX cluster, an Ethernet LAN is used to interconnect a number of separate VAX systems to provide computing system users with the image of a single processor that has the combined power of the clustered VAX processors as shown in Fig. 1.1.

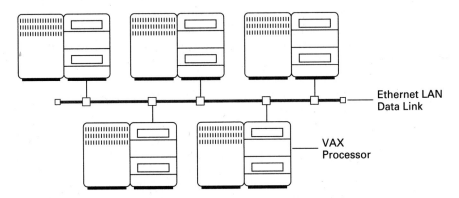

Figure 1.1   VAX cluster using Ethernet data link technology.

LAN data links are often used in the computer room to provide a simplified method of interconnecting computing devices. For example, in the IBM mainframe environment, a Token Ring LAN might be used to connect a number of terminal cluster controllers to a communication controller to avoid the need for a separate high-speed point-to-point connection for each cluster controller as illustrated in Fig. 1.2.

LAN data links have also been used to support alarm and security systems. They are also used in the factory environment for process control and monitoring applications.

The many uses of high-speed local area networking technology is limited only by the ingenuity of system designers.

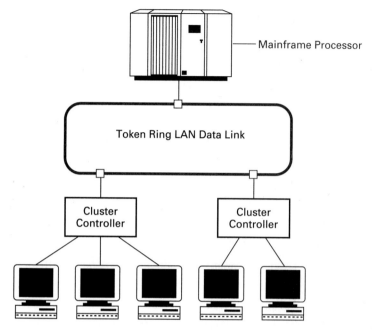

Figure 1.2   Using a LAN data link to interconnect devices in the mainframe environment.

CLIENT-SERVER COMPUTING

A typical application of the high transmission speeds provided by a LAN is to implement a *client-server* environment. In its most general sense, the client-server computing paradigm supports an environment in which an application component called a *client* issues requests for services. Another application component called a *server*, which may run in some other computing system, provides the requested service. A communication network, such as a LAN, provides the means of transporting information back and forth between the client component and the server component. This is illustrated in Fig. 1.3. There can be multiple clients sharing the services of a single server, and the client applications need not be aware that processing is not being performed locally.

    The term *client-server computing* has many interpretations, and the term is often used in the personal computer environment to refer to client-server database systems. In a client-server database environment, desktop computers operating in the role of clients make requests for data that is maintained on another computing system operating in the role of a database server. Our definition of the client-server environment described in the foregoing section is a much broader definition than this.

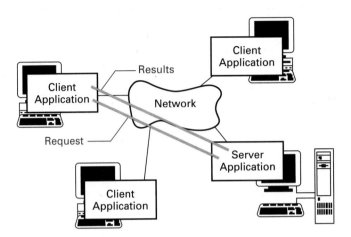

Figure 1.3   Client-server computing.

The client-server computing paradigm permits many different types of server systems to be built. The following are a few types of server systems that are possible in the client-server environment:

- **File Server.** Provides file access and management services.
- **Print Server.** Provides printing services.
- **Database Server.** Provides database services.
- **Communications Server.** Provides access to modems or other communication facilities that provide networked computing systems with access to specialized communication capabilities.
- **Application Server.** Provides access to application logic, allowing an application to be distributed among more than one computing system.

LAN COMPONENTS

Local area networks are typically implemented by a combination of hardware and software components. The components used to implement LANs, shown in Fig. 1.4 include computing devices, network interface cards, a cabling system, hubs or concentrators, and networking software.

Computing Devices

A local area network is typically used to interconnect general-purpose computing devices, such as personal computers or workstations, which may be of the same or different types. Special-purpose devices, such as intelligent printers and devices used to interconnect individual LANs, may also be directly attached to a LAN.

Simple peripheral devices, such as hard disks and simple line printers, are not typically attached directly to the LAN. Instead, such peripheral devices are attached to one of

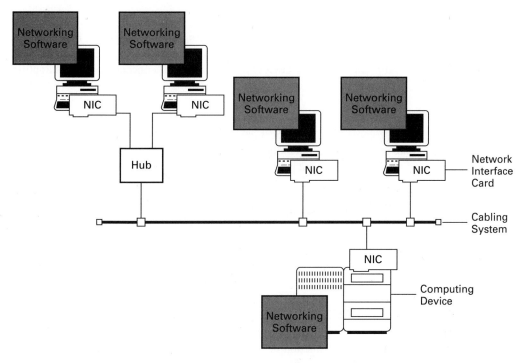

Figure 1.4   Local area network components.

the networked computer systems. Peripheral devices can, however, be made accessible to other systems on the network and can be shared by all network users.

Network Interface Cards

A *network interface card* (NIC) is typically installed in each computing device that is directly attached to the LAN. A NIC is sometimes called a *network adapter* or *LAN adapter*. A NIC performs the hardware functions that are required to provide a computing device with physical communication capabilities.

Some types of computing devices that are designed for use on specific types of networks, such as a network printer, have the functions of a NIC integrated directly into them. Other types of computing devices, such as general-purpose computing systems, typically allow various types of NICs to be installed in them.

Cabling Systems

A LAN cabling system includes the cable used to interconnect the NICs installed in the networked computing devices. Various types of electrical cable or fiber-optic cable are used to implement LANs. The cabling system also typically includes *attachment units* that allow the devices to attach to the cable. In some cases, the cabling system is replaced with some form of wireless communication, such as radio, microwave, or infrared signaling.

Access Units or Concentrators

Some local area network implementations use devices called *access units*, *concentrators*, or *hubs* that allow multiple network devices to be connected to the LAN cabling system through a central point. Attaching devices through a central concentrator often simplifies the installation and maintenance of the local area network.

Networking Software

Network interface cards (NICs) perform low-level functions that allow physical communication to take place between interconnected devices. High-level functions that end users employ for doing useful work are generally handled by networking software that accesses a NIC on behalf of an end user. Software products that provide end user facilities are often called *network operating systems*. Network operating systems augment a computer system's conventional system software by providing networking facilities, such as remote file and printer access. Some literature uses the term network operating system to refer to the system software that runs on a network server computing system, but in this book we will use it more generically to refer to the networking software running on either a client or a server system.

TWO LOCAL AREA NETWORK PERSPECTIVES

It is important to make a distinction between two very different ways of looking at local area networking technology. We must make a clear distinction between the *LAN data link technology* that is used to implement a computer network and the *LAN networking software* that is used to provide users with local area networking facilities.

LAN Data Link Technology

LAN data link technology is used to implement a flexible, high-speed form of networking data link. This is a low-level perspective in which we view LAN technology as providing a simple communication path between any source system and any destination system. The source system generates a message and uses the facilities of a LAN data link to deliver that message to the destination system.

When we look at local area network technology from the data link perspective, we view a LAN data link in the same way as we view any other type of data link, such as a data link implemented using an ordinary point-to-point telecommunications facility. However, as we have already pointed out, a major difference between a LAN data link and other forms of data links that have been used for data communication is that a LAN data link typically implements a many-to-many communication facility. A LAN data link allows any device attached to the LAN to communicate with any other attached device.

There are four characteristics that have become important in describing a particular form of LAN data link technology. These characteristics allow us to compare one type of LAN data link with another. We will introduce these four characteristics here, and we will describe them further in the first two chapters in Part I:

- **Transmission Medium.** The *transmission medium* is the cable or other physical circuit that is used to interconnect systems. Typical LAN transmission media are twisted-wire-pair telephone wire, coaxial cable, fiber-optic cable, and various forms of wireless transmission. LAN data link transmission media are described further in Chapter 2.

- **Transmission Technique.** The *transmission technique* refers to the type of signals that are exchanged over the physical transmission medium. The most common techniques used with LAN data links are called *baseband* and *broadband* transmission. LAN data link transmission techniques are described further in Chapter 2.

- **Network Topology.** The *network topology* identifies the logical shape that device interconnections take. Common LAN data link topologies are the *bus,* the *ring,* and the *star.* LAN data link topologies are described further in Chapter 3.

- **Access Control Method.** The *access control method* describes the method by which communicating systems control their access to the transmission medium. Devices on a LAN data link share the cabling system that connects them and the transmission facilities it provides. However, a LAN data link generally allows only one system to transmit at a time. Some method must be used to control when each system can use the transmission facilities. Commonly used access control methods are *contention, token passing,* and *circuit switching.* LAN data link access control methods are described in Chapter 3.

When we look at LAN technology from a data link perspective, we typically discuss the low-level technology that is used to implement the LAN data link. A wide variety of LAN data link technologies are in common use. Some of the most commonly used LAN data link technologies are as follows:

- **Ethernet.** A LAN data link technology in which systems are attached to a common transmission facility, such as a coaxial cable or twisted-pair cable. A system typically attempts to transmit whenever it has data to send. Ethernet is the most widely used form of LAN data link technology. Ethernet technology is described in Chapters 10 and 11.

- **Token Bus.** A LAN data link technology in which systems are connected to a common transmission medium, in a similar manner as an Ethernet LAN. A system is allowed to transmit only when it has a special data unit, called the *token,* that is passed from one system to another. Token Bus LANs are sometimes used in factory automation environments. Token Bus technology is described in Chapter 12.

- **ARCnet.** A relatively low-speed form of LAN data link technology in which all systems are attached to a common coaxial cable. Like the Token Bus form of LAN, a system transmits when it has the token. ARCnet technology is described in Chapter 12.

- **Token Ring.** A LAN data link technology in which systems are connected to one another using point-to-point twisted-pair cable segments to form a ring structure. A system is allowed to transmit only when it has the token, which is passed from one system to another around the ring. Token Ring technology is described in Chapter 13.

- **Fiber Distributed Data Interface (FDDI).** A high-speed LAN data link technology in which systems are connected to one another using point-to-point fiber-optic cable segments to form a ring structure. A system is allowed to transmit only when it has the token. FDDI technology is described in Chapter 14.

- **LocalTalk.** A low-speed LAN data link technology—part of Apple Computer's AppleTalk networking scheme—in which systems are attached to a common cable. LocalTalk technology has been built into most of the computing devices that Apple Computer has manufactured, although Apple has been building Ethernet technology as well into much of its more recent equipment. LocalTalk technology is described in Chapter 15.

When networking literature references a specific LAN data link technology, such as an Ethernet LAN or a Token Ring LAN, the literature is typically viewing the LAN from the perspective of the NICs and the cabling system that are used to interconnect network systems.

Most of the chapters in Parts I, II, and III of this book concentrate on the low-level technology that is used to implement LAN data links.

LAN Networking Software

End users are not ordinarily concerned with the individual data links that are used to implement a computer network. A typical network user views a local area network simply as a collection of computing systems that are capable of communicating with one another. A user ordinarily interacts with high-level networking software that allows them to use the networked computers to perform useful work.

The most useful kind of networking software makes the network totally transparent to the user. A user should be able to access a file, send an electronic mail message, or print a spreadsheet without having to be aware that a network is being used.

When we are discussing local area networks from the viewpoint of the facilities they provide to end users, we typically discuss the high-level networking software that end users employ. This software typically runs in a user's own desktop computing system and in the other systems they access, such as file and print servers. A wide variety of networking software is available that uses LAN data link technology.

The following are some of the most commonly used networking software systems:

- **NetWare.** *NetWare* is a family of network operating system software that is marketed by Novell. At the time of writing, NetWare is by far the most popular of all networking software used in the personal computer environment. NetWare provides file and print sharing facilities as well as a broad range of other networking services. NetWare is described further in Chapters 17 and 22.

- **LAN Manager and LAN Server.** *LAN Manager* and *LAN Server* refer to a family of network operating systems codeveloped by Microsoft and IBM. LAN Manager refers to the Microsoft products and LAN Server refers to the IBM products. LAN Manager and LAN Server, and the interfaces they implement, are described further in Chapters 17 and 21.

- **VINES.** *VINES* is a family of network operating system software that is marketed by Banyan Systems. It provides many of the same facilities as NetWare, LAN Server, and LAN Manager and also provides many facilities that are especially well suited for large networks.

- **LANtastic.** *LANtastic* is a family of network operating systems for the personal computer environment that is marketed by Artisoft. LANtastic server software can be run on personal computers that can also be used as ordinary desktop systems.

- **TCP/IP.** *TCP/IP, Transmission Control Protocol/Internet Protocol,* refers to a set of communication protocols that grew out of a research project that was funded by the U. S. Department of Defense. The TCP/IP networking scheme implements a peer-to-peer client-server architecture. Any computing system in the network can run TCP/IP server software and can provide services to any other computing system that runs complementary TCP/IP client software. TCP/IP is described further in Chapters 17 and 23.

- **AppleTalk.** *AppleTalk* is Apple Computer's networking scheme that has been used for many years to network Apple equipment. Apple system software contains integrated AppleTalk networking support that allows Apple computing systems to participate in peer-to-peer computer networks and to also access the services of AppleTalk servers. NICs and networking software are available for a variety of other types of computing systems, including personal computers and UNIX workstations, that allow them to participate in AppleTalk networks. AppleTalk is described further in Chapters 17 and 24.

- **DECnet.** *DECnet* is a term that Digital Equipment Corporation uses to refer to its proprietary networking software. DECnet networking facilities are typically used in the DEC minicomputer and workstation environments. A DECnet network typically consists of a wide area network made up of interconnected LAN data links. DECnet is described further in Chapter 17.

- **PATHWORKS.** *PATHWORKS* is a family of personal computer network operating system software marketed by Digital Equipment Corporation. The original goal of PATHWORKS was to provide personal computers with access to DECnet networking capabilities. However, PATHWORKS now supports access to other forms of networking as well.

- **Systems Network Architecture.** *Systems Network Architecture* (SNA) is IBM's proprietary networking scheme that has been widely used in the mainframe environment. A form of SNA called *Advanced Peer-to-Peer Networking* (APPN) provides SNA communication support for smaller systems. SNA is described further in Chapter 17.

When networking literature refers to a networking software system, such as a *NetWare LAN*, a *LANtastic LAN*, or an *SNA network*, the literature is typically viewing the network from the viewpoint of the networking software that a user employs. Chapter 5 and the chapters in Parts IV and V of this book view local area networks from the high-level perspective of the networking software.

In many cases, networking capabilities are being integrated directly into the system software that is used with small computers. This has been common with TCP/IP support in the UNIX workstation environment for many years, and this trend is continuing in the personal computer environment. For example, the Windows for Workgroups and Windows NT system software from Microsoft contain integrated networking support that makes it unnecessary to install separate networking software.

INTERCONNECTED NETWORKS

Most networking software can be used to construct local area networks that allow users to access the facilities of networked computing systems that are located relatively close together, often in a small work group. However, what is becoming more important in today's networking environment is that networking software also typically allows the local area networks implemented by different work groups to be interconnected to form larger *enterprise internetworks*.

An important goal of computer networking technology is to remove the distinction between local area networks and wide area networks from the perspective of the end user.

A user should be able to access the facilities of a networked computing system in the same manner whether the system is located across the room or on the other side of the globe. Much networking software that was used a few years ago only in the local area networking environment now has the capability for allowing such enterprise internetworks to be built.

SUMMARY

Computer networking technologies can be classified according to the distances they are designed to span. Wide area networks cover large geographic areas, metropolitan area networks span a few miles, and local area networks serve the needs of a single building or campus of buildings.

Local area networks have been put to a wide variety of uses, and the transmission speeds they support are allowing applications to be built that would not be possible without the high bandwidth they make available. The client-server environment is becoming increasingly important, in which small computers are networked together to implement applications in which the computing load is spread over a number of cooperating systems.

The components making up a typical local area network consist of the networked computing devices, network interface cards that provide the computing devices with physical communication capabilities, cabling systems that interconnect the network interface cards, access units that permit groups of devices to be connected to the transmission medium, and networking software that provides end users with access to communication capabilities.

Local area networks can be viewed from two perspectives—from the viewpoint of the data link technology that is used to provide groups of computing systems with physical communication capabilities and from the viewpoint of the networking software that provides computer users with access to high-level communication services.

Chapter 2 begins Part I of this book that investigates the concepts underlying local area networks. Chapter 2 concentrates on the transmission technologies that are employed in local area networks for sending signals from one system to another.

LOCAL AREA NETWORK CONCEPTS

The technology used to construct local area networks has unique terminology associated with it. Part II defines some of the terms that are used to describe LAN technology and introduces some of the important concepts associated with local area networks.

The exchange of signals over a physical medium is fundamental to all forms of computer communication. Chapter 2 discusses the data transmission techniques that are used in local area networks for sending signals between networked devices.

The communication links that interconnect intelligent devices in a LAN can take on a number of different shapes, or topologies. Chapter 3 explores the physical and logical structures that the various forms of LAN data link technology employ and describes the methods that networked machines use for controlling access to the shared transmission medium.

Standards are important in all forms of electronic communication. Chapter 4 examines information technology standardization and discusses architectures for computer networking, including the international standard *Reference Model for Open Systems Interconnection* (OSI model) on which standards for local area network data links are based.

End users are not ordinarily concerned with the underlying technologies that are used to construct computer networks. Instead, they are interested in what the network can do for them. Chapter 5 introduces the general functions of the networking software that end users employ for accessing the facilities of local area networks.

Physical Transmission

Different LAN data link technologies use different methods for transmitting data across a physical transmission medium. The various types of physical transmission that LAN data link technologies use can be compared using two categories of characteristics—characteristics concerning the physical nature of the transmission medium itself and characteristics concerning the signaling technique that is used to send data over the transmission medium. We begin this chapter on physical transmission by examining the four general types of transmission media that are used most often in constructing local area networks. We then look at the different types of signaling techniques that are used.

TRANSMISSION MEDIA

The telecommunications industry has employed a wide variety of physical media for the transmission of information. These media range from the open-wire pairs that were carried on poles in the early days of telecommunications to the high-speed, fiber-optic links that are today used to connect distant points on the globe. Although most of the media employed in conventional telecommunications could be employed in the construction of local area networks, four media are used most often in today's LAN implementations. These are *twisted-wire pairs*, *coaxial cable*, *fiber-optics links*, and *wireless transmission*. These four general types of physical media each have different transmission characteristics and different costs associated with them.

Twisted-Pair Cable

A twisted-wire pair consists of two insulated strands of copper wire that have been twisted spirally around each other. A number of twisted-wire pairs are often grouped together and enclosed within a protective sheath or jacket to form a twisted-pair cable. Figure 2.1 illustrates twisted-wire pairs.

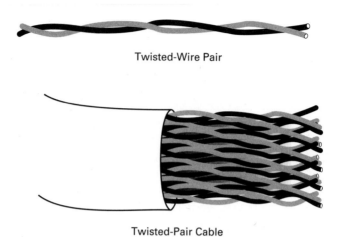

Twisted-Wire Pair

Twisted-Pair Cable

Figure 2.1   Twisted-wire pairs.

The wiring often used within buildings for telephone systems consists of twisted-pair cable. One of the reasons that this type of cable is being used to implement local area networks is that it is already installed in many locations. Many local area network products are available that use ordinary telephone wire for LAN communication, and most forms of LAN data link technology have been adapted for use over twisted-pair cable. Some high-performance LAN data link implementations that use twisted-wire pairs employ a special, higher-quality form of twisted-wire-pair cable, called *shielded-twisted-wire-pair cable*, that uses a protective sheath. Shielded cable is less subject to electrical interference and can more reliably support high transmission rates over long distances.

Twisted-pair cable remains one of the most versatile forms of transmission media, and it is often the best choice when new construction must be wired for LAN communication.

Coaxial Cable

Figure 2.2 shows the construction of a typical coaxial cable. Coaxial cable consists of a central conducting copper core that is surrounded by insulating material. The insulation is surrounded by a second conducting layer, which can consist either of a braided wire mesh or a solid sleeve. A protective jacket of nonconducting material protects the outer conductor. Coaxial cable is less subject to interference and crosstalk than a twisted-pair cable and is more easily able to reliably support high data rates over long distances.

Coaxial cable has been used for many years for television transmission. The same cable and electronic components that are used by the cable television industry is used in some LAN data link implementations. In others, a form of coaxial cable is used that has different electrical characteristics.

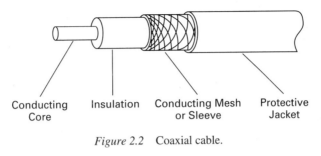

Conducting Core   Insulation   Conducting Mesh or Sleeve   Protective Jacket

Figure 2.2   Coaxial cable.

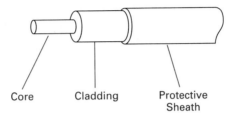

Core   Cladding   Protective Sheath

Figure 2.3   Optical fiber construction.

Fiber-Optic Cable

An optical fiber can be used to carry data signals in the form of modulated light beams. An optical fiber consists of an extremely thin cylinder of glass, called the *core*, surrounded by a concentric layer of glass, called the *cladding*. The construction of a typical optical fiber is shown in Fig. 2.3. The refractive index of the cladding is lower than that of the core, which causes light that is traveling down the core to be reflected back into the core when it strikes the cladding. In practice, a number of such optical fibers are often bound together into a fiber-optic cable, with all of the individual fibers surrounded by a protective sheath.

Fiber-optic cables have the potential for supporting very high transmission rates. Transmission rates of up to 565 Mbps are routinely employed in commercially available systems, and data rates of up to 200,000 Mbps have been demonstrated. Signals transmitted over fiber-optic cables are not subject to electrical interference. A fiber-optic cable is also typically smaller in size and lighter in weight than electrical cable. However, optical fiber is sometimes more expensive to install than electrical cable, although the cost is dropping.

Wireless Transmission

Local area network transmission that does not depend on a physical cable is becoming more prevalent in the LAN marketplace. Wireless transmission can be used in a number of different ways. One way is to interconnect individual local area network cable segments where it would be difficult to physically interconnect two sites. For example, instead of interconnecting two buildings with a cable, a point-to-point microwave or infrared transmission link might be used. Such a point-to-point link would appear no different from a physical cable connection to other local area network equipment.

A more flexible way in which wireless transmission is sometimes used is to use radio transmission or infrared links to replace the physical cables that are used to connect individual computer systems to the LAN. Wireless forms of local area networks make it very easy to move computer systems and other types of network devices from one location to another without having to change physical wiring.

Wireless transmission has disadvantages as well. Wireless LANs that employ radio transmission are often subject to interference, which can cause error rates to be high. Also, the distances that can be spanned are often quite limited. Wireless transmission is often used to attach individual systems to concentrators, with physical cabling used to interconnect the concentrators. Wireless LANs that employ transmission techniques other than radio transmission, such as LANs that use infrared links, often require that there be no physical barrier between the transmitter and the receiver and depend on line-of-site transmission. Errors are often experienced on such local area networks when transmission is intermittently interrupted because of normal traffic in the work area.

WIRING FOR LOCAL AREA NETWORKS

Each form of LAN technology that we describe in this book defines its own requirements for physical transmission media. A major factor in choosing a particular local area network data link technology concerns the types of physical cabling system that the LAN supports. In a very simple case, a local area network may be used to link a number of computers and other intelligent devices that are in close physical proximity, sometimes in the same room. In such a case, the type of wiring the local area network employs may be of little concern. In more complex environments, an enterprise might want to interconnect devices in an entire building or even throughout a group of buildings. In such cases, the type of cabling a particular LAN technology uses may be the most important characteristic of the network, and the installation of the cabling plant may have a high cost associated with it.

As we mentioned earlier, many different forms of LAN technology can use ordinary twisted-pair cable for data transmission. Such LAN technologies may be of interest to an enterprise that already has its offices interconnected with sufficient telephone wiring so that existing wiring can be used for local area network communication. Installing a LAN is then a matter of gaining access to the various wiring closets in which the telephone wiring terminates and locating the unused telephone circuits that are to be used for installing the local area network.

However, in some installations, especially where telephone wiring has been installed for many years, finding the unused wiring and locating the end points can be a daunting task. In many situations, it has proven less costly to pull new cables than to attempt to use existing cabling.

EIA Cabling Architecture

Work is being done in various standards bodies, with the Electronic Industries Association (EIA) playing a leadership role, in developing architectures to govern the way in which electrical and optical cables should be installed in buildings to support flexible, integrated networking.

Wiring Environments

The EIA technical report TR 48.1 describes one such standard that defines a hierarchy of three different types of environments in which network cabling can be used:

- **Work Area Environment.** A *work area environment* consists of an open area within a building in which walls and cabling are not typically considered permanent. In any given work area, the distances spanned by cabling are relatively short, and relatively few devices are installed. One type of work area might be a general office area in which typical network equipment consists of devices that are employed directly by end users and connected to some form of LAN data link. Typical devices installed in such a work area might be personal computers, graphics workstations, printers, and various types of server systems. Another type of work area might be a computer room in which various types of larger computer systems are installed.

- **Building Environment.** A *building environment* is a building, or a collection of floors in a building, in which the walls and the wiring are considered relatively permanent. In a building environment, the distances spanned by cable runs are moderate, and a relatively large number of devices must be interconnected.

- **Campus Environment.** A *campus environment* involves a number of buildings connected by cable segments making up what is often called a *backbone* network. In a campus environment, distances are relatively great and cables are often permanently installed in underground tunnels. The number of different points of interconnection is relatively small.

Local area network data links typically form the basis of device interconnection in work area, building, and campus environments, with common carrier facilities most often linking multiple, widely-separated building and campus environments. Most early local area networks were installed only in work area environments, where a relatively small number of network devices were connected in an ad hoc manner. In today's environment, building and campus environments are increasingly important as organization-wide networks are being created to link together all parts of an enterprise. Careful planning is of the greatest importance in building and campus environments because of the relative permanence of the wiring and its greater cost relative to the wiring installed in a work area environment.

Equipment Rooms

The EIA cable plant architecture defines three types of *equipment rooms*, which are those physical places in the three environments at which cables are physically terminated, as shown in Fig. 2.4. An equipment room is a dedicated space for

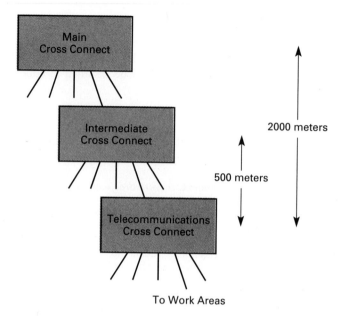

Figure 2.4   Hierarchy of equipment rooms.

facility wiring in which all types of wiring might be terminated, including wiring for data, telephone, electrical power, security, and various alarm systems. Network cabling is terminated in each type of equipment room using various types of patch panels that facilitate wiring documentation, maintenance, and reconfiguration. Equipment rooms are normally kept locked and are accessed only by qualified service personnel.

The three different types of equipment rooms defined by the EIA cabling architecture are as follows:

- **Main Cross Connect Equipment Room.** The *main cross connect* equipment room is at the top of the hierarchy. A campus of buildings has a single main cross connect equipment room used to terminate cabling running to each individual building or collection of building floors in the campus environment.

- **Intermediate Cross Connect Equipment Room.** For each building, or for each collection of floors making up an individual building environment, there is a single *intermediate cross connect* equipment room. It terminates the cabling running from the main cross connect equipment room to a particular building or collection of floors.

- **Telecommunications Cross Connect Equipment Room.** Cabling is run from an intermediate cross connect equipment room to as many *telecommunications cross connect* equipment rooms as are needed to serve the needs of the building environment. Cabling runs from a telecommunications cross connect equipment room to the individual work areas it serves.

Cabling Systems

In many cases, an enterprise may decide to install wiring specifically for the purpose of handling the data communication needs of the organization. Various organizations now market general-purpose cabling systems that can serve a wide range of communication needs. These cabling systems provide the capability for handling voice, low-speed data communication, high-speed local area network communication, and also video signal distribution. Integrated cabling systems are particularly attractive to organizations that are constructing new facilities and that wish to provide for future growth.

We next introduce two examples of widely used cabling systems—the *IBM Cabling System* and Digital Equipment Corporation's *DECconnect Communication System*. Other competing cabling systems are also available, including the AT&T SYSTIMAX Premises Distribution System, the AMP NETCONNECT Open Wiring System, and the Thomas & Betts/Nevada Western Wire Management System.

The IBM Cabling System

In 1984, before it even offered local area network products in its product line, IBM recognized the future importance of local area networks. At that time it began marketing the *IBM Cabling System*. The IBM Cabling System offers several types of physical cables, including the following:

- **Type 1 Cable.** Type 1 cable consists of two solid, #22 AWG twisted-wire pairs surrounded by an outer braided shield. Both twisted-wire pairs are suitable for data use. Several varieties of Type 1 cable are available, including cable for indoor use in conduits, cable suitable for installation in wiring plenums, and cable for outdoor installation.

- **Type 2 Cable.** Type 2 cable contains two solid, #22 AWG twisted-wire pairs surrounded by an outer braided shield. Between the braided shield and the outer protective sheath are four additional solid #22 AWG twisted-wire pairs suitable for use in telephone communication. Several varieties of Type 2 cable are also available for indoor use in conduits or in wiring plenums.

- **Type 5 Cable.** Type 5 cable contains two optical fibers within a single outer cover. Type 5 cable can be installed indoors, outdoors, and in dry, waterproof underground conduits.

- **Type 6 Cable.** Type 6 cable is similar to Type 1 cable, except that it uses stranded #26 AWG wire. Type 6 cable is typically used for constructing patch cables that interconnect longer lengths of Type 1 and Type 2 cable.

In addition to the above types of cable, the IBM Cabling System includes a variety of accessories, including connectors, wiring face plates, surface-mounted outlets, distribution panels, and patch cables. IBM recommends that cable be installed so that the wiring from each individual office or workplace terminates in a central *wiring closet*, thus creating a star configuration, as shown in Fig. 2.5. Since all wiring terminates in easily accessible wiring closets, patch cables can be used to create networks having any desired physical structure.

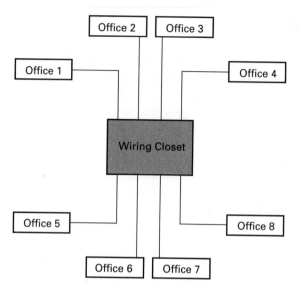

Figure 2.5   Star configuration using a wiring closet.

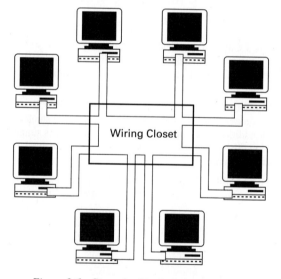

Figure 2.6   Star-wired logical ring structure.

Much of the LAN equipment that IBM markets uses Token Ring LAN data link technology, so many of the networks that are typically constructed using the IBM Cabling System are logically ring structured but are laid out physically in the shape of a star, as shown in Fig. 2.6. The various network structures, or topologies, to which local area networks conform are described in Chapter 3.

The DECconnect Communication System

The cabling system offered by the Digital Equipment Corporation is called the *DEC-connect Communication System*. The DECconnect system uses the following types of cable to interconnect offices and workplaces:

- **ThinWire Ethernet Cable.** *ThinWire Ethernet cable* is a flexible coaxial cable, about a quarter-inch thick, that is similar to the type of coaxial cable used for closed circuit television transmission. It is used for relatively short distance communication at 10 Mbps transmission using Ethernet LAN data link technology. Ethernet technology is described in detail in Chapters 10 and 11.

- **Standard Ethernet Cable.** *Standard Ethernet cable* is relatively rigid, half-inch-thick coaxial cable that is typically used to interconnect several smaller networks that use the ThinWire Ethernet cable.

- **Twisted-Pair Data Communication Cable.** *Twisted-pair data communication cable* is unshielded and contains four twisted-wire pairs. It is used for data communication of various types.

- **Telephone Cable.** *Telephone cable* contains four unshielded twisted-wire pairs. It is used for ordinary voice telephone communication.

- **Video Cable.** *Video cable* is standard closed-circuit television coaxial cable and is used for video applications.

The DECconnect system centers around a single type of faceplate that is designed to serve all the communication needs of a particular office or workplace. As shown in Fig. 2.7, the DECconnect faceplate has the following four connectors:

- A BNC connector that gives access to a ThinWire Ethernet network.

- A modified modular connector, similar to a telephone connector, that is used to connect computer equipment to the twisted-wire-pair data communication cable.

- A standard modular telephone jack that is used to connect telephone equipment to the telephone system.

- An F-type connector for connecting video equipment to the video coaxial cable.

DEC recommends that the four types of cable that terminate in the faceplate be installed between each office or workplace and a central *Satellite Equipment Room* (SER). One or more satellite equipment rooms can be installed on each floor of a building, with the satellite equipment rooms interconnected using standard, thick Ethernet cable as shown in Fig. 2.8. Like the IBM Cabling System, patch cables can be used to create networks having any desired structure. The DECconnect system includes a variety of accessories, including connectors, wiring faceplates, surface mounted outlets, patch panels, and patch cables.

Like the IBM Cabling System, the DECconnect system uses a physical star configuration to interconnect workplaces with the satellite equipment room. However, the DECconnect system is typically used to construct bus- or tree-structured

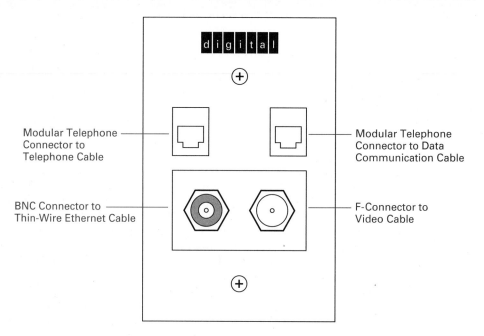

Modular Telephone Connector to Telephone Cable

Modular Telephone Connector to Data Communication Cable

BNC Connector to Thin-Wire Ethernet Cable

F-Connector to Video Cable

Figure 2.7 DECconnect faceplate.

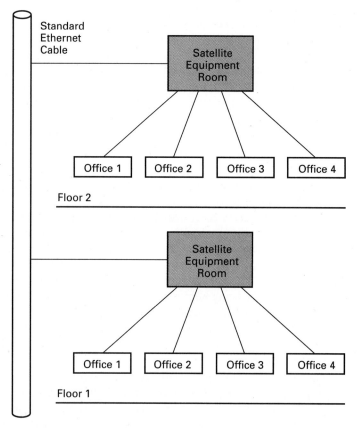

Standard Ethernet Cable

Satellite Equipment Room

Office 1 Office 2 Office 3 Office 4

Floor 2

Satellite Equipment Room

Office 1 Office 2 Office 3 Office 4

Floor 1

Figure 2.8 Interconnecting satellite equipment rooms with standard Ethernet cable.

local area networks. Local area network structures, or topologies, are introduced in Chapter 3.

SIGNALING TECHNIQUES

Now that we have discussed the physical transmission media that are used to construct local area networks, we next discuss the techniques that are used for transmitting signals over those media. There are two general techniques that can be used for transmitting signals over a physical communication medium: *baseband* and *broadband*. Baseband transmission uses *digital* signaling while broadband transmission uses *analog* techniques. Equipment can be designed to transmit either digital or analog signals over any of the types of physical transmission media we have described.

In discussing signaling techniques, we refer to the medium over which data is transmitted as a *communication channel*. By communication channel, we mean a circuit of arbitrary construction that has certain characteristics. These characteristics can be defined apart from the physical media that are used to implement the channel. Equivalent channels can be constructed using any desired transmission medium, and in many cases the physical methods that are used to transmit data can be made transparent to the communicating systems.

In the following sections, we will discuss the differences between baseband and broadband transmission and the related differences between digital and analog signaling.

Baseband Transmission

With baseband transmission, data signals are carried over the physical communication medium in the form of discrete pulses of electricity or light. With this form of transmission, a sending device sends data pulses directly over the communication channel, and the receiving device detects them.

As the data pulses travel along the communication medium, they become distorted. The pulses received at the other end are far from their original shape, and if the channel is too long, the signals too weak, or the transmitting speed too great, the received signal may be unrecognizable and wrongly interpreted by the machine at the other end. To overcome these difficulties, devices called *repeaters* can be used that receive the digital signal and then retransmit them at their original strength and sharpness. Since the repeater totally regenerates the signal, the result of any noise that might have crept into the signal is nullified. Noise and interference are not a problem with baseband transmission unless they corrupt the signal sufficiently to prevent a bit from being correctly identified as a 0 or a 1. Communicating systems attached to a network may themselves act as repeaters in some types of LAN implementations so that separate, specialized equipment is not needed for signal regeneration.

With baseband transmission, the entire channel capacity is used to transmit a single data signal. Local area networks use a variety of techniques, called *medium access control methods*, to control access to the transmission medium. The various medium access control methods used with local area networks are discussed in Chapter 3.

Broadband Transmission

Broadband transmission typically employs analog transmission using a wider range of frequencies than baseband transmission. With analog transmission, the signals employed are continuous and nondiscrete. Signals flow across the transmission medium in the form of *electromagnetic waves*. Figure 2.9 illustrates the characteristics of an electromagnetic wave.

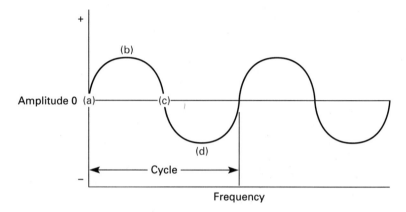

Figure 2.9   Characteristics of an electromagnetic wave.

Electromagnetic Wave Characteristics

Electromagnetic waves have three characteristics that are useful in telecommunications:

- **Amplitude.** With an electrical wire, a wave's *amplitude* is associated with the *level of voltage* carried on the wire; with an optical fiber, the wave's amplitude is concerned with the *intensity of the light beam.*

- **Frequency.** The *frequency* of a wave concerns the number of cycles or oscillations that the wave makes per second. A frequency rate of one oscillation per second is defined as one *Hertz* (Hz).

- **Phase.** A wave's *phase* refers to the point to which the wave has advanced in its cycle. In Fig. 2.9, (a) identifies the beginning of the cycle, (b) is 1/4 of the cycle, (c) is 1/2 the cycle, and (d) is 3/4 of the cycle. A wave's phase is generally described in terms of degrees, with the beginning of the cycle being 0°, 1/4 of the cycle being 90°, 1/2 of the cycle being 180°, 3/4 of the cycle being 270°, and completion of the cycle being 360°.

Modulation Techniques

With analog transmission, a data signal is superimposed on a carrier signal by varying, or *modulating*, any one of the three wave characteristics of the carrier signal. For example, a particular value of the carrier signal's amplitude, frequency, or phase might represent the value 0, and some other amplitude, frequency, or phase value might represent the value 1. In this way a data signal can be *carried* by the carrier signal.

Measurements of Channel Capacity

In general, the higher the frequency of the carrier signal, the greater its information carrying capacity. In telecommunications literature, the term *bandwidth* is often used to refer to the capacity of a communication channel. A channel's bandwidth is the difference between the highest and the lowest frequencies that are carried over the channel. The higher the bandwidth, the more information can be carried. For example, a telephone channel supporting voice communication transmits frequencies ranging from about 300 Hertz (Hz) to 3100 Hz. So the range of frequencies, or *bandwidth*, supported is 3100 − 300 = 2800 Hz, or about 3 kHz. The transmission media used with local area networks support bandwidths much larger than this.

A channel's bandwidth has a direct relationship to its *data rate*, or the number of *bits per second* (bps) that can be carried over it. Since local area networks deal mainly with data transmission, we will find bits per second to be a more useful measure of a channel's capacity than bandwidth. However, in telecommunications literature, the term bandwidth is often used to mean data transmission capacity.

Another term that is used to express channel capacity is *baud*. Baud is a measurement of the *signaling speed* of a channel; a certain communication channel is said to have a speed of so many *baud*. Signaling speed, or baud, refers to *the number of times in each second the line condition changes.*

Suppose we are using amplitude modulation and that one amplitude value is used to represent the binary value 0 and another amplitude binary value 1. In this particular case, the line's signaling speed in *baud* is the same as the line's data rate in *bits per second*. Suppose, however, that we use four different amplitudes to represent the binary values 00, 01, 10, or 11 (called *dibits*). In this case the data rate in bits per second will be twice the signaling speed in baud. If the signals are coded into eight possible states, then one line condition represents a *tribit* and the data rate in bits per second is three times the signaling speed in baud. Some literature mistakenly uses the term baud to mean *bits per second*. Since the term *baud* can be confusing, we will avoid using it in this book.

Signal Amplification

Another issue that must be dealt with as part of physical data transmission is that of signal strength. When an electrical signal is transmitted along a wire, it gradually decreases in strength—a process known as *attenuation*. With analog transmission, *amplifiers* may be included as part of the network. An amplifier receives a signal and then retransmits it at its original strength. Placing amplifiers at appropriate points along the physical transmission medium allows devices to be more widespread geographically and still be able to detect the signals that are transmitted over the physical medium. However, if any noise or interference has crept into the signal along the way, the noise is typically amplified along with the signal. Thus, with analog transmission, the quality of the signal tends to deteriorate with distance even when amplifiers are used.

Frequency-Division Multiplexing

When analog transmission is used, the available bandwidth of the physical transmission medium is often divided up into multiple channels. Different transmissions can then take place simultaneously over the different channels using a technique called *frequency-division multiplexing* (FDM).

With broadband transmission, the multiple channels are often used in entirely different ways. For example, data can be transmitted on some channels, video signals on others, voice telephone calls on still others, and so on. For data transmission, one channel can be used by devices for data flowing in one direction and another channel for data flowing in the opposite direction. When multiple devices share the same channel for data transmission, a method of determining when a device is allowed to transmit must be employed, as with baseband transmission.

A limited form of broadband transmission is possible, where the entire bandwidth is used to make up a single channel. This is known as single-channel broadband. Single-channel broadband provides a relatively inexpensive way to initially construct a network that can later be converted to multichannel broadband without requiring rewiring.

Direction of Transmission

Another difference between baseband and broadband transmission is in the direction of signal flow. With baseband transmission, signal flow is bidirectional; that is, the signal travels away from the sending device in both directions on the physical medium. This is illustrated in Fig. 2.10. When device B transmits data, the signal goes out in both directions and eventually reaches all other devices along the wire or cable. When the signal reaches either end of the cable, terminators employed at the ends of the cable absorb the signal. Generally, the single-channel broadband technique also uses bidirectional transmission.

With full broadband signaling, transmission is unidirectional; the signal moves in one direction along the cable. In order for a signal to reach all devices on the network,

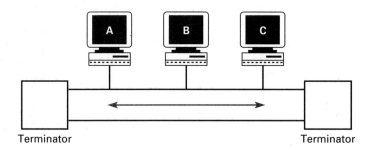

Figure 2.10   Bidirectional flow.

then, there must be two paths for data flow. Figure 2.11 shows the two most common approaches used to provide the two paths.

The configuration shown in the top of Fig. 2.11 is called *midsplit broadband*. Here the bandwidth of the cable is divided into two channels, each using a different range of frequencies. One channel is used to transmit signals and the other is used to receive. When a signal is transmitted, it travels to one end of the cable, called the *head end*. At the head end, a frequency converter changes the frequency of the signal from the send channel range to the receive channel range, and retransmits it in the opposite direction along the cable. The signal is then received by all devices on the cable.

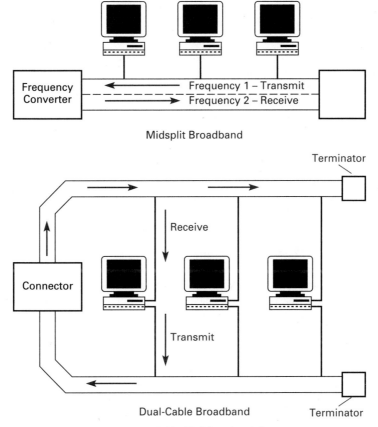

Figure 2.11   Unidirectional flow.

The second configuration is called *dual-cable broadband*. In this configuration, each device is attached to two cables. One cable is used to send and the other to receive. When a signal is transmitted, it reaches the head end and is passed on via a connector to the other cable, without any change in the frequency of the signal. The signal can then be received by any of the devices as it passes along the second cable.

Digital Transmission Over An Analog Channel

In the previous sections, we have discussed the differences between analog and digital signaling. Although analog transmission is often used over a communication medium, it is important to realize that the communicating systems that are attached to the network are digital in nature, whether the network uses baseband (digital) or broadband (analog) signaling.

Modems

When analog signaling techniques are used to implement the communication channel, the digital signals that communicating systems generate must be converted to and from analog form. This conversion is often performed by devices called *modems*, short for *modulator-demodulator*. Modems are routinely employed in conventional data transmission for transmitting digital data over ordinary analog telecommunications channels. Modems are also employed on local area networks when analog signaling techniques are used over the physical communication medium.

With broadband transmission, the carrier frequencies employed are very-high-frequency radio waves. Thus, radio frequency (RF) modems must be used to attach devices to the transmission medium. Commonly available equipment used for cable television, including coaxial cable, amplifiers, and signal distribution equipment, can be used for constructing broadband data networks. The use of existing technology can help to keep down the cost of network components.

Virtual Channels

Figure 2.12 shows a configuration that might be used in order for two digital devices to communicate over a physical communication medium that uses analog transmission. It is important to realize that the use of modems and analog signaling techniques is transparent to the two communicating devices. The two communicating systems send and receive digital bit streams, whether the physical transmission medium uses digital or analog techniques. The modems automatically convert these digital bit streams to and from analog form. To the two communicating devices, it appears as though a digital channel connects them. This apparent digital channel is often referred to as a *virtual channel*.

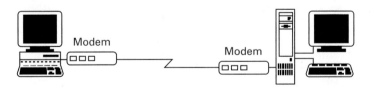

Analog Communication Facility

Figure 2.12   Digital transmission over an analog communication facility.

ENCODING SCHEMES

Communicating systems can use a variety of encoding schemes to represent binary values for transmission over the communication channel. With one simple encoding scheme, used for many years over some telegraph circuits, the presence of a pulse indicates the value 1 and the absence of a pulse represents the value 0, as shown in Fig. 2.13.

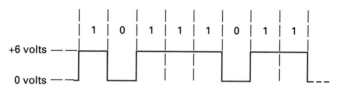

Figure 2.13 Telegraph signaling.

Local area networks generally use a more sophisticated encoding scheme than the above for representing binary values. The two most commonly used LAN encoding schemes are *Manchester encoding* and *differential Manchester encoding*. A number of commonly used encoding schemes, including the two Manchester variations, are described in Box 2.1.

BOX 2.1   Encoding schemes.

RS-232-D Encoding

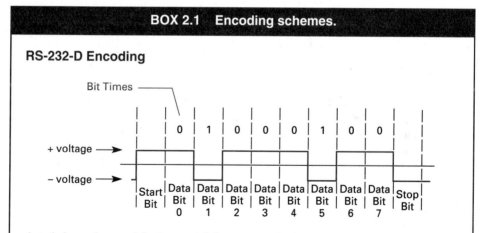

A technique often used for low-speed data communication is defined in a standard called RS-232-D, which is published by the Electronics Industry Association (EIA). With RS-232-D transmission, a negative voltage on the line for a bit time represents the value 1 and a positive voltage the value 0.

(Continued)

BOX 2.1 *(Continued)*

Zero-complemented Differential Encoding

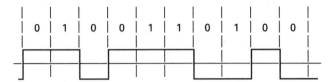

Many high-performance line control procedures often employ a more complex encoding scheme called zero-complemented differential encoding to represent bit values. With this technique, a transition on the line from negative to positive or from positive to negative within a bit time indicates the value 0; the lack of a transition during a bit time represents the value 1.

Manchester Encoding

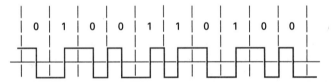

For electrical purposes, it is desirable in many local area network implementations that transitions from positive to negative and from negative to positive occur often with predictable regularity. A form of encoding, called Manchester encoding, produces the desired number of transitions and is used on many types of LAN data links. With a typical implementation of Manchester encoding, a negative voltage for the first half of the bit time followed by a positive voltage for the second half of the bit time represents the value 1; a positive voltage followed by a transition to a negative voltage represents the value 0. Thus, with Manchester encoding, a transition from negative to positive or from positive to negative occurs every bit time.

With Manchester encoding, bit times in which the signal is held either positive or negative for the entire bit time are used to represent something other than a bit value, for example the beginning or ending of a transmission block.

Differential Manchester Encoding

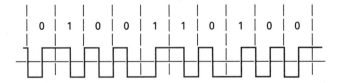

BOX 2.1 *(Continued)*

A form of Manchester encoding, called differential Manchester encoding, is used with some forms of LAN technology. With this technique, illustrated above, a transition occurs during each bit time, as with conventional Manchester encoding. However, the interpretation of the transition from positive to negative or from negative to positive depends on whether the previous bit time represented a 0 or a 1. To represent the value 1, the polarity remains the same as it was at the end of the previous bit time and then changes in polarity at the midpoint of the bit time only. To represent the value 0, the polarity changes at the beginning of the bit time and also at the midpoint of the bit time. With this form of encoding, a change from positive to negative can represent either a 0 or a 1 depending on the state of the line at the end of the previous bit time. It is the transition that occurs, or does not occur, at the beginning of the bit time that indicates the value. No transition at the beginning of the bit time indicates the value 1; a transition at the beginning of the bit time indicates the value 0.

As with conventional Manchester encoding, bit times in which no transition occurs at the midpoint of the bit time are often used for control purposes.

Synchronization

In order for communication to take place between two digital devices, a particular length of time is generally associated with the transmission of each bit. This is known as the *bit duration*, or *bit time*. Both the sending and receiving systems must be in synchronization with one another and must be able to determine when the beginning and the ending of each bit time occurs. In order to properly interpret received data, the receiving device must be able to recognize when data is being transmitted and to identify the portion of the signal that corresponds to each bit. There are several ways in which this can be done.

Start/Stop Bits

When a simple encoding scheme is used, such as with RS-232-D transmission, described in Box 2.1, *start bits* and *stop bits* can be used to identify the beginning and ending of sequences of data. When start and stop bits are employed, each group of bits generally corresponds to a single character, usually 7 or 8 bits in length.

RS-232-D transmission uses start and stop bits to control transmission. This type of transmission is referred to as *asynchronous*, or *start/stop transmission*. Between transmissions of each individual data character, the line is kept in an idle state, normally indicated by the continuous transmission of a signal having a negative voltage. A start bit precedes any group of data bits and consists of a change to a signal of positive voltage. A predetermined number of data bits (on which both sender and receiver must agree) then follow, where a negative voltage level indicates a 1 bit and a positive signal level a 0 bit. Following the data bits there will be at least one stop bit, which is indicated by at least one bit time at which the line remains at the negative voltage. This guarantees that there will be a transition in the signal level when the next start bit is sent.

The occurrence of start bits at the beginning of each data character allows the communicating devices to establish synchronization with one another to ensure that the receiver samples the signal at appropriate points to identify data bit values correctly. If long strings of data bits are sent between start and stop bits, it is possible that the receiver might slip out of synchronization with the sender, and the data bit values would be interpreted incorrectly.

With some types of transmission, the receiver uses the occurrence of transitions in the signal to help in maintaining synchronization. In such a system, it is important that transitions occur relatively frequently. If long strings of 0 or 1 bit values are sent, it is difficult for the receiver to remain in synchronization with the sender. Various schemes have been used to insert transitions into the transmitted data at intervals in the event that long strings of 0 or 1 bits randomly occur in the data.

However, start/stop transmission is typically used with low data rates and with transmissions where only a single data character at a time is transmitted. Under these conditions start and stop bits are sent frequently enough so that a lack of adequate transitions does not occur.

Delimiter Bits

In more advanced data transmission systems, signal patterns representing other than a 0 or a 1 bit are typically used to identify the beginning and end of data blocks being transmitted. These signal patterns are known as *delimiter signals* or *delimiters*. For example, with Manchester encoding, values of 0 and 1 are both associated with a transition in signal level occurring at the midpoint of the bit time. Bit times in which a transition does not occur can represent delimiters that mark the beginning and the end of a data block, with no possibility of data bits being confused with delimiters. These delimiters can also be used to initially synchronize processing. Since Manchester encoding employs a signal transition for every data bit, it is easy for the receiver to maintain synchronization even when long strings of data are transmitted.

Synchronization Characters

Another approach to synchronization is to use a group of bits having a predefined bit configuration as a synchronization character. In this case, a data block is preceded by one or more of these synchronization characters. The receiving device looks for this pattern, and when it finds it, recognizes that data will follow. The receiving device uses the synchronization characters to synchronize its processing with that of the sender. The synchronization characters are discarded before the data is actually processed. Synchronization characters may also be inserted within a message if needed for the receiver to maintain synchronization.

When synchronization characters are used, provision must be made for carrying characters of actual data that may correspond to the same bit configuration as the delimiter character.

SUMMARY

Data signals are carried over a local area network using a physical transmission medium. The transmission media employed in implementing LAN data links include twisted-pair cable, coaxial cable, fiber-optic cable, and wireless transmission. A number of architectures and cabling systems have been developed to facilitate the wiring of buildings to support local area networks.

Transmission can be classified as either baseband or broadband. With baseband transmission, the entire bandwidth is used to transmit a single digital signal, and data is carried on the transmission medium in its original form. With broadband transmission, analog techniques are used in which the available bandwidth may be sliced up into a number of channels. Data is superimposed upon a carrier signal that is modulated by varying either its amplitude, frequency, or phase.

A variety of encoding schemes, such as Manchester encoding, can be used to encode data signals. Depending on the encoding scheme used, synchronization can be accomplished using start/stop bits, delimiters, or synchronization characters.

In addition to the physical transmission media that are used and the types of signals that are employed, LAN technology can be categorized according to the general shape, or topology, of the network and by the way in which computing devices gain access to the transmission medium. Chapter 3 examines network topologies and introduces various methods that LAN data link technology uses to control access to the transmission medium.

Chapter **3**

Medium Access Control

A characteristic common to all local area network data link technology is that there are multiple communicating devices that must share access to a single physical transmission medium. There are several different methods that can be employed to control this sharing, and an important way that different forms of LAN technologies can be classified is by the particular method that is used to control access to the shared medium. Principal issues that concern the designers of LAN technology in choosing a particular medium access control method include the network topology that is employed and whether control to the transmission medium is random, distributed, or centralized.

We begin this chapter by examining the various topologies that networks can use and then look at the different forms of medium access control that are in common use for those different topologies.

NETWORK TOPOLOGIES

The topology of a communication network concerns both the *physical* configuration of the cabling that is used to interconnect communicating systems and the *logical* way in which systems view the structure of the network. There are three principle topologies that are employed by LAN data link technology—*star*, *bus*, and *ring*.

Star Topology

In a *star* configuration, shown in Fig. 3.1, there is a central point to which a group of systems is directly connected. With the star topology, all transmissions from one system to another pass through the central point, which may consist of a device that plays a role in managing and controlling communication.

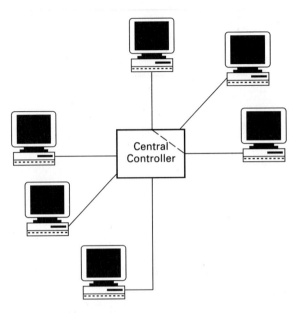

Figure 3.1   Star topology.

The device at the center of the star may act as a switching device. When one system wishes to communicate with another system, the central switch might establish a *circuit*, or dedicated path, between the two systems that wish to communicate. One such path is represented by the red line in Fig. 3.1. Once a circuit is established, data can be exchanged between the two systems as if they were linked by a dedicated point-to-point link.

The star topology has been employed for many years in dial-up telephone systems, in which individual telephone sets are the communicating systems and a *private branch exchange* (PBX) acts as the central controller. Although it is not common, local area networking can be accomplished using PBX-type technology.

Figure 3.2 illustrates a more complex version of the star topology, often called a *snowflake* configuration. Here a system in the basic star configuration is a star itself, with subsidiary systems attached to it.

Bus Topology

With the *bus* topology, shown in Fig. 3.3, each system is directly attached to a common communication channel. Signals that are transmitted over the channel make up messages. As each message passes along the channel, each system receives it. Each system then examines a destination address contained in the message. If the destination address tells a particular system that the message is addressed to it, that system accepts and processes the message. If the message address tells a system that the message is intended for some other system, that system ignores the message.

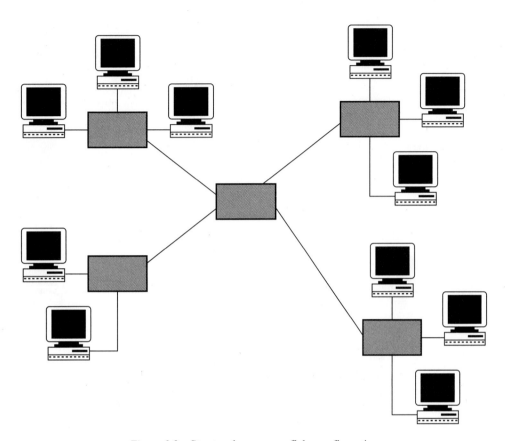

Figure 3.2   Star topology—snowflake configuration.

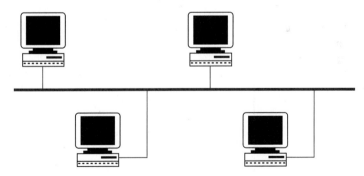

Figure 3.3   Bus topology.

An extension of the bus topology is the tree structure, shown in Fig. 3.4. With the tree topology, the common communication channel takes the form of a cable having mul-

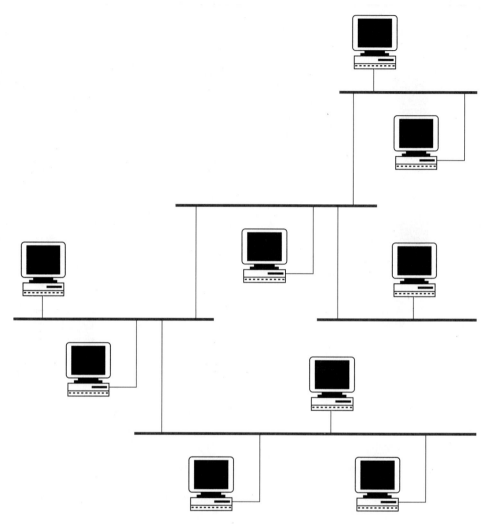

Figure 3.4   Tree topology.

tiple branches, with the systems attached like leaves to the branches. As with a simple bus topology, all systems in the tree structure receive all transmissions.

Bus- and tree-structured networks are examined further in Chapters 10 and 11.

Ring Topology

The *ring* topology is illustrated in Fig. 3.5. Here the cabling forms a loop, with a simple, point-to-point connection attaching each system to the next around the ring. Each system acts as a repeater for all signals it receives and retransmits them to the next system in the ring at their original signal strength.

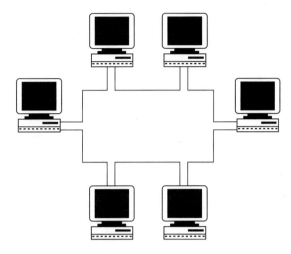

Figure 3.5   Ring topology.

Again, signals that are transmitted around the ring make up messages. All messages transmitted by any system are received by all other systems, but not simultaneously. A message is received by each system in turn. As with the bus topology, a system determines, based on a destination address contained in each message, whether to copy and process a given message. The system that originates a message is generally responsible for determining that a message has made its way all the way around the ring and then not repeating that message, thus removing it from the ring.

Figure 3.6 shows a more complex form of ring topology, where multiple rings are interconnected.

LAN technologies that use a ring topology are examined further in Chapters 13 and 14.

Different Physical and Logical Topologies

Many LAN technologies employ network topologies in which the physical layout of the cabling can be different from the logical topology of the network that systems on the LAN perceive. For example, the most commonly used LAN technologies employ either a bus-structured or a ring-structured logical topology. But most LAN products allow the physical wiring for the local area networks to be laid out in a physical star configuration for ease of installation and maintenance.

Star-Wired Tree Structures

LAN technology that employs a bus- or tree-structured logical topology often employs devices called hubs or repeaters that allow individual systems to be attached to centrally located points. Each hub and its attached systems form an individual star structure. Each hub can be located in a wiring closet or equipment room, and the hubs can be

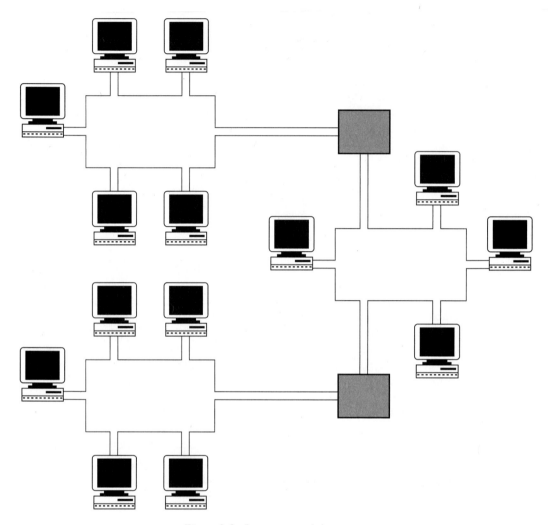

Figure 3.6   Interconnected rings.

interconnected to create a larger tree structure. A simple star-wired tree structure is shown in Fig 3.7.

Star-Wired Ring Structures

LAN technology that employs a ring-structured logical topology also often employs centrally located access units that allow individual systems to be wired using a star configuration. With ring-structured LANs, a single cable supporting two communication paths is generally used to connect each system to the central access unit, as illustrated in Fig. 3.8. The cabling is interconnected so that the systems on the LAN

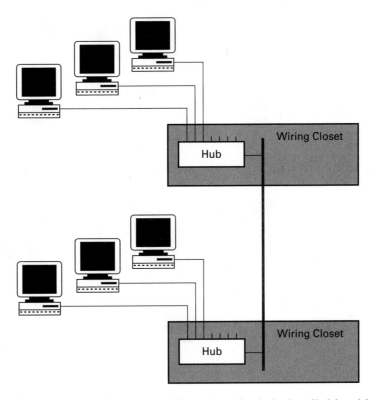

Figure 3.7   Star-wired tree configuration using hubs installed in wiring closets.

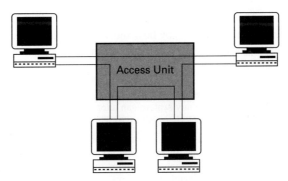

Figure 3.8   Star-wired ring configuration using a central access unit.

perceive a ring structure, but the physical wiring appears as though there is a simple point-to-point connection between each system and the central access unit.

Individual access units can be interconnected to extend the ring structure, as shown in Fig. 3.9.

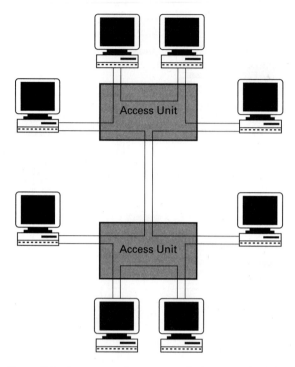

Figure 3.9   Interconnecting access units in a star-wired ring.

MEDIUM ACCESS CONTROL TECHNIQUES

One way in which the various medium access control methods that LAN technology employs can be categorized is by how the medium access control function is managed. A medium access control method can manage access to the transmission medium in one of three ways:

- **Random Management.** With *random* management, explicit permission for transmission is not required, and any system can attempt to transmit at any time. With random control, a system might check the medium to see if it is free before beginning to transmit.

- **Distributed Management.** With *distributed* management, all the systems participate in a distributed algorithm for managing access to the transmission medium. The intent with distributed control is that the systems themselves cooperate to ensure that only one system at a time has the right to transmit.

- **Centralized Management.** With *centralized* management, one system controls the entire network and other systems must receive explicit permission from the controlling system in order to transmit.

In this chapter we will examine each of the above forms of medium access control. Before beginning, however, it is important to point out that there is no one *best* method for handling transmission control. Rather, the various methods each offer different advantages, and the developer of LAN technology must make tradeoffs in choosing a particular form of medium access control to use.

The forms of transmission control that are discussed in this chapter are listed in Box 3.1.

BOX 3.1 Medium access control techniques.

Random Medium Control

- Carrier sense multiple access with collision detection (CSMA/CD)
- Slotted ring
- Register insertion

Distributed Medium Access Control

- Token passing
  —Token ring
  —Token bus
- Carrier sense multiple access with collision avoidance (CSMA/CA)

Centralized Medium Access Control

- Polling
- Circuit switching
- Time division multiple access (TDMA).

Of the techniques listed in Box 3.1, four are of primary importance. The following medium access control methods are employed by the mainstream LAN technologies, introduced in Chapter 1, that are in the most widespread use:

- **Carrier Sense Multiple Access with Collision Detection (CSMA/CD).** The medium access control method used with Ethernet LAN data link technology. (See Chapters 10 and 11)

- **Token Bus.** The medium access control method used with Token Bus and ARCnet LAN data link technologies. (See Chapter 12)

- **Token Ring.** The medium access control method used with Token Ring and Fiber Distributed Data Interface (FDDI) LAN technologies. (See Chapters 13 and 14)

- **Carrier Sense Multiple Access with Collision Avoidance (CSMA/CA).** The medium access control method used with LocalTalk LAN data link technology. (See Chapter 15)

Much mathematical analysis has been done of the various possible types of access control to determine which are the most efficient. The optimum choice varies depending on factors such as the number of systems served, the length and distribution of lengths of the messages, the speed of the channel, and the ratio of propagation time to message transmission time. It was once fashionable to compare one LAN data link technology against another based on the type of medium access control the technology employed. Today, it is clear that all the forms of LAN data link technology that have come into widespread use have proven themselves in actual operation, and the various forms of medium access control they employ, although different, are all efficient and reliable.

We will next briefly describe each of the access control methods listed in Box 3.1.

RANDOM MEDIUM ACCESS CONTROL

With medium access control methods that manage access to the physical transmission medium in a *random* fashion, any system is allowed to transmit whenever the transmission medium is available. The three access control methods discussed next that employ random control are *carrier sense multiple access with collision detection (CSMA/CD)*, *register insertion*, and *slotted ring*.

Carrier Sense Multiple Access With Collision Detection

The *carrier sense multiple access with collision detection* (CSMA/CD) access method has been in use in Ethernet technology for many years and is the most commonly used access method for local area networks that employ a bus or tree topology.

The basic principle involved with CSMA/CD is that before a system transmits, it first *listens* to the transmission medium to determine whether or not another system is currently transmitting a message. The term *carrier sense* indicates that a system listens before it transmits. If the transmission medium is *quiet*, meaning that no other system is transmitting, the system then sends its message.

When a message is transmitted, it travels to all other systems on the network. As the message arrives at each receiving system, that system examines the destination address attached to the message. If the destination address indicates that the message applies to that system, the system receives and processes the message.

With CSMA/CD, it occasionally happens that two (or more) systems send their messages close to simultaneously, resulting in a garbled transmission called a *collision*. All systems on the network, including the transmitting systems, continually listen to the transmission medium and are able to detect that a collision has occurred. Receiving systems ignore the garbled transmission, and the transmitting systems immediately stop transmitting as soon as they detect the collision. Following a collision, each transmitting system waits for a varying period of time and then attempts to transmit again.

A key advantage of the CSMA/CD method is that access to the physical medium is typically very fast as long as traffic is not heavy, since a system can transmit any time the carrier is idle. Under heavier traffic loads, the number of collisions increases and the time spent responding to collisions and retransmitting may cause performance to degrade. However, collisions do not typically cause a significant problem unless traffic is very heavy. Up to about 90 percent utilization of the channel capacity is possible with the CSMA/CD technique.

The technical details concerning the CSMA/CD form of medium access control, as it is used in conjunction with Ethernet technology, are described further in Chapter 10.

Slotted Ring and Register Insertion

Two other access control techniques that use random control have been used with ring-structured LAN technology. However, these methods, described briefly in Box 3.2, are not used with any of today's mainstream LAN technologies.

BOX 3.2   Slotted ring and register insertion medium access control.

Slotted Ring

With the *slotted-ring* technique, the various systems on the ring continuously send several fixed-length transmissions, called *slots,* from one system to the next around the ring. Each slot has a marker at the beginning that indicates whether the slot is empty or contains data. If a system has a message to transmit, it waits for an empty slot, changes the marker, inserts the destination address and as much of the message as will fit in the slot, and transmits the slot to the next system on the ring.

When a slot containing data is received by a system, the system checks the destination address to see if it should copy the message. If so, the system copies the data and then retransmits the slot to the next system on the ring. A system that does not accept the data does not copy it and simply transmits the slot to the next system on the ring. When the message returns to the original sender, the sender removes the message from the ring and transmits an empty slot. With this method, a system must wait until it receives an empty slot before it can transmit a message of its own.

As we have seen, it is the responsibility of the sending system to mark a slot as empty. However, transmission errors may affect a slot so that the sending system no longer recognizes a message, or a failure may make a system unable to perform its function. In order to prevent problems like these from causing a slot to remain marked as full indefinitely, one of the systems on the ring is designated as a *monitor.* The monitor watches for slots that have traversed the entire ring because they have not been reset properly and causes those slots to be removed from the ring.

The slotted ring technique works well for short messages and has the advantage of simplicity, thus making the network interface hardware and software required for each system relatively simple. For long messages that require multiple slots to transmit, the need for addressing and control information in each slot can drive overhead up and make the method less efficient than it is for short messages.

(Continued)

BOX 3.2 *(Continued)*

Register Insertion

With the *register insertion* method, each system has a shift register equal in size to the maximum-length message that is used on the network. Each system also has a buffer of the same size that it uses for storing a message that it wishes to send.

Each system receives each message from the ring and sends it on to the next system. An input pointer initially points to the rightmost position in the shift register. As each bit in the message is received, it is stored in the shift register and the input pointer moves to the left. When enough bits have been received to identify the destination address, the system determines if it needs to copy the message. If not, the system begins sending bits to the next system on the ring. The rightmost bit is sent and the other bits are shifted one to the right. The next incoming bit is then inserted in the spot indicated by the input pointer, which now remains stationary. When the end of the message is reached, bits continue to shift right and the input pointer moves with them.

If during the process of examining the destination address the system recognizes the address in the message as its own address, the system copies the message for processing. The message may be erased from the shift register at this point, and thus removed from the ring, or it may be retransmitted. Retransmission may be necessary if the message is to be processed by multiple systems.

When the system's shift register is empty, the contents of the system's buffer are transferred in parallel to the shift register. Bits are then shifted out to the ring, just as if a message had been received from the ring. When a message is of less than the maximum size, it can be placed in the shift register before the shift register is completely empty. The transmitting system waits until the shift register has a large enough empty portion following the end of a message that it is already sending. The new message then shifts out and is transmitted following the message just received.

With register insertion, a system is allowed to transmit whenever its shift register has enough empty space for the message. This method is very efficient in its use of the transmission medium, since a system may transmit any time the ring is idle at its location. However, since there may be multiple messages on the ring, a message must be positively identified before it can be removed. With this technique, a transmission error that damages the address portion of a message can cause problems with message removal. Various techniques can be used to handle this type of situation.

DISTRIBUTED MEDIUM ACCESS CONTROL

With access control methods that use *distributed* management, all systems on the network cooperate in performing the job of controlling access to the transmission medium. There are two commonly used access control methods that use distributed techniques: *token passing* and *carrier sense multiple access with collision avoidance (CSMA/CA)*.

Token Ring

With networks that employ a ring topology, the most commonly used access method is *token passing*. The Token Ring and FDDI forms of LAN data link technology both use variations of the token-ring form of medium access control.

With a typical token-ring method, a short message, called the *token*, is passed from one system to the next around the ring. If the token is marked as free, a system that receives it can transmit a message. It then marks the token as busy, appends the token to the message, and transmits the message along with the busy token. The message, with the attached busy token, circulates around the ring, passing from system to system.

Each system that receives the message checks the destination address in the message to see if the system should copy and process the message. Whether or not the system copies the message, it transmits the message and the busy token to the next system on the ring. When the message finally reaches the system that originally sent it, that system removes the message from the ring, changes the token back to a free token, and transmits only the free token to the next system on the ring. The free token then circulates around the ring again until another system wishes to transmit.

Error conditions might prevent a sending system from recognizing and being able to remove its message when the message comes back around to the originating system. To handle this, one of the systems on the ring is designated as a monitor. The monitor is responsible for detecting a busy token that is not being reset properly, removing it from the ring, and transmitting a new free token.

With the token-ring approach, each system is always guaranteed a chance to transmit a message within some predetermined period of time. The method allows for different priorities to be assigned to systems on the ring. High priority systems can be given the opportunity to transmit before lower priority systems. A system may also be allowed to send multiple messages while it has the token. In this case, there is usually a time limit on how long a system can continue transmitting new messages. The principle disadvantages of the token-ring technique are the complexity of the algorithm and the overhead involved in token processing and monitoring.

The variation of the token-ring form of medium access control that is used with Token Ring LAN technology is described further in Chapter 13, and the variation used with FDDI LAN technology is described further in Chapter 14.

Token Bus

Token passing is also used in the access control method used by the Token Bus form of LAN technology. With the token-bus method, a token is transmitted from one system to the next. When a system receives the token, it is allowed to transmit messages until a maximum amount of time has been reached. It then transmits the token to the next system. If a system has no messages to transmit it immediately passes the token to the next system.

With token bus, systems are physically connected using a *physical* bus or tree topology. However, the systems use a *logical* ring topology for determining how to pass the token. This is illustrated in Fig. 3.10. The logical ring is generally implemented based

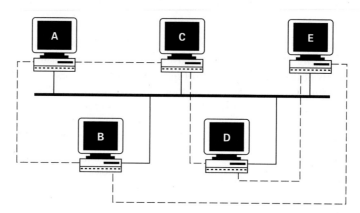

Figure 3.10   Token bus.

on descending system address values. Physically, the systems are attached to the transmission medium in a linear sequence of A, B, C, D, and E. The token, however, may be passed in the sequence shown by the dashed line. It may go from A, to C, to D, to E, to B, and back to A, forming a logical ring. The ring is always passed to the system having the next lowest address until the system having the lowest address on the network receives the token. The token is then passed to the system having the highest network address and the cycle begins again.

As with the token-ring technique, the token-bus method can provide for a high degree of control over each system's access to the transmission medium. Also as with token ring, there is additional complexity. Removing messages from the network is not a problem because messages do not circulate from system to system as they do in a physical ring. However, provision must be made for detecting problems with the token, including loss of the token, duplication of the token, or monopolization of the token by one system. Also, as systems are added to or removed from the network, adjustments must be made to the logical sequence of the token passing to include or remove these systems.

Further details concerning the token-bus forms of medium access control that are used with the Token Bus and ARCnet LAN technologies are included in Chapter 12.

Carrier Sense Multiple Access With Collision Avoidance

Another distributed form of medium access control is called *carrier sense multiple access with collision avoidance* (CSMA/CA). This is the form of medium access control that is used with LocalTalk LAN data link technology. With CSMA/CA, each system *listens* to the carrier while each transmission is in progress. After the transmission ends, each system waits for a specified period of time, based on its relative position in a logical list of systems. If no other system has started transmitting by the time a particular system's waiting time has elapsed, it may begin sending.

Different methods can be used to handle the situation that can occur when the end of the allotted time is reached and no system has a message to send. In one approach, the highest priority system (highest in the list) sends a dummy message, which then triggers another time period where systems have an opportunity to transmit. Another approach allows the systems to enter a free-for-all mode, where any system can transmit, and collision detection techniques are employed to handle conflicting transmissions.

There are also variations related to prioritization. With one variation, the first transmission slot is reserved for the system that has just received a message. This allows the system to send a response and the two systems to maintain an efficient dialog. In another variation, a system that has just transmitted must wait until all the other systems have had an opportunity to transmit before it can transmit again. This ensures that the systems that are lower in the list do have an opportunity to transmit.

The particular form of CSMA/CA medium access control that is used with LocalTalk LAN technology is described further in Chapter 15.

CENTRALIZED MEDIUM ACCESS CONTROL

With centralized control over access to the transmission medium, a single network device controls when other systems on the network can begin transmitting. This form of access control is more commonly used on wide area network data links rather than on local area networks. None of today's mainstream LAN technologies employ centralized medium control.

Typical access control methods that employ a centralized approach include *polling*, *circuit switching*, and *time-division multiple access (TDMA)*. Each of these is briefly described in Box 3.3.

BOX 3.3   Centralized medium access control methods.

Polling

One centralized way of controlling access to a shared transmission medium is through polling. With polling, one system is designated the master system; all other systems are secondary systems. The master system sends a message to each of the secondary systems in turn, notifying the system it has the opportunity to transmit. If the polled secondary system has a message to transmit, it sends the message to the master system, which in turn relays the message to the system or systems indicated by the message's destination address. If a polled system has no message to transmit, it responds negatively to the poll. When the master system completes the polling of one system, it consults a polling list to determine the next secondary system to poll.

Polling is often used on a multipoint wide area networking data link where a computer acting as the master system uses a single circuit to connect to a number of terminals acting as secondary systems.

(Continued)

BOX 3.3 *(Continued)*

The polling method allows for flexibility of control, since a system can be permitted to send multiple messages before the next system is polled. Also, priorities can be assigned to systems, with higher priority systems being polled more frequently than lower priority systems. With polling, the secondary systems have very simple requirements, and their interface to the network can be implemented simply and for a low cost. However, the master system is more complex than secondary systems, and when the master system fails, the entire network fails. Also, messages may need to be sent twice, first to the master system and then to the receiving system, thus requiring more bandwidth than other access control methods.

Circuit Switching

Another centralized control technique, which is well suited for use with a star-structured network, is circuit switching. With circuit switching, a system wishing to begin transmitting requests the establishment of a physical connection, or circuit, with another system. A central controller is responsible for establishing requested circuits. Once a circuit has been established between a pair of systems, the two systems can transmit messages back and forth, with the circuit they are using remaining dedicated to their use. When the two systems finish their dialog, they are disconnected and the circuit is released. This technique is used by private branch exchanges (PBXs) in conventional telephone systems.

The central controller is typically able to support multiple circuits between pairs of systems that can be used simultaneously. If the controller uses digital techniques, there are mechanisms that allow a large number of circuits to share access to the transmission facilities managed by the controller. Transmission access is switched among the different circuits at very high speed relative to the data transmission rates, giving each circuit the appearance of having continuous access.

With circuit switching, as with polling, systems other than the central controller have simpler requirements and can be implemented less expensively. However, there can be higher overhead associated with the establishment and disconnection of circuits, and, again, the entire network goes down if the central controller fails.

Time-Division Multiple Access

Time-division multiple access (TDMA) is a centralized control method that can be used with a bus-structured network. With the TDMA technique, each system on the bus has a specific time slot during which only it can transmit. If a system has nothing to transmit during its time slot, that transmission time goes unused.

The cycle is started by a master system that sends out a short timing message. Each system synchronizes itself with the master system and then transmits when its time interval arrives. If a new system is added to the network, the master system lengthens the total time interval and assigns the new system the time interval at the end of the cycle.

Prioritization can be implemented by assigning priorities to systems and inserting a priority value in the timing message. Only systems with a priority equal to or higher than the

(Continued)

BOX 3.3 *(Continued)*

priority value contained in the timing message participate in the sequence of transmissions following that timing message.

The TDMA technique allows for centralized control over access to the transmission medium, but there may be large amounts of unused transmission capacity if only a few systems have messages to transmit. Also, a system that miscalculates the timing interval, because of some malfunction, may cause interference with another system's transmission. The TDMA method is also vulnerable to master system failures and may require alternate master systems that can be activated if the current master system fails.

ASYNCHRONOUS TRANSFER MODE

Circuit switching is not used in any of the mainstream LAN technologies as a way of controlling access to the transmission medium. However, it is interesting to note that it is likely that circuit switching will play a much more important role in future networking technologies. The *asynchronous transfer mode* (ATM) technology, introduced in Appendix C, uses a form of medium access control that gives any pair of communicating systems the appearance of a dedicated circuit between them.

Asynchronous transfer mode, not yet standardized at the time of writing, has the potential of eliminating the distinctions between wide area networking and local area networking. It provides a single networking technology that provides very high transmission speeds over both short-distance and long-distance transmission facilities.

SUMMARY

The three principle topologies used for local area networks are the bus, ring, and star. Many LAN technologies employ combinations of logical and physical topologies, such as star-wired tree structures and star-wired ring structures.

Control of access to the local area network transmission medium can be random, distributed, or centralized. The four most commonly used methods of medium access control used with today's LAN technology include carrier sense multiple access with collision detection (CSMA/CD), a random form of control on a bus- or tree-structured network; token bus, a token-passing form of distributed control on a bus- or tree-structured network; token ring, a token-passing form of distributed control on a ring-structured network; and carrier-sense multiple access with collision avoidance (CSMA/CA), a form of distributed control on a bus- or tree-structured network.

Asynchronous transfer mode (ATM) uses a high-speed form of circuit switching to provide pairs of systems with the appearance of a dedicated circuit between them. ATM technology has the potential for eliminating the distinctions between local area networking and wide area networking technologies.

Chapter 4 discusses information technology standardization, examines architectures for computer networking, and introduces the international standard *Reference Model for Open Systems Interconnection* (OSI model) on which standards for local area network data links are based.

Chapter **4**

Network Architectures

Part of the power of local area networks comes from their ability to allow a wide variety of different types of devices, from different vendors, to interoperate with one another. Supporting a wide variety of devices, however, can present substantial compatibility problems. For widely varying devices to be linked together, the hardware and software of these devices need to be compatible or else complex interfaces have to be built for meaningful communication to take place. In order to facilitate this compatibility, *network architectures* have been developed that allow complex networks to be built using a variety of equipment.

Before we discuss the nature of network architectures, we will introduce the functions of a computer network by using an analogy to describe the benefits of independent functional layers in complex systems.

HUMAN COMMUNICATION ANALOGY

We can make an analogy between the communication functions performed in a computer network and the functions performed in ordinary human communication. Figure 4.1 shows how we might divide the functions performed during ordinary human communica-

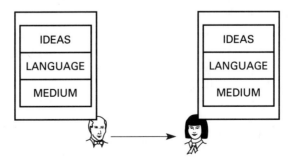

Figure 4.1   Levels of human communication.

tion into three independent layers—a Medium layer, a Language layer, and an Ideas layer.

The Medium Layer

In the *Medium* layer, the two parties must select and use a common communication medium. A typical communication medium used in human communication might be sound waves in air. For example, Fig. 4.2 shows the physical medium used when two parties are involved in a face-to-face conversation.

In human communication, it is important that both parties agree upon and use the same communication medium. For example, if one party is speaking, but the other party is deaf and can only read written words, no communication takes place.

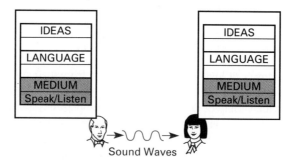

Figure 4.2   Medium level: human speech.

The Language Layer

Once a common medium has been chosen, each party involved in a conversation must use a language understood by the other. If one party speaks only French and the other only English, little communication will take place. Figure 4.3 shows the *Language* layer when two parties are conducting a conversation using the English language.

With no common language, there is no successful dialog, even though both parties may have agreed to use the same communication medium. If I enter a Tokyo hotel and

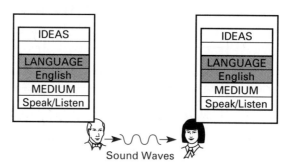

Figure 4.3   Language level: English.

walk up to a clerk who does not speak English, I will not be able to book a room, even though we can both easily hear each other.

The Ideas Layer

We might think of the highest layer in human communication as the *Ideas* layer. In this layer, each person involved in a conversation must have some idea of what the conversation is about and must understand the concepts being discussed. Figure 4.4 shows the Ideas layer when two parties are discussing horticulture.

If an English-speaking gardener enters into a conversation with another English-speaking person and begins a technical discussion on horticulture, little real communication is likely to take place if the second party is a 2-year-old child.

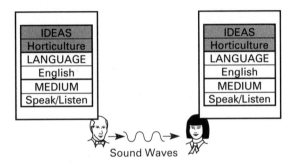

Figure 4.4   Ideas level: horticulture.

Protocols

In each layer in any communication system, a set of precisely defined *rules* must be agreed to and followed by both parties for communication to be successful. The rules governing communication at a given layer are called *protocols*. Each set of protocols can be thought of as a *rule book* that specifies a set of procedures governing communication. Each layer on one side communicates with a complementary layer on the other side using a protocol. Both parties must adhere exactly to the protocol; otherwise, communication is not possible.

Human Communication Protocols

The protocols involved in the Medium layer of human communication are simple and involve mechanical procedures. When two parties agree to use a common communication medium, they must both observe the same rules in using that medium. For example, in polite conversation, both parties should not talk at the same time. If both people speak at once, little communication takes place.

For the Language layer, the protocols involve procedures described by the rules of grammar and syntax for the common language. When two parties agree to use English, they agree to abide by the rules of grammar and syntax that govern the English language.

For the Ideas layer, the protocols involve procedures described by the body of knowledge concerning the subject being discussed. If two parties are discussing horticulture, the protocols might involve technical details concerning botany and agriculture.

Layer Independence

When people communicate, the protocol used for one layer is independent of the protocols used at other layers. For example, a business communication between two people might begin with an exchange of letters and then proceed to a telephone conversation. The two people may then decide that a face-to-face meeting is required to continue the discussion. The rules, or protocols, governing the Ideas and Language layers remain the same each time the discussion is resumed, even though the protocol governing the Medium layer may be different. Similarly, communication in any language—French, Russian, Chinese, Arabic—can take place using a face-to-face conversation at the Medium layer. As long as both parties agree to use the same language, the protocol used for the Language layer does not affect the protocol used at the Medium or Ideas layer.

NETWORK ARCHITECTURES AND PROTOCOLS

A *network architecture* is a comprehensive plan and a set of rules that governs the design and operation of the hardware and software components used to create computer networks. Network architectures define sets of *communication protocols* that govern how communication takes place.

A software system for communicating in a computer network generally conforms to a particular network architecture and uses a particular set of communication protocols. There are a great many different network architectures and systems of communication protocols that are in use today in computer networks.

The following are some of the most commonly used computer networking schemes that are used in conjunction with LAN data links:

- Xerox Networking System
- Novell NetWare
- TCP/IP
- DECnet Phase IV
- DECnet/OSI
- AppleTalk
- NetBIOS
- SNA Subarea Networking
- SNA Advanced Peer-to-Peer Networking

Chapter 17 describes each of the foregoing computer networking systems.

Layered Approach

An important characteristic common to all network architectures is the use of a layered approach. In modern computer networks, data transmission functions are performed by complex hardware and software in the various devices that make up the network. In order to manage this complexity, the functions performed in network devices are divided into independent *functional layers*, analogous to the layers we described in the human communication analogy.

The layered approach offers three key advantages:

- **Ease of Modification.** If a new technology becomes available for use in a particular layer, it can be incorporated without having a major impact on any of the other layers, as long as the interfaces between that layer and the layers above it and below it remain the same.

- **Diversity.** Two devices can be built using completely different hardware and software technologies. They will be able to communicate successfully as long as both devices employ the same communication protocol in a given layer.

- **Transparency.** Through the use of the layering concept, the technical details of the lower layers can be hidden from the higher layers. At the top of the structure, the user perceives an easy-to-use interface to the network, even though the details of the layers below may be quite complex.

Services and Protocols

A network architecture defines the *services* that each layer provides to the layer above it and also the *protocols* that each layer uses to provide those services. Figure 4.5 illustrates a general model for a layered network architecture.

There is an *interface* between each pair of layers, and each functional layer provides a set of *services* to the layer above it. This is represented by the solid vertical arrows in Fig. 4.5. A network architecture also defines *protocols* that are used by corresponding layers in different systems. This is represented by the dashed horizontal arrows in Fig. 4.5. In a communication system, a protocol defines the formats of the data units

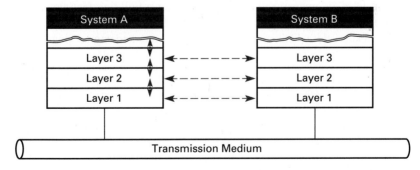

Figure 4.5 A network architecture defines two different types of interfaces between layers.

that are exchanged by two complementary layers in different machines and the rules that govern how they are exchanged.

Goals of a Network Architecture

Network architectures are important to both users and vendors. An architecture must provide users with a variety of choices in the configuration of networks, and it must allow them to change a configuration with relative ease as their systems evolve. It should provide the precise coordination between intelligent machines required if the advantages of networks are to be realized.

For providers of networking products and services, network architectures should permit mass production of hardware or software building blocks that can be used in a variety of different networks. Network architectures also provide standards and definitions that facilitate the development of new devices and software that will be compatible with existing systems. These new products can then be integrated into existing networks without the need for costly interfaces and program modifications.

The Nature of Architecture

Although network architectures provide rules for the development of new products, these rules can change. This is because the term *architecture* in the computer industry often implies an overall scheme or plan that may be evolving. An architecture defines an overall framework that permits evolution and change to support new technologies. An architecture should also define sufficient detail to guide implementors in creating products that will fully conform to the architecture and, therefore, that will interoperate with all other implementations of the architecture. As one network architect has said

> An architecture must be always complete, but it is never finished. It must provide a framework that permits change.

A good architecture should relate primarily to the needs of users rather than to enthusiasms for particular techniques. A well-architected house reflects the desired lifestyle of its owners rather than exploiting a building technique that is currently in vogue. Fred Brooks, author of *The Mythical Man-Month*, defined architecture in a way that makes a clear distinction between architecture and engineering:

> By the *architecture* of a system, I mean the complete and detailed specification of the user interface. For a computer this is the programming manual. For a compiler it is the language manual. . . . For the entire system it is the union of the manuals the user must consult to do his entire job.

> The architect of a system, like the architect of a building, is the user's agent. It is his job to bring professional and technical knowledge to bear in the unalloyed interest of the user, as opposed to the interests of the salesman, the fabricator, etc.*

*Frederick P. Brooks, Jr., *The Mythical Man-Month: Essays on Software Engineering* (Reading, MA: Addison-Wesley, 1982), p. 45.

STANDARDS ORGANIZATIONS

Many of today's network architectures and computer networking systems have been developed by independent hardware and software vendors. However, it is a major goal of today's network architecture development to allow diverse equipment from many different vendors to be interconnected using standard interfaces and protocols. Because of this, widely accepted standards will play an increasingly important role in network architecture development.

A number of standards organizations around the world are actively involved in developing standards and architectures for data communication and computer networking. Three important standards organizations that are playing important roles in the standardization of local area network technologies are the International Organization for Standardization (ISO), the Institute of Electrical and Electronic Engineers (IEEE), and the American National Standards Institute (ANSI).

International Organization for Standardization

The *International Organization for Standardization* (ISO) is the largest standards organization in the world.* ISO produces large numbers of standards on nearly every subject, from humane animal traps to screw threads. It is also the dominant information technology standardization organization in the world. The members of ISO are individual national standards organizations. Only national positions—positions representing an entire country—are discussed in ISO. The ISO member organization from the United States is the *American National Standards Institute* (ANSI); all major industrialized countries have a similar standards organization that represents its national interests in ISO. ISO technical meetings take place at various locations around the world.

The Secretariat of ISO, located in Geneva, Switzerland, is the organization charged with running the day-to-day affairs of ISO, including keeping track of its numerous Technical Committees (TCs) and publishing the standards the Technical Committees produce. The Technical Committees, which not only create the standards but also determine what standards to produce, are composed of thousands of volunteers from computer manufacturers, suppliers of communication products, major computer users, governments, and consulting organizations. To participate, these delegates operate under the aegis of the national body. So a delegate from the United States not only brings technical expertise to the committee but also represents his or her sponsoring organization, ANSI, and the United States itself. A TC is ordinarily divided into Subcommittees (SCs) and Working Groups (WGs), which write the standards. The standards then receive the approval of the Technical Committee as a whole before they finally become accepted as international standards.

---

*ISO is an acronym whose letters do not match up with its spelled out name. This is because the acronym is based on the "official" name of the organization, which is in the French language. We are using the English translation of the French name as it appears in translated standards documents. Another example of such an acronym is CCITT, which is the acronym for International Telegraph and Telephone Consultative Committee.

Many important standards for local area network technology that have been developed by other organizations, such as IEEE and ANSI have been adopted by ISO as international standards.

Institute of Electrical and Electronic Engineers

The *Institute of Electrical and Electronic Engineers* (IEEE) is a professional society whose members are individual engineers rather than companies. The IEEE operates under ANSI guidelines when it develops standards and ordinarily concentrates on product standards.

The IEEE Computer Society Local Network Committee (Project 802) has focused on standards related to local area networks and has produced a set of LAN standards. The IEEE LAN standards have been accepted by ISO as international standards and are published by ISO as well. ANSI standards for local area networks also conform to the IEEE Project 802 LAN architecture. The IEEE Project 802 standards are described in detail in the chapters in Parts II and III.

American National Standards Institute

Virtually every country in the world has a national standards organization responsible for publishing standards to guide that nation's industries. In the United States, this organization is the *American National Standards Institute* (ANSI). ANSI is a nonprofit organization that writes the rules for standards bodies to follow and publishes standards produced under its rules of consensus. ANSI accredits standards committees to write standards in areas of their expertise. The major accredited standards committees (ASCs) in the information technology arena are as follows:

- **JTC1 TAG.** This is the U.S. technical advisory group (TAG) for the ISO/IEC JTC1. This group provides U.S. positions on JTC1 standards and is the single interface to ISO/IEC JTC1 in the United States.

- **ASC X3.** This committee produces approximately 90 percent of the standards for U.S. information technology and provides the technical expertise for a majority of U.S. technical advisory groups to the subcommittees and working groups in ISO/IEC JTC1. A subcommittee of ANSI X3 is responsible for standardizing the Fiber Distributed Data Interface (FDDI) LAN data link technology described in Chapter 14.

- **ASC T1.** This group is the voluntary standards-making body for the U.S. telecommunications industry and sets U.S. national telecommunications standards. T1 helps the State Department with CCITT positions.

- **ASC X12.** This group is responsible for standards relating to electronic data interchange (EDI) in the United States. It acts to set national positions for the United Nations EDI-FACT group, which establishes EDI standards worldwide.

ANSI has a small secretariat located in New York City whose function is organizational and administrative rather than technical. ANSI is not a government organization; it is funded by its members and through the sale of standards. ANSI standards can be obtained directly from ANSI or from Global Engineering Documents.

National standards organizations from other countries include

- **France.** Association Française de Normalisation (AFNOR)
- **United Kingdom.** British Standards Institute (BSI)
- **Canada.** Canadian Standards Association (CSA)
- **Germany.** Deutsches Institut für Normung e.V. (DIN)
- **Japan.** Japanese Industrial Standards Committee (JISC)

These standards organizations have the same general role and organization as ANSI and provide a discussion forum for individuals. Some of those individuals then participate in international meetings and represent the agreed upon views of their countries. It is the national bodies that vote in the formal approval process for standards.

Other important standards organizations are described briefly in Box 4.1. Some important terms relevant to information systems standardization are defined in Box 4.2.

BOX 4.1   Other standards organizations.

- **International Electrotechnical Commission (IEC).** The International Electrotechnical Commission (IEC) is closely associated with ISO. IEC has a role similar to that of ISO but is restricted to electrical and electronic matters. There is an agreement between ISO and IEC to ensure that their work does not overlap. In the field of information technology standards, IEC's role is limited to physical aspects, such as electrical safety. ISO and IEC have recently merged their Technical Committees working on information technology into a single organization, called ISO/IEC Joint Technical Committee 1 (JTC1), to ensure and improve continued close cooperation. JTC1 is the ISO/IEC technical committee responsible for a particularly important framework for a computer network architecture called the *Reference Model for Open Systems Interconnection* or the *OSI model,* which we describe later in this chapter.

- **International Telegraph and Telephone Consultative Committee (CCITT).** The International Telegraph and Telephone Consultative Committee (CCITT) is the leading organization involved in the development of standards relating to telephone and other telecommunications services. CCITT is a part of the International Telecommunications Union (ITU), which in turn is a body of the United Nations. The delegation to the ITU from the United States is the Department of State. In other countries, the ITU delegation is often the governmentally controlled Postal, Telephone, and Telegraph (PTT) organization. CCITT deals with standards for interconnecting the world's telephone networks and for the signaling systems used by modems in sending computer data over telephone lines. The principal contributors to CCITT are individuals representing the public and private telecommunications organizations, although nonvoting memberships are also open to

---

(Continued)

BOX 4.1   *(Continued)*

industrial organizations. CCITT maintains a secretariat in Geneva, where most of the meetings take place. ISO, IEC, and CCITT cooperate quite closely. ISO and CCITT, in particular, have a strong interest in aligning their standards and thus try not to duplicate work between them. Standards of mutual interest typically are developed in one organization and then published by both. The technical people participating in committees of ISO are very often the same people on CCITT committees, and the technical development activities associated with information systems standardization are often undertaken jointly by ISO and CCITT.

- **European Computer Manufacturers Association (ECMA).** ECMA was originally formed by a group of European companies. Since then, its membership has grown to become international and includes representatives from such organizations as IBM, Digital, AT&T, British Telecom, and Toshiba. ECMA is considered a regional standards organization and develops information technology standards for the European region. ECMA standards are often forwarded to ISO/IEC JTC1 for development as international standards. Such cooperation between organizations can result in a faster standards development process, since consensus has already been demonstrated. ECMA has a small secretariat in Geneva, and its members meet in various places throughout Europe.

- **Comité Européan de Normalization (CEN) and Comité Européan de Normalisation dans le domain Electrique (CENELEC).** CEN and its associated organization CENELEC have a relationship similar to that between ISO and IEC. They are concerned with the adoption of standards by the countries of the European Economic Community (EEC) and other European countries. Standards adopted by CEN/CENELEC are called European Norms (ENs) and are binding for procurement purposes on the CEN's member countries. CEN normally does not develop its own standards but instead relies heavily on standards developed by other organizations, especially ISO. Where there is no ISO or IEC standard, however, CEN will develop its own standard and forward it to ISO for development as an international standard.

- **National Institute for Science and Technology (NIST).** NIST (formerly known as the National Bureau of Standards) is a U.S. government organization. ISO standards often cover broad ranges of function and allow many choices to be made by individual implementors. The NIST has taken a leadership role in creating *profiles* that define preferred groups of choices from among the many options documented in ISO standards. Initially this was done in an informal workshop that developed *implementors agreements*. As the importance of these profiles has increased and other organizations have started similar work internationally, the NIST workshop has become more formally organized. NIST is one of the three major international contributors to the development of Internationally Standardized Profiles (ISPs), which are the profiles formally ratified by ISO.

- **European Workshop on Open Systems (EWOS).** EWOS has the same role in Europe as the NIST workshop has in the United States. EWOS was started primarily by members of SPAG (see below) to ensure that Europe had a voice in the development of profiles. It also serves as the technical committee to support the technical activity of CEN. EWOS and NIST work closely together to achieve and maintain harmonization of their profiles. EWOS is located in Brussels.

- **Promotion of OSI/Asia and Oceania Workshop (POSI/AOW).** AOW is another organization that contributes to the international adoption of profiles. POSI is a Japanese

BOX 4.1 *(Continued)*

organization concerned with promoting the adoption of ISO standards for the OSI model, while AOW is an open workshop that includes Australia and other Pacific countries as well as Japan.

- **Corporation for Open Systems (COS).** COS was initiated as a consortium of computer manufacturers and others to encourage the adoption of ISO information systems standards. It has initially directed its efforts toward the development of testing procedures to allow vendors to demonstrate conformance to ISO standards. COS operates as a nonprofit organization funded by its members. It does not produce standards nor does it contribute to the development of standards. COS is located in McLean, VA.

- **Standards Promotion and Application Group (SPAG).** SPAG was initially a private consortium of European companies, set up with objectives similar to those of the COS. Like COS, it has now directed its efforts primarily toward the development of testing procedures, and it cooperates closely with COS in that regard. Membership in SPAG is now open, and many U.S. companies are members.

- **Electrical Industries Association (EIA).** EIA is an association of companies involved in electrical and related industries. EIA undertakes some standardization projects and operates in that capacity as an accredited organization (AO) under the rules of consensus standards formulated by ANSI. The standards developed by the EIA are concerned primarily with physical communication interfaces and electrical signaling. A well-known EIA standard is EIA-232-D, which documents the way in which a terminal or computer is attached to a modem.

- **Conference of European PTTs (CEPT).** CEPT was established by the European PTTs primarily to develop technical standards that could be used in Europe prior to the development of corresponding CCITT standards. With the establishment of ETSI (see below), CEPT remains a closed forum that is concerned mainly with marketing and lobbying.

- **European Telecommunications Standards Institute (ETSI).** ETSI was established by the European Economic Commission to formalize many of the activities formerly undertaken by CEPT. Membership is open to suppliers of telecommunications equipment and services, PTTs, and other industrial organizations, with formal voting on a national basis. ETSI develops European telecommunications standards (ETSs). Some of these are intended as a basis for the provision of services and as a foundation for CCITT work, while others are oriented toward permission to connect testing for the attachment of equipment to public networks. ETSI is based in Sophie Antipolis, France. It has its own permanent technical staff and depends on the participation of its members.

- **Open Systems Foundation (OSF).** OSF is a nonprofit organization established by a number of computer manufacturers to develop a common foundation for open computing. It is not directly concerned with standards but rather with the development of an agreed collection of software around a UNIX-like operating system kernel. OSF has its own permanent technical staff and depends on the participation of its members.

- **X/Open.** X/Open was set up by European computer manufacturers to develop a consistent UNIX-like suite of application programming interfaces to permit application portability. Membership is open and worldwide.

BOX 4.2   Other standards terminology.

- **Manufacturing Automation Protocol (MAP).** MAP is a project started in the United States by General Motors to develop a single standard for communication between devices in a factory automation environment. Its work has been based on U.S. national and ISO standards and also defines additional standards specific to factory automation applications.

- **Technical and Office Protocol (TOP).** TOP is a complementary project to MAP started by Boeing to extend the applicability of MAP into other environments, such as office information systems and computer-aided design.

- **Government Open Systems Interconnection Profile (GOSIP).** GOSIP is a name for procurement-oriented standard profiles specifying how ISO standards will be used for U.S. government computing. The acronym GOSIP has been adopted by other countries to describe their own government procurement specifications.

- **European Procurement Handbook for Open Systems (EPHOS).** EPHOS is a project similar to GOSIP for government computing throughout Europe.

- **Open Distributed Processing (ODP).** ODP is a project started within ISO to develop standards for a heterogeneous distributed computing environment. It is defining an overall reference model for distributed computing that goes beyond the OSI model.

- **POSIX.** POSIX is a standard developed by IEEE under its Project 1003 that defines a UNIX-like interface to basic operating system functions to provide application portability.

OSI REFERENCE MODEL

During the time that today's network architectures and communication protocols were being developed, an ambitious project was underway in ISO to develop a single international standard set of communication protocols that could be used in a communication network. By 1984, ISO had defined an overall model of computer communication called the *Reference Model for Open Systems Interconnection*, or *OSI model*. The OSI model, described in international standard ISO 7498, documents a generalized model of system interconnection.

Purpose of the OSI Model

The OSI model is designed to provide a common basis for the coordination of standards development for the purpose of interconnecting *open systems*. The term *open* in this context means systems open to one another by virtue of their mutual use of applicable standards.

The OSI model describes how machines can communicate with one another in a standardized and highly flexible way by defining the functional layers that should be incorporated into each communicating machine. The OSI model does not define the networking software itself, nor does it define detailed standards for that software; it simply defines the broad categories of function each layer should perform.

The OSI Network Architecture

ISO has also developed a comprehensive set of standards for the various layers of the OSI model. These standards together make up the *OSI architecture* for computer networking.

Currently, the standards making up the OSI architecture are not widely implemented in commercial products for computer networking. However, the OSI model is still important. The concepts and terminology associated with the OSI model have become widely accepted as a basis for discussing and describing network architectures. The OSI model is often used in categorizing the various communication protocols that are in common use today and in comparing one network architecture with another.

The remainder of this chapter introduces the seven functional layers defined by the OSI model.

OSI MODEL FUNCTIONAL LAYERS

The OSI model defines the seven functional layers shown in Fig. 4.6. Each layer performs a different set of functions, and the intent was to make each layer as independent as possible from all the others. The following sections briefly describe each of the seven layers of the OSI model, working from the bottom up.

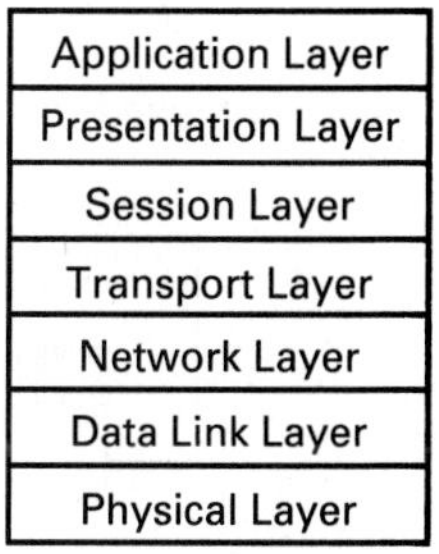

Application Layer
Presentation Layer
Session Layer
Transport Layer
Network Layer
Data Link Layer
Physical Layer

Figure 4.6   OSI model functional layers.

The Physical Layer

The *Physical* layer is responsible for the actual transmission of a bit stream across a physical circuit. It allows signals, such as electrical signals, optical signals, or radio signals, to be exchanged among communicating machines. The Physical layer, shown in Fig. 4.7, typically consists of hardware permanently installed in the communicating devices. The Physical layer also addresses the cables, connectors, modems, and other devices used to permit machines to physically communicate.

Physical layer mechanisms in each of the communicating machines typically control the generation and detection of signals that are interpreted as 0 bits and 1 bits. The Physical layer does not assign any significance to the bits. For example, it is not concerned with how many bits make up each unit of data, nor is it concerned with the meaning of the data being transmitted. In the Physical layer, the sender simply transmits a signal and the receiver detects it.

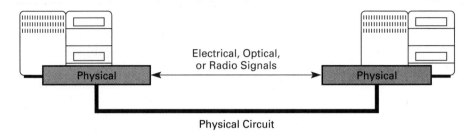

Figure 4.7   The Physical layer is concerned with sending and receiving signals.

The Data Link Layer

The *Data Link* layer is responsible for providing data transmission over a single connection from one system to another. Control mechanisms in the *Data Link* layer handle the transmission of data units, often called *frames*, over a physical circuit. Functions operating in the Data Link layer allow data to be transmitted, in a relatively error-free fashion, over a sometimes error-prone physical circuit, as illustrated in Fig. 4.8. This layer is concerned with how bits are grouped into frames and performs synchronization functions with respect to failures occurring in the Physical layer. The Data Link layer implements error-detection mechanisms that identify transmission errors. With some types of data links, the Data Link layer may also perform procedures for flow control, frame sequencing, and recovery from transmission errors.

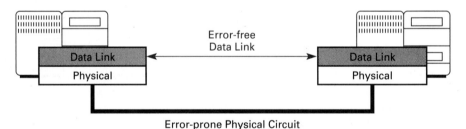

Figure 4.8   The Data Link layer is responsible for the transmission of data units over a physical circuit.

The Network Layer

The *Network* layer is concerned with making routing decisions and relaying data from one device to another through the network. The OSI model classifies each system in the network as one of two types—*end systems* act as the source or the final destination of data, and *intermediate systems* perform routing and relaying functions, as shown in Fig. 4.9.

The facilities provided by the Network layer supply a service that higher layers employ for moving data units, often called *packets*, from one end system to another, where the packets may flow through any number of intermediate systems.

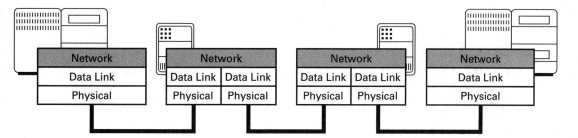

Figure 4.9 The Network layer allows communication across multiple data links.

End systems generally implement all seven layers of the OSI model, allowing application programs to exchange information with each other. It is possible for intermediate systems performing *only* routing and relaying functions to implement only the bottom three layers of the OSI model.

In a complex network, the path between any two systems may at one instant be via a number of data links. The application programs running in two end systems that wish to communicate should not need to be concerned with the route packets take nor with how many data links they must cross. The Network layer functions operating in end systems and in intermediate systems together handle these routing and relaying functions.

Whereas the Data Link layer provides for the transmission of frames between *adjacent* systems across a single data link, the Network layer provides for the much more complex task of transmitting packets between *any* two end systems in the network, regardless of how many data links may need to be traversed.

The Transport Layer

The Transport layer builds on the services of the Network layer and the layers below it to form the uppermost layer of a reliable end-to-end data transport service. The Transport layer hides from the higher layers all the details concerning the actual moving of packets and frames from one computer to another and shields network users from the complexities of network operation.

The lowest three layers of the OSI model implement a common physical network many machines can share independently of one another, just as many independent users share the postal service. It is possible for the postal service to occasionally lose a letter. To detect the loss of a letter, two users of the postal service might apply their own end-to-end controls, such as sequentially numbering their letters. The functions performed in the Transport layer can include similar end-to-end integrity controls to recover from lost, out-of-sequence, or duplicate messages.

Transport layer functions handle addressing of the processes, such as application programs, that use the network for communication. The Transport layer can also control the rate at which messages flow through the network to prevent and control congestion. Whereas the Network layer is concerned with the interface between network systems and

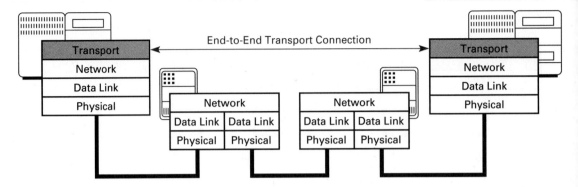

Figure 4.10   The Transport layer is the lowest layer required *only* in the computers that are communicating.

operates in end systems and intermediate systems, the Transport layer provides an end-to-end service that programs can use for moving data back and forth between them. The Transport layer, shown in Fig. 4.10, is the lowest layer required *only* in the computers running the programs that use the network for communication.

The Session Layer

There is a fundamental difference in orientation between the bottom four layers and the top three layers, as illustrated in Fig. 4.11. The bottom four layers are concerned more with the network itself and provide a general data transport service useful to any application. The top three layers are more concerned with services that are oriented to the application programs themselves.

The Session layer is the lowest of the layers that are associated with the application programs, as shown in Fig. 4.12. It is responsible for organizing the dialog between two application programs and for managing the data exchanges between them. To do this, the Session layer imposes a structure on the interaction between two communicating programs.

The Session layer defines three types of dialogs: two-way simultaneous interaction, where both programs can send and receive concurrently; two-way alternate interaction, where the programs take turns sending and receiving; and one-way interaction, where one

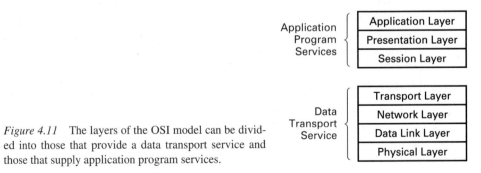

Figure 4.11   The layers of the OSI model can be divided into those that provide a data transport service and those that supply application program services.

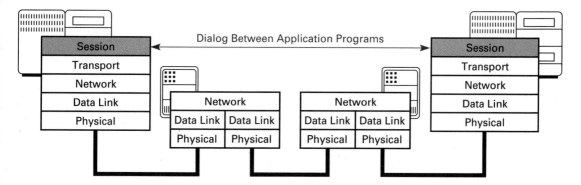

Figure 4.12 The Session layer organizes the dialog between two application programs.

program sends and the other only receives. In addition to organizing the dialog, Session layer services include establishing synchronization points within the dialog, allowing a dialog to be interrupted, and resuming a dialog from a synchronization point.

The Presentation Layer

The five layers below the Presentation layer are all concerned with the orderly movement of a stream of bits from one program to another. The Presentation layer, shown in Fig. 4.13, is the lowest layer interested in the *meaning* of those bits and deals with preserving the *information content* of data transmitted over the network.

The Presentation layer is concerned with three types of *data syntax* that can be used for describing and representing data:

- **Abstract Syntax.** An *abstract syntax* consists of a formal definition of the information content of the data two programs exchange. An abstract syntax is concerned only with information content and not with how that information content is represented in a com-

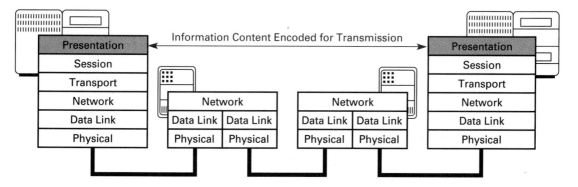

Figure 4.13 The Presentation layer is responsible for preserving the information content of the data transmitted over the network.

puter or how it is encoded for transmission. For example, an abstract syntax might define a data type called AccountNumber, values of which consist of integers. ISO 8824 *Abstract Syntax Notation One* (ASN.1) defines an international standard notation that is often used in practice to define abstract syntaxes in the OSI environment.

- **Transfer Syntax.** A *transfer syntax* defines how the information content of data is encoded for transmission over the network. A value of the AccountNumber type might be transferred over the network using some form of encoding scheme that identifies the value as being of the AccountNumber type, specifies that it consists of an integer, and encodes that integer's value using a minimum number of bits.

- **Local Concrete Syntax.** A *local concrete syntax* defines how the information content of data is actually represented in a computing system. Two communicating systems might use different local concrete syntaxes. For example, one system might represent the integers in an account number in the form of a binary number using two's complement notation; another system might use a string of decimal digits. The OSI model is not concerned with the local concrete syntax, and programs are free to represent data internally in any desired way.

The OSI model defines two major functions for the Presentation layer. First, the Presentation layer in the two communicating systems must negotiate a common transfer syntax to be used to transfer the messages defined by a particular abstract syntax. Second, the Presentation layer must ensure that one system does not need to care what local concrete syntax the other system is using. If the local concrete syntaxes in the two communicating systems are different, an implementation of the Presentation layer is responsible for transforming from the local concrete syntax to the transfer syntax in the sending system and from the transfer syntax to the local concrete syntax in the receiving system.

If both computers are running COBOL programs in IBM mainframes, the Presentation layer has little to do, since both programs use the same local concrete syntax. However, if a FORTRAN program running in a VAX is communicating with a COBOL program running in an IBM mainframe, the Presentation layer becomes more important. The FORTRAN program may represent an integer using a 32-bit binary number and the COBOL program may represent an integer using packed-decimal notation. The Presentation layer performs the necessary conversions that allow each program to work with data in its own preferred format without having to be aware of the data formats that its partner uses.

The Application Layer

The topmost layer, the one user processes plug into, is the Application layer, shown in Fig. 4.14. The Application layer is concerned with high-level functions that provide support to the application programs using the network for communication. The Application layer provides a means for application programs to access the system interconnection facilities to exchange information. It provides all functions related to communication between systems that are not provided by the lower layers.

The *Application* layer provides a means for application programs to exchange information with each other. Communication services provided by the Application layer hide the complexity of the layers below from the communicating programs. As far as the Application layer is concerned, a program running in one computer sends a message, and a program running in some other computer receives it. The Application layer is not con-

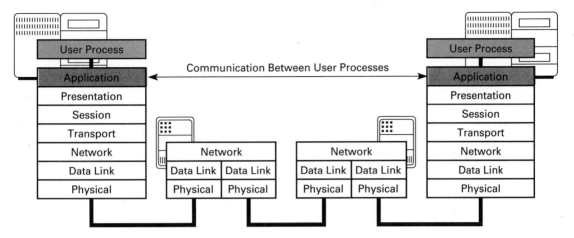

Figure 4.14   The Application layer is the topmost layer into which user processes plug.

cerned with any of the details related to how the message gets from the source computer to the destination computer.

The Application layer is more open-ended than the layers below. Due to the wide variety of applications that will ultimately use networks for communication, many standards for the Application layer are likely to be developed.

SUMMARY

Network architectures define plans and rules for constructing computer networks in which the functions performed in networked devices are divided into independent functional layers. A layered approach to computer networking provides for ease of modification, diversity, and transparency.

A number of standards organizations around the world develop standards and architectures for computer communication, with the International Organization for Standardization (ISO), the Institute of Electrical and Electronic Engineers (IEEE), and the American National Standards Institute (ANSI) playing a leadership role in local area networking standardization.

The Reference Model for Open Systems Interconnection (OSI Model) provides a common basis for the coordination of standards development for interconnecting computer systems. The OSI model defines seven functional layers that can be implemented in communicating systems—the Physical layer, the Data Link layer, the Network layer, the Transport layer, the Session layer, the Presentation layer, and the Application layer.

A number of different software subsystems have been developed for computer networking. Chapter 5 introduces the general functions of the networking software used with local area networks.

Chapter **5**

Networking Software

In the previous three chapters, we introduced the technical aspects of LAN data link technology and discussed the nature of the network architectures to which communicating systems conform. These issues are not ordinarily of great concern to the typical user of a computing system attached to a local area network. The end user typically only perceives the high-level networking software that provides a set of useful services. The networking software takes advantage of the facilities that local area network data links provide for communication between systems and typically implements a particular network architecture. This chapter introduces the capabilities of the networking software that users employ.

As we introduced in Chapter 1, a typical local area network consists of a number of hardware and software components. Box 5.1 reviews the components of a typical local area network.

NETWORKING SOFTWARE

The first four components listed in Box 5.1 make up the LAN physical data link technology that we introduced in Chapters 2 and 3. We describe LAN data link technology further in the chapters in Parts II and III. The final component listed in Box 5.1 is the networking software that provides services to end users. The functions of high-level networking software is introduced in this chapter and is described further in Parts IV and V.

A variety of different types of software subsystems are used in computer networking. LAN networking support is typically provided by two software components:

- **High-Level Networking Software.** High-level networking software provides end-user-oriented functions that are associated with the Application layer through the Network layer of the OSI model. This is the software that the end user perceives. Some types of high-level networking software subsystems, especially in the personal computer environment, are called *network operating systems.*

BOX 5.1   Local area network components.

- **Computing Devices.** A local area network is typically used to interconnect general-purpose computing devices, such as personal computers or workstations. Special-purpose devices, such as intelligent printers and devices used to interconnect individual LANs, may also be directly attached to a LAN.

- **Network Interface Cards.** A *network interface card* (NIC) is typically installed in each computing device that is directly attached to the LAN. A NIC performs the hardware functions that are required to provide a computing device with physical communication capabilities.

- **Cabling Systems.** A LAN cabling system includes the cable used to interconnect the NICs installed in the networked computing devices. Various types of electrical cable or fiber-optic cable, or wireless communication mechanisms, are used to implement LANs. The cabling system also typically includes *attachment units* that allow the devices to attach to the cable.

- **Access Units or Concentrators.** Some local area network implementations use devices called *access units, concentrators,* or *hubs* that allow multiple network devices to be connected to the LAN cabling system through a central point.

- **Networking Software.** Network interface cards (NICs) perform low-level functions that allow physical communication to take place between interconnected devices. High-level functions that end users employ for doing useful work are generally handled by networking software that accesses a NIC on behalf of an end user.

- **Network Driver Software.** Network driver software provides an interface between the high-level networking software and the particular network interface card (NIC) that is being used for physical LAN communication. Like the NIC itself, the driver software is generally transparent to the end user.

High-level networking software is provided by a number of networking product vendors. A particular networking software subsystem often supports a variety of different types of network drivers and different forms of LAN technology. Box 5.2 further describes some of the commonly used high-level networking software systems that we introduced in Chapter 1.

NETWORKING ENVIRONMENTS

Networking software systems can be used to construct either a peer-to-peer or a server-based environment. Both types of environments can be used to implement the client-server computing paradigm.

Peer-to-Peer Environments

In a *peer-to-peer* environment, any system in the network can make resources under its control available for use by other systems. All systems operate as peers and can all pro-

BOX 5.2   Networking software.

- **NetWare.** *NetWare* is a family of network operating system software that is marketed by Novell. At the time of writing, NetWare is by far the most popular of all networking software used in the personal computer environment. NetWare implements a client-server architecture in which NetWare *server* software typically runs in one or more dedicated server systems. NetWare *client* software runs in the individual desktop systems that access the NetWare servers. A NetWare server provides file and print sharing facilities as well as a broad range of other networking services. NetWare is described further in Chapters 17 and 22.

- **LAN Manager and LAN Server.** *LAN Manager* and *LAN Server* refer to a family of network operating systems codeveloped by Microsoft and IBM. LAN Manager refers to the Microsoft products and LAN Server refers to the IBM products. Like NetWare, LAN Manager and LAN Server software runs on a dedicated server system and allows desktop client systems to access server facilities, such as file and print sharing. Among the interfaces that LAN Manager and LAN Server implement are the *NetBIOS, Server Message Block* (SMB), and *Named Pipes* interfaces, which are three widely implemented interfaces for requesting networking services. Many other network operating systems, including NetWare, also implement the interfaces codeveloped by Microsoft and IBM. LAN Manager and LAN Server, and some of the interfaces they implement, are described further in Chapters 17 and 21.

- **VINES.** *VINES* is a family of network operating system software that is marketed by Banyan Systems. It provides many of the same facilities as NetWare, LAN Server, and LAN Manager.

- **LANtastic.** *LANtastic* is a family of network operating systems for the personal computer environment that is marketed by Artisoft. LANtastic server software can be run on personal computers that can also be used as ordinary desktop systems. LANtastic networking software consumes small amounts of memory and processor resources and is well suited for use in smaller networks.

- **TCP/IP.** *TCP/IP,* which stands for *Transmission Control Protocol/Internet Protocol,* refers to a set of communication protocols that grew out of a research project that was funded by the United States Department of Defense. The TCP/IP protocols are widely implemented on many different types of computers and are used in a great number of computer networks. A TCP/IP computer network is typically called a *TCP/IP internet.* The largest TCP/IP internet is called the *Worldwide Internet,* or simply the *Internet.* Today's Worldwide Internet interconnects thousands of networks containing hundreds of thousands of computers in universities, national laboratories, and commercial organizations. The TCP/IP networking scheme implements a peer-to-peer client-server architecture. Any computing system in the network can run TCP/IP server software and can provide services to any other computing system that runs complementary TCP/IP client software. Many network operating systems, such as NetWare, support the TCP/IP communication protocols. TCP/IP is described further in Chapters 17 and 23.

- **AppleTalk.** *AppleTalk* is Apple Computer's networking scheme that has been used for many years to network Apple equipment. Apple system software contains integrated AppleTalk networking support that allows Apple computing systems to participate in peer-to-peer computer networks and to also access the services of dedicated AppleTalk

(Continued)

BOX 5.2   *(Continued)*

servers. NICs and networking software are available for a variety of other types of computing systems, including personal computers and UNIX workstations, that allow them to participate in AppleTalk networks. AppleTalk is described further in Chapters 17 and 24.

- **DECnet.** *DECnet* is a term that Digital Equipment Corporation uses to refer to its proprietary networking products. DECnet networking facilities are widely used in the DEC minicomputer and workstation environments. A DECnet network typically consists of a wide area network made up of interconnected LAN data links. DECnet is described further in Chapter 17.

- **PATHWORKS.** *PATHWORKS* is a family of personal computer network operating system software marketed by Digital Equipment Corporation. The original goal of PATHWORKS was to provide personal computers with access to DECnet networking capabilities. However, PATHWORKS now supports access to other forms of networking as well, and a PATHWORKS client can interoperate with servers running other types of networking software, including NetWare, LAN Manager, LAN Server, and TCP/IP.

- **Systems Network Architecture.** *Systems Network Architecture* (SNA) is IBM's proprietary networking scheme that has been widely used in the mainframe environment. A form of SNA called *Advanced Peer-to-Peer Networking* (APPN) provides SNA communication support for smaller systems. SNA is primarily a networking system for wide area networking, although it does support the use of LAN data links for local connection of networked devices. SNA is described further in Chapter 17.

---

vide other systems with access to the resources they control. TCP/IP networking software typically operates in a peer-to-peer environment.

Server-Based Environments

In a server-based environment, one or more systems on the network are designated as dedicated servers and run specialized server software. The servers provide services to other systems on the network that typically run simpler networking software than the servers. Novell NetWare products are typically used in a server-based environment.

Client-Server Computing

Both peer-to-peer and server-based networking software can be used to implement the client-server computing paradigm. As we introduced in Chapter 1, a system operating in the role of a server provides one or more services to other systems. A system operating in the role of a client requests the services that are provided by servers.

With peer-to-peer networking software, any system can play the role of a server and any system can play the role of a client. Systems often change their roles depending on the task being performed. With server-based networking the dedicated servers typically function in the role of servers with user systems typically operating in the role of clients.

NETWORK APPLICATIONS

Application programs that run in a networking environment can use a number of methods for taking advantage of the functions offered by the networking software. Application programs can be classified as being either network transparent or network aware.

Network-Transparent Applications

Many application programs have not been specifically designed to take advantage of networking facilities. We call these *network transparent* applications. Networking software typically provides services that allow network transparent programs to use the services of the network without being aware that they are doing so. For example, all applications can access files stored on local storage devices. Networking software typically implements functions that allow the I/O requests that a program makes to be redirected so they access the files stored on systems operating as file servers. The application program need not be aware that requests are not being processed locally. This allows a network transparent program to use print servers and file servers without being specifically designed to do so.

Network-Aware Applications

Each networking software subsystem also defines application programming interfaces (APIs) that allow applications to explicitly invoke network services. A networking API typically consists of a set of function calls and associated parameters or data formats that define the requests and responses that are exchanged in providing networking services. The specific calls and data formats used vary from one type of networking software to another. Programs that explicitly invoke networking services are called *network-aware* applications. An application may need to be network aware if it allows multiple users to have access to a resource such as a spreadsheet or document and needs to accept requests, coordinate processing, or send replies to different users across the network.

Standard Application Programming Interfaces

At the time of writing, application programming interfaces have been defined and proposed as standards for some types of networking services. However, these interfaces have not yet been widely implemented and used. Because of the differences in the APIs from one networking software subsystem to another, network-aware applications are typically developed for a specific environment, and porting the application to a different environment often involves making significant changes to it.

The Open System Foundation (OSF) has developed specifications for a *Distributed Computing Environment* (DCE) that includes interfaces for accessing file services, naming services, program-to-program communication services, security services and time services. A number of vendors have indicated that they will provide implementations of these specifications, allowing applications to be developed that can be moved more easily from one network environment to another.

Several vendors have developed interfaces for accessing messaging services suitable for developing mail-based applications. These include the *Mail Application Programming Interface* (MAPI), developed by Microsoft; *Vendor Independent Messaging*, developed and supported jointly by Lotus, Novell, Apple, and Borland; and the *Open Collaborative Environment* from Apple. It has yet to be determined if any of these interfaces will become a standard.

To some extent, the APIs associated with the *NetBIOS* and *Server Message Block* (SMB) protocols used in IBM and Microsoft local area networking products have become a de facto standard. Many local area network products offer support for these interfaces and allow an application developed using them to run in many environments. Another IBM and Microsoft application program interface that is developing wide-spread support is *Named Pipes*. All three of these application program interfaces are discussed in Chapter 21.

NETWORKING SOFTWARE SERVICES

Different networking software subsystems vary widely in their capabilities and in the services they provide. However, certain types of functions have now become commonplace in generally available high-level networking software subsystems.

Networking software typically provides an interface that allows network users and network administrators to invoke various network facilities and services. This interface typically consists of a combination of commands that can be issued via a user's computer system and various menus that can be used to select options and enter information. The commands and menus that make up the user/administrator interface typically conform to the user interface implemented by a particular computing platform and are specific to each vendor's networking software product.

The following sections introduce some of the application-oriented services that most high-level networking software systems provide.

Print Services

Print services allow any system on the network to use a printer attached to some other system. Output can be sent to a remote printer exactly as if the printer were attached directly to the user's own system. Queuing facilities are generally provided so that output can be sent to the printer even when it is busy. Print queues or print jobs can have different priorities, thus allowing certain print jobs to be scheduled ahead of others. Printers can be grouped in pools, with output printed by the first printer in the pool that becomes available. Print services can also be used to start, end, cancel, or flush a print job in a queue.

File Services

File services allow users to access the disks and files that are controlled by other systems in the network. Remote file access can be implemented in various ways. It can be done at the device level, where a user can access a particular hard disk on another system as if the hard disk were directly attached to the user's local system. It can be done on a directory or subdirectory basis, where the user is allowed to access only particular directories on a shared disk. Sharing can also be controlled at the file level, where users are granted the authority to access only particular files on the shared disk.

When multiple applications are able to concurrently access the same file, updates to the file that are made by one application can interfere with another application's use of the file. A file sharing system must be able to take measures to preserve file integrity. One way of preventing potential problems is through the use of file access rights. For example, a file may be limited to having only one user at any given time that is allowed to have update access to the file. Other users may then be restricted to read-only access or to no access at all while the file is in use. Record locking can be used to restrict access to a particular record or portion of a file, so that only one application is allowed to update that record at a given time.

Electronic Mail Services

Networking software often provides electronic mail applications that allow end users to compose, send, receive, and store messages and documents. Some electronic mail applications provide messaging facilities only within the local network. Other electronic mail applications provide users with access to the messaging facilities provided by other networks and with public electronic mail services as well.

Directory Services

Network users and application programs that use networking software often request services based on *network names*. Network names are used to represent other network users and the shared resources that are available on the network. A network directory service translates a network name into a network address so that requests and responses can be properly delivered to the appropriate remote system.

There are different approaches that can be taken to name translation in a computer network:

- Each system can keep track of its own mappings between network names and network addresses and perform network name translations using its own local capabilities.

- A central facility can maintain a table of mappings between network names and network addresses and can perform network name translations for other systems.

- The directory of network name to network address mappings can be distributed among a number of different systems in the network that all work cooperatively to provide name translation services.

Network Administration Services

Networking software subsystems commonly offer management facilities that can be used for monitoring and controlling the network. Some of the network management services that network software provides include the following:

- Defining users and network resources to the network.
- Monitoring and controlling the status of network resources.
- Managing user access to network resources.
- Performing diagnostic tests on network resources.
- Monitoring and reporting performance.
- Implementing security.
- Recording and reporting accounting information.

SUMMARY

Networking software can be divided into two categories—the high-level networking software with which the end user interacts and the network driver software that interfaces with a specific network interface card. Commonly used high-level networking software subsystems and architectures that use LAN data links include NetWare, LAN Manager, LAN Server, VINES, LANtastic, TCP/IP, AppleTalk, DECnet, PATHWORKS, and Systems Network Architecture.

Networking software can be used to implement the client-server computing paradigm using two different environments. In a peer-to-peer environment, any system can operate as a server and provide services to other systems operating as clients. In a server-based environment, dedicated systems operate in the role of servers that supply services to other systems operating as clients.

Application programs that operate in a networking environment can be either network-transparent or network-aware. Network-transparent applications are programs that use conventional I/O mechanisms to access networked resources as if they were local. Network-aware applications explicitly invoke networking services using an API implemented by the networking software. Common services provided by networking software include print services, file services, electronic mail services, directory services, and network administration services.

Part II begins a discussion of the important standards for local area network data link technology that have been developed by IEEE and accepted as international standards by ISO. Chapter 6 describes the IEEE/ISO/ANSI LAN architecture and introduces the standards for the Logical Link Control sublayer of the OSI model Data Link layer.

PART II

LOGICAL LINK CONTROL

Much of the LAN data link technology in use today in local area networks conforms to the international standards published by IEEE, ISO, or ANSI. All of these standards support a common interface to the services that a local area network data link provides to a user of the LAN data link. This interface is described by the IEEE/ISO *Logical Link Control* (LLC) standard defined by IEEE 802.2 and ISO 8802-2. The chapters in Part II describe the IEEE/ISO LLC standard.

The IEEE, ISO, and ANSI standards for LAN data link technology are based on the principles of information technology standardization defined by the OSI model. Chapter 6 introduces OSI concepts and describes the overall architecture behind the international standards for local area networks.

International standards for computer networking document both *service definitions* and *protocol specifications*. Chapter 7 concentrates on the LLC service definition and describes the services that a local area network data link conforming to international standards provides to a user of the data link. Chapter 8 examines the LLC protocol specification and describes the procedures that govern how a LAN data link provides its services.

Chapter 9 describes how some actual software subsystems have implemented the IEEE 802.2/ISO 8802-2 Logical Link Control standard to provide LAN data link services.

Chapter 6

Local Area Network Architecture

As we discussed in Chapter 4, the IEEE has undertaken a major role in local area network standards development. IEEE Project 802 has defined a flexible architecture that is oriented specifically to the standardization of local area network data link technology. The approach the IEEE has taken in developing its LAN architecture is in conformance with the OSI model. However, IEEE Project 802 addresses only the lowest two layers of the OSI model, the *Physical* and *Data Link* layers.

The IEEE Project 802 LAN architecture has subsequently been accepted by ISO and ANSI to form the underlying basis for their own LAN standardization efforts, and we refer to the IEEE Project 802 LAN architecture in this book as the IEEE/ISO/ANSI LAN architecture. Figure 6.1 illustrates the relationships between the OSI model and the LAN architecture that underlies IEEE, ISO, and ANSI standards for local area network technology.

OSI CONCEPTS

The standards that make up the IEEE/ISO/ANSI LAN architecture are based on the OSI model and use much of the terminology that ISO has adopted in documenting communication services and protocols. In order to understand the standards that IEEE, ISO, and ANSI have documented for local area network technology, some understanding is necessary of concepts underlying the OSI model.

The OSI model is concerned with the interconnection of systems—the way in which they exchange information—and not the internal functions performed by a given system. In OSI terminology, a system is defined as follows:

> A *system* is a set of one or more computers, the associated software, peripherals, terminals, human operators, physical processes, transfer means, etc., that forms an autonomous whole capable of performing information processing and/or information transfer.

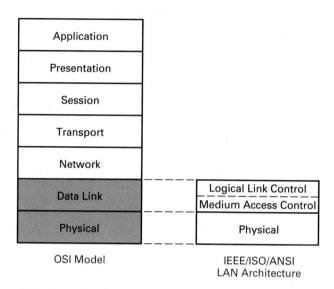

Figure 6.1   Comparing the layers of the OSI model with the layers and sub-layers of the IEEE/ISO/ANSI LAN architecture.

The OSI model provides a generalized view of a layered architecture. With the broad definition given for a system, the architecture can apply to a very simple system, such as a point-to-point connection between two computers, or to a very complex system, such as the interconnection of two entire computer networks.

Entities and Service Access Points

The notions of entities and service access points are important to understanding how interactions take place between layers in communicating systems.

- **Entity.** An *entity* is an active element within a layer. Two communicating entities within the same layer, but in different network systems, are called *peer entities*. Entities in the Application layer are called *Application entities,* entities in the Presentation layer are called *Presentation entities,* and so on. A particular layer provides services to entities running in the layer above.

- **Service-Access-Point.** A *service-access-point* (SAP) is the point at which the services of a layer are provided. Each layer provides service-access-points at which entities in the layer above request the services of that layer. Each service-access-point has an *SAP address,* by which the particular entity that is employing a layer service can be differentiated from all other entities that might also be able to use that layer service.

Abstract Interfaces

The OSI model defines an interface between any two pairs of adjacent layers in the same system. At any point in the architecture, layer *N* can be viewed as a *service provider*, and layer *N* + 1 can be viewed as the *service requester* or *service user*, as shown in Fig. 6.2. An entity in layer *N* provides a set of services to entities running in layer *N* + 1 via a ser-

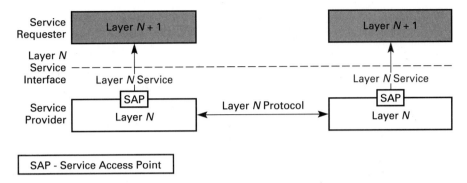

Figure 6.2   A service provides a defined set of services to a service requester via a service-access-point. The set of services provided by layer N defines an abstract interface between layer N and layer $N + 1$.

vice-access-point into layer N. The set of services provided by layer N defines the *abstract interface* between layer N and layer $N+1$.

    An abstract interface describes the semantics of the interactions that can occur between two architectural layers. An abstract interface does not specify implementation details, nor does it describe the syntax that must be used to implement the interface. The interactions between two adjacent layers are described only in terms of an abstract set of services that layer N provides to layer $N + 1$.

Concrete Interfaces

In addition to abstract interfaces, *concrete interfaces* are also important at some points in the architecture, especially in the Physical layer and at points where application programming interfaces (APIs) must be specified. A concrete interface might describe a point in the architecture at which a physical connector is used, for example, to connect a device to a cable. A concrete interface might provide specific electrical and mechanical specifications for the cables and connectors that must be used to properly implement the architecture. A concrete interface might also define an application programming interface a programmer must adhere to in writing programs to request the services of a layer.

Services and Protocols

The ISO standards for the OSI model define for each layer a single service definition and one or more protocol specifications. A *service definition* defines the specific services a layer provides to the layer above it. A service definition specifically does not say anything about how those services are to be provided. A *protocol specification* describes the formats of the data units exchanged and specifies the procedures a layer must perform in exchanging those data units in providing the services of that layer.

    The relationship between the services layer N provides and the protocol governing its operation are shown in Fig. 6.3. As shown there, the layer N protocol uses the services of layer $N - 1$ to provide a defined set of services to layer $N + 1$ above it.

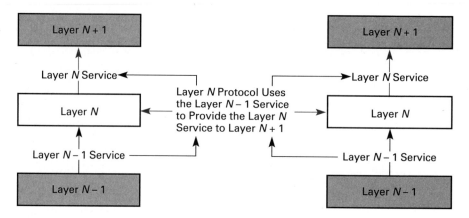

Figure 6.3   Relationship between a layer's *service definition* and its *protocol specification.*

Service Definitions

The ISO service definition for a layer documents the services a layer provides to the layer above it in terms of a set of *service primitives*, each of which has a defined set of *parameters*. The service primitives precisely define the abstract interface between a layer and the layer above it.

Service Primitives

The ISO standards define four general types of service primitives:

- **Request.** Issued by a service requester to request that a particular service be performed by a service provider and to pass parameters needed to fully specify the requested service.

- **Indication.** Issued by the service provider to notify a service requester that a significant event has occurred.

- **Response.** Issued by the service requester to acknowledge or complete some procedure previously invoked by the service provider through an *indication* primitive.

- **Confirm.** Issued by a service provider to notify the service requester of the results of one or more *request* primitives the service requester previously issued.

A particular service typically uses two or more service primitives. Figure 6.4 shows two *time-sequence diagrams* that illustrate the sequence in which service primitives might be issued using the ISO model of service primitives. In a time-sequence diagram, service primitives are represented by arrows, and time flows down.

The first diagram in Fig. 6.4 shows an example of a *nonconfirmed service*, in which the service requester is not informed of the completion of the service request. In the normal case, a request invoked at one end results in an indication being invoked at the other end.

The second service shown in Fig. 6.4 is a *confirmed service*, in which the service requester is informed by the distant peer entity of the success or failure of the service request.

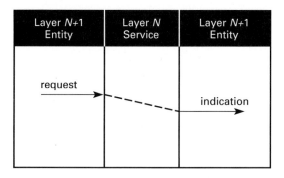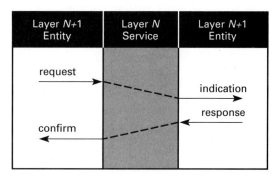

Nonconfirmed Service   Confirmed Service

Figure 6.4   Time-sequence diagrams for a nonconfirmed service and a confirmed service.

Service-Data-Units

Some layer services are intended to be used to transmit units of data from a layer entity in one system to a peer layer entity in another system. A layer does this by issuing a data transfer request service primitive to the layer below and passing the data unit to be transferred as a parameter of the request primitive. Data units passed from a service requester to a service provider are called *service-data-units* (SDUs).

The name of the SDU passed from a layer to the layer below begins with the name of the layer to which the SDU is passed. For example, the SDUs passed from the Transport layer to the Network layer are called *network-service-data-units* (NSDUs), the SDUs passed from the Network layer to the Data Link layer are called *data-link-service-data-units* (DLSDUs), and so on.

Protocol Specifications

Another principle of the OSI model is that when two network systems are communicating with one another, an entity in each layer in the first system communicates with its peer entity in the second system using a *protocol*. Figure 6.5 illustrates protocols operating in each of the seven layers of the OSI model.

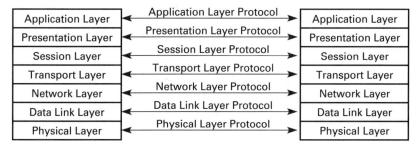

Figure 6.5   A separate protocol controls the operation of each of the layers in the OSI model.

A protocol specification describing the procedures layer N performs in supplying its services to layer $N + 1$ defines the following:

- The formats of the data units exchanged between peer layer N entities.
- The interactions that occur between peer layer N entities in exchanging data units.
- The way in which layer N and layer $N + 1$ interact in exchanging the service primitives defined in the service definition for layer N.
- The way in which the layer N and layer $N - 1$ interact in exchanging the service primitives defined in the service definition for layer $N - 1$.

Protocol-Data-Units

Data units sent from a layer entity in one system to a peer layer entity in another system are called *protocol-data-units* (PDUs). PDUs appear to flow from a layer $N + 1$ entity in the sending system to a layer $N + 1$ entity in the receiving system using the layer $N + 1$ protocol. From this perspective, functions performed in layer N and below are hidden from layer $N + 1$.

Protocol Control Information

A layer constructs a protocol-data-unit from the service-data-unit passed down from the layer above by adding *protocol-control-information* (PCI) to it, as shown in Fig. 6.6. Some of the information making up the protocol information may be passed down from layer $N + 1$ to layer N in the form of service primitive parameters. The PCI is used to control the operation of the protocol operating in a particular layer. Protocol-control-information is carried in the form of a header (and in the case of the Data Link layer, also a trailer) that is added to the SDU.

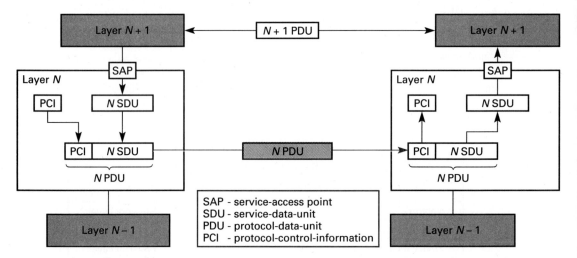

Figure 6.6   A layer accepts a service-data-unit (SDU) from the layer above and adds protocol-control-information (PCI) to it to create a protocol-data-unit (PDU) that it sends to its peer entity.

Segmentation and Blocking

In some cases, a layer might implement a *segmentation* facility in which a single SDU is used to create a number of individual PDUs. It is also possible for a layer to implement a *blocking* facility that allows multiple SDUs to be grouped together and transported across the network in a single PDU.

Generated PDUs

A layer N entity can also itself generate PDUs apart from the PDUs it creates from the SDUs it receives from layer $N + 1$. Such generated PDUs are typically transmitted between peer layer N entities to control the operation of the layer N protocol. The layer $N + 1$ service requester is not directly aware of the existence of these PDUs.

LAN ARCHITECTURE FUNCTIONAL LAYERS

As we have already pointed out, the IEEE/ISO/LAN architecture describes the functions that are performed in the OSI model Data Link and Physical layers for a LAN data link. The functions performed by layers above the OSI Data Link layer are defined by the particular network architecture with which the local area network data link is used. In discussing local area network facilities, we will often use OSI terminology and refer to the layer above the Data Link layer as the *Network layer*, even though this layer has different names in different network architecture.

The following sections describe the functions of the OSI model Data Link and Physical layers, especially as they relate to communication over a LAN data link.

DATA LINK LAYER

As we introduced in Chapter 4, the Data Link layer of the OSI model is responsible for the transmission of data from one system to another. ISO has defined a Data Link layer protocol, used extensively in wide area networks, called *High-level Data Link Control* (HDLC). The Data Link layer protocols that are used in local area networks are different from those used in wide area networks; however, they all use HDLC principles. Readers who have some familiarity with the HDLC protocol will see many parallels between HDLC and the protocols used in implementing LAN communication. HDLC is described briefly in Appendix B.

Box 6.1 lists some of the general functions that the OSI model defines for the Data Link layer.

In the IEEE/ISO/ANSI LAN architecture, the Data Link layer is divided into two sublayers—the *Logical Link Control* (LLC) sublayer and the *Medium Access Control* (MAC) sublayer. Before we examine each of the sublayers of the Data Link layer, we must discuss the *user* of LAN data link services.

BOX 6.1   OSI model data link layer functions.

- **Data Link Connection Establishment and Release.** Dynamically establishes, for a connection-oriented Data Link layer service, a logical data link connection between two users of the Data Link layer service (typically Network layer entities) and releases the connection when it is no longer required. These functions are not provided for a connectionless Data Link layer service, in which connections are not used. (Chapter 7 discusses the differences between a connection-oriented Data Link layer service and a connectionless Data Link layer service.)

- **Service-Data-Units.** Defines the service-data-unit (SDU) passed down from the user of the Data Link layer service to a Data Link layer entity in the sending system and up from a Data Link layer entity to the user of the Data Link layer service in the receiving system.

- **Framing.** Creates a single protocol-data-unit (PDU) from each SDU passed from a user of the Data Link layer service, marks the beginning and the end of the PDU when sending, and determines the beginning and ending of frames when receiving. The term *frame* is often used as an informal name for the PDU exchanged between peer Data Link layer entities.

- **Data Transfer.** Transfers frames over a physical circuit, extracts the SDU from each frame by removing the protocol-control-information (PCI), and passes SDUs up to the user of the Data Link layer service in the receiving system.

- **Frame Synchronization.** Establishes and maintains synchronization between the sending system and the receiving system. This means the receiving system must be capable of determining where each frame begins and ends.

- **Frame Sequencing.** Uses sequence numbers, for a connection-oriented Data Link service, to ensure that frames are delivered in the same order in which they were transmitted. Frame sequencing does not apply to a connectionless Data Link layer service.

- **Error Detection.** Detects transmission errors, frame format errors, and procedural errors on the data link connection using redundant bits carried in the PCI in the frame.

- **Error Recovery.** Recovers from errors detected on data links using connection-oriented operation. Error recovery does not apply to a connectionless Data Link layer service.

- **Identification and Parameter Exchange.** Performs a set of identification and parameter exchange functions, typically prior to the exchange of frames carrying user data. Some types of Data Link services allow parameter values to be negotiated.

- **Flow Control.** Controls the rate at which a user of a connection-oriented Data Link layer service receives frames to prevent a user of the Data Link layer service from being overloaded. Flow control does not apply to a connectionless Data Link layer service.

- **Physical Layer Services.** Uses the services of the Physical layer to transmit and receive data and to control the operation of the physical transmission medium.

- **Network Management.** Monitors and controls the operation of the Data Link layer. Management functions might include setting Data Link layer protocol operating characteristics, enabling and disabling data link connections, monitoring the status of enabled connections, and performing loopback tests for verifying correct operation of the data link.

LAN DATA LINK USERS

The user of a LAN data link employs a specific implementation of local area networking technology, such as an Ethernet or Token Ring LAN, for communication with some other user. It is important to point out that when we refer to the user of a LAN data link, we normally do not mean the end user. Rather, we mean a mechanism, process, or protocol operating at the level of the OSI model Network layer that is requesting LAN data link services.

As we introduced in Chapter 1, we make a distinction between an individual *LAN data link* that is used for communication at the level of the Data Link layer and a complete *local area network* that end users employ to request networking services, such as file and printer sharing. The user of a LAN data link is typically a component in a network operating system (NOS) or other high-level networking software subsystem—such as Novell NetWare, TCP/IP, or DECnet—that supplies network services to end users. This relationship is shown in Fig. 6.7.

Notice that, as shown in Fig. 6.2, the network operating system typically consists of software implementing the upper layers, typically the Application layer through the Logical Link Control sublayer. The Medium Access Control sublayer and the Physical layer are typically implemented in hardware in a network interface card (NIC). However, in some cases, a network operating system may implement the Application layer through

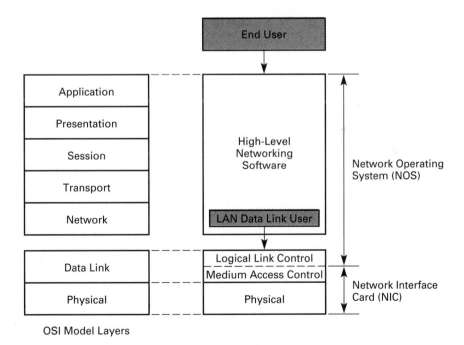

Figure 6.7 Comparing an *end user* with a *LAN data link user*.

the Network layer, with a separate software component implementing the Logical Link Control sublayer. Such minor implementation details need not concern us here.

It is possible for an end user to write an application program that requests the services directly of a LAN data link, and most LAN data link implementations provide application programming interfaces (APIs) for this purpose. Examples of these are described in Chapter 9. However, it is much more common for end users to employ the services that are provided by high-level networking software. Such software accesses one or more LAN data links *on behalf* of end users. End users who have occasion to write application programs that use networking facilities typically use an API that is also defined by high-level networking software rather than by a specific LAN data link implementation.

It is important to keep in mind as you read this book that the chapters in Parts II and III concentrate on the services that local area networking products provide to implement *LAN data links*. Parts IV and V then concentrate on the services that are provided to end users by high-level networking software. Such high-level networking software subsystems employ LAN data links to implement the *local area networks* and *enterprise internetworks* that end users perceive.

We next examine the two sublayers that make up the Data Link layer in the IEEE/ISO/ANSI LAN architecture.

LOGICAL LINK CONTROL SUBLAYER

The Logical Link Control sublayer is responsible for medium-independent data link functions. It allows a LAN data link user to access the services of a local area network data link without having to be concerned with the form of medium access control or physical transmission medium that is used. The LLC sublayer is shared by a variety of different medium access control technologies, many of which are described in the chapters in Part III. The LLC sublayer presents a common interface to the LAN data link user.

LLC-Protocol-Data-Units

The data unit that LLC sublayer entities exchange is called the *logical-link-control-protocol-data-unit* (LLC-PDU). As shown in Fig. 6.8, the LLC sublayer adds protocol-control-information (PCI) in the form of a header to each message it receives from the LAN data link user to create an LLC-PDU. The format of the LLC-PDU is described later in this chapter. The procedures that are used to exchange LLC-PDUs are described in Chapter 8.

LLC Service-Access-Points

The user of a LAN data link requests data transmission services through a *service-access-point* (SAP) into the LLC sublayer. It is possible for an implementation of Logical Link Control in a system to allow more than one user to concurrently access the services of the LAN data link. Each does so through a separate SAP having a different SAP identifier, as shown in Fig. 6.9.

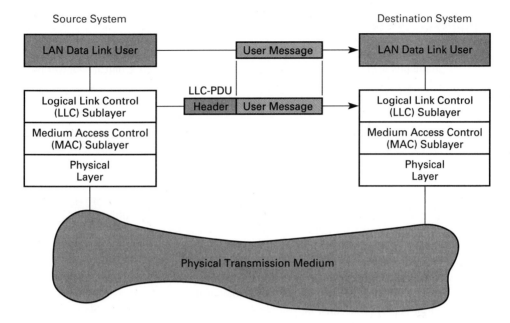

Figure 6.8 Relationship between the LAN data link user message and the LLC-PDU.

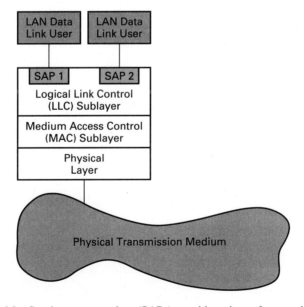

Figure 6.9 Service-access-points (SAPs) provide points of access into the LLC sublayer.

MEDIUM ACCESS CONTROL SUBLAYER

A local area network typically supports multiple devices that all contend for access to a single physical transmission medium. The Medium Access Control sublayer provides services to a user of the MAC sublayer service, which is typically the LLC sublayer.

MAC-Protocol-Data-Units

The data unit that MAC sublayer entities exchange is called the *medium-access-control-protocol-data-unit* (MAC-PDU). The MAC-PDU is often called a *MAC frame*. The purpose of the MAC frame is to carry the LLC-PDU across a specific type of physical transmission medium from one network device to another.

Figure 6.10 illustrates the relationship between the LLC sublayer, the MAC sublayer, and the PDUs that are associated with them. The MAC sublayer adds PCI in the form of a header and a trailer to each LLC-PDU that it receives from the LLC sublayer to create a MAC-PDU (MAC frame). The formats of the MAC frame for each particular form of medium access control technology and the specific procedures that are used to exchange MAC frames are described in the chapters in Part III.

The standards defining the functions of the MAC sublayer are primarily concerned with the rules that must be followed for network devices to be able to share access to a common transmission medium. The MAC sublayer performs a framing function that adds header and trailer information to each MAC frame that is sent. The header and trailer

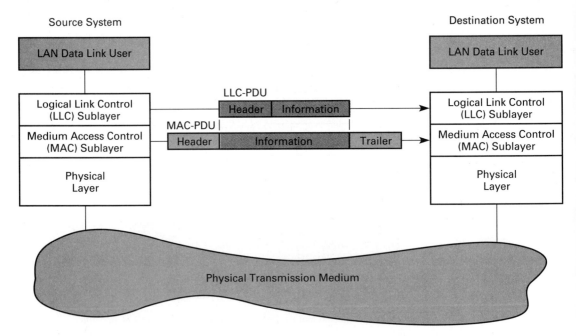

Figure 6.10   Relationship between the LLC-PDU and the MAC-PDU.

contain information necessary to identify the beginning and end of a frame, specify the source and destination of a message, synchronize the sender and receiver, and provide for error detection.

PHYSICAL LAYER

The lowest layer in the IEEE/ISO/ANSI LAN architecture corresponds directly to the Physical layer of the OSI model. It provides services to a user of the Physical layer, which is typically the MAC sublayer. Box 6.2 lists some of the functions that the OSI model defines for the Physical layer. The PDUs that are exchanged by the Physical layer consist of signals that represent the individual bits making up a MAC frame.

The Physical layer is concerned with the physical transmission of signals across a transmission medium. This layer defines procedures for establishing physical connections to the transmission medium and for transmitting and receiving signals over it. Physical layer specifications also include descriptions of the types of cabling, plugs, and connectors to be used and the characteristics of the signals that are exchanged.

BOX 6.2　OSI model physical layer functions.

- **Circuit Establishment and Release.** Allow a physical circuit to be dynamically established when it is required and released when the circuit is no longer needed. This function is typically used for a circuit implemented by a temporary facility, such as a dial-up line in the telephone network. It is typically not used with local area networks that use dedicated cabling.

- **Bit Synchronization.** Establishes synchronization in a receiving device with a stream of bits coming in and clocks data in from the communication circuit at the correct rate.

- **Service-Data-Units.** Defines the service-data-unit (SDU) passed down from a user of the Physical layer in the sending device and up from the Physical layer to its user in the receiving device. A Physical layer SDU typically consists of a signal representing a single bit.

- **Data Transfer and Sequencing.** Allow electrical signals to be exchanged over the circuit connecting two communicating devices and allow bits to be accepted by the receiving device in the same order in which they are delivered by the sending device.

- **Fault Condition Notification.** Notifies the Physical layer user when fault conditions occur.

- **Network Management.** Controls and monitors the operation of functions operating in the Physical layer. Network management functions include setting the operating characteristics of the communication link, activating and deactivating physical circuits, monitoring the status of physical links, and performing diagnostic procedures, such as loopback tests.

- **Medium Specific Control Functions.** Provides control functions for specific forms of transmission media, such as encoding/decoding, carrier sensing, collision detection, collision announcement, and detection of illegal cabling topologies.

IEEE/ISO/ANSI LAN STANDARDS

Early in its work on the development of local area network standards, IEEE Project 802 determined that it would not be able to develop a single local area network standard to meet the needs of all users. In recognition of this, the project developed a *family* of LAN standards. This family initially included a single standard for the LLC sublayer and three standards for the MAC sublayer and Physical layer—*CSMA/CD (Ethernet)*, *Token Bus*, and *Token Ring*. The IEEE standards for local area networking technology were subsequently accepted by ISO as international standards and are now also described by ISO standards. ANSI then developed the *Fiber Distributed Data Interface* (FDDI) form of medium access control that has also been accepted as a MAC sublayer and Physical layer standard by ISO.

Box 6.3 briefly describes each of the LAN standards that are described in the remaining chapters in Part II and in Part III.

We next look at the addressing mechanisms that are used in conjunction with LAN data links to identify users of the data link and to identify individual network devices.

LOCAL AREA NETWORKING ADDRESSING

An important aspect of the IEEE/ISO/LAN architecture concerns the addressing mechanisms that are implemented by a LAN data link. In discussing addressing, we will use the term *station* instead of the more general term *system* to refer to a device attached to the LAN data link. This is because a system can implement more than one station.

LAN Stations

A *station* is defined as a collection of hardware, firmware, and software that appears to other stations as a single functional and addressable unit on the LAN data link. A station implements a single physical point of connection to the transmission medium. A station is a collection of one or more hardware and/or software components that performs the functions of the LLC sublayer, the MAC sublayer, and the Physical layer.

Many types of computing devices, such as desktop computing systems and host computers, need to implement only one station and may have only one point of attachment to the network. However, many types of network devices routinely implement a number of stations. Examples of these are bridges and routers that are used to interconnect multiple LANs. Such devices must implement at least one separate station for each physical LAN to which it is attached. Bridges and routers are described in the chapters in Part IV.

Station Components

A station typically consists of a software component that implements the Logical Link Control layer and a hardware component that implements the Medium Access Control sublayer and the Physical layer. The software component of a station is often part of a

BOX 6.3 IEEE/ISO/ANSI LAN standards.

- **Logical Link Control.** The *Logical Link Control* standard describes the functions of the LLC sublayer of the IEEE/ISO/ANSI LAN architecture. It is defined by the IEEE 802.2 and ISO 8802-2 standards. The Logical Link Control standard describes the function of the LLC sublayer for all three forms of medium access control defined by the IEEE and can be used in conjunction with the FDDI standard as well. The Logical Link Control standard is described in Chapters 6, 7, and 8.

- **Carrier Sense Multiple Access with Collision Detection (Ethernet).** The *Carrier Sense Multiple Access with Collision Detection* (CSMA/CD) standard describes the MAC sublayer and Physical layer functions for a bus- or tree-structured LAN using CSMA/CD as an access protocol. It is defined by the IEEE 802.3 and ISO 8802-3 CSMA/CD standards. Equipment conforming to the CSMA/CD standard is most often called *Ethernet* equipment. The CSMA/CD standard has its roots in the *Ethernet Version 2 Specification* for local area networking technology that was jointly developed by Digital Equipment Corporation, Xerox, and Intel. The IEEE 802.3/ISO 8802-3 CSMA/CD standard is described in Chapter 10, and the older *Ethernet Version 2 Specification* is described in Chapter 11.*

- **Token Bus.** The *Token Bus* standard describes the MAC sublayer and Physical layer functions for a bus-structured LAN using token passing as an access protocol. It is defined by the IEEE 802.4 and ISO 8802-4 standards. The Token Bus form of LAN was designed to meet the needs of factory automation applications. The Token Bus standard is described in Chapter 12.

- **Token Ring.** The *Token Ring* standard describes the MAC sublayer and Physical layer functions for a ring-structured LAN using a token-passing access protocol. It is defined by the IEEE 802.5 and ISO 8802-5 standards. The Token Ring standard is an outgrowth of the development work that IBM did for its *Token-Ring Network* family of LAN products. The Token Ring standard is described in Chapter 13.

- **Fiber Distributed Data Interface.** The *Fiber Distributed Data Interface* (FDDI) standard defines a high-speed form of LAN that was standardized by a subcommittee of ANSI. It is defined by the ANSI X3T9.5 and ISO 9314 standards. FDDI uses a logical ring-structured topology using a timed token-passing access protocol that is substantially different from the token-passing protocol defined by the Token Ring standard. The FDDI standard is described in Chapter 14.

* Most Ethernet equipment that is available today implements the IEEE 802.3/ISO 8802-3 CSMA/CD standard. However, some LAN data links are in use that employ equipment that implements the older *Ethernet Version 2 Specification*. It is important to note that IEEE 802.3/ISO 8802-3 MAC frames and Ethernet Version 2 MAC frames are slightly different. Therefore, equipment implementing only the IEEE 802.3/ISO 8802-3 standard is incompatible with equipment implementing only the Ethernet Version 2 Specification. However, techniques for interoperating between them are discussed in Chapter 10. In this book, the term *Ethernet,* when used without qualification, refers to an implementation of the IEEE 802.3/ISO 8802-3 standard. The term *Ethernet Version 2* is used to refer to an implementation of the older *Ethernet Version 2 Specification*.

network operating system (NOS) subsystem. The hardware component often takes the form of a network interface card (NIC). A typical implementation of the layers and sublayers of the IEEE/ISO/ANSI LAN architecture is shown in Fig. 6.11.

As we introduced in Chapter 1, some computing devices, such as certain desktop workstations and printers, have integrated into them all the hardware functions required to implement a NIC. Other computing systems, including many types of desktop systems and larger computing systems, implement NICs in the form of separate circuit boards that are installed into the computing system. Different manufacturers have different terms for NICs. For example, IBM typically calls them *network adapters* or *LAN adapters*.

A computing device that implements more than one station, possibly by having more than one NIC installed, has more than one point of physical attachment to the network. Such a computing device can transmit information over the LAN data link using each station independently.

Two Levels of Data Link Addressing

The IEEE/ISO/ANSI LAN architecture provides for two levels of addressing—service-access-point (SAP) addressing and Medium Access Control (MAC) addressing:

- **SAP Addressing.** A *service-access-point (SAP) address* identifies an individual service-access-point into the LLC sublayer. SAP addressing is the concern of the Logical Link

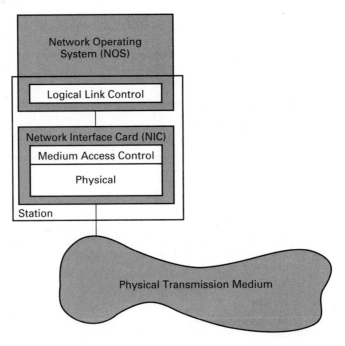

Figure 6.11   Typical station component implementation.

Control sublayer. A SAP address represents a particular mechanism, process, or protocol that is requesting LLC sublayer services through the associated SAP. As we introduced earlier, each mechanism, process, or protocol that is concurrently using the services of the LLC sublayer in a given station must use a different SAP address.

- **MAC Addressing.** A *Medium Access Control (MAC) address* uniquely identifies an individual station that implements a single point of physical attachment to a LAN data link. MAC addressing is the concern of the Medium Access Control sublayer. Each station attached to a LAN data link must have a unique MAC address on that LAN data link.

The MAC addressing mechanism is used by the MAC sublayer to deliver each MAC frame to the appropriate station or stations on the LAN data link. The SAP addressing mechanism is used by the LLC sublayer to deliver LLC-PDUs to the appropriate user or users of the LLC sublayer service within a particular destination station. It will be easier to see how these two separate addressing mechanisms work together if we examine them one by one, from the bottom up.

MAC ADDRESSING

The main role of MAC addressing is to make it possible to move a MAC frame from the station that originates it to the correct destination station or stations. MAC address fields in the MAC frame are used to make this happen. As we introduced earlier, each of the forms of medium access control that we examine in this book defines its own MAC frame format. However, the MAC frames for all of the medium access control technologies that we describe in this book have the same general format.

The general format of the MAC frame is shown in Fig. 6.12. Each type of MAC frame carries a header and a trailer that contains, among other things, destination MAC address and source MAC address fields. MAC frame formats for the different MAC sublayer and Physical layer technologies are examined in the chapters in Part III.

As shown in Fig. 6.12, the *destination MAC address* field in a MAC frame identifies the station or stations that are intended to receive the frame. The destination MAC address can refer to an individual station or to a group of stations. The *source*

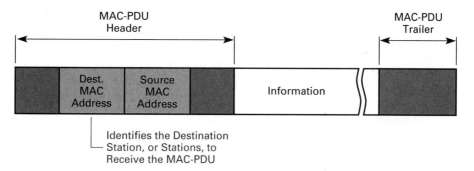

Figure 6.12 MAC sublayer protocol-data-unit (MAC-PDU) format.

MAC address refers to the station that transmitted the frame and always refers to an individual station.

MAC Address Formats

The IEEE/ISO/ANSI LAN standards allow MAC addresses to be either 16 bits or 48 bits in length. The formats of destination MAC address fields and source MAC address fields are shown in Fig. 6.13 and are described below:

- **Destination MAC Address.** The *destination MAC address* identifies the destination station, or stations, that are to receive the MAC frame. If the first bit of a destination MAC address is 0, the address identifies an individual station; if the first bit is 1, the address refers to a group of stations. A destination address value of all 1 bits is the broadcast address and refers to all active stations on the LAN data link. A station that sends MAC frames containing group destination MAC addresses implements a *multicasting* function that allows it to deliver each frame to more than one destination station in a single transmission. In a 48-bit destination MAC address, the second bit indicates whether the address is a locally-administered address or a globally-administered address.

- **Source MAC Address.** The *source MAC address* identifies the station that originated the MAC frame. The first bit of a source MAC address is always 0. In a 48-bit MAC address, the second bit indicates whether the address is a locally-administered address or a globally-administered address.

For a given LAN data link, the source and destination address fields must be the same size in all MAC frames that are generated.

MAC Address Administration

The IEEE/ISO/ANSI LAN standards define both locally administered MAC addressing and globally administered MAC addressing. All 16-bit addresses are locally administered. For 48-bit addressing, if the second bit is 0, addressing is globally administered; if the second bit is 1, addressing is locally administered.

- **Locally Administered MAC Addressing.** With *locally administered MAC addressing,* it is the responsibility of the organization installing the network to assign a unique MAC address to each network station. This is often done with DIP switches on the NIC or it might be done using a software function.

- **Globally Administered MAC Addressing.** With *globally administered MAC addressing,* each LAN manufacturer assigns a unique address to each NIC it manufactures, thus guaranteeing that no two stations in the world have the same address, as long as they use globally administered MAC addressing. With globally-administered MAC addressing, each NIC has a permanent address, and DIP switches or software functions are not required to set the NIC's MAC address.

MAC Address Value Assignment

The IEEE is the organization responsible for coordinating the assignment of address values for globally-administered MAC addresses. The IEEE, upon request and upon payment of a small fee, assigns a value for the high-order 24 bits of MAC addresses to any organization that manufactures networking equipment. The manufacturer is then respon-

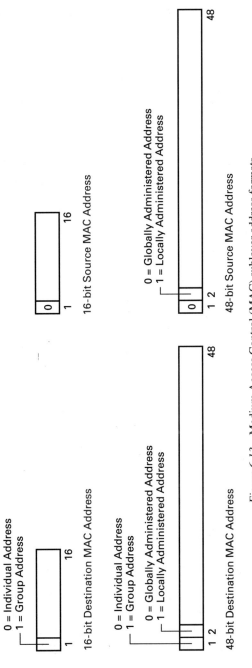

Figure 6.13 Medium Access Control (MAC) sublayer address formats.

sible for guaranteeing that a different address value is placed in the low-order 24 bits of the MAC address for each NIC that it manufactures.

The use of globally-administered addresses simplifies address management for networks; but it does increase transmission overhead, since more addressing bits must be sent in each frame. The majority of LAN product vendors today use globally-administered addresses in the NICs they manufacture. However, vendors of network products can choose whether to support one or both forms of addressing as part of their NIC products. For example, some NICs have a factory-set, globally administered MAC address but allow the preset address to be overridden by a software function should the organization installing the LAN decide to use its own locally administered address values.

MAC Address Filtering

The LLC sublayer always receives the LLC-PDUs that are carried in MAC frames having that station's own MAC address. However, many implementations of the Logical Link Control standard often provide a *MAC address filtering mechanism*. Such a mechanism allows the LLC sublayer to request that MAC frames having other destination MAC addresses also be delivered to it.

For example, a MAC address filtering mechanism may implement a multicasting capability by allowing an LLC user to specify a list of group destination MAC addresses. The station will then copy all MAC frames having those group destination MAC addresses. A MAC address filtering mechanism is often used in conjunction with a SAP address filtering mechanism, which we describe later in this chapter. Implementations of MAC address filtering mechanisms are described further in Chapter 9.

SAP ADDRESSING

The LLC sublayer has the overall responsibility of controlling the exchange of messages between individual users of the LLC sublayer service. Once a MAC frame carrying an LLC-PDU arrives at an appropriate destination station, the Logical Link Control sublayer in that station uses SAP addressing to ensure that the LLC-PDU is delivered to the appropriate LAN data link user or users.

SAP Addresses

As we have seen, the data unit that LLC sublayer entities exchange is the LLC-PDU. It is placed within a MAC frame for transmission across the LAN data link.

Figure 6.14 shows the format of the LLC-PDU and illustrates how the LLC-PDU is carried within a MAC frame. The Information field of the LLC-PDU carries the data unit that is passed down from a user of the LAN data link. This data unit is often called a *packet*. The header of the LLC-PDU contains two 1-octet SAP address values—the destination-service-access-point (DSAP) address and source-service-access-point (SSAP) address.

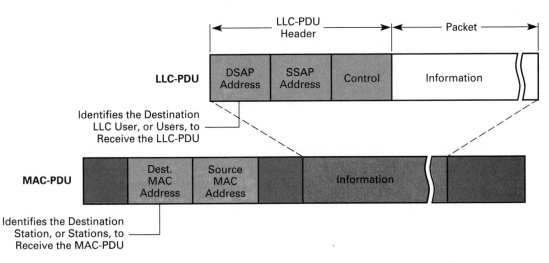

Figure 6.14   LLC sublayer and MAC sublayer protocol-data-unit (LLC-PDU and MAC-PDU) formats.

The formats of DSAP and SSAP address fields are shown in Fig. 6.15 and are described below:[*]

- **DSAP Address.** The *destination-service-access-point (DSAP) address* identifies the LLC sublayer user, or users, that are to receive the LLC-PDU. The destination-service-access-point address can be either an *individual* address, which identifies a single SAP, or it can be a *group* address, which identifies a set of SAPs. If the first bit of a DSAP address contains a 0, the address refers to an individual SAP; if the first bit contains a 1, the address is a group address. The group address consisting of all 1 bits is the *global SAP address* that specifies all active SAPs in the station.

- **SSAP Address.** The *source-service-access-point (SSAP) address* is always an individual address that identifies a single SAP—the SAP that is responsible for originating the LLC-

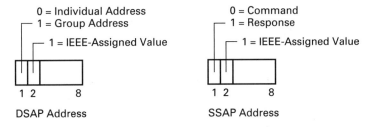

Figure 6.15   Service-access-point (SAP) address formats.

* International standards for the OSI model typically use the term *octet* to refer to a collection of 8 bits. Even though the term *byte* is today more common than *octet,* we will adopt the OSI terminology and use the term *octet* to refer to an arbitrary collection of 8 bits, such as when describing a communication protocol. But we will continue to use the term *byte* when referring to a collection of 8 bits in a storage system.

PDU. If the first bit of a SSAP address contains a 0, the LLC-PDU is a *command;* if the first bit contains a 1, the LLC-PDU is a *response.* A command is sent by an LLC sublayer entity that is initiating a data transfer operation; a response is sent by the opposite LLC sublayer entity in reply to a command. Commands and responses are discussed further in Chapter 7.

As we have seen, SAP address values are used to distinguish one user of the LAN data link from another user of the same LAN data link that might be active at the same time in the same station. The LLC sublayer standard itself does not define what is meant by a user that requests services of an LLC sublayer entity. Some further discussion of this point will be helpful.

LAN Data Link LLC Sublayer Users

As we introduced earlier, when we use the term *user* in the context of a user of a LAN data link, we generally are not referring to an *end user.* Rather, the term *LAN data link user* refers to a mechanism, process, or protocol operating in the layer above the LLC sublayer—at the level of the Network layer of the OSI model—that is requesting services of the Logical Link Control sublayer.

The specific process that requests LLC sublayer services depends on the network architecture that is being employed in the higher layers. If the higher layer software conforms to the OSI architecture, then the user of the LAN data link is a process that implements an OSI model Network layer entity. That process will typically be running a Network layer protocol that is defined by an ISO standard. If the higher layer software conforms to some other network architecture, then the user of the LAN data link is a process running in the layer that sits above the LLC sublayer in that network architecture. For example, in IBM's SNA architecture, the layer above the LLC sublayer is the *Path Control* layer; in the TCP/IP architecture, the layer above the LLC sublayer is the *Internet* layer, and so on. Higher-layer protocols are introduced in Chapter 17.

As we have already mentioned, it is possible for an implementation of the Logical Link Control standard to allow more than one user to concurrently request LAN data link services, each through a separate service-access-point into the LLC sublayer.

As we will see, SAP addresses are often used to identify the specific protocols that are being used by the layer above the LLC sublayer. However, it is important to realize that the LLC standard itself allows specific implementations of Logical Link Control to use SAP address values for any desired purpose. As far as the LLC sublayer is concerned, SAP address values can be used to identify users of the LLC sublayer service in any way the implementor chooses.

We will next look at some examples of how SAP address values are often used in practice.

LLC Sublayer User Multiplexing

LLC sublayer SAP addresses allow stations to implement *user multiplexing* facilities that allow different types of users in the layer above the LLC sublayer to coexist on the same LAN data link. For example, an LLC sublayer user in station A might be employing the international standard ISO 8473 Internet protocol in the Network layer to communicate with a user in station B. Another LLC sublayer user in station A might be using the Internet Protocol (IP) of the TCP/IP protocol suite to communicate with a user in station C. Still another LLC sublayer user in station A might be using a Network layer protocol from yet another architecture, such as AppleTalk or Novell NetWare, to exchange information with a user in station D.

SAP Address Assigned Values

All SAP address values that have the second bit position set to 1 are reserved for definition by the IEEE, and specific meanings have been assigned to a number of these reserved SAP values. For example, the SAP address value X'FE' has been assigned by the IEEE to the ISO 8473 Internet protocol that operates in the OSI Network layer. Networking products that conform to the OSI model—such as Digital's *DECnet/OSI* and IBM's *OSI/Communications Subsystem* products—use LLC SAP address values of X'FE' to exchange ISO 8473 Internet protocol packets over LAN data links. With such networking products, the SAP address value X'FE' differentiates LLC-PDUs carrying ISO 8473 Internet protocol packets from LLC-PDUs carrying the traffic conforming to other Network layer protocols.

Figure 6.16 shows an LLC-PDU carrying an ISO 8473 Internet protocol packet. Notice that both the DSAP and SSAP address fields carry a value of X'FE'. In a later section we will see how LLC-PDUs can also carry packets associated with Network layer protocols that are not described by international standards.

SAP Address Filtering

A LAN data link user that is employing a particular implementation of LLC typically receives packets that are carried in LLC-PDUs that have the SAP address of the user's own service-access-point in the DSAP address field. However, many implementations of the Logical Link Control standard provide a *SAP address filtering* mechanism that allows

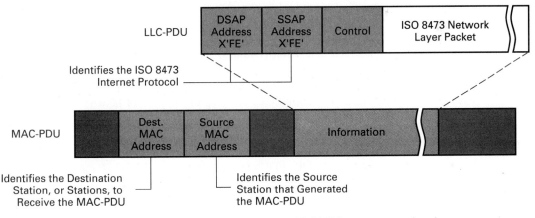

Figure 6.16   LLC-PDU carrying an ISO 8473 Internet protocol packet.

a LAN data link user to also receive the packets carried in LLC-PDUs having other DSAP address values.

For example, a SAP address filtering mechanism may implement a multicasting capability by allowing a LAN data link user to specify a list of the group DSAP addresses in which that user is interested. Then, for all MAC frames that station accepts, the LLC sublayer will pass to a user the packets carried in all LLC-PDUs having DSAP addresses that correspond to that user's SAP address list. A SAP address filtering mechanism is often used in conjunction with a MAC address filtering mechanism, which we described earlier.

An LLC implementation typically allows only one LLC user in a particular station to receive the packets carried in LLC-PDUs having a particular *individual* DSAP address. But multiple LLC users in the same station can typically receive the packets carried in LLC-PDUs having a particular *group* DSAP address. Implementations of SAP address filtering mechanisms are described further in Chapter 9.

SUBNETWORK ACCESS PROTOCOL

Very little of the traffic on today's LAN data links carries packets that conform to international standard protocols, such as the ISO 8473 Internet protocol. IEEE has defined a protocol called the *Subnetwork Access Protocol* (SNAP) that many networking products use to carry traffic that does not conform to international standards. The SNAP protocol implements another mechanism that can be used for the purpose of distinguishing LLC-PDUs that are carrying packets associated with one Network layer protocol from LLC-PDUs that are carrying packets associated with some other Network layer protocol.

Private Protocols

The SNAP mechanism is intended for use with *private* Network layer protocols. By this we mean protocols that operate in the layer above the LLC sublayer but do not conform to international standards for the OSI model Network layer. Examples of such protocols are the Internet Protocol (IP) used in the TCP/IP protocol suite and the Internet Packet Exchange (IPX) Protocol used by Novell NetWare networking products. Such protocols do not have IEEE-assigned SAP address values. Therefore, a mechanism is needed that goes beyond SAP addressing to distinguish one private protocol from another. This is especially important when packets associated with one private Network layer protocol are carried over a LAN data link that may be carrying other types of network traffic at the same time.

SNAP LLC-PDU Format

Figure 6.17 shows the format of the PDUs that are defined by the SNAP mechanism. The data unit carried inside the LLC-PDU when the SNAP mechanism is used is often called a *SNAP PDU*. Notice that LLC-PDUs carrying SNAP PDUs have SSAP and DSAP address values of hex 'AA'.

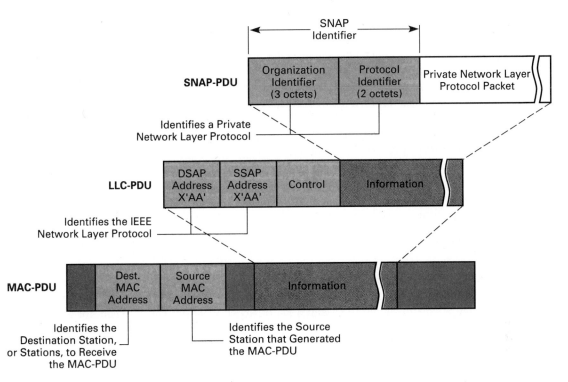

Figure 6.17 LLC-PDU format for the IEEE Subnetwork Access Protocol (SNAP).

The SNAP mechanism provides a level of multiplexing over and above that provided by SAP addressing to differentiate one private Network layer protocol from other private Network layer protocols. The first 5 octets of a SNAP PDU contain a SNAP identifier value that uniquely identifies the protocol associated with the packet the SNAP PDU is carrying. The first 3 octets of the SNAP identifier contain a value assigned to a particular organization; the remaining 2 octets identify a specific protocol that has been defined by that organization.

Protocol Coexistence

Any organization that defines one or more private Network layer protocols, and chooses to implement the IEEE SNAP mechanism, can apply to the IEEE for an organization identifier that it can use to distinguish its private protocols from the private protocols defined by other organizations. For example, private Network layer protocols that are associated with the TCP/IP protocol suite all have 5-octet protocol identifiers that begin with the TCP/IP 3-octet organization identifier, and all Novell Network layer protocols use Novell's 3-octet organization identifier. Computing equipment vendors that have defined proprietary network architectures, such as IBM and DEC, also have unique values that distinguish their private Network layer protocols from those of other organizations.

LLC-PDUs containing SNAP PDUs that carry traffic for different private Network layer protocols and LLC-PDUs that carry traffic conforming to international standard Network layer protocols can all coexist on the same LAN data link without interfering with one another. The SAP address values carried in all LLC-PDUs and the SNAP identifier values carried in SNAP PDUs allow LLC-PDUs carrying packets associated with one Network layer protocol to be easily distinguished from LLC-PDUs carrying packets associated with other Network layer protocols.

Applications for the various addressing mechanisms and protocol identification schemes used in modern networks are discussed further in Chapters 17 and 18 and in Appendix B, when we discuss techniques that are used for interconnecting individual LANs to form enterprise internetworks.

SNAP Protocol Identifier Filtering

An implementation of the LLC sublayer that provides the SNAP mechanism may provide a *SNAP protocol identifier filtering* mechanism that is similar to the MAC address and SAP address filtering mechanisms described earlier. For example, a LAN data link user might be able to supply LLC with a list of SNAP identifier values. Then, for all SNAP PDUs the LLC sublayer receives, the user will only receive the packets carried by SNAP PDUs having the SNAP protocol identifier values in that user's list. A SNAP protocol filtering mechanism is often used in conjunction with SAP address and MAC address filtering mechanisms.

LAN ARCHITECTURE SERVICES AND PROTOCOLS

The standards making up the IEEE/ISO/ANSI LAN architecture, like all standards that are based on the OSI model, define two aspects of the operation of each layer and sublayer—a service definition and a protocol specification.

Service Definitions

As we pointed out earlier in this chapter, the *service definition* for a layer or sublayer defines the interactions that take place between adjacent layers and sublayers in the same system. LLC sublayer services consist of those services that the LLC layer provides to a LAN data link user in the layer above the LLC sublayer. This is indicated by the vertical arrows in Fig. 6.18. MAC sublayer services consist of those services that the MAC layer provides to the LLC sublayer. As described earlier, service definitions are described in terms of time-sequence diagrams, service primitives, and service primitive parameters.

The Logical Link Control sublayer service definition is described in Chapter 7. The service definitions associated with the MAC sublayer and the Physical layer for various forms of medium access control are described in the chapters in Part III.

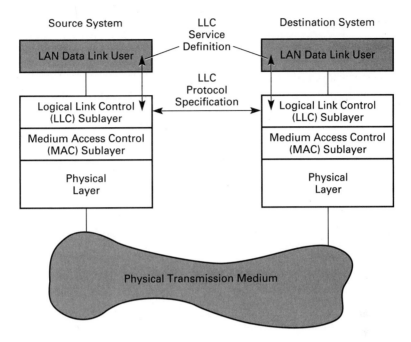

Figure 6.18   Service definition and protocol specification.

Protocol Specifications

The *protocol specification* for a layer or sublayer describes the interactions that take place between complementary layers or sublayers in two communicating devices. The protocol specification for the LLC sublayer is indicated by the horizontal arrow in Fig. 6.18.

A layer or sublayer protocol specification defines both protocol-data-unit (PDU) formats and the rules that govern the way in which those PDUs are exchanged. As we have seen, the PDU exchanged by LLC sublayer entities is called the logical-link-control-protocol-data-unit (LLC-PDU), and the PDU exchanged by MAC sublayer entities is called the medium-access-control-protocol-data-unit (MAC-PDU), or MAC frame.

The Logical Link Control sublayer protocol specification is described in Chapter 8. The protocol specifications associated with the MAC sublayer for various forms of medium access control are described in the chapters in Part III.

Service and Protocol Relationships

The LLC sublayer service definition and protocol specification are separate but interrelated. For example, the relationship between the services the LLC layer provides to a LAN data link user and the protocol that governs its operation are shown in Fig. 6.19. As shown there, the LLC sublayer protocol uses the services of the MAC sublayer to provide a defined set of services to a user of the local area network data link.

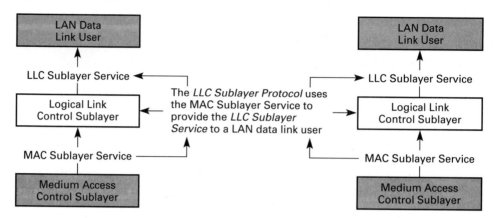

Figure 6.19   Relationship between the LLC sublayer *service definition* and the LLC sublayer *protocol specification.*

LLC Sublayer Data Transmission

The major service that the LLC sublayer provides to its users is a data transmission service. In the context of the OSI model, the user of the LAN data link is an entity operating in the OSI model Network layer. A Network layer entity exchanges *network-protocol-data-units* (NPDUs) with its peer Network layer entity. Figure 6.20 illustrates how a Network layer entity uses the services of the LLC sublayer to transmit data from one system to another. As we have seen, the data unit exchanged by the layer above the LLC sublayer is often called a packet.

A user of the LAN data link requests a data transfer service of the LLC sublayer and passes the packet to the LLC sublayer entity in the form of a *logical-link-control-service-data-unit* (LLC-SDU). The LLC sublayer entity adds protocol-control-information (PCI) to the LLC-SDU in the form of a header to create an LLC-PDU.

The LLC sublayer then uses the services of the MAC sublayer to transmit the LLC-PDU to a destination station or stations. The LLC sublayer entity in a destination station removes the PCI and delivers the enclosed LLC-SDU to the LAN data link user there.

MAC Sublayer Data Transmission

To transmit an LLC-PDU over the network, an LLC sublayer entity passes the LLC-PDU down to a MAC sublayer entity in the form of a *medium-access-control-service-data-unit* (MAC-SDU), as shown in Fig. 6.21. The MAC sublayer entity encapsulates the MAC-SDU with additional PCI—which takes the form of a header and a trailer—to create a MAC-PDU, or MAC frame. The MAC sublayer then uses the services of the Physical layer to transmit the individual bits of the MAC frame over the physical transmission medium.

The formats of the MAC frames and the protocol mechanisms that are used in the MAC sublayer are described for each individual form of medium access control technology in the chapters in Part III.

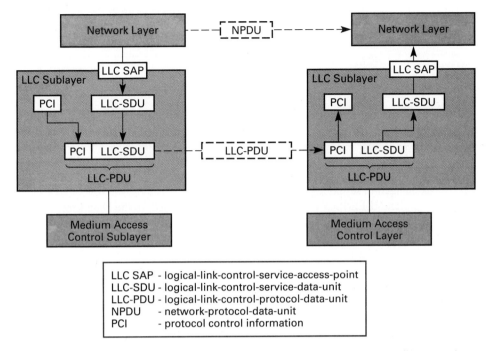

LLC SAP - logical-link-control-service-access-point
LLC-SDU - logical-link-control-service-data-unit
LLC-PDU - logical-link-control-protocol-data-unit
NPDU - network-protocol-data-unit
PCI - protocol control information

Figure 6.20 Providing the Logical Link Control sublayer service.

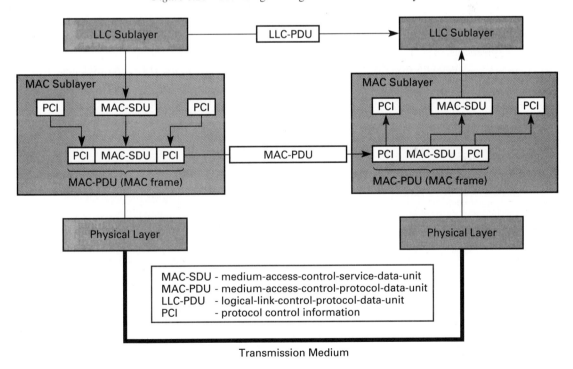

MAC-SDU - medium-access-control-service-data-unit
MAC-PDU - medium-access-control-protocol-data-unit
LLC-PDU - logical-link-control-protocol-data-unit
PCI - protocol control information

Transmission Medium

Figure 6.21 Providing the Medium Access Control sublayer service.

SUMMARY

The standards developed by IEEE and ANSI for LAN data link technology are based on the OSI model and conform to the conventions adopted by ISO for communication standards. ISO standards for the layers of the OSI model document both a service definition and a protocol specification. A service definition defines an abstract interface between two layers in the terms of the services a layer provides to the layer above. A protocol specification defines the formats of data units and the rules by which those data units are exchanged in supplying a layer's services.

The IEEE/ISO/ANSI LAN architecture is based on the Data Link and Physical layers of the OSI model and divides the Data Link layer into a Logical Link Control (LLC) sublayer and a Medium Access Control (MAC) sublayer. The IEEE/ISO/ANSI standards for LAN data link technology include IEEE 802.2/ISO 8802-2 Logical Link Control, IEEE 802.3/ISO 8802-3 Carrier Sense Multiple Access with Collision Detection (Ethernet), IEEE 802.4/ISO 8802-4 Token Bus, IEEE 802.5/ISO 8802-5 Token Ring, and ANSI X3T9.5/ISO 9314 Fiber Distributed Data Interface.

The IEEE/ISO/ANSI LAN architecture defines two levels of addressing. Station addressing, or MAC addressing, is used to uniquely identify an individual network interface card, attached to a LAN data link. Service access point (SAP) addressing is used to identify an individual user of the LAN data link service in a particular station and is used to differentiate between Network layer protocols. IEEE defines a subnetwork access protocol (SNAP) that can be used to distinguish between different private Network layer protocols.

Chapter 7 describes the service definition contained in the IEEE and ISO standards for the Logical Link Control sublayer and examines the three types of data transfer services that the LLC sublayer can supply to the user of a LAN data link.

Chapter **7**

LLC Service Definition

As we introduced in Chapter 6, the Logical Link Control sublayer is the uppermost of the two sublayers in the IEEE/ISO/ANSI LAN architecture that make up the Data Link layer in the OSI model. International standards describe two aspects of the operation of the Logical Link Control sublayer—a service definition and a protocol specification. This chapter describes the LLC sublayer service definition; Chapter 8 examines the protocol specification.

The Logical Link Control sublayer service definition precisely documents the services that the LLC sublayer provides to a LAN Data Link layer user. It also describes the information that the user must provide to the LLC sublayer in requesting its services. As we described in Chapter 6, the LLC sublayer allows a LAN data link user to request the services of a LAN data link without having to be aware of the type of medium access control technology that is implemented in the Medium Access Control sublayer and Physical layer.

TYPES OF LAN DATA LINK SERVICE

The Logical Link Control sublayer service definition specifies two general types of LAN data link service:

- Connectionless service.
- Connection-oriented service.

There is also a third type of data link service that is under consideration for possible addition to the Logical Link Control standard:

- Acknowledged connectionless service.

A particular implementation of the LLC standard might provide only one of the above services, two of them, or all three. All LAN implementations must provide the connectionless service, and many of them provide only the connectionless service.

Before we describe each of the above types of services, we will briefly describe their functions.

Connectionless Service

The *connectionless LLC service* incurs the least amount of protocol overhead. With the connectionless LLC service, there is no need to establish a prior association between the source and destination system before data transmission can take place. Each LLC-PDU sent using the connectionless LLC service is processed independently of any other LLC-PDU. No sequence checking is done to ensure that LLC-PDUs are received in the same sequence in which they were sent, and the receiving system sends no acknowledgment that it has received an LLC-PDU. No flow control or error recovery is provided as part of connectionless service. A connectionless data transfer service is sometimes referred to as *datagram* service.

We can think of the connectionless LLC service as a black box. A user of the LAN data link on the source end inserts an LLC-PDU into the black box. If no errors occur during transmission to corrupt the LLC-PDU, an identical copy emerges from the black box on the destination end. If data is corrupted during the transmission of an LLC-PDU, the LLC service detects the error, discards the erroneous PDU, and nothing emerges at the destination end of the black box. The source and destination users are not informed that anything went wrong; the destination user simply does not receive the PDU that the source user sent. When the connectionless service is used, all necessary flow control and error recovery services that are required must be provided in the layers above Logical Link Control.

Connectionless service is the most commonly used LLC service in LAN implementations. With the connectionless LLC service, LLC-PDUs can be sent to either individual or group SAP addresses. The connectionless LLC sublayer service uses group SAP addresses to provide a multicasting capability that a source user can employ to send an LLC-PDU to more than one destination user in a single transmission.

Connection-Oriented Service

With the *connection-oriented LLC service*, delivery of LLC-PDUs is guaranteed by the LLC service itself as long as an *LLC connection* is maintained between a source LLC service-access-point and a destination LLC service-access-point. An LLC connection consists of a logical association between a pair of LLC sublayer entities. With the connection-oriented LLC service, a connection between the source and the destination LLC sublayer entities must be established before data transfer can begin, the connection must be maintained while data transfer proceeds, and the connection can be terminated when data transfer is no longer required.

We can think of the connection-oriented LLC service as a pair of pipes that connect two LAN data link users, one for data flowing in each direction. A user of the LLC sublayer service at the source end inserts an LLC-PDU into the appropriate pipe, and an identical copy of the LLC-PDU emerges at the destination end. The protocol that provides the connection-oriented LLC service attempts to correct any errors that are detected by retransmitting LLC-PDUs that are corrupted by transmission errors. With the connection-oriented LLC service, an identical copy of an LLC-PDU emerges from the pipe for each LLC-PDU transmitted, whether or not transmission errors occur. The protocol that provides the connection-oriented LLC service handles necessary PDU retransmissions. If an error occurs from which the LLC sublayer service cannot recover, the LLC sublayer releases the connection and informs the two LAN data link users that the connection has been broken.

The connection-oriented LLC service supports two functions related to error correction—sequence checking and message acknowledgment. LLC-PDUs being sent are assigned sequence numbers. As LLC-PDUs are received, the sequence number of each incoming LLC-PDU is checked to ensure that LLC-PDUs have arrived in the sequence sent and that no LLC-PDUs are missing or duplicated. Periodically, the receiving LLC sublayer entity sends an acknowledgment so the source LLC sublayer entity knows that the LLC-PDUs have arrived successfully. If problems occur and the destination LLC sublayer entity informs the source LLC sublayer entity that LLC-PDUs were not successfully received, the source LLC sublayer entity is able to retransmit them. The protocol mechanisms that are associated with sequence checking and acknowledgments are described later in this chapter.

Since the connection-oriented LLC service always involves a *pair* of LLC sublayer entities, there is no provision for delivering an LLC-PDU to more than one destination service-access-point. Therefore, the connection-oriented LLC service does not provide a multicasting mechanism. If the source user of the LAN data link wishes to send an LLC-PDU to more than one destination user, a separate connection must be established with each destination SAP, and a copy of the LLC-PDU must be sent in a separate transmission to each destination user.

Acknowledged Connectionless Service

The *acknowledged connectionless LLC service* is somewhat of a compromise between the completely unacknowledged connectionless service and the connection-oriented service. At the time of writing, it is being considered for incorporation into the LLC standard to support certain types of process control applications. Few LAN implementations provide the acknowledged connectionless service. Many authorities doubt whether it is really necessary, since it is quite complex and incurs almost as much protocol overhead as using the full connection-oriented service to provide the same capability. It is described in this chapter for completeness.

With the acknowledged connectionless LLC service, no connection is established between the source and destination systems, and there is no relationship between one LLC-PDU transmitted by a source system and any other LLC-PDU. But each LLC-PDU that is transmitted by a source system is acknowledged by the destination system. The acknowledged connectionless service is considered to be a guaranteed delivery service because the entity that requests a data transmission service is informed if the LLC-PDU fails to be delivered.

Connectionless versus Connection-Oriented Service

At first glance, it may appear as though the connection-oriented service or the acknowledged connectionless service are to be preferred because of their ability to handle errors that may occur during transmission. However, the vast majority of LAN implementations employ only the connectionless LLC service. This is because in a typical network architecture, error correction procedures are implemented in a higher layer of the architecture no matter what type of service is provided by the Data Link layer. Also, most LAN data links are highly reliable, and very few errors typically occur during physical transmission.

The terms *reliable* and *unreliable* are often used to differentiate a connection-oriented data transfer service from a connectionless service. A connection-oriented service is referred to as a *reliable* service while a connectionless service is often termed *unreliable*. It is important to realize that the terms *reliable* and *unreliable* in this context are not meant to have *good* or *bad* connotations. For example, a connection-oriented service, although considered reliable, would provide a very poor service if large numbers of failures caused the connection to be frequently broken. On the other hand, a connectionless service may deliver 999,999 messages out of every 1,000,000 sent. However, we cannot consider it reliable because we don't know for sure.

The service that the LLC sublayer itself is providing must not be confused with the service that the network as a whole provides to an end user when all the layers of a particular architecture are considered. To make good use of an unreliable data transfer service in a lower layer of the architecture it is only necessary to ensure that the required reliability controls are implemented in a higher layer. This ensures that the end user is ultimately provided with a reliable message delivery service, whether or not a reliable data transfer service is provided by the LLC sublayer. Most modern networking systems provide such controls in a higher layer and allow a connectionless data transfer service to be used in the LLC sublayer.

We will next describe in detail the service primitives that define each of the three general types of LLC service we have introduced.

ISO SERVICE PRIMITIVES

As we introduced in Chapter 4, international standards—including those for local area networking technology—typically document service definitions using the ISO scheme of *service primitives*. The four general types of ISO service primitives introduced in Chapter 4 are reviewed in Box 7.1.

A particular Logical Link Control sublayer service employs one or more service primitives to provide that service. The LLC sublayer service definition defines the service primitives that are used in providing each LLC service.

Semantics versus Syntax

It is important to realize that the Logical Link Control standard defines only the *semantics*, or the *meaning*, of service primitives, using an abstract form of representation. The

BOX 7.1　ISO service primitive types.

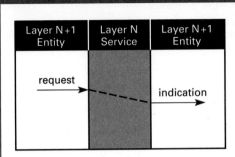

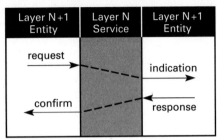

Nonconfirmed Service　　　　　　　　Confirmed Service

- **Request.** Issued by a service requester to request that a particular service be performed by a lower-level layer and to pass parameters needed to fully specify the requested service.

- **Confirm.** Issued by the service provider to notify the higher-level layer service requester of the results of one or more *request* primitives that the service requester previously issued.

- **Indication.** Issued by the lower-level service provider to notify a higher-level service requester that a significant event has occurred.

- **Response.** Issued by the higher-level service requester to acknowledge or complete some procedure previously invoked by the lower-level service provider through an *indication* primitive.

standard does not specify a particular application programming interface (API) coding *syntax* for invoking a particular service, nor does it define how a service is to be implemented. For example, a particular service primitive might be implemented using a procedure call mechanism in a particular programming language, or it might be implemented in hardware possibly using an interrupt mechanism.

Issues of an application programming interface and other implementation details are the responsibility of the vendors that build LAN hardware and software products. Chapter 9 examines two specific implementations of the LLC sublayer standard as examples of how LLC sublayer services can be provided.

We next look at the service primitives that are defined for the three general types of LLC sublayer service.

SERVICE PRIMITIVES FOR THE CONNECTIONLESS LLC SERVICE

The connectionless service defines a single DL_UNITDATA data transfer service that involves the following two service primitives:

- **DL_UNITDATA.request.** Issued by a LAN data link user in the sending system to pass data to a Logical Link Control sublayer entity for transmission to one or more destination service-access-points in one or more destination stations.

- **DL_UNITDATA.indication.** Issued by an LLC sublayer entity in the destination system in order to notify the LAN data link user in the destination system that data has been received by the LLC sublayer entity and to pass that data up to the LAN data link user.

Figure 7.1 shows a time-sequence diagram illustrating the sequence in which the two service primitives are issued in providing the DL_UNITDATA data transfer service. The DL_UNITDATA data transfer service is a nonconfirmed service in which the LAN data link user is not informed of the success or failure of an attempt to transmit an LLC-PDU.

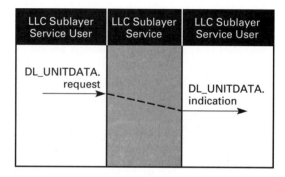

Figure 7.1   Time-sequence diagram for the DL_UNITDATA data transfer service.

Each of the two DL_UNITDATA service primitives has a set of parameters associated with it. These parameters define the information that is passed across the interface between the LAN data link user and the LLC sublayer itself as part of a service request. The parameters that are associated with the DL_UNITDATA.request and DL_UNITDATA.indication service primitives are described in Box 7.2.

SERVICE PRIMITIVES FOR THE CONNECTION-ORIENTED LLC SERVICE

For the connection-oriented service, the LLC standard defines the following services, each of which involves a separate set of service primitives:

- **DL_CONNECT.** A connection establishment service.
- **DL_DATA.** A data transfer service.
- **DL_DISCONNECT.** A connection release service.
- **DL_RESET.** A connection reset service.
- **DL_CONNECTION_FLOWCONTROL.** A flow control service.

BOX 7.2   DL_UNITDATA service primitive parameters.

DL_UNITDATA.request   (
                        source_address,
                        destination_address,
                        data,
                        priority
)

DL_UNITDATA.indication   (
                        source_address,
                        destination_address,
                        data,
                        priority
)

- **source_address.** Specifies a source data link address consisting of a combination of the source-service-access-point (SSAP) address and the source MAC address. The SSAP address is used by the LLC sublayer to identify the source LAN data link user, and the source MAC address is used by the MAC sublayer to identify the source station.

- **destination_address.** Specifies a destination data link address consisting of a combination of the destination-service-access-point (DSAP) address and the destination MAC address. This parameter can specify either individual or group addresses. The DSAP address is used by the LLC sublayer to identify the destination LAN data link user or users, and the destination MAC address is used by the MAC sublayer to identify the destination station or stations. Full source and destination data link addresses must be specified for each data transmission request.

- **data.** Specifies the information to be transmitted.

- **priority.** Specifies the priority desired for the transmission. Note that not all medium access control technologies support a priority mechanism.

DL_CONNECT Service

The DL_CONNECT connection establishment service is used to establish a logical link connection between two users of the LLC sublayer service. The DL_CONNECT service is provided through the following four service primitives:

- **DL_CONNECT.request.** Issued by a LAN data link user in the source system to request that a connection be established with a LAN data link user in a destination system. This primitive causes an LLC-PDU that carries information about the connection establishment request to be sent from the source LLC-entity to the destination LLC-entity.

- **DL_CONNECT.indication.** Issued by the LLC sublayer entity in the destination station to notify the LAN data link user in the destination system that a connection has been requested by a LAN data link user in the source system.

- **DL_CONNECT.response.** Issued by a LAN data link user in the destination system to indicate that it has received a connection establishment request. This primitive causes an acknowledgment to be sent from the destination station to the source station.

- **DL_CONNECT.confirm.** Issued by the LLC sublayer entity in the source station to notify a LAN data link user in the source system of the results of the connection establishment request.

Figure 7.2 includes four time-sequence diagrams showing various ways in which the four DL_CONNECT service primitives are used in attempting to establish an LLC connection. DL_CONNECT is a confirmed service in which the LAN data link user that is attempting to establish a connection is informed of the success or failure of the connection establishment request.

The parameters that are associated with the DL_CONNECT service primitives are described in Box 7.3. The three parameters included with the primitives are the same as the corresponding ones included in the service primitives for connectionless service. No data parameter is included, since these primitives are not used for data transfer but only for the management of connections.

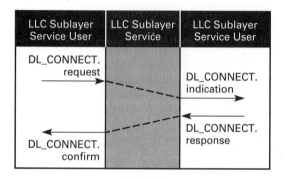

Successful Connection Establishment

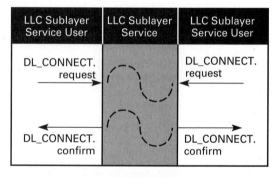

Connection Establishment Collision

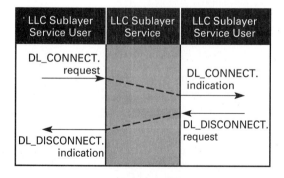

User Rejection of an Attempt
to Establish a Connection

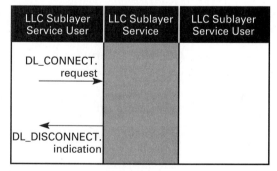

LLC Service Rejection of an Attempt
to Establish a Connection

Figure 7.2 Time-sequence diagrams for the DL_CONNECT connection establishment service.

BOX 7.3   DL_CONNECT service primitive parameters.

DL_CONNECT.request   (
                      source_address,
                      destination_address,
                      priority
)

DL_CONNECT.indication   (
                        source_address,
                        destination_address,
                        priority
)

DL_CONNECT.response   (
                       source_address,
                       destination_address,
                       priority
)

DL_CONNECT.confirm   (
                      source_address,
                      destination_address,
                      priority
)

- **source_address.** Specifies a source data link address consisting of a combination of the source service-access-point (SSAP) address and the source MAC address.

- **destination_address.** Specifies a destination data link address consisting of a combination of the destination service-access-point (DSAP) address and the destination MAC address. For the connection establishment service, full data link addresses must be provided in the source and destination address parameters in the same manner as for the connectionless data transmission service. The connection establishment service may assign a shorter connection identifier to the connection to differentiate the connection from other connections that may be active in the same system. The connection identifier may then be used in place of full data link addresses in the other services that make up the connection-oriented LLC service.

- **priority.** Specifies the priority desired for the transmission. Not all forms of medium access control technology support a priority mechanism.

DL_DATA Service

The DL_DATA service is a data transfer service that can be employed by two LAN data link users after a connection has been successfully established using the DL_CONNECT service. The DL_DATA service is provided using the following two service primitives:

- **DL_DATA.request.** Issued by a LAN data link user in the source system to pass an LLC-SDU to an LLC sublayer entity for transmission over a previously established connection.

- **DL_DATA.indication.** Issued by an LLC sublayer entity in the destination station to indicate to the LAN data link user that data has been received and to pass the data up to the LAN data link user.

Figure 7.3 shows the sequence in which the two DL_DATA data transfer service primitives are issued in carrying out a data transfer operation.

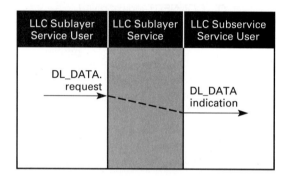

Figure 7.3   Time-sequence diagram for the DL_DATA data transfer service.

Notice that the LAN data link user that requested the data transfer is not informed of the success or failure of the data transfer operation. However, the connection-oriented data transfer service is a guaranteed delivery service, and the LAN data link user can assume that delivery was accomplished. The term *guaranteed delivery* can be misleading because it is possible for the data transfer operation to fail. In the case of the DL_DATA service, the data transfer will either be successful, in which case the LAN data link user is told nothing and can assume that delivery has taken place, or the LAN data link user will be informed of the failure by having the connection either reset or disconnected using one of the two services described next.

Box 7.4 describes the parameters that are associated with the two service primitives that make up the DL_DATA data transfer service.

DL_DISCONNECT Service

The DL_DISCONNECT service is used to release a connection that was previously established by the DL_CONNECT service. The DL_DISCONNECT service is provided through the following two service primitives:

- **DL_DISCONNECT.request.** Issued by either a LAN data link user or the LLC sublayer entity to initiate a request for the release of a connection.

- **DL_DISCONNECT.indication.** Issued by an LLC sublayer entity to notify a LAN data link user of the results of a DL_DISCONNECT.request primitive.

BOX 7.4　DL_DATA service primitive parameters.

DL_DATA.request　（
　　　　　　　　　source_address,
　　　　　　　　　destination_address,
　　　　　　　　　data
　　　　　　　　　）

DL_DATA.indication　（
　　　　　　　　　source_address,
　　　　　　　　　destination_address,
　　　　　　　　　data
　　　　　　　　　）

- **source_address.** Specifies a source data link address consisting of a combination of the source-service-access-point (SSAP) address and the source MAC address.

- **destination_address.** Specifies a destination data link address consisting of a combination of the destination-service-access-point (DSAP) address and the destination MAC address. The destination_address parameter can specify either individual or group addresses. If the connection establishment service assigns a connection identifier to a connection, this service might support the use of the connection identifier in place of full data link addresses.

- **data.** Specifies the information to be transmitted.

Figure 7.4 shows four time-sequence diagrams that illustrate how the two DL_DIS-CONNECT service primitives might be issued to release an existing LLC connection. The DL_DISCONNECT service is a nonconfirmed service.

Box 7.5 describes the parameters that are associated with the DL_DISCONNECT service.

DL_RESET Service

The DL_RESET service can be used to reset an LLC connection to its initial state while data is being transferred. The reset operation can be issued by either the LAN data link user or the LLC sublayer entity on either end of the LLC connection. The DL_RESET service is provided through the following four service primitives:

- **DL_RESET.request.** Requests that a connection be reset.
- **DL_RESET.indication.** Issued by an LLC sublayer entity to notify a LAN data link user of a request to reset the connection.
- **DL_RESET.response.** Issued by the LAN data link user to acknowledge receipt of the DL_RESET.indication primitive.
- **DL_RESET.confirm.** Issued by an LLC sublayer entity to notify the LAN data link user of the results of a reset request.

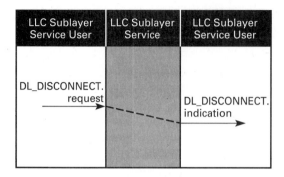

Connection Release Requested
by an LLC Sublayer Service User

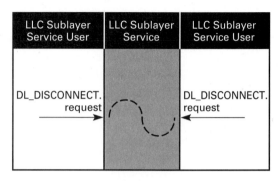

Connection Release Requested
Simultaneously by Both LLC Sublayer
Service Users

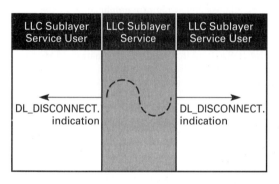

Connection Release Requested
by the LLC Sublayer Service

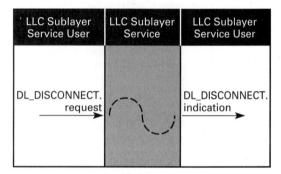

Connection Release Requested Simultaneously by
an LLC Sublayer Service
User and the LLC Sublayer Service

Figure 7.4 Time-sequence diagrams for the DL_DISCONNECT connection release service.

Figure 7.5 shows a possible sequence in which the four DL_RESET service primitives might be issued in resetting an existing LLC sublayer connection. The DL_RESET service is a confirmed service that is explicitly confirmed by the distant LAN data link user.

Box 7.6 describes the parameters that are associated with the DL_RESET service.

DL_CONNECTION_FLOWCONTROL Service

The DL_CONNECTION_FLOWCONTROL service can be used to control the amount of data that is passed between a LAN data link user and an LLC sublayer entity. The DL_CONNECTION_ FLOWCONTROL service is provided through the following two service primitives:

- **DL_CONNECTION_FLOWCONTROL.request.** Issued by a LAN data link user to an LLC sublayer entity to control the flow of data from the LLC sublayer entity to the LAN data link user over a particular connection.

- **DL_CONNECTION_FLOWCONTROL.indication.** Issued by an LLC sublayer entity to a LAN data link user to control the flow of data from the LAN data link user to the LLC sublayer entity over a particular connection.

BOX 7.5   DL_DISCONNECT service primitive parameters.

DL_DISCONNECT.request   (
                             source_address,
                             destination_address
)

DL_DISCONNECT.indication   (
                             source_address,
                             destination_address,
                             reason
)

- **source_address.** Specifies a source data link address consisting of a combination of the source-service-access-point (SSAP) address and the source MAC address.

- **destination_address.** Specifies a destination data link address consisting of a combination of the destination-service-access-point (DSAP) address and the destination MAC address. It can specify either individual or group addresses. As with the data transfer service, a connection identifier may be used in place of full data link addresses.

- **reason.** Indicates to the LAN data link user which entity initiated the disconnect request.

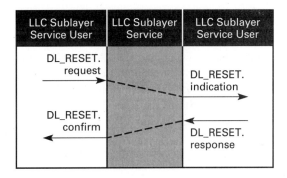

Figure 7.5   Time-sequence diagram for the DL_RESET connection reset service.

BOX 7.6   DL_RESET service primitive parameters.

DL_RESET.request   (
source_address,
destination_address
)

DL_RESET.indication   (
source_address,
destination_address,
reason
)

DL_RESET.response   (
source_address,
destination_address
)

DL_RESET.confirm   (
source_address,
destination_address
)

- **source_address.** Specifies a source data link address consisting of a combination of the source-service-access-point (SSAP) address and the source MAC address.

- **destination_address.** Specifies a destination data link address consisting of a combination of the destination-service-access-point (DSAP) address and the destination MAC address. It can specify either individual or group addresses. As with the data transfer service, a connection identifier may be used in place of full data link addresses.

- **reason.** Indicates to the LAN data link user which entity initiated the reset request.

Figure 7.6 shows how a DL_CONNECTION_FLOWCONTROL service primitive can be issued independently by either the LAN data link user or the LLC sublayer service provider to control the flow of data in either direction. The DL_CONNECTION_FLOW-CONTROL service is a nonconfirmed service.

Box 7.7 describes the parameters that are associated with the DL_CONNECTION_FLOWCONTROL service.

SERVICE PRIMITIVES FOR THE ACKNOWLEDGED CONNECTIONLESS SERVICE

The primitives used with the *acknowledged connectionless service* can be used to provide two related but independent services:

- **DL_DATA_ACK.** A data transfer service.
- **DL_REPLY.** A reply and reply update service.

Neither of the above two services requires that a connection be established between communicating users before they are used.

DL_DATA_ACK Service

The DL_DATA_ACK service is a service in which an LLC-PDU is sent from a LAN data link user in the source system to a LAN data link user in the destination system. With this service, only one LLC-PDU can be outstanding at a time, and it must be acknowledged before the next LLC-PDU can be transmitted. The DL_DATA_ACK service is provided through the following three service primitives:

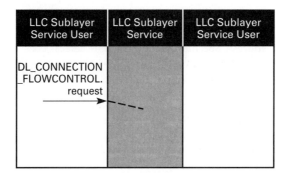

Controlling the Flow from the LLC
Sublayer to the LLC Sublayer User

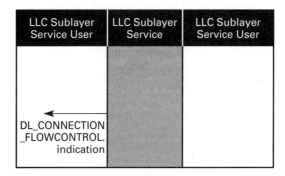

Controlling the Flow From the LLC
Sublayer User to the LLC Sublayer

Figure 7.6 Time-sequence diagrams for the DL_CONNECTION_FLOW-CONTROL flow control service.

BOX 7.7   DL_CONNECTION_FLOWCONTROL service primitive parameters.

DL_CONNECTION_FLOWCONTROL.request
(
source_address,
destination_address,
amount
)

DL_CONNECTION_FLOWCONTROL.indication
(
source_address,
destination_address,
amount
)

- **source_address.** Specifies a source data link address consisting of a combination of the source-service-access-point (SSAP) address and the source MAC address.

- **destination_address.** Specifies a destination data link address consisting of a combination of the destination-service-access-point (DSAP) address and the destination MAC address. It can specify either individual or group addresses. As with the data transfer service, a connection identifier may be used in place of full data link addresses.

- **amount.** Specifies the amount of data that can be passed. The value can be changed in each request or indication primitive that is issued. Specifying an amount value of 0 causes the data flow to stop in the specified direction.

- **DL_DATA_ACK.request.** Issued by a LAN data link user to pass an LLC-SDU to the LLC sublayer entity in the source station for transmission to the destination station.

- **DL_DATA_ACK.indication.** Issued by an LLC sublayer entity in the destination station to indicate to the LAN data link user that an LLC-PDU has been received and to pass the LLC-SDU up to the LAN data link user in the destination system.

- **DL_DATA_ACK_STATUS.indication.** Issued by an LLC sublayer entity in the source station to the LAN data link user to indicate whether or not the LLC-PDU sent as a result of a DL_DATA_ACK.request primitive was successfully received and, if not, what was the cause of the failure to deliver the LLC-PDU.

Figure 7.7 shows the sequence in which the three DL_DATA_ ACK service primitives are issued. The DL_DATA_ACK service, while not confirmed by the distant LAN data link user, is a guaranteed delivery service. This is because the distant LLC sublayer entity informs the source data link user of the success or failure of the data delivery attempt.

Box 7.8 describes the parameters that are associated with the DL_DATA_ACK service.

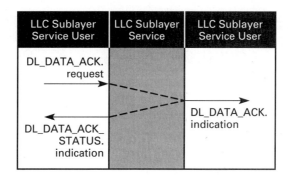

Figure 7.7 Time-sequence diagram for the DL_DATA_ACK acknowledged delivery data transfer service.

DL_REPLY Service

The DL_REPLY service consists of a poll with a guaranteed response to the poll. This service allows a LAN data link user to pass an LLC-SDU to an LLC sublayer entity in the user's station to be held for later transmission to one or more other users. It then allows LAN data link users in other systems in the network to request delivery of the LLC-SDU that the first system is holding. The DL_REPLY service implements two sub-services that are together provided through five service primitives.

Reply Update Subservice

The first two service primitives are used to provide a *reply update* subservice and are issued to pass an LLC-SDU to the LLC sublayer to be held for later delivery to those systems that request it:

- **DL_REPLY_UPDATE.request.** Issued by a LAN data link user to pass an LLC-SDU to an LLC sublayer entity to be held by that entity for later delivery to users that request it. Each time the LAN data link user issues this service primitive, the LLC-SDU the LLC sublayer is currently holding is replaced by the new LLC-SDU.

- **DL_REPLY_UPDATE_STATUS.indication.** Issued by an LLC sublayer entity to indicate to the LAN data link user the success or failure of a DL_REPLY_UPDATE.request primitive.

Figure 7.8 shows the sequence in which the two DL_REPLY_ UPDATE service primitives are issued.

Reply Subservice

The remaining three service primitives are used to provide a *reply* subservice and are issued to request delivery of an LLC-SDU that the destination station is holding and, optionally, to transmit an LLC-PDU to the destination station:

- **DL_REPLY.request.** Issued by a LAN data link user to request delivery of the LLC-SDU that the destination station is holding as a result of a DL_REPLY_UPDATE.request

BOX 7.8 DL_DATA_ACK service primitive parameters.

DL_DATA_ACK.request
(
source_address,
destination_address,
data,
priority,
service_class
)

DL_DATA_ACK.indication (
source_address,
destination_address,
data,
priority,
service_class
)

DL_DATA_ACK_STATUS.indication
(
source_address,
destination_address,
priority,
service_class,
status
)

- **source_address.** Specifies a source data link address consisting of a combination of the source-service-access-point (SSAP) address and the source MAC address. The SSAP address is used by the LLC sublayer to identify the source LAN data link user, and the source MAC address is used by the MAC sublayer to identify the source station.

- **destination_address.** Specifies a destination data link address consisting of a combination of the destination-service-access-point (DSAP) address and the destination MAC address. This parameter can specify either individual or group addresses. The DSAP address is used by the LLC sublayer to identify the destination LAN data link user, and the destination MAC address is used by the MAC sublayer to identify the destination station. Full source and destination data link addresses must be specified for each data transmission request.

- **data.** Specifies the information to be transmitted.

- **priority.** Specifies the priority desired for transmission. Not all forms of medium access control technology supports a priority mechanism.

- **status.** Indicates the results of the previous DL_DATA_ACK. request primitive.

- **service_class.** Specifies whether an acknowledge capability in the MAC entity is used for LLC-PDU transmission. Only the Token Bus standard supports this capability, which is discussed in Chapter 12.

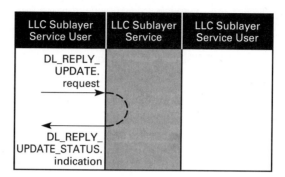

Figure 7.8   Time-sequence diagram for the DL_REPLY_UPDATE reply update service.

primitive that the destination station issued previously. This service primitive can option-ally also be used to send an LLC-PDU to the destination station.

- **DL_REPLY.indication.** Issued by an LLC sublayer entity in the destination station to indicate to the LAN data link user that a request has been received to transmit the LLC-SDU the LLC sublayer entity is holding. It also causes the LLC-SDU that the LLC sub-layer entity is holding to be transmitted to the source LLC entity.

- **DL_REPLY_STATUS.indication.** Issued by an LLC sublayer entity in the source sta-tion to indicate to the LAN data link user the success or failure of a DL_REPLY.request primitive and to pass the LLC-SDU that was received as a result of that request up to the LAN data link user.

Figure 7.9 shows the sequence in which the three DL_REPLY service primitives are issued. The example assumes that the system on the left has the reply data ready to deliver as a result of a previous DL_REPLY_UPDATE sequence, and so shows the sequence proceeding in the opposite direction from the other examples. The DL_REPLY service is a guaranteed delivery service in which the LAN data link user is informed of the success or failure of the data delivery attempt by the distant LLC sublayer entity.

Box 7.9 shows the parameters that are associated with the service primitives for the DL_REPLY service.

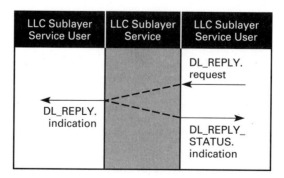

Figure 7.9   Time-sequence diagram for the DL_REPLY reply request service.

BOX 7.9   DL_REPLY service primitive parameters.

DL_REPLY_UPDATE.request
(
source_address,
data
)

DL_REPLY_UPDATE_STATUS.indication
(
source_address,
status
)

DL_REPLY.request
(
source_address,
destination_address,
data,
priority,
service_class
)

DL_REPLY.indication
(
source_address,
destination_address,
data,
priority,
service_class
)

DL_REPLY_STATUS.indication
(
source_address,
destination_address,
data,
priority,
service_class,
status
)

- **source_address.** Specifies a source data link address consisting of a combination of the source-service-access-point (SSAP) address and the source MAC address. The SSAP address is used by the LLC sublayer to identify the source LAN data link user, and the source MAC address is used by the MAC sublayer to identify the source station.

BOX 7.9   *(Continued)*

- **destination_address.** Specifies a destination data link address consisting of a combination of the destination-service-access-point (DSAP) address and the destination MAC address. This parameter can specify either individual or group addresses. The DSAP address is used by the LLC sublayer to identify the destination LAN data link user, and the destination MAC address is used by the MAC sublayer to identify the destination station. Full source and destination data link addresses must be specified for each data transmission request.

- **data.** Specifies the information to be transmitted.

- **priority.** Specifies the priority desired for the transmission. Not all forms of medium access control technology support a priority mechanism.

- **status.** Indicates the results of the previous request primitive.

- **service_class.** Specifies whether an acknowledge capability in the MAC entity is used for the LLC-PDU transmission.

SUMMARY

The Logical Link Control sublayer service definition precisely documents the services that the LLC sublayer provides to a user of the LAN data link. It also describes the information that the user software must provide to the LLC sublayer in requesting its services. The Logical Link Control sublayer defines two types of services with a third proposed for possible addition to the standard.

The connectionless LLC service delivers LLC-PDUs on a best-efforts basis and provides no error correction or flow control. The connectionless LLC service is provided through the DL_UNITDATA data transfer service.

The connection-oriented LLC service can be used for reliable data transmission in which a logical association is established between the source and destination systems. The connection-oriented LLC service defines sequence checking and acknowledgment mechanisms for flow control and error recovery. The connection-oriented LLC service is provided by the DL_CONNECT connection establishment service, the DL_DATA data transfer service, the DL_DISCONNECT connection release service, the DL_RESET connection reset service, and the DL_CONNECTION_FLOWCONTROL flow control service.

The acknowledged connectionless service is a proposed addition to the LLC standard that defines a compromise between the connectionless service and the connection-oriented service. The acknowledged connectionless service is provided by the DL_DATA_ACK data transfer service and the DL_REPLY reply and reply update service.

Chapter **8**

LLC Protocol Specification

In Chapter 7, we examined the LLC *services* that define the interface between the LLC sublayer and the LAN data link user. Another important part of the Logical Link Control sublayer standard concerns the *protocols* that enable an LLC sublayer entity in one system to communicate with an LLC sublayer entity in another system. The Logical Link Control protocol specifies the means by which the LLC sublayer service is provided.

We begin by reviewing the format of the logical-link-control-protocol-data-unit (LLC-PDU) that flows between LLC sublayer entities. We then describe the protocol mechanisms that are used by the Logical Link Control sublayer in controlling the flow of LLC-PDUs to provide the three types of LLC service described in Chapter 7.

LLC-PROTOCOL-DATA-UNIT

In transmitting an LLC-PDU from a source LLC sublayer entity to a destination LLC sublayer entity, the source LLC sublayer entity passes the LLC-PDU down to the Medium Access Control sublayer. Box 8.1 shows the format of the LLC-PDU and describes its fields.

Note that the DSAP field can contain either an individual address value or a group address value. A group DSAP value allows an LLC-PDU to be delivered to a group of service-access-points in a destination station. Such a multicasting mechanism can be implemented in a variety of ways, such as through a SAP address filtering mechanism, as described in Chapter 6.

Commands and Responses

An LLC-PDU can take the form of either a *command* or a *response*. A command is sent by an LLC sublayer entity that is initiating a data transfer operation. A response is sent by the distant LLC sublayer entity in reply to a command. The first bit of the SSAP value indicates whether the LLC-PDU is a command or a response. A 0 bit indicates a command and a 1 bit indicates a response.

DSAP Address	SSAP Address	Control	Information
1 octet	1 octet	1 or 2 octets	0 – *n* octets

BOX 8.1   Logical-link-control-protocol-data-unit (LLC-PDU).

- **Source- and Destination-Service-Access-Point Address Fields.** A 1-octet destination-service-access-point (DSAP) address followed by a 1-octet source-service-access-point (SSAP) address. The formats of DSAP and SSAP addresses are described in Chapter 6.

- **Control Field.** A 1- or 2-octet field that describes the LLC-PDU's type and contains control information. The formats of LLC-PDU control fields are described later in this chapter.

- **Information Field.** A variable-length field that typically contains the packet passed down from the layer above the LLC sublayer. The Information field is supplied by the LLC sublayer itself for LLC-PDUs that are generated by the LLC sublayer. It can consist of 0 octets for some LLC-PDU types.

LLC-PDU Types

There are three general types of LLC-PDUs. The following are brief descriptions of each of them:

- **Information LLC-PDUs.** The primary function of an *Information* LLC-PDU (I-format LLC-PDU) is to carry user data. However, I-format LLC-PDUs sometimes also perform control functions.

- **Supervisory LLC-PDUs.** *Supervisory* LLC-PDUs (S-format LLC-PDUs) are used to carry information necessary to control the operation of the LLC sublayer protocol.

- **Unnumbered LLC-PDUs.** *Unnumbered* LLC-PDUs (U-format LLC-PDUs) are sometimes used to carry data and are sometimes used for special functions, such as performing initialization procedures and invoking diagnostic sequences.

I-format LLC-PDUs and S-format LLC-PDUs carry 2-octet control fields; U-format LLC-PDUs carry 1-octet control fields.

Each of the three types of LLC protocol operation uses a different set of LLC-PDUs to carry out its functions. The specific LLC-PDUs that are used for each type of protocol operation are described later in this chapter.

LLC-PDU Names and Mnemonics

Each of the LLC-PDUs that are used to provide the LLC sublayer service has a *full name* and a shorthand *mnemonic*. For example, one of the LLC-PDUs employed in the protocol for supplying the connectionless LLC service is the Exchange Identification (XID) LLC-PDU. Its full name is *Exchange Identification*, and its mnemonic is *XID*.

I-Format LLC-PDU Control Field Format

Figure 8.1 illustrates the format of the I-format LLC-PDU control field. Bit positions 1 and 2 in the first control field octet identify the LLC-PDU's type. An I-format LLC-PDU

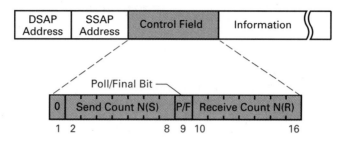

Figure 8.1 I-format LLC-PDU control field format.

always has a 0 in bit position 1. The remainder of the bits in the I-format LLC-PDU control field are used to contain a receive count [N(R)], a send count [N(S)], and a poll/final (P/F) bit. The count fields and the Poll/Final bit are used in implementing error-detection mechanisms that are described later in this chapter.

S-Format LLC-PDU Control Field Format

Figure 8.2 shows the format of the S-format LLC-PDU control field for the various S-format LLC-PDUs that are used to implement the LLC protocol. The use of each LLC-PDU is described later in this chapter.

When bit position 1 of the first control field octet is 1, bit position 2 further identifies the LLC-PDU as being either an S-format LLC-PDU or a U-format LLC-PDU. A 10 in bit positions 1 and 2 identifies the LLC-PDU as an S-format LLC-PDU. The remainder of the bits in the S-format LLC-PDU control octet are interpreted as containing a receive count [N(R)], a poll/final bit, and a 2-bit function code. The function code bits identify the type of command or response the LLC-PDU represents.

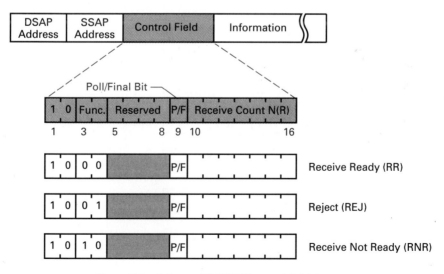

Figure 8.2 S-format LLC-PDU control field format.

U-Format LLC-PDU Control Field Format

Figure 8.3 shows the format of the U-format LLC-PDU control field for the various S-format LLC-PDUs that are used to implement the LLC protocol. The use of each LLC-PDU is described later in this chapter.

A 11-bit configuration in bit positions 1 and 2 of the first control field octet identifies the LLC-PDU as a U-format LLC-PDU and indicates that the control field is only 1 octet in length. The remainder of the bits are interpreted as a poll/final bit and function

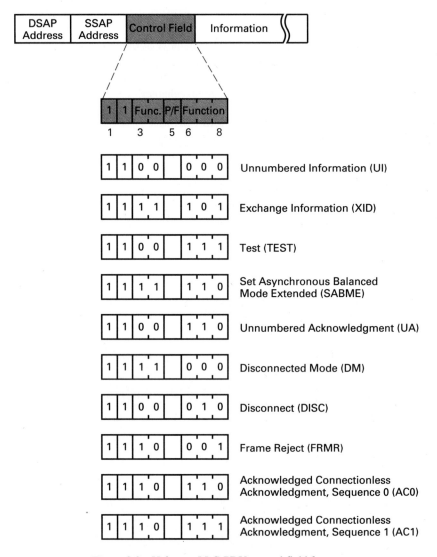

Figure 8.3   U-format LLC-PDU control field format.

code bits. The function code bits in a U-format LLC-PDU identify the type of command or response the LLC-PDU represents. Some U-format LLC-PDU commands and responses have information fields; others do not.

LLC PROTOCOL OPERATIONAL MODES

In Chapter 7, we described the service primitives that are defined for the three forms of service that the Logical Link Control sublayer can implement. Each of the three forms of LLC service are provided by a different type of LLC protocol operation.

Types of LLC Protocol Operation

The Logical Link Control standard describes two types of LLC protocol operation that correspond to the first two forms of LLC service that we examined in Chapter 7:

- **Type 1 Operation.** With *Type 1 Operation*, the LLC protocol provides the connectionless LLC service.
- **Type 2 Operation.** With *Type 2 Operation*, the LLC protocol provides the connection-oriented LLC service.

A third type of LLC protocol operation has been proposed for addition to the Logical Link Control standard:

- **Type 3 Operation.** With *Type 3 Operation*, the LLC protocol provides the acknowledged connectionless LLC service.

Implementation Classes

Implementations of the Logical Link Control standard are classified according to the types of LLC protocol operation they support. The Logical Link Control standard defines two LLC implementation classes:

- **Class I LLC.** A *Class I LLC* implementation supports only Type 1 operation and provides only the connectionless LLC service.
- **Class II LLC.** A *Class II LLC* implementation supports Type 1 and Type 2 operation and provides both the connectionless LLC service and the connection-oriented LLC service.

Two additional LLC implementation classes have been proposed as possible additions to the Logical Link Control standard:

- **Class III LLC.** A *Class III LLC* implementation supports Type 1 and Type 3 operation and provides both the connectionless LLC service and the acknowledged connectionless LLC service.
- **Class IV LLC.** A *Class IV LLC* implementation supports Type 1, Type 2, and Type 3 service and provides the connectionless LLC service, the connection-oriented LLC service, and the acknowledged connectionless LLC service.

Notice that all implementations of Logical Link Control, to be considered in conformance with the Logical Link Control standard, must support Type 1 operation at a minimum and must provide the connectionless LLC service. Most implementations of LLC are Class I LLC implementations and provide only the connectionless LLC service.

We next examine the specific LLC-PDUs and the protocol mechanisms that apply to each of the three types of LLC operation.

PROTOCOL FOR TYPE 1 CONNECTIONLESS OPERATION

The protocol for Type 1 operation provides the connectionless LLC service. Three U-format LLC-PDUs that are used to support Type 1 operation are listed in Box 8.2.

BOX 8.2   LLC-PDUs for type 1 operation.

- **Unnumbered Information (UI).** Unnumbered Information (UI) commands and responses are used to convey user data between a pair of LLC entities.

- **Exchange Identification (XID).** Exchange Identification (XID) commands and responses are used to exchange identification information between a source and a destination LLC entity.

- **Test (TEST).** Test (TEST) commands and responses are used to conduct a loopback test of the transmission path between two LLC entities.

The protocol mechanisms for Type 1 operation provide for a data transfer service and simple station identification and loopback testing procedures. The following are descriptions of each of the procedures that are used during Type 1 operation.

Data Transfer

An LLC sublayer entity carries out a request for a data transfer operation by encapsulating each received LLC-SDU in an Unnumbered Information (UI) LLC-PDU command and then uses the MAC sublayer service to transmit the UI command over the transmission medium. An LLC sublayer entity receiving a UI command passes it up, in the form of an LLC-SDU, to the appropriate LAN data link user or users in the layer above. When a UI command is received by an LLC sublayer entity in the destination station, no sequence checking is done, and the LLC sublayer entity in the destination station sends no acknowledgment.

Error Detection

Error detection is implemented by the MAC sublayer on behalf of the LLC sublayer. The error detection mechanism that the MAC sublayer uses is described here, since a similar error detection mechanism is used for all the various medium access control technologies.

When the MAC sublayer receives an LLC-PDU from the LLC sublayer in the form of a MAC-SDU, the MAC sublayer encapsulates the MAC-SDU in a MAC frame. As part of the encapsulation process, the MAC sublayer places the frame through an algorithm that calculates a cyclical redundancy check (CRC) value. This CRC value becomes part of the MAC frame the MAC sublayer sends over the transmission medium. When the MAC sublayer in a destination system accepts a frame, it places the frame through an identical algorithm to calculate its own CRC value. The destination system then compares the calculated CRC value with the received value. If the values match, the MAC sublayer assumes that no errors have occurred. If the values do not match, the MAC sublayer assumes that the MAC frame was corrupted during transmission.

When the MAC sublayer detects a transmission error, it discards the corrupted frame. The MAC sublayer that detects a corrupted frame need not notify either the source or destination LLC sublayer entity of the error. The LLC sublayer receives only error-free LLC-PDUs. The LLC sublayer does not receive LLC-PDUs that were corrupted by transmission errors. An error correction mechanism operating in a higher layer typically detects missing frames that were corrupted during transmission and requests their retransmission.

Exchanging Identification Information

Any LLC sublayer entity that receives an Exchange Identification (XID) LLC-PDU command is required to generate an XID LLC-PDU response specifying the class of service it can support.

The exact way in which the XID command is used is left as an implementation option. However, the Logical Link Control standard suggests possible uses for exchanging identification information using XID commands and responses. These include the following:

- Determining if a particular station is available on the network.
- Announcing the presence of a station on the network.
- Determining the stations assigned to a particular group address.
- Checking for duplicate addresses.
- Determining the implementation class an LLC implementation supports and choosing a type of protocol operation to use.
- For LLC entities supporting Type 2 operation, exchanging information concerning window sizes to implement error detection and flow control procedures.

Loopback Testing

When an LLC sublayer entity receives a TEST LLC-PDU command, it is required to send a TEST LLC-PDU response back to the user that sent the TEST command. An optional Information field can be included in the TEST command. If one is included, the TEST response must echo the Information field back. Exchanges of TEST commands and responses can be used to perform a basic test of the presence of a transmission path between LLC sublayer entities.

PROTOCOL FOR TYPE 2 CONNECTION-ORIENTED OPERATION

The protocol for Type 2 operation provides the connection-oriented LLC service. I-format, S-format, and U-format LLC-PDUs are used to support Type 2 operation. These are shown in Box 8.3.

The protocol mechanisms for Type 2 operation provide for a data transfer service and for performing LLC-PDU acknowledgments and sequence checking. The fol-

---

BOX 8.3   LLC-PDUs for type 2 operation.

I-Format LLC-PDU

- **Information (I).** I-format LLC-PDU commands and responses are used to transfer user data between two communicating LLC entities.

S-Format LLC-PDUs

- **Receive Ready.** A Receive Ready (RR) response is used as an acknowledgment to Information LLC-PDUs when there is no reverse traffic. An RR command can also be used to indicate that the LLC sublayer entity is able to receive additional LLC-PDUs after LLC-PDU transmission has been halted.

- **Receive Not Ready.** A Receive Not Ready (RNR) response is used to acknowledge receipt of an LLC-PDU and also to ask the sending LLC sublayer entity to stop transmitting I-format LLC-PDUs. The RNR response is used to handle possible internal constraints, such as lack of buffer space.

- **Reject.** A Reject (REJ) response is used to reject an LLC-PDU and to ask that it and any subsequent LLC-PDUs be retransmitted.

U-Format LLC-PDUs

- **Set Asynchronous Balanced Mode Extended.** A Set Asynchronous Balanced Mode Extended (SABME) command is used to request the establishment of a connection between a pair of LLC entities.

- **Disconnected Mode.** A Disconnected Mode (DM) response is used to reject a request for an establishment of an LLC connection.

- **Disconnect.** A Disconnect (DISC) command is used to request the release of a connection that was previously established using the SABME command.

- **Frame Reject.** A Frame Reject (FRMR) response is sent by a destination LLC sublayer entity to indicate that it has received an LLC-PDU that it is unable to handle, such as one that is invalid or unimplemented, has an invalid sequence number, or has an Information field that exceeds the maximum size.

- **Unnumbered Acknowledgment.** An Unnumbered Acknowledgment (UA) response is sent by a destination LLC sublayer entity as a positive acknowledgment. It is sent in response to an SABME LLC-PDU that requests a connection or to a DISC LLC-PDU that requests a connection release.

---

lowing are descriptions of the major protocol mechanisms that are used during Type 2 operation.

Sequence Checking

Transmission errors are detected using the error detection mechanism described for Type 1 operation, and erroneous frames are discarded by the MAC sublayer. The I-format and S-format commands and responses that are sent during Type 2 operation contain sequence numbers. These sequence numbers are used to detect the missing frames that result from discarded LLC-PDUs, to ensure that LLC-PDUs are received in the order in which they were sent, and to ensure that LLC-PDUs are not duplicated.

The *send count* [N(S)] field contains the sequence number of the LLC-PDU the LLC sublayer entity is sending, and the *receive count* [N(R)] field contains the sequence number the LLC sublayer entity expects to find in the next LLC-PDU it receives. Each LLC sublayer maintains a send counter and a receive counter. After an LLC sublayer entity sends each I-format LLC-PDU, the LLC entity updates its send counter. When an LLC sublayer entity receives an I-format command, it compares the send count [N(S)] value in the LLC-PDU with its own receive counter. If the LLC-PDU's N(S) field value matches the value in the LLC entity's own receive counter, it accepts the LLC-PDU and adds 1 to its receive counter. If the counter values do not match, the LLC entity assumes that there may be one or more missing frames, and it rejects the LLC-PDU.

Box 8.4 illustrates a data flow that shows how LLC sublayer entity send and receive counter values and the N(S) and N(R) count values in LLC-PDUs are used to detect missing frames.

Acknowledgments

There are several factors that determine when acknowledgments are required. One is the poll/final bit carried in each LLC-PDU's control field. When an LLC sublayer entity sends an I-format LLC-PDU that has its poll/final bit set to 1, the destination LLC sublayer entity must send back an acknowledgment immediately. If the destination LLC sublayer entity does not have an Information LLC-PDU ready to send at that time, it responds by sending an S-format Receive Ready (RR) response.

If an LLC sublayer entity receives an Information LLC-PDU that does not have the poll/final bit set to 1, the action taken by the LLC sublayer entity depends on several factors. If the LLC sublayer entity has already received a number of LLC-PDUs that is equal to a value called the *window size*, the LLC sublayer entity sends an acknowledgment; otherwise, the LLC sublayer entity waits for additional LLC-PDUs to arrive. If no additional LLC-PDUs arrive immediately, the LLC sublayer entity waits a period of time before sending an acknowledgment. The length of time is based on an *acknowledgment timer* that the LLC sublayer entity starts each time it receives a new Information LLC-PDU.

When the LLC sublayer entity starts sending LLC-PDUs, it also starts an acknowledgment timer. If no acknowledgment is received before the acknowledgment timer runs out, it sends an S-format LLC-PDU with the poll/final bit set to 1 to request an immediate acknowledgment. Depending on the response received, the LLC sublayer entity may resume sending, retransmit previously sent LLC-PDUs, or perform a reset procedure.

BOX 8.4　LLC data transfer data flow.

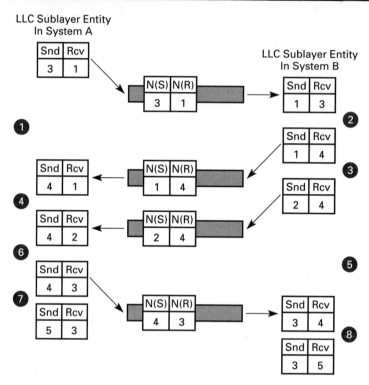

1. The LLC sublayer entity in system A sends an I-format command containing the current values of its send counter [N(S) = 3] and receive counter [N(R) = 1]. The LLC sublayer entity in system A adds 1 to the current value of its send counter making its new send counter value 4.

2. The LLC sublayer entity in system B receives the I-format LLC-PDU and checks that the N(S) field value in the received LLC-PDU matches its receive counter value. Since the two values match, the LLC entity in system B accepts the LLC-PDU and adds 1 to its receive counter. The value of 1 in the N(R) field in the LLC-PDU indicates that the LLC sublayer entity in system A expects the next LLC-PDU it receives from system B will have an N(S) field value of 1. This LLC-PDU acknowledges receipt of the LLC-PDU having an N(S) field value of 0.

3. The LLC sublayer entity in system B formats an LLC-PDU with an N(S) field value equal to its own send counter (1) and an N(R) field value equal to its own receive counter (4) and sends it. The LLC sublayer entity in system B then adds 1 to its send counter.

4. The LLC sublayer entity in system A receives the LLC-PDU, sequence checks it, and adds 1 to its receive counter. This LLC-PDU acknowledges receipt of the LLC-PDU sent by the LLC sublayer entity in system A having the N(S) value of 3.

BOX 8.4   (Continued)

5. The LLC sublayer entity in system B sends another LLC-PDU. This one has an [N(S)] field value of 2. The LLC sublayer entity in system B adds 1 to its send counter.

6. The LLC sublayer entity in system A receives the LLC-PDU, sequence checks it, and adds 1 to its receive counter.

7. The LLC sublayer entity in system A sends an LLC-PDU with N(S) = 4 and adds 1 to its send counter.

8. The LLC sublayer entity in system B receives the LLC-PDU, sequence checks it, and updates its receive counter. This LLC-PDU acknowledges receipt of LLC-PDUs with N(S) = 1 and N(S) = 2 sent by the LLC sublayer entity in system B.

Flow Control

The window size maintained by an LLC entity places a limit on the number of LLC-PDUs an LLC sublayer entity can send before it must wait for an acknowledgment. The window size value that source and destination LLC entities maintain acts as a flow control mechanism.

The window size has a maximum value of 127, reflecting the 7-bit size of the N(S) and N(R) count fields in an I-format LLC-PDU's control field. Window sizes can be set smaller than this. In some implementations of the Logical Link Control standard, LLC entities exchange XID commands and responses prior to establishing a connection to negotiate window size values. When an LLC sublayer entity sends the number of LLC-PDUs specified by the window size without receiving an acknowledgment, it stops sending until it receives an acknowledgment.

The window size limits the number of LLC-PDUs the source LLC sublayer entity transmits and thus prevents the destination LLC sublayer entity from being overloaded. If the LLC sublayer entity in the destination system waits for multiple LLC-PDUs to arrive, the number of LLC-PDUs that are allowed to accumulate before a response is sent depends on the window size. The destination LLC sublayer entity can also use acknowledgments and Receive Not Ready (RNR) commands to control the rate at which it receives LLC-PDUs. In this way the destination LLC sublayer entity can ensure that it does not receive more data than it has the resources to handle.

PROTOCOL FOR TYPE 3 ACKNOWLEDGED CONNECTIONLESS OPERATION

The protocol for Type 3 operation provides the acknowledged connectionless LLC service. The two U-format LLC-PDUs that are used to support Type 3 operation are shown in Box 8.5.

Type 3 operation is a proposed addition to the Logical Link Control standard and is implemented very rarely. Specific protocol mechanisms that are used in providing Type 3 operation are beyond the scope of this book.

BOX 8.5   LLC-PDUs for type 3 operation.

- **Acknowledged Connectionless Information, Sequence 0 (AC0).** Used to send user data in either direction between a pair of LLC entities.

- **Acknowledged Connectionless Information, Sequence 1 (AC1).** Also used to send user data in either direction between a pair of LLC entities. Each sender alternates the use of AC0 and AC1 LLC-PDUs. A receiver acknowledges an AC0 with an AC1 and acknowledges an AC1 with an AC0.

SUMMARY

The Logical Link Control sublayer protocol specification defines the format of the logical-link-control-protocol-data-unit (LLC-PDU) exchanged by peer LLC entities and describes the procedures by which LLC-PDUs flow between communicating systems in providing the LLC sublayer service.

The LLC standard defines two operational modes with a third proposed for addition to the standard. LLC Type 1 operation provides the connectionless LLC service. The protocol for Type 1 operation uses U-format LLC-PDUs to supply an unreliable data transfer service, an error detection mechanism, an exchange identification function, and a loopback testing facility. LLC Type 2 operation provides the connection-oriented service. The protocol for Type 2 operation uses I-format, S-format, and U-format LLC-PDUs to supply a reliable data transfer service using sequence checking, acknowledgments, and flow control mechanisms. The proposed LLC Type 3 operation provides the acknowledged connectionless service. The protocol for Type 3 operation uses U-format LLC-PDUs to supply a reliable data transfer service using acknowledgments.

The LLC standard defines two implementation classes, with two additional classes proposed for addition to the standard. A Class I LLC implementation supports only Type 1 operation, and a Class II LLC implementation supports both Type 1 and Type 2 operation. The proposed Class III LLC supports Type 1 and Type 3 operation, and the proposed Class IV LLC supports Type 1, Type 2, and Type 3 operation.

Chapter **9**

LLC Implementations

The preceding two chapters described standards for the services and protocols that have been defined for the Logical Link Control sublayer of the IEEE/ISO/ANSI LAN architecture. The Logical Link Control standard does not contain information specifying how the LLC sublayer should be implemented in an actual computer system. Implementation details are intentionally left to the ingenuity of those who design and build local area networking equipment and software. It is instructive to look at examples of actual implementations of the LLC standard to see how vendors have interpreted the standard and build actual products based on it.

This chapter begins by describing some of the issues that differentiate an architecture for communications from specific implementations of that architecture. It then examines Logical Link Control sublayer specifications that Digital Equipment Corporation and IBM have developed to guide the development of their own local area networking products.

ARCHITECTURE VERSUS IMPLEMENTATION

A communications architecture, and the standards that support that architecture, must describe both service definitions and protocol specifications. In some network architectures, the two are so closely related that they cannot be separated. In other architectures—such as the architecture based on the OSI model and the IEEE/ISO/LAN architecture—service definitions and protocol specifications are described separately. This is so services can be described in a way that is as independent as possible from the means by which those services are provided.

In the IEEE/ISO/ANSI LAN architecture, the service definition for the LLC sublayer defines the services that the LLC sublayer provides to a user of the LAN data link service. The protocol specification describes the formats of the LLC-PDUs that are exchanged by communicating LLC sublayer entities and the rules by which those PDUs are exchanged.

Service Definitions

A service definition is defined in terms of service primitives and is an *abstract* specification. The LLC service definition describes only the semantics of the services that the LLC sublayer provides and does not specify any concrete syntax that must be employed by a user of an LLC sublayer implementation to actually request LLC sublayer services.

Each local area network equipment vendor is able to implement the LLC service definition in any desired way, as long as all the services described in the standard are provided in some manner.

Protocol Specifications

A protocol specification describes the means by which the services in the service definition are provided. A protocol specification is relatively *concrete*. In order for an implementation to conform to the LLC standard, the LLC-PDUs that flow over the transmission medium must conform exactly with those defined in the LLC sublayer protocol specification, and they must flow back and forth in the prescribed manner.

The LLC sublayer protocol specification forms the basis for conformance to the LLC sublayer standard. An important role for the LLC protocol specification is to ensure that one vendor's implementation of the LLC standard will successfully interoperate with some other vendor's implementation.

Even though the LLC sublayer protocol specification is relatively concrete, the designer of local area networking equipment and software still has considerable latitude in implementing the procedures that are described in the protocol specification.

Layer Boundaries

The layer and sublayer boundaries that are described in an architecture, such as in the IEEE/ISO/ANSI LAN architecture, are often quite different than the layer boundaries that can be identified in an actual implementation of the architecture.

For example, in a local area network product, the MAC sublayer and the Physical layer are often implemented totally in hardware in the form of a network interface card (NIC). It is often difficult to find an actual layer boundary between the MAC sublayer and the Physical layer when examining a particular vendor's NIC products.

There must usually be a cleaner dividing line between the LLC sublayer and the MAC sublayer because the LLC sublayer is often implemented in software.

There is also generally a clean dividing line between the user of the LAN data link service and the LLC sublayer itself. This is because the LLC sublayer of a particular LAN product implementation may be used by different higher level software products, each of which may conform to a different network architecture. For example, a LAN product vendor might manufacture a NIC for a particular medium access control technology—such as for a Token Ring LAN—and might also supply a software implementation of the LLC sublayer. The NIC vendor's implementation of the LLC sublayer might then be used in an SNA network, a Novell NetWare network, or a TCP/IP network. In each case, different higher level software might access the services of the same implementation of the LLC sublayer.

LLC Sublayer Implementations

The LLC sublayer is often implemented as a component in a high-level networking software subsystem, such as a network operating system. Alternatively, it can be a separate software component that is supplied by the LAN equipment vendor and is accessed by other high-level networking software. These two alternatives are shown in Fig. 9.1.

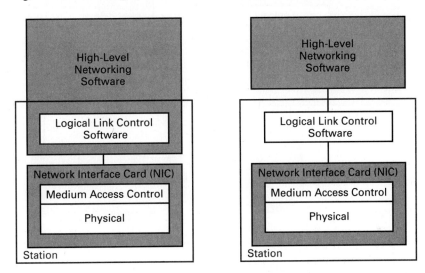

Figure 9.1   Logical Link Control sublayer software implementations.

In either case, an implementation of the LLC sublayer must provide an application programming interface (API) that the LAN data link user employs to request LAN data link services. The LLC sublayer API can be implemented in any desired manner, as long as it provides the services described in the Logical Link Control standard.

The remainder of this chapter examines specifications for Digital Equipment Corporation's and IBM's Logical Link Control sublayer implementations.

DEC'S LOGICAL LINK CONTROL SUBLAYER SPECIFICATION

Digital Equipment Corporation has developed a specification for the Logical Link Control sublayer of the IEEE/ISO/ANSI LAN architecture as part of Phase V of the Digital Network Architecture (DNA Phase V). DNA Phase V is the architecture on which Digital's DECnet/OSI networking products are based. DEC's specification for the LLC sublayer is designed to guide the development of actual DECnet/OSI product implementations of the LLC sublayer.

An architectural model for DEC's specification for the LLC sublayer is shown in Fig. 9.2.

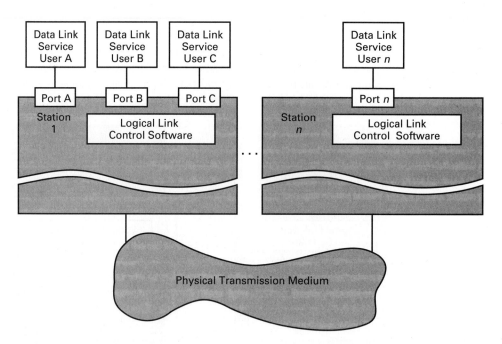

Figure 9.2   DECnet/OSI Logical Link Control architectural model.

DEC LLC Architectural Model

In the DEC LLC sublayer specification, an LLC sublayer entity resides in a component called a *station*. A station represents a physical point of attachment to the LAN transmission medium. A user requests the services of a LAN data link through a *port* into a station.

An LLC sublayer *port* is a data structure representing a particular user of an LLC sublayer entity. Each port is associated with a separate LLC sublayer service-access-point (SAP) and has its own unique SAP address within the station. A port's SAP address is assigned when the port is opened. Each user of the LLC sublayer has its own port and, thus, its own SAP that it uses to request LAN data link services. A particular station can implement multiple ports, and a user can employ more than one port concurrently. However, a port can service only a single user at a time.

DEC LLC Service Interface

DEC's specification for the Logical Link Control layer describes implementation details for a Class I LLC implementation. DEC implementations of the LLC sublayer that are based on this specification implement only Type 1 protocol operation and provide only the connectionless LLC service. However, the service interface also defines a user-supplied service that can be employed by the LAN data link user to implement any desired LLC sublayer protocol. This service allows a LAN data link user to build an implementation of Type 2 or Type 3 protocol operation. However, details concerning protocol operation beyond Type 1 operation is not addressed by the DEC LLC service interface itself.

BOX 9.1   DEC LLC Service interface procedure declarations.

Port Control Functions

- **OpenPort.** Opens a port into an LLC entity allowing an LLC user to transmit and receive LLC-SDUs. A port is a data structure that represents a particular LLC user's service-access-point and contains information needed by the LLC entity to service that user's requests.

- **Close.** Deallocates a port that was allocated with the OpenPort function.

Data Transfer Functions

- **Transmit.** Passes an LLC-SDU to the LLC sublayer for transmission.

- **TransmitPoll.** Checks for completion of a Transmit request.

- **TransmitAbort.** Aborts all outstanding Transmit requests for a port.

- **Receive.** Provides a receive buffer for use by an LLC sublayer entity.

- **ReceivePoll.** Checks for the completion of a Receive request.

- **ReceiveAbort.** Aborts all incomplete receive requests for a port.

Control Functions

- **EnablePromiscuous.** Indicates that a port is to receive LLC-PDUs contained in MAC frames having any destination MAC address value.

- **DisablePromiscuous.** Indicates that a port is no longer to receive LLC-PDUs contained in MAC frames having any destination MAC address value.

- **EnableProtocolType.** Adds an Ethernet frame protocol type value to the list of Ethernet frame protocol types a port maintains and begins receiving Ethernet frames having that protocol type value.

- **DisableProtocolType.** Removes an Ethernet frame protocol type value from the list of Ethernet frame protocol types a port maintains and stops receiving Ethernet frames having that protocol type value.

- **EnableProtocolIdentifier.** Adds a SNAP identifier value to the list of SNAP identifiers a port maintains and begins receiving SNAP PDUs having that SNAP identifier value.

- **DisableProtocolIdentifier.** Removes a SNAP identifier value from the list of SNAP identifiers a port maintains and stops receiving SNAP PDUs having that SNAP identifier value.

- **EnableLLCSap.** Adds a group or individual SAP address value to the list of SAP address values a port maintains and begins receiving LLC-PDUs having that DSAP address value.

- **DisableLLCSap.** Removes a group or individual SAP address value from the list of SAP address values a port maintains and indicates that the port can no longer send or receive LLC-PDUs having that SAP address value.

- **EnableMACAddress.** Adds a group or individual MAC address value to the list of MAC address values a port maintains and begins receiving LLC-PDUs contained in frames having that destination MAC address value.

- **DisableMACAddress.** Removes a group or individual MAC address value from the list of MAC address values a port maintains and stops receiving LLC-PDUs contained in frames having that destination MAC address value.

- **GetLinkAttributes.** Reads the attributes of the data link.

DEC's specification for the Logical Link Control sublayer is based on a set of procedure declarations that define the interface between an LLC sublayer entity and its users. While DEC's interface is still considered an abstract interface, it is expressed in terms of procedure declarations in a Pascal-like notation that is close to an actual programming language. The function and procedure declarations defining DEC's LLC service interface are listed in Box 9.1.

The DEC service interface provides functions that closely match the service primitives for Type 1 operation defined in the LLC standard. DEC's LLC service interface also defines specifications for MAC address, SAP address, and protocol identification filtering mechanisms. In addition, functions are defined that deal with MAC frames that conform to the *Ethernet Version 2 Specification* described in Chapter 11. These functions allow DEC implementations of the LLC sublayer to interoperate with other stations that implement only the *Ethernet Version 2 Specification* as well as with other stations that implement the Logical Link Control sublayer standard.

IBM'S LOGICAL LINK CONTROL SUBLAYER SPECIFICATION

IBM local area network products include both hardware devices and software subsystems. A typical IBM LAN hardware product consists of a network interface card (NIC) that is installed in a computer system, such as a personal computer. IBM typically uses the term *LAN adapter* instead of *network interface card*. An IBM LAN adapter consists of hardware and firmware that together implement the Physical layer and MAC sublayer for a particular form of medium access control technology. A separate IBM software product typically implements the Logical Link Control sublayer standard and often software for the higher layers of a particular network architecture as well.

IBM LAN Architectural Model

IBM's Logical Link Control sublayer specification defines a Class II LLC implementation and includes support for both Type 1 and Type 2 protocol operation. As described in Chapter 7, Type 1 operation provides the connectionless LLC service, and Type 2 operation provides the connection-oriented LLC service.

IBM's architectural model for LAN communication is based on *service-access-points* (SAPs) and *link stations*. For Type 1 operation, only SAPs are used. Any SAP can exchange data using the connectionless LLC service with any other SAP. For Type 2 operation, a link station must be set up within each SAP, and a connection must be established between a pair of link stations. There can be multiple SAPs in one system and multiple link stations for each SAP. This is illustrated in Fig. 9.3.

The SAPs for a particular system are assigned 1-octet SAP address values. Link stations for a particular SAP are assigned 1-octet link station identifiers. A SAP can have more than one connection established at one time. However, a given *pair* of SAPs can have only one connection established between them. Given this restriction, the MAC address and SAP address values for the two SAPs are sufficient to identify a particular

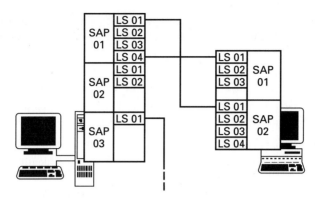

Figure 9.3　　IBM Logical Link Control service-access-points and link stations.

connection. Thus, IBM's use of service-access-points is a valid use of the IEEE/ISO SAP addressing scheme described in Chapter 6.

Data Link Control Interface

IBM's Logical Link Control sublayer interface is called the *Data Link Control* (DLC) interface. Like the DEC LLC specification, IBM's DLC interface is a specification that is implemented in a number of actual software products. Unlike the DEC LLC specification, which is an abstract interface, the DLC interface is a concrete interface that defines an actual application programming interface (API). The IBM DLC API defines an implementation of all the service primitives that are described in the LLC sublayer service definition for the connectionless LLC service and the connection-oriented LLC service.

Command Control Blocks

The DLC API is implemented in the form of data structures called *command control blocks* (CCBs). A program using the DLC interface creates a CCB containing the appropriate information and then passes it to the LLC sublayer implementation. The information in the CCB identifies the particular command to be executed and provides any information needed to execute the command, such as the addresses of data areas. Certain commands also use parameter lists to provide additional information.

　　　　The exact format of the CCB, and the way in which it is passed to the LLC software, varies with the operating system environment and the particular type of high-level networking software that is used. The differences generally reflect programming differences between the various software environments and the types of processors that IBM LAN products support. IBM LAN products support the SNA networking environment for larger systems as well as network operating systems for smaller systems, including IBM's LAN Server, Microsoft's LAN Manager, Novell's NetWare, and TCP/IP. Processors supported range from personal computers to mainframes.

　　　　The major commands making up IBM's DLC command control block interface are listed in Box 9.2.

BOX 9.2   IBM DLC interface commands.

Data Transmission Commands

- **Transmit.I.Frame.** Transmit an Information (I) LLC-PDU.
- **Transmit.UI.Frame.** Transmit an Unnumbered Information (UI) LLC-PDU.
- **Transmit.TEST.Cmd.** Transmit a Test (TEST) LLC-PDU.
- **Transmit.XID.Cmd.** Transmit an Exchange Identification (XID) LLC-PDU command.
- **Transmit.XID.Resp.Final.** Transmit an Exchange Identification (XID) LLC-PDU response with the poll/final bit on.
- **Transmit.XID.Resp.Not.Final.** Transmit an Exchange Identification (XID) LLC-PDU response with the poll/final bit off.

SAP and Link Station Management Commands

- **DLC.Open.SAP.** Activate a SAP and reserve a number of link stations for it.
- **DLC.Close.SAP.** Deactivate a SAP.
- **DLC.Open.System.** Reserve resources for a link station.
- **DLC.Connect.System.** Send the command/response sequence needed to establish a connection between two link stations.
- **DLC.Close.System.** Deactivate a link station.
- **DLC.Flow.Control.** Control the flow of data across a link station by setting and resetting its busy status.
- **DLC.Modify.** Modify values associated with a link station or SAP.
- **DLC.Reallocate.** Adjust the number of link stations allocated to a SAP.
- **DLC.Reset.** Return link station or SAP values to their original setting.
- **DLC.Set.Threshold.** Set the threshold for application program notification for the SAP buffer pool.
- **DLC.Statistics.** Read and reset DLC log information.

General Management Commands

- **Dir.Close.Adapter.** Terminate network communication for the adapter.
- **Dir.Define.MIF.Environment.** Define the environment needed for a NetBIOS emulation program.
- **Dir.Initialize.** Initialize work areas, tables, and buffers associated with the adapter.
- **Dir.Interrupt.** Force an adapter interrupt.
- **Dir.Modify.Open.Parms.** Modify values set by Dir.Open.Adapter.
- **Dir.Open.Adapter.** Prepare the adapter for network communication.
- **Dir.Read.Log.** Read and reset the adapter logs.

BOX 9.2   (Continued)

- **Dir.Restore.Open.Parms.** Restore parameters modified by Dir.Modify.Open.Parms to their original values.
- **Dir.Set.Exception.Flags.** Define user notification appendages and flags.
- **Dir.Set.Functional.Address.** Set functional addresses for the adapter.
- **Dir.Set.Group.Address.** Set the group address for the adapter.
- **Dir.Set.User.Appendage.** Change appendage addresses.
- **Dir.Status.** Read the general status information.
- **Dir.Timer.Cancel.** Cancel a timer set by Dir.Set.Timer.
- **Dir.Timer.Cancel.Group.** Cancel timers set by a group of Dir.Set.Timer commands.
- **Dir.Timer.Set.** Set a timer.
- **PDT.Trace.Off.** Terminate a trace started by PDT.Trace.On.
- **PDT.Trace.On.** Start a trace of all adapter traffic.
- **Purge.Resources.** Purge resources owned by a terminating application process.

SUMMARY

Networking hardware and software vendors have implemented the IEEE/ISO Logical Link Control standard in a variety of ways. An implementation of the LLC standard must conform to the LLC protocol specification and must define an application programming interface that LAN data link users employ to invoke LLC services.

Digital Equipment Corporation's specification for the LLC sublayer is defined in the documentation for Phase V of the Digital Network Architecture. DECnet/OSI products are based on DNA Phase V. The DEC LLC specification is for a Class I implementation that provides only Type 1 protocol operation to supply the connectionless LLC service. The DEC LLC sublayer service interface is defined using a Pascal-like notation that is close to an actual program language. The DEC LLC service interface is meant to be an abstract specification that is used to guide the developers of actual APIs to provide LLC services in software products. The DEC LLC service interface defines port control functions, data transfer functions, and control functions.

IBM's specification for the LLC sublayer is defined by its Data Link Control (DLC) interface. IBM's DLC interface defines a Class II LLC implementation that provides both Type 1 protocol operation to supply the connectionless LLC service and Type 2 protocol operation to supply the connection-oriented LLC service. IBM's DLC interface defines an actual application programming interface that is implemented in a variety of software subsystems that provide LLC services. The DLC interface defines data structures called command control blocks (CCBs) that a LAN data link user employs to request LLC services. The CCBs that the DLC interface defines includes those for controlling data transmission, service access points, and station management.

Chapter 10 begins Part III of this book and concentrates on the functions of the Medium Access Control sublayer of the IEEE/ISO/ANSI LAN architecture. Chapter 10 describes the carrier sense multiple access with collision detection (CSMA/CD), or Ethernet, form of medium access control technology. CSMA/CD uses contention techniques to implement bus- or tree-structured LAN data links.

PART **III**

MEDIUM ACCESS CONTROL

The members of IEEE Project 802 understood that it would not be possible to standardize a single form of LAN technology that would meet the needs of all users. For this reason, a single standard for the Logical Link Control sublayer supports the use of a variety of LAN data link technologies in the Medium Access Control sublayer. The Medium Access Control sublayer of the IEEE/ISO/ANSI LAN architecture is the subject of this part of the book.

Chapter 10 describes the carrier sense multiple access with collision detection (CSMA/CD), or Ethernet, form of LAN data link technology. CSMA/CD uses contention techniques to implement a bus- or tree-structured LAN.

Chapter 11 examines the *Ethernet Version 2 Specification*, jointly developed by Digital Equipment Corporation, Intel, and Xerox, on which the CSMA/CD standard is based.

Chapter 12 discusses the Token Bus form of LAN data link technology. The Token Bus medium access control method uses a token-passing technique to implement a bus- or tree-structured LAN.

Chapter 13 examines the Token Ring form of LAN data link technology. The Token Ring medium access control method uses a token-passing technique to implement a bus- or tree-structured LAN using twisted-pair cable.

Chapter 14 describes the Fiber Distributed Data Interface (FDDI) form of LAN data link technology. The FDDI medium access control method uses a timed token-passing technique to implement a ring-structured LAN using fiber-optic cable.

Chapter 15 discusses the LocalTalk form of LAN data link that is defined by AppleTalk, Apple's networking system. LocalTalk uses carrier sense multiple access with collision avoidance (CSMA/CA) to implement a bus- or tree-structured LAN.

Chapter 10

CSMA/CD (Ethernet)

This chapter describes the medium access control method called *carrier sense multiple access with collision detection* (CSMA/CD) that is defined in the IEEE 802.3/ISO 8802-3 standard. A LAN data link conforming to this standard is often called an *Ethernet* LAN because the CSMA/CD standard is based on the older *Ethernet Version 2 Specification* jointly developed by DEC, Intel, and Xerox. At the time of writing, Ethernet is the most commonly used LAN data link technology.

An Ethernet LAN uses building blocks of individual cable segments to which one or more end-user stations is attached in a bus-structured topology. Various types of cabling are supported, and an individual cable segment has a limited length, which depends on the cable's type. *Repeaters* or *hubs* can be used to propagate the signal from one cable segment to another, thus creating a branching, nonrooted tree topology, an example of which is shown in Fig. 10.1. The CSMA/CD standard places a number of restrictions on the types of tree structures that can be formed. An important restriction is that there can be no more than one physical path between any two stations.

An Ethernet LAN implements a multiaccess form of data link in which all stations on the LAN receive the transmissions of all other stations. All MAC frames broadcast over the transmission medium reach every station, and each station is responsible for interpreting the destination MAC address contained in a frame and for accepting frames addressed to it.

The CSMA/CD standard defines both a service definition and a protocol specification for the MAC sublayer. It also defines architectural models for the MAC sublayer and Physical layer and describes specifications for various types of transmission media that can be used to implement the standard.

MAC SUBLAYER SERVICE DEFINITION

Medium Access Control sublayer services allow an LLC entity in one station to exchange LLC-PDUs with LLC sublayer entities in other stations. The MAC sublayer service definition is specified in terms of service primitives and service primitive parameters and describes a single MA_UNITDATA unconfirmed data transfer service.

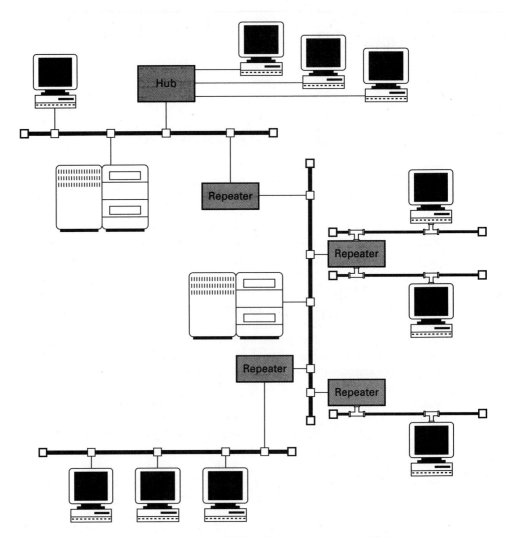

Figure 10.1   Ethernet LAN data link using repeaters and hubs.

MAC Sublayer Service Primitives

The following are descriptions of the service primitives that make up the MA_UNITDA-TA service:

- **MA_UNITDATA.request.** Issued by the LLC sublayer entity to the MAC sublayer entity in the source station to request that a MAC-SDU be sent to one or more destination stations.
- **MA_UNITDATA_STATUS.indication.** Issued by the MAC sublayer entity in the source station to the LLC entity to provide information about the success or failure of an attempt to transmit an LLC-PDU.

- **MA_UNITDATA.indication.** Issued by the MAC entity in the destination station to the LLC entity to indicate that an LLC-PDU has been received and to pass the LLC-PDU up to the LLC entity.

Figure 10.2 shows a time-sequence diagram that documents the sequence in which the three service primitives are issued during normal MAC frame transmission. Notice that the MA_UNITDATA service is an unconfirmed service. The MA_UNITDATA_STATUS.indication primitive tells the LLC sublayer entity in the source station only that the transmission attempt was successful. It does not tell the LLC sublayer entities in either the source or the destination station whether the MAC frame was received successfully by the distant station.

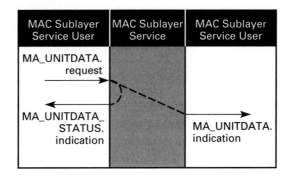

Figure 10.2 Time-sequence diagram for the MA_UNITDATA data transfer service.

Service Primitive Parameters

Box 10.1 describes the parameters that are included in the service primitives for the MA_UNITDATA data transfer service.

MAC SUBLAYER PROTOCOL SPECIFICATION

The data unit the MAC sublayer receives from the LLC sublayer is the *medium-access-control-service-data-unit* (MAC-SDU). The MAC-SDU contains the LLC-PDU that the two LLC sublayer entities are exchanging.

MAC Sublayer Functions

During MAC frame transmission, the Medium Access Control sublayer entities in all stations on the LAN data link perform the following functions:

- **Source Station MAC Sublayer Functions.** The MAC sublayer in a source station accepts each LLC-PDU from the LLC sublayer entity in the form of a MAC-SDU. A data encapsulation function in the source MAC sublayer entity adds protocol-control-information (PCI) to the MAC-SDU to form a *medium-access-control-protocol-data-unit* (MAC-PDU) or *MAC frame*. The MAC sublayer then uses the services of the Physical layer to broadcast the MAC frame onto the transmission medium.

- **Receiving Station MAC Sublayer Functions.** The MAC sublayer in a receiving station uses the Physical layer to receive MAC frames from the transmission medium. It interprets the destination MAC address in each frame it receives and accepts only frames that are addressed to that station. For each frame that it accepts, the MAC sublayer entity removes the PCI from the MAC frame and passes the resulting MAC-SDU to the LLC sublayer.

BOX 10.1   MA_UNITDATA service primitive parameters.

MA_UNITDATA.request   (
destination_address,
m_sdu,
service_class
)

MA_UNITDATA_STATUS.indication
(
transmission_status
)

MA_UNITDATA.indication
(
destination_address,
source_address,
m_sdu,
reception_status
)

- **destination_address.** Specifies a destination MAC address defining the station or stations to which the MAC-SDU is to be delivered. The MAC addressing scheme is described in Chapter 6.

- **source_address.** Specifies a source MAC address identifying the station originating the MAC-SDU.

- **m_sdu.** Specifies the MAC-SDU passed down from the LLC sublayer for transmission from the source station to the destination station or stations.

- **service_class.** Only one class of service is currently defined by the CSMA/CD standard, and this parameter is ignored by a CSMA/CD MAC sublayer entity. This parameter is included for conformance with other standards for the Medium Access Control sublayer.

- **transmission_status.** Indicates to the source LLC entity whether or not the previous MA_UNITDATA.request primitive was accepted by the MAC sublayer entity.

- **reception_status.** Indicates to a destination LLC sublayer entity whether the MAC-SDU was received without error.

MAC Frame Format

The protocol specification for the CSMA/CD MAC sublayer defines the format of the MAC frame that is exchanged between MAC sublayer entities in source and destination stations. Box 10.2 shows the format of the CSMA/CD MAC frame and describes its fields.

BOX 10.2   CSMA/CD (Ethernet) MAC frame.

Preamble	Start Frame Delimiter	Dest. MAC Address	Source MAC Address	Length	LLC Data	Pad	Frame Check Sequence
7 octets	1 octet	2 or 6 octets	2 or 6 octets	2 octets	0 – n octets	0 – p octets	4 octets

- **Preamble.** A sequence of 56 bits having alternating 1 and 0 values that are used for synchronization.

- **Start Frame Delimiter.** A sequence of 8 bits having the bit configuration 10101011 that indicates the beginning of the MAC frame.

- **Station Addresses.** A *Destination MAC Address* field followed by a *Source MAC Address* field. The Destination MAC Address field identifies the station or stations that are to receive the MAC frame. The Source MAC Address field identifies the station that originated the frame. Address fields can be either 16 bits or 48 bits in length, although the great majority of Ethernet implementations use 48-bit addresses. (The MAC addressing mechanism is described in Chapter 6.) The destination MAC address field can specify either an individual address or a group address. A group destination MAC address is called a *multicast-group address*. The group destination MAC address value of all 1 bits refers to all stations on the LAN data link and is called the *broadcast address*.

- **Length.** A 2-octet field that indicates the length of the LLC Data field that follows.

- **LLC Data.** Contains the MAC-SDU that was passed from the LLC sublayer entity in the source station and is to be delivered to the LLC sublayer entity in the destination station or stations.

- **Pad.** Octets used to bring a short frame up to the minimum allowable size. Each MAC frame must contain some minimum number of octets, which is determined by the characteristics of the Physical layer. If a MAC frame being assembled for transmission does not have the requisite number of octets, a Pad field is added to bring it up to the minimum length.

- **Frame Check Sequence.** A cyclical redundancy check (CRC) value used for error checking. When the source station assembles a MAC frame, it performs a CRC calculation on the bits in the MAC frame. The specific algorithm that is used is described in the IEEE and ISO documentation and always results in a 32-bit value. The source station stores this value in the Frame Check Sequence (FCS) field and then transmits the MAC frame. When the destination station receives the MAC frame, it performs the identical CRC calculation. If the calculated value does not match the value in the FCS field, the destination station assumes that a transmission error has occurred and discards the MAC frame.

MAC Frame Length Restrictions

MAC sublayer specifications for the CSMA/CD standard do not restrict the length of the LLC Data field of the MAC frame. However, the standard does state that for a 10 Mbps implementation using 48-bit address fields, the combination of the LLC Data and Pad fields must be a minimum of 46 octets and a maximum of 1500 octets. This size range is determined by Physical layer specifications for the medium specification allowing the longest span between any two stations. Adhering to the size range of 46-1500 octets allows Ethernet equipment to interoperate over all commonly used transmission media. Medium specifications are described later in this chapter.

MAC Frame versus Physical Layer PDU

The MAC sublayer itself is concerned only with the fields from the Destination MAC Address field through the Frame Check Sequence field. The standard recommends that the length of these fields together range from 64 octets to 1518 octets, resulting in the range described above of 46-1500 octets for the LLC Data plus Pad fields. The Preamble and Start Frame Delimiter fields are added to the MAC frame by the Physical layer.

Some authorities distinguish between the MAC frame itself—which can be considered to range from the Destination MAC Address through the Frame Check Sequence field—and the Physical layer PDU, which includes the Preamble and the Start Frame Delimiter. The Physical layer PDU is sometimes called a *packet*.* However, in this book we will not make a distinction between MAC frames and Physical layer PDUs.

MAC Frame/LLC-PDU Relationship

Figure 10.3 shows the relationship between the LLC-PDU that is passed to the MAC sublayer in a MAC-SDU and the CSMA/CD MAC frame. Notice that the LLC-PDU is carried in a CSMA/CD MAC frame; all fields in the LLC-PDU are treated by the MAC sublayer as data.

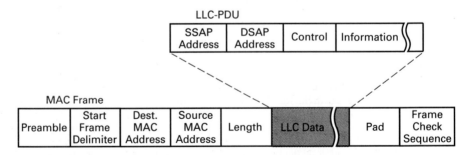

Figure 10.3   CSMA/CD (Ethernet) MAC frame and LLC-PDU relationship.

* This is an unfortunate choice of terminology, since most authorities use the term *packet* to refer to the PDU exchanged by the layer above the LLC sublayer.

MAC PROTOCOL OPERATION

As we introduced in Chapter 3, Ethernet technology uses the carrier sense multiple access with collision detection (CSMA/CD) method for medium access control. The CSMA/CD form of medium access control is one of a class of protocols that uses random access or contention techniques to solve the problem of "who goes next" in a system where all stations share a common multiaccess transmission medium. The following sections explain the operation of the IEEE 802.3/ISO 8802-3 variation of the CSMA/CD form of access control and describe its evolution.

The ALOHA System

The earliest of the contention techniques was used in an experimental packet radio broadcasting system called ALOHA, developed at the University of Hawaii in the early 1970s. The protocol used by the ALOHA system is a *free-for-all* technique. When a station has a frame to transmit, it does so. It then waits for a period of time that is equal to twice the *propagation delay*, which is the length of time it takes a frame to travel between two stations that are furthest apart in the network. Twice the propagation delay is called the *slot time*. (On an Ethernet LAN, the maximum distance between stations is 2800 meters, giving a slot time of 51.2 microseconds.)

If the source station receives an acknowledgment to its MAC frame within the slot time, it knows that the MAC frame was correctly received. If the source station does not hear an acknowledgment in that time, it assumes something has gone wrong and retransmits the frame. After repeated retransmissions without an acknowledgment, the source station gives up.

If two stations attempt to transmit frames at the same time, the two transmissions interfere, creating a condition called a *collision*. When collisions occur, frames are damaged. Receiving stations detect collisions through a collision detection mechanism and ignore MAC frames damaged through collisions. Both stations then attempt to retransmit.

This protocol is simple but inefficient during high channel utilization. The maximum utilization of the transmission medium with the pure ALOHA protocol is less than 18 percent.

Carrier Sense Multiple Access

With the ALOHA protocol, collisions often occur when a station begins transmitting a frame while another station is already transmitting. A protocol that evolved from the pure ALOHA protocol added the technique of *carrier sensing* to form the *carrier sense multiple access* (CSMA) protocol. With CSMA, a source station first listens to the transmission medium before sending (carrier sense). If the medium is busy, the station waits, thus avoiding a collision. The station sends a frame only when the medium is quiet.

Even with the CSMA technique, two or more stations can listen at exactly the same time, transmit simultaneously, and still cause a collision. When frame transmission times are long compared to the propagation time, a significant portion of channel capacity can be lost due to collisions because each station transmits its entire frame before it discovers that a collision has occurred.

Collision Detection

The final refinement to the CSMA technique is to add the *collision detection* (CD) function, resulting in *CSMA/CD*. In addition to listening to the transmission system before transmitting, a source station continues to listen during the time the frame is being sent. If two or more stations have begun transmitting within a sufficiently short time interval, a collision occurs quickly. When this happens, the transmitting stations immediately detect the collision, cease transmitting data, and all send out a short *jamming signal*. The jamming signal ensures that all stations on the network detect the collision. Any station that has been transmitting then stops transmitting, waits for a time, and, if the carrier is free, transmits its frame again.

Deference Process

The process of monitoring the status of the transmission medium and determining when to begin retransmission is called the *deference process*. If all stations waited the same length of time before checking the carrier and restarting transmission, then another collision would inevitably occur. The deference process avoids this. In executing the deference process, each station generates a random number that determines the length of time it must wait before testing the carrier. This time period is known as the station's *backoff delay*.

Backoff delay is calculated in multiples of slot time. Each station generates a random number that falls within a specified range of values. It then waits that number of slot times before attempting retransmission. The smaller the range of values from which the random number is selected, the greater the likelihood that two stations will select the same number and have another collision. However, if the range of numbers is large, all the stations may wait for several slot times before any station transmits, causing transmission time to be wasted.

Truncated Binary Exponential Backoff

To achieve a balance between these two considerations, the CSMA/CD deference process uses an approach called *truncated binary exponential backoff*. The range of numbers (r) is defined as $0 < r < 2^k$, where k reflects the number of transmission attempts the station has made. For the first attempt the range is 0 to 1; for the second attempt, 0 to 3; for the third, 0 to 7 and so on. If repeated collisions occur, the range continues to expand until k reaches 10 (with r ranging from 0 to 1023), after which the value for k stays at 10. If a station is unsuccessful in transmitting after 16 attempts, the MAC sublayer entity reports an *excessive collisions* error condition.

Binary exponential backoff results in minimum delays before retransmission when traffic on the LAN is light. When traffic is high, repeated collisions cause the range of numbers to increase, thus lessening the chance of further collisions. Of course, when the traffic is extremely high, repeated collisions can still begin to cause excessive collisions error conditions to be generated. However, the CSMA/CD technique, combined with a deference process using truncated binary exponential backoff, results in utilizations that are extremely high, better than 90 percent in many cases.

CSMA/CD ARCHITECTURAL MODEL

The IEEE/ISO CSMA/CD standard defines the architectural model illustrated in Fig. 10.4. In conformance with the overall IEEE/ISO/ANSI LAN architecture, the Data Link layer is divided into the Logical Link Control (LLC) sublayer and the Medium Access Control (MAC) sublayer.

The MAC sublayer provides services to the MAC sublayer user, which is normally a Logical Link Control (LLC) sublayer entity. The LLC sublayer standard is described in the chapters in Part II.

The Physical layer in the CSMA/CD specification is divided into a Physical Signaling sublayer and a Physical Medium Attachment sublayer.

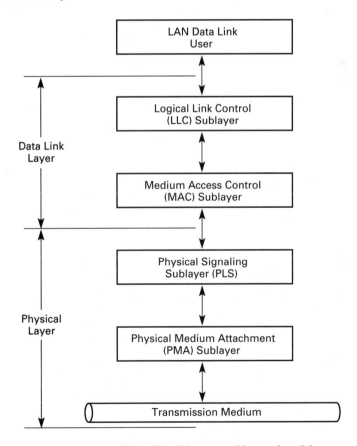

Figure 10.4   CSMA/CD (Ethernet) architectural model.

Physical Signaling Sublayer

The *Physical Signaling sublayer* (PLS) is responsible for encoding data passed down from the MAC sublayer in a transmitting station. Data encoding involves translating bits into proper electrical signals for broadcast over the transmission medium. In a destination station, the Physical Signaling sublayer decodes the signals it receives and translates electrical signals back into a bit stream that is passed up to the MAC sublayer.

Physical Medium Attachment Sublayer

The *Physical Medium Attachment* (PMA) sublayer provides services to the Physical Signaling sublayer. It performs a translation function between the Physical Signaling sublayer and the transmission medium itself and defines the characteristics of a particular transmission medium.

MAC SUBLAYER FUNCTIONAL MODEL

The CSMA/CD standard defines a functional model that includes the six functions shown in Fig. 10.5. Three of the functions are associated with transmitting data, and three parallel functions are concerned with receiving data. The *data encapsulation/decapsulation* and *medium access management* functions shown in Fig. 10.5 are performed by the Medium Access Control sublayer; the *data encoding/decoding* function is performed by the Physical Signaling sublayer.

Data Encapsulation/Decapsulation

Data encapsulation applies to a source station and provides for adding protocol-control-information (PCI) to the beginning and end of the MAC-SDU that is received from the LLC sublayer to form a MAC-PDU, or MAC frame. The PCI in the MAC frame is used to perform the following functions:

- Synchronize the destination station with the signal.
- Delimit the start and end of the MAC frame.
- Carry the MAC addresses of the source and destination stations.
- Detect transmission errors.

When a MAC frame is received, a *data decapsulation* function in the destination station is responsible for recognizing the destination MAC address and determining if the station should accept and copy a MAC frame having that address. For an accepted frame, the data decapsulation function removes the PCI that was added by the data encapsulation function in the source station and passes the resulting MAC-SDU up to the Logical Link Control sublayer.

Medium Access Management

The medium access management function in a sending station receives a MAC frame from the data encapsulation function once the necessary protocol-control-information has

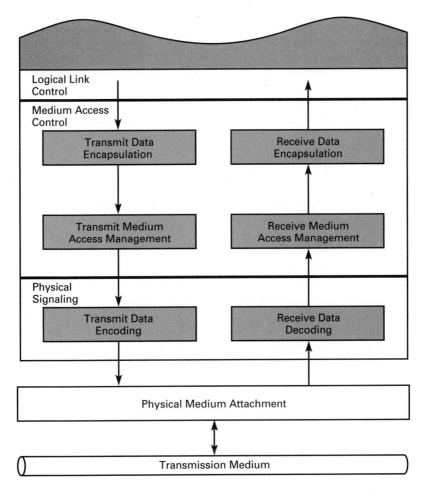

Figure 10.5   CSMA/CD (Ethernet) functional model.

been added. Medium access management is then responsible for handling the physical transmission of the MAC frame. As described earlier, the approach used by CSMA/CD involves *carrier sensing*, or listening for a free transmission medium before transmitting.

Medium access management determines, through the services of the PLS sublayer, whether or not the transmission medium (carrier) is currently being used. If the carrier is free, medium access management passes the MAC frame to the PLS sublayer for transmission. If the transmission medium is busy, medium access management continues monitoring the carrier until no other stations are transmitting. Medium access management then waits a specified time to allow the LAN to clear and begins transmission.

Medium access management continues to monitor the carrier after transmission of the MAC frame starts. If two stations have begun transmission at the same time, their signals will result in a collision. When this happens, each transmitting station detects the collision, ceases transmitting data, and sends out a jamming signal. All stations that have been transmitting cease their transmission, wait a period of time, and if the carrier is free, attempt retransmission of the MAC frame. Medium access management uses the deference process described earlier to determine the time interval to wait before attempting retransmission.

In a destination station, medium access management performs validity checks on a MAC frame before passing it on to the data decapsulation function.

PHYSICAL LAYER SPECIFICATIONS

The specifications in the CSMA/CD standard for the Physical layer concern issues such as the physical characteristics of the transmission medium (typically an electrical wire or cable, although fiber optics or wireless transmission is used in some implementations) and the mechanical connection from the station to the transmission medium. These specifications address physical specifications, including plug dimensions, the number of pins in the plug, and the placement of the pins. They also address electrical issues, such as the voltage levels of the signals that flow on the wire, and functional issues, such as the meaning of a particular voltage level on a given wire.

PHYSICAL LAYER ARCHITECTURAL MODEL

The CSMA/CD standard defines the Physical layer architectural model shown in Fig. 10.6. The following are descriptions of each Physical layer component and interface shown in the model.

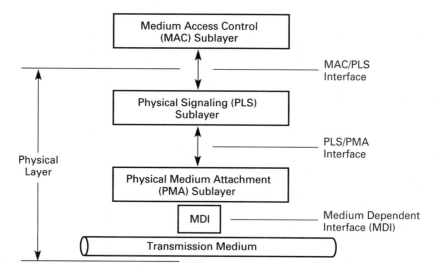

Figure 10.6   CSMA/CD (Ethernet) Physical layer architectural model.

Physical Signaling Sublayer

The *Physical Signaling* (PLS) sublayer provides services to the MAC sublayer. The PLS sublayer in a source station is responsible for encoding the data passed down from the MAC sublayer in a transmitting station. The data encoding function is responsible for translating the bits being transmitted into the proper electrical signals that are then broadcast over the transmission medium.

The bits are encoded using the Manchester encoding scheme, illustrated in Fig. 10.7. As described in Chapter 2, with Manchester encoding, the signal state changes at roughly the midpoint of each bit time. The signal for a 1 bit changes from low to high, and the signal for a 0 bit changes from high to low. This type of signaling allows data and clocking signals to be combined, since the destination station can use the state change that occurs during each bit time for synchronization purposes.

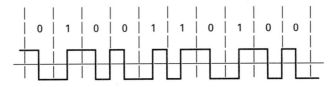

Figure 10.7   Manchester encoding.

The PLS sublayer in a destination station is responsible for decoding the signal it receives. The decoding function translates received signals into an appropriate bit stream and passes the resulting data up to the MAC sublayer. The PLS sublayer is also responsible for listening to the transmission medium, notifying the MAC sublayer whether the carrier is free or busy, and detecting collisions.

Physical Medium Attachment Sublayer

The *Physical Medium Attachment* (PMA) sublayer provides services to the PLS sublayer. It performs a translation function between the PLS sublayer and the transmission medium itself and defines the characteristics of a particular type of transmission medium. The interface between the MAC sublayer and the PLS sublayer (the PLS-PMA interface) defines the services that a PMA sublayer entity supplies to a PLS sublayer entity.

The CSMA/CD standard allows the PLS and PMA sublayers to be implemented in the same device or in separate devices, as shown in Fig. 10.8. A device implementing both the PLS and PMA sublayers is attached directly to the transmission medium. In such a device, the PLS-PMA interface is an abstract interface that defines services only.

The CSMA/CD standard anticipates that in many implementations the station will be located a short distance away from the transmission medium, which is often installed behind a wall or in a ceiling. So the CSMA/CD standard allows the PMA sublayer to be implemented in a separate device called a *Medium Attachment Unit* (MAU). The MAU described in the standard is often called a *transceiver* in an implementation of the standard.

An MAU provides the physical and electrical interface between a cable segment and a CSMA/CD station. The MAU handles all functions that depend on the specific

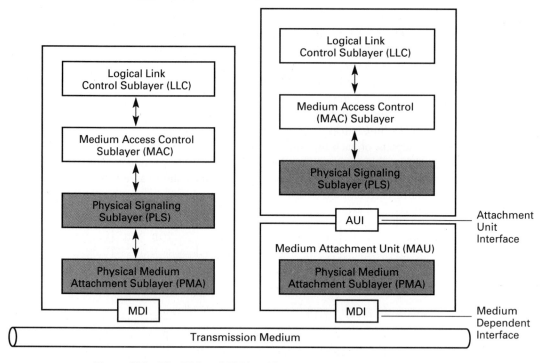

Figure 10.8 The PLS and PMA sublayers can be implemented in the same device or in different devices.

transmission medium being used. By having an MAU separate from the station itself, the same station can be used with different transmission media simply by changing the MAU.

Attachment Unit Interface

When a separate MAU is used to implement the PMA sublayer, the PLS-PMA interface consists of a concrete interface called the *Attachment Unit Interface* (AUI). The AUI defines the cable and the connectors used to connect the MAU to the device implementing the PLS sublayer. The AUI also specifies the characteristics of the signals exchanged across the interface. The cable that connects the device implementing the PLS sublayer to an MAU is called an *AUI cable*. The AUI cable is called a *transceiver cable* in many Ethernet implementations.

Medium Dependent Interface

The interface between the PMA sublayer and the transmission medium (the PMA-Medium interface) is a concrete interface called the *Medium Dependent Interface* (MDI). The MDI for a particular form of transmission medium defines the characteristics of *cable segments* (sometimes called the *trunk cable*), *connectors* for joining cable segments and connecting cable segments to equipment, and *terminators* used at the ends of cable segments. Although the transmission medium ordinarily consists of a physical cable, such as coaxial cable, twisted-pair cable, or fiber-optic cable, it can also consist of a microwave link, or other wireless link, in some Ethernet implementations.

Repeaters

The CSMA/CD standard also describes an architectural model and Physical layer specifications for *repeaters*. As described earlier, a repeater is a device that is used to interconnect two or more CSMA/CD cable segments. A repeater regenerates the signal by receiving it from one cable segment and then retransmitting it at its original strength over all other cable segments to which it is attached. Repeaters are used to create longer cable spans between stations than can be supported using a single cable segment and also to create branching tree structures.

The architectural model for a repeater is shown in Fig. 10.9. A repeater can implement any number of physical attachment points to the same or different types of cable segments. Each attachment point can implement a Medium Dependent Interface (for attachment directly to a cable segment) or the Attachment Unit Interface (for attachment to an external Medium Attachment Unit), as required.

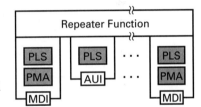

Figure 10.9   CSMA/CD (Ethernet) repeater architectural model.

Notice that a repeater implements only the repeater function and Physical layer components. Repeaters do not implement any of the functions of the Medium Access Control sublayer and so are not considered as addressable stations on the LAN. Stations are not aware of the presence of repeaters on an Ethernet LAN data link.

PHYSICAL LAYER MEDIUM-INDEPENDENT SPECIFICATIONS

The standards that define the components and interfaces that we just described can be grouped into two parts—a medium-independent part and a medium specification. The *medium-independent* part deals with services and interface specifications that are provided by the Physical layer regardless of the particular type of transmission medium used. The *medium specification* addresses the parts of the Physical layer operation that are specific to a particular type of transmission medium.

The CSMA/CD standard defines several different medium specifications, and more are being added to the standard over time. A local area network vendor decides which of the medium specifications to support in a given Ethernet implementation.

The medium-independent part of the Physical layer specification defines the following:

- The services that the Physical Signaling sublayer of the Physical layer provides to the Medium Access Control sublayer.
- The functions that the Physical Signaling sublayer performs in supplying services to the MAC sublayer.
- The optional Attachment Unit Interface that defines the interface between the Physical Signaling sublayer and the Physical Medium Attachment sublayer of the Physical layer.

Physical Signaling Sublayer Functions

The primary functions that the Physical Signaling sublayer performs are as follows:

- Accept a bit from the MAC sublayer, encode it, and transmit it.
- Receive a bit signal from the MAU, decode it, and pass it to the MAC sublayer.
- Provide the MAC sublayer with information concerning the status of the carrier, occurrences of collisions, and the success or failure of transmissions.

Physical Signaling Sublayer Services

The services provided by the Physical Signaling sublayer for the Medium Access Control sublayer are defined in terms of four service primitives, each of which has a single parameter. The following are descriptions of these service primitives:

- **PLS_DATA.request (output_unit).** Issued by the MAC sublayer to cause PLS to transmit a single bit of data onto the transmission medium. The **output_unit** parameter can be set to **1** or **0** to transmit a bit or to **data_complete** to indicate that there is no more data to send.
- **PLS_DATA.indication (input_unit).** Issued by PLS to the MAC sublayer in each station that receives a bit. The **input_unit** parameter reflects the **output_unit** parameter of the sending PLS_DATA.request primitive.
- **PLS_CARRIER.indication (carrier_status).** Issued by PLS to the MAC sublayer whenever the status of the transmission medium changes. The **carrier_status** parameter is set to **carrier_off** when the status changes to idle and to **carrier_on** when signal activity exists and input is being received.
- **PLS_SIGNAL.indication (signal_status).** Issued by PLS to the MAC sublayer with a **signal_status** parameter value of **signal_error** when an improper signal or a collision is first detected by PLS. PLS then issues this primitive with a **signal_status** parameter value of **no_signal_error** when the error condition ends.

Physical Signaling Sublayer Functional Specification .

The CSMA/CD standard provides a narrative description of the CSMA/CD algorithm and a more formal specification written in the Pascal programming language. The functions of the Physical Signaling sublayer are defined in terms of a single function, two procedures, and three boolean variables.

Function and Procedures

The following are descriptions of the single function and the two procedures that are defined in the PLS functional specification:

- **ReceiveBit Function.** Issued by the MAC entity to pass one bit from PLS to the MAC sublayer.

- **TransmitBit Procedure.** Each invocation passes one bit from the MAC sublayer to PLS, where it is broadcast onto the transmission medium.

- **Wait Procedure.** Each invocation allows the MAC sublayer to wait a specified number of bit times. The slot time used for back-off following a collision is defined in bit times. This procedure is used to wait the appropriate number of slot times following a collision.

Boolean Variables

The following are descriptions of the boolean variables that are defined by the Physical Signaling sublayer functional specification:

- **CollisionDetect Boolean Variable.** Used to signal the MAC sublayer that a collision has been detected by PLS.

- **CarrierSense Boolean Variable.** Used to inform the MAC sublayer whether or not data is currently being transmitted on the transmission medium.

- **Transmitting Boolean Variable.** Used by the MAC sublayer to signal PLS that it has bits ready to transmit.

Attachment Unit Interface Specification

The optional Attachment Unit Interface is the interface between the Physical Signaling sublayer and the Physical Medium Attachment sublayer when a separate Medium Attachment Unit is used. For the Attachment Unit Interface, the CSMA/CD standard defines signal characteristics, electrical characteristics, interchange circuits, and mechanical characteristics. When an implementation does not use a separate Medium Attachment Unit, the interface between the Physical Signaling sublayer and the Physical Medium Attachment sublayer can be implemented in any desired way within the station itself.

The Attachment Unit Interface consists physically of a number of circuits that are implemented by a shielded cable that connects the Physical Signaling sublayer to the Medium Attachment Unit. Box 10.3 lists the circuits that implement the AUI interface.

Two modes of operation have been defined for the Medium Attachment Unit in the CSMA/CD standard. In *normal* mode, the MAU is able to both send and receive. In *monitor* mode, which is an optional feature that not all CSMA/CD implementations support, the MAU is unable to send but is still able to receive signals from the carrier. The optional **control_out** circuit is primarily related to the monitor mode.

The interface between the Medium Attachment Unit and the station can be logically defined in terms of two sets of signals that flow over the wires that connect the station to the Medium Attachment Unit, one set flowing in each direction. Box 10.4 lists the signals that flow between the station and the MAU.

BOX 10.3　Attachment Unit Interface (AUI) circuits.

- **data-out.** Transmits data signals from the station to the Medium Attachment Unit.
- **data-in.** Transmits data signals from the Medium Attachment Unit to the station.
- **control-out (optional).** Transmits control signals from the station to the Medium Attachment Unit.
- **control-in.** Transmits control signals from the Medium Attachment Unit to the station.
- **voltage-plus.** Supplies the Medium Attachment Unit with power from the station.
- **voltage-common.** Serves as a return for the **voltage-plus** circuit.
- **protective-ground.** Connects the chassis ground of the PLS sublayer to the chassis ground of the MAU via the cable shield.

BOX 10.4　Medium Attachment Unit (MAU) signals.

Signals Sent from the Station to the MAU

- **output.** Sent over the data-out circuit whenever PLS receives a data bit from the MAC sublayer.
- **output_idle.** Sent over the data-out circuit at all times when the MAC sublayer is not sending PLS data bits to transmit.
- **normal.** Sent over the control-out circuit to indicate that the MAU should operate in normal mode and both transmit and receive data.
- **mau_request (optional).** Sent over the control-out circuit when the MAU has indicated the medium is not available, and the MAU wants it to be made available because the MAC sublayer has a data bit to transmit.
- **isolate (optional).** Sent over the control-out circuit to indicate that the MAU should operate in monitor mode and should only receive data.

Signals Sent from the MAU to the Station

- **input.** Sent over the data-in circuit when the MAU has received a bit from the transmission medium and wants to transfer it to the station.
- **input_idle.** Sent over the data-in circuit whenever the MAU does not have a data bit ready to transfer to the station.
- **mau_available.** Sent over the control-in circuit to indicate that the MAU is available for transmission.
- **signal_quality_error.** Sent over the control-in circuit whenever the MAU detects a collision or improper signal on the transmission medium.
- **mau_not_available (optional).** Sent over the control-in circuit whenever the MAU is not available for transmission.

MEDIUM SPECIFICATIONS

A medium-dependent part of the CSMA/CD standard, called a *medium specification*, defines the following:

- Functions performed by the Physical Medium Attachment sublayer of the Physical layer for a particular type of transmission medium.
- The interface between the Physical Medium Attachment sublayer and the transmission medium in terms of the signals that are exchanged with the transmission medium.
- Physical characteristics of the transmission medium.

For the Medium Attachment Unit (MAU) and the physical transmission medium, the CSMA/CD standard defines functional specifications, electrical characteristics, cable and connector specifications, and environmental specifications. Attachment unit standards are designed to encompass signaling rates from 1 Mbps to 20 Mbps. All devices attached to a given LAN data link must operate at a single signaling rate. However, stations and MAUs may be designed to operate at more than one possible rate and may provide the ability to be manually set to a specific rate when attached to a particular LAN data link.

Although the standard allows for a range of signaling rates, virtually all Ethernet implementations of the CSMA/CD standard employ a signaling rate of 10 Mbps. However, work is being done on new medium specifications, often referred to as *Fast Ethernet*, that allow for a data rate of 100 Mbps.

CSMA/CD Transmission Media

The CSMA/CD standard includes medium specifications for many different types of transmission media, each of which has a different set of specifications for the Physical Medium Attachment sublayer. Local area network vendors often develop and market Ethernet products that use other medium specifications in anticipation of future standardization. The following are some of the types of Ethernet transmission media that are commonly used today:

- Baseband signaling over 50-ohm coaxial cable, approximately 10 mm thick (often called *Standard Ethernet* or *Thick Ethernet* cable).
- Baseband signaling over 50-ohm coaxial cable, approximately 5 mm thick (often called *Thin Ethernet* or *ThinNet* cable).
- Broadband signaling over 75-ohm CATV coaxial cable.
- Baseband signaling over unshielded twisted-pair telephone wiring.
- Baseband signaling over fiber-optic cable.
- Baseband signaling using microwave transmission.

The IEEE and ISO are working on standards for many forms of transmission media, and the most current IEEE 802.3 and ISO 8802-3 standards documents should be consulted to see what new transmission media have been included in the standard since this was written.

Physical Medium Attachment Functions

The functional specification of the Physical Medium Attachment sublayer is different for each medium specification. Typical functions performed by PMA for a typical medium specification are as follows:

- **Transmit.** Transmit serial data bit streams on the transmission medium.
- **Receive.** Receive serial data bit streams from the transmission medium.
- **Collision Presence.** Detect the presence of two or more stations transmitting concurrently.
- **Monitor Inhibit.** Inhibit the Transmit function while the Receive and Collision Presence functions remain operational.
- **Jabber Interrupt.** Interrupt the Transmit function when an abnormally long data bit stream is being transmitted.

Through the above five functions, the MAU sees that signals received from the Physical Signaling sublayer (PLS) are placed on the transmission medium and that signals received from the transmission medium are passed to PLS. The MAU also detects collisions and notifies PLS when a collision occurs.

The remainder of this chapter describes some of the most commonly used CSMA/CD medium specifications.

10BASE5—STANDARD ETHERNET

The oldest of the CSMA/CD medium specifications is based on the *Ethernet Version 2 Specification* developed by DEC, Intel, and Xerox. This medium specification defines baseband transmission using coaxial cable supporting a data rate of 10 Mbps. Cable segments may be up to 500 meters in length. The data rate (**10** Mbps), the transmission technique (**BASE**band), and maximum cable segment length (**500** meters) are combined to give a shorthand medium specification name of *10BASE5*. With the 10BASE5 medium specification, the original, thick (10 mm) form of 50-ohm coaxial cable is used. This type of cable is often referred to as *thick Ethernet* or *Standard Ethernet* cable.

Electrical characteristics are defined for the Medium Attachment Unit and for its interface to a cable segment. Electrical, mechanical, and physical characteristics are also defined for the coaxial cable and the connectors and terminators used with it. Environmental specifications related to safety, electromagnetic environment, temperature and humidity, and regulatory requirements are also included in the standard.

10BASE5 Configurations

With the 10BASE5 specification, repeaters can be used to create longer cable runs and to build tree-structured configurations. A sample 10BASE5 configuration using repeaters is shown in Fig. 10.10.

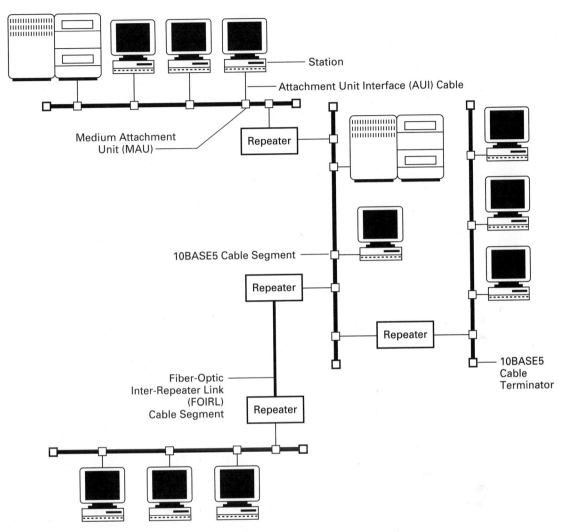

Figure 10.10   Typical 10BASE5 network configuration using repeaters.

According to the 10BASE5 specification, a cable segment that has stations attached to it is called a *coax cable segment* or *multiaccess cable segment*. A cable segment that is used simply to connect two repeaters and does not have stations attached to it is called a *point-to-point link cable segment*, or an *inter-repeater link* (IRL) cable segment. An inter-repeater link cable segment implemented using fiber optics, called a *Fiber-Optic Inter-Repeater Link* (FOIRL) can be up to 1000 meters in length. Of the five cable segments that can lie in the path between two stations, only three can be coax cable segments; the other two must be point-to-point link cable segments. A particular

CSMA/CD data link must be configured so that there is never more than one physical path between any two stations.

10BASE5 Medium Attachment Unit

The 10BASE5 medium specification describes the use of a separate Medium Attachment Unit (MAU) to attach a station to a cable segment. The MAU is most often implemented in a device called a *transceiver* that is clamped directly onto the coaxial cable. The transceiver has a contact that pierces the thick Ethernet coaxial cable shielding and makes appropriate contact with both the shielding and the central conductor.

Maximum Distance between Stations

There can be up to five cable segments, and thus up to four repeaters, in the path between any two stations. The attachment unit interface (AUI) cable connecting a station to its MAU can be up to 50 meters in length. The 10BASE5 medium specification allows for up to 1500 meters of coax cable segments, up to 1000 meters of inter-repeater link, and up to six AUI cables connecting stations or repeaters to MAUs. This allows the total distance between two stations to be up to 2800 meters. Figure 10.11 shows an example of an Ethernet configuration that implements the 2800-meter maximum cable span between two stations.

10BASE5 Collision Detection

Collisions are detected when the signal level on the cable equals or exceeds the combined signal level of two transmitters. As a signal travels along the cable, it gradually attenuates, or weakens. If the signal is allowed to weaken too much, when it combines with the signal from another transmitter the combined signal might not be recognized as a collision.

Figure 10.12 illustrates worst-case collision detection on a CSMA/CD data link that uses 10BASE5 cable segments. Assume that stations 1 and 2 have the maximum allowable distance between them. Station 1 begins transmitting, and just before its signal reaches station 2, station 2 also begins transmitting. The collision occurs near station 2, causing a signal that must travel back the full length of the LAN data link to reach station 1. The MAC frame that station 1 is transmitting must be large enough to ensure that station 1 is still transmitting when it detects the collision with station 2's transmission. Otherwise, it will assume that its MAC frame got through without a collision. The maximum allowable distance between stations of 2800 meters results in the minimum size of 46 octets that the CSMA/CD standard recommends for the LLC Data and Pad fields in the MAC frame.

The maximum time that it takes to detect a collision is twice the propagation time for the maximum cable length defined in the specification. This represents the time it takes station 1's signal to reach the far end plus the time it takes the collision signal to travel the length of the LAN data link to reach station 1.

Another collision detection problem can arise if stations are not spaced properly. Signal reflection may give a false collision indication. To avoid this, the 10BASE5 standard specifies that Medium Attachment Units must be located in such a way that the distance between them is a multiple of 2.5 meters, and no more than 100 stations can be

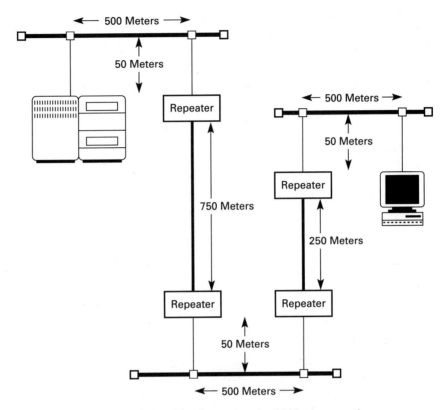

Figure 10.11   Example of implementing the 2800-meter maximum span between two Ethernet stations.

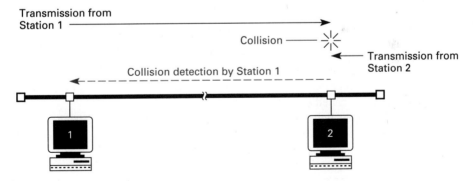

Figure 10.12   Worst-case 10BASE5 collision detection.

attached to any one 500-meter cable segment. The cable jacket on Standard Ethernet cable generally has markings at 2.5 meter intervals to facilitate the placement of Medium Attachment Units at the proper intervals.

10BASE2—THIN ETHERNET

The 10BASE2 medium specification is similar to the 10BASE5 specification. The main difference is that a less expensive, thinner (5 mm) 50-ohm coaxial cable is used. With this specification, baseband transmission is used with the same data rate as the 10BASE5 specification—10 Mbps. With 10BASE2, the maximum cable segment length is 185 meters, and up to 30 stations are supported per cable segment. As with the 10BASE5 specification, longer cable spans and tree structures can be created using repeaters.

The 10BASE2 specification allows lower cost Ethernet implementations to be constructed, and the 10BASE2 specification is often used in personal computer Ethernet implementations. In most implementations of the 10BASE2 medium specification, the transmission medium is brought directly to the network interface card (NIC), and no separate Medium Attachment Unit is used. The 10BASE2 standard, however, does not specifically preclude the use of a separate Medium Attachment Unit.

A standard T-type BNC connector is typically used to attach two cable segments directly to the NIC, allowing stations to be connected together in a daisy-chain fashion, as shown in Fig. 10.13. The final station in a daisy chain must have a short cable segment to which a cable terminator is attached. Station spacing is not critical with the 10BASE2 specification, but the minimum amount of cable that must separate two stations is .5 meters.

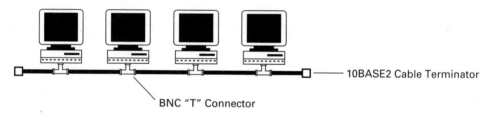

Figure 10.13   10BASE2 daisy chain configuration.

Devices called *multiport repeaters* are often used with 10BASE2 configurations. An individual station, or a daisy chain of multiple stations, is connected to each port of the multiport repeater in a star configuration, as shown in Fig. 10.14. Multiport repeaters are sometimes called *hubs*.

Intelligent hubs and switches that allow stations to be switched from one LAN cable segment to another are also available for Ethernet LANs. The functions of intelligent hubs and switches are discussed in Chapter 16.

10BASE-T—TWISTED PAIR

The 10BASE-T medium specification is similar to 10BASE5 and 10BASE2. With 10BASE-T, ordinary twisted-pair telephone cabling is used instead of coaxial cable. With this specification, baseband transmission is used with a 10 Mbps data rate, making signal-

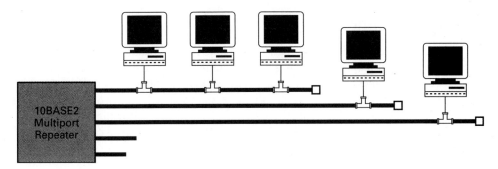

Figure 10.14 10BASE2 star configuration using a multiport repeater.

ing on a 10BASE-T cable segment compatible with signaling on 10BASE5 and 10BASE2 cable segments.

With 10BASE-T, each station is connected using a single length of cable to a device called a *hub*. A hub generally supports a number of stations in a star configuration, as shown in Fig. 10.15, in a similar manner as a 10BASE2 multiport repeater configuration. A single port on a 10BASE-T hub connects to only one station; 10BASE-T stations are not ordinarily daisy chained as in a 10BASE2 configuration. Up to 100 meters of cabling can be used to connect a station to its hub.

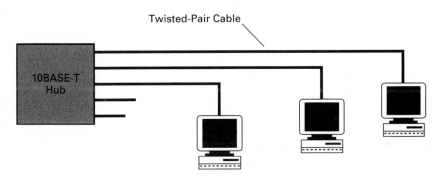

Figure 10.15 10BASE-T star configuration using a hub.

The type of connector most often used with 10BASE-T cabling is the *RJ-45 modular connector*. The RJ-45 modular connector is similar to the standard RJ-11 modular connector commonly used in telephone wiring but allows for up to eight conductors rather than six.

10BASE-T hubs can be interconnected to form larger LANs using 10BASE-T, 10BASE2, or 10BASE5 cable segments, depending on the implementation. Adapters are also available that allow stations already having 10BASE5 AUI interfaces or 10BASE2 connectors to be connected to a 10BASE-T hub.

FOIRL—FIBER OPTIC

The medium specification for a *Fiber-Optic Inter-Repeater Link* (FOIRL) cable segment is a special-purpose medium specification that defines a data rate of 10 Mbps using baseband signaling over a fiber-optic cable. An FOIRL cable segment is used to implement a relatively long-distance, point-to-point connection between two repeaters. FOIRL cable segments can be up to 1000 meters in length, thus allowing longer distances to be spanned between repeaters than can be spanned using a coaxial cable link.

10BROAD36—BROADBAND

A less commonly used CSMA/CD medium specification than 10BASE5, 10BASE2, or 10BASE-T uses broadband transmission over the inexpensive 75-ohm coaxial cable typically used to carry cable television signals. With the 10BROAD36 specification, the maximum length of a cable segment is 1800 meters. Both the dual-cable and split transmission techniques described in Chapter 2 are allowed. The head end can be at the end of a single cable segment, or it can be the root of a branching tree. Thus, the maximum cable span between any two stations is 3600 meters.

Collision detection is performed by the source station's Medium Attachment Unit. The MAU keeps a copy of the MAC frame it is transmitting and compares the bits received to the bits sent as it transmits the frame. If the bits match for the time interval required for all other stations to have received the signal, the source station assumes that no collision has occurred.

For broadband transmission, worst-case collision detection involves two stations that are farthest from the head end. This is illustrated in Fig. 10.16. Here station 2 begins transmitting just before it receives a transmission from station 1, and a collision occurs.

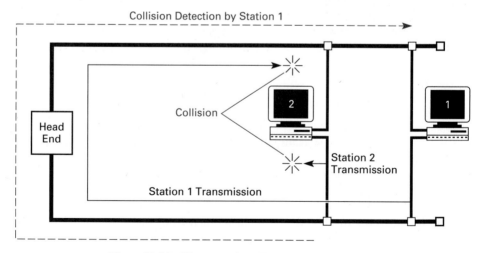

Figure 10.16   Worst-case broadband collision detection.

The collision signal must then travel to the head end and down the other cable until it is received by station 1. Here the time to detect the collision is approximately four times the propagation time from station 1 to the head end. Station 1's signal travels to the head end and back almost to the far end before station 2 begins transmitting and the collision occurs. The collision signal must then travel to the head end and back to the far end for station 1 to receive it.

100BASE-X—FAST ETHERNET

At the time of writing, work is being done in IEEE Project 802 on a new set of CSMA/CD medium specifications that will support a data rate of 100 Mbps using baseband signaling. These new medium specifications are typically referred to as *100BASE-X* or *Fast Ethernet*. Currently, not enough standardization work has been completed on these specifications to include any details. However, Fast Ethernet is likely to be an important form of local area networking during the latter part of the 1990s and into the twenty-first century.

ETHERNET PRODUCTS

As we described earlier, the CSMA/CD standard is based on the *Ethernet Version 2 Specification* that was jointly developed by DEC, Intel, and Xerox. The *Ethernet Version 2 Specification*, and the name *Ethernet*, were made publicly available, and any local area networking product vendor is free to produce Ethernet LAN equipment conforming to either the CSMA/CD standard or the *Ethernet Version 2 Specification*. By far the majority of the Ethernet equipment manufactured today conforms to the IEEE/ISO CSMA/CD standard. The older Ethernet Version 2 Specification is very close to the CSMA/CD standard and differs from it mainly in the use that is made of one of the fields in the MAC frame. The *Ethernet Version 2 Specification* is described in Chapter 11.

A variety of Ethernet equipment is marketed by a large number of different local area networking equipment vendors. These vendors manufacture a wide range of Ethernet equipment, including network interface cards (NICs), repeaters, transceivers, hubs, and cabling systems. The most widely available Ethernet equipment today implements the 10BASE5, 10BASE2, or 10BASE-T medium specifications.

The components used to connect a station to the LAN in a typical 10BASE5 Standard Ethernet coaxial cable implementation are shown in Fig. 10.17. Notice that the external Medium Access Unit (MAU) used with Standard Ethernet cable is often called a *transceiver*. The Attachment Unit Interface (AUI) cable is often called a *transceiver cable*.

Standard Ethernet cable segments conforming to the 10BASE5 medium specification are often used in practice to form the basis of a high-quality backbone in an Ethernet LAN. This is because Standard Ethernet cable segments can be longer than thin Ethernet and twisted-pair cable segments and are more resistant to noise. However, it is more common today, especially in personal computer LANs, for individual stations to be connected to the LAN using the lower cost thin Ethernet coaxial cable or twisted-pair cable.

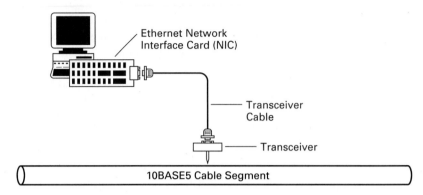

Figure 10.17   Typical Ethernet 10BASE5 implementation.

Network interface cards are available that support multiple medium specifications. For example, NICs are widely available that have an MAU cable connector for an external transceiver and also an internal MAU. The internal MAU often terminates in both an RJ-45 connector for twisted-pair cable and a BNC connector for thin Ethernet cable. Such a NIC could be used with Standard Ethernet, thin Ethernet, or twisted-pair cabling.

Ethernet Network Configurations

The 10BASE5, 10BASE2, and 10BASE-T medium specifications all use the same data rate and the same collision detection scheme. Thus, Standard Ethernet, thin Ethernet, and twisted-pair cable segments can be combined using the repeaters and hubs that are available from a number of different vendors. A possible combination is shown in Fig. 10.18, in which a Standard Ethernet cable segment is used as a backbone for a number of thin Ethernet and twisted-pair cable segments.

A guideline that should be followed in creating such combinations is that a thin Ethernet or twisted-pair cable segment should not be used between two Standard Ethernet cable segments. This is because thin Ethernet and twisted-pair cable is not as resistant to noise as Standard Ethernet cable, and a cable segment used as a backbone should be at least as resistant to noise as the cable segments it connects.

Wiring Closets

The Ethernet form of local area networking has sometimes been criticized because of the difficulties involved in wiring a building using a pure bus topology. In many cases, the best solution to local area network wiring is to create a star-wired configuration using a system of *wiring closets*. All the wiring closets in a building might be interconnected with one another in a bus configuration, possibly using Standard Ethernet cable, and each station is then directly connected to the nearest wiring closet.

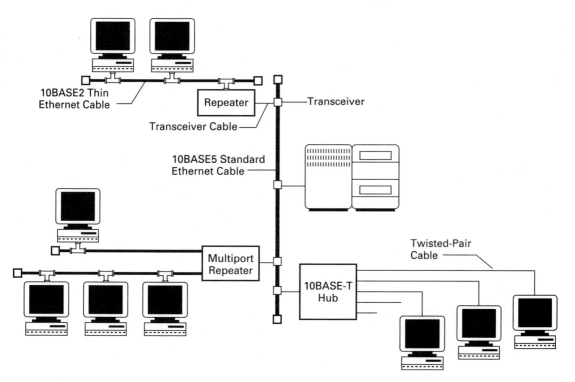

Figure 10.18   Interconnecting 10BASE2 and 10BASE-T cable segments using a 10BASE5 backbone.

The hubs and multiport repeaters used with thin Ethernet and twisted-pair wiring are ideally suited to creating the star-wired configurations that are used with systems of wiring closets. Hubs or multiport repeaters are often installed in the wiring closets and allow a separate cable to connect each station to the wiring closet. Figure 10.19 shows such a star-wired configuration using thin Ethernet cable, with multiport repeaters installed in wiring closets.

IBM PC NETWORK PRODUCTS

Most products that implement the CSMA/CD standard take the form of the widely used Ethernet equipment. However, IBM implements many aspects of the CSMA/CD standard in two product lines that are not compatible with Ethernet equipment. The *PC Network—Broadband* product line implements the CSMA/CD medium access control method using broadband transmission, and the *PC Network—Baseband* product line implements it using baseband transmission. Both versions of the product use different medium specifications than are defined in the CSMA/CD standard and support a data rate of 2 Mbps.

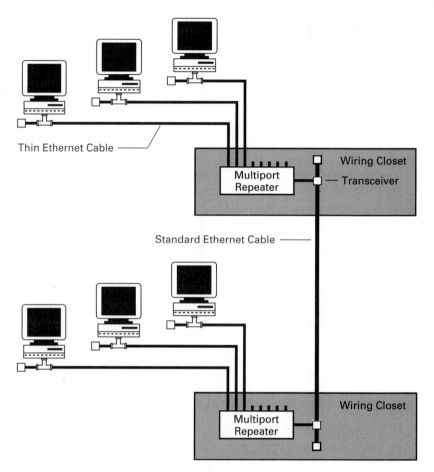

Figure 10.19   Star-wired tree configuration using multiport repeaters installed
in wiring closets.

Medium Access Management

PC Network products implement the CSMA/CD medium access control method essentially as it is described in the CSMA/CD standard. The approach used involves listening
to the transmission medium before transmitting. Medium access management determines,
via the Physical layer, whether or not the transmission medium, or carrier, is currently
being used. If the carrier is free, medium access management initiates transmission of the
MAC frame. If the carrier is busy, medium access management continues monitoring the
carrier until the carrier is free. Medium access management then waits a specified time to
allow the LAN to clear and begins transmission. Collision detection techniques are used
to recover from the collisions that occur.

Box 10.5 shows how the IBM PC Network MAC frame compares to that defined
by the CSMA/CD standard and describes the fields in the PC Network MAC frame.

BOX 10.5   IBM PC network MAC frame.

Preamble	Start Frame Delimiter	Dest. MAC Address	Source MAC Address	Length	LLC Data	⟩⟩	Pad	Frame Check Sequence
7 octets	1 octet	2 or 6 octets	2 or 6 octets	2 octets	0 – n octets		0 – p octets	4 octets

CSMA/CD (Ethernet) Frame Format

Preamble	Start Frame Delimiter	Dest. MAC Address	Source MAC Address	Length	Routing Info.	LLC Data	⟩⟩	Frame Check Sequence
7 octets	1 octet	2 or 6 octets	2 or 6 octets	2 octets	0 – r octets	0 – n octets		4 octets

IBM PC Network Frame Format

- **Preamble.** A sequence of 56 bits of alternating 1 and 0 bits, used to allow destination stations to synchronize with the signal.

- **Start Frame Delimiter.** An octet containing the bit sequence 10101011, used to identify the beginning of the MAC frame.

- **Address Fields.** A Destination MAC Address field and a Source MAC Address field, used to identify the receiving and sending stations, respectively. PC Network products employ 6-octet addresses, allowing for either locally administered or universal addresses. The Destination MAC Address can specify either an individual station or a group of stations.

- **Length.** A 2-octet field that is not used but is included for consistency with the CSMA/CD standard.

- **Routing Information.** An optional field that contains information about the path a frame should take from the source station to the destination station. If the high-order bit in the source MAC address field is 1, routing information is present; if it is 0, the routing information field is not present. For conformance to the CSMA/CD standard, the Routing Information field can be considered to be part of the CSMA/CD LLC Data field. (The use of routing information is discussed in Chapter 19 in the section on source routing bridges.)

- **LLC Data.** Contains the MAC-SDU being transmitted. There is no Pad field defined.

- **Frame Check Sequence.** A CRC value used for error checking.

Collision Detection

Medium access management continues to monitor the carrier after MAC frame transmission begins. If two stations have begun transmitting at the same time, the transmitting station detects the collision, and the station stops transmitting data and sends a jamming signal to ensure that all other stations detect the collision. All stations that have been transmitting stop their transmissions, wait a period of time, and if the carrier is free, attempt retransmission of their frames.

Two different methods are used to detect a collision. One is to monitor the incoming signal to see if any code violations are detected. A code violation is a bit time that does not fit the encoding rules and has a signal transition in an invalid place. The second method is based on the fact that data sent out is received by every station on the LAN, including the station that sent it. The source station does a comparison of the data it sent with the data it receives. This comparison is done by calculating a cyclical redundancy check (CRC) value for a specified number of bits for the data being sent. The CRC value is saved. When the data is received, a CRC value is again calculated on the specified number of bits, and the two CRC values are compared. If they are not equal, the station assumes that a collision has occurred.

IBM PC Network—Broadband Products

The basic components of the broadband version of the IBM PC Network include the following:

- **Adapter Card.** The *adapter card* is a NIC that is installed in a personal computer and contains the logic required to implement communication functions using the CSMA/CD medium access control method.

- **Translator Unit.** The *translator unit* is responsible for receiving any signal transmitted by a station on the LAN and retransmitting it at a different frequency. The translator unit also comes with an 8-way splitter that allows the attachment of eight stations.

- **Cabling Components.** The *cabling components* include splitters and the cable required to add additional stations to the LAN.

LAN Topology

The above components are used to construct a configuration that has a tree topology, as shown in Fig. 10.20. The translator forms the root of the tree. A transformer is used to supply power to the translator. One 8-way splitter attaches to the translator through a directional coupler, and up to eight personal computers can be attached to the first splitter. Additional splitters can be used to attach additional personal computers to the LAN. Up to 72 stations can be attached to a given broadband LAN, using the IBM components, with a maximum cable span of 1000 feet from any station to the translator. Larger LAN data links, of up to 1000 stations located up to 5 km from the translator, can be constructed using non-IBM translators and cable.

Transmission Characteristics

Standard 75-ohm, CATV-type coaxial cable is used as the transmission medium for broadband PC Network components. Transmission on the cable is frequency modulated, using continuous-phase frequency-shift keying with a transmission rate of 2 Mbps. Two channels are used, each with a 6-MHz bandwidth. When a station transmits, it sends out the data at a frequency of 50.75 MHz. When the transmission reaches the translator, the translator retransmits it on the same cable at a frequency of 219 MHz. Every station on the

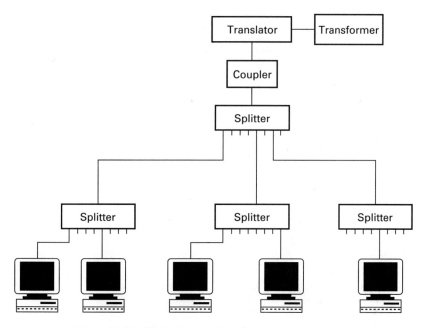

Figure 10.20   PC Network—Broadband network topology.

LAN *listens* to the transmission medium at a frequency of 219 MHz, so when the retransmission arrives, it is received by all the stations on the LAN data link. Having the translator retransmit ensures that the signal will be of sufficient strength throughout the LAN.

IBM PC Network—Baseband

The basic components of the baseband version of the IBM PC Network include the following:

- **Adapter Card.** The *adapter card* is a NIC that is installed in each personal computer on the LAN and provides the logic required to implement communication.
- **Extender.** An *extender* is used to create larger, star-wired configurations.
- **Cabling System.** The cabling used for the baseband version of the PC Network is twisted-pair cable.

The baseband version of the PC Network can use one of two topologies, shown in Fig. 10.21. Up to eight stations can be connected together serially in a daisy-chain topology. An extender can be used to connect together up to ten daisy chains in a star configuration, providing for up to 80 stations in a single LAN.

PC Network Direct Interface API

The service definition that we described earlier for the CSMA/CD MAC sublayer consists of an abstract definition of the services that the MAC sublayer provides to the LLC sublayer software. Each vendor that manufactures a NIC product can define its own

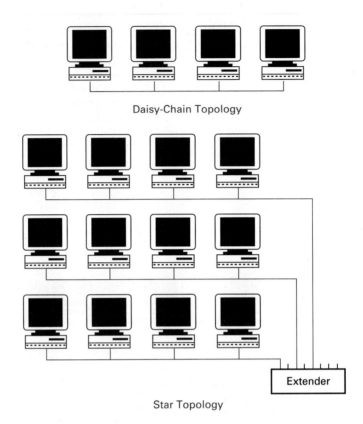

Figure 10.21   PC Network—Baseband network topologies.

application programming interface (API) that a software subsystem can use to request MAC sublayer services. If the NIC vendor supplies a software implementation of the LLC sublayer, that vendor may or may not publish the API that the LLC sublayer uses to request MAC sublayer services.

We end this chapter by describing IBM's MAC sublayer API for its local area networking products, called the *IBM Direct Interface*. Each type of IBM LAN adapter product supports a slightly different Direct Interface. The version described here is for IBM's PC Network line of LAN adapters.

Like IBM's DLC interface, described in Chapter 9, the Direct Interface is based on the use of command control blocks (CCBs) A CCB provides the information necessary to execute a particular command and contains a command code that identifies the particular function to perform. A CCB also specifies information about work areas and parameters. The specific format of the CCB, and the way it is passed to the MAC sublayer implementation, varies depending on the computing system hardware and operating system environment.

Box 10.6 lists the commands that the Direct Interface defines for IBM's PC Network LAN adapter products.

BOX 10.6   Direct interface commands.

Frame Transmission Commands

- **Buffer.Free.** Return one or more buffers to the direct station buffer pool.
- **Buffer.Get.** Acquire one or more buffers from the direct station buffer pool.
- **Read.** Accept received data from the direct station.
- **Receive.** Receive data from the direct station.
- **Receive.Cancel.** Stop receiving data from the direct station.
- **Receive.Modify.** Receive data and put some of the data in a buffer other than the direct station buffer.
- **Transmit.Dir.Frame.** Transmit a MAC frame of data using the direct station.

General Commands

- **Dir.Close.Adapter.** Terminate communication for the adapter.
- **Dir.Close.Direct.** Terminate application program's use of the direct station.
- **Dir.Define.MIF.Environment.** Define the environment needed for a NETBIOS emulation program.
- **Dir.Initialize.** Initialize work areas, tables, and buffers associated with the adapter.
- **Dir.Interrupt.** Force an adapter interrupt.
- **Dir.Modify.Open.Parms.** Modify values set by Dir.Open.Adapter.
- **Dir.Open.Adapter.** Prepare the adapter for communication.
- **Dir.Open.Direct.** Give the application program use of the direct station for communication.
- **Dir.Read.Log.** Read and reset the adapter logs.
- **Dir.Restore.Open.Parms.** Restore parameters modified by Dir.Modify.Open.Parms to their original values.
- **Dir.Set.Exception.Flags.** Define user notification appendages and flags.
- **Dir.Set.Functional.Address.** Set functional addresses for the adapter.
- **Dir.Set.Group.Address.** Set the group address for the adapter.
- **Dir.Set.User.Appendage.** Change appendage addresses.
- **Dir.Status.** Read the general status information.
- **Dir.Timer.Cancel.** Cancel a timer set by Dir.Set.Timer.
- **Dir.Timer.Cancel.Group.** Cancel timers set by a group of Dir.Set.Timer commands.
- **Dir.Timer.Set.** Set a timer.
- **PDT.Trace.Off.** Terminate a trace started by PDT.Trace.On.
- **PDT.Trace.On.** Start a trace of all adapter traffic.
- **Purge.Resources.** Purge resources owned by a terminating application process.

SUMMARY

The IEEE/ISO carrier sense multiple access with collision detection (CSMA/CD) standard is based on the Ethernet Version 2 technology. CSMA/CD, or Ethernet, medium access control technology implements a multiaccess data link that uses a bus- or tree-structured network topology in which all stations receive all transmissions within a period of time determined by the propagation delay of the network.

The CSMA/CD MAC service definition defines a single MA_UNITDATA unconfirmed data transfer service. The CSMA/CD protocol specification defines the format of the MAC-SDU, specifies how the MAC-SDU is encapsulated in a MAC-PDU, and documents the procedures controlling the exchange of MAC-PDUs between communicating stations.

The CSMA/CD form of medium access control uses a contention technique to determine which station transmits next. Each station having a frame to send listens to the transmission medium and transmits when the medium is free. If two or more stations transmit simultaneously, a collision results. A station detecting a collision stops transmitting and sends out a jamming signal to ensure that other stations also detect the collision. The station then uses a deference process based on a binary exponential backoff procedure to wait for a period of time before retransmitting.

The CSMA/CD architectural model divides the Physical layer into a Physical Signaling (PLS) sublayer and a Physical Medium Attachment (PMA) sublayer. Both sublayers can be implemented in the station, or a separate Medium Attachment Unit (MAU), located a short distance from the station, can be used to implement the PMA sublayer. The CSMA/CD standard also documents Physical layer specifications for a repeater that can be used to interconnect two or more cable segments.

Medium specifications for the CSMA/CD standard supporting a 10 Mbps transmission speed include 10BASE5 for Standard Ethernet coaxial cable, 10BASE2 for thin Ethernet coaxial cable, 10BASE-T for twisted-pair cable, FOIRL for fiber-optic interrepeater link cable segments, and 10BROAD36 for broadband transmission over CATV-type coaxial cable. Work is underway on Fast Ethernet specifications that support 100 Mbps transmission using CSMA/CD techniques.

Chapter 11 describes the *Ethernet Version 2 Specification*, jointly developed by Digital Equipment Corporation, Intel, and Xerox, on which the CSMA/CD standard is based.

Chapter **11**

The Ethernet Version 2 Specification

In 1972, the Palo Alto Research Center of Xerox Corporation (Xerox PARC) began developing a local area network system called *Experimental Ethernet*. Later, Digital Equipment Corporation, Intel, and Xerox worked together to jointly define and publish a revised and improved *Ethernet Specification*. This was further refined in Version 2 of the specification. The work done on Ethernet Version 2 contributed substantially to the IEEE/ISO CSMA/CD standard, which we described in Chapter 10. The CSMA/CD standard is compatible in most ways with Ethernet Version 2.

This chapter introduces the *Ethernet Version 2 Specification* and describes how it is different from the CSMA/CD standard. Keep in mind, however, as you read this chapter that very little new Ethernet equipment is being marketed today that implements the *Ethernet Version 2 Specification*. Almost all of today's Ethernet equipment conforms to the IEEE/ISO CSMA/CD standard.

TERMINOLOGY

An Ethernet Version 2 LAN data link uses building blocks of individual coaxial cable segments to which one or more stations is attached in a bus-structured topology. The only form of coaxial cable described in the *Ethernet Version 2 Specification* is Standard Ethernet cable. This is the 10 mm, 50-ohm coaxial cable that is defined in the 10BASE5 medium specification of the CSMA/CD standard.

Ethernet Version 2 is a form of LAN data link technology that provides a best-efforts datagram service with error detection but not error correction. An Ethernet Version 2 LAN is defined as a multiaccess network that uses a passive broadcast medium with no central control. Frames transmitted over the LAN data link reach every station, and each station is responsible for interpreting the destination address contained in a frame and for accepting frames addressed to it. Access to the transmission medium is governed by the individual stations using a statistical arbitration scheme.

The *Ethernet Version 2 Specification* does not divide the Data Link layer into sub-layers. The software layer operating above the Data Link layer is called the *Client layer* and works with data units called *packets*. The Client layer passes packets to the Data Link layer, which encapsulates them in *frames* for transmission over the LAN.

The goals that the original designers articulated early in the design of Ethernet Version 2 are listed in Box 11.1.

BOX 11.1   Ethernet Version 2 goals.

- **Simplicity.** Features that would complicate the design without substantially contributing to meeting the other goals were excluded.

- **Low cost.** Since technological improvements will continue to reduce the overall cost of stations wishing to connect to the Ethernet, the cost of the connection itself should be minimized.

- **Compatibility.** All implementations of the Ethernet should be capable of exchanging data at the Data Link level. For this reason, the specification avoids optional features to eliminate the possibility of incompatible variants of the Ethernet.

- **Addressing flexibility.** The addressing mechanisms should provide the capability to target frames to a single station, a group of stations, or to all stations on the network.

- **Fairness.** All stations should have equal access to the network when averaged over time.

- **Progress.** No single station operating in accordance with the protocol should be able to prevent the progress of other stations.

- **High speed.** The network should operate efficiently at a data rate of 10 Megabits per second.

- **Low delay.** At any given level of offered traffic, the network should introduce as little delay as possible in the transfer of a frame.

- **Stability.** The network should be stable under all load conditions, in the sense that the delivered traffic should be a monotonically nondecreasing function of the total offered traffic.

- **Maintainability.** The Ethernet design should allow for network maintenance, operation, and planning.

- **Layered architecture.** The Ethernet design should be specified in layered terms to separate the logical aspects of the Data Link protocol from the physical details of the communication medium.

SERVICE DEFINITION

The *Ethernet Version 2 Specification* does not explicitly define a service definition and a protocol specification in the same manner as for IEEE, ISO, and ANSI standards. It defines services in terms of *functions* that a higher layer can request of a lower layer.

The two services that the Data Link layer provides to the Client layer are the transmission and reception of frames. These services are defined by the following functions:

- **TransmitFrame.** The *TransmitFrame* function is performed by a source station to send a frame to one or more destination stations. This function defines a service that is roughly equivalent to that performed by a combination of the DL_UNITDATA.request service primitive defined by the Logical Link Control sublayer standard and the MA_UNITDATA.request service primitive defined by the CSMA/CD standard.

- **ReceiveFrame.** The *ReceiveFrame* function is performed by a destination station to receive a frame that has been sent by a source station. This function defines a service that is roughly equivalent to that performed by the DL_UNITDATA.indication service primitive defined by the Logical Link Control sublayer standard and the MA_UNITDATA.indication service primitive defined by the CSMA/CD standard.

PROTOCOL SPECIFICATION

The *Ethernet Version 2 Specification* describes a single protocol to carry out the procedures that the IEEE/ISO LAN standards specify in the protocols for the Logical Link Control and Medium Access Control sublayers.

Frame Format

Box 11.2 compares the format of the MAC frame format described by the CSMA/CD standard with the Ethernet Version 2 frame and describes the fields in the Ethernet Version 2 MAC frame.

Protocol Operation

The *Ethernet Version 2 Specification* defines only a connectionless Data Link layer service that is equivalent to that provided by Type 1 operation defined in the IEEE/ISO Logical Link Control sublayer standard. It also defines a protocol that is equivalent to that defined by the CSMA/CD Medium Access Control sublayer standard for controlling access to the transmission medium and for detecting and recovering from collisions.

FUNCTIONAL MODEL

Figure 11.1 shows the Ethernet Version 2 functional model and compares it to the functional model documented in the IEEE/ISO CSMA/CD standard. Although there are some differences in terminology, the functions of the Data Link and Physical layers are similar to those defined in the IEEE and ISO standards:

- **Data Encapsulation/Decapsulation.** When a packet is received from the Client layer for transmission, it is encapsulated with the control information necessary for transmission, thus forming a frame. When the frame is received, the control information is removed before the enclosed packet is passed up to the Client layer.

- **Link Management.** The link management function is responsible for collision handling in a similar manner as for the CSMA/CD standard.

- **Data Encoding/Decoding.** The encoding/decoding functions use the same Manchester encoding scheme as described in the CSMA/CD standard.

- **Channel Access.** The channel access function transmits bits to and receives bits from the coaxial cable. It also senses the carrier (the presence of data transmission on the medium) and detects collisions.

BOX 11.2   Ethernet Version 2 MAC frame.

Preamble	Start Frame Delimiter	Dest. MAC Address	Source MAC Address	Length	LLC Data	Pad	Frame Check Sequence
7 octets	1 octet	2 or 6 octets	2 or 6 octets	2 octets	0 – n octets	0 – p octets	4 octets

CSMA/CD (Ethernet) Frame Format

Preamble	Dest. Address	Source Address	Type	LLC Data	Frame Check Sequence
8 octets	2 or 6 octets	2 or 6 octets	2 octets	0 – n octets	4 octets

Ethernet Version 2 Frame Format

- **Preamble.** Eight octets used to provide synchronization and to mark the start of a frame. The same bit pattern is used for the Ethernet Version 2 Preamble field as for the CSMA/CD Preamble and Start Frame Delimiter fields.

- **Address Fields.** A *Destination Address* field followed by a *Source Address* field. A destination address can reference an individual station or a group of stations, and globally-administered or locally-administered addresses can be used. Xerox Corporation provides vendors of Ethernet Version 2 products with blocks of addresses to use in assigning unique addresses to individual network interface cards (NICs).

- **Type.** A Type value that is used in place of the Length field of the CSMA/CD MAC frame. The Type field is meaningful to the higher layers and is ordinarily used to identify a Network layer protocol.

- **Information.** Contains the packet passed to the Data Link layer by the Client layer. The *Ethernet Version 2 Specification* defines a minimum frame size of 72 octets and a maximum frame size of 1526 octets, including all header and trailer fields. This is equivalent to the recommended 46-1500 octet limitation of the LLC Data plus Pad fields described in the CSMA/CD standard. If the data to be sent is smaller or larger, it is the responsibility of the Data Link layer user to pad it or to break it into multiple packets.

- **Frame Check Sequence (FCS).** A CRC value used for error checking in the same manner as for the CSMA/CD standard.

IMPLEMENTATION MODEL

A typical Ethernet Version 2 implementation uses similar components as an implementation of the IEEE/ISO CSMA/CD 10BASE5 medium specification. The Data Link layer functions, and the data encoding/decoding function of the Physical layer, are assumed to be packaged in a NIC that is installed in a computing device, such as a personal computer.

A separate device called a *transceiver* is attached to the coaxial cable. The trans-

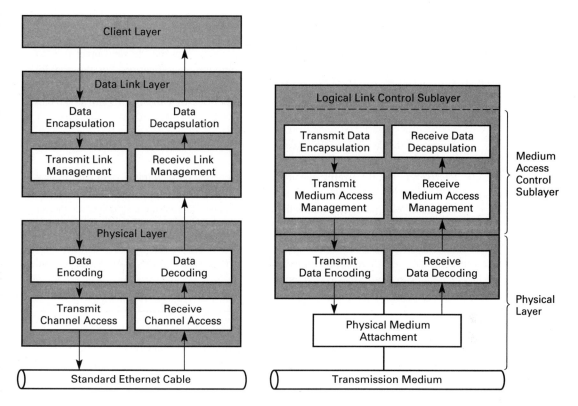

Figure 11.1   Ethernet Version 2 Specification and IEEE/ISO CSMA/CD functional model comparison.

ceiver implements the channel access function and corresponds to the medium attachment unit defined in the CSMA/CD standard. A *transceiver cable* is used to connect the transceiver to the NIC and corresponds to the Attachment Unit Interface of the CSMA/CD standard.

In Ethernet Version 2, the functions of the Physical layer are referred to as the *physical channel*, or simply the *channel*. This includes the logic in the NIC that does encoding and decoding, preamble generation and removal, and carrier sensing. The transceiver contains the logic required to send and receive bits over the coaxial cable and to detect collisions.

The channel access function is performed within the transceiver. The facilities provided by the channel access function include the following:

- Accepting encoded bits from the controller and putting them onto the coaxial cable.
- Taking bits from the coaxial cable and passing them to the controller.
- Detecting collisions and passing an appropriate signal to the controller.

PHYSICAL LAYER SPECIFICATIONS

The *Ethernet Version 2 Specification* defines the functions that the Physical layer uses to supply services to the Data Link layer. It also documents specifications for the coaxial cable that is used as the transmission medium.

The Physical layer provides the following functions that the Data Link layer can request:

- **TransmitBit.** The TransmitBit procedure passes one bit of a frame from the Data Link layer to the Physical layer for transmission.
- **ReceiveBit.** The ReceiveBit function is used to pass a bit of a frame from the Physical layer to the Data Link layer.
- **Wait.** The Wait procedure allows the Data Link layer to measure a specified number of bit times. This is used to wait the proper amount of time after a collision before attempting retransmission.

The foregoing services match very closely the interface between the MAC sublayer and the Physical layer in the CSMA/CD standard.

MEDIUM SPECIFICATION

The *Ethernet Specification* defines electrical, mechanical, and other physical characteristics for the components making up the physical channel. These characteristics include the following:

- Physical configuration limits, such as coaxial cable segment length, number of repeaters, total path length, and transceiver cable length.
- Coaxial cable component specifications, including the cable itself, connectors, and terminators.
- Interface specifications for the transceiver cable and the transceiver.
- Configuration requirements and environmental specifications.

The most commonly used implementation of the specification uses baseband transmission over coaxial cable with a data rate of 10 Mbps. The maximum cable length is 500 meters, thus conforming to the 10BASE5 medium specification as described in the IEEE/ISO CSMA/CD standard. Thin Ethernet cable and twisted-pair cable have also been used in some implementations, although these are not addressed by the *Ethernet Version 2 Specification*.

INTEROPERATION OF ETHERNET VERSION 2 AND IEEE/ISO CSMA/CD STATIONS

The *Ethernet Version 2 Specification* and the IEEE/ISO CSMA/CD standard are quite similar. However, the difference in frame formats is enough to make a NIC that conforms only to one specification incompatible with one that conforms only to the other specification. There are techniques, however, that LAN vendors have employed to allow devices of the two types to coexist on the same LAN data link.

Digital Equipment Corporation faced a requirement for such interoperation when making the transition from DECnet Phase IV to DECnet/OSI. DECnet Phase IV LAN products conform to the *Ethernet Version 2 Specification*, while the newer DECnet/OSI LAN products support the IEEE/ISO CSMA/CD local area network standard.

To permit interoperation, DECnet/OSI LAN devices are designed to normally transmit IEEE/ISO CSMA/CD frames but to accept incoming frames in either the CSMA/CD or Ethernet Version 2 format. When a DECnet/OSI LAN station receives an IEEE/ISO CSMA/CD frame from a station, it replies to that station with CSMA/CD frames; when it receives an Ethernet Version 2 frame, it replies to that station with Ethernet Version 2 frames.

A DECnet/OSI device distinguishes between an Ethernet Version 2 frame and an IEEE/ISO CSMA/CD frame by examining the 2-octet Length field, which corresponds to the Type field in an Ethernet Version 2 frame. Because of the maximum frame size restriction, the Length field value in a CSMA/CD frame must contain a value that falls within the range of 3 to 1500. Therefore, if the Length field value falls within the range of 3 to 1500, the frame is a CSMA/CD frame; if the Length field value falls outside of this range, it is an Ethernet Version 2 frame.

LAN product vendors other than DEC have also used this simple scheme to build Ethernet equipment that can accept frames in both formats. Such equipment can interoperate with Ethernet devices that conform to either the IEEE/ISO standard or the *Ethernet Version 2 Specification*.

SUMMARY

The *Ethernet Version 2 Specification*, jointly developed by Digital Equipment Corporation, Intel, and Xerox, was based on the original *Ethernet Specification* defined by Xerox. An Ethernet Version 2 data link uses coaxial cable segments to which stations are attached in a bus- or tree-structured topology.

The *Ethernet Version 2 Specification* does not divide the Data Link layer into separate sublayers. The services that are provided to a user of an Ethernet data link include the transmission and reception of frames. The protocols defined by the *Ethernet Version 2 Specification* combine the procedures performed in the LLC and MAC sublayers for IEEE/ISO/ANSI LAN data link technology. The MAC frame format is similar to the frame format for the CSMA/CD standard except that the Length field is replaced by a Type field that identifies the protocol associated with the data unit contained in the MAC frame.

The *Ethernet Version 2 Specification* includes a single medium specification defining 10 Mbps baseband transmission over 50-ohm standard Ethernet coaxial cable.

Chapter 12 describes the token-bus form of medium access control technology. The token-bus medium access control method uses a token-passing technique to implement bus- or tree-structured LAN data links.

Token Bus

The IEEE/ISO/ANSI LAN standards include three medium access control methods that are based on the token-passing technique. The IEEE 802.4/ISO 8802-4 Token Bus standard, the subject of this chapter, uses token passing in conjunction with a network that has a bus- or tree-structured topology. The IEEE/ISO Token Ring and the ANSI/ISO Fiber Distributed Data Interface (FDDI) standards are both based on a network that has a ring-structured topology.

The Token Bus network topology can be described as a combination of a *logical ring* with a *physical bus or tree*. This is illustrated in Fig. 12.1.

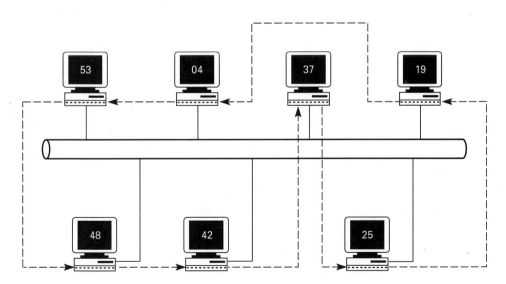

Figure 12.1 Token Bus network topology—logical ring on a physical bus.

A Token Bus LAN implements a multiaccess form of data link in which all stations on the LAN receive the transmissions of all other stations. All MAC frames broadcast over the transmission medium reach every station, and each station is responsible for interpreting the destination MAC address contained in a frame and for accepting frames addressed to it.

The token bus form of medium access control is the LAN technology adopted by the General Motors *Manufacturing Automation Protocol* (MAP) architecture developed for use in factory automation environments. The MAP architecture is introduced later in this chapter.

The Token Bus standard defines both a service definition and a protocol specification for the MAC sublayer. It also defines an architectural model for the MAC sublayer and Physical layer and describes specifications for various types of transmission media that can be used to implement the standard.

MAC SUBLAYER SERVICE DEFINITION

Medium Access Control sublayer services allow an LLC entity in one station to exchange LLC-PDUs with LLC sublayer entities in other stations. The MAC sublayer service definition is specified in terms of service primitives and service primitive parameters and describes an MA_UNITDATA unconfirmed data transfer service and an optional response capability.

MAC Sublayer Service Primitives

The following are descriptions of the service primitives that make up the MA_UNITDATA service:

- **MA_UNITDATA.request.** Issued by the LLC sublayer entity to the MAC sublayer entity in the source station to request that a MAC-SDU be sent to one or more destination stations.

- **MA_UNITDATA_STATUS.indication.** Issued by the MAC sublayer entity in the source station to the LLC entity to provide information about the success or failure of an attempt to transmit an LLC-PDU.

- **MA_UNITDATA.indication.** Issued by the MAC entity in the destination station to the LLC entity to indicate that an LLC-PDU has been received and to pass the LLC-PDU up to the LLC entity.

Figure 12.2 shows a time-sequence diagram that documents the sequence in which the three service primitives are issued during normal MAC frame transmission. Notice that the MA_UNITDATA service is ordinarily an unconfirmed service. The MA_UNITDATA_STATUS. indication primitive tells the LLC sublayer entity in the source station only that the transmission attempt was successful. It does not tell the LLC sublayer entities in either the source or the destination station whether or not the MAC frame was received successfully by the distant station.

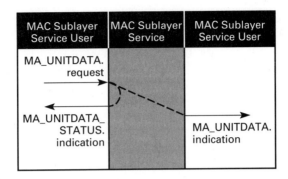

Figure 12.2 Time-sequence diagram for the MA_UNITDATA data transfer service.

Optional Response Capability

When the optional response capability is implemented, the MA_UNITDATA.request and MA_UNITDATA.indication service primitives can also be issued in the opposite direction for the purposes of returning a response. Figure 12.3 shows a time-sequence diagram illustrating the use of the service primitives when the optional response mechanism is used.

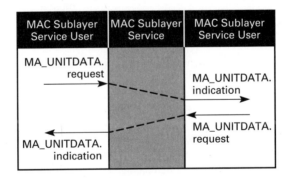

Figure 12.3 Time-sequence diagram for the MAC sublayer optional response facility.

Service Primitive Parameters

Box 12.1 describes the parameters that are included in the service primitives for the MA_UNITDATA data transfer service.

MAC SUBLAYER PROTOCOL SPECIFICATION

The data unit the MAC sublayer receives from the LLC sublayer is the *medium-access-control-service-data-unit* (MAC-SDU). The MAC-SDU contains the LLC-PDU that the two LLC sublayer entities are exchanging.

BOX 12.1   MA_UNITDATA service primitive parameters.

MA_UNITDATA.request   (
                         destination_address,
                         source_address,
                         m_sdu,
                         desired_quality
)

MA_UNITDATA_STATUS.indication
                         (
                         destination_address,
                         source_address,
                         status,
                         provided_quality
)

MA_UNITDATA.indication
                         (
                         destination_address,
                         source_address,
                         m_sdu,
                         quality
)

- **destination_address.** Specifies a destination MAC address defining the station or stations to which the MAC-SDU is to be delivered. The MAC addressing scheme is described in Chapter 6.

- **source_address.** Specifies a source MAC address identifying the station originating the MAC-SDU.

- **m_sdu.** Specifies the MAC-SDU passed down from the LLC sublayer for transmission from the source station to the destination station or stations.

- **desired_quality.** Contains two components that specify the requested priority and the type of service requested. This parameter can request that a MAC-SDU be delivered to its destination or that an optional response mechanism be used to verify that the delivery actually took place.

- **status.** Indicates to the source LLC entity whether or not the previous MA_UNITDATA.request primitive was accepted by the MAC sublayer entity.

- **provided_quality.** Indicates the quality of service that was used to satisfy the previous MA_UNITDATA.request primitive.

- **quality.** Indicates the quality of service that was actually used to deliver the MAC-SDU.

MAC Sublayer Functions

During MAC frame transmission, the Medium Access Control sublayer entities in all the stations on the LAN data link perform the following functions:

- **Interface to the LLC Sublayer.** The MAC sublayer must receive MAC-SDUs from the LLC sublayer and prepare them for transmission. On the receiving side, the MAC sublayer must receive MAC-SDUs that have been transmitted across the network and pass them to the LLC sublayer.

- **Token Handling.** This includes passing the token from one station to the next, recognizing a token when it is received and, optionally, providing for the prioritization of data units.

- **Ring Maintenance.** The logical ring that the stations form must be initialized when the network is powered up and modified as stations are added or deleted.

- **Fault Detection and Recovery.** Possible faults include multiple tokens, lost tokens, token pass failures, stations with inoperative receivers, and duplicate station addresses. These must be detected and, where possible, corrected.

- **Sending and Receiving Data.** In a source station, MAC frames are passed from the MAC sublayer to the Physical layer for transmission across the network; in a destination station, MAC frames must be received by the MAC sublayer from the Physical layer. These functions include adding and removing the control information necessary to form MAC frames in the format described in the Token Bus standard.

MAC Frame Format

The protocol specification for the Token Bus MAC sublayer defines the format of the MAC frame that is exchanged between MAC sublayer entities in source and destination stations. Box 12.2 shows the format of the Token Bus MAC frame and describes its fields.

MAC Frame/LLC-PDU Relationship

Figure 12.4 shows the relationship between the LLC-PDU and the Token Bus MAC frame. All fields in the LLC-PDU exchanged by the Logical Link Control sublayer entities are treated by the Token Bus MAC sublayer as data.

MAC PROTOCOL OPERATION

With the Token Bus approach to medium access control, access to the transmission medium is determined by possession of a special data unit called the *token*, which is passed from station to station.

When a station receives the token, it is allowed to transmit data units until a maximum amount of time has been reached. It then transmits the token to the next station. If a station that receives the token has no data units to transmit, it passes the token immediately to the next station.

The network stations are physically attached in a *bus* topology. However, the token, as indicated by the dashed line in the diagram, follows a *logical ring* around the network. The token is passed from one station to the next based on descending order of MAC addresses. When the station having the lowest MAC address value is reached, the token passes back to the station having the highest MAC address.

BOX 12.2   Token Bus MAC frame.

Preamble	Start Frame Delimiter	Frame Control	Dest. MAC Address	Source MAC Address	Information	Frame Check Sequence	Frame End Delimiter
	1 octet	2 octets	2 or 6 octets	2 or 6 octets	0 – n octets	4 octets	1 octet

- **Preamble.** A sequence of octets used by the receiving station for synchronization. The length of this field and its contents vary with the modulation method and the data rate used in the particular implementation of the standard.

- **Start Frame Delimiter.** An octet containing a signaling pattern that is always distinguishable from data. (For example, with Manchester encoding, this might be an octet containing one or more bit times in which no transition takes place.)

- **Frame Control.** An octet that identifies the type of frame being sent. Possible types are LLC data frames, token control frames, MAC management data frames, and special-purpose data frames.

- **Station Addresses.** A *Destination MAC Address* field followed by a *Source MAC Address* field. The destination address identifies the station or stations that are to receive the MAC frame. The source address identifies the sending station. Address fields can be either 16 bits or 48 bits in length. (The MAC addressing mechanism is described in Chapter 6.) The destination MAC address field can specify either an individual station or a group of stations.

- **Information.** A MAC-SDU, token control data, management data, or special-purpose data, as indicated by the frame control field. The Information field can be 0 octets in length for some types of MAC frames.

- **Frame Check Sequence.** A cyclic redundancy check (CRC) value used for error checking. When the sending station assembles a frame, it performs a CRC calculation on the bits in the frame. The specific algorithm that is used is described in the IEEE/ISO Token Bus standard. The sending station stores this value in the Frame Check Sequence field and then transmits the frame. When the receiving station receives the frame, it performs an identical CRC calculation and compares the results with the value in the Frame Check Sequence field. If the two values do not match, the receiving station assumes that a transmission error has occurred.

- **End Frame Delimiter.** An octet containing a signaling value that is always distinguishable from data. It marks the end of the frame and also identifies the position of the Frame Check Sequence field.

Token Addressing

Because the physical topology of a Token Bus LAN takes the form of a bus, the token and all other frames are sent in a broadcast fashion and are received by all stations on the network. Every frame, including the token, contains a destination MAC address field that identifies the station or stations that are to receive it. Each station then accepts and processes only frames that are addressed to it. A station passes the token by changing the

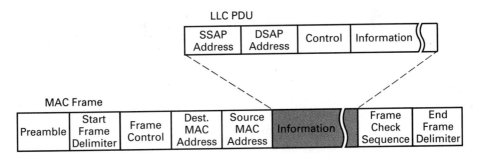

Figure 12.4   Token Bus MAC frame and LLC-PDU relationship.

destination MAC address field in the token to that of the next logical station in the ring before it transmits the token.

Since a station transmits only when it has received the token, two stations can never transmit at the same time and collisions cannot occur. Because there can be no collisions, there is no minimum length requirement for frames, and the token can be a very short data unit. It contains only the control information required for proper processing.

Control Frames

The MAC sublayer generates its own control frames that are transmitted across the network and are used to control the operation of the MAC sublayer protocol. These control frames are in addition to the frames that are used to transmit the MAC-SDUs that are passed down from the LLC sublayer. With control frames, no information is exchanged with the LLC sublayer, either in the sending or the receiving station.

Control frames are used for token-passing and ring-maintenance functions. Listed below are the control frames that are defined in the Token Bus standard. The binary control field value is included in parentheses after the name of each frame.

- **Claim_token (00000000).** Used to initiate token-passing operations when a network is initialized or when the token is lost.
- **Solicit_successor_1 (00000001).** Used to invite new stations to be added to the network. Invited stations are those whose addresses are between the holder of the token and its current successor.
- **Solicit_successor_2 (00000010).** Used to invite new stations to be added to the network. Invited stations are those whose addresses are not between the holder of the token and its current successor.
- **Who_follows (00000011).** Used when a successor station does not respond to being passed the token. Based on the response to this frame, the station sending the token acquires a new successor.
- **Resolve_contention (00000100).** Used when multiple stations respond to a Solicit_successor frame.
- **Token (00001000).** The holder of the token is the station that is allowed to transmit.
- **Set_successor (00001100).** Used in response to a Who_follows frame or a Solicit_successor frame to supply the address of the new successor station.

Optional Priority Scheme

The Token Bus standard allows each MAC frame to be assigned to one of four classes of service: 6, 4, 2, and 0, with 6 being the highest priority service class. The **priority** parameter that is included by the LLC sublayer in the DL_UNITDATA.request service primitive is passed to the MAC sublayer to specify the class of service to assign to the MAC frame. If an odd priority value is specified, the value is mapped to the service class that is one lower than the specified priority value.

When the optional priority scheme is not implemented, the MAC sublayer treats all MAC frames as if they are assigned to service class 6, no matter what priority value is assigned to them. When the optional priority scheme is implemented, the MAC sublayer stores MAC-SDUs that it receives from the LLC sublayer in four queues according to the service class to which each MAC-SDU is assigned, as shown in Fig. 12.5. MAC-SDUs that are held in the queue for service class 6 are treated as though the priority system were not in operation. A station that receives the token is always allowed to transmit MAC-SDUs in service class 6 until its timer expires.

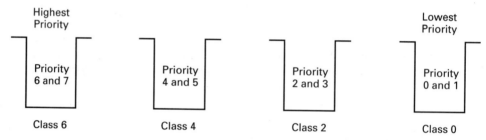

Figure 12.5   Token Bus priority values and service classes.

Target Token Rotation Times

When the priority scheme is implemented, each of the three lower-priority service classes has a *target token rotation time* assigned to it, with higher-priority classes having longer target token rotation times than the lower-priority classes. Each station sets three rotation timers to the three target rotation time values each time it transmits the token. These timers all begin to count down as soon as the token begins to circulate around the ring as illustrated in Fig. 12.6.

Suppose a station has transmitted all of the MAC-SDUs assigned to service class 6 that it has queued up. It then examines the rotation timer for service class 4 to see if that time limit has expired. If the timer for service class 4 has not yet expired, the station is able to transmit any MAC-SDUs that it might have queued up in service class 4. It transmits these until either it has no more service class 4 MAC-SDUs or until the rotation timer assigned to service class 4 expires. If the station transmits all of the MAC-SDUs assigned to service class 4, and the timer for service class 4 has still not expired, the station checks the timer for service class 2, and if that timer has not yet expired, it transmits any available MAC-SDUs from that queue. The station then moves down to service class 0 if the timer for service class 2 has not yet expired.

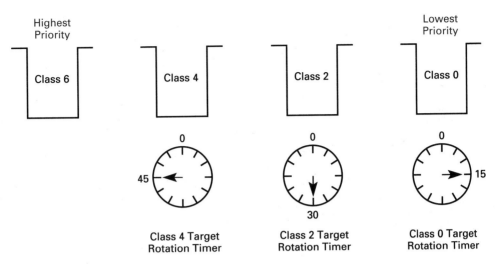

Figure 12.6   Token Bus target rotation timers.

Priority Algorithm Intent

The priority algorithm is designed so that transmission capacity is assigned to the highest-priority MAC-SDUs as long as there are MAC-SDUs assigned to service class 6 available for transmission by any station on the network. Lower-priority MAC-SDUs are sent only when there is sufficient capacity available for them. If there are many stations that have MAC-SDUs in service class 6 to transmit, it is likely that by the time a station finally receives the token, all of its rotation timers will already have expired. The station will then be allowed to transmit only MAC-SDUs assigned to service class 6. On the other hand, if traffic on the network is light, a station may receive the token before any of its rotation timers have expired, and the chances are better that lower-priority MAC-SDUs will be transmitted.

Ring Maintenance

In order to control the operation of the ring, each station knows the address of its *predecessor*, the station from which it received the token, and its *successor*, the station to which it transmits the token. When a Token Bus network is initialized, or when it is reestablished following a major failure, each station must establish its predecessor and successor. As stations are added to or deleted from the ring, stations update their predecessor and successor values accordingly.

Adding a Station to the Ring

In order to allow for additions to the ring, each station must periodically provide an opportunity for new stations to be added to the ring. To do this, a station that has received the token transmits a special control frame, called a Solicit_successor frame, that contains the station's own MAC address and the MAC address of its current successor. Any station on the network that has an address that falls within the range of these two MAC addresses can request that it be added to the ring.

Ring maintenance procedures are designed so that new stations are added to the ring only when traffic on the network is relatively light. A station consults a timer, called the *ring maintenance rotation timer*, before transmitting a Solicit_successor frame. If the current value of the ring maintenance rotation timer is greater than the maximum ring maintenance rotation time, the station does not transmit a Solicit_successor frame for that rotation of the token.

After a station holding the token transmits a Solicit_successor frame, it waits a period of time called the *response window* to see if any station responds. The response window is the maximum amount of time it would take a response to reach the transmitting station, and is equal to the *slot time*—twice the end-to-end propagation delay of the network. If the token holder detects no response during the response window, it assumes that no new station wishes to be added to the ring.

A station that wishes to be added to the ring, and has an address within the range specified in Solicit_successor frame, responds to that frame. If only one station responds, that station is added to the ring. The addition process involves the following steps:

1. The token holder changes its successor MAC address to be that of the station being added. The token holder also transmits the token to the station being added.

2. The station being added sets its successor and predecessor MAC addresses appropriately and proceeds to process the token.

3. When the old successor receives a frame from the station just added, it saves that station's MAC address as its new predecessor MAC address.

If more than one new station responds to the Solicit_successor frame, their responses collide and cause a garbled transmission. If the token holder detects a garbled transmission, it uses a contention resolution procedure to determine which station to add. The token holder begins the contention resolution procedure by transmitting a Resolve_contention frame. A station wishing to be added must wait 0, 1, 2, or 3 response windows before responding, depending on the value of its address. If a station detects a response from another station while it is waiting, that station does not respond.

If another conflict occurs, and the token holder again detects a garbled transmission, it sends out another Resolve_contention frame. This time, only stations that responded to the first Resolve_contention frame are allowed to respond. They wait 0, 1, 2, or 3 response windows again based on the values of their addresses. This process continues until a single station responds or a maximum number of retries have been attempted. If the retry maximum is reached, the token holder passes the token on to its successor without adding a station to the ring.

Deleting a Station from the Ring

The process of deleting a station from the ring is simpler than the addition process. When a station wishes to be deleted, it waits until it receives the token. It then sends a Set_successor frame to its predecessor, notifying it to change its successor address to the successor address of the station being deleted. Now its predecessor will pass the token directly to the deleted station's successor, bypassing the station being deleted. When the new successor receives a MAC frame from its new predecessor, it saves that address as its predecessor address.

Fault Management

The Token Bus standard defines how certain error conditions are to be detected and corrected. Among these conditions are the following:

- A station failure that breaks the logical ring.
- The presence of multiple tokens on the ring.
- The loss of the token from the ring.

Station Failure

After a station transmits the token, it listens for a period of time equal to the response window to be sure its successor station has received the token and is transmitting. If a station detects a transmission within the response window, it assumes that its successor station is operating properly.

If the issuing station does not detect a transmission within the response window period, it assumes that its successor station has not received its transmission and then retransmits the token. If the station detects no activity following the second token transmission, the station assumes that its successor station has failed. The station then transmits a Who_follows frame, which asks the station that follows the failed station to identify itself. The station that follows the failed station identifies itself by transmitting a Set_successor frame.

When the issuing station receives the Set_successor frame, it changes its successor station address and passes the token to its new successor station, thus deleting the failed station from the ring. If there is no response to the Who_follows frame, the station sends the Who_follows frame a second time. If no response is received the second time, the issuer transmits a Solicit_successor frame that contains a range of addresses that includes all stations on the network.

Responses to the Solicit_successor frame are handled according to the procedure for adding a new station to the ring. The end result is to establish a two-station ring. The process is then repeated to add a third station to the ring, and so on until the entire ring is reestablished. If no response is received to the Solicit_successor frame, the issuer transmits the frame a second time. If no response is received after the second attempt, the issuing station reverts to listening mode.

Multiple Tokens

If a station that has received a token detects another transmission on the network, this indicates that some other station is also holding a token and is currently transmitting. To eliminate a multiple-token condition, the station that received a token and has detected a transmission drops the token and reverts to a receiving state. This reduces the number of token holders to either one or zero. If a station drops the token and there is no other token circulation around the ring, the lost token procedure starts a new token circulating.

Lost Token

If a station detects a lack of activity on the transmission medium that lasts longer than a predetermined period of time, the station assumes that the token has been lost. When this happens, the station transmits a Claim_token frame that invites any station on the ring to claim the token and begin processing. Contending responses to the Claim_token frame are handled in the same way as an addition to the ring. In this way, a single claimant is identified and is issued the token.

There are several conditions that can trigger lost token processing, including failure of the token-holding station and a corrupted token. When the network is being initially powered up, there will be no token. Lost token processing provides the ring initialization necessary to start up the network.

TOKEN BUS ARCHITECTURAL MODEL

The Token Bus standard employs the architectural model shown in Fig. 12.7. In conformance with the overall IEEE/ISO/ANSI LAN architecture, the Data Link layer is divided into the Logical Link Control (LLC) sublayer and the Medium Access Control (MAC) sublayer. The MAC sublayer provides services to the MAC sublayer user, which is normally a Logical Link Control (LLC) sublayer entity. The LLC sublayer standard is described in the chapters in Part II.

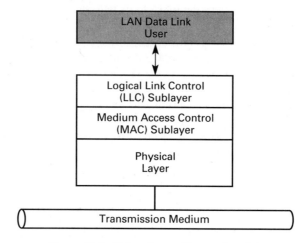

Figure 12.7   Token Bus architectural model.

PHYSICAL LAYER SPECIFICATIONS

The Physical layer standards for the Token Bus form of medium access control include a specification for the interface between the MAC sublayer and the Physical layer. The standard also documents functional specifications for the Physical layer and describes different medium specifications. Two of the medium specifications are for baseband coaxial cable transmission, and one is for broadband coaxial cable transmission. A fiber-optic implementation is also described in the standard.

Physical Layer Services

The interface between the MAC sublayer and the Physical layer provides for the passing of bits and control information between them. It is defined in terms of the following set of service primitives and parameters:

- **PHY_UNITDATA.request (symbol).** Issued by the MAC sublayer to the Physical layer to request that a symbol, which can be a 0 bit, a 1 bit, or a nondata bit, be transmitted.
- **PHY_UNITDATA.indication (symbol).** Issued by the Physical layer to the MAC sublayer to indicate that a symbol has been received and to pass the symbol up to the MAC sublayer.
- **PHY_MODE.invoke (mode).** Issued by the MAC sublayer to the Physical layer to select a mode of operation. The mode selected can be either originating-MAC if the entity is originating signals or repeating-MAC if the station is functioning as a repeater.
- **PHY_NOTIFY.invoke.** Issued by the MAC sublayer to the Physical layer to notify it that an end-of-frame delimiter has been detected.

These primitives provide for the transmission and reception of 0 and 1 bits, and also for nondata bits that are used in the start and end delimiter fields.

Medium Attachment Physical Model

The Token Bus standard defines a physical model for the way in which a station is attached to the transmission medium. This model is illustrated in Fig. 12.8. The transmission medium itself is called the *trunk cable*, and a *trunk coupling unit* is used to tap into the trunk cable. A *drop cable* is then used to attach the trunk coupling unit to the component in the network interface card (NIC) that implements the Physical layer.

MEDIUM SPECIFICATIONS

The Token Bus standard defines medium specifications for three different types of transmission. For each transmission type, there is a specification for the Physical layer and a description of the physical transmission medium. Physical layer specifications include detailed descriptions of functional, electrical, and physical characteristics as well as environmental specifications related to safety, electromagnetic and electrical environment, temperature, humidity, and regulatory requirements. Transmission medium descriptions

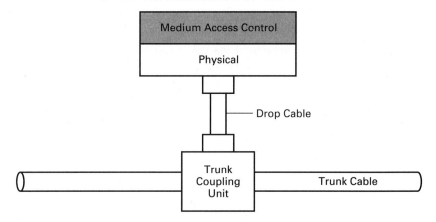

Figure 12.8   Physical model for station attachment.

also specify transmission path delay considerations and, in some cases, network sizing considerations.

The three most commonly implemented forms of transmission defined by the standard are as follows:

- **Baseband—Single-channel Phase-continuous FSK.** This is the lowest cost implementation type.

- **Baseband—Single-channel Phase-coherent FSK.** An implementation of this type is typically more expensive than single-channel phase-continuous FSK but less expensive than a full broadband implementation.

- **Broadband.** This is typically the most expensive of the three types of transmission to implement.

Baseband—Single-channel Phase-continuous FSK

The single-channel phase-continuous FSK medium specification uses baseband transmission. Frequency-shift keying (FSK) is used as the modulation technique, where the changes in frequency occur continuously (phase-continuous).

Manchester Encoding

This medium specification defines the use of Manchester encoding. With the form of Manchester encoding used with single-channel phase-continuous FSK, a low-high signal combination represents a 1 bit, and a high-low combination represents a 0 bit. The other possible combinations, low-low and high-high, are used to represent nondata bits. These nondata bits are used to identify start and end frame delimiters. By using signals that are different from data signals, the beginning and end of a frame are always clearly identifiable, and no combination of bits in a frame can be mistaken for a frame delimiter.

Repeater and Jabber-Inhibit Functions

In addition to the basic signal transmission and reception functions, the Physical layer specification for single-channel phase-continuous FSK includes the following functions:

- **Repeater Function.** The repeater function allows a station to act as a repeater only, connecting two cable segments and regenerating the signal as it passes from one segment to the other.

- **Jabber-Inhibit Function.** The jabber-inhibit function allows a station to interrupt a transmission and disable the transmitter if the transmission continues for too long a time.

Transmission Medium and Data Rate

A 75-ohm, CATV-type coaxial cable is used for the trunk cable. Devices are attached to the trunk cable using a very short 35- to 50-ohm drop cable, no more than 35 cm in length. The data rate is 1 Mbps. The carrier frequency ranges from 3.75 MHz to 6.25 MHz.

Baseband—Single-channel Phase-coherent FSK

With the single-channel phase-coherent FSK medium specification, baseband transmission is used and the modulation technique is frequency modulation. Here, the frequency varies between two discrete values rather than varying continuously.

Manchester Encoding

The encoding technique used is another variation of Manchester encoding. A low-low combination represents a 1 bit, and a high-high combination a 0 bit. The other combinations, low-high and high-low, are used for nondata bits that are employed in the frame delimiters. The repeater and jabber-inhibit functions are also supported with this transmission specification.

Transmission Medium and Data Rates

This specification also uses 75-ohm, CATV-type coaxial cable for the trunk cable. Two data rates are supported—5 Mbps and 10 Mbps. For the 5 Mbps rate, the frequencies used are 5 MHz and 10 MHz. For the 10 Mbps rate, the frequencies are 10 MHz and 20 MHz. A 75-ohm cable is also used for the drop cable and can be up to about 30 meters in length.

Broadband

The broadband medium specification uses broadband transmission over a bus-structured network. Either a single-cable, midsplit, or a dual cable configuration can be used, although the single-cable is recommended. The modulation technique used is called multilevel duobinary AM/PSK. This modulation technique uses amplitude modulation (AM) combined with phase-shift keying (PSK).

Signaling Technique

The signaling technique, which is called *multilevel duobinary*, allows for three distinct amplitude levels. The three levels are symbolically represented as {0}, {2}, and {4}. Nondata bits are represented by the signal value {2}, 0 bits by {0}, and 1 bits by {4}. A scrambler function is also used when there is a long sequence of 0 bits or a long sequence of 1 bits, in which a pseudorandom function is used to convert certain 0 bits to 1 bits and vice-versa. This prevents long sequences of a given bit value from affecting synchronization. On the receiving end, a reverse descrambling function restores the bits to their original values.

Transmission Medium and Data Rates

The transmission medium is standard 75-ohm, CATV coaxial cable. Three data rates are supported—1 Mbps, 5 Mbps, and 10 Mbps. With 1 Mbps, a 1.5 MHz channel bandwidth is required. With 5 Mbps, a 6 MHz channel bandwidth is required. With 10 Mbps, a 12 MHz channel bandwidth is required.

MAP AND TOP SPECIFICATIONS

A complication with networking standards as they are defined by IEEE, ISO, ANSI, and CCITT is that they permit a great many options. If different vendors implement entirely different sets of options, it may be difficult for any two vendors to achieve interoperability, even though all vendors adhere to the standards.

A number of groups have been formed to address the development of network communications conventions suitable for specific application areas. These groups select specific groups of options from standards for implementation. Among these are two groups that are having much influence in the development of standards in two key application areas for local area networks. The first group, the *Manufacturing Automation Protocol* (MAP) task force, was formed under the leadership of General Motors to address the area of factory automation. The second group, the *Technical and Office Protocols* (TOP) task force, sponsored by The Boeing Company, was formed to address engineering, manufacturing, and general office applications.

OSI Standards

The MAP and TOP task forces share a similar approach toward developing a networking environment in which there is a high degree of compatibility in the equipment offered by different vendors. The approach involves developing a specification that defines a uniform set of protocols to be used in the network structure. By having a common set of protocols to which all vendors adhere, complete interoperability between them can be achieved.

Both the MAP and TOP groups use the OSI model as a basis for their architectures. The OSI model provides guidelines within which specific standards and protocols must fit. The model itself allows any number of standards and protocols to be created for any of the seven layers of the architecture, and a wide range of protocols and features can be selected for any of the seven layers. Implementors of products that conform to the OSI architecture can then choose which protocols and features their products will implement.

The MAP and TOP approach is to define a selected set of protocols and features for implementation and to rigorously document these choices. By limiting the number of protocols and features available for implementation, adherence to the MAP and TOP specifications increase the likelihood that individual vendors will develop products that will interoperate and that can be interconnected in the same network. Both the MAP and TOP specifications define similar sets of protocols in their specifications, making it possible for MAP and TOP networks to also be interconnected with one another. Of importance in this book is that the MAP and TOP specifications specify the use of the IEEE and ISO standards as the basis for the Physical and Data Link layers of the architecture.

Both the MAP and the TOP specifications define protocols to be used at each of the layers of the OSI model. Both MAP and TOP specify the use of the IEEE/ISO Logical Link Control standard. But each of the two task forces has chosen a different LAN standard for the Medium Access Control sublayer and the Physical layer.

Logical Link Control Sublayer

At the level of the Logical Link Control sublayer, only Type 1 operation that provides the connectionless LLC service is required by the MAP and TOP specifications. With the connectionless LLC service, no sequence checking, message acknowledgment, flow control, or error recovery functions are performed at the level of the Logical Link Control sublayer. These functions are left to higher-level layers.

Type 3 operation that provides the acknowledged connectionless service can be optionally supported. With acknowledged connectionless service, a sending station transmits a frame, and the receiving station acknowledges it with a response. There is no sequence checking or flow control with this type of service, but the acknowledgment allows for detection of nondelivery and for retransmission at the level of the Logical Link Control sublayer.

MAP MAC Sublayer

MAP has endorsed the Token Bus standard, using 48-bit addresses, as its choice for the MAC sublayer.

The MAP specification endorses two of the Physical layer standards described in this chapter:

- **Broadband.** Provides for broadband transmission using multilevel duobinary AM/PSK modulation with a data rate of 10 Mbps.
- **Single-channel Phase-coherent FSK.** Specifies baseband, or single channel transmission, using coaxial cable. The modulation technique is phase coherent frequency modulation with a data rate of 5 Mbps.

TOP MAC Sublayer

TOP has endorsed the CSMA/CD standard, with 48-bit addressing, as its choice for the MAC sublayer.

For the Physical layer, baseband transmission over coaxial cable at the rate of 10 Mbps with 500 meter segments (10BASE5) is specified.

ARCNET PRODUCTS

ARCnet, developed by Datapoint, is a popular form of LAN technology that uses a token-bus form of medium access control. However, ARCnet products were first released before the IEEE/ISO Token Bus standard was finalized and does not conform to it. ARCnet is a popular, low-cost form of LAN data link, and products that conform to ARCnet specifications are available from a number of vendors.

The data rate supported on an ARCnet LAN data link is 2.5 megabits per second, although a variation of the ARCnet specification supporting a data rate of 20 Mbps has been developed.

Network Topology

ARCnet uses a bus- or tree-structured network topology, in which all stations on the LAN data link receive the transmissions of all other stations. An ARCnet implementation typically uses RG-62 coaxial cable, in conjunction with hubs or repeaters, to create physical star structures. Twisted-pair cable and fiber-optic cable have been used in some ARCnet implementations.

The ARCnet specification allows up to a maximum of 20,000 feet of cable to lie between the most distant points in the network, and up to about 2,000 feet of cable can be used to connect active hubs or repeaters.

Medium Access Control

A token-passing protocol, similar to that defined for Token Bus, is used on an ARCnet LAN data link to determine when stations are allowed to transmit. Token passing is based on station addresses, which range in value from 1 to 255. Station addresses are normally manually set on an ARCnet LAN data link. If a station currently holding the token has data to transmit, it is allowed to send it.

Token Retransmission

When the station finishes sending data, or if it has no data to send, it transmits the token to the station that has the next sequentially higher address. When a station receives the token, it either sends data or passes the token to the next station. In either case, there will be activity on the transmission medium. The station that previously sent the token monitors the transmission medium. If it detects activity within a certain time period, it assumes the token was successfully received. If there is no activity within this time period, it increments the address used previously and sends the token again. This continues until the token is sent to a station that successfully receives it. The sending station then continues to use this address in subsequent processing as the next station address.

Station Failure

The failure of a station is a condition that causes a station to increment its next station address. When a station fails or is powered down, the preceding station will detect this after it transmits the token. It will then continue transmitting the token until it reaches the next station in sequence. When a station fails to receive a token after a period of time, it triggers a process called *reconfiguration* by generating a noise burst to destroy the token being passed. This causes token passing to stop and the network to become temporarily idle.

Reconfiguration Timeout

All stations in the network monitor the transmission medium. If a period of time equal to the maximum delay between transmissions expires and no transmission is detected, the network goes through a reconfiguration process. Each station waits a period of time based on its station address, with a station having a higher address waiting a shorter period of time. When the time period elapses, the station sends a token to the address that is its own address plus one. If it detects no activity after waiting the appropriate period, it increments the address by one and sends the token again. This continues, with the address wrapping around to 1 if necessary, until the station detects activity after it has sent the token.

Activity indicates that the token has been successfully received and recognized by another station. The original sending station then saves the address used when the token was successfully transmitted. Each station on the network follows this same procedure, sending the token to each address in sequence, until the token is successfully received. From that point on, stations transmit the token to the saved address.

Triggering Reconfiguration

There are several conditions that will trigger the reconfiguration process. When the network is initially powered up, the reconfiguration process prepares the network for operation. When a new station is powered up and wants to be added to the network, it transmits a reconfiguration burst. This is a transmission that interferes with any other transmission on the network. The reconfiguration burst is long enough in duration to ensure that it will interfere with any data being transmitted and with the token following it. After the token is destroyed through this interference, a reconfiguration timeout occurs and the reconfiguration process takes place. Since the token is sent to each possible address, the new station will be included in the network following the reconfiguration process.

Lost Token

A reconfiguration will also occur if the token is inadvertently destroyed by noise on the network. The sending station interprets the noise as a transmission and does not attempt to retransmit the token. When no further transmission takes place, the stations begin the reconfiguration process.

VISTALAN/1 PRODUCTS

VistaLAN/1 is a family of LAN products, available from Allen-Bradley, that also uses a token-bus form of medium access control. VistaLAN/1 products use broadband transmission over a bus- or tree-structured network. The specifications for VistaLAN/1 are similar to those defined in the Token Bus standard but do not conform exactly to it.

Various types of devices can be attached to a VistaLAN/1 network, including mainframe computers, minicomputers, terminals, printers, and personal computers used to emulate terminals. Devices are attached to the network through a *network interface unit* (NIU). The NIU contains the logic necessary to implement local area network station functions.

Terminal Server Network

VistaLAN/1 is primarily a terminal server network. Through the network, a given terminal can access different mainframes or minicomputers, and a given printer can be used to print data from different systems. Each NIU implements 2, 4, or 8 ports. These ports can be used to attach multiple terminals or printers to a single NIU or to provide a mainframe or minicomputer with multiple ports through which it can access the network.

Sessions

In order to communicate, a session, or virtual circuit, is established between two ports. These ports can be in different NIUs or in the same NIU. Each NIU can establish up to 12 concurrent sessions and can switch between them to transmit or receive data. A session can be established directly between two communicating parties. For example, a terminal user can establish a session with a mainframe and then use the session to interact with a program running on the mainframe. A third party can also establish a session between two other parties. For example, a terminal user can establish a session between a computer and a printer so that the printer can be used to print data from the computer.

Network Names and Addresses

A network address consists of an NIU number and a port number. When a session is established, the network address of the port with which the connection is to be made can be specified directly. There is also a facility that allows a table of network names and their corresponding addresses to be built. If such a table has been built, then a name can be specified when a session is being established, and the table is used to translate the name into an address. On a given network, NIU addresses range from 1 to 255. Address 0 is reserved for a system broadcast function.

Certain ports can be specified as *protected*. When a session is established with a protected port, a user name and password must be specified. These are checked, and the session is not established unless they are correctly entered.

Internets

If a network interconnection device is used to interconnect VistaLAN/1 networks, then an *Internet* address must also be used. An *Internet* address consists of two parts:

- The first part consists of three fields that identify the network.
- The second part identifies the port within the network (NIU number and port number).

Names in the name-address table can correspond either to a local network address or a full Internet address.

Medium Access Control

The medium access control protocol used by VistaLAN/1 products is similar to the medium access control protocol used with the ARCnet LAN technology described previously.

Physical Specifications

VistaLAN/1 uses broadband transmission with a single cable configuration. Data is transmitted at one frequency. When the signal reaches the head end, the head end translator translates the signal to a second frequency and retransmits the signal. The transmit and receive frequencies are each 6 MHz wide. The broadband cable used for VistaLAN/1 supports up to five different transmit/receive channel pairs coexisting on the same cable. Each NIU operates using only one channel pair. Up to 255 NIUs, supporting up to 2040 users, can communicate on a given channel pair. With the five possible channel pairs, this allows up to 10,200 users on the same broadband cable. Data is transmitted using continuous phase frequency shift keying at a data rate of 2.5 Mbps.

SUMMARY

The Token Bus standard defines a multiaccess form of data link that uses a bus- or tree-structured network topology. All stations receive all transmissions within a period of time determined by the propagation delay of the network, but the right to transmit is granted by passing a special data unit from station to station in a sequence based on station addresses.

The Token Bus MAC service definition describes an MA_UNITDATA service that provides an unconfirmed data transfer service and an optional response capability. The Token Bus protocol specification defines the format of the MAC-SDU, specifies how the MAC-SDU is encapsulated in a MAC-PDU, and documents the procedures controlling the exchange of MAC-PDUs between communicating stations.

The token-bus form of medium access control uses a control frame, called the token, that is passed in a logical ring structure from one station to the next. When a station receives the token, it is allowed to transmit for a specified period of time. Different priorities can be assigned to frames, and token rotation timers are used to allow transmission based on priority values. Each station knows the address of its predecessor and successor on the logical ring. When a station is added to or deleted from the LAN or the LAN is initialized, stations use control frames to update predecessor and successor addresses. Fault management procedures are defined to detect multiple tokens, the loss of the token, and inactive stations.

The Token Bus Physical layer specifications define three types of transmission—baseband transmission using single-channel phase-continuous FSK, baseband transmission using single-channel phase-coherent FSK, and broadband transmission.

Chapter 13 describes the token-ring form of medium access control technology. The Token Ring medium access control method uses a token-passing technique to implement bus- or tree-structured LAN data links using twisted-pair cable.

Token Ring

The IEEE 802.3/ISO 8802-3 Token Ring standard defines a LAN data link technology in which stations are connected to one another in a ring structure using a series of point-to-point physical circuits. Each station is connected to both the next station and to the previous station to form a physical ring around which data circulates. The logical structure of a simple Token Ring network is shown in Fig. 13.1.

A Token Ring LAN implements a multiaccess form of data link in which all stations on the LAN data link eventually receive the transmissions of all other stations. All MAC frames are repeated all the way around the ring and reach every station on the LAN data link. Each station is responsible for interpreting the destination MAC address contained in a frame and for copying those frames addressed to it.

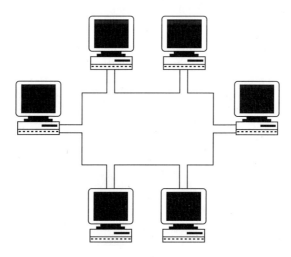

Figure 13.1   Token Ring LAN basic topology.

The Token Ring architecture is the basis for IBM's *Token-Ring Network* product family, IBM's mainstream local area network product line. Many other vendors also market equipment and software that are compatible with IBM's Token-Ring Network products and with the IEEE/ISO Token Ring standard.

The Token Ring standard defines both a service definition and a protocol specification for the MAC sublayer. It also defines an architectural model for the MAC sublayer and Physical layer and describes specifications for the transmission media that can be used to implement the standard.

MAC SUBLAYER SERVICE DEFINITION

Medium Access Control sublayer services allow an LLC entity in one station to exchange LLC-PDUs with LLC sublayer entities in other stations. The MAC sublayer service definition is specified in terms of service primitives and service primitive parameters and describes a single MA_UNITDATA unconfirmed data transfer service.

MAC Sublayer Service Primitives

The following are descriptions of the service primitives that make up the MA_UNITDATA service:

- **MA_UNITDATA.request.** Issued by the LLC sublayer entity to the MAC sublayer entity in the source station to request that a MAC-SDU be sent to one or more destination stations.
- **MA_UNITDATA_STATUS.indication.** Issued by the MAC sublayer entity in the source station to the LLC entity to provide information about the success or failure of an attempt to transmit an LLC-PDU.
- **MA_UNITDATA.indication.** Issued by the MAC entity in the destination station to the LLC entity to indicate that an LLC-PDU has been received and to pass the LLC-PDU up to the LLC entity.

Figure 13.2 shows a time-sequence diagram that documents the sequence in which the three service primitives are issued during normal MAC frame transmission. Notice

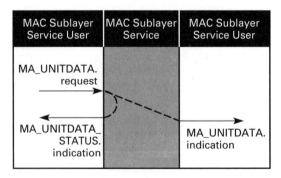

Figure 13.2 Time-sequence diagram for the MA_UNITDATA data transfer service.

that the MA_UNITDATA service is ordinarily an unconfirmed service. The MA_UNIT-DATA_STATUS. indication primitive tells the LLC sublayer entity in the source station only that the transmission attempt was successful. It does not tell the LLC sublayer entities in either the source or the destination station whether or not the MAC frame was received successfully by the distant station.

Service Primitive Parameters

Box 13.1 describes the parameters that are included in the service primitives for the MA_UNITDATA data transfer service.

Station Management Service Primitives

The Token Ring standard defines an interface between the MAC sublayer and a *station management* function. The station management function is responsible for control functions, such as resetting the MAC sublayer, specifying values for constants (such as timer values) used in the network, and so on.

The interface between the MAC sublayer and the station management function is defined in terms of the following set of service primitives:

- **MA_INITIALIZE_PROTOCOL.request.** Sent by station management to reset the MAC sublayer and to change MAC operational parameters.
- **MA_INITIALIZE_PROTOCOL.confirm.** Sent by the MAC sublayer to indicate the success or failure of an initialization request.
- **MA_CONTROL.request.** Sent by station management to control the operation of the MAC sublayer.
- **MA_SMT_STATUS.indication.** Sent by the MAC sublayer to report errors and significant status changes.
- **MA_SMT_UNITDATA.request.** Sent by station management when it has a data unit to transmit.
- **MA_SMT_UNITDATA.indication.** Sent to station management to notify it that a station management data unit has arrived and to transfer the data unit to station management.
- **MA_SMT_UNITDATA_STATUS.indication.** Sent by the MAC sublayer to indicate the success or failure of a data transfer request.

MAC SUBLAYER PROTOCOL SPECIFICATION

The data unit the MAC sublayer receives from the LLC sublayer is the *medium-access-control-service-data-unit* (MAC-SDU). The MAC-SDU contains the LLC-PDU that the two LLC sublayer entities are exchanging.

MAC Sublayer Functions

During MAC frame transmission, the Medium Access Control sublayer entities in all stations on the ring perform the following functions:

BOX 13.1   MA_UNITDATA service primitive parameters.

MA_UNITDATA.request

(
destination_address,
source_address,
data,
priority,
service_class
)

MA_UNITDATA_STATUS.indication

(
destination_address,
source_address,
transmission_status,
provided_priority,
provided_service_class
)

MA_UNITDATA.indication

(
destination_address,
source_address,
data,
priority,
service_status
)

- **destination_address.** Specifies a destination MAC address defining the station or stations to which the MAC-SDU is to be delivered. The MAC addressing scheme is described in Chapter 6.

- **source_address.** Specifies a source MAC address identifying the station originating the MAC-SDU.

- **data.** Specifies the MAC-SDU passed down from the LLC sublayer for transmission from the source station to the destination station or stations.

- **priority.** Specifies the priority that the source LLC entity is requesting for data transmission.

- **service_class.** This parameter is ignored by the MAC entity since only one class of service is currently defined by the Token Ring standard. It is included for conformance with other MAC sublayer standards.

- **transmission_status.** Indicates to the source LLC entity whether or not the previous MA_UNITDATA.request primitive was accepted by the MAC sublayer entity.

- **provided_priority.** Specifies the actual priority that was used for transmission.

- **provided_service_class.** This parameter is ignored by the LLC entity, since only one class of service is currently defined by the Token Ring standard. It is included for conformance with other MAC sublayer standards.

- **service_status.** Indicates to a destination LLC sublayer entity whether the MAC-SDU was received without error.

- **Source Station MAC Sublayer Functions.** The MAC sublayer in a source station accepts each LLC-PDU from the LLC sublayer entity in the form of a MAC-SDU. A data encapsulation function in the source MAC sublayer entity adds protocol-control-information (PCI) to the MAC-SDU to form a *medium-access-control-protocol-data-unit* (MAC-PDU) or *MAC frame*. The MAC sublayer then uses the services of the Physical layer to transmit the MAC frame to the next station on the ring.

- **Receiving Station MAC Sublayer Functions.** The MAC sublayer in a receiving station uses the Physical layer to receive MAC frames from the previous station on the ring. It interprets the destination MAC address in each frame it receives and copies only frames that are addressed to that station. For each frame that it copies, the MAC sublayer entity removes the PCI from the MAC frame and passes the resulting MAC-SDU to the LLC sublayer. The MAC sublayer in a receiving station also interprets the source address in each MAC frame that it receives to identify frames that it originally placed onto the ring. When a receiving station identifies one of its own frames, it does not repeat that frame, thus removing it from the ring. A receiving station repeats all other MAC frames, whether it copied them or not, to the next station on the ring.

MAC Frame Format

The protocol specification for the Token Ring MAC sublayer defines the format of the MAC frame that is exchanged between MAC sublayer entities in source and destination stations. Box 13.2 shows the format of the Token Ring MAC frame and describes its fields.

MAC Frame/LLC-PDU Relationship

Figure 13.3 shows the relationship between the LLC-PDU and the Token Ring MAC frame. All fields in the LLC protocol data unit created by the Logical Link Control sublayer are treated by the Token Ring MAC sublayer as data.

MAC Sublayer Control Frames

As discussed earlier, a MAC frame can contain either an LLC-PDU passed from the Logical Link Control sublayer or control information generated by the Medium Access Control sublayer. The following is a list of the MAC control frames defined by the standard. The control frame mnemonic and the value of the control bit (ZZZZZZ) portion of the frame control field are shown in parentheses following each frame's name.

- **Claim Token (CL_TK—000011).** Used by a station to become the active monitor when no active monitor is present on the ring.

- **Duplicate Address Test (DAT—000000).** Used when a station is added to the ring to ensure that its address is unique.

- **Active Monitor Present (AMP—000101).** Used to notify all stations that an active monitor is present.

- **Standby Monitor Present (SMP—000110).** Used to notify all stations that a standby monitor is present.

- **Beacon (BCN—000010).** Sent when a serious ring failure occurs to help identify the location of the failure.

- **Purge (PRG—000100).** Sent by the active monitor after claiming the token or to reinitialize the ring.

BOX 13.2   Token Ring MAC frame.

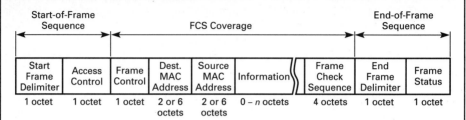

Start Frame Delimiter	Access Control	Frame Control	Dest. MAC Address	Source MAC Address	Information	Frame Check Sequence	End Frame Delimiter	Frame Status
1 octet	1 octet	1 octet	2 or 6 octets	2 or 6 octets	0 – n octets	4 octets	1 octet	1 octet

- **Start Frame Delimiter.** An octet containing a unique signal pattern that identifies the start of a frame. The Token Ring medium access control method uses differential Manchester encoding, which allows for signal values that do not correspond to either a 0 or a 1 bit. These are called the nondata J signals and the nondata K signals. The use of nondata signals ensures that no data sequence will ever be mistaken for a delimiter. The signal configuration for a Start Frame Delimiter field is JK0JK000.

- **Access Control.** A field used to control the operation of the MAC protocol. The Access Control field bits are interpreted as PPPTMRRR:

  — **PPP.** *Priority* bits containing a value from 0 through 7 indicating the transmission priority of the frame or token.

  — **T.** A *token* bit containing a 0 in a token and a 1 in a MAC frame.

  — **M.** A *monitor* bit that is set to 1 by the active monitor to detect and avoid an endlessly circulating frame or a persistent high-priority token.

  — **RRR.** *Reservation* bits that are set to a value from 0 through 7 by a station that has frames to send to request that the token be issued at the specified priority.

- **Frame Control.** Identifies the type of frame and, for certain control frames, the particular function to be performed. The Frame Control field bits are interpreted as FFZZZZZZ:

  — **FF.** *Frame type* bits containing 00 if the frame is a control frame generated by the MAC sublayer or 01 if the frame contains an LLC-PDU. Bit values of 10 and 11 indicate an undefined format and are reserved for future use.

  — **ZZZZZZ.** *Control bits* that are interpreted differently in MAC frames containing LLC-PDUs and in MAC control frames. In a MAC frame that contains an LLC-PDU, the bits are interpreted as rrrYYY. The YYY bits contain the same value as specified in the priority parameter of the MA_UNITDATA.request primitive that was used to pass the LLC-PDU to the MAC sublayer in the source station. For a MAC control frame, the control bits indicate the MAC control frame type. MAC control frames are described later in this chapter.

- **Station Addresses.** A *Destination MAC Address* field and a *Source MAC Address* field. The Destination MAC Address field identifies the station or stations that are to receive the MAC frame. The Source MAC Address field identifies the source station. Address fields can be either 16 bits or 48 bits in length. (The MAC addressing mechanism is described in Chapter 6.) The destination address can specify either an individual station or a group of stations.

BOX 13.2 *(Continued)*

- **Information.** Contains either a MAC-SDU passed from the Logical Link Control sublayer or control information supplied by the Medium Access Control sublayer.

- **Frame Check Sequence.** A cyclical redundancy check (CRC) value used for error checking. When the sending station assembles a frame, it performs a CRC calculation on the bits in the frame. The specific algorithm that is used is described in the IEEE/ISO Token Ring standard. The source station stores this value in the Frame Check Sequence field and then transmits the frame. When a receiving station receives the frame, it performs an identical CRC calculation and compares the results with the value in the Frame Check Sequence field. If the two values do not match, the receiving station assumes that a transmission error has occurred.

- **End Frame Delimiter.** A value that identifies the first octet of the end-of-frame sequence. The End Frame Delimiter bits are interpreted as JK1JK1IE:

  — **JK1JK1.** Bits that identify this octet as the ending delimiter and contain a unique combination of data and nondata signals.

  — **I.** An *intermediate frame* bit that is set to 0 if this is the last or only frame the station is transmitting or 1 if more frames follow this one.

  — **E.** An *error* bit that is set to 1 by a station that detects an error in frame reception so that subsequent stations know that this frame has been damaged by a transmission error.

- **Frame Status.** The final octet of the frame. The bits of the Frame Status field are interpreted as ACrrACrr:

  — **A.** An *address recognized* bit that is set by a station recognizing the frame as being addressed to it.

  — **C.** A *packet copied* bit that is set by a station copying the packet contained in the frame.

  — **rr.** Bits reserved for future use.

  Because the Frame Status field is outside the scope of the FCS bits, the ACrr bits are included twice in this octet to provide a redundancy check to help in detecting transmission errors in this octet.

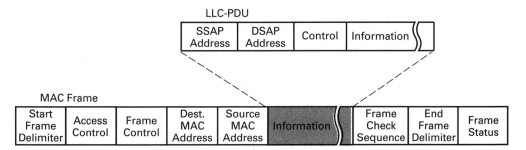

Figure 13.3   Token Ring MAC frame and LLC-PDU relationship.

Information Field Vector Format

In MAC control frames that include an Information field, the Information field is format-ted in the form of a data structure called a *vector*, which in turn contains one or more data structures called *subvectors*. The vector and subvector structure of a MAC control frame Information field is shown in Fig. 13.4.

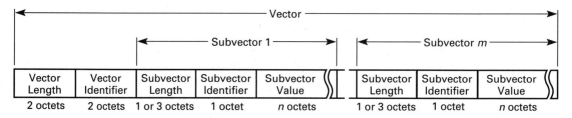

Figure 13.4   Information field vector and subvector format.

The length of the entire Information field is defined by the 2-octet vector length field that begins the vector. The length of each subvector is defined by the length field that begins each subvector. If the first octet of the subvector is less than hexadecimal FF, the length field is a single octet in length. If the first octet of the subvector contains hexa-decimal FF, the length field is three octets in length and the subvector length is defined by the value in the second and third octets of the length field.

Abort Sequence

In addition to tokens and MAC frames, a special frame format called the *abort sequence* is used to prematurely terminate the transmission of a frame. Figure 13.5 shows the for-mat of the abort sequence.

Start Frame Delimiter	End Frame Delimiter
1 octet	1 octet

Figure 13.5   Abort sequence.

MAC PROTOCOL OPERATION

The Token Ring network structure consists of a logical ring implemented using a physi-cal ring topology. Data units are passed from one station to the next, in a single direction, in physical sequence along the ring. Each station transmits the data unit to the next sta-tion, acting as a repeater. Data units that flow from station to station around the ring con-sist of tokens and MAC frames. MAC frames are of two types:

- Frames that contain LLC-PDUs that were passed down from the LLC sublayer.
- Control frames that are generated by the MAC sublayer to control network operation.

The right to transmit frames is controlled by a token, which is passed from one sta-tion to the next around the ring.

A station sends a frame by waiting for the token to arrive. It then changes the token to transform it into a start-of-frame sequence. It next attaches the remainder of the frame to the start-of-frame sequence to create a complete MAC frame and then transmits the MAC frame to the next station on the ring. A station that has MAC frames to send starts a timer and can then send frames until either it has no more frames to send or until the timer expires.

MAC frames travel from station to station around the ring. Each station that receives a frame checks the address in it to see if it should copy that frame. Whether or not a station copies a MAC frame, it sends the frame to the next station. When a frame returns to the station that originally sent it, that station removes the frame from the ring and sends a token to the next station. Figure 13.6 illustrates this procedure.

Notice that a new token is issued only after a frame has made its way all the way around the ring to the station that originated it. This means that there can be only one frame outstanding on the ring at any given time.

Since a frame travels to all stations and then returns to the sending station, it is possible for destination stations to set control bits in the frame as they pass it on to the next station, indicating whether or not the frame was processed and whether any errors were detected. Three control bits have been defined for these purposes:

- **Address Recognized.** The destination station identified this frame as being addressed to it.
- **Packet Copied.** The destination station passed a copy of the frame up to the Logical Link Control sublayer for processing.
- **Error.** An error condition was detected. This bit can be set by any station on the ring, not only by a station that has copied the frame.

Different combinations of the Address Recognized and Packet Copied bits allow the source station to differentiate between different circumstances. Possible circumstances are as follows:

- The frame was copied by one or more destination stations.
- The destination station recognized the frame as being addressed to it but was not able to copy it.
- The destination station either did not recognize the frame or is nonexistent or inactive.

Fault Management

There are two error conditions that can seriously impact the operation of a Token Ring network—the loss of the token or an endlessly circulating frame. The approach taken to detecting and correcting these conditions is to have one of the stations on the network function as an *active monitor*.

Active Monitor Functions

The station designated as the active monitor continuously monitors the network. If a predetermined period of time elapses with no token being detected, the monitor assumes the token has been lost and issues a new token.

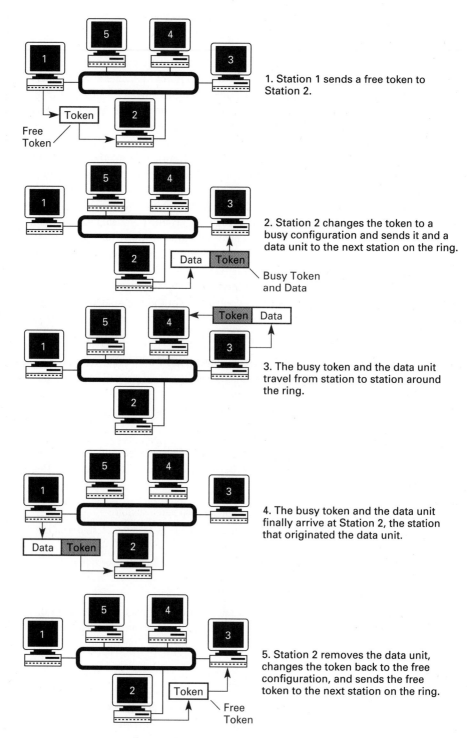

1. Station 1 sends a free token to Station 2.

2. Station 2 changes the token to a busy configuration and sends it and a data unit to the next station on the ring.

3. The busy token and the data unit travel from station to station around the ring.

4. The busy token and the data unit finally arrive at Station 2, the station that originated the data unit.

5. Station 2 removes the data unit, changes the token back to the free configuration, and sends the free token to the next station on the ring.

Figure 13.6   Token Ring protocol operation.

To check for an endlessly circulating frame, the monitor sets a Monitor bit in each frame it receives. If a frame returns to the active monitor station with the Monitor bit still set, the monitor knows the source station failed to remove the frame from the network. The active monitor removes the frame by changing the start-of-frame sequence into a new token, discarding the remainder of the frame, and starting the new token circulating. Two situations can cause an endlessly circulating frame. A transmission problem may have damaged the frame so that the source station does not recognize it as its own, or the source station may have failed.

All other stations on the network act as *passive monitors*. They monitor the operation of the active monitor. If for some reason the active monitor fails, the passive monitors use a contention resolution procedure to determine which station should take over the role of active monitor.

Bypassing a Failed Station

When a station fails, it may no longer be able to transmit data units, thus causing the ring to be broken. The approach used to deal with this is to provide a *bypass switch* as part of each station. If a station fails, the bypass switch can be closed, either manually or automatically, removing the station from the ring and allowing data units to again circulate around the ring.

If the bypass switch is combined with a physical-star wiring configuration, physical failures in the ring can be much simpler to correct. Figure 13.7 illustrates the use of star wiring and bypass switches. With star wiring, each device is attached to a centrally located access unit, which contains the bypass switches. If a failure occurs in a device or a dis-

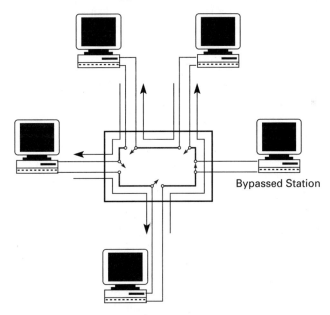

Figure 13.7   Star wiring and bypass switches.

ruption occurs in the cable attaching the device, the bypass switch is closed, and the ring remains unbroken.

Notice that the topology of the network is still a ring and not a star, since the central panel does not have the intelligence to act as a network station. It is simply a passive wiring concentrator. However, by having a portion of the wiring centrally located, it is much easier to attach a new device or to identify and isolate a fault.

Optional Priority Scheme

Token Ring access control can be operated on either a nonpriority or a priority basis. When the optional priority scheme is not implemented, a station can send frames whenever it receives a token.

When the priority scheme is implemented, three bits in each frame are used to represent its *priority*. A token also has a priority value. When a station receives a token, it compares the priority value in the token against the priority of any frames it has to transmit. If a frame's priority is equal to or higher than the token priority, the station transmits that frame. If the frame's priority value is lower than that of the token, the station does not transmit that frame.

Each frame also contains three *reservation* bits. If a station has a frame to transmit that has a priority greater than 0, when it receives and retransmits a frame, it checks the reservation bits in the frame. If the reservation bits are not already set to a higher value, it sets them to the priority value of the frame it has waiting to send. When the original sending station removes the frame and generates a token, it checks the reservation bits. If the priority of the reservation bits is higher than the current token priority, it sets the token priority to the higher value. When a station raises the token's priority value, it saves the previous lower value of the token's priority and is responsible for eventually restoring the token priority to the original lower value. This allows higher priority frames to be sent first.

TOKEN RING ARCHITECTURAL MODEL

The IEEE/ISO Token Ring standard defines the architectural model shown in Fig. 13.8. In conformance with the IEEE/ISO/ANSI LAN architecture, the Token Ring architectural model defines a Logical Link Control sublayer, a Medium Access Control sublayer, and a Physical layer. A Token Ring network interface card (NIC) is attached to the transmission medium using a *trunk coupling unit*. The trunk coupling unit has two point-to-point links attached to it—one leading to the next station in the ring and the other leading to the previous station in the ring.

PHYSICAL LAYER SPECIFICATIONS

The Physical layer standards for the token-ring form of medium access control include a specification for the interface between the MAC sublayer and the Physical layer. The standard also documents functional specifications for the Physical layer and includes medium specifications.

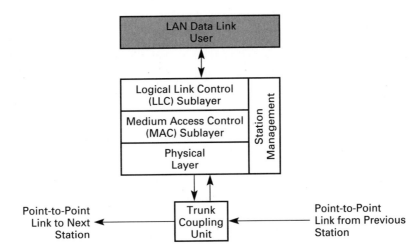

Figure 13.8   Token Ring architectural model.

Physical Layer Service Primitives

The interface between the MAC sublayer and the Physical layer provides for the passing of bits and control information between them. It is defined in terms of the following set of service primitives and parameters:

- **PH_UNITDATA.request (symbol).** Issued in a sending station by the MAC sublayer to the Physical layer to request that a symbol, which can be a 0 bit, 1 bit, or nondata bit, be transmitted. All stations on the network eventually receive the data transmitted with a PH_UNITDATA.request primitive.

- **PH_UNITDATA.indication (symbol).** Issued in a receiving station by the Physical layer to the MAC sublayer to indicate that a symbol has been received and to pass the symbol up to the MAC sublayer.

These primitives provide for the transmission and reception of 0 and 1 bits and also for nondata bits that are used in the starting and ending delimiters.

Physical Layer Station Management Service Primitives

An interface is also defined between the Physical layer and the station management function. The service primitives that apply to this interface are:

- **PH_CONTROL.request (control_action).** Issued by station management to the Physical layer to request that the Physical layer insert the station onto the ring or remove the station from the ring.

- **PH_SMT_STATUS.indication (status_report).** Issued by the Physical layer to station management to inform station management of errors or significant status changes.

Station Attachment Specification

The physical model defined by the Token Ring standard for station attachment is shown in Fig. 13.9. The transmission medium is implemented in the form of *trunk cable* segments that connect stations to form the physical and logical ring. A *trunk coupling unit* (TCU) is used to connect each station to an incoming and outgoing trunk cable segment. The station itself is connected to the trunk coupling unit via a cable called the *medium interface cable*. The medium interface cable itself can consist of multiple segments of cable connected together using a *medium interface connector* (MIC). The medium interface cable is shielded and contains two balanced, 150-ohm twisted pairs.

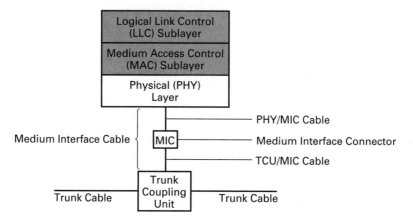

Figure 13.9   Token Ring physical model.

Differential Manchester Encoding

The Token Ring standard uses differential Manchester encoding. As with Manchester encoding, differential Manchester encoding always has a transition in the middle of a bit frame, which allows the encoded data to be self-clocking. The differential Manchester encoding system used with the Token Ring standard is illustrated in Fig. 13.10. A signal that has a transition at the beginning of a bit time is interpreted as a 0 bit; a signal that has no transition at the beginning of a bit time is considered a 1 bit.

If there is no transition at the midpoint of a bit signal, this is considered a code violation. There are two types of code violations, called J and K. If there is no transition at the start of the bit time and no transition at the midpoint, it is a J violation. If there is a transition at the start but none in the middle, it is a K violation. These two types of code

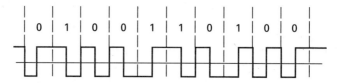

Figure 13.10   Differential Manchester encoding.

violations, illustrated in Fig. 13.11, are used in the starting and ending frame delimiters to distinguish the delimiters from data.

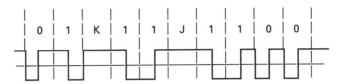

Figure 13.11   J and K code violations.

MEDIUM SPECIFICATIONS

The Token Ring standard currently defines functional, electrical, and mechanical characteristics for baseband transmission using 150-ohm shielded, twisted-pair cable. With this form of transmission medium, data rates of 1 Mbps or 4 Mbps can be supported. A variation of the standard that has also been implemented allows for a transmission rate of 16 Mbps over shielded twisted-pair cable. Some LAN vendors also offer implementations of both the 4 Mbps and 16 Mbps variations of the Token Ring standard that run over unshielded twisted-pair cable, although these are not described in the current version of the Token Ring standard.

IBM TOKEN-RING NETWORK PRODUCTS

The *IBM Token-Ring Network* is a product family that implements the IEEE/ISO Token Ring standard. It uses a physical ring that is wired in a star-type configuration using central access units.

Network Components

The components that make up the IBM Token-Ring Network product family include the following:

- **IBM Token-Ring Network Adapter Card.** The Token-Ring Network adapter card is a NIC that provides the logic and control functions necessary to implement the Medium Access Control sublayer and Physical layer for a station and enables the computing device in which it is installed to send and receive information across the network.

- **IBM Token-Ring Network Multistation Access Unit.** The multistation access unit allows up to eight stations to be attached to form a star-wired subnetwork, as shown in Fig. 13.12. The cable used to connect a device to the access unit is called a *lobe.* The red line traces the physical and logical ring that is formed with this type of attachment. Access units can be wired together to allow for a ring having more than eight network stations. This is illustrated in Fig. 13.13. Again, the red line traces the ring that is formed. The use of a star-wired ring structure simplifies the maintenance of the network. When an attaching device is to be added or removed, there is a central point where this can be done. It also is easier to bypass a failing portion of the network while the problem is being repaired, since the bypass can be done at the central point.

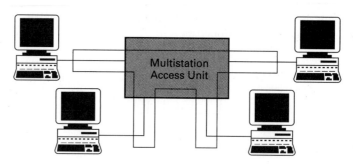

Figure 13.12 Star-wired IBM Token-Ring Network LAN using a multistation access unit.

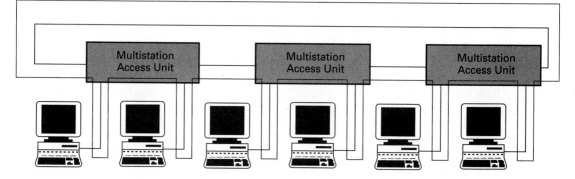

Figure 13.13 Multiple access units.

- **Cabling System.** The IBM Token-Ring Network uses baseband transmission and a data rate of 4 Mbps or 16 Mbps over a cabling system that uses twisted-pair cable. Data grade, or shielded, twisted-pair cable is recommended for reliable transmission; however, unshielded cable can be used with certain limitations.

Medium Access Management

IBM Token-Ring Network products use the method of medium access control defined in the IEEE/ISO Token Ring standard. The optional priority scheme defined for the Token Ring standard is supported.

Medium Access Control Commands

The interface between the Logical Link Control (LLC) sublayer and the Medium Access Control (MAC) sublayer is defined in terms of three commands. These commands are implementations of the MAC sublayer service primitives defined in the Token Ring standard. These commands are as follows:

- **SEND_AC_DATA.** Issued in a sending station by the LLC sublayer to transfer an LLC-PDU from the LLC sublayer to the MAC sublayer for transmission across the network. It is an implementation of the MA_UNITDATA.request service primitive and also includes a parameter to provide routing information.

- CONFIRM_AC_DATA. Issued in a sending station by the MAC sublayer to the LLC sublayer as a response to a SEND_AC_DATA command. It signals whether or not the data unit was accepted by the MAC sublayer for transmission. It is an implementation of the MA_UNITDATA_STATUS. indication service primitive.

- RECEIVE_AC_DATA. Issued in a receiving station by the MAC sublayer to transfer a received LLC-PDU from the MAC sublayer to the LLC sublayer. It is an implementation of the MA_UNITDATA.indication service primitive.

MAC Frame Format

The MAC frame format used by IBM Token-Ring Network products is in conformance with the Token Ring standard. Box 13.3 compares the format of the MAC frame defined by the Token Ring standard with the IBM Token-Ring MAC frame and describes the fields in the IBM Token-Ring MAC frame.

Station Addressing

IBM Token-Ring Network products support three types of station addressing—*individual*, *group*, and *functional*.

Individual Addresses

An individual address identifies a particular station on a ring. An individual address can be either universal or locally administered. If it is universal, then it will be unique across all networks. Each IBM LAN adapter comes with a unique universal address already installed. However, software can assign a different individual address to the adapter if desired. If an alternate individual address is assigned, it must be a locally-administered address.

Group Addresses and Functional Addresses

Each station can also have a group address and a functional address associated with it. A group address identifies a group of stations on a ring. A functional address identifies a particular set of functions that a station is able to perform. Each bit in the functional address corresponds to a different function, and if the bit is on, the station implements that function. A functional address can be used to identify a station as an active monitor, an error monitor, a bridge, and so on.

Address Type Bits

The Destination MAC Address field in a MAC frame contains bits that indicate which type of addressing is being used. Bit 0 of octet 0 in an address indicates whether the frame is being sent to an individual address or a group address. Bit 1 of octet 0 indicates whether the address is universal or locally administered. When a locally-administered group address is specified, bit 0 of octet 2 specifies whether this is a functional address or a normal group address. Based on these bits in the destination MAC address, a station uses its individual, group, or functional address to determine if it should process the frames that it receives.

BOX 13.3   IBM Token-Ring MAC frame.

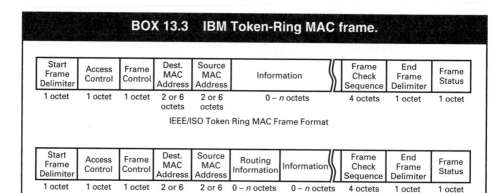

Start Frame Delimiter	Access Control	Frame Control	Dest. MAC Address	Source MAC Address	Information	Frame Check Sequence	End Frame Delimiter	Frame Status
1 octet	1 octet	1 octet	2 or 6 octets	2 or 6 octets	0 – n octets	4 octets	1 octet	1 octet

IEEE/ISO Token Ring MAC Frame Format

Start Frame Delimiter	Access Control	Frame Control	Dest. MAC Address	Source MAC Address	Routing Information	Information	Frame Check Sequence	End Frame Delimiter	Frame Status
1 octet	1 octet	1 octet	2 or 6 octets	2 or 6 octets	0 – n octets	0 – n octets	4 octets	1 octet	1 octet

IBM Token-Ring MAC Frame Format

- **Start Frame Delimiter.** Marks the beginning of a frame or token and has the same format as the Token Ring standard Start Frame Delimiter.

- **Access Control.** An octet included in both frames and tokens having the same bit format (PPPTMRRR) as the Token Ring standard Access Control field.

- **Frame Control.** Identifies the purpose of the frame. As with the Token Ring standard, currently defined frame types are MAC control frames and MAC frames containing LLC-PDUs.

- **Station Addresses.** Six-octet source and destination MAC addresses. The first bit of the *Source MAC Address* field is used to identify whether or not routing information is present in the frame.

- **Routing Information.** A variable-length field used when a frame is to travel across a bridge to another ring in a multiring network. Since routing is not defined as part of the Token Ring standard, this field represents an extension to the Token Ring standard frame format. It can be considered to be a part of the Information field for conformance with the Token Ring standard. Routing in a multiring network is discussed in detail in Chapter 19.

- **Information.** Contains data that is being transmitted across the network. The Information field can contain a MAC-SDU or control information.

- **Frame Check Sequence.** A cyclic redundancy check (CRC) value used for error checking.

- **End Frame Delimiter.** An octet identifying the end of the frame. It conforms to the Token Ring standard frame format.

- **Frame Status.** Used by receiving stations to send status information back to the sending station. It conforms to the Token Ring standard frame format.

Broadcast Addresses

There are two special addresses defined that act as all-stations broadcast addresses when specified as a destination MAC address. These addresses specify that the frame should be received by all stations. The address X'C000 FFFF FFFF' specifies that the frame should be received by all stations on the sending station's ring. The address X'FFFF FFFF FFFF' specifies that the frame should be received by all stations on all rings on a multiring network.

Physical Layer Specifications

The IBM Token-Ring Physical layer conforms to the Token Ring standard and is responsible for providing attachment to the transmission medium and for encoding, transmitting, and recognizing signals. The Physical layer in a sending station accepts 0 and 1 bits and nondata J and nondata K code violations from the Medium Access Control sublayer and transmits them to the next station on the ring. The Physical layer in a receiving station recognizes 0 and 1 bits and signal violations on the transmission medium and passes them to the Medium Access Control sublayer. It also recognizes signal losses.

The IBM Direct Interface

There are a number of possible ways for a program to interface with an IBM Token-Ring Network LAN adapter. Programs can be written using interfaces that are defined by high-level networking software. A program can also interface directly with the Medium Access Control sublayer using the *IBM Direct Interface*.

The IBM Direct Interface is based on the use of a control block called a *Command Control Block* (CCB). This control block provides the information necessary to execute a particular command. The CCB contains a command code that identifies the particular function to perform. It also specifies information such as work areas and parameters that are used as part of the function. The format of the CCB and the way it is passed to the MAC sublayer implementation is the same as for the DLC interface described in Chapter 9 and varies depending on the computing hardware and operating system environment.

Box 13.4 lists the commands that are available as part of the direct interface.

SUMMARY

The Token Ring standard defines a multiaccess form of data link that uses a ring-structured network topology. Stations are connected to one another using point-to-point cable segments to form a ring, and stations pass frames from one station to the next so that all stations eventually receive all frames that are transmitted.

The Token Ring service definition defines a single MA_UNITDATA unconfirmed data transfer service. The Token Ring protocol specification defines the format of the MAC-SDU, specifies how the MAC-SDU is encapsulated in a MAC-PDU, and documents the procedures controlling the exchange of MAC-PDUs between communicating stations.

With the Token Ring access control method, a data unit, called the token, is passed from one station to the next around a physical ring. When a station receives the token, it is allowed to transmit MAC frames for a specified time. The station that originates a frame is responsible for removing that frame from the ring after it has circulated all the way around and then sending a token to the next station. Each station that receives a frame can set bits in the frame that indicate whether the destination MAC address was recognized, the frame was copied, or an error was detected. Different priorities can be assigned to frames. The priority value associated with the token then determines when different frames can be transmitted.

BOX 13.4   IBM direct interface commands.

Frame Transmission Commands

- **Buffer.Free.** Return one or more buffers to the direct station buffer pool.
- **Buffer.Get.** Acquire one or more buffers from the direct station buffer pool.
- **Read.** Accept received data from the direct station.
- **Receive.** Receive data from the direct station.
- **Receive.Cancel.** Stop receiving data from the direct station.
- **Receive.Modify.** Receive data and put some of the data in a buffer other than the direct station buffer.
- **Transmit.Dir.Frame.** Transmit a frame of data using the direct station.

General Commands

- **Dir.Close.Adapter.** Terminate network communication for the adapter.
- **Dir.Close.Direct.** Terminate application program use of the direct station.
- **Dir.Define.MIF.Environment.** Define the environment needed for a NetBIOS emulation program.
- **Dir.Initialize.** Initialize work areas, tables, and buffers associated with the adapter.
- **Dir.Interrupt.** Force an adapter interrupt.
- **Dir.Modify.Open.Parms.** Modify values set by Dir.Open.Adapter.
- **Dir.Open.Adapter.** Prepare the adapter for network communication.
- **Dir.Open.Direct.** Give the application program use of the direct station for communication.
- **Dir.Read.Log.** Read and reset the adapter logs.
- **Dir.Restore.Open.Parms.** Restore parameters modified by Dir.Modify.Open.Parms to their original values.
- **Dir.Set.Exception.Flags.** Define user notification appendages and flags.
- **Dir.Set.Functional.Address.** Set functional addresses for the adapter.
- **Dir.Set.Group.Address.** Set the group address for the adapter.
- **Dir.Set.User.Appendage.** Change appendage addresses.
- **Dir.Status.** Read general status information.
- **Dir.Timer.Cancel.** Cancel a timer set by Dir.Timer.Set.
- **Dir.Timer.Cancel.Group.** Cancel timers set by a group of Dir.Timer.Set commands.
- **Dir.Timer.Set.** Set a timer.
- **PDT.Trace.Off.** Terminate a trace started by PDT.Trace.On.
- **PDT.Trace.On.** Start a trace of all adapter traffic.
- **Purge.Resources.** Purge resources owned by a terminating application process.

A station designated as the active monitor is responsible for detecting and recovering from the loss of the token or a persistently busy token. Stations designated as passive monitors oversee the active monitor station, and take over its functions if it fails.

The Token Ring standard defines a medium specification for shielded, 150-ohm twisted-pair cable, although unshielded twisted-pair cable is used in many implementations of the standard. Data rates of 1, 4, and 16 Mbps can be supported.

Chapter 14 describes the Fiber Distributed Data Interface (FDDI) form of medium access control technology. The FDDI medium access control method uses a timed token-passing technique to implement ring-structured LAN data links using a fiber-optic transmission medium.

Chapter **14**

Fiber Distributed Data Interface

The *Fiber Distributed Data Interface* (FDDI) standard defines a ring-structured network that uses a token-passing form of medium access control. The FDDI standard specifies the use of full-duplex, point-to-point fiber-optic physical links to interconnect stations, although implementations based on twisted-pair cable have also been developed. (The variation of the FDDI standard adapted for twisted-pair cable is often called CDDI, for *copper distributed data interface*.) An FDDI LAN operates at a data rate of 100 Mbps. A special data unit called the *token* circulates around the ring, and a station can transmit frames only when it is in possession of the token. Figure 14.1 shows the basic topology of an FDDI LAN data link.

An FDDI LAN implements a multiaccess form of data link in which all stations on the LAN eventually receive the transmissions of all other stations. All MAC frames are

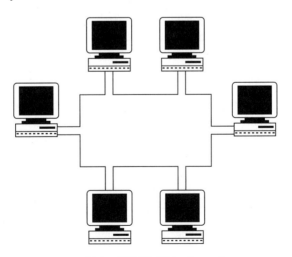

Figure 14.1   FDDI LAN basic topology.

repeated all the way around the ring and reach every station on the LAN data link. Each station is responsible for interpreting the destination MAC address contained in a frame and for copying those frames addressed to it.

FDDI has many similarities with the IEEE/ISO LAN standards described in the preceding chapters. However, the FDDI standard was developed by the Accredited Standards Committee (ASC) X3T9.5 of the American National Standards Institute (ANSI). It has been accepted by ISO as an international standard and is also published as ISO 9314.

The FDDI standard is designed to meet requirements for both high-performance individual networks and high-speed connections between networks. It addresses the requirements associated with a variety of different types of local networks, including *backend local networks*, *high-speed local networks*, and *backbone local networks*. The characteristics of these are described in Box 14.1.

BOX 14.1   Potential uses for FDDI LANs.

- **Backend Local Networks.** *Backend local networks* are used to interconnect enterprise computing systems and large data storage devices where there is a need for high-volume data transfer operations. In a backend local network there will typically be a small number of devices to be connected, and they will be close together. This was the original use for which FDDI was intended, but FDDI LANs will probably be used much more extensively for the other two uses, described next.

- **High-Speed Local Networks.** The need for *high-speed local networks* has arisen from the increased use of image and graphics processing devices in the computing environment. The use of graphics and images can increase the amount of data that needs to be transmitted on a network by orders of magnitude. A typical data processing transaction may involve 500 bits, while a document page image may require the transmission of half a million bits or more.

- **Backbone Local Networks.** *Backbone local networks* are used to provide a high-capacity LAN data link that can be used to interconnect other, lower-capacity LAN data links.

Like the other LAN technologies already discussed, the FDDI standard defines both a service definition and a protocol specification for the MAC sublayer. It also defines architectural models for the MAC sublayer and Physical layer and describes specifications for the fiber-optic transmission media used to implement the standard.

MAC SUBLAYER SERVICE DEFINITION

Medium Access Control sublayer services allow an LLC entity in one station to exchange LLC-PDUs with LLC sublayer entities in other stations. The MAC sublayer service definition is specified in terms of service primitives and service primitive parameters. The

service definition describes an MA_UNITDATA unconfirmed data transfer service and
an MA_TOKEN token request service.

MA_UNITDATA Service Primitives

The MA_UNITDATA data transfer service uses the following three service primitives:

- **MA_UNITDATA.request.** Issued by the LLC sublayer entity to the MAC sublayer entity
  to request that a MAC-SDU be sent to one or more destination stations.
- **MA_UNITDATA.indication.** Issued by the MAC sublayer entity in a destination station
  to the LLC sublayer entity to indicate that a MAC-SDU has been received and to pass the
  MAC-SDU up to the LLC sublayer entity.
- **MA_UNITDATA_STATUS.indication.** Issued by the MAC sublayer entity in the
  source station to the LLC sublayer entity to provide information about the success or failure of an MA_UNITDATA.request to transmit a MAC-SDU.

Figure 14.2 shows a time-sequence diagram that documents the sequence in which
the three service primitives making up the MA_UNITDATA data transfer service are
issued during normal MAC frame transmission.

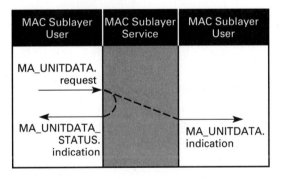

Figure 14.2   Time-sequence diagram for the MA_UNITDATA data transfer
service.

The MA_UNITDATA_STATUS.indication primitive is issued by the MAC sublayer to the LLC sublayer in the source station to indicate the success or failure of an
attempt to transmit a frame. It does not indicate whether the frame was successfully
received by the destination station. As with the MAC sublayer service for the other types
of LAN data links we have described, the FDDI MAC sublayer data transfer service is an
unconfirmed service in which data transfer is not guaranteed.

MA_TOKEN Service Primitives

The MA_TOKEN token request service is an optional service that can be used by the
LLC sublayer to request the capture of the next token. The FDDI standard states that this
service is meant to be used only in certain special cases when time-critical data must be
transmitted. Its use can minimize the effects of ring latency and can reduce the waiting

time for the next token for an individual station. However, this is ordinarily at the expense of reducing transmission capacity on the network as a whole.

The following is the single service primitive for the MA_TOKEN service.

- **MA_TOKEN.request.** Issued by the LLC sublayer entity to request the capture of the next token.

Figure 14.3 shows a time-sequence diagram that documents how the service primitive for the MA_TOKEN token request service is issued.

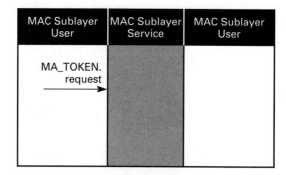

Figure 14.3 Time-sequence diagram for the MA_TOKEN token request service.

Service Primitive Parameters

Box 14.2 describes the parameters that are included in the MA_UNITDATA and MA_TOKEN service primitives. A single MA_UNITDATA.request primitive can include multiple sets of parameters, one for each MAC-SDU that is to be transmitted. Thus, a single service request can cause multiple MAC-SDUs to be sent.

MAC SUBLAYER PROTOCOL SPECIFICATION

The data unit the MAC sublayer receives from the LLC sublayer is the *medium-access-control-service-data-unit* (MAC-SDU). The MAC-SDU contains the LLC-PDU that the two LLC sublayer entities are exchanging.

MAC Sublayer Functions

The general functions performed by the FDDI MAC sublayer are similar to the functions performed by the MAC sublayer in other LAN standards. During MAC frame transmission, the Medium Access Control sublayer entities in all stations on the ring perform the following functions:

- **Source Station MAC Sublayer Functions.** The MAC sublayer in a source station accepts each LLC-PDU from the LLC sublayer entity in the form of a MAC-SDU. A data encapsulation function in the source MAC sublayer entity adds protocol-control-informa-

MA_UNITDATA.request   (
                         FC_value(1),
                         destination_address(1),
                         M_SDU(1),
                         requested_service_class(1),
                         stream(1),
                         ...
                         FC_value(n),
                         destination_address(n),
                         M_SDU(n),
                         requested_service_class(n),
                         stream(n),
                         Token_class
)

MA_UNITDATA_STATUS.indication
                         (
                         number_of_SDUs,
                         transmission_status,
                         provided_service_class
)

MA_UNITDATA.indication
                         (
                         FC_value,
                         destination_address,
                         source_address,
                         M_SDU,
                         reception_status
)

MA_TOKEN.request
                         (
                         requested_Token_class
)

- **FC_value.** Provides a value for the Frame Control field of the MAC frame. This field is described later in this chapter.
- **destination_address.** Specifies a destination MAC address defining the station or stations to which the MAC-SDU is to be delivered. The MAC addressing scheme is described in Chapter 6.

(Continued)

BOX 14.2 *(Continued)*

- **source_address.** Specifies a source MAC address identifying the station originating the MAC-SDU.

- **M_SDU.** Specifies the MAC-SDU passed down from the LLC sublayer for transmission from the source station to the destination station or stations.

- **requested_service_class.** Specifies whether the normal synchronous service or the optional asynchronous service is requested for the data transfer. Synchronous and asynchronous service are described later in this chapter.

- **stream.** Specifies whether or not multiple MAC-SDUs are to be transmitted in a single MA_UNITDATA.request operation. The parameter is set in all but the last group of parameters and reset in the last group of parameters.

- **Token_class.** Specifies the class of token that should be issued following the transmission of the MAC-SDU or MAC-SDUs.

- **number_of_SDUs.** Indicates the number of MAC-SDUs actually transmitted as a result of this request.

- **transmission_status.** Indicates to the source LLC sublayer entity whether or not the previous MA_UNITDATA.request primitive was accepted by the MAC sublayer entity.

- **provided_service_class.** Specifies whether synchronous or asynchronous service was actually provided for the data transfer.

- **reception_status.** Indicates to a destination LLC sublayer entity whether the MAC-SDU was received without error.

- **requested_Token_class.** Specifies the class of token that should be issued.

---

tion (PCI) to the MAC-SDU to form a *medium-access-control-protocol-data-unit* (MAC-PDU) or *MAC frame*. The MAC sublayer then uses the services of the Physical layer to transmit the MAC frame to the next station on the ring.

- **Receiving Station MAC Sublayer Functions.** The MAC sublayer in a receiving station uses the Physical layer to receive MAC frames from the previous station on the ring. It interprets the destination MAC address in each frame it receives and copies only frames that are addressed to that station. For each frame that it copies, the MAC sublayer entity removes the PCI from the MAC frame and passes the resulting MAC-SDU to the LLC sublayer. The MAC sublayer in a receiving station also interprets the source address in each MAC frame that it receives to identify frames that it originally placed onto the ring. When a receiving station identifies one of its own frames, it does not repeat that frame, thus removing it from the ring. A receiving station repeats all other MAC frames, whether it copied them or not, to the next station on the ring.

MAC Frame Format

The MAC frame format is described in the FDDI standard using the term *symbol* to refer to a group of 4 bits. Symbols are encoded in a way that allows both data and nondata values to be represented. The FDDI symbol encoding scheme is described later in this chapter when we discuss Physical layer specifications. Box 14.3 shows the format of the FDDI MAC frame and describes its fields.

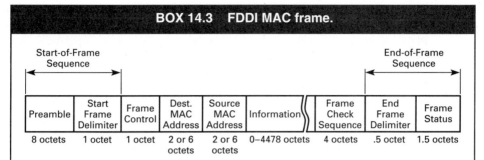

BOX 14.3   FDDI MAC frame.

- **Preamble.** A minimum of 16 symbols used to synchronize each station's clock with frame transmission.

- **Start Frame Delimiter.** A unique signal pattern, using nondata symbols, that identifies the start of the frame.

- **Frame Control.** Identifies the frame's type. It has the bit format CLFFZZZZ, interpreted as follows:

  — **C.** Identifies this as a synchronous or asynchronous frame.
  — **L.** Specifies whether 16- or 48-bit addresses are used.
  — **FF.** Indicates the frame's type.
  — **ZZZZ.** Provides control information for MAC frames.

- **Station Addresses.** A *Destination MAC Address* field and a *Source MAC Address* field. Station addresses can be either 16 bits or 48 bits in length. A ring may contain a mixture of stations using 16-bit and 48-bit addresses. The destination address can specify an individual address, a group address, or the broadcast address. The source address must identify an individual station. The MAC addressing scheme is described in Chapter 6.

- **Information.** Contains a MAC-SDU passed from the LLC sublayer or control information supplied by the MAC sublayer. FDDI Physical layer specifications limit the maximum length of a frame to 9000 symbols, including four symbols of the Preamble. This limits the length of the Information field to a maximum of 8956 symbols or 4478 octets.

- **Frame Check Sequence.** Contains a cyclic redundancy check (CRC) value used for error checking. The value is calculated by the source station based on the contents of the Frame Control, Destination MAC Address, Source MAC Address, and Information fields. A destination station performs the same CRC calculation as the source station. If the calculated CRC value does not match the value in the FCS field, the frame is considered to be in error and is discarded.

- **End Frame Delimiter.** Identifies the end of the frame. The ending delimiter for a token consists of two symbols (1 octet). For all other frames, it consists of a single symbol (1/2 octet).

- **Frame Status.** Contains information about the status of a frame, including whether an error was detected, the address was recognized, or the frame was copied. Additional implementation-defined indicators may also be included in this field.

Some authorities distinguish between the MAC frame itself and the Physical layer PDU. The MAC frame can be considered to range from the Frame Control field through the Frame Check Sequence. The Physical layer PDU can be considered to be the MAC frame plus a Start of Frame Sequence (Preamble and Start Frame Delimiter) and an End of Frame Sequence (End Frame Delimiter and Frame Status field). The Physical layer PDU is sometimes called a *packet*.* In this book we are not making a distinction between MAC frames and Physical layer PDUs.

MAC Frame/LLC-PDU Relationship

Figure 14.4 shows the relationship between the LLC-PDU that is passed to the MAC sublayer in a MAC-SDU and the FDDI MAC frame. Notice that the LLC-PDU is carried in an FDDI MAC frame; all fields in the LLC-PDU are treated by the MAC sublayer as data.

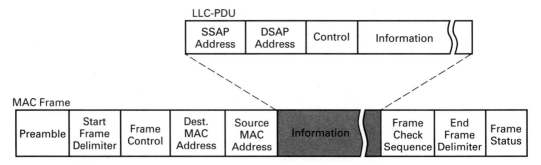

Figure 14.4 FDDI MAC frame and LLC-PDU relationship.

Frame Types

The Frame Control field contains bits that indicate a frame's type. The FDDI specification defines eight types of frames:

- **Void Frame.** A data unit that is considered logically not to be a frame; its contents are ignored.
- **Token.** The token, used to grant permission to transmit.
- **Restricted Token.** The restricted token, used to control transmission in multiframe dialogs.
- **SMT Frames.** Data units sent by station management components to control their operation.
- **MAC Frames.** Data units used to control the operation of the MAC protocol, including the Claim and Beacon frames.
- **LLC Frames.** Data units containing a MAC-SDU passed down from the LLC sublayer.
- **Implementor Frames.** Data units reserved for the implementor.
- **Reserved Frames.** Data units intended for use in future versions of the FDDI standard.

Token Format

A special data unit format, illustrated in Fig. 14.5, is used for the token. A token consists of a Preamble, Start Frame Delimiter, Frame Control field, and End Frame Delimiter.

*As mentioned in Chapter 9, this is an unfortunate choice of terminology, since most authorities use the term *packet* to refer to the PDU exchanged by the layer above the LLC sublayer.

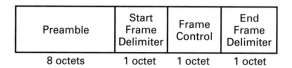

Preamble	Start Frame Delimiter	Frame Control	End Frame Delimiter
8 octets	1 octet	1 octet	1 octet

Figure 14.5 FDDI Token format.

MAC PROTOCOL OPERATION

The FDDI MAC sublayer uses a timed Token Ring access protocol that governs the way in which a MAC sublayer entity gains access to the ring to transmit data. Although FDDI uses a *token-ring* form of medium access control, the timed Token Ring access protocol used by FDDI is quite different from the access protocol defined in the IEEE/ISO Token Ring standard and is not compatible with it.

The protocol implemented by the FDDI MAC sublayer performs the following functions in supplying its services:

- Ring initialization.
- Providing fair and deterministic access to the transmission medium.
- Address recognition and address filtering.
- Generation and verification of frame check sequence (FCS) fields.
- Frame transmission and reception.
- Frame repeating.
- Frame stripping (removal of frames from the ring).

During operation of the FDDI timed Token Ring access control protocol the token is passed from station to station around the ring. When the token arrives at a station, it is passed up to the MAC sublayer entity in that station. A MAC sublayer entity holding the token is allowed to transmit frames. If the MAC sublayer entity has frames to send, it holds the token and transmits as many frames as desired onto the ring until the station runs out of frames to send or reaches a predefined time limit. The station then transmits the token to the next station on the ring.

After a frame circulates all the way around the ring and returns to the station originating it, that station is responsible for stripping the frame from the ring by not repeating it. As a station repeats each frame around the ring, it sets bits in the Frame Status field of the frame indicating whether the station detected an error in the frame, recognized the address in the frame's destination MAC address field, or copied the frame for processing. The FDDI token-passing procedure is illustrated in Fig. 14.6.

Notice that a station transmits the token immediately after it finishes transmitting frames. This makes it possible for a station to transmit new frames while frames that were transmitted by other stations are still circulating around other parts of the ring. Thus, there can be multiple frames, from multiple stations, on the ring at any given time.

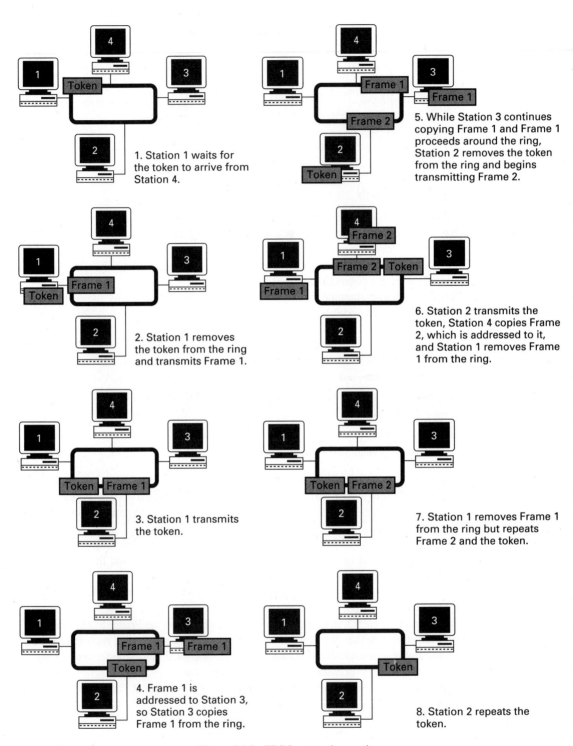

Figure 14.6 FDDI protocol operation.

Ring Monitoring Functions

All stations on the ring participate in distributed algorithms that monitor the operation of the ring to check for invalid conditions that may require the ring to be reinitialized. An example of an invalid condition is a ring that currently has no token circulating. To detect the absence of a circulating token, each station maintains a *token rotation timer* (TRT), which the station resets each time it receives the token. If the timer expires twice before the station next receives the token, the station assumes the token has been lost and begins the ring initialization procedure.

Other types of incorrect activity can also cause a station to begin the station initialization procedure. A station begins the ring-initialization process by performing a claim token procedure.

Claim Token Procedure

In performing the *claim token* procedure, a station bids for the right to initialize the ring. The station begins the claim token procedure by issuing a continuous stream of control frames, called Claim frames. Each Claim frame contains a suggested *Target Token Rotation Time* (TTRT) value. If a station sending Claim frames receives a Claim frame from another station, it compares TTRT values. If the station's own TTRT value is lower, it keeps transmitting Claim frames. If the TTRT value in a Claim frame a station receives is lower than its own TTRT value, it passes on the received Claim frame instead of its own. If the values are the same, MAC addresses are used to determine which station takes precedence.

Eventually, the Claim frame with the lowest TTRT value will be passed on by other stations and will return to the station that sent it. At this point the source station recognizes itself as the winner in the claim token procedure. That station has won the right to initialize the ring and continues by performing the ring initialization procedure. As a result of the claim token procedure, all stations now have the TTRT value to be used in subsequent ring operation because all stations have seen the TTRT value in the Claim frame sent by the winning station.

The claim token procedure sounds complex and time consuming, but with a data rate of 100 Mbps, the procedure takes only a millisecond or two to complete, even on a large ring.

Ring Initialization

The station winning the claim token procedure sets its own token rotation timer (TRT) to the negotiated TTRT and transmits a token onto the ring. Each station that receives the token then sets its own TTRT to the negotiated value and transmits the token to the next station. No frames are transmitted until the token has passed once all the way around the ring. The purpose of the initial token rotation is to align TTRT values and TRT times in all stations on the ring.

Beacon Process

When a serious failure occurs, such as a break in the ring, stations use a *beacon process* to locate the failure. Each station's station management (SMT) component can initiate the beacon process. When a station that has been sending Claim frames recognizes that a defined time period has elapsed without the claim token process being resolved, it begins the beacon process by transmitting a continuous stream of Beacon frames. If a station receives a Beacon frame from another station, it stops sending its own Beacon frames and passes on the Beacon frames it has received. Eventually, Beacon frames from the station immediately following the break will be propagated to all stations in the network. Some process external to the MAC sublayer entity must then be invoked to diagnose the problem and to reconfigure the ring to bypass the failure. If during the beacon process a station receives its own Beacon frames, it assumes the ring has been restored and initiates the claim token procedure.

Optional FDDI MAC Protocol Features

The FDDI standard specifies optional mechanisms that implement a capacity allocation scheme. This scheme is designed to support a mixture of stream and burst transmissions and transmissions involving dialogs between pairs of stations.

Synchronous and Asynchronous Frames

Two types of MAC frames are defined by the FDDI standard—*asynchronous* frames and *synchronous* frames. In normal FDDI protocol operation, only asynchronous frames are transmitted. The use of synchronous frames is optional, and an FDDI implementation need not support them.

Each station may be allocated a certain length of time during which it can transmit synchronous frames. This time interval is called its *synchronous allocation* (SA). The target token rotation time (TTRT) must be large enough to accommodate the sum of all the station synchronous transmission times plus the time it takes for a frame of maximum size to travel around the ring.

Each station keeps track of the time that has elapsed since it last received the token. When a station next receives the token, it records the elapsed time since the last token was received. The station is then allowed to transmit synchronous frames for its synchronous allocation time. Then, if the elapsed time, as recorded when the token was received, is less than the TTRT, the station is allowed to send asynchronous frames for a time interval equal to that time difference.

All stations that have a synchronous allocation are guaranteed an opportunity to transmit synchronous frames, but a station sends asynchronous frames only if time permits. Asynchronous frames can optionally be subdivided using levels of priority that are then used to further prioritize the sending of asynchronous traffic.

Multiframe Dialogs

FDDI provides another optional mechanism for implementing *multiframe dialogs* between pairs of stations. When a station needs to enter into a dialog with another station, it can do so using its asynchronous transmission capacity. After the station transmits the first frame in the dialog, it transmits a *restricted token*. Only the station receiving the first frame is allowed to use the restricted token for transmitting asynchronous frames. The two stations can then exchange data frames and restricted tokens for the duration of the dialog. During this time, other stations are able to send synchronous frames but no asynchronous frames.

FDDI ARCHITECTURAL MODEL

The FDDI specification defines an architectural model describing the organization of the Data Link and Physical layers. This architectural model is illustrated in Fig. 14.7. The components in the architectural model can be divided among those components associated with the Data Link layer, those associated with the Physical layer, and those associated with the station management (SMT) function.

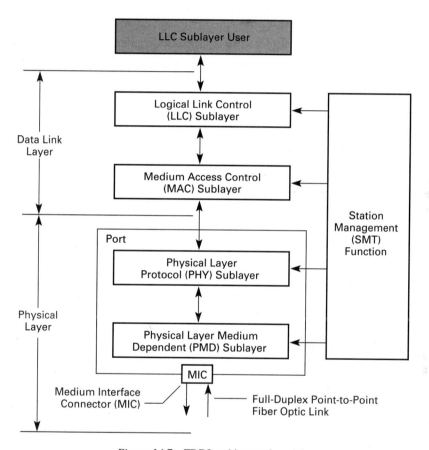

Figure 14.7   FDDI architectural model.

Data Link Layer Components

The Data Link layer is divided into a *Logical Link Control* (LLC) sublayer and a *Medium Access Control* (MAC) sublayer. The FDDI standard does not define the LLC sublayer but permits the use of the IEEE/ISO Logical Link Control standard for this sublayer. The Medium Access Control (MAC) sublayer of the Data Link layer is concerned with the protocol used to handle the transmission of tokens and data frames around the logical ring.

Physical Layer Components

The FDDI Physical layer is divided into a *Physical Layer Protocol* (PHY) sublayer and a *Physical Layer Medium Dependent* (PMD) sublayer.

In FDDI terminology, a *station* is an addressable network component that is capable of generating and receiving frames. Each instance of a PHY sublayer entity and a PMD sublayer entity within a station is called a *port*. A station can implement one or more ports. Each port is attached to the transmission medium through a *Medium Interface Connector* (MIC).

Station Management Component

A station has a single *station management* (SMT) component, which is responsible for monitoring the operation of the station and for controlling the various management-oriented attributes of other station components. The SMT component implements the following functions:

- Initializing, inserting, and removing stations.
- Managing a station's configuration, its attachment to the FDDI transmission medium, and its connections with other stations.
- Isolating and recovering from faults.

STATION TYPES AND NETWORK TOPOLOGIES

A station contains one or more MAC sublayer entities, one or more ports, and a single station management (SMT) entity. There are various ways in which stations and other devices can be configured to form an FDDI network, and various types of MICs are defined for attaching a device to the network. We will look next at the station configurations and MIC types that are defined by the FDDI standard and examine the various types of network topologies that can be formed using the different station configurations.

Dual-Attachment Station

A *dual-attachment station* (DAS) is designed to connect to two separate full-duplex transmission medium segments. A dual-attachment station has one SMT entity, one or more MAC sublayer entities, and exactly two ports. Each of the ports is associated with its own MIC. The architectural model for a dual-attachment station is shown in Fig. 14.8.

Dual-attachment stations are used to form a structure that is commonly called a *dual-ring*, or *trunk-ring* structure. The two rings are called the *primary ring* and the *secondary ring*. In a dual-ring structure, when each MIC is properly connected, two physical and logical rings are formed.

To properly form a dual ring, each dual-attachment station must implement exactly two MICs—one MIC of type A and one MIC of type B. The type A and type B MICs are defined as follows:

- **MIC Type A.** A MIC of type A is defined to be the *input* of the path for the primary ring.
- **MIC Type B.** A MIC of type B is defined to be the *output* of the path for the primary ring.

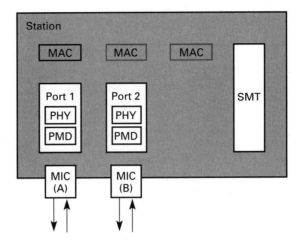

Figure 14.8　FDDI dual-attachment station (DAS) architectural model.

Figure 14.9 shows a simple FDDI network consisting of four dual-attachment stations. The network is formed by connecting the type A MIC of one station to the type B MIC of the next station with a single transmission medium segment. Since each transmission medium segment is full-duplex, transmissions can flow in both directions simultaneously over each segment, thus forming a dual, counter-rotating ring structure.

FDDI MICs and transmission medium segments are designed to facilitate the connection of MICs in the proper manner. For example, the connectors at the end of transmission medium segments do not allow one type A MIC to be attached to another type A MIC.

The FDDI standard does not specify how the primary and secondary rings are to be used. This is left to the implementors. Normally, the primary ring is used to carry data, and the secondary ring is idle and is used to recover from physical link and station failures. However, it is possible, although not common, for an FDDI implementation to employ both rings simultaneously for data transmission.

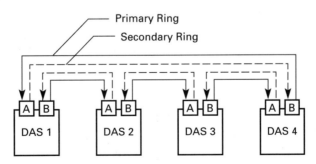

Figure 14.9　Simple ring of dual-attachment stations.

Dual-Attachment Concentrator

A *concentrator* is an FDDI device that has more ports than are needed to simply attach the concentrator itself to the FDDI network. The additional ports can be used to attach other stations to the network. A *dual-attachment concentrator* (DAC) is a station that has three or more ports, each associated with its own MIC.

A dual-attachment concentrator is used to create a network topology called a *dual ring of trees*, in which tree structures branch off the dual counter-rotating ring to connect *single-attachment stations* (SASs). (The architecture of a single-attachment station is described later in this chapter.) A dual-attachment concentrator implements one MIC of type A, one of type B, and one or more MICs of type M. Each MIC of type M (short for *master*) in a concentrator is attached to a MIC of type S (short for *slave*), implemented in a single-attachment station.

Notice that the type A and type B MICs are interconnected in exactly the same way as in the example in Fig. 14.7. A simple concentrator network—made up of dual-attachment stations, dual-attachment concentrators, and single-attachment stations—is shown in Fig. 14.10.

The numbers next to each station in Fig. 14.10 indicate the path the token takes as it travels from station to station around the primary ring. In this example, we are assuming that each concentrator implements a MAC sublayer entity and also acts as a station. When a concentrator is also a station, it logically follows any slave stations to which it is attached.

An architectural model of the dual-attachment concentrator is shown in Fig. 14.11. A dual-attachment concentrator can implement zero or more MAC entities. If a device

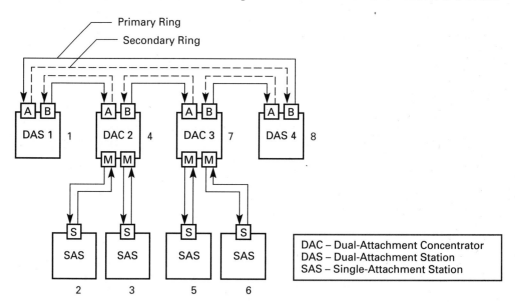

Figure 14.10 A simple concentrator network showing token flow on the primary ring. Bold numbers indicate the sequence in which the MAC sublayer entities receive the token.

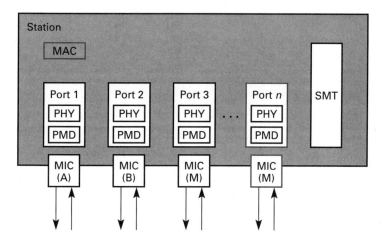

Figure 14.11   FDDI dual-attachment concentrator (DAC) architectural model.

performs a concentrator function only, it implements no MAC entities, and the concentrator will not be the source or the final destination of any frames. In this case, the concentrator is not addressable and is not considered to be a station on the network; it performs a concentrator function only. A concentrator can contain MAC entities, however, and then also function as a station.

Single-Attachment Station

A single-attachment station implements a single MIC of type S. A single-attachment station is typically connected, via a single transmission medium segment, to a concentrator implementing a MIC connector of type M.

Figure 14.12 shows the architectural model of a single-attachment station. It contains an SMT entity, a MAC sublayer entity, and one port having a MIC of type S.

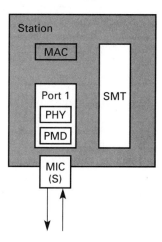

Figure 14.12   FDDI single-attachment station (SAS) architectural model.

Single-Attachment Concentrator

A *single-attachment concentrator* (SAS) can be used to create a hierarchy of trees. This configuration is illustrated in Fig. 14.13.

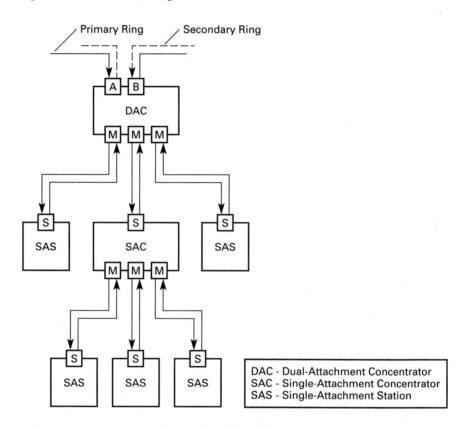

Figure 14.13   Hierarchy of trees.

The architectural model of the single-attachment concentrator is shown in Fig. 14.14.

Null-Attachment Concentrator

It is also possible to have an FDDI network that consists only of a tree structure with no dual ring. In such a configuration, as shown in Fig. 14.15, the topmost concentrator is a *null-attachment concentrator*. A null-attachment concentrator has no MICs of type A or B for connection to a dual ring and no MIC of type S for connection to a higher-level concentrator. It contains only MICs of type M, for attachment of stations and concentrators at a lower level.

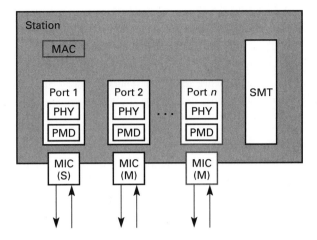

Figure 14.14 FDDI single-attachment concentrator (SAC) architectural model.

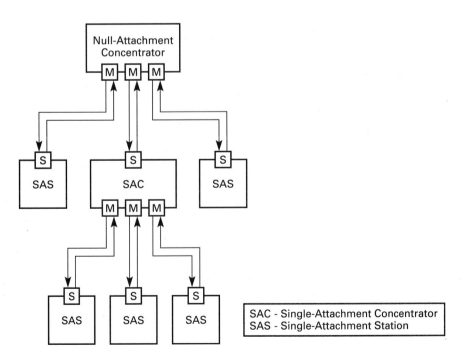

Figure 14.15 Hierarchy of trees using a null-attachment concentrator.

NETWORK RECONFIGURATION

In addition to supporting high data transfer rates, FDDI has been designed to provide a high level of reliability. One way in which it does this is by including the secondary ring as part of the basic network topology. The secondary ring can be used to recover from physical failures of links or stations by allowing the network to be dynamically reconfigured to bypass a failed component.

Physical Link Failures

If a physical link failure occurs, stations can perform procedures to detect the failure and set bypass switches to use the secondary ring to bypass the problem. This is shown in Fig. 14.16. The redundant physical links that implement the secondary ring can be used to bypass the missing physical link, thus reconfiguring the primary ring. The numbers in the diagram show the sequence in which the token flows around the ring both before and after the link failure.

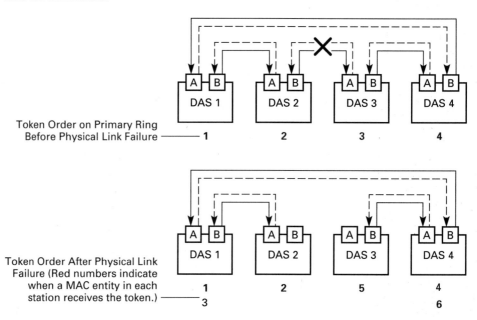

Figure 14.16   Reconfiguration after physical link failure.

Station Failures

The secondary ring can also be used to bypass a station that either fails or is disconnected from the ring. This is shown in Fig. 14.17. Stations on either side of the physical links to the failed station can reconfigure the network using the secondary ring. Again, numbers show the sequence in which the token flows around the ring both before and after the station failure.

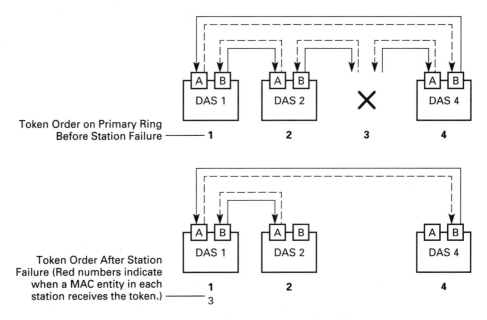

Figure 14.17   Reconfiguration after station failure.

PHYSICAL LAYER SPECIFICATIONS

As we described earlier, the FDDI Physical layer is divided into a Physical Layer Protocol (PHY) sublayer and a Physical Layer Medium Dependent (PMD) sublayer. Each sublayer performs a different set of functions and has its own service definition.

PHY Sublayer

The *Physical Layer Protocol* (PHY) sublayer performs the following functions:

- Encoding and decoding data and control information.
- Transmitting data received from the MAC sublayer.
- Performing clock synchronization and recovering the data coming in from the PMD sublayer.
- Transmitting and receiving groups of code bits, called *line states,* that are used to initialize and condition the transmission medium.

The PHY sublayer provides a well-defined set of services to a MAC sublayer entity and enables the local MAC sublayer entity to exchange MAC frames with other stations. The interface between the MAC sublayer and the PHY sublayer is an abstract interface defining the services that a PHY sublayer entity supplies to a MAC sublayer entity.

The following are the service primitives that define the interface between the MAC sublayer and the PHY sublayer:

- **PH_UNITDATA.request(symbol).** Issued by the MAC sublayer entity in the sending station to transfer one symbol from the MAC sublayer to the PHY sublayer for transmission to the next station on the ring.

- **PH_UNITDATA.indication(symbol).** Issued by the PHY sublayer entity in the receiving station to transfer one symbol from the PHY sublayer to the MAC sublayer.

- **PH_UNITDATA_STATUS.indication(transmission_status).** Issued by the PHY sublayer in the sending station to indicate readiness to accept another symbol for transmission.

- **PH_INVALID.indication(PH_invalid).** Issued by the PHY sublayer to indicate to the MAC sublayer that an invalid symbol stream has been detected.

PMD Sublayer

The *Physical Layer Medium Dependent* (PMD) sublayer performs the following functions:

- Providing the services required to transport an encoded digital bit stream from one station to the next over a point-to-point transmission medium.

- Defining requirements for the *Medium Interface Connector* (MIC) and the keying of various types of MIC receptacles. The MIC is a fiber-optic connector that connects the fiber-optic transmission medium to the FDDI attachment.

- Specifying the characteristics of fiber-optic drivers and receivers, fiber-optic transmission media, connectors, power budgets, and other physical, hardware-related characteristics.

- Determining when an actual signal is being received by a receiver.

The PMD sublayer provides services to the PHY sublayer. The interface between the PHY sublayer and the PMD sublayer is an abstract interface defining the services that a PMD sublayer entity supplies to a PHY sublayer entity.

The following are the service primitives that define the interface between the PHY sublayer and the PMD sublayer:

- **PM_DATA.request(PM_Request).** Issued by the PHY sublayer in the sending station to transfer an encoded NRZI bit stream to the PMD sublayer for transmission to the next station on the ring.

- **PM_DATA.indication(PM_indication).** Issued by the PMD sublayer in the receiving station to transfer an encoded NRZI bit stream to the PHY layer.

- **PM_SIGNAL.indication(Signal_Detect(status).** Issued by the PMD sublayer to indicate to the PHY sublayer whether the optical signal being received by PMD is of satisfactory or unsatisfactory quality.

The PMD sublayer is responsible for translating the NRZI-encoded bit stream used by the PHY sublayer to and from signals that are transmitted over the transmission medium to the next station on the ring. The transmission medium consists of the portion of the physical communication channel to which two or more PMD sublayer entities are connected. Each transmission medium segment implements a full-duplex transmission path.

Each transmission medium segment ordinarily implements two optical fibers, one for transmission in each direction. The PMD specification contains definitions for the physical characteristics of the optical signal and of the fiber-optic cable used to implement the transmission medium. It also defines the physical characteristics of the MIC receptacle that is used to physically connect a port to the transmission medium.

The only transmission medium specified in the FDDI standard at the time of writing is a fiber-optic medium. However, as we mentioned earlier, other transmission media, such as twisted-pair cable, have been used in FDDI implementations. It is possible that the FDDI standard will be extended over time to include additional media.

Symbol Encoding

A key service provided by the PHY sublayer is the encoding and decoding of data. The encoding system used by FDDI is designed to provide ease of synchronization as well as reliable data transmission. Data and control information is carried on the transmission medium in the form of code bits. A *code bit* is the smallest signaling entity and is represented using *nonreturn to zero inverted* (NRZI) encoding. With NRZI, a 1 code bit is represented by a transition in the signal and a 0 code bit by no transition. A *code group* is a consecutive sequence of 5 code bits that is used to represent a *symbol* on the transmission medium.

A *4b/5b code* is used to assign interpretations to the various code groups. The FDDI 4b/5b code is shown in Fig. 14.18. Each 5-bit data symbol corresponds to a 4-bit

Code Group	Symbol	Interpretation
Data		
11110	0	hex 0
01001	1	hex 1
10100	2	hex 2
10101	3	hex 3
01010	4	hex 4
01011	5	hex 5
01110	6	hex 6
01111	7	hex 7
10010	8	hex 8
10011	9	hex 9
10110	A	hex A
10111	B	hex B
11010	C	hex C
11011	D	hex D
11100	E	hex E
11101	F	hex F
Control		
00000	Q	Quiet
11111	I	Idle
00100	H	Halt
11000	J	Start Delimiter (1st symbol)
10001	K	Start Delimiter (2nd symbol)
01101	T	Ending Delimiter
00111	R	Reset
11001	S	Set

Figure 14.18   FDDI 4b/5b symbol encoding.

binary data value. The code groups used to represent data symbols were chosen so there are never more than three consecutive 0 bits and thus no more than three bit times without a transition. An additional eight symbols are used for control purposes. Other possible 5-bit values are invalid.

STATION MANAGEMENT SPECIFICATIONS

The *station management* (SMT) component provides services to the MAC, PHY, and PMD sublayers. The interfaces between the SMT component and the MAC, PHY, and PMD sublayers are abstract interfaces defining the services that an SMT entity supplies to a particular sublayer entity.

Station Management Service Definition

The following are service definitions for the three major SMT interfaces.

SMT-MAC Interface Service Definition

The following are the service primitives that define the interface between SMT and the MAC sublayer.

- **SM_MA_INITIALIZE_PROTOCOL.request.** Sent by station management to reset the MAC sublayer and change MAC operational parameters.
- **SM_MA_INITIALIZE_PROTOCOL.confirm.** Sent by the MAC sublayer to indicate the success or failure of an initialization request.
- **SM_MA_CONTROL.request.** Sent by station management to control the operation of the MAC sublayer.
- **SM_MA_SMT_STATUS.indication.** Sent by the MAC sublayer to report errors and significant status changes.
- **SM_MA_SMT_UNITDATA.request.** Sent by station management when it has one or more data units to transmit.
- **SM_MA_SMT_UNITDATA.indication.** Sent to station management to notify it that a station management data unit has arrived and to transfer the data unit to station management.
- **SM_MA_SMT_UNITDATA_STATUS.indication.** Sent by the MAC sublayer to indicate the success or failure of a data request.
- **SM_MA_TOKEN.request.** Sent by station management to request the capture of the next token.

SMT-PHY Interface Service Definition

The following are the service primitives that define the interface between SMT and the PHY sublayer.

- **SM_PH_LINE_STATE.request.** Issued by station management to the PHY sublayer to request the transmission of a continuous stream of similar symbols.
- **SM_PH_SMT_STATUS.indication.** Issued by the PHY sublayer to station management to inform station management of Line-State activity and status changes.

- **SM_PH_CONTROL.request.** Issued by station management to the PHY sublayer to control the operation of the PHY sublayer.

SMT-PMD Interface Service Definition

The following are the service primitives that define the interface between SMT and the PMD sublayer.

- **SM_PM_CONTROL.request.** Issued by station management to the PMD sublayer to force the transmission of a particular signal.
- **SM_PM_BYPASS.request.** Issued by station management to the PMD sublayer to indicate that SMT wants to join or leave the FDDI network.
- **SM_PM_SIGNAL.indication.** Issued by the PMD sublayer to station management to indicate the status of the signal level being received by PMD.

Station Management Functions

SMT functions are divided into two categories—connection management and ring management. *Connection management* is responsible for the management of Physical layer components and their interconnection. *Ring management* is responsible for the management of MAC layer components and the rings to which they are logically attached.

Connection Management

Connection management is subdivided into the following three areas:

- **Entity Coordination Management (ECM).** Entity coordination management manages the physical connection of a port to the transmission medium. This involves controlling the optical bypass switch and notifying physical connection management when an acceptable connection has been made and the transmission medium is available.
- **Physical Connection Management (PCM).** Physical connection management manages the interconnection of ports that are attached to the same transmission medium segment. This involves the recognition and transmission of different signals between the ports. The different signals are used to perform a handshaking process when the interconnection is initialized and to signal the presence of information or changes in line state after the interconnection has been established.
- **Configuration Management (CFM).** Configuration management manages interconnections between MAC sublayer entities and PHY sublayer entities within a station, which determines the station's internal configuration. Configuration management also controls the connection and disconnection of ports to the primary, secondary, and local transmission paths. Port connection configurations are defined for dual-attachment stations, single-attachment stations, dual-attachment concentrators, and single-attachment concentrators. Configuration management also manages changes in port connection required for ring reconfiguration in the event of a physical failure.

Ring Management

Ring management performs MAC-level fault detection and recovery, including recovery from a stuck Beacon condition and detection and resolution of duplicate MAC addresses on the network. Ring management also signals changes in MAC availability.

FDDI II

At the time of writing, an upwardly compatible extension of FDDI, called *FDDI II*, is undergoing standardization in ISO. The original FDDI specification is now sometimes called *FDDI I*. The original intent of FDDI technology was to provide a higher-speed alternative to other types of LAN technology, such as Ethernet and Token Ring, for data applications. However, since standardization work on FDDI was begun, there has been an increasing need to use integrated networks that carry both data and nondata traffic, such as voice and video.

An FDDI I LAN uses packet-switching technology to carry user data in variable-length frames. As discussed earlier in this chapter FDDI I defines a capacity allocation scheme, using synchronous frames, that can be used to control the amount of time any single station has access to the transmission medium. This mechanism can be used to guarantee a certain minimum sustained data rate to a user, but it does not provide for a uniform data stream between two communicating stations. Packet-switching mechanisms are not well suited for communication applications in which a constant, uniform data stream is required. Circuit-switching technologies are better suited for such applications.

Isochronous Transmission

FDDI II defines additional optional protocol mechanisms that allow an FDDI data link to be used to provide circuit-switched services in addition to packet-switched services. The mode of transmission that is used to provide circuit-switched services is called *isochronous transmission*. The FDDI II isochronous transmission mechanisms impose a 125-microsecond frame structure on the ring. The frame structure is used to divide the total transmission capacity into a number of discrete channels by allocating regularly repeating time slots to users that require them. These discrete channels are used to provide virtual circuit between pairs of communicating stations.

Basic and Hybrid Operation

An FDDI II network can operate in either *basic* or *hybrid* mode. In basic mode, the network functions in an identical fashion to an FDDI I network and provides only packet-switching services. In hybrid mode, the capacity of the transmission medium is split between packet-switching and circuit switching.

Figure 14.19 illustrates the FDDI II architectural model. A new sublayer structure imposes a *Hybrid Ring Control* (HRC) function between the conventional FDDI I Medium Access Control (MAC) sublayer and the Physical layer. The HRC function contains a new *Isochronous Medium Access Control* (IMAC) sublayer and a *Hybrid Multiplexor* (HMUX) function. The IMAC sublayer provides services to a circuit-switched multiplexor component that operates at the level of the LLC sublayer. The HMUX function provides an interface between the Physical layer and the two alternative MAC sublayer functions and divides the transmission capacity into channels that can be split between packet-switching and circuit-switching applications.

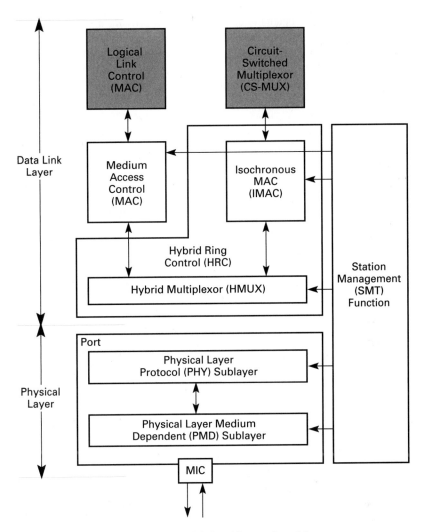

Figure 14.19   FDDI II architectural model.

Wideband Channels

When an FDDI II network is operating in basic mode, the entire 100 Mbps transmission capacity is used for packet-switching services. When the network is operating in hybrid mode, the transmission capacity is split between a *packet-data channel* and several *wideband channels* (WBCs). Up to 16 wideband channels can be used that each supports a data rate of 6.144 Mbps. The minimum capacity of the packet-data channel is .768 Mbps. A total of .928 Mbps of channel capacity is devoted to overhead functions, making the total capacity of an FDDI II network operating in hybrid mode 99.072 Mbps.

A wideband channel can be devoted to proving a single virtual circuit between a pair of communicating stations, or the capacity of a single wideband channel can be split to provide lower capacity virtual circuits that can be used by different pairs of communicating stations. Any number of the wideband channels can also be devoted to packet-switching service and can be used to increase the capacity of the packet-data channel. Thus, the capacity of the packet-data channel can grow in 6.144 Mbps increments.

Future Direction

FDDI II represents a refinement of the shared access technology used in local area networks that allows the LAN to be used for applications that are better suited to circuit switching. However, the future direction of networking technology to support both data and nondata applications most probably lies in the use of Asynchronous Transfer Mode (ATM) technology in which any pair of communicating stations is always provided with a high-speed virtual circuit. ATM technology is described in Appendix C

FDDI PRODUCTS

A number of vendors, including Digital Equipment Corporation and IBM, are marketing, or planning to market, FDDI concentrators, network interface cards (NICs), and FDDI network infrastructure components. As mentioned earlier, networking equipment vendors are implementing FDDI products using the fiber-optic transmission medium described in the standard and also other transmission media, such as twisted-pair cable.

DEC FDDI Architectural Model

As an example of one vendor's approach to FDDI product implementation, we will look at the architecture of Digital Equipment Corporation's FDDI product line.

Figure 14.20 shows the FDDI architectural model that DEC has defined. It is based on the architectural model defined in the FDDI standard and is in conformance with the standard but has a few extra elements. The following are descriptions of the components that have been added to or are different from the architectural model defined in the FDDI standard.

Station

DEC's definition of an FDDI station is slightly different from the definition in the FDDI standard. In DEC's FDDI architecture, a station is considered to be an instance of an SMT component and the components that an SMT component controls. Different types of stations can be implemented that contain the other architectural components in various combinations. A device that is used as a concentrator only, and has no LLC or MAC sublayer components, is still considered a station in DEC's architecture, even though it is not an addressable component and is transparent to other stations on the network.

Link Component

The DEC FDDI architectural model defines a *link* component as being an instance of the LLC and MAC sublayers in a station. A DEC FDDI station can implement zero, one, or two link components, depending on the use to which the station is put.

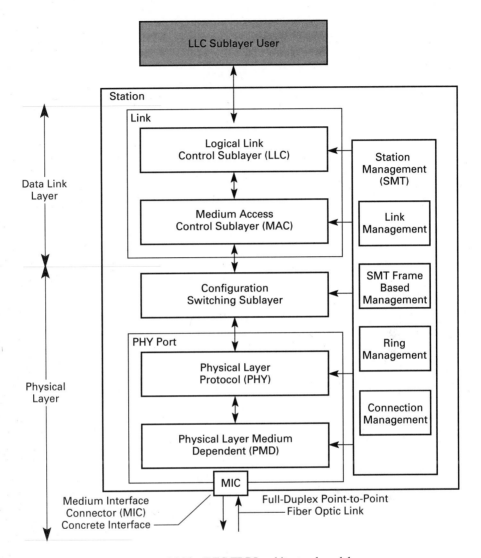

Figure 14.20   DEC FDDI architectural model.

Configuration and Switching Sublayer

The DEC FDDI architectural model also adds an explicit *Configuration and Switching* sublayer between the MAC sublayer and the PHY sublayer. It allows the ports (called *PHY ports* in the DEC architectural model) and link components in a station to be interconnected in various ways. This allows the station configuration to be changed to determine the local topology of the network and allows any link component or PHY port to be enabled or disabled as a result of a network management action. The Configuration and Switching sublayer can determine the path that information takes through the station when new connections become available or when connections are removed.

Station Management Component

The station management (SMT) component is responsible for monitoring the operation of the station and for controlling the various management-oriented attributes of other station components. The DEC SMT component implements the following functions:

- **Link Management.** Monitors and controls the link components in a station.

- **SMT Frame-Based Management.** Monitors and controls functions associated with the transmission of SMT MAC frames used by SMT components in communicating with each other over the network.

- **Ring Management.** Monitors and controls functions associated with ensuring the proper operation of the logical ring, such as identifying when a break in the logical ring has occurred.

- **Connection Management.** Monitors and controls the operation of the various PHY Ports implemented in a station.

Station Configurations

The architectural models of the specific station types that DEC specifies are similar to those specified in the FDDI standard. Figure 14.21 shows the DEC architectural models for three commonly used station types:

- **Single-Attachment Station.** A DEC single-attachment station (SAS) implements a single link component and a single PHY port with a MIC of type S. A single-attachment station is ordinarily connected to a concentrator that implements a MIC of type M.

- **Dual-Attachment Station.** A DEC dual-attachment station (DAS) can implement either one or two link components and implements exactly two PHY ports, one with a MIC of type A and another with a MIC of type B. A configuration switch component is provided in a dual-attachment station to control the data paths between the two PHY ports and the link components to direct the flow of data through the station.

- **Dual-Attachment Concentrator.** A DEC dual-attachment concentrator (DAC) can implement zero, one, or two link components and three or more PHY ports, one with a MIC of type A, another with a MIC of type B, and one or more with MICs of type M. A dual-attachment concentrator that is designed to provide only a concentrator function is likely to implement zero link components. Like a dual-attachment station, a dual-attachment concentrator provides a configuration switch component to control the data paths between the PHY ports and the link components (if any) to direct the flow of data through the concentrator.

Network Topology

DEC recommends using the dual ring of trees topology in which individual single-attachment stations are attached to concentrators that are interconnected using the dual ring. The primary ring is used for data transmission, and the secondary ring is used for recovering from link and station failures. The Configuration and Switching sublayer of the DEC FDDI architecture defines functions that can be used for dynamically recovering from failures using the reconfiguration techniques described earlier in this chapter.

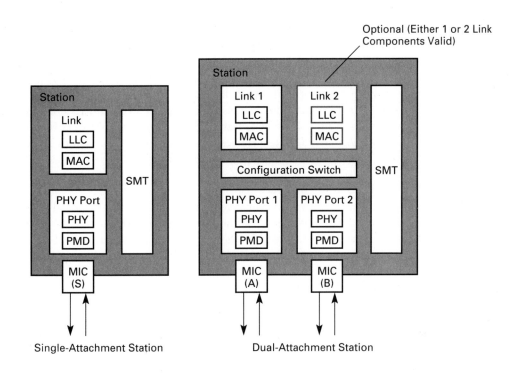

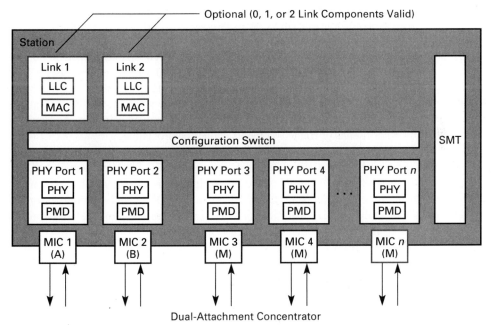

Figure 14.21   DEC FDDI station architectural models.

Interconnecting FDDI and Ethernet LANs

The DEC FDDI architecture provides provision for using an FDDI LAN as a backbone for individual Ethernet LAN data links. To handle such extended LANs, the LLC sublayer in DEC's FDDI architecture provides for handling *mapped Ethernet frames*. A mapped Ethernet frame is encapsulated within an IEEE/ISO SNAP PDU, which is, in turn, enclosed in an FDDI MAC frame for transmission across an FDDI data link. This allows frames originating from FDDI NICs, frames originating from NICs conforming to the IEEE/ISO CSMA/CD standard, and frames originating from NICs conforming to the *Ethernet Version 2 Specification* to all coexist in the same network.

Frame Stripping and Purging

One of the properties of a local area network that uses a ring topology and a token-passing access protocol is that it is possible for a frame to circulate indefinitely. A frame that is not removed after its first traversal of the ring is called a *no-owner frame*.

The FDDI standard specifies a single method for removing frames from the ring, a process called *frame stripping*. The frame stripping procedure defined in the FDDI standard does not guarantee that no-owner frames will always be removed from the ring. With the frame stripping procedure defined in the standard, a MAC sublayer entity that transmits a frame onto the ring has the responsibility of removing it when the frame has circulated all the way around the ring and returns to the source MAC sublayer entity. A MAC sublayer entity does this by recognizing the source MAC address in a frame it receives as being equal to its own MAC address. This method for stripping frames from the ring is adequate when a transmitting MAC sublayer entity transmits only frames having its own MAC address as the source MAC address.

However, in an extended LAN that implements bridges, a MAC sublayer entity in a bridge may transmit frames onto a ring that have originated in a station on some other LAN data link. (Bridges are discussed in Chapters 16 and 19.) In such a case, a MAC sublayer entity in a bridge may transmit frames onto the ring with source MAC addresses that are different from the bridge's own MAC address. Such frames have the potential of becoming no-owner frames. Other conditions, such as transmission errors, may also result in no-owner frames or frame fragments endlessly circulating.

DEC's FDDI architecture defines a *frame content independent stripping* (FCIS) algorithm and a *ring purging* algorithm, that are used in DEC FDDI products. MAC sublayer entities in DEC FDDI products use these algorithms to remove frames from the ring. Although these algorithms are not specified in the FDDI standard, they perform no operations that violate FDDI specifications. They also operate properly on a ring that contains stations that do not implement the DEC algorithms.

Frame Content Independent Stripping

To implement the FCIS algorithm, each DEC MAC sublayer entity maintains a local count of the frames it has transmitted onto the ring but has not yet stripped since the last time it received the token. The station also transmits a Void frame after it finishes transmitting a set of MAC frames onto the ring. Stations that do not implement the FCIS algorithm ignore Void frames and simply repeat them around the ring.

  The MAC sublayer entity transmitting a Void frame sets the Void frame's source MAC address field equal to the MAC sublayer entity's own MAC address. The MAC sublayer entity then strips from the ring any frame it receives—even if the frame's source MAC address field value is not equal to its own MAC address—and reduces its transmitted frame count by one for each error-free frame it strips. The MAC sublayer entity continues stripping the frames it receives until one of three termination conditions occurs:

- The station's transmitted frame count reaches 0.
- It receives a token.
- It receives its own error-free Void frame, a Claim frame, or a Beacon frame.

DEC's FCIS algorithm guarantees that a station will always strip the frames that it transmitted, no matter what source MAC addresses they contain, but will not inadvertently strip frames transmitted by other stations. The algorithm works because the frames a station receives first after it has transmitted the token will always be the frames that *it* transmitted. Frames generated by stations downstream on the ring must always follow the frames the station itself transmitted. The three termination conditions guarantee that there is a low probability of stripping too many frames from the ring and a *very* low probability of not stripping enough frames, even when one or more frames are corrupted as they circulate around the ring.

Ring Purging

  In addition to the FCIS algorithm, DEC's FDDI products also include an additional *ring purger algorithm* that reliably removes no-owner frames from the ring. The ring purger algorithms consist of an election algorithm and a purging algorithm.

- **Election Algorithm.** The *election algorithm* is used to choose one of the stations on the ring to be the *ring purger.* The primary purpose of the ring purger election algorithm is to ensure that there is one and only one ring purger operating on the ring at any given time. It recovers from ring initializations and from failure of the station acting as the ring purger. Each time the ring is initialized, a station becomes the ring purger if it is the winner of the claim token procedure or if it was the ring purger prior to ring initialization. A ring purger periodically announces its presence on the ring by transmitting a Purger Hello frame. If there is no ring purger after ring initialization, or at any time during the operation of the ring, a new ring purger is elected using a broadcast election protocol. The election algorithm is designed to elect one and only one station to be the ring purger.

- **Purging Algorithm.** The station designated as the ring purger runs the *purging algorithm* to remove no-owner frames and frame fragments from the ring. In running the purging algorithm, the station designated as the ring purger waits for a token. Once that station captures a token, it transmits any frames it has to transmit. After the ring purger's transmissions are completed, it transmits two Void frames. The Void frames mark the end of transmission of the ring purger's frames. When the ring is operating normally, the ring purger should receive only the frames it sent, followed by its own Void frames. The ring purger strips from the ring all frames and frame fragments that it receives until it receives its Void frames. It then strips the two Void frames and ceases stripping frames from the ring. If there are any no-owner frames circulating on the ring, the ring purger will strip these from the ring while stripping the frames that precede its own Void frames. The ring purger does not begin another purging operation until it receives the token. The ring purger also stops the purging algorithm if it receives a Beacon frame or a Claim frame. With a ring purger active on the ring, no frame will circulate as a no-owner frame for more than one traversal around the ring. These frames will therefore be received at most only twice by any destination station.

SUMMARY

The Fiber Distributed Data Interface (FDDI) standard defines a multiaccess form of data link that uses a ring-structured network topology. Stations are connected to one another using point-to-point fiber-optic cable segments to form a ring, and stations pass frames from one station to the next so that all stations eventually receive all frames that are transmitted.

The FDDI service definition defines an MA_UNITDATA unconfirmed data transfer service and an MA_TOKEN token request service. The FDDI protocol specification defines the format of the MAC-SDU, specifies how the MAC-SDU is encapsulated in a MAC-PDU, and documents the procedures controlling the exchange of MAC-PDUs between communicating stations.

With the FDDI access control method, a data unit, called the token, is passed from one station to the next around a physical ring. When a station receives the token, it is allowed to transmit MAC frames for a specified time. After a station finishes transmitting frames, it immediately transmits a token granting the next station on the ring the right to transmit frames. Frames from multiple stations can all be circulating at any time around the ring. Each station that receives a frame can set bits in the frame that indicate whether the destination MAC address was recognized, the frame was copied, or an error was detected. The station that originates a frame is responsible for removing that frame from the ring after it has circulated all the way around.

The FDDI standard defines optional procedures for implementing a capacity allocation scheme using synchronous and asynchronous frames and a multiframe dialog mechanism using restricted tokens.

The FDDI standard defines architectural models for various types of stations, including dual-attachment stations, dual-attachment concentrators, single-attachment stations, single-attachment concentrators, and null-attachment concentrators. Stations are connected using full-duplex transmission medium segments that allow dual ring and tree structures to be formed. The dual ring formed by dual-attachment stations and concentrators allow the ring structure to be dynamically reconfigured to recover from station and link failures.

The FDDI standard defines a fiber-optic transmission medium supporting baseband transmission at a 100 Mbps data rate. Some implementations of the standard use twisted-pair cable.

Chapter 15 describes the LocalTalk form of LAN data link that is defined by AppleTalk, Apple's networking system. LocalTalk uses the carrier sense multiple access with collision avoidance (CSMA/CA) medium access control method to implement bus- or tree-structured LAN data links.

Chapter **15**

Apple LocalTalk

The popularity of Apple computer systems in the business environment has led to increased use of Apple's networking protocol family, called *AppleTalk*. Support for many of the AppleTalk protocols have been included as a standard part of Apple hardware and system software so that basic networking capability is included in every machine. The protocols are also built into other devices, such as many laser printers, so that Macintosh networks with shared printer capability can be built simply by plugging the devices together with the appropriate cables.

The AppleTalk protocol family does not conform completely to the OSI model or to the IEEE/ISO/ANSI LAN architecture. However, AppleTalk includes protocols that correspond to many of the functions defined by the Data Link and Physical layers of the IEEE/ISO/ANSI LAN architecture as well as protocols that operate in the upper layers of the OSI model. In this chapter, we describe the protocols that AppleTalk defines for the Data Link and Physical layers. Chapters 17 and 24 describe the AppleTalk protocols that operate in the upper layers of the OSI model.

The AppleTalk protocol family includes its own LAN data link protocol, called the *LocalTalk Link Access Protocol* (LLAP). It defines operations that are associated with the Physical and Data Link layers of the OSI model and performs functions that are analogous to the protocols described in the previous chapters.

AppleTalk also supports the use of Ethernet and Token Ring LAN data links in the Data Link and Physical layers. The use of Ethernet and Token Ring LAN data links are also described in this chapter.

NETWORK CONNECTION

A typical Apple computer includes serial ports that can be used for a variety of purposes, including attaching the computer to a LocalTalk network. The serial port is connected to the network using an inexpensive external connector that interfaces with the LAN transmission medium. LocalTalk Network Interface Cards (NICs) are also available for computing systems other than Apple computers, such as IBM-compatible personal computers and various types of workstations. LocalTalk NICs allow the same external connectors used with Apple computer systems to connect to a LocalTalk LAN data link. A typical small LocalTalk LAN consisting of Apple personal computers, an IBM-compatible personal computer, and a printer is shown in Fig. 15.1.

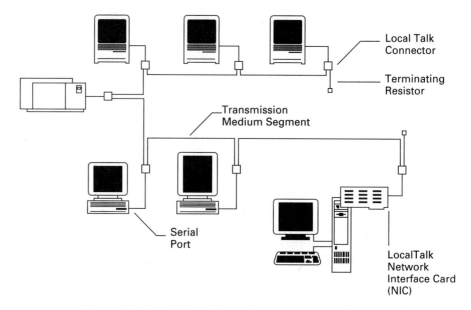

Figure 15.1   LocalTalk LAN data link daisy-chain configuration.

NETWORK TOPOLOGY AND TRANSMISSION MEDIUM

LocalTalk uses a bus- or tree-structured topology using twisted-pair cable as the most commonly used form of transmission medium. Optical fiber is also used with some LocalTalk implementations. The LocalTalk specification defines a data rate of 230.4 Kbps, but some LocalTalk implementations support a higher data rate. LocalTalk is designed to allow up to 32 devices to be attached to a single LocalTalk data link; however, larger AppleTalk networks can be constructed using network interconnection devices.

LocalTalk Connectors

The original form of transmission medium defined for use with LocalTalk data links used an external connector that attached to shielded twisted-pair cable segments to create a daisy-chain configuration. These external connectors are often called *LocalTalk connectors*. The maximum total cable length defined by the LocalTalk specification is 300 meters, but each implementation defines its own cable-length limitations.

PhoneNet Connectors

Different external connectors are available from a variety of vendors to support ordinary telephone wiring as a transmission medium. These connectors are sometimes called PhoneNet or PhoneTalk connectors. Cable length limitations when using external connectors that support unshielded telephone wiring are defined by the vendor supplying the external connector.

LOCALTALK DATA LINK ADDRESSING

On a LocalTalk LAN data link, each system is identified by a unique 8-bit Data Link address, called a *node ID* value. Node IDs are not assigned externally or hard coded in network devices. Instead, the LocalTalk specification defines a mechanism that is used to dynamically assign a unique node ID to each system when it physically attaches itself to an LLAP LAN data link.

Node ID Assignment

When a system is activated, the LocalTalk process running in a system makes a *guess* at the system's node ID value by extracting a value from some form of long-term memory, such as nonvolatile RAM or disk, or by generating a random number. It then checks to see if the guessed node ID value is already in use by some other device on the network. LLAP does this by placing its guessed node ID value in an Enquiry control frame and broadcasting it to all systems on the data link. If another system is using the guessed node ID value, it sends back an acknowledgment, indicating that the guessed node ID value is already in use. The new system then generates a new node ID value and repeats the verification process.

If the system receives no acknowledgment to its Enquiry frame, it assumes that its guessed node ID value is unique and accepts that value as the system's permanent node ID value. Since LLAP does not provide a reliable data transfer service, there is no guarantee that all systems will receive an Enquiry frame. Therefore, a system broadcasts a series of Enquiry control frames to increase the chances that all systems on the data link will receive it. Mechanisms are provided that recover from situations in which a system inadvertently assigns a nonunique node ID value because of a delay in receiving an acknowledgment to an Enquiry frame.

AppleTalk systems are divided into two classes—*server systems* and *client systems*. Client systems are sometimes referred to as *workstations* in AppleTalk documentation. Each class of system uses a different range of node ID values. Server systems use node ID values that range from 128 to 254; client systems use node ID values that range from 1 to 127. A server system implements more extensive checking in assigning its own node ID value than do client systems. This is because network operation can be disrupted if a system inadvertently acquires a node ID value that is the same as that of some active server in the network.

LLAP FRAME FORMAT

LLAP frames are used to carry user data and are also generated by LLAP itself to control frame transmission. Box 15.1 shows the format of the LLAP frame and describes its fields.

BOX 15.1 LocalTalk link access protocol (LLAP) frame.

Preamble	Dest. Node ID	Source Node ID	LLAP Type	Data	Frame Check Sequence	Flag	Abort Sequence
At least 2 octets	1 octet	1 octet	1 octet	0–596 octets	2 octets	1 octet	12–18 bits

- **Preamble.** A sequence of at least 12 octets containing flag values having the bit configuration 01111110.
- **Station Addresses.** A Destination Node ID value and a Source Node ID value that identify the destination and source stations.
- **LLAP Type.** Identifies the frame's type.
- **Data.** Contains 0-600 octets of user data or control information.
- **Frame Check Sequence.** A cyclical redundancy check (CRC) value used for error detection. A CRC value is calculated by the source system based on the contents of the LLAP frame. In the destination system, the CRC value is calculated based on the contents of the received frame. If the calculated value does not match the received value, the frame is discarded as being in error.
- **Flag.** A single flag octet containing the bit configuration 01111110.
- **Abort Sequence.** A sequence of 12-18 1 bits.

The AppleTalk specifications make a distinction between the *LLAP packet* and the *LLAP frame*. The LLAP packet consists of the Station Address, Type, and Data fields. The LLAP frame consists of the LLAP packet encapsulated by the Preamble field and a *trailer* that consists of the Frame Check Sequence, Ending Flag, and Abort Sequence fields.*

LLAP MEDIUM ACCESS CONTROL

The medium access control method used on an LLAP data link is designed for the purpose of transmitting frames across a single AppleTalk LAN data link. Delivery of frames is on a best-efforts basis, with no acknowledgments or retransmissions of corrupted frames.

CSMA/CA

An LLAP data link uses a *carrier sense multiple access with collision avoidance* (CSMA/CA) technique for controlling access to the transmission medium, which we

---

*Again, this is an unfortunate choice of terminology, since most authorities use the term *packet* to refer to the data unit exchanged by the layer above the Data Link layer, which is carried in the LLAP frame's Data field.

introduced in Chapter 3. With the LLAP variation of CSMA/CA medium access control, a transmitting system uses the Physical layer to sense the link and see if it is busy. If the link is busy, the system *defers* (waits until the link becomes idle). Once the transmitting system determines that the link is idle, it waits for a period of time called the minimum *interdialog gap* (IDG), which is typically 400 microseconds. If the link continues to be idle for this period, the system waits a further randomly generated length of time. If the link is still idle after the second wait, the system sends its frame.

The use of a random wait period reduces the chances of a collision occurring by making it relatively unlikely that two systems will attempt to transmit at the same time. LLAP does not perform functions to directly detect collisions. A system assumes that a collision has occurred if it does not receive an expected response within 200 microseconds, a period of time called the maximum *interframe gap* (IFG).

When a transmitting system does not receive an expected response, it retransmits the previous frame sent using the same waiting process. The method used to determine the random wait time is based on recent transmission history, using the number of deferrals and number of presumed collisions that have occurred while attempting to send the current frame. As the number of deferrals and collisions increases, the range from which the random number is chosen increases. Thus, when transmission loads are heavy and there is high contention for the transmission medium, the random wait time is selected from a relatively large range. This has the affect of spreading out over time the attempted transmissions of all the systems that are contending for access to the transmission medium. If the number of deferrals and collisions is small, the range is also small so that little time is spent waiting.

Transmission Dialogs

LLAP defines two types of frame transmission dialogs that are used:

- **Directed Transmission Dialogs.** A *directed transmission dialog* is used when a frame is being sent to a single destination system. The source system waits until the carrier has been idle for both the minimum IDG time and the random wait time. It then sends a Request-to-Send control frame to the intended destination. The destination system returns a Clear-to-Send control frame to the source system if it is able to receive the transmission. If the source system receives a Clear-to-Send frame within the expected response time, it then transmits the Data frame. If the source system does not receive the Clear-to-Send frame within the expected time, the source system assumes a collision has occurred and repeats the process.

- **Broadcast Transmission Dialogs.** A *broadcast transmission dialog* is used when a source system is sending a frame to all active systems on the network using the broadcast destination address. With a broadcast transmission dialog, the source system waits the minimum IDG time and a random wait time and then sends out a Request-to-Send control frame with a destination address value of 255. It then waits the maximum IFG time. If the source station receives no transmission during that time, it transmits the Data frame. If the source station detects a transmission during the maximum IFG time, the source system repeats the process.

With either of the foregoing forms of transmission dialog, if the source system is unable to transmit the data frame after 32 attempts, the Data Link layer reports a failure condition to the user of the LLAP service.

PHYSICAL LAYER SPECIFICATIONS

The LocalTalk Physical layer specifies the functions of bit encoding/decoding, signal transmission/reception, and carrier sensing. The encoding method specified is called *FM-0*. With FM-0, there is always a transition at the beginning of each bit time. For a 0 bit, there is also a transition in the middle of the bit time; for a 1 bit, there is no transition in the middle. Signal transmission is differential, balanced-voltage and is based on the EIA-422 signaling standard. The Physical layer carrier sensing function provides an indication to the Data Link layer of whether or not a transmission is in progress on the transmission medium.

ETHERTALK AND TOKENTALK LINK ACCESS PROTOCOLS

In addition to LocalTalk, the data link protocol defined in the AppleTalk specification, the AppleTalk protocol family supports the use of the IEEE/ISO CSMA/CD (Ethernet) and Token Ring protocols in the Data Link and Physical layers.

Ethernet support is provided through the *EtherTalk Link Access Protocol* (ELAP), and Token Ring support is provided through the *TokenTalk Link Access Protocol* (TLAP). In both cases, standard IEEE/ISO Logical Link Control (LLC) interfaces and data formats are used. Only the connectionless Type 1 LLC service is supported.

ELAP and TLAP Frame Formats

Figure 15.2 shows the frame formats used with EtherTalk and TokenTalk. They are the same as those defined in the IEEE/ISO Logical Link Control, CSMA/CD, and Token Ring standards. AppleTalk specifies the use of the IEEE/ISO Subnetwork Access Protocol (SNAP). Therefore, the DSAP and SSAP fields in the LLC header always carry the hexadecimal value 'AA'. A SNAP Identifier value of hex '080007809B' identifies the higher level protocol as the AppleTalk Datagram Delivery Protocol (DDP), the AppleTalk Network layer protocol.

AppleTalk Address Resolution Protocol (AARP)

As we have seen, each system on an AppleTalk data link is identified by a unique 8-bit node ID value. In order to send data using CSMA/CD or Token Ring frames, however, the destination address and source address values contained in the CSMA/CD or Token Ring frame must contain station address values as defined by the IEEE/ISO standards. CSMA/CD and Token Ring NICs employed on AppleTalk networks use 48-bit universal addressing and have globally-unique station addresses assigned to them. Therefore, a translation function is required to convert between 48-bit station addresses and the 8-bit node ID values that are used on an LLAP data link. This translation function is performed by the *AppleTalk Address Resolution Protocol* (AARP). AARP has other functions as well, which are described in Chapter 24.

With respect to the EtherTalk and TokenTalk protocols, the AppleTalk Address Resolution Protocol (AARP) provides the following services:

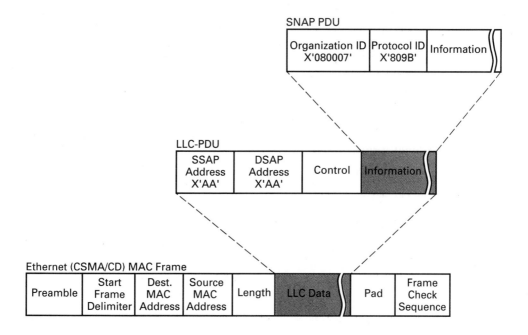

EtherTalk Frame Format

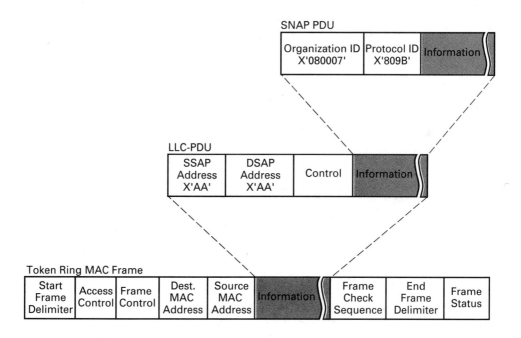

TokenTalk Frame Format

Figure 15.2 EtherTalk and TokenTalk frame formats.

- Translating between AppleTalk node ID values and CSMA/CD or Token Ring station addresses.
- Dynamically assigning a unique node ID value to a system when it is activated.
- Checking that a frame received has a destination node ID value that is addressed to the receiving system.

Broadcast Addresses

When an EtherTalk or TokenTalk system needs to send a frame to all systems on the network using the AppleTalk broadcast address, it translates the AppleTalk broadcast address into an appropriate group destination address. The broadcast group address is not used by EtherTalk and TokenTalk. Instead, an AppleTalk-defined group address is used that refers only to the AppleTalk stations on the LAN. When an AppleTalk system is activated, it must register itself as part of the AppleTalk broadcast group. This allows the AppleTalk protocols to operate correctly when the EtherTalk or TokenTalk protocols are used on a LAN on which traffic conforming to other protocols also exists.

SUMMARY

The LAN data link protocol defined by Apple's AppleTalk protocol family is the LocalTalk Link Access Protocol (LLAP). LocalTalk implements a multiaccess form of data link in which stations are attached, using LocalTalk connectors, in a bus- or tree-structured configuration using twisted-pair cable. A data rate of 230.4 Kbps is supported. A LocalTalk station dynamically chooses an 8-bit node ID value for use as a station address when the station is powered on and attached to the data link.

A LocalTalk LAN data link uses a carrier sense multiple access with collision avoidance (CSMA/CA) form of medium access control. With CSMA/CA, a station having a frame to transmit listens to the carrier and transmits when it determines that the medium is available. Stations use a deference process to reduce the likelihood of two stations transmitting at the same time. Stations retransmit frames when they determine that frames have been damaged by collisions. Collisions are assumed when expected responses to transmitted frames are not received.

The AppleTalk protocol family also supports the use of Ethernet LAN data links through the EtherTalk Link Access Protocol (ELAP) and Token Ring LAN data links through the TokenTalk Link Access Protocol (TLAP).

Chapter 16 begins Part IV of this book that discusses how multiple LAN data links can be interconnected to form enterprise internetworks, or internets. Chapter 16 introduces the internetworking environment and describes the functions of various types of devices that can be used to interconnect data links to form extended LANs and internets.

ENTERPRISE INTERNETWORKING

Local area network data links can be used in conjunction with network interconnection devices and wide area networking data links to form internets. Issues surrounding the construction of enterprise internetworks are the subject of this part of the book.

Chapter 16 introduces the internetworking environment and describes the functions of the different types of network interconnection devices that can be used to combine data links to form internets.

An internet can carry the data traffic generated by end systems that implement different high-level protocol families. Chapter 17 introduces the most commonly used Network layer and Transport layer protocols employed in computer networks.

Enterprise internetworks can be constructed that implement different data link technologies and can carry the data traffic conforming to multiple high-level protocol families. Issues relating to the construction of heterogeneous internets are discussed in Chapter 18.

Chapter 19 examines the operation of bridges in an extended LAN and discusses the differences between transparent bridges and source routing bridges.

Routers are used to construct enterprise internetworks that consist of two or more independent subnetworks. Chapter 20 describes the operation of routers in an internet.

Chapter 16

The Internetworking Environment

As we have seen in earlier chapters, it is becoming common in most organizations to use local area networks to give users access to computing power beyond that provided by their own desktop systems. LANs are often used to interconnect a number of computers in a particular location for the purpose of resource sharing. A challenge today in many organizations is to expand the reach of the LANs that have been created for individual workgroups so that they may serve the needs of the entire enterprise. In this chapter, we will see how various types of network interconnection devices and wide area networking data links can be used to interconnect individual LANs to create networks that span the entire enterprise.

INTERNETS AND SUBNETWORKS

A computer network, in which a number of relatively small physical networks are tied together to form a single, large logical network, is called an *enterprise internetwork*, or *internet* for short. The structure of a simple enterprise internetwork is shown in Fig. 16.1.

The systems making up an internet are interconnected by *data links*. Systems and data links together form *subnetworks*. We define a subnetwork as a collection of systems that are attached to a single virtual transmission medium so that each system in the subnetwork is one hop from any other system on that subnetwork. A *hop* is defined as a traversal from one system to another across a single data link.

A subnetwork employing a broadcast form of data link technology, such as a local area network, can contain two or more systems—a subnetwork employing a point-to-point form of data link technology, such as wide area networking data link, has exactly two systems. An important characteristic of a subnetwork is that it appears to software operating in layers above the Data Link layer of the OSI model as if any device in the subnetwork can communicate directly with any other device in the subnetwork.

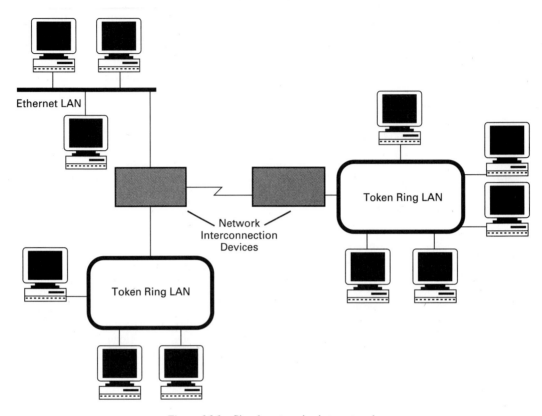

Figure 16.1   Simple enterprise internetwork.

ENTERPRISE INTERNETWORKS

As we have seen, networking facilities are often used to implement a client-server environment in which individuals using desktop systems can access the facilities of server systems also attached to the LAN. A client-server environment can be useful in an individual workgroup that is served by a single LAN. However, a client-server environment that operates between departments within an enterprise, and with other enterprises as well, can be even more powerful. Enterprise internetworks can also provide an organization with access to general sources of public information. This chapter introduces the technologies that are used to construct enterprise internetworks.

Growth of Enterprise Internetworks

An important characteristic of enterprise internetworks is that, in most cases, they are not explicitly designed and coordinated from a single centralized location. Enterprise internetworks typically grow and evolve over time as the organization's networking needs change and mature, and the planning for them often occurs on an ad hoc basis.

Heterogeneity

Another characteristic of enterprise internetworks is that a variety of networking technologies are often employed in constructing the network. Heterogeneity also applies to the software that uses the physical network for communication. An enterprise internetwork may need to carry traffic generated by different types of networking software. Different types of high-level networking software conform to different network architectures and employ different communication protocols. The most widely used of these are described in Chapter 17.

For example, one user who is employing communication software that conforms to the TCP/IP protocol suite, a popular set of communications protocols used in many environments, may be operating in the role of a client and may be accessing server software running on other TCP/IP systems. In the same internet, a user who is employing Novell NetWare client software may be requesting access to a NetWare server also attached to the internet, as shown in Fig. 16.2.

Chapter 18 examines many of the factors involved in constructing heterogeneous enterprise internetworks.

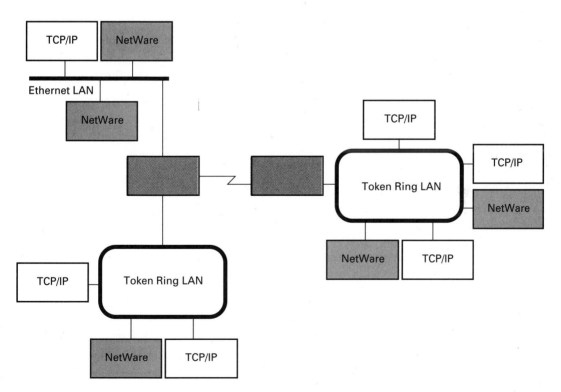

Figure 16.2   Heterogeneous enterprise internetwork.

INTERCONNECTED LAN CONFIGURATIONS

Local area networks can be interconnected in a number of different ways to form internets, some of which are illustrated in Fig. 16.3:

- **Direct Interconnection.** Two or more physical LANs in the same geographical location can be directly connected to one another to form a larger subnetwork, sometimes called an *extended LAN*. The individual LANs can be of the same or of different types. For example, some of the LANs may be Ethernet, others may be Token Ring, and still others may be LocalTalk.

- **WAN Data Link Interconnection.** Two or more physical LANs in different geographical locations can be connected by telecommunications facilities that support transmission over arbitrary distances. In some cases, the telecommunications facilities may support lower transmission speeds than the LANs. For example, a T1 telecommunications facility, supporting a transmission speed of 1.544 Mbps, may be used to connect two Ethernet LANs.

- **Backbone LAN Interconnection.** Individual physical LANs can be connected to a backbone LAN. A backbone LAN often consists of one LAN to which two or more other LANs are attached. Individual systems are not attached directly to the backbone but to the attached LANs. In some cases, the backbone LAN may support a higher transmission speed than the individual LANs that are attached to it. For example, individual Ethernet and Token Ring LANs may be connected to an FDDI backbone.

Backbone Networks

Interconnecting individual physical LANs using a backbone LAN offers many advantages over other network interconnection methods:

- The individual LANs are able to operate in parallel. Each individual LAN can continue to operate if one of the other individual LANs or the backbone LAN fails.

- The backbone LAN can filter message traffic and only forward messages to a particular individual LAN if those messages are destined for stations on it.

- A backbone LAN can be optimized to provide high bandwidth, to transmit across long distances, and to be highly reliable.

- Each individual LAN attached to the backbone can be optimized for flexibility and can support low-cost user connections.

Optical fiber and microwave-based links are particularly suited for use in a backbone LAN because of their ability to provide high bandwidth and to support long transmission distances.

INTERNETWORKING ELEMENTS

Enterprise internetworks are typically constructed using three different elements: *local area network data links*, *wide area networking data links*, and *network interconnection devices*.

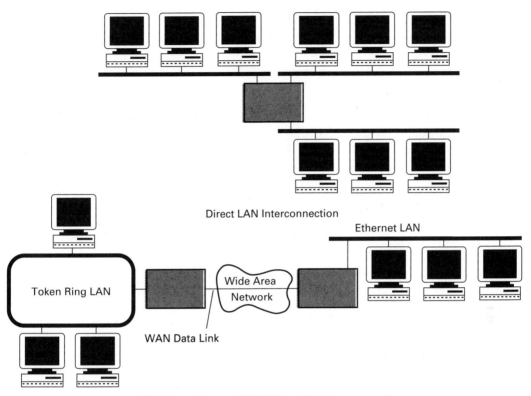

Direct LAN Interconnection

Wide Area Network (WAN) Data Link Interconnection

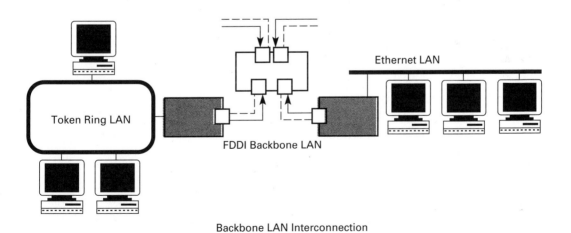

Backbone LAN Interconnection

Figure 16.3   LAN interconnection configurations.

Local Area Network Data Links

The preceding chapters have described the local area networking data link technologies that are typically employed to interconnect computing systems in individual work groups. As we have seen, local area networks have evolved as a way to meet the requirements for high-speed, relatively short-distance communication among computing systems. LAN data links are normally constrained to being within a single building or within a campus of buildings. They do not ordinarily cross public thoroughfares and normally operate over private cabling. Local area networking facilities are generally used to create many-to-many networks that allow any device on the data link to physically communicate with any other device on the data link.

Wide Area Network Data Links

When local area networks are located close together, network interconnection devices alone (described later) can be used to hook them together. But when the LANs are located in widely separated locations, *wide area network* (WAN) data links are often used in conjunction with network interconnection devices to interconnect the LANs. Wide area network data links are most often used to implement point-to-point connections between pairs of network interconnection devices.

Commonly used data transfer speeds supported over common carrier telecommunications facilities include 9600 bps, 14,400 bps, 19,200 bps, and 56,000 bps. Digital T1 and T3 facilities, also available from common carriers, are also widely used in enterprise internetworks. T1 and T3 facilities provide bit rates of 1.544 and 45 megabits per second (Mbps) respectively. Common carriers also provide fractional T1 data links that allow multiple users to share a single T1 communication facility. A number of other types of public telecommunications facilities are also coming into common use.

Some of the commonly used wide area networking facilities that are used in computer networks include

- Common Carrier Telecommunications Data Links
- X.25 Packet Switched Public Data Network Links
- Frame Relay Links
- Narrowband ISDN Links
- Wideband ISDN Links
- Distributed Queue Dual Bus (DQDB) Links
- Switched Multimegabit Data Service (SMDS) Links

The characteristics of these various types of wide area networking data link technologies are described in Appendix B. A future networking technology, called *Asynchronous Transfer Mode* (ATM), is described in Appendix C. ATM has the potential for integrating LAN and WAN transmission.

Network Interconnection Devices

To create flexible enterprise internetworks, it is necessary to interconnect individual local area network data links and wide area networking facilities. There are a number of different types of devices that can be used to accomplish this. Each has its own unique uses and is appropriate for different forms of network interconnection. The types of devices that are available for network interconnection can be divided into the following general categories:

- Repeaters
- Bridges
- Routers
- Switches
- Converters

This chapter introduces the differences between the various categories of network interconnection devices. Note that some actual network interconnection devices available from networking infrastructure vendors perform more than one of the foregoing network interconnection functions.

Of the five categories of network interconnection devices, it is generally easy to determine when to use repeaters, switches, and converters in an internetworking situation. But the decision concerning when to use a bridge and when to use a router is more difficult to make. Therefore, the functions of bridges are explored in detail in Chapter 19, and the functions of routers are examined more thoroughly in Chapter 20.

The following sections describe each of the five major types of network interconnection devices.

REPEATERS

The simplest facility used for network interconnection is the *repeater*. The major function of a repeater is to receive a signal from one LAN cable segment and to retransmit it, regenerating the signal at its original strength over one or more other cable segments. A repeater operates in the OSI model Physical layer and is transparent to all the protocols operating in the layers above the Physical layer, as shown in Fig. 16.4.

A specific local area network implementation usually places a limit on the physical size of any single cable segment. This limit is based on the physical medium and transmission technique used. Repeaters allow a network to be constructed that exceeds the size limit of a single physical cable segment. The number of repeaters that can be used in tandem is generally limited by a particular LAN implementation.

Using a repeater between two or more LAN cable segments requires that the same Physical layer protocols be used to send signals over all the cable segments. For example, as shown in Chapter 10, two LAN cable segments in an Ethernet LAN that both use base-

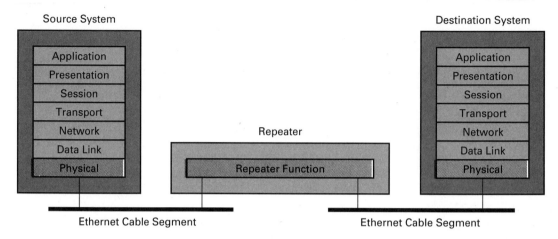

Figure 16.4   A repeater performs its function in the Physical layer.

band transmission could be connected with a repeater. Different types of physical transmission media can be connected using a properly designed repeater, as long as they all handle similar types of signals. For example, Ethernet repeaters are available that allow all the various types of baseband Ethernet transmission media—including 10BASE5 coaxial cable segments, FOIRL inter-repeater link cable segments, 10BASE2 coaxial cable segments, and 10BASE-T twisted-pair cable segments—to be interconnected in the same LAN.

Bus and Tree Structures

Repeaters are used in bus-structured local area networks, such as an Ethernet LAN, to connect individual cable segments to form a larger local area network. In ring-structured local area networks, such as a Token Ring LAN, every station performs the function of a repeater, and separate repeaters are not used.

A repeater can retransmit the signal over a single cable segment to create a longer bus structure. Or a repeater might retransmit the signal over multiple cable segments to create a tree-structured LAN. Repeaters are typically used to interconnect cable segments that are located relatively close together. Repeaters cannot be used to interconnect a LAN data link and a wide area network data link.

Transparency

Repeaters are generally transparent to the networking software operating in the individual computers attached to a local area network. The main characteristics of a repeater is that all the signals that are generated on the cable segment on one side of the repeater are propagated to the cable segment or segments on the other side of the repeater. A repeater implements no form of filtering capability.

The chief advantages of repeaters are simplicity and low cost. The chief disadvantage is that repeaters provide no method for isolating the traffic generated on one cable segment from traffic generated by the others. When a repeater is used to connect cable segment A to cable segment B, all the signals that are generated on segment A are forwarded to segment B, whether or not there is a station on segment B that is the destination of those signals.

BRIDGES

A bridge also forwards frames from one LAN segment to another, but bridges can be more flexible and intelligent than repeaters. A *bridge* interconnects separate LAN or WAN data links rather than just cable segments. Some bridges learn the addresses of the stations that can be reached over each data link they bridge so they can selectively relay only traffic that needs to flow across each bridge. The bridge function operates in the Medium Access Control sublayer and is transparent to software operating in the layers above the MAC sublayer, as shown in Fig. 16.5.

A bridge can interconnect networks that use different transmission techniques and/or different medium access control methods. For example, a bridge might be used to interconnect an Ethernet LAN using broadband transmission with an Ethernet LAN using baseband transmission. A bridge might also be used to interconnect an Ethernet LAN with a Token Ring or FDDI LAN. A bridge must be able to resolve any differences in frame formats among the data links it interconnects.

Multiple bridges can be used to interconnect a series of networks. A bridge can also be designed to connect a LAN data link to a wide area networking telecommunications

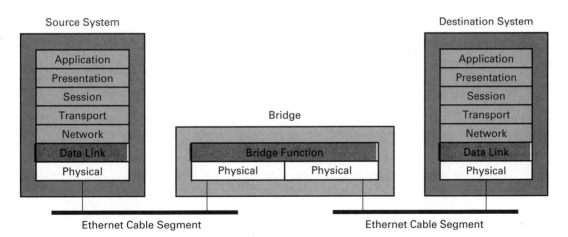

Figure 16.5 A bridge performs its functions in the Data Link layer.

facility. A pair of bridges with a telecommunications facility between them can be used to interconnect two LANs that are located in different geographical locations.

The mechanism implemented by a bridge is often called a *store-and-forward* facility, since messages are temporarily *stored* in the bridge and then *forwarded* to a station on some other LAN.

Extended LANs

As with repeaters, the collection of individual LAN data links that are interconnected by bridges are considered to be a single subnetwork. Each of the station addresses throughout the subnetwork must be unique and must use the same station address format. A LAN subnetwork constructed using bridges is sometimes called an *extended LAN* to differentiate it from a single physical LAN. Software operating in the layers above the MAC sublayer view the extended LAN as if it were a single LAN data link.

Frame Filtering

A bridge can implement a *frame filtering* mechanism. Such a bridge, often called a *filtering bridge*, receives all frames that are transmitted over each data link to which it is attached. The bridge then determines, based on each frame's destination address, whether or not the frame should be transmitted across the bridge to any of the other data links to which it is also attached. Thus, a bridge can isolate some of the network traffic that is generated on one LAN data link from the other LAN data links in the extended LAN.

Broadcast traffic generated on one LAN, however, is typically always transmitted across a bridge to all the other data links to which it is attached. Therefore, broadcast traffic generated by any station is received by all the stations on the extended LAN.

Bridge Types

Two types of bridges are in common use in enterprise internetworks—*spanning tree* bridges and *source routing* bridges—and are described below:

- **Spanning Tree Bridges.** Spanning tree bridges are used to form tree structures in which only one active path connects any two stations in the extended LAN. Spanning tree bridges are transparent to ordinary stations on the interconnected LANs. A spanning tree bridge learns appropriate routes for frames by observing transmissions that take place on the data links to which the bridge is connected. It then forwards frames over the appropriate data links when required.

- **Source Routing Bridges.** Source routing bridges are typically used only with Token Ring LANs. More than one path through source routing bridges can interconnect any two LAN stations. With source routing bridges, each station is expected to know the route over which to send each frame. If a station does not know the route, or if a previously known route is no longer active, the station broadcasts Route Discovery frames over the extended LAN and then determines from the responses that come back the appropriate route to use.

The mechanisms used by transparent bridges and source routing bridges are described further in Chapter 19.

ROUTERS

Routers provide the ability to route messages from one system to another where there may be multiple paths between them. A router performs its function in the OSI model Network layer, as shown in Fig. 16.6. Routers typically have more intelligence than bridges and can be used to construct enterprise internetworks of almost arbitrary complexity. Interconnected routers in an internet all participate in a distributed algorithm to decide on the optimal path over which each message should travel from a source system to a destination system. However, routers must have more detailed knowledge than bridges about the protocols that are used to carry messages through the internet.

Traffic Isolation

On an individual LAN data link, each station on the LAN typically receives all messages that are transmitted. A receiving station uses the destination MAC address field in each frame it receives to determine if it should process the frame. With an extended LAN implemented using bridges, the bridges can filter some of the frames, but broadcast traffic generated on one LAN is propagated to all the stations on the extended LAN.

Routers can be used to interconnect a number of individual LANs or extended LANs in such a way that the traffic generated on one LAN is better isolated from the traffic generated on other LANs in the internet. Like bridges, routers can be used to interconnect different types of data links. For example, a router can be used to connect two unlike local area networks or to connect a LAN data link to a WAN data link.

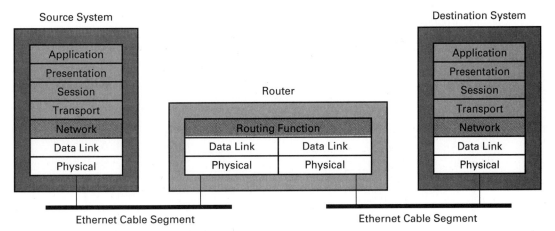

Figure 16.6   A router performs its functions in the Network layer.

Subnetworks

If two or more LANs are interconnected by routers, each of the individual LANs is considered to be a separate subnetwork. Although station addresses may be unique across the entire internet, this is not a requirement. Station addresses need only be unique within each subnetwork. A network addressing scheme, over and above the station addressing scheme employed on individual data links, must be implemented in an internet that uses routers for subnetwork interconnection. Addressing schemes used in the internetworking environment are described in Chapter 17.

Routing Function

In an enterprise internetwork implemented using routers, a message may pass through a series of routers in arriving at its final destination. There may be more than one possible sequence of systems through which a message might pass in traveling from the source system to the destination system.

A system of routers can implement multiple active paths between any two subnetworks. In some network implementations, it is possible for different messages traveling from a source system to a destination system to take different routes, and messages may arrive at the destination system out of sequence. The higher-level layers in such networks must have the capability for resequencing message segments.

End Systems and Intermediate Systems

In the internetworking environment, a router is often called an *intermediate system*. By contrast, systems that originate data traffic and serve as the final destination for that traffic are called *end systems*, as shown in Fig. 16.7.

In general, a router performs the routing function by determining the next system to which a message should be sent. It then transmits the message to the next system over the appropriate data link to bring the message closer to its final destination.

Routers are described further in Chapters 18 and 20.

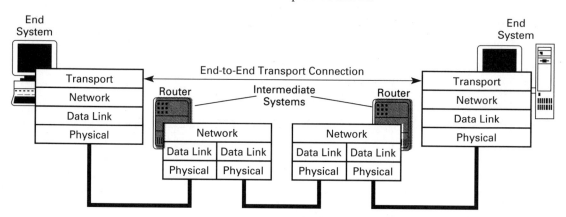

Figure 16.7   Routers act as intermediate systems between end systems.

SWITCHES

In addition to repeaters, bridges, and routers, a variety of different types of switching facilities can be used in constructing internets. The main purpose of interconnecting LAN data link segments using interconnection devices, such as repeaters and bridges, is to allow a greater degree of sharing of a common communication medium. Network interconnection devices allow a larger number of different network devices to be attached to the same LAN. All the systems attached to a LAN or extended LAN created using repeaters and bridges share the same physical transmission medium.

Switching devices are designed for the opposite purpose of repeaters and bridges. In some cases, when the number of devices attached to the same common transmission medium gets too large, the transmission capacity can be exceeded, especially when systems are transmitting large quantities of data between them. One of the ideas of routers is to allow network segments to be interconnected but to isolate one physical group of systems from another. Routers provide a good solution to this type of interconnection when the systems forming one workgroup are physically separated from the systems forming other workgroups. Figure 16.8 shows how three Ethernet LAN segments, each serving the needs of a different physical workgroup, can be interconnected using routers. Each workgroup can use almost the entire 10 Mbps capacity of its own LAN segment, with traffic flowing over the router only when a system in one workgroup needs to access a system in another workgroup.

In many cases, it is necessary to form logical workgroups among systems that may be in different physical locations. To accomplish this, the organization can install multiple, parallel transmission medium segments to which different systems can be attached, as illustrated in Fig. 16.9. Routers can still be used to interconnect the parallel transmission medium segments so that a system attached to one segment can communicate with a system attached to another segment. The router still isolates most of the network traffic generated on one transmission medium segment from traffic generated on the others.

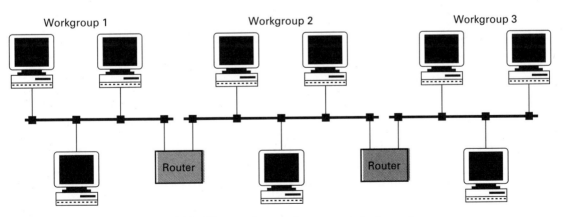

Figure 16.8   Three workgroups interconnected using routers.

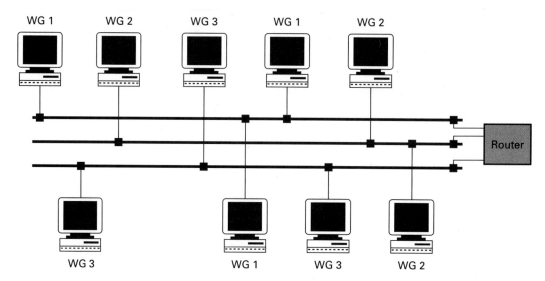

Figure 16.9   Multiple, parallel transmission medium segments.

Using multiple, parallel transmission medium segments provides a method for increasing the total transmission capacity that is available to the systems that are attached to each of the segments.

      Individual devices can be connected to an appropriate transmission medium segment, or hubs that implement switching facilities can be used to facilitate connecting systems to the appropriate transmission medium segments. The different types of hubs that can be used to connect those systems are module assignment hubs, bank assignment hubs, and port assignment hubs.

Module Assignment Hubs

With *module assignment* hubs, shown in Fig. 16.10, no switching facility is used within a hub to assign LAN bandwidth. Module assignment hubs, ordinary hubs, or multiport repeaters are used to connect groups of systems to an appropriate transmission medium segment.

Bank Assignment Hubs

With a *bank assignment* hub, a switching facility is implemented in the hub to allow each of the multiple banks of ports to be interconnected to one of the transmission medium segments, as shown in Fig. 16.11. With a bank assignment hub, an entire bank of ports in the hub is attached to the same transmission medium segment.

      The component that connects the hub to the transmission medium segments is sometimes called a *backplane*. Each bank of ports may be implemented on a circuit card that plugs into the backplane. A bank assignment hub allows switches to be set, either physically or through network management software, to determine the transmission medium segment in the backplane to which each bank of ports in the hub is connected.

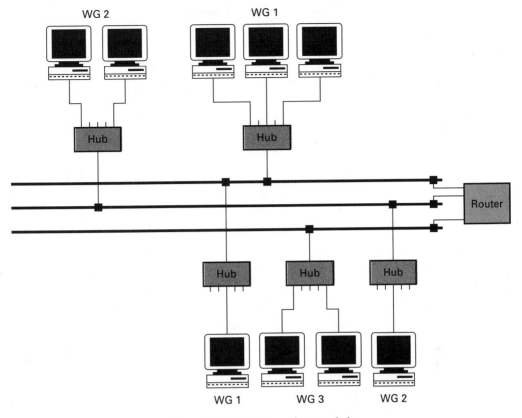

Figure 16.10 Module assignment hubs.

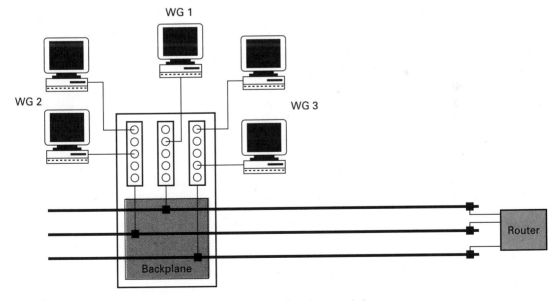

Figure 16.11 Bank assignment hub.

Port Assignment Hubs

With a *port assignment* hub, sometimes called an intelligent hub, a more sophisticated switching facility in the hub allows each individual port to be assigned to an appropriate transmission medium segment, as shown in Fig. 16.12. Such hubs allow for great flexibility in workgroup assignment, especially when transmission medium segment assignment can be selected for each port through network management software and can be changed dynamically as workgroup assignments change.

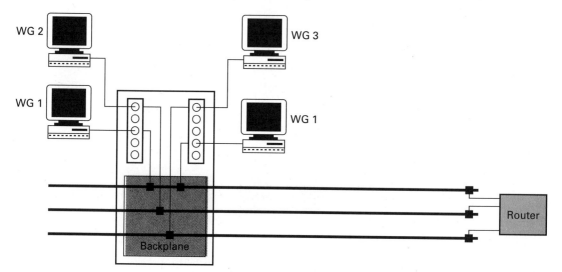

Figure 16.12   Port assignment hub.

Asynchronous Transfer Mode

The use of LAN switching facilities makes it possible for smaller groups of systems to have a higher percentage of the total transmission capacity available to them for data transmission. A new technology for networking, called *Asynchronous Transfer Mode* (ATM) is undergoing standardization at the present time. ATM will extend the notion of LAN switching even further and make it possible for virtual LANs to be set up so that any two systems can have the full available transmission capacity to them each time they need to exchange data with one another. ATM technology is introduced in Appendix C.

CONVERSION FACILITIES

Repeaters, bridges, routers, and switches are used strictly to interconnect LANs in various ways to form a larger internet. Additional devices are available that perform conversion functions that allow a system conforming to one network architecture to use the services of a network or a device conforming to some other network architecture. Many different types of conversion devices are available, and there is no consistent terminology that is used by all vendors for referring to devices that allow networks and systems conforming to different network architectures to interoperate. However, most devices that perform conversion services can be categorized as either *gateways* or *encapsulation facilities*.

Gateways

A *gateway* is a fundamentally different type of device than a repeater, bridge, router, or switch and can be used in conjunction with them. A gateway makes it possible for an application program running on a system conforming to one network architecture to communicate with an application program running in a system conforming to some other network architecture.

A gateway performs its function in the Application layer of the OSI model, as shown in Fig. 16.13. The function of a gateway is to convert from one set of communication protocols to some other set of communication protocols. Protocol conversion may include the following functions:

- **Message Format Conversion.** Different networks may employ different message formats, maximum message sizes, or character codes. The gateway must be able to convert messages to an appropriate format, size, and coding.

- **Address Translation.** Different networks may employ different network addressing mechanisms and network address structures. The gateway must be able to interpret network addresses in one network and convert them into appropriate network addresses in the other network.

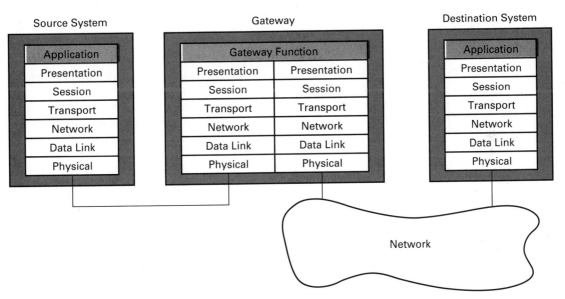

Figure 16.13   A gateway performs a protocol conversion function in the Application layer.

- **Protocol Conversion.** When a message is prepared for transmission, each layer adds control information unique to the protocol used in that layer. The gateway must be able to convert control information used by each layer so that the receiving system receives control information in the format it expects. Services affected may include message segmentation and reassembly, data flow control, and error detection and recovery.

Encapsulation Facilities

An *encapsulation* facility allows two systems that conform to a given network architecture to communicate using a network that conforms to some other network architecture. The encapsulation facility at each end is sometimes referred to as a *portal*. A pair of portals, one on each end of the network, can be viewed as implementing what is sometimes called a *tunnel*. The tunnel transports messages through a network conforming to a foreign network architecture, as shown in Fig. 16.14.

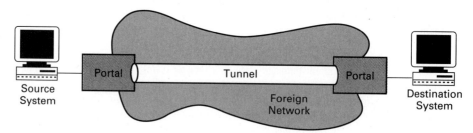

Figure 16.14 An encapsulation facility consists of two portals implementing a tunnel through a network conforming to an architecture that is foreign to the source and destination systems.

Unlike a gateway, an encapsulation facility does not perform actual protocol conversions. Instead, a portal operating on behalf of the source system encapsulates a message conforming to the source system's network architecture within a protocol message capable of being carried across the network. A complementary portal operating on behalf of the destination system extracts the original message and passes it to the destination system.

SUMMARY

An enterprise internetwork, or internet, is a collection of subnetworks, each of which consists of two or more systems connected by a LAN data link or a point-to-point telecommunications facility. Internets can be implemented using a variety of different physical data link technologies and can transport data traffic conforming to multiple high-level protocol families. The elements making up enterprise networks include LAN data links, WAN data links, and network interconnection devices. Network interconnection devices can be divided into five categories.

Repeaters perform their function in the OSI model Physical layer and relay signals from one cable segment to another in a LAN.

Bridges perform their function in the Data Link layer and can interconnect separate LAN data links. Bridges are used to build extended LANs and often implement a filtering function that limits the flow of nonmulticast traffic over the bridge.

Routers perform their function in the Network layer and are used to interconnect separate subnetworks. Routers have more intelligence than bridges and can be used to isolate both multicast and nonmulticast traffic to individual subnetworks.

Switches are used to implement multiple, parallel transmission medium segments to which different groups of stations can be attached. Switches can be used to provide full network bandwidth to multiple groups of systems.

Conversion facilities include gateways and encapsulation techniques. A gateway is used to provide a protocol conversion function that allows a program running in a system conforming to one network architecture to communicate with a program running in a system conforming to some other network architecture. An encapsulation facility allows two systems conforming to a given network architecture to communicate over a network conforming to some other network architecture.

Enterprise internetworks can be designed to carry the data traffic generated by end systems that implement different high-level protocol families. Chapter 17 introduces the most commonly used high-level communication protocols employed in computer networks.

Chapter **17**

Protocols for Internetworking

Networking software products that are used to provide communication services to end users and application programs use particular families of protocols for communicating. These protocols are typically associated with the layers of the OSI model that are above the Data Link layer. As we introduced in Chapter 16, a typical enterprise internetwork must often be designed to carry data traffic generated by end user systems that use various networking software products and, thus, that conforms to multiple high-level protocol families. This chapter introduces the various high-level protocol families, each associated with a particular networking architecture, that can be used for communication in an enterprise internetwork.

OSI MODEL LAYERS

The specific protocols that are described in this chapter are associated with the OSI Network and Transport layers. These are the protocols that are concerned with moving user data from one computing system to another in a network.

Physical and Data Link Layer Protocols

Most of the networking software in use today allows a variety of protocols to be used at the level of the Physical and Data Link layers. Typically, any type of physical data link can carry the traffic associated with any of the protocol families. The data link technologies that are used to implement the various physical LANs and the WAN data links between them are transparent to the protocols that operate at the level of the OSI Network and Transport layers.

Application Protocols

All networking products also provide application-oriented protocols that provide facilities that operate in the layers above the Transport layer of the OSI model. These application facilities provide services to application programs and to end users, such as electronic mail services, remote file access, remote login capabilities, remote procedure call facilities, and so on. The characteristics of the application-level facilities provided by networking software are beyond the scope of this chapter. However, the application facilities provided by a few representative networking products are described in Part V. Detailed information on the application facilities provided by other networking software products can be found in documentation available from their respective vendors.

CATEGORIES OF PROTOCOL FAMILIES

The protocol families, or networking architectures, that are commonly used by the networking software most often employed today in computer networks, can be divided into two categories—*routable* protocol families and *unroutable* protocol families.

Routable Protocol Families

In the *routable protocol family* category are those protocol families that use a layering structure that is close to that defined by the OSI model and contain a layer that is closely associated with the OSI Network layer. These protocol families are specifically designed to be used to construct internets in which a number of individual subnetworks, such as individual LANs and WAN data links, can be connected using a system of routers. They are specifically designed to carry data traffic beyond the confines of a single LAN or extended LAN. The routable protocol families introduced in this chapter are as follows:

- Xerox Networking System
- Novell NetWare
- TCP/IP
- DECnet Phase IV
- DECnet/OSI
- AppleTalk

Unroutable Protocol Families

In the *unroutable* protocol family category are those protocol families that use a layering structure that is different from the OSI model and either do not implement a routing scheme or implement a routing scheme that is substantially different from the scheme used by the routable protocol families. Some unroutable protocols are designed to carry data traffic only within the confines of a single LAN or extended LAN and are not designed to carry traffic from one LAN to another through routers. Although some protocol families are categorized as unroutable, technologies are available for routing the data traffic associated with them in an enterprise internetwork. The unroutable protocol families that are of interest in this chapter are as follows:

- NetBIOS
- SNA Subarea Networking
- SNA Advanced Peer-to-Peer Networking

This chapter discusses all of the above protocol families individually and describes their characteristics.

HETEROGENEOUS ENTERPRISE INTERNETWORKS

It is possible for computers that implement different high-level protocol families to coexist in the same enterprise internetwork. However, it is important to realize that a computer that implements a particular high-level protocol family is aware only of other computers in the network that implement that same high-level protocol family. For example, TCP/IP systems are aware only of other TCP/IP systems, and NetWare systems are aware only of other NetWare systems. Therefore, a heterogeneous enterprise internetwork can be viewed as a number of separate logical networks, each of which consists of all the computers implementing a particular high-level protocol family. This characteristic of enterprise internetworks will be explored in more detail in Chapter 18.

The reason that computers implementing different high-level protocol families cannot interoperate is that they use different high-level communication protocols and different network addressing schemes.

INTERNET ADDRESSING MECHANISMS

All of the routable protocol families provide a mechanism in the Network layer for uniquely identifying each of the systems associated with a particular protocol family that is attached to an internet. In an internet, a Network layer addressing mechanism is used in addition to a Data Link layer station addressing mechanism to identify and locate systems.

The following describes the differences between Network layer addressing and MAC sublayer station addressing:

- **Network Layer Addressing.** Network layer addressing mechanisms are used to assign a unique *network address,* or *internet address,* to each system in the entire internet. A different Network layer addressing mechanism is associated with each high-level protocol family, and each family uses a different network address structure. For example, each system in an enterprise internetwork that implements TCP/IP networking software must have a unique internet address that conforms to the TCP/IP network address structure. Each system in the network that implements Novell NetWare software also has a unique network address that conforms to the NetWare network address structure.

- **Data Link Station Addressing.** A Data Link layer station address identifies a particular network interface card (NIC) that is used to attach a system to a data link. The MAC sublayer station addressing mechanism described in Chapter 6 is the Data Link layer station addressing mechanism used to identify stations on an IEEE/ISO/ANSI LAN data link. For example, on an Ethernet LAN data link, each Ethernet NIC attached to the data link has a unique MAC address.

Packet Transmission

Routable protocol families typically employ a Network layer packet that is carried within a Data Link layer frame for transmission through an internet. In an IEEE/ISO/ANSI local area network, the Network layer packet is also contained within an LLC-PDU, as shown in Fig. 17.1.

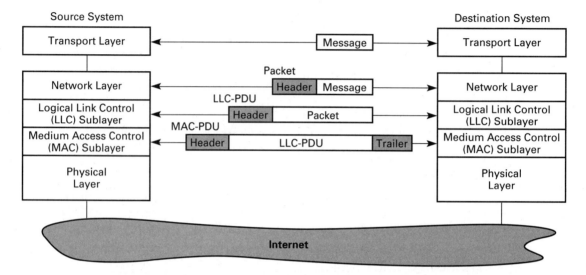

Figure 17.1 Message encapsulation by the Network layer and the LLC and MAC sublayers.

Figure 17.2 shows an IEEE/ISO/ANSI MAC frame carrying an LLC-PDU. The LLC-PDU, in turn, carries a Network layer packet that is generated by the international standard ISO 8473 Internet protocol.

Figure 17.3 shows how the subnetwork access protocol (SNAP) mechanism described in Chapter 6 is used to carry a Network layer packet conforming to a private Network layer protocol, in this case the AppleTalk Datagram Delivery Protocol (DDP).

Figure 17.4 illustrates the general procedure that is used to deliver user data through the internet from a source system to a destination system. The following describes each of the steps in the procedure:

1. A Transport layer process in the source end system passes a message down to a Network layer process for transmission to some destination end system in the internet.

2. The Network layer in the source system formats one or more packets, which each include a source network address and a destination network address. The Network layer then passes each packet down to the Data Link layer in the source system. (In an IEEE/ISO/ANSI LAN, the Data Link layer combines the LLC sublayer and the MAC sublayer.)

3. The Data Link layer encloses each packet in a frame for transmission across a data link to the next system along the route the packet takes through the internet. If the data link being traversed is a LAN data link, the frame's header contains the MAC address of the sending station and the MAC address of the receiving station.

4. The Network layer in each system that receives a packet then determines the packet's destination for the next hop. The original packet is enclosed in a new frame for each data link it traverses in reaching its final destination. The Data Link layer in the destination system eventually receives a frame containing the original packet.

5. The Network layer in the final destination system then passes the original packet up to the Transport layer there.

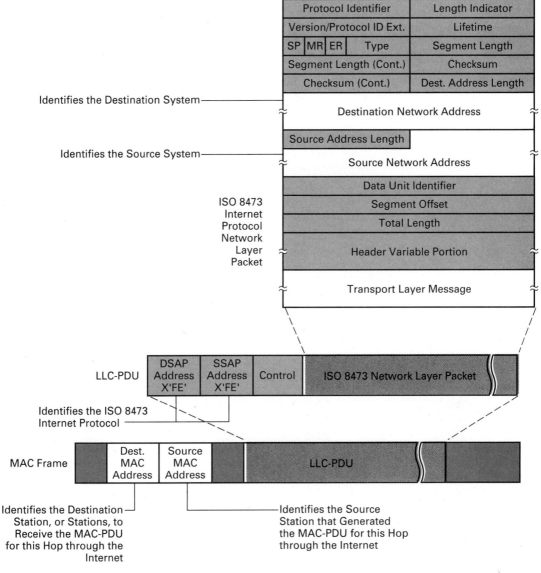

Figure 17.2   MAC frame and LLC-PDU carrying an ISO 8473 Internet protocol packet.

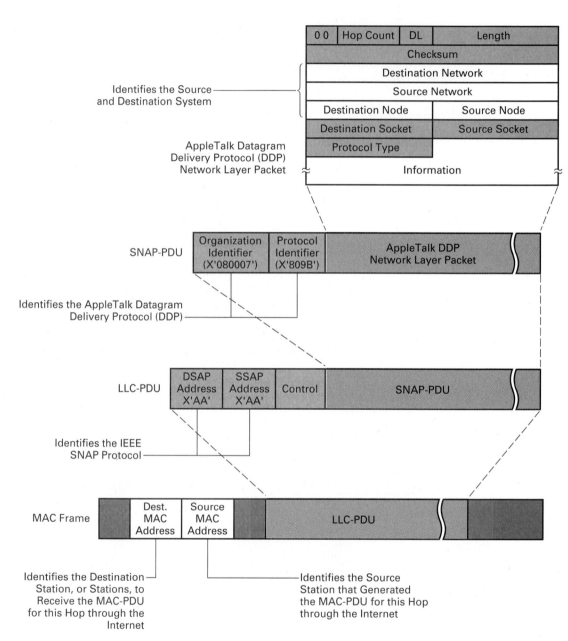

0 0	Hop Count	DL	Length

Checksum

Destination Network

Source Network

Destination Node	Source Node
Destination Socket	Source Socket
Protocol Type	

Information

Identifies the Source
and Destination System

AppleTalk Datagram
Delivery Protocol (DDP)
Network Layer Packet

SNAP-PDU

Organization Identifier (X'080007')	Protocol Identifier (X'809B')	AppleTalk DDP Network Layer Packet

Identifies the AppleTalk Datagram
Delivery Protocol (DDP)

LLC-PDU

DSAP Address X'AA'	SSAP Address X'AA'	Control	SNAP-PDU

Identifies the IEEE
SNAP Protocol

MAC Frame

	Dest. MAC Address	Source MAC Address		LLC-PDU	

Identifies the Destination
Station, or Stations, to
Receive the MAC-PDU
for this Hop through the
Internet

Identifies the Source
Station that Generated
the MAC-PDU for this Hop
through the Internet

Figure 17.3 MAC frame, LLC-PDU, and SNAP PDU carrying an AppleTalk
Network layer packet.

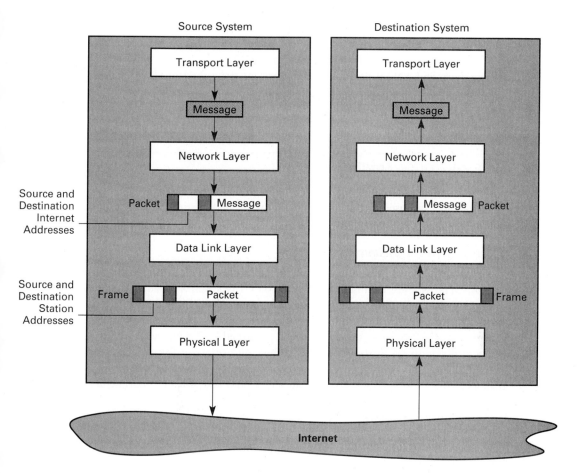

Figure 17.4   Message transmission through an internet.

To summarize this process, each packet that travels through an internet always carries in its header the internet addresses of the source end system and the destination end system. The source and destination internet addresses remain unchanged as the packet travels through the network to its destination. The packet is enclosed in a frame for each hop it makes across a data link in traveling to its final destination, and the source and destination station addresses contained in the frame are different for each hop.

Protocol Identification Mechanisms

It is common for a single enterprise internetwork to handle traffic that corresponds to multiple high-level protocol families. Therefore, there must be a method for determining the protocol that is associated with the packet contained in each frame that is transmitted over each data link in the internet. For example, in an enterprise internetwork that has Novell NetWare equipment, TCP/IP equipment, and AppleTalk equipment attached to it, each type of data link technology employed in the internet must provide a means of identifying which packets correspond to which protocol family.

Protocol identification on an IEEE/ISO/ANSI LAN is handled using LLC SAP identifiers and SNAP protocol identifiers, as described in Chapter 6. Appendix B describes the protocol addressing and station addressing schemes that are used with the most widely used WAN data link technologies that are employed in enterprise internetworks.

ROUTABLE PROTOCOL FAMILIES

The following sections describe the characteristics of the important routable protocol families that are used in enterprise internetworks and examine their packet formats and network address structures.

Xerox Network System

The *Xerox Network Systems* (XNS) architecture was initially developed by Xerox in the 1970s to provide for communication between various Xerox products using Ethernet networking. XNS facilities include the interconnection of individual Ethernet LAN data links with each other and for connecting Ethernet LANs with packet-switched public data networks. The XNS architecture has been published by Xerox and has been generally available to the public. The XNS architecture is one of the earliest of the published architectures for internetworking, and a number of local area network vendors have adopted forms of the XNS protocols and have built additional routing facilities on top of the XNS protocols for use in their own products.

Many networking schemes—such as that developed by Novell for its NetWare protocol family—have been adapted from the original XNS specifications. However, it is important to note that devices implementing these newer protocol families cannot interoperate with devices implementing the original XNS protocols. Each vendor has added its own enhancements to the original XNS protocols making them incompatible with XNS.

Box 17.1 shows how the layering structure of the XNS architecture compares with the OSI model and lists the major Transport and Network layer protocols that are part of the XNS protocol family.

The unit of data that routers are concerned with in moving user data through an XNS internet is the IDP packet that IDP handles at the level of the OSI Network layer. Figure 17.5 shows an Ethernet Version 2 frame carrying an XNS IDP packet.

The destination network address of the packet is contained in two fields in the IDP packet header:

- **Destination Network.** Contains a value that identifies the particular physical network (subnetwork) to which the destination system is attached. The network administrator assigns a unique value to each subnetwork in the internet.

- **Destination Host.** Contains the 48-bit MAC address of the NIC installed in the destination system.

BOX 17.1   Xerox Network System (XNS) protocols.

Application		Application Layer				
Presentation		Control Layer				
Session						
Transport		PEP	SPP	Echo	Error	Transport Layer
Network		IDP		RIP		Internet Layer
Data Link		Network Access and Transmission Medium Layer				
Physical						

Transport Layer Protocols

- **Packet Exchange Protocol (PEP).** PEP uses the services of IDP to provide application programs with an unreliable, end-to-end connectionless data transport service.

- **Sequenced Packet Protocol (SPP).** SPP also uses the services of IDP to provide application programs with a reliable, sequenced, connection-oriented data transport service that applications can use as an alternative to PEP.

- **Echo Protocol.** The Echo protocol allows an end system to verify the existence of a route between one end system and another end system in the internet.

- **Error Protocol.** The Error protocol provides for detecting errors and for exchanging information about them between end systems and routers.

Network Layer Protocols

- **Internetwork Datagram Protocol (IDP).** IDP provides an unreliable, connectionless, datagram delivery service.

- **Routing Information Protocol (RIP).** RIP allows routers to communicate with one another for the purposes of determining routes to be used for relaying user traffic from one router to another through the internet.

Since the XNS network addressing scheme uses the MAC address of the NIC installed in the destination system as part of the network address, it may appear on first glance that this simply duplicates the MAC address contained in the Ethernet frame carrying the packet. However, keep in mind that the destination MAC address in the frame indicates only the destination of the frame for a single hop across a data link.

The destination network address in the packet header remains the same as the packet moves through the internet and always identifies the final destination system. The destination MAC address in the frame carrying the packet changes for each hop the packet makes and always indicates the destination of the next hop the packet is to make. The

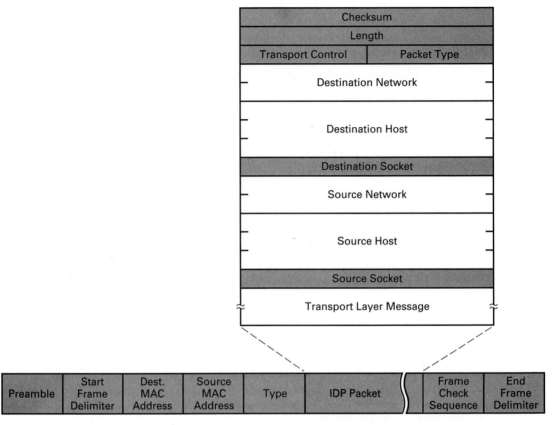

Figure 17.5   XNS Internetwork Datagram Protocol (IDP) packet carried in an
Ethernet Version 2 frame.

IDP packet may also be enclosed in frames of different types for each hop depending on
the type of LAN or WAN data link the frame is traversing for each hop.

Novell NetWare

Novell Corporation markets a family of local area networking software products called
NetWare. NetWare products implement the NetWare protocol family, which is often
called the *IPX* protocol family after the name of the Network layer protocol in the Net-
Ware family. Most of the products in the NetWare family are used to implement a client-
server computing environment in which user systems functioning as clients communicate
with servers over a single local area network or over an internet of interconnected LANs.
In the NetWare environment, one or more computing systems are ordinarily designated
as dedicated NetWare servers that typically provide file server, print server, and electronic mail services. NetWare software is also available for creating peer-to-peer networks in
which user systems can play the role of servers.

The protocols that are used by the NetWare family of products are derivations of the XNS protocols described previously. Novell has added functions to many of the XNS protocols, and so Novell NetWare protocols are essentially incompatible with the original XNS protocols, even though some of them have the same names.

Box 17.2 shows how the layering structure of the Novell NetWare architecture compares with the OSI model and lists the major Transport and Network layer protocols that are part of the Novell NetWare protocol family.

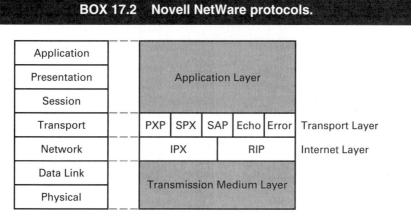

BOX 17.2   Novell NetWare protocols.

Transport Layer Protocols

- **Packet Exchange Protocol (PXP).** PXP provides application programs with an unreliable end-to-end connectionless data transport service.

- **Sequenced Packet Exchange (SPX) Protocol.** SPX uses the services of IPX to provide application programs with a reliable, sequenced, connection-oriented data transport service.

- **Service Advertising Protocol (SAP).** SAP is a broadcast protocol that NetWare servers employ to inform NetWare clients of the services that are available.

- **Echo Protocol.** Echo allows an end system to verify the existence of a route between one end system and another end system in the internet.

- **Error Protocol.** Error provides for detecting and reporting on errors between an end system and a router to which it is directly attached.

Network Layer Protocols

- **Internet Packet Exchange (IPX) Protocol.** IPX operates at the level of the OSI Network layer and provides an unreliable, connectionless, datagram delivery service.

- **Routing Information Protocol (RIP).** RIP allows routers to communicate with one another for the purposes of determining routes and for relaying user traffic from one router to another through the internet.

The unit of data that routers are concerned with, in moving user data through a Novell NetWare internet, is the IPX packet. Figure 17.6 shows a Token Ring MAC frame carrying an IPX packet.

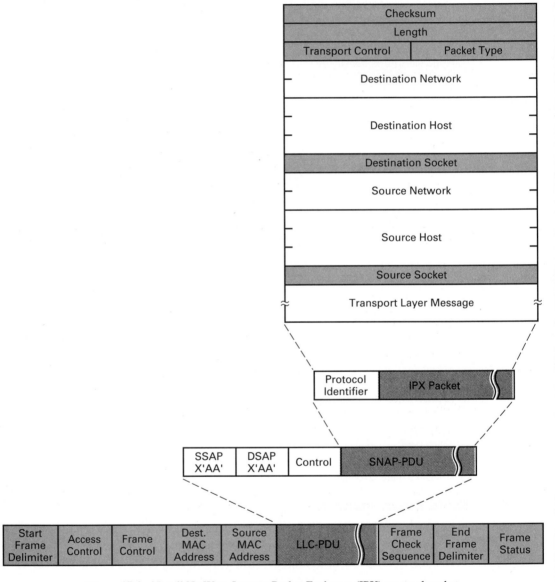

Figure 17.6   Novell NetWare Internet Packet Exchange (IPX) protocol packet carried in a Token Ring frame.

Since IPX is not an international standard Network layer protocol, it is carried in a SNAP frame. The destination network address of the packet is contained in two fields in the IPX packet header:

- **Destination Network.** Contains a value that identifies the particular subnetwork to which the destination system is attached. The network administrator assigns a unique value to each subnetwork in the internet.

- **Destination Host.** Contains the 48-bit MAC address of the NIC installed in the destination system.

As with the XNS network addressing scheme, the MAC address of the NIC in the destination system is used in the network address to identify the destination system.

The protocols that are used by Novell NetWare networking software products are described further in Chapter 22.

TCP/IP

The term TCP/IP, which is an acronym for *Transmission Control Protocol/Internet Protocol*, refers to a set of protocols that grew out of a research project that was funded by the United States Department of Defense. The original idea behind the TCP/IP protocol suite was to define a standard set of procedures to allow individual computer networks—such as the local area networks run by individual organizations—to be interconnected. The TCP/IP protocols allow the interconnected individual networks to give the appearance of a single, unified internet in which all systems can freely exchange data with each other as if they were all directly connected.

The TCP/IP protocols are used throughout the world in a great number of computer networks operated by individual organizations. The largest internet is called the *Worldwide Internet*, or simply the *Internet*. Today's Worldwide Internet interconnects many thousands of networks containing millions of computers in universities, national laboratories, and commercial organizations.

The TCP/IP protocol family implements a peer-to-peer client-server environment. Any computing system in the internet can run TCP/IP server software that can provide services to any other computing system that runs complementary TCP/IP client software.

Box 17.3 shows how the layering structure of the TCP/IP architecture compares with the OSI model and lists the major Transport and Network layer protocols that are part of the TCP/IP protocol family.

There are a number of alternative routing protocols that can be used to communicate with end systems and with other routers to perform routing functions and to relay user data through the internet. The routing protocols that are actually used depends on the size and complexity of the internet. Large TCP/IP internets are often divided into what are called *autonomous systems*, each of which is a collection of end systems, routers, and data links that are maintained by a single organization. Some TCP/IP routing protocols are designed to route traffic within a single autonomous system, while others are designed to route traffic between autonomous systems.

BOX 17.3   TCP/IP protocols.

Application		
Presentation		Application Layer
Session		
Transport		UDP / TCP — Transport Layer
Network		IP ICMP ARP RARP RIP OSPF EGP BGP — Internet Layer
Data Link		Network Interface Layer
Physical		Hardware Layer

Transport Layer Protocols

- **User Datagram Protocol (UDP).** UDP operates at the level of the OSI Transport layer and uses the services of IP to provide application programs with a best-efforts, connectionless datagram delivery service.

- **Transmission Control Protocol (TCP).** TCP is a more powerful connection-oriented Transport layer protocol that also uses the services of IP to provide for reliable, sequenced stream data delivery.

Network Layer Protocols

- **Internet Protocol (IP).** IP is the core protocol of the TCP/IP protocol suite. It provides a connectionless, best-efforts datagram delivery service that operates at the level of the OSI Network layer.

- **Internet Control Message Protocol (ICMP).** ICMP employs the services of IP to allow end systems to report on error conditions and to provide information about unexpected circumstances.

- **Address Resolution Protocol (ARP).** ARP helps a source end system deliver data to a destination system on the same LAN data link. ARP can also be used by an end system to determine the physical hardware address of a router.

- **Reverse Address Resolution Protocol (RARP).** RARP allows an end system that does not yet have its network address to obtain it. RARP is typically used to support workstations and intelligent terminals that do not have their own disk storage.

- **Routing Information Protocol (RIP).** The TCP/IP version of RIP is a simple routing protocol that provides for the transmission of routing control information between TCP/IP routers within a single autonomous system. Note that the XNS and NetWare implementations of RIP are incompatible with the TCP/IP version.

- **Open Shortest Path First (OSPF).** OSPF is a routing protocol that also operates within a single autonomous system but implements a more complex routing algorithm than RIP. OSPF is better suited for routing in large networks.

- **Exterior Gateway Protocol (EGP).** EGP is used by routers that must communicate with routers in other autonomous systems.

- **Border Gateway Protocol (BGP).** BGP can be used as an alternative to EGP to allow routers to communicate between autonomous systems. It employs a more sophisticated routing algorithm than EGP.

The unit of data that routers are concerned with in moving user data through a TCP/IP internet is the IP packet that IP handles at the level of the OSI Network layer. Figure 17.7 shows a Point-to-Point Protocol frame carrying an IP packet over a WAN data link. (See Appendix B for a description of the Point-to-Point Protocol.)

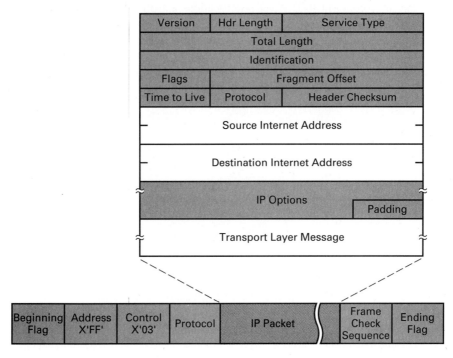

Figure 17.7   TCP/IP Internet Protocol (IP) packet carried in a Point-to-Point protocol frame.

The network address of the destination system is contained in the Destination Internet Address field. TCP/IP network addresses are 32 bits in length. The initial bits of the address identify a particular data link in the internet, and the remaining bits identify the destination system on that data link. The number of bits that are used to identify the data link and the number of bits that are used to identify the particular system are variable. The way in which address bits are allocated can be set by the TCP/IP network administrator.

The individual protocols making up the TCP/IP protocol suite are described further in Chapter 23.

DECnet Phase IV

The term *DECnet* is used by Digital Equipment Corporation to refer to its own line of networking products. DECnet products conform to a proprietary networking architecture called the *Digital Network Architecture* (DNA). Since DECnet is the more familiar term, the term DECnet will be used to refer to Digital's protocol families.

DECnet products have evolved through a series of phases, beginning with Phase I. The most current phase of DECnet products is DECnet Phase V, usually referred to as *DECnet/OSI*. However, at the time of writing, most installed DECnet networks conform to Phase IV of the architecture, and most networking products that today state that they conform to DECnet specifications actually conform to the DECnet Phase IV specifications.

Box 17.4 shows how the layering structure of the DECnet Phase IV architecture compares with the OSI model and lists the two major Transport and Network layer protocols that are part of the DECnet Phase IV protocol family.

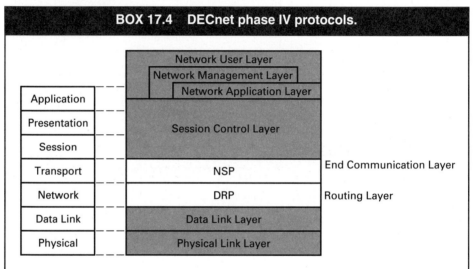

BOX 17.4   DECnet phase IV protocols.

Transport Layer Protocol

- **Network Services Protocol (NSP).** NSP provides a reliable, sequenced, connection-oriented end-to-end data delivery service.

Network Layer Protocol

- **Digital Routing Protocol (DRP).** DRP uses a distributed adaptive routing algorithm that implements hierarchical routing. Hierarchical routing is a technique that allows adaptive routing to operate efficiently in large networks by dividing the network into subdivisions called *areas*.

The unit of data that routers are concerned with in moving user data through a DECnet Phase IV internet is the packet that DRP works with at the level of the OSI Network layer. Figure 17.8 shows an Ethernet MAC frame carrying a DECnet Phase IV DRP Data packet.

Phase IV of DECnet defines a 16-bit network address that allows networks to be constructed that theoretically contain up to about 64,000 nodes.

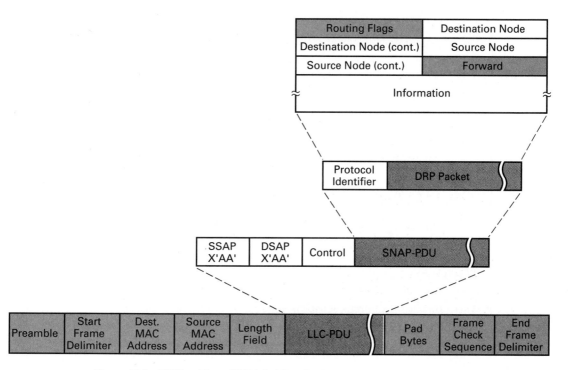

Figure 17.8   DECnet Phase IV Digital Routing Protocol (DRP) packet carried in a CSMA/CD (Ethernet) frame.

DECnet/OSI

A major characteristic of DECnet/OSI is that it is a fairly complete implementation of the major protocols that are published by ISO to support the OSI model. A major benefit of DECnet/OSI is that DECnet/OSI products can interoperate with the equipment of any vendor that also implements the ISO standards for the OSI model. Another major benefit of DECnet/OSI products is that they can be used to construct internets of almost unlimited size, into the millions of systems.

Box 17.5 shows how the layering structure of the DECnet/OSI architecture compares with the OSI model and lists the major Transport and Network layer protocols that are part of the DECnet/OSI protocol family.

The four lower layers of the DECnet/OSI protocol stack are identical to the layers of the OSI model. Above the Transport layer, DECnet/OSI gives the user the option of using the protocols that are defined for the three upper layers of the OSI model or Digital's own proprietary protocols.

The unit of data that routers are concerned with in moving user data through an OSI internet is the packet that the ISO 8473 Internet protocol works with in the Network layer. Figure 17.9 shows an Ethernet MAC frame carrying an ISO Internet protocol Data packet.

BOX 17.5   DECnet/OSI protocols.

Application		Application Layer	DEC Session Control Layer	
Presentation		Presentation Layer		
Session		Session Layer		
Transport		ISO 8073	NSP	Transport Layer
Network		ISO 8473 / ISO 8878 / ISO 9542 / ISO 10589 / DRP		Network Layer
Data Link		Data Link Layer		
Physical		Physical Link Layer		

Transport Layer Protocols

- **ISO 8073—Connection-Oriented Transport Protocol.** ISO 8073 provides a reliable, sequenced data transport service using the services of the underlying Network layer.

- **Network Services Protocol (NSP).** NSP is also provided for compatibility with DECnet Phase IV networks and equipment.

Network Layer Protocols

- **ISO 8473—Protocol for Providing the Connectionless-Mode Network Service.** ISO 8473 is often called the ISO Internet protocol and provides an unreliable, datagram data delivery service.

- **ISO 8878—Use of X.25 to Provide the OSI Connection-Mode Network Service.** Although the normal operating mode of the DECnet/OSI Network layer is to provide a connectionless Network service, DECnet/OSI uses ISO 8878 to provide the connection-oriented Network service under certain circumstances.

- **ISO 9542—End System to Intermediate System Routing Exchange Protocol.** ISO 9542 allows an end system to exchange messages with a router for the purposes of automatically configuring an end system into an OSI internet. ISO 9542 allows an end system to be connected to an OSI internet without requiring manual network management intervention.

- **ISO 10589—Intermediate System to Intermediate System Intra-Domain Routing Exchange Protocol.** ISO 10589 implements a link-state routing algorithm for automatically calculating optimum routes for relaying traffic from one router to another through an OSI internet.

- **Digital Routing Protocol (DRP).** The DECnet Phase IV DRP routing protocol is also implemented for compatibility with DECnet Phase IV networks and equipment.

Since DECnet/OSI uses an international standard Network layer protocol, the packet is not carried in a SNAP frame; the source and destination SAP address fields in the LLC-PDU directly identify the ISO 8473 protocol.

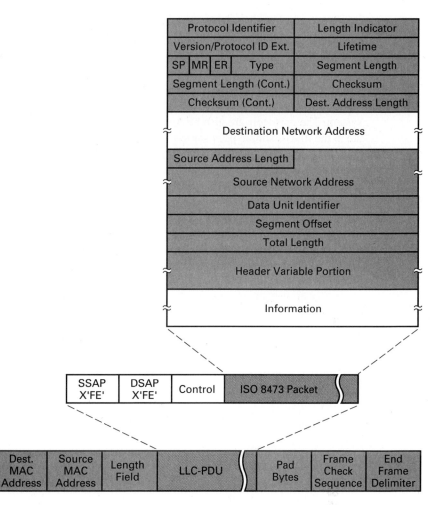

Figure 17.9   DECnet/OSI ISO 8473 Internet protocol packet carried in a CSMA/CD (Ethernet) frame.

DECnet/OSI networks use the network addressing scheme that has been developed by ISO for use in networks that employ international standard Network layer protocols. ISO network addresses are up to 20 octets in length. The intent of the ISO addressing scheme is that no two computers in the world should have the same network address, thus allowing the eventual creation of a global computer network in which computers throughout the world can participate. With the ISO addressing scheme, an organization applies to an addressing authority for a unique value to use in the high-order bits of all the network addresses it assigns in its networks. This ensures that all the network addresses that an organization generates are different from the network addresses that any other organization in the world generates.

Like DECnet Phase IV networks, DECnet/OSI networks are divided by network administrators into subdivisions called *areas* that consist of one or more interconnected subnetworks.

AppleTalk

The AppleTalk protocols are implemented in Apple hardware and system software so that basic client-server networking capabilities are included in almost every Apple computer system. The protocols are also built into many laser printers, which allows them to operate in the role of simple print servers. Client-server networks with shared printer capability can be built simply by interconnecting Apple computers and printers with the appropriate cables. Software is also available from Apple that allows an Apple computer to function as a file server on an AppleTalk network. Apple's latest system software provides built-in client-server networking support so that internets can be built that allow any computer on the network to operate in the role of a file server for other computers that operate in the role of file service clients.

Box 17.6 shows how the layering structure of the AppleTalk architecture compares with the OSI model and lists the major Transport and Network layer protocols that are part of the AppleTalk protocol family.

The AppleTalk architecture defines Physical and Data Link protocols for a relatively low-speed bus-structured form of physical LAN called *LocalTalk*, discussed in Chapter 15. However, the high-level protocols defined for the AppleTalk protocol family are often used over other forms of LAN data links, including Ethernet and Token Ring.

The unit of data that routers are concerned with in moving user data through an AppleTalk internet is the DDP packet that the Datagram Delivery Protocol handles at the level of the OSI Network layer. Figure 17.10 shows an Ethernet MAC frame carrying a DDP packet.

The destination network address of the packet is contained in two fields in the DDP packet header:

- **Destination Network.** Contains a 16-bit value that identifies the particular subnetwork to which the destination system is attached.

- **Destination Node.** Contains an 8-bit value that identifies the destination system on the destination network.

AppleTalk network address values are assigned dynamically when an AppleTalk computer is physically attached to the network and is powered on. An address assignment protocol ensures that no two systems in the same AppleTalk network have the same network address.

The protocols making up the AppleTalk networking system are described further in Chapter 24.

UNROUTABLE PROTOCOL FAMILIES

The three protocol families described next are often described as *unroutable*. This is because they either do not provide a routing capability at the level of the OSI Network layer or they implement routing using techniques that are different from the protocol families described thus far and pose special problems for routing in an internet.

```
┌─────────────────────────────────────────────────────────────────────┐
│                  BOX 17.6   AppleTalk protocols.                      │
```

Application		Presentation Layer				
Presentation						
Session		Session Layer				
Transport		ATP	AEP	RTMP	NBP	Transport Layer
Network		DDP		AARP		Network Layer
Data Link		Data Link Layer				
Physical		Physical Layer				

Transport Layer Protocols

- **AppleTalk Transaction Protocol (ATP).** ATP uses the services of DDP to provide a reliable, connection-oriented, sequenced data transfer service that operates at the level of the OSI Transport layer.

- **AppleTalk Echo Protocol (AEP).** AEP provides for a system reachability test function.

- **Routing Table Maintenance Protocol (RTMP).** RTMP allows routers to communicate with one another for the purposes of determining routes and for relaying user traffic from one router to another through the internet. It provides for establishing and maintaining routing tables used by DDP.

- **Name Binding Protocol (NBP).** NBP provides a directory service in which names can be assigned to objects, such as application programs and services available over the network. The service then translates between names and the network addresses of the systems associated with those names.

Network Layer Protocols

- **Datagram Delivery Protocol (DDP).** DDP provides an unreliable, connectionless datagram delivery service at the level of the OSI Network layer.

- **AppleTalk Address Resolution Protocol (AARP).** AARP helps a source end system to deliver data to a destination system on the same subnetwork. AARP can also be used by an end system to determine the physical hardware address of a router.

NetBIOS

NetBIOS is the name of an application programming interface (API) and communication protocol that was developed by IBM and Microsoft for use in the personal computer networking environment. The NetBIOS protocol operates in the OSI model Transport layer and provides data delivery services to application programs and higher-level protocols. The NetBIOS Transport protocol is sometimes called NETBEUI after the program module that first implemented it.

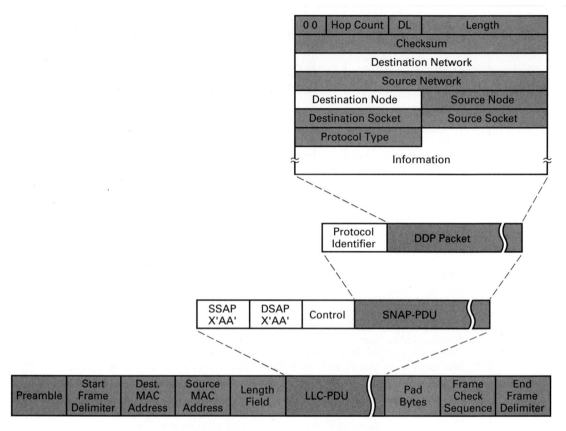

Figure 17.10   AppleTalk Datagram Delivery Protocol (DDP) packet carried in
a CSMA/CD (Ethernet) frame.

The NetBIOS protocol defines the format of packets that are exchanged between the communicating stations and the sequences in which the packets are sent and received. In a NetBIOS packet, the source and destination systems are specified by identifier values that take the form of unique names. These identifiers should not be considered network addresses in the same sense as the network addresses that are used by the routable protocol families.

The NetBIOS facility was never meant to operate outside the confines of a single local area network, and NetBIOS assumes that all the stations with which a source station wishes to communicate are on the same LAN data link or extended LAN. Therefore, the NetBIOS networking scheme defines no specific routing facilities. The NetBIOS protocols use the multicast capability of a local area network to convert the identifier of the destination system into the appropriate NIC destination MAC address. Because routers block multicast traffic, NetBIOS protocols cannot operate in an internet implemented using routers. Therefore, special techniques must be used for routing NetBIOS traffic. These techniques are examined in Chapter 18.

Some routers have been developed that use proprietary schemes to dynamically build and maintain tables of NetBIOS names and their associated destination networks. These types of routers can handle the routing of NetBIOS traffic in a way that is similar to the way traffic associated with routable traffic is handled.

NetBIOS and the overall personal computer networking environment for which it was designed are described further in Chapter 21.

Systems Network Architecture

IBM's own network architecture, widely used in the IBM large-system environment, is SNA. Many networks built using IBM equipment and software conform to SNA specifications. SNA defines specifications for constructing the hardware and software components that make up an SNA network. These specifications include definitions of the formats of data units and the protocols that govern how data units flow over the network.

Logical Units

Of key importance in understanding SNA is the concept of the *logical unit*. A logical unit can be considered as a logical *port* by which a user of the SNA network accesses SNA communication facilities. An SNA user can be a *person*, such as a person entering data at a terminal, or a *program* running in an intelligent device, such as a personal computer or a large-system processor. Users communicate with each other over an *LU-LU session* that is set up between the pair of logical units representing the two users who wish to communicate. SNA defines a number of different types of logical units that can be used to represent different types of users. For example, a terminal user accessing an SNA network using a 3270-type display terminal uses an LU type suitable for that type of communication.

The most important LU type in today's SNA networks is *LU Type 6.2*, or *LU 6.2* for short. LU 6.2 provides a set of communication services that are suitable for use by two programs that wish to communicate with one another over the network. The LU 6.2 architecture defines a set of communication services, such as SEND_DATA and RECEIVE_AND_WAIT, that programs can use to exchange messages with one another in a standardized manner.

SNA Nodes

The physical building blocks that make up an SNA network are intelligent devices of various types, called *nodes*. SNA nodes run software that is divided into the seven functional layers illustrated in Fig. 17.11.

SNA provides two different types of facilities for constructing SNA networks that can be used either alone or in combination:

- Subarea Networking
- Advanced Peer-to-Peer (APPN) Networking

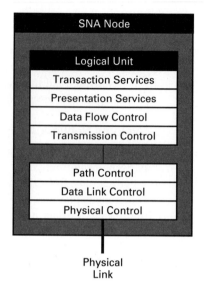

Figure 17.11 SNA functional layers in an SNA node.

SNA Subarea Networking

A subarea network is a hierarchical network constructed using three types of nodes. IBM large-system processors (Type 5 nodes) are at the top of the hierarchy. Communications controllers (Type 4 nodes) are at the second level. IBM midrange processors, personal computers, and intelligent terminals (Type 2.0 nodes) are at the bottom of the hierarchy. In a subarea network, application programs run in large-system processors at the top of the hierarchy (in Type 5 nodes) and in computers and terminals at the bottom of the hierarchy (in Type 2.0 nodes).

    Subarea networking services include a comprehensive routing function that allows an application program running in any device at the bottom of the hierarchy, to communicate with an application program running in any large-system processor at the top of the hierarchy. Subarea network facilities do not allow an LU-LU session to be set up between one Type 2.0 node and some other Type 2.0 node. An example of a simple subarea network is shown in Fig. 17.12.

    The routing facilities that are used in SNA subarea networks are quite different from the routing facilities used by the routable protocol families described earlier in this chapter. SNA routing protocols are also proprietary, and vendors of routers that are used to construct enterprise networks do not typically attempt to route SNA traffic using native SNA subarea network routing techniques. Instead, special techniques, described in Chapter 18, are often used to route SNA subarea network traffic.

SNA Advanced Peer-to-Peer Networking

Advanced Peer-to-Peer network (APPN) facilities use an enhanced version of the Type 2.0 node, called a *Type 2.1 node*. A major enhancement of the Type 2.1 node over the Type 2.0 node is that it allows LU-LU sessions to be established between programs run-

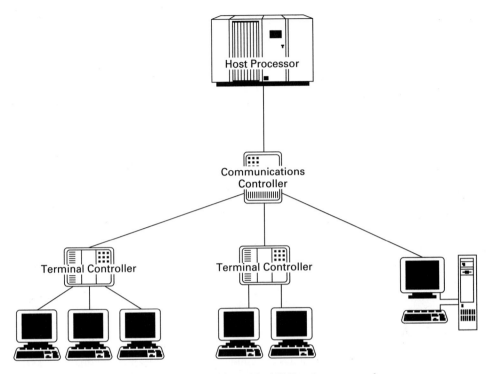

Figure 17.12   Simple hierarchical SNA subarea network.

ning in two peer Type 2.1 nodes. APPN allows networks to be constructed entirely of Type 2.1 nodes implemented in large system processors, midrange systems, and personal computers without requiring the use of the SNA subarea network routing facilities. An example of a simple APPN network is shown in Fig. 17.13.

The Type 2.1 node has undergone architectural enhancements over time, and there are now three variations of the Type 2.1 node: *APPN Network Nodes* (NNs), *APPN End Nodes* (ENs), and *Low Entry Network* (LEN) *Nodes*. APPN End Nodes can automatically configure themselves into an APPN network. To attach a LEN Node to an APPN network requires manual system configuration to be performed. APPN Network Nodes perform the routing function and can be used as intermediate systems to which APPN End Nodes and LEN Nodes can be attached.

The routing techniques that are used in APPN Network Nodes to provide routing capabilities are similar to the routing techniques employed by the routable protocol families. IBM licenses the information that describes APPN Network Node routing protocols, and the vendors of routers can provide the ability to route APPN traffic in an enterprise internetwork in the same manner as other network traffic.

In some cases, however, APPN is treated as an unroutable protocol, and similar techniques to those used to route NetBIOS and SNA subarea network traffic are used to route SNA APPN traffic.

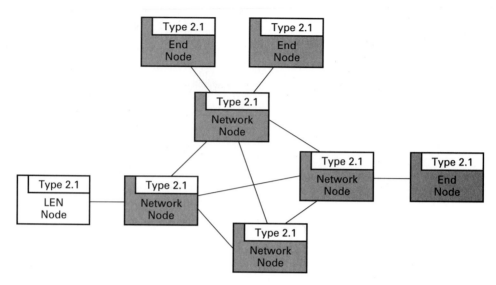

Figure 17.13   Simple SNA Advanced Peer-to-Peer Networking (APPN) network.

SUMMARY

The protocol families that are commonly used today can be categorized as routable protocol families and unroutable protocol families. In the routable protocol family category are those protocol families that use a layering structure that is close to that defined by the OSI model. In the unroutable protocol family category are those protocol families that use a layering structure that is different from the OSI model and either do not implement a routing scheme or implement a routing scheme that is substantially different from the scheme used by the routable protocol families. All of the protocol families define a number of Network and Transport layer protocols that work together to make internetworking possible.

The first protocol families described in this chapter are classified as routable protocol families. The Xerox Network Systems (XNS) architecture is an early protocol family for internetworking that has been adopted for use in many networking software subsystems. The NetWare protocol family is implemented by Novell NetWare software products that allow devices to communicate with one another in a client-server relationship over a single local area network or over an internet of interconnected LANs. The TCP/IP protocols allow a number of interconnected individual networks to give the appearance of a single, unified internet in which all systems can freely exchange data with each other as if they were all directly connected. TCP/IP implements a peer-to-peer, client-server environment in which any computing system in the internet can operate in the role of a server. DECnet products have evolved through a series of phases. Most installed DECnet networks conform to Phase IV of the architecture. The most current phase of DECnet products is DECnet/OSI. A major characteristic of DECnet/OSI is that it is a fairly complete implementation of the major protocols that have been developed by ISO to support the OSI model. The AppleTalk protocols are implemented in Apple hardware and system software and by a number of third-party software vendors.

The remaining protocol families described in this chapter are classified as unroutable protocol families. NetBIOS is the name of an API and transport mechanism, developed by IBM and Microsoft, that is implemented in many personal computer networking software subsystems. IBM's proprietary network architecture, widely used in the IBM large-system environment, is SNA. SNA defines two forms of networking—subarea networking and advanced peer-to-peer networking.

Enterprise internetworks can be constructed that consist of data links implementing a number of different technologies and can carry the data traffic conforming to multiple high-level protocol families. Considerations in constructing heterogeneous internets are discussed in Chapter 18.

Chapter **18**

Heterogeneous Internetworking

This chapter introduces ways in which individual LAN data links can be interconnected to form enterprise internetworks. It concentrates on the differences between bridges and routers in forming internets and also shows how traffic associated with unroutable protocols can be carried through a system of routers.

SINGLE LAN ENVIRONMENT

Figure 18.1 shows a simple network consisting of a single LAN data link. All systems run similar communication software that implements a single protocol family—in this case TCP/IP. In this network, any system can communicate with any other system. A TCP/IP Transport layer protocol is responsible for handling end-to-end communication between a program in one system and a program in another system. To establish communication, the Transport layer in the source system must know the network address (called an *internet address* in TCP/IP terminology) of the destination system. A TCP/IP Network layer protocol is responsible for using Data Link layer functions to move data from a source system on the LAN to a destination system on the LAN.

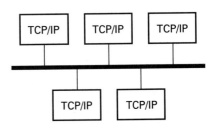

Figure 18.1   Single homogeneous local area network.

Box 18.1 summarizes the steps a source system performs in transmitting a message to a destination system:

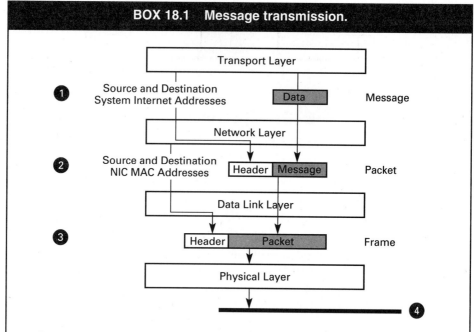

BOX 18.1   Message transmission.

1. The Transport layer passes a message down to the Network layer along with the destination network address of the system to which the message is being sent.

2. The Network layer constructs packets, each of which contains header information that includes the packet's source and destination internet addresses. In the single-LAN environment, the Network layer in the source system simply converts the destination internet address in each packet into the MAC address of the network interface card (NIC) in the destination system. The Network layer also passes each packet down to the Data Link layer along with the destination MAC address.

3. The Data Link layer adds additional header and trailer information to each packet to create a MAC frame and passes the frame to the Physical layer for transmission. Each frame contains the packet's source and destination MAC address.

4. The appropriate NIC in the destination system finally receives the frame. Data Link, Network, and Transport layer functions in the destination system then interpret and remove the header and trailer information and extract the original message.

HETEROGENEOUS LANS

Adding systems to the LAN that run software implementing other protocol families, such as Novell NetWare IPX/SPX and NetBIOS, increases the complexity of the single LAN environment, as shown in Fig. 18.2.

At the level of the Data Link layer, the NIC in any system is still capable of communicating with the NIC in any other system in the network. But the networking software that implements the layers above the Data Link layer will be aware only of other compat-

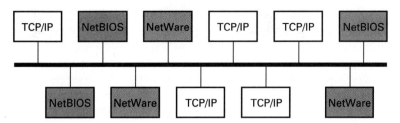

Figure 18.2   Systems implementing different higher-level protocols sharing a single physical LAN.

ible systems in the network and cannot communicate with systems running incompatible networking software. Transport and Network layer functions in each TCP/IP system are aware only of the other TCP/IP systems on the LAN, NetWare systems perceive only other NetWare systems, and NetBIOS systems see only other NetBIOS systems. Therefore, we can view the LAN as if it actually consisted of three completely separate logical networks superimposed on the same LAN data link, as illustrated in Fig. 18.3.

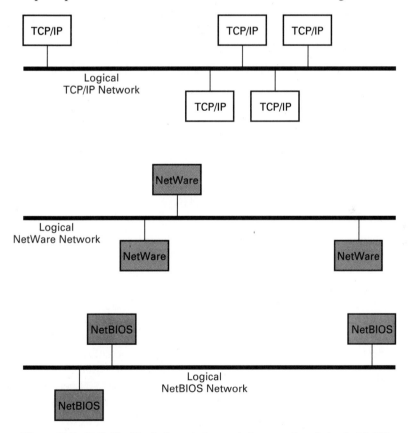

Figure 18.3   Individual logical networks coexisting on a shared physical LAN.

The Network layer protocol identification facility implemented by each system on the LAN allows each NIC to determine the Network layer protocol that is associated with the packet contained in each MAC frame it accepts. It is not possible for a system supporting only TCP/IP protocols to exchange messages with a system supporting only NetWare IPX/SPX protocols, nor can it communicate with a system supporting only NetBIOS.

Figures 18.2 and 18.3 illustrate the simplest form of heterogeneity, where each system supports only one higher-level protocol family. However, even here, the NIC in each system must be prepared to receive frames carrying packets conforming to all the various protocol types and to determine which of those frames that system should actually process. The various LAN medium access control protocols all support the ability to send a frame using a multicast address that causes the frame to be received and accepted for processing by all stations on the LAN. So, for example, a NetWare system could transmit a frame using the all-stations broadcast address, and the frame would be received by all the systems on the LAN. However, the TCP/IP and NetBIOS systems would be unable to successfully process the packet contained in the frame because the packet conforms to the IPX protocol format and not to the IP or NetBIOS format. The TCP/IP and NetBIOS systems must be able to recognize and discard frames carrying packets associated with other Network layer protocols.

On a LAN that conforms to the IEEE/ISO/ANSI LAN architecture, the service-access-point (SAP) addresses and the subnetwork access protocol (SNAP) protocol identifier values described in Chapter 6 are often used to provide the protocol identification function. Other mechanisms are used to perform the protocol identification function when packets are sent across wide area networking data links.

Multiple Protocol End Systems

It is possible to construct heterogeneous internets in which different end systems in the internet may employ multiple higher-level protocols for communication. A general goal in networking today is to provide any-to-any connectivity, where a user at one system can communicate with any other computing system in the internet. Many products have been developed that are designed to interconnect unlike systems. However, the more limited standardization that has taken place at the higher layers increases the complexity of interconnection when differences exist above the Data Link layer.

Multiple Protocol Clients

A given client end system may contain software supporting more than one higher-level protocol family. For example, an end system might implement more than one network operating system and may be configured to be both a NetWare client and a TCP/IP client. Such an end system implements separate protocol stacks for each supported protocol family.

It is also becoming more common for a single LAN network operating system to support more than one protocol family. A NetWare client end system, for example, through the use of various network loadable modules (NLMs), can support both AppleTalk and TCP/IP protocols in addition to its own native IPX/SPX based protocols.

Multiple-Protocol Servers

Server systems on a network can also support multiple protocol stacks. For example, a Macintosh client might request standard AppleTalk file and print services from a NetWare server. The server may implement the AppleTalk protocol stack in addition to IPX/SPX to service both AppleTalk clients and IPX/SPX clients. Similarly, a UNIX client implementing a TCP/IP protocol stack might submit print jobs to a NetWare server, transfer files to or from a NetWare server and use TCP/IP services for file sharing to access files stored on a NetWare server.

Protocol Stack and Network Driver Interfaces

In the single protocol environment, different network drivers are often used to support different higher-level protocols and attachments to different types of LAN data links. This is illustrated in Fig. 18.4. In such a situation, the network administrator chooses an appropriate network driver depending on the higher-level protocols supported by the network operating system installed in the system and the type of LAN to which the system is attached. The three configurations in Fig. 18.4 show three systems running network operating systems that use the NetWare IPX/SPX protocols to communicate on a Token Ring LAN, the IPX/SPX protocols over an Ethernet LAN, and the TCP/IP protocols over an Ethernet LAN. Each system uses different network driver software.

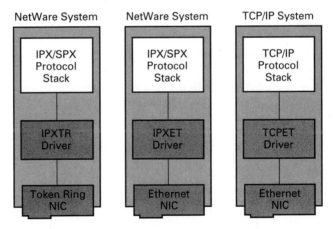

Figure 18.4 Protocol-specific and network-specific driver software is sometimes used to support a particular combination of a high-level protocol stack and a network interface card (NIC).

In a system that supports multiple higher-level protocol families, a network driver must be used that supports all the protocol families that will be used. Figure 18.5 shows a configuration in which a single system supporting three protocol stacks uses a single network driver and a single NIC.

Vendors of NICs and networking software have had to support many different combinations of high-level protocol stacks and network drivers to handle the many combinations that are possible.

Multiple Protocol System

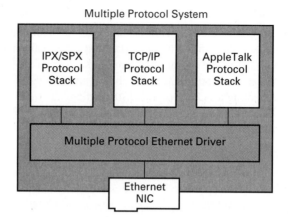

Figure 18.5 A system implementing multiple protocol stacks must use network driver software capable of handling all supported protocol stacks.

As support for multiple protocols has become more widespread, an approach that involves standard interfaces is coming into more widespread use. Standard interfaces can eliminate the need for supporting large numbers of different network drivers. This approach is illustrated in Fig. 18.6. With this approach, standards are defined for two interfaces:

- **Protocol Stack Interface.** This is the interface between a high-level protocol stack and the network driver software.

- **Network Driver Interface.** This is the interface between the network driver software and the NIC.

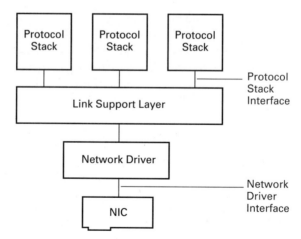

Figure 18.6 The use of standard interfaces provides a method of supporting multiple combinations of protocol stacks and network interface cards (NICs).

A layer of code called the *link support layer* is often used between the protocol stacks and the network driver to allow multiple protocol stacks to share the same network driver software.

The use of standard interfaces allows a network operating system that implements the standard protocol stack interface to use any network driver that also implements that interface. This approach also allows any network driver that implements the standard network driver interface to be used with any NIC that also conforms to that interface. The use of standard interfaces allows multiple protocol stacks to share a single NIC, without requiring the user to switch from one network driver to another.

Ideally, there would be a single standard for each of the two interfaces, thus providing maximum interoperability between network driver/NIC combinations and network operating systems. Unfortunately, competing standards have been developed. The Open Data Link Interface (ODI) was codeveloped by Novell and Apple and has been implemented in NetWare software. The Network Driver Interface Specification (NDIS) was codeveloped by Microsoft Corp. and 3Com Corp. and has been implemented in a variety of products, such as IBM LAN Server, Microsoft LAN Manager, Banyan VINES, and DEC PATHWORKS. ODI and NDIS provide essentially the same services but have defined different protocol stack and network driver interfaces.

INTERNETWORKING USING BRIDGES

Interconnecting three LANs that are in close proximity increases the complexity of the network. Assume, first, that all the systems on the three LANs run only TCP/IP communication software. As we discussed in Chapter 16, a bridge can be used to combine the three LANs to create an extended LAN. An example of a simple extended LAN consisting of three bridged LANs is shown in Fig. 18.7.

Since all of the systems on the extended LAN implement TCP/IP networking software, any system can communicate with any other system. As shown in Fig. 18.8, a bridge performs its functions in the Data Link layer, so all networking software functions operating in the Network and Transport layers will be unaware of the presence of the bridge. The Network and Transport layer functions operate in the same manner on an extended LAN as they do on a single LAN data link.

Heterogeneous Extended LAN

Like individual LAN data links, extended LANs can also accommodate communication among systems implementing different high-level protocol families. Systems that use networking software that implements the NetBIOS protocols can be added to the extended LAN, as shown in Fig. 18.9. Now TCP/IP systems can communicate with other TCP/IP systems anywhere on the extended LAN, and NetBIOS systems can communicate with other NetBIOS systems.

Adding a fourth LAN to the extended LAN, all of whose systems implement Novell NetWare, adds another dimension to the internetworking situation, as shown in Fig. 18.10.

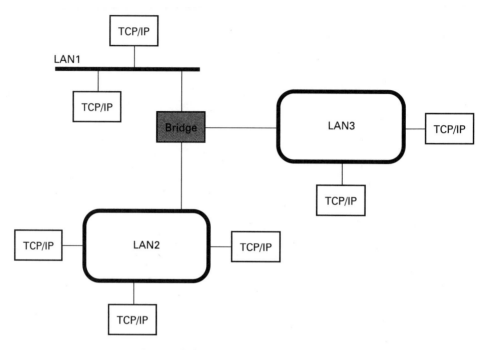

Figure 18.7 Homogeneous extended LAN.

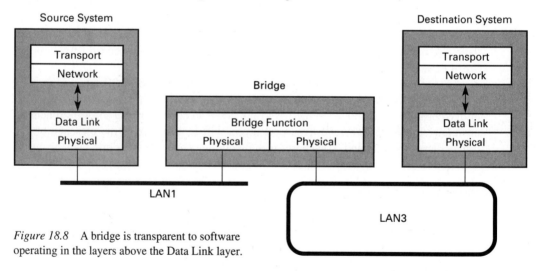

Figure 18.8 A bridge is transparent to software
operating in the layers above the Data Link layer.

Since there are no systems implementing NetWare on the first three LANs, the fourth
bridge connection serves no real purpose at this time. The three NetWare systems on LAN4
will not be able to communicate with any of the other systems in the extended LAN.

If we were to later add NetWare systems to the first three LANs and TCP/IP and
NetBIOS systems to LAN4, as shown in Fig. 18.11, all the NetWare systems in the

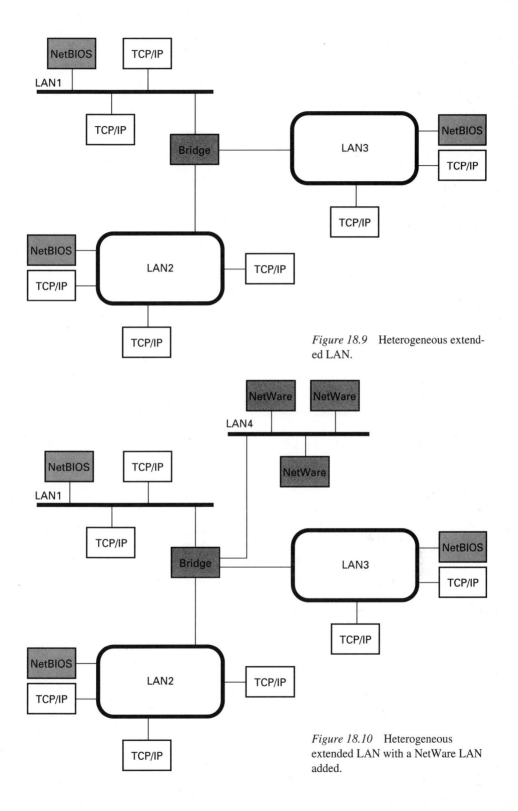

Figure 18.9 Heterogeneous extended LAN.

Figure 18.10 Heterogeneous extended LAN with a NetWare LAN added.

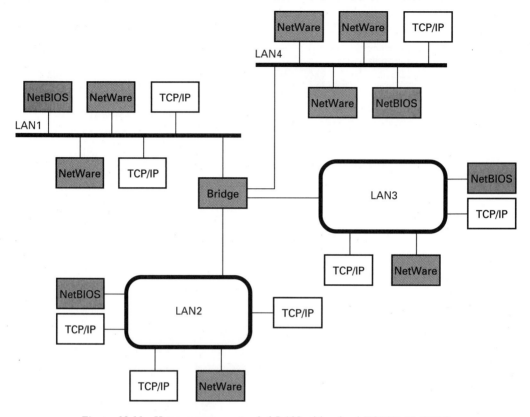

Figure 18.11   Heterogeneous extended LAN with mixed TCP/IP, NetBIOS, and NetWare systems.

extended LAN would be able to freely communicate, as would all the TCP/IP systems and all the NetBIOS systems. Again, the single extended LAN consists of a logical TCP/IP network containing only the TCP/IP systems, a logical NetWare network containing only the NetWare systems, and a logical NetBIOS network containing only the NetBIOS systems.

Bridges and WAN Data Links

As we introduced in Chapter 16, bridges are available that can be connected to wide area networking data links in addition to LANs. A pair of bridges can be connected by a point-to-point communication facility, as shown in Fig. 18.12. Such an extended LAN operates in an identical manner as an extended LAN consisting of closely-located LAN data links. However, depending on the speed of the point-to-point communication facility, there may be longer delays experienced when communicating between systems that are located at opposite ends of the point-to-point WAN data link.

Because the extended LAN may be carrying traffic corresponding to multiple protocol families, it is necessary that the data link protocol being used to carry traffic over

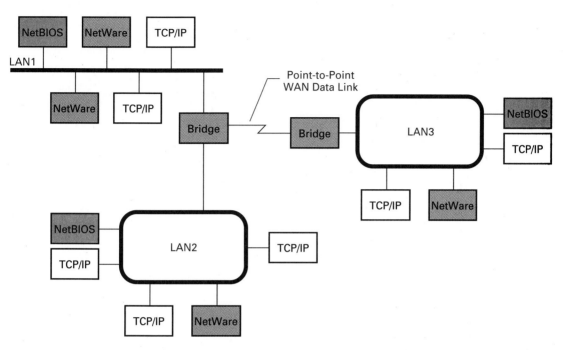

Figure 18.12   Extended LAN with a point-to-point WAN data link connecting bridges.

the WAN data link implement a Network layer protocol identification facility. The characteristics of various types of WAN data links that are useful in the internetworking environment are discussed in Appendix B.

INTERNETWORKING USING ROUTERS

A primary advantage of using bridges to interconnect LANs is that they are transparent to Transport and Network layer functions. From the viewpoint of high-level network software functions, an extended LAN constructed using bridges operates in an identical manner to a single LAN data link. This characteristic, however, can also be a drawback. Bridges allow all multicast traffic to be propagated throughout the entire extended LAN. Therefore, as the extended LAN grows, the amount of multicast traffic that is transmitted over the entire extended LAN also grows. At some point, the extended LAN may grow so large that the individual LANs become saturated with multicast traffic. Routers can be used instead of bridges to interconnect LANs when it is desirable to isolate multicast traffic to individual LANs.

Homogeneous Internets Using Routers

Figure 18.13 shows three LAN data links, containing only TCP/IP systems, interconnected using a router. The router effectively isolates each of the individual LANs from one

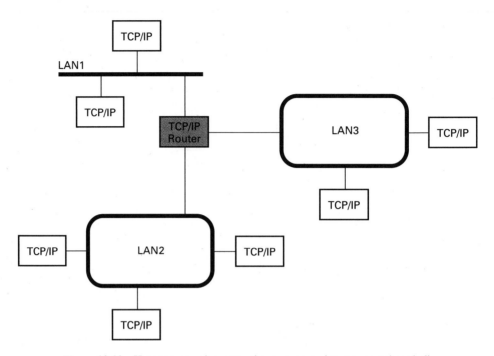

Figure 18.13 Homogeneous internet using a router to interconnect three individual TCP/IP subnetworks.

another. Each LAN data link now constitutes a separate subnetwork. The NICs in the systems on LAN1 can communicate only with the NICs in other systems on LAN1. The LAN1 NICs have no knowledge of the NICs in the systems on LAN2 or LAN3. Because there is no direct communication possible at the level of the Data Link layer, the Network layer must be involved in the communication when routers are used to interconnect LANs.

Message Transmission Through a Router

Figure 18.14 summarizes the process of sending a message from a system on LAN1 to a system on LAN3. The source system uses the services of the Network layer to create one or more packets containing the internet addresses of the source and destination systems. In transmitting each packet, the Network layer in the source system examines the destination internet address in the packet header and determines that the destination system is not on the source system's own LAN data link. The source system then encloses the packet in a MAC frame and delivers the frame to its local router.

The router's Data Link layer receives the frame from the source system, extracts the packet, and passes it up to the Network layer. The Network layer in the router interprets the packet's header, determines the packet's destination internet address, and uses its routing tables to determine the next hop the packet should take through the internet. In this case, the destination system is on a LAN with which the router can communicate

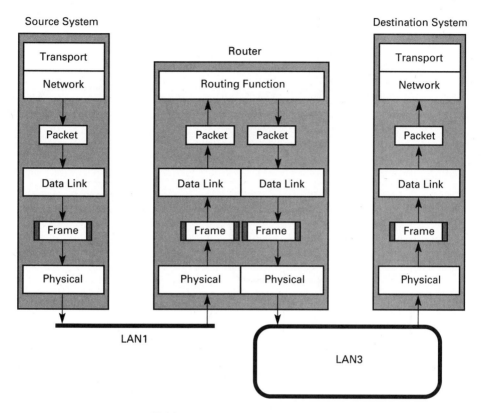

Figure 18.14   Message transmission through a router.

directly. Therefore, the router converts the destination internet address to the MAC address of the destination system's NIC. The router then uses the services of the Data Link layer to enclose the packet in a new transmission frame and delivers the frame to the appropriate NIC in the destination system. The Data Link layer then passes the enclosed packet up to the destination system's Network layer, which, in turn, delivers the original message to the Transport layer there.

Figure 18.15 shows that when a router is interposed between two different LAN data links containing the source and destination systems, the packet is transmitted between the source system and the destination system in two separate hops, across two separate data links. The packet is enclosed in a separate MAC frame for each hop. The destination of the first MAC frame is the router; the destination of the second MAC frame is the destination system.

Systems of Interconnected Routers

In large internets, individual LAN data links are often interconnected by systems of routers that are interconnected in a mesh configuration by point-to-point data links that may span long distances. In such an internet, a packet may have to travel over a number

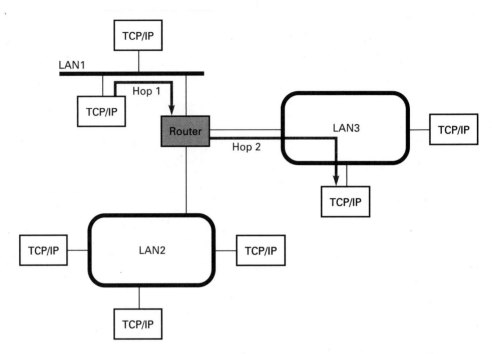

Figure 18.15   A message sent from a system on LAN1 to a system on LAN3 takes two hops through the internet.

of point-to-point links and through a number of routers. In such internets, routing decisions can be quite complex, and the routers must maintain routing tables that help them make routing decisions. The routers may use a routing protocol to periodically exchange information with one another to keep their routing tables up-to-date, and the routing tables may change as systems are added and removed from the individual LANs and as the topology of the interconnected system of routers changes. Routing is described further in Chapter 20 and in the chapters in Part V.

Heterogeneous Internets with Routers

As with bridges, it is possible to have systems that implement different protocol families attached to an internet implemented using routers. Figure 18.16 shows a three-LAN internet implemented using a router. Both TCP/IP and NetWare systems are attached to the internet. As before, on each LAN data link, TCP/IP systems can communicate only with other TCP/IP systems, and NetWare systems can communicate only with other NetWare systems.

With a router interconnecting the three LANs, the communication that is possible between LANs depends on the capabilities of the router. If the router is capable only of routing TCP/IP packets, as is the case in Fig. 18.16, any TCP/IP system in the internet can communicate with any other TCP/IP system in the internet. Since the router can interpret only TCP/IP packets, the NetWare systems will be unaware of the presence of

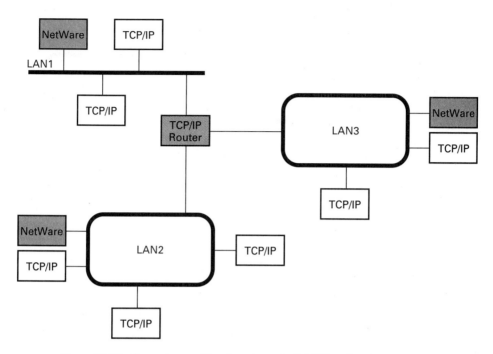

Figure 18.16　If a router capable of routing only TCP/IP packets interconnects subnetworks, the NetWare systems cannot exchange messages with one another through the router.

the router, and a NetWare system on one LAN will be unable to communicate with Net-Ware systems on the other LANs.

One way to handle a heterogeneous internet is to install separate routers to handle each protocol family, as illustrated in Fig. 18.17. A NetWare router—or a NetWare server that can perform the NetWare routing function—can operate side-by-side with the TCP/IP router. The NetWare systems use the NetWare router for communication over the internet, and the TCP/IP systems use the TCP/IP router. As with bridges, the physical internet consists of two completely separate logical networks. One consists of all the NetWare systems and the other all the TCP/IP systems.

Multiple-Protocol Routers

An alternative to installing a separate router for each protocol family is to use a single router that is capable of routing traffic for all desired protocol families. Such a router is called a *multiple-protocol router*, as shown in Fig. 18.18. A router capable of routing both TCP/IP and IPX/SPX traffic would be known to both the TCP/IP and the NetWare systems and would be capable of handling both TCP/IP and IPX/SPX packets. The router would accept a packet, use the SAP address and possibly a SNAP identifier to determine the Network layer protocol associated with the packet, and hand that packet to the appropriate routing routine.

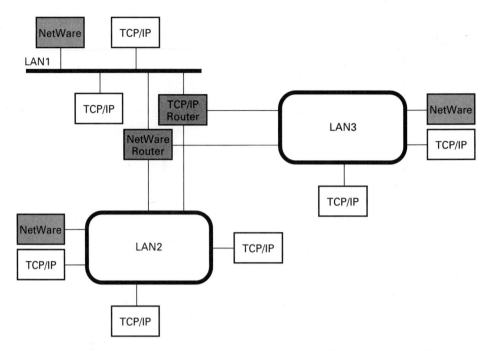

Figure 18.17 Separate routers can be used to route traffic associated with different protocol types.

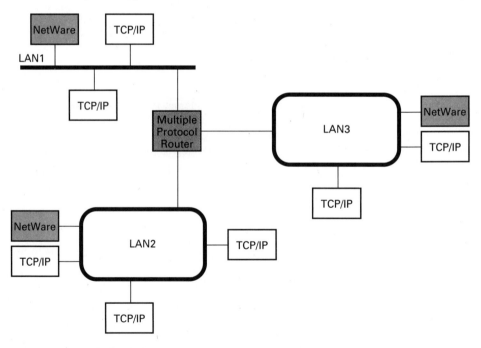

Figure 18.18 A single multiple-protocol router can be used to route the traffic associated with different protocol types.

The router must maintain different routing tables for each protocol family it is designed to process and will use the appropriate routing tables for routing packets associated with each protocol family. The selected routing routine would then interpret the packet's header, extract the destination network address, repackage the packet in a new MAC frame, and relay the new frame to the appropriate destination.

HANDLING UNROUTABLE PROTOCOLS

Adding NetBIOS systems to each of the LANs in the internet adds an additional complication, as shown in Fig. 18.19. In a previous example, when we used a bridge to interconnect three LANs, NetBIOS systems were able to freely communicate across the bridge because the internet appeared to the NetBIOS systems as if it were a single LAN data link.

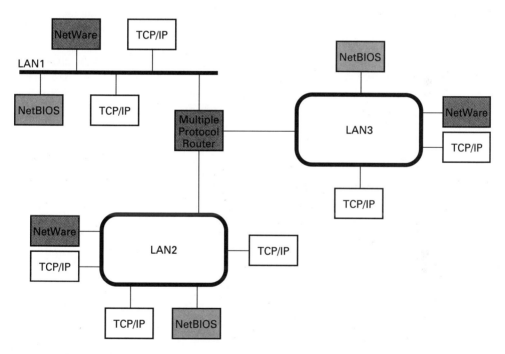

Figure 18.19   Special techniques must be used to route traffic associated with an unroutable protocol, such as NetBIOS.

When using a router to interconnect the LANs, it is more difficult to make it possible for the NetBIOS systems to communicate. This is because the NetBIOS protocols do not implement a system of network addresses and were designed to allow communication only over a single LAN. This is why in Chapter 17 we categorized the NetBIOS protocol family as an unroutable protocol family.

Brouters

One way to handle unroutable protocols is to use a device called a *brouter*, which combines the functions of a bridge and a router. A brouter handles the routing function for one or more designated protocol families and performs a bridge function for traffic associated with all other protocol families. For example, we might replace the multiple protocol router in Fig. 18.19 with a brouter that routes TCP/IP and NetWare traffic and bridges all other traffic. The brouter would allow multicast frames generated by TCP/IP and NetWare systems to be isolated to each individual LAN but still allow all the NetBIOS multicast traffic to flow across the brouter from one LAN to the others.

A disadvantage of a brouter is that if a high percentage of traffic is bridged instead of routed, undesirably large amounts of multicast traffic can be propagated over the internet and can cause individual LAN data links to become overloaded.

Encapsulation Facilities

Some multiple protocol routers use an encapsulation facility to handle the routing of network traffic associated with unroutable protocols. Figure 18.20 shows routers implementing NetBIOS portals that perform an encapsulation function for carrying NetBIOS traffic over a TCP/IP internet. Such routers accept unroutable NetBIOS traffic and enclose each NetBIOS packet within a TCP/IP packet. The TCP/IP packets are delivered, using TCP/IP routing, to a complementary router/portal on the destination LAN subnetwork. The portal then removes the NetBIOS packets from their TCP/IP packets and delivers

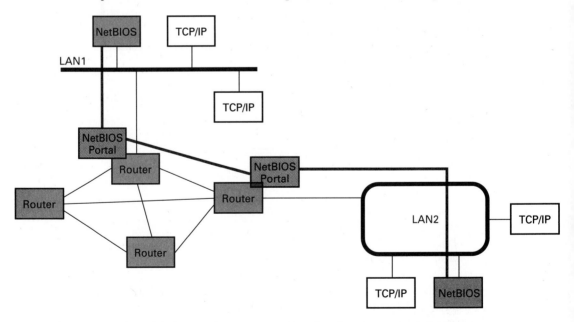

Figure 18.20   Routers that act as portals and perform an encapsulation function can be used to transport traffic associated with unroutable protocols.

them to the destination NetBIOS system. As we described in Chapter 16, the portals on each end can be viewed as implementing a tunnel through the system of routers that run the TCP/IP routing protocol.

USING GATEWAYS FOR PROTOCOL CONVERSION

In the examples we have looked at thus far, we have assumed that the source and destination systems both use the same higher-level protocols. However, there may be times when the end systems are unlike. For example, a NetWare client end system may need to communicate with a host in an SNA network. In this type of situation, shown in Fig. 18.21, a gateway can be used to perform a protocol conversion function. The gateway processes and removes all the control information that was added to a packet by the NetWare client and converts it to the SNA control information necessary for the message to reach and be processed by the designated SNA host.

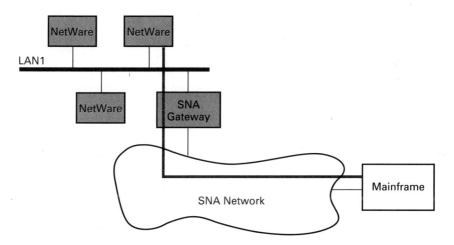

Figure 18.21   A gateway can be used when the source system and the destination system run networking software that conforms to different network architectures.

Gateways could also be used in a similar manner as an encapsulation technique when an intermediate network must be crossed. In order for two NetBIOS systems to exchange messages over a TCP/IP internet, a pair of complementary gateways could be used, as shown in Fig. 18.22. Although the gateway functions are shown as running in separate systems in Fig. 18.22, the gateway functions could run in devices that also function as routers, or they could run in the two end systems themselves.

The first gateway translates from NetBIOS format to TCP/IP format when the TCP/IP network is entered, and the second gateway translates from TCP/IP back to NetBIOS when the packet leaves the TCP/IP network.

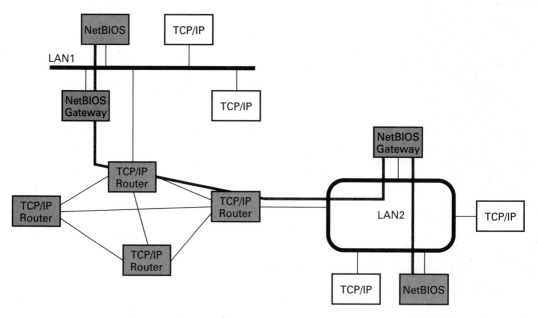

Figure 18.22   A pair of complementary gateways can be used instead of an encapsulation facility to carry traffic associated with unroutable protocols.

SUMMARY

The simplest form of computer network is one in which all systems are connected to a single LAN data link and in which all systems run similar network software conforming to a single high-level protocol family. Any system in such a network can interoperate with any other system. A more complex single-LAN environment is one in which systems conforming to different network architectures coexist on the same LAN data link. Such networks form multiple logical LANs in which different sets of systems can interoperate. Multiple-protocol client and server systems increase the level of interoperation that is possible in heterogeneous networks.

More complex networks can be formed by interconnecting multiple LAN data links of the same or different types to form extended LANs or internets. Extended LANs are constructed by interconnecting LAN data links using bridges. Systems employing different high-level protocols can coexist on an extended LAN. Internets consisting of multiple independent subnetworks can be formed using routers. When routers are used, the routers must be capable of routing the data traffic that systems on the internet generate. Multiple-protocol routers are often used to route traffic conforming to different network architectures. Specialized equipment, such as brouters, are often used when traffic conforming to unroutable protocol families must travel through an internet.

Chapter 19 examines the operation of bridges in an extended LAN and discusses the differences between transparent bridges and source routing bridges.

Chapter **19**

Bridges

As we introduced in Chapter 16, a *bridge* is a network interconnection device used to join together two or more separate LAN data links to create a larger local area network, sometimes called an *extended LAN*.

A bridge typically performs a filtering function and passes frames from one LAN to another only when necessary.

A bridge performs its function in the OSI model Data Link layer, as shown in Fig. 19.1. An extended LAN is viewed as a single subnetwork by the layers above the Data Link layer. Software operating in the layers above the Data Link layer in end systems are not aware of the presence of bridges.

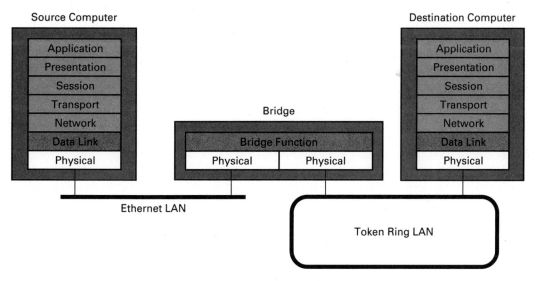

Figure 19.1 A bridge performs its function in the Data Link layer.

Box 19.1 lists some of the advantages and disadvantages of using bridges instead of routers to interconnect LAN data links in an extended LAN.

BOX 19.1   Advantages and disadvantages of bridges.

Bridge Advantages

- **Cost.** Bridges are relatively simple devices that are typically less expensive than routers.
- **Ease of Use.** Bridges tend to be easier to install and easier to maintain than routers.
- **Protocol Independence.** Bridges operate in the OSI Data Link layer and are independent of any protocol operating in the Network layer and above. This makes it relatively easy to create an internet containing systems that run networking software implementing different higher-level protocol families.
- **Performance.** Since bridges are relatively simple devices, they introduce little processing overhead into the network and tend to support higher traffic throughput than routers.

Bridge Disadvantages

- **Traffic Volume.** Bridges are best suited to networks in which the total traffic volume is relatively low and that support low numbers of total users (less than a few hundred). Problems can occur when bridging two LANs that are already experiencing high traffic volumes.
- **Flow Control.** Bridges simply pass frames from one LAN to another and do not implement flow control procedures to control the rate at which frames flow through the bridge.
- **Bridge Choking.** In a large internet, a bridge has a tendency to choke as a result of heavy traffic loads. This can result in the loss of frames.
- **Broadcast Storms.** Broadcast frames are passed over a bridge from one LAN to another. In a large internet generating a large amount of multicast traffic, broadcast storms can result in which the capacity of an individual LAN data link is exceeded by the broadcast traffic alone.
- **Loops.** Some types of bridged network configurations can result in endless loops around which frames can endlessly circulate.
- **Bottlenecks.** Bridges do not share problem information with one another, and network bottlenecks that occur can remain undetected.
- **Duplicate Addresses.** Physical station addresses must be unique within bridged networks. This can sometimes be a problem where locally-administered MAC addresses are used in two or more LANs that are being bridged.
- **Duplicate Names.** When the same network names are employed by users on two or more bridged networks, excessive traffic can result from attempts to resolve naming conflicts.
- **Effect of Failures.** The failure of some types of bridges requires that all communication sessions using a failed bridge be terminated and reestablished.

EXTENDED LANS

An extended LAN can contain LAN data links that are all of the same type, or the various LAN data links can be of different types. For example, an Ethernet LAN and a Token Ring LAN can be connected using an appropriately designed bridge. However, whether the individual LANs are the same or different, all station addresses on the extended LAN must be unique and must all use the same format.

A bridge can also be used to connect a local area network to a wide area networking data link. In many cases, a pair of bridges connected by a telecommunication facility is used to interconnect two or more LANs that are installed at different geographic locations. Therefore, an extended LAN can be created using bridges that span any desired distance.

BRIDGE TYPES

There are two basic methods that are used by bridges to determine how to forward frames through the extended LAN when frames must flow from one data link to another in reaching their destinations:

- **Transparent Bridges.** A *transparent* bridge observes transmissions that take place on each data link and learns which stations can be reached over which data links.
- **Source Routing Bridges.** *Source routing* bridges use routing information that has been included in the data link header by the source station to determine the path the frame should take through the extended LAN.

The following sections describe the operation of each type of bridge.

TRANSPARENT BRIDGES

The operation of transparent bridges is covered by an international standard and is documented in ISO 8802-1d *MAC Bridges*. The term *transparent* is used to describe this type of bridge because ordinary stations on an extended LAN constructed using transparent bridges communicate with one another as if the bridges did not exist. An extended LAN looks to the source and destination end systems as if they were both attached to the same LAN data link. The fact that the local area network consists of an extended LAN having transparent bridges is hidden from ordinary stations.

A transparent bridge is sometimes called a *spanning tree* bridge after the name of one of the algorithms used to implement the transparent bridging function.

A transparent bridge performs three basic functions:

- Forwarding frames.
- Building address tables that list the MAC addresses of stations that can be reached over each data link to which the bridge is attached.
- Converting an arbitrary extended LAN physical topology into a spanning tree.

Each of the above functions is described next.

Forwarding Frames

A transparent bridge receives and examines all the frames that are sent over all the data links to which it is attached. The bridge then takes one of the following actions for each frame that it receives:

- If the frame has a group destination MAC address, the bridge forwards the frame over all the data links to which it is attached except the one from which the bridge originally received the frame. This ensures that all stations on the extended LAN eventually see all multicast traffic.

- If the frame has an individual destination MAC address, the bridge looks up the address in its address tables. If the bridge finds the address and determines that the frame can reach the destination station over the same data link as the one from which the bridge received the frame, the destination station is on the same LAN data link as the source station, and no bridging function is required. The bridge simply discards the frame.

- If the bridge finds the destination MAC address in its address tables and determines that the destination station can be reached over a different data link from the one over which the bridge received the frame, the bridge forwards the frame over that data link.

- If the bridge does not find the destination MAC address in its address tables, it forwards the frame over all the data links to which it is attached, except the one over which the bridge originally received the frame.

The algorithms implemented by a transparent bridge ensure that the bridge forwards multicast traffic and traffic for unknown destinations over the entire extended LAN. This guarantees that a frame will be seen by the destination station wherever that station may be, as long as the destination station is active and functioning properly. However, if the bridge knows the location of the destination station, it avoids unnecessarily forwarding traffic over those data links that do not lead to the destination station.

Building Address Tables

When a bridge first becomes operational, its MAC address tables are empty. A bridge builds its address tables by examining the source MAC address fields in all the frames it receives over all the data links to which it is attached. If a bridge receives a frame having a source MAC address not currently in its address tables, it adds the address to the address table associated with the data link over which the bridge received the frame. The bridge then knows over which data link to forward a frame when it next receives a frame having that destination MAC address.

If the bridge receives a frame from a station whose MAC address is already in one of the bridge's address tables, it updates the table entry for that station. This handles the situation where a station is moved from one LAN data link to another. A bridge stores each MAC address table entry for only a predetermined period of time. If a bridge receives no new frames from a particular station, the bridge eventually removes the entry for that station from its address tables. This handles the situation where a station is powered down or is removed from the network.

Creating a Spanning Tree

Individual data links can be physically connected in any desired way using transparent bridges. For example, networks can be physically interconnected, if desired, in an arbitrary mesh topology such that more than one physical path exists between any two stations. However, during the operation of an extended LAN using transparent bridges, the bridges ensure that there is never more than one *active* path that is used at any given time to carry traffic between any two stations. The bridges do this by converting the physical topology of the extended LAN into a *logical* topology that always consists of a *spanning tree*. A spanning tree is a graph structure that includes all the bridges and stations on the extended LAN but in which there is never more than one active path connecting any two stations.

Figure 19.2 illustrates the formation of a spanning tree. The top of the figure shows the physical topology of a simple extended LAN. The bottom of the figure shows a possible logical topology that may result from the process of creating a spanning tree. As part

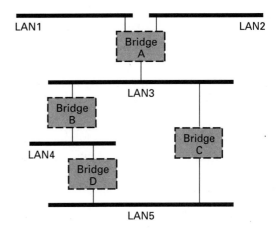

Extended LAN—Physical Topology

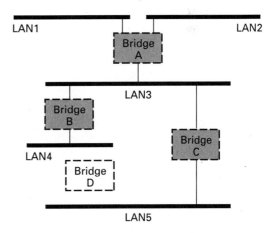

Figure 19.2   Creating a spanning tree structure.

Extended LAN—Spanning Tree Logical Topology

of the process, one of the bridges, in this case bridge A, is chosen as the root bridge. Where there are multiple paths from the root bridge to one of the other LANs, the root bridge chooses one of the paths as the active path, based on factors associated with each of the bridges in the path. In this example, there are two paths to LAN 5, through bridges B and D and through bridge C. In this case, the path through bridge C has been chosen as the active path, and the redundant path through bridge D is not used.

To create and maintain the spanning tree, bridges run a distributed algorithm in which each bridge periodically multicasts Hello frames to all other bridges in the extended LAN. The Hello frames each bridge receives are used by that bridge to calculate the spanning tree and to ensure that all bridges are using the same topology. Redundant links not part of the spanning tree are treated as spares and are not used. If a bridge or link failure occurs, the Hello frames the bridges periodically transmit allow them to quickly calculate a new spanning tree, possibly using links that were previously not used.

Work is being done in an ISO committee to standardize the operation of another type of

SOURCE ROUTING BRIDGES

bridge, called a *source routing* bridge, as an alternative to transparent bridges. At the time of writing, this standardization work has not yet been completed. The operation of source routing bridges that are in use today typically conforms to specifications developed by IBM for its own Token-Ring Network product family. Many vendors who supply token ring LAN products also supply bridges that conform to IBM's source routing bridge specifications. Source routing bridges are typically used only with token ring LANs.

Stations on an extended LAN that uses source routing bridges employ a routing mechanism in relaying traffic from one data link to another. The term *routing* used in context of a source routing bridge should not be confused with the functions performed by routers. The function performed by a router takes place in the OSI Network layer and involves network addresses; the source routing function takes place in the Data Link layer and involves MAC addresses.

When source routing bridges are used in an extended LAN, the source station is expected to know the route over which to send each frame it transmits. If a source station does not know the route, or if the source station determines that a previously-known route is no longer active, the station multicasts a Route Discovery frame. A Route Discovery frame contains the MAC address of the destination station the source station is attempting to reach. The Route Discovery frame is propagated by the bridges throughout the entire extended LAN. As a Route Discovery frame travels across the interconnected networks, each bridge that receives the frame adds routing information to the frame header. When the Route Discovery frame finally reaches its final destination, the destination station sends a response back to the source station. The response contains information that describes the route that the original Route Discovery frame used to reach that destination station. The original source station then uses the source routing information that is contained in the response to its Route Discovery frame to send Data frames to the destination station.

The following sections further describe the functions that are performed by stations and bridges in an extended LAN that is implemented using Token Ring LAN data links and source routing bridges.

Route Discovery Function

Figure 19.3 illustrates one way in which three Token Ring LAN data links might be interconnected using source routing bridges. Any two rings can be interconnected by a bridge attached to each of the two rings. The bridge copies frames from the first ring and retransmits them over the second ring, as well as retransmitting them to the next station on the first ring.

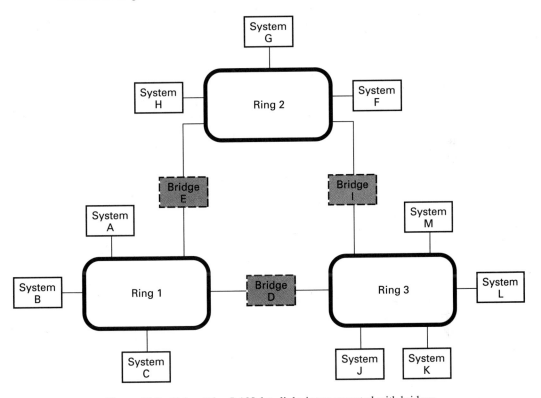

Figure 19.3   Token Ring LAN data links interconnected with bridges.

Depending on how rings are interconnected, there may be more than one possible route over which a frame can travel to a destination station. For example, in Fig. 19.3 a frame going from station B to station J could travel across bridge D or across bridges E and I through ring 2.

As we have seen, if a source station wishes to send a frame to a station on a ring other than its own, it must supply information that specifies the route over which the frame must travel to reach the destination station. As we introduced earlier, in order to determine the route to use, the source station begins by sending a Route Discovery frame addressed to the destination station around the source station's own ring. The Route Discovery frame takes the form of either a TEST or XID frame. If the source station receives a response to the Route Discovery frame, it knows the destination station is on its own ring and does not need to supply routing information for the subsequent frames it transmits.

If the source station does not receive a response to the TEST or XID frame that it sends on its own ring, the station then multicasts a TEST or XID frame using the broadcast destination MAC address. As the frame is forwarded by bridges and passes through the interconnected rings, the bridges add routing information to the frame's header as described previously. If there is more than one possible path to the destination station, multiple copies of the TEST or XID frame will eventually reach the destination station, each containing a different set of routing information. The destination station sends back a response for each TEST or XID frame it receives. Each response contains routing information for one possible path that can be used to reach the destination station. Each response travels back to the source station over the same path used by the original TEST or XID frame but in the reverse direction.

After receiving all the responses to its Route Discovery frame, the source station chooses one of the paths to use in sending subsequent Data frames to the destination station. It then includes routing information for the chosen path in each Data frame that it sends. The destination station uses that path in reverse if it has responses to return to the source station.

Routing Information

When source routing is used in an extended LAN, each MAC frame sent over the extended LAN contains a Routing Information field. If a frame contains routing information, a bit in the source address field is set to 1. Figure 19.4 shows the format of the Routing Information field contained in the IBM Token-Ring Network MAC frame.

The Routing Information field begins with two octets of control information and is followed by a series of segment numbers. Each separate ring in the extended LAN is

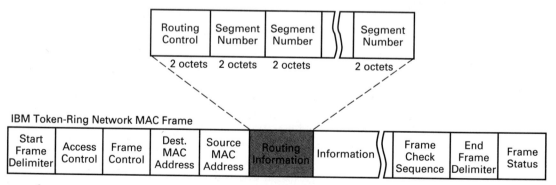

Figure 19.4   IBM Token-Ring Network MAC frame Routing Information field format.

assigned a ring number, and each bridge is assigned a bridge number. The combination of a ring number and a bridge number forms a segment number. The collection of segment numbers contained in a frame's Routing Information field defines the path over which the frame travels through the extended LAN.

Figure 19.5 illustrates the contents of the Routing Control field in the Routing Information field. The Broadcast bit identifies the frame as either a broadcast frame or a nonbroadcast frame. This bit affects the way a bridge treats the routing information— whether it adds a segment number and forwards the frame or uses the existing information to determine whether to forward it. The Length field contains the length of the Routing Information field, which enables stations to determine where the frame's Information field begins.

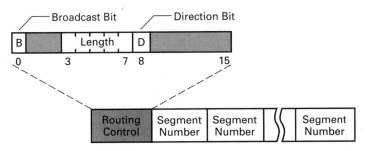

Figure 19.5   IBM Token-Ring Network routing control information.

When a bridge adds a segment number as part of forwarding a broadcast frame, the length value indicates where to add it. After adding it, the bridge updates the length value to reflect the new size of the Routing Information field. The Direction bit indicates whether a frame is traveling from the station that originated the routing process or back to that station. Depending on this value, the segment numbers are used either left-to-right or right-to-left.

Handling Nonmulticast Frames

The segment numbers in the Routing Information field of a nonbroadcast frame are used to route the frame from the source station to the destination station. When a bridge receives a nonbroadcast frame, it checks the segment numbers in the Routing Information field. If a segment number in the frame's Routing Information field matches one of the bridge's own segment numbers, the bridge copies the frame to the indicated ring. If there is no match, the bridge does not copy the frame to another ring.

Handling Multicast Frames

IBM's source routing specification defines two group destination MAC addresses that are used in implementing the source routing function. A frame containing the destination group address value X'C000 FFFF FFFF' is received by all stations on the sending station's ring. A frame containing the broadcast address value X'FFFF FFFF FFFF' is received by all stations on all rings in a multiring network.

When a bridge receives an all-rings broadcast frame, it checks the segment numbers in the frame's Routing Information field. If none of the segment numbers match any of the bridge's own segment numbers, the bridge adds a segment number to the Routing Information field in that frame and copies the frame to the appropriate ring. If there is a match, the bridge discards the frame because that frame has already circled the ring.

Returning to Fig. 19.3, suppose system B sends an all-rings broadcast frame. When the frame reaches bridge D, bridge D adds a segment number to the frame, based on bridge D's bridge number and ring 3's ring number, and copies the frame to ring 3. The frame also continues around ring 1 to bridge E. Bridge E then adds a segment number for bridge E/ring 2 and copies the frame to ring 2. When the frame traveling around ring 2 reaches bridge I, bridge I adds another segment number to the frame for bridge I/ring 3.

SOURCE ROUTING BRIDGES VERSUS TRANSPARENT BRIDGES

Source routing bridges are typically used when bridging individual Token Ring LANs to create a larger Token Ring extended LAN. An advantage of using source routing bridges is that multiple bridges can be installed to create parallel, active paths between individual rings. Multiple active paths allow for higher throughput and load balancing through the various bridges.

A disadvantage of the source routing technique is that source routing bridges often cannot be used to interconnect Token Ring LANs with other types of LANs. Problems can sometimes occur in extended LANs that include both source routing bridges and transparent bridges.

SUMMARY

A bridge is a network interconnection device used to interconnect two or more LAN data links to form a single extended LAN subnetwork. A bridge typically performs a filtering function and passes nonmulticast frames from one LAN data link to another only when necessary. The two types of bridges most often used in constructing internets are transparent bridges and source routing bridges.

The operation of transparent bridges, sometimes called spanning tree bridges, is hidden from end systems on the extended LAN. A transparent bridge learns the addresses of stations that can be reached over each data link to which the bridge is attached and forwards frames based on address tables that it builds. Transparent bridges convert an arbitrary network topology into a spanning tree structure in which there is one active path between any two stations in the extended LAN.

With source routing bridges, typically used only with Token Ring LANs, end systems participate in a routing mechanism to relay traffic through the extended LAN. Source routing bridges can implement multiple active paths between end systems. With source routing bridges, a source system is expected to know the route over which to send frames to a destination system. A source system learns the route to use by multicasting

Route Discovery frames on its own LAN data link. Source routing bridges add routing information to the frame headers of a Route Discovery frame as it travels to the destination station. When the destination system receives a Route Discovery frame, it sends a response back to the original source system containing information about the route to use in sending frames to that destination station.

Routers are used to construct enterprise internetworks that consist of two or more independent subnetworks. Chapter 20 describes the operation of routers in an internet.

CHAPTER **20**

Routers

Routers provide an alternative to bridges for interconnecting local area network and wide area network data links. Bridges are used to construct an extended LAN consisting of a single subnetwork. When LANs are interconnected using routers, each of the LANs forms a separate subnetwork that is better isolated from the other LANs in the internet. An internet can also be implemented using some combination of bridges and routers.

Routers provide the ability to route messages from one system to another where there may be multiple active paths between them. A router performs its function in the OSI model Network layer, as shown in Fig. 20.1. The data units processed by the Network layer are commonly referred to as packets.

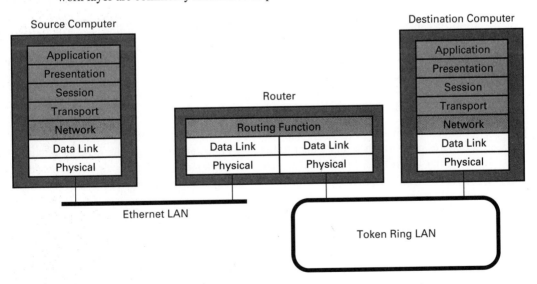

Figure 20.1 The routing function operates in the Network layer.

Routers typically have more intelligence than bridges in deciding how to relay traffic from one LAN to another and permit networks of great complexity to be built. However, routers are typically more complex and more expensive than bridges, and routers must have more detailed knowledge than bridges about the Network layer protocols that are used to carry messages through the internet. Routers also provide the advantage that multicast traffic is typically not forwarded from one LAN to another by a router. Therefore, a router can reduce the amount of multicast traffic that each individual LAN experiences.

Box 20.1 summarizes the major advantages and disadvantages of routers over bridges.

SUBNETWORKS

The systems making up an internet are interconnected by *data links*, and systems and data links together form *subnetworks*. In Chapter 16, we defined a subnetwork as a collection of systems that are attached to a single virtual transmission medium so that each system in the subnetwork is one hop from any other system on that subnetwork. A *hop* is defined as a traversal from one system to another across a single data link, as viewed from the perspective of software operating in the OSI Network layer.

We view traversing from one station to any other in a local area network as a single hop, even though a data unit may be relayed many times from one device to another through the LAN. Relaying functions that are performed by stations, repeaters, or bridges in a LAN or extended LAN is a Data Link layer function and is hidden from the Network layer.

A subnetwork employing a broadcast form of data link technology, such as a local area network, can contain two or more systems; a subnetwork employing a point-to-point form of data link technology, such as wide area networking data link, has exactly two systems. Each of the local area networks in Fig. 20.2 constitutes a separate subnetwork. The two routers connected by the WAN data link also constitutes a subnetwork.

ROUTING ALGORITHMS

Routing algorithms concern how routers acquire the information they need to determine the routes over which to relay data traffic. This chapter introduces the general functions of routing algorithms. Some representative examples of the routing algorithms used in conjunction with specific types of networking software are examined further in the chapters in Part V.

There are several different types of algorithms that can be used for routing. These are summarized in Fig. 20.3 and are described below.

Static Routing

With *static routing*, all routing information is precomputed and is provided to each router through a management action. Static routing has the advantage that sophisticated compu-

BOX 20.1   Advantages and disadvantages of routers.

Advantages of Routers

- **Isolation of Broadcast Traffic.** A major advantage of routers over bridges is that routers prevent the flow of broadcast traffic from one local area network to another, thus reducing the amount of network traffic that the internet as a whole experiences.

- **Flexibility.** Routers can support any desired network topology. Internets that use routers are also less susceptible to time delay problems that sometimes occur in large bridged networks.

- **Priority Control.** Routers can implement priority schemes in which traffic conforming to certain protocols can be given a higher priority than traffic conforming to other protocols.

- **Configuration Control.** Routers are typically more configurable than bridges and allow network administrators to more easily tune network performance.

- **Problem Isolation.** Routers form natural barriers between individual LANs and allow problems that occur in one LAN to be isolated to that LAN. In general, large internets that use routers are easier to maintain and troubleshoot than large bridged extended LANs.

- **Path Selection.** Routers are generally more intelligent than bridges and allow optimal paths to be selected for traffic that flows across the internet. Some routers also allow for load balancing over redundant paths between source and destination systems.

Disadvantages of Routers

- **Protocol Dependence.** Routers operate in the OSI Network layer and must be aware of the protocol or protocols they are designed to route. A router will ignore traffic associated with protocols that it is not designed to handle.

- **Cost.** Routers are typically more complex devices than bridges and are generally more expensive.

- **Throughput.** The use of routers generally involves more overhead in processing each packet, and routers typically provide lower levels of throughput than bridges.

- **Address Assignment.** A bridged internet consists, logically, of a single local area network. Therefore, a user device can be moved from one location to another without requiring that its network address be changed. In an internet constructed using routers, moving a user machine from one LAN to another often requires that a new network address be assigned to that system.

- **Unreachable Systems.** Routing table entries must be accurate in order for a system on one LAN data link to send data to a system on another LAN data link. When using routers that do not dynamically configure their routing tables, inaccurate routing table entries can result in systems being unreachable.

- **Unroutable Protocols.** Some protocols, such as SNA subarea network traffic and Net-BIOS traffic, do not lend themselves to traditional routing and must be handled using specialized techniques.

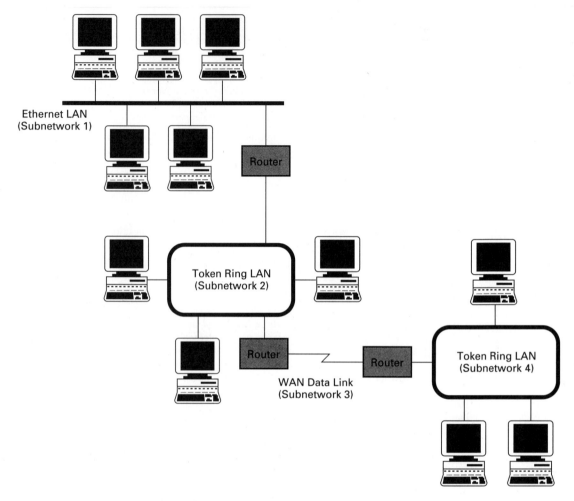

Figure 20.2 Subnetworks interconnected with routers.

tational methods can be used for computing routes, since routes are not computed in real time. However, with static routing techniques, routing information must be recomputed and provided to the routers each time the network topology changes. Thus, static routing techniques are generally not well suited to large internets that may be constantly changing. Static routing techniques are, however, appropriate for small internets that require few routers and have a simple, relatively unchanging topology.

Quasi-Static Routing

Quasi-static routing is similar to static routing except the routing information that is computed and provided to each router includes information about alternative paths that can be used when certain types of failures occur. Quasi-static routing techniques can handle

Method	Collection	Distribution	Computation	Adaptability
Static	Through network management.	Through network management.	Routes computed offline.	None in real time.
Quasi-static	Through network management.	Through network management.	Routes computed offline.	Limited adaptability to failures.
Centralized	Routers report information about the local environment to a central facility.	Central facility distributes forwarding information to each router.	Routes computed by central facility.	Can adapt to any changes to the central facility, but routers have difficulty finding the central facility.
Distributed Distance Vector	Routers report current routes to each neighbor router.	Routers accept routing information from neighbor routers and redistribute their view of local neighborhood.	Routes computed individually by each router upon receipt of information that changes their routing decisions.	Adapts to any changes that are reported by neighbors.
Link State	Routers collect globally-provided information to obtain a table describing the routing domain.	Routers globally distribute information about their local environments to all other routers.	Routes computed individually by each router upon receipt of information that changes their routing domain tables.	Adapts to any changes that are reported in the link state information.

Figure 20.3   Characteristics of five types of routing algorithms.

some kinds of topological changes, such as links becoming unavailable, but major changes to the network topology still require routing information to be recomputed offline for the routers.

Centralized Routing

With *centralized routing*, end systems and routers report information about their local environments to a centralized facility. The centralized facility accumulates routing information from all the systems in the network, computes routes, and sends to each router the information it needs to make routing decisions. In effect, only the centralized facility has complete knowledge of the network topology.

Although, in theory, a centralized routing scheme can respond to topological changes, it has two major drawbacks. First, a way must be found for relaying the routing information to the centralized facility after a topological change occurs. This is difficult because the routing information maintained by the centralized facility cannot be reliably used for this purpose after the network topology changes. Second, the delays inherent in propagating routing information to and from the centralized facility can cause the calculated routes to be different from the optimal routes that should be used.

Distributed Adaptive Routing

With *distributed adaptive routing*, systems dynamically sense their local environments and exchange this information with each other in a distributed fashion. Each router then periodically computes new routes for relaying packets from one system to the next. Distributed adaptive algorithms are robust, and they can quickly adapt to changing network topologies.

A system of routers that use distributed adaptive routing all participate in a distributed algorithm to decide on the optimal path over which each packet should travel from a source system to a destination system. Distributed adaptive routing protocols govern how routers exchange packets with each other in an internet to maintain the routing information they use.

Two forms of distributed adaptive routing are in common use in computer networks: *distance-vector* routing and *link-state* routing. Each of these is described in the following sections. The routing algorithms used by specific networking software are described in the chapters in Part V.

DISTANCE-VECTOR ROUTING

With a *distance-vector* routing algorithm, also called a *Bellman-Ford* algorithm, each router in the internet learns about the network topology by exchanging routing information packets with its neighbor routers. A router initializes its routing table by storing information for each subnetwork to which it is directly attached. It stores information that identifies the subnetwork and the distance to that network, typically measured in hops. For a subnetwork that is directly attached to the router, the number of hops is zero. Periodically the router sends out a copy of its routing table to all the other routers it can reach directly.

When the router receives routing information from another router, it uses that information to update its own routing table. The router adds entries to its own routing table for subnetworks that are not currently in the table but that can be reached through the other router. If the router determines that there is a shorter route to a subnetwork already referenced in its routing table, the router updates that entry. Any other changes in distance or availability are also reflected.

By exchanging routing information with each other, each router learns what its neighbors think the topology of the internet looks like. Each router then constructs a new description of the network topology and communicates this new picture to its neighbor routers. The process is continually repeated and eventually stabilizes when all the routers learn that they have the same description of the network topology.

A distance-vector algorithm is a relatively simple algorithm and is relatively easy to design and implement. A major problem with distance-vector routing, however, is that the computational complexity of the algorithm grows rapidly as the internet grows in size. Distance-vector routing is well suited to internets having a maximum size in the thousands of systems, but it does not scale well much beyond this to, say, internets with millions of systems. The algorithm can take many iterations to converge in a large network after a topology change occurs. Also, in a network containing routers having varying levels of performance, and links having varying bandwidths, the slowest routers in the network and the slowest links tend to become convergence bottlenecks.

LINK-STATE ROUTING

The other major form of distributed adaptive routing algorithm is called a *link-state* routing algorithm, sometimes called a *shortest path first* (SPF) algorithm. The routing algorithm chosen for the OSI architecture, and the only routing algorithm currently documented in an international standard (ISO 10589), is a link-state routing algorithm.

With link-state routing, each router knows the complete topology of the internet in terms of the existence of all other routers and the links between them. Each router broadcasts information about the routers to which it is directly attached and the status of the data links between them. A router constructs a map of the internet from this information, consisting of a graph with routers as systems and links as edges. Routers are then able to calculate routes from this graph using the Dijkstra shortest path algorithm.

Routers continually monitor the status of their links by exchanging packets with neighboring routers. If a router does not respond after a certain number of tries, the link is assumed to be down. Periodically, each router sends out link status information that other routers use to update their topology maps. If the status of a router or a link changes, routes are recalculated. Since each router broadcasts information about its own local environment to all the other routers, all the routers quickly receive a complete description of the network topology. Each router then knows where all the other routers are and what links interconnect them.

In contrast with distance-vector routing, a link-state algorithm converges in a single iteration after any topology change. Link-state routing also involves the transmission of less information than distance-vector routing. With distance-vector routing, each router broadcasts information from its entire routing table, which reflects all subnetworks in the internet. With link-state routing, a router broadcasts information only about its own directly-attached links.

The main disadvantage of link-state algorithms is that they are more difficult to design and build than distance-vector algorithms.

GUIDELINES FOR CHOOSING BETWEEN BRIDGES AND ROUTERS

It is difficult to provide a set of guidelines that can be used in all cases to assist in making the decision between using a router versus using a bridge in implementing an enterprise internetwork. In most cases, traffic modeling must be performed to determine the true requirements of each LAN in the internet that is being designed.

In general, however, if two LANs are to be interconnected that carry exclusively traffic conforming to one or more of the routable protocols, such as TCP/IP or NetWare, then it is generally preferable to interconnect them using a router. A router prevents the broadcast traffic generated on one LAN from flowing across the router to the other LAN.

On the other hand, traffic conforming to some protocols is carried correctly only in the single-LAN environment. NetBIOS and the Local Area Transport (LAT) protocol used by some Digital Equipment Corporation equipment are examples of these. For such protocols to work properly across interconnected LANs, a bridge instead of a router should be used to interconnect them.

In general, a good design strategy with relatively low volume networks is often to bridge traffic within a building or small campus and to route traffic between locations that are separated by larger distances. Such a strategy allows a network topology to be created that combines LAN and WAN technology in an optimal manner. As traffic volumes go up, it may become necessary to replace certain bridges with routers, even for traffic flowing within the same building, to adequately isolate the multicast traffic.

When designing networks that must carry large volumes of traffic conforming to the unroutable protocols, such as SNA or NetBIOS, bridges must sometimes be used when routers might otherwise be advisable. In designing networks that must carry traffic conforming to the routable protocols and also traffic conforming to one or more unroutable protocols, special considerations apply. Devices categorized as brouters can be used that route traffic conforming to certain protocols, such as TCP/IP and Novell NetWare, and bridge traffic conforming to all other protocols.

SUMMARY

Routers provide an alternative to bridges for interconnecting LAN and WAN data links. In an internet consisting of independent subnetworks, multicast traffic does not flow through routers from one subnetwork to another. Routers implement a routing algorithm in making decisions about how to relay packets through the internet. Routers can employ static routing, quasi-static routing, centralized routing, or distributed adaptive routing. Most routers use distributed adaptive routing techniques, of which there are two major types—distance-vector and link-state.

With a distance-vector routing algorithm, sometimes called a Bellman-Ford routing algorithm, each router in the internet learns about the network topology by exchanging routing information packets with its neighbor routers. The routing information packets a router sends contain information about each subnetwork the router can reach including the distance to that subnetwork, typically measured in hops. A distance-vector routing algorithm typically takes many iterations to stabilize after a topology change occurs.

With a link-state routing algorithm routers also exchange routing information packets. The routing information packets that a router sends consist of information about the data links to which that router is directly attached. A link-state routing algorithm converges in a single iteration after a topology change occurs.

Chapter 21 begins Part V of the book in which we explore representative examples of the networking software that is employed in constructing local area networks and internets. Chapter 21 examines the protocols and mechanisms that IBM and Microsoft have implemented in networking software for the personal computer environment.

NETWORKING SOFTWARE

A wide variety of networking software is available in the various computing environments for making use of LAN data links in local area networks and in enterprise internetworks. This part of the book describes four widely-used, representative approaches to network software.

Chapter 21 examines the protocols and mechanisms that IBM and Microsoft have implemented in networking software for the personal computer environment.

Chapter 22 introduces the Novell NetWare family of networking software that is also used in the personal computer networking environment.

Chapter 23 describes the TCP/IP approach to computer networking that is used in a wide variety of computing environments.

Chapter 24 describes AppleTalk, Apple's approach to computer networking.

IBM and Microsoft Networking Software

IBM and Microsoft have worked together on a number of different approaches to integrating personal computer networking into the MS-DOS operating system. IBM's earliest hardware products for personal computer networking were its PC Network LAN adapter products, which we described in Chapter 10. To support the PC Network LAN products, IBM developed a number of relatively simple software subsystems. Today, IBM and Microsoft both offer far more sophisticated networking software subsystems for both the MS-DOS, OS/2, Windows, and Windows/NT system software environments.

The various networking software products offered by IBM and Microsoft offer a wide range of networking capabilities, including support for the NetWare and TCP/IP architectures described in Chapters 22 and 23. However, the IBM and Microsoft products all continue support for the basic architecture on which IBM's early networking support was based.

IBM'S PERSONAL COMPUTER NETWORKING ARCHITECTURE

IBM's fundamental architecture for personal computer networking, and the way in which it relates to the OSI model, is shown in Fig. 21.1. The following sections briefly describe the functions of the three major layers making up IBM's approach to PC networking. Later sections in this chapter further describe each of the major services and protocols that have been defined for the upper layers.

LAN Adapter Layer

IBM uses the term *LAN adapter* to refer to the network interface card (NIC) that is installed in a personal computer to provide it with physical LAN communication capabilities. Although IBM's initial support for personal computer networking was based on its PC Network product family, IBM's approach to personal computer networking now also supports the IEEE/ISO/ANSI LAN architecture through its *Data Link Control* (DLC)

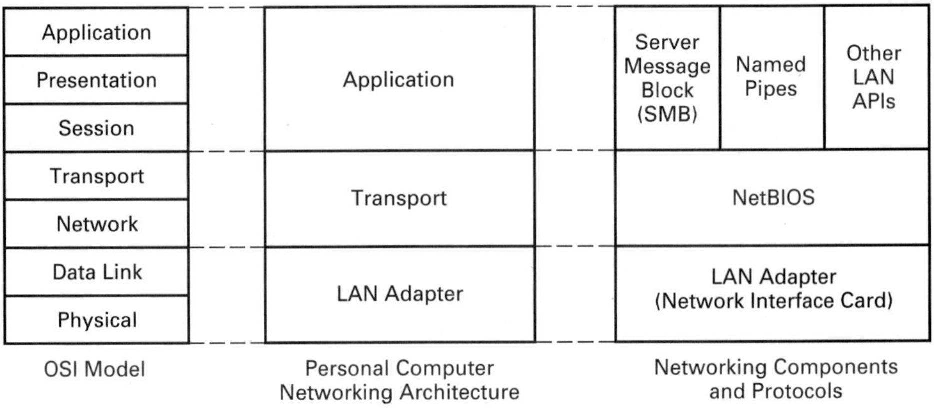

Application			Server Message Block (SMB)	Named Pipes	Other LAN APIs
Presentation		Application			
Session					
Transport		Transport	NetBIOS		
Network					
Data Link		LAN Adapter	LAN Adapter (Network Interface Card)		
Physical					
OSI Model		Personal Computer Networking Architecture	Networking Components and Protocols		

Figure 21.1 IBM personal computer networking architecture.

interface. The DLC Interface is described in Chapter 9. IBM's and Microsoft's networking software supports the major LAN technologies in common use today, including Token Ring, Ethernet, and FDDI.

Transport Layer

The basic function of the Transport layer in IBM's approach to personal computer networking is to perform an end-to-end data delivery service. IBM's and Microsoft's current networking software subsystems support many approaches to data transport. However, early in the development of the MS-DOS operating system environment, IBM and Microsoft cooperatively defined an approach to data transport in a local area networking environment, called *NetBIOS*, that allowed IBM-compatible personal computers to exchange data over a LAN data link.

NetBIOS defines both an application programming interface (API) for requesting Transport layer communication services and a communication protocol for supplying those services. Many networking software subsystems from third-part software vendors also support the NetBIOS APIs and Transport layer protocol.

Application Layer

The fundamental purpose of the Application layer in the IBM approach to personal computer networking is to provide end users at personal computers with transparent access to communication facilities. The Application layer provides facilities that application programs operating on behalf of end users can employ for requesting network facilities.

As with the Transport layer, IBM's and Microsoft's network operating systems support a wide range of application services and protocols. Three important sets of application services and protocols include the following:

- **Server Message Blocks.** The term *Server Message Block* (SMB) refers to an API that application programs use to request high-level application services and a protocol for providing those services. The SMB services and protocol were originally developed for networking software that operated in the MS-DOS environment. Many newer networking software subsystems for the OS/2, Windows, and Windows/NT environments continue to support the SMB interface and protocol.

- **Named Pipes.** Named pipes is a more powerful interface for interprocess communication than is provided by the NetBIOS and SMB interfaces. Named Pipes was originally developed for the IBM LAN Server and Microsoft LAN Manager network operating system products. It is also implemented in many other networking software subsystems that operate in the OS/2, Windows, and Windows/NT environments.

- **Additional LAN APIs.** This is an additional collection of application-oriented API services that IBM has defined for accessing networking services. These APIs are implemented in many networking software subsystems, including those that operate in the OS/2, Windows, and Windows/NT environments.

The following sections further describe the major services and protocols that operate in the Application and Transport layers of IBM's architecture for personal computer networking. We begin with the Application layer.

APPLICATION SERVICES AND PROTOCOLS

The services and protocols that operate in the Application layer of the IBM personal computer networking architecture are designed to provide services to end users and to application programs with which end users interact. The three sets of application services and protocols described in this section include the Server Message Block protocol, Named Pipes, and a set of additional LAN APIs identified by IBM for the personal computer networking environment.

Server Message Blocks

IBM's local area networking products support an API for requesting communication services and a protocol for supplying those services that is based on data structures called *Server Message Blocks* (SMBs). SMBs are transported between communicating systems in providing networking services. The SMB protocol supports many of the services that are commonly provided by a networking software subsystem, such as electronic mail and file and print server functions.

The SMB protocol defines the formats of SMBs and the rules governing how SMBs are sent between systems. In SMB terminology, a user system operating in the role of a client is called a *redirector*. A redirector communicates with a server by exchanging SMBs between the redirector and the server. An SMB sent from a redirector to a server is called a Request; an SMB flowing from a server to a redirector is called a Response. SMBs are carried between systems using the services of an underlying Transport layer service, such as NetBIOS.

The SMB protocol has been designed to be extensible, and different dialects of it have been developed for various different networking software subsystems. In this chapter, we will examine a base dialect of the SMB protocol that is supported in most environments that use SMBs for communication.

SMB Format

Box 21.1 shows the general format of an SMB data structure and describes its fields. The contents of the parameter and buffer fields are dependent on the particular SMB function being invoked and on whether the SMB is functioning as a Request or a Response.

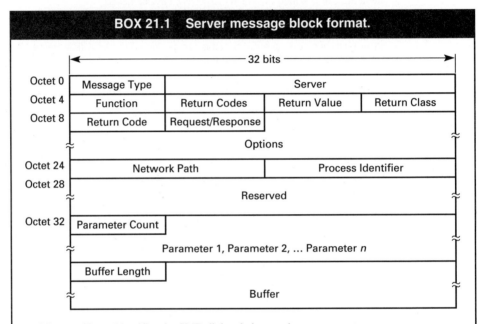

BOX 21.1   Server message block format.

- **Message Type.** Identifies the SMB dialect being used.
- **Server.** Identifies the server being addressed.
- **Function.** Identifies the SMB function requested.
- **Return Class.** Identifies a class of error that has occurred.
- **Return Value.** Contains the value returned by a 24H interrupt.
- **Return Code.** Further identifies completion status.
- **Request/Response.** Identifies an SMB as a Request to a server or a Response to a redirector.
- **Network Path.** The path ID for the resource being accessed.
- **Process Identifier.** Identifies a process used to clean-up a connection.
- **Parameter Count.** Gives the number of parameters that follow.
- **Parameter.** Contains a function-specific parameter.
- **Buffer Length.** Gives the length of the buffer that follows.
- **Buffer.** Contains function-specific data.

SMB Services

A variety of SMB formats are defined to perform different functions. SMBs can be divided into four categories:

- Session Control
- File Access Management
- Print Server Support
- Message Delivery

The major SMBs in each of the four SMB categories are listed in Box 21.2.

Redirecting I/O Requests

The primary way in which SMB services are requested is by redirecting local I/O requests that an application program executing in a redirector issues. A conventional application program executing in a system operating as a redirector need not be aware that it is operating in a networking environment and that its I/O requests are being redirected. An application that is unaware of network redirection is called a *network-transparent* application.

An application program requests I/O services by issuing function calls. The redirector function intercepts all I/O function call interrupts and checks to see if the call applies to a resource under the control of a server rather than to a local resource.

If the interrupt is associated with a server, the redirector sends the request across the network to the appropriate server. This is done by creating an appropriate SMB and by using a transport service, such as NetBIOS, to send it across the network to the server. The server processes the request using normal operating system facilities to handle the processing and sends the results of the request back to the original redirector system using another SMB. The redirector function then returns the results to the application program. To the user at the local system, and to the application program, it appears as if the request had been processed locally.

Explicitly Requesting SMB Services

A *network-aware* application program is one that is designed to perform network-based processing directly. For example, an application that provides electronic mail services to users on the network must be network-aware and able to explicitly send and receive SMBs across the network.

SMB services are explicitly requested by an application program by formatting appropriate SMB data structures, and then executing a function call that sends the SMB across the network.

Named Pipes

The SMB interface and protocol was specifically designed to meet the needs for interprocess communication in the MS-DOS operating system environment. More powerful interfaces and protocols designed for more advanced operating system environments have

BOX 21.2   System message block (SMB) services.

Session Control SMBs

Session control SMBs perform two major functions—controlling connections between a redirector and a server resource, such as a printer or file directory, and determining the particular set of SMBs to be supported. The session control SMBs are as follows:

- **Verify Dialect.** Establishes the dialect to be used on a session.
- **Start Connection.** Establishes a redirector/server connection.
- **End Connection.** Terminates a redirector/server connection.

File Access Management SMBs

The file access management SMBs allow applications using the network to share files and directories. There are file access SMBs for managing directories, maintaining files, accessing files, and locking files.

The SMBs for managing directories are as follows:

- **Create Directory.** Implements the DOS MKDIR function.
- **Remove a Directory.** Implements the DOS RMDIR function.
- **Check Directory.** Determines if a directory exists at the server.

The SMBs for file maintenance are as follows:

- **Create File.** Creates a new file or truncates an old file to zero length and establishes a handle for the file for subsequent access.
- **Create New File.** Creates a new file and guarantees that the file name of a file being created is unique.
- **Create Unique File.** Creates a unique file.
- **Delete File.** Deletes a file.
- **Rename File.** Renames an existing file within a network resource.
- **Get File Attributes.** Obtains information about a file.
- **Set File Attributes.** Sets a file's attributes for subsequent access.
- **Get Disk Attributes.** Gets storage sizes and disk layout.
- **Search Multiple Files.** Implements the FCB and ASCIIZ search function.

The SMBs for accessing files are as follows:

- **Open File.** Establishes a handle to an existing file for subsequent access. Supports file sharing and allows access mode and sharing mode to be specified in the Open File request.
- **Close File.** Closes a file.

BOX 21.2 *(Continued)*

- **Commit File.** Causes all buffers for a file to be written to the media.
- **Read Octet Block.** Reads a block of data from a file.
- **Write Octet Block.** Writes a block of data to a file.
- **LSEEK.** Moves the file read/write pointer.
- **End of Process.** Ends all work within this connection that belongs to a given process.

The SMBs for file locking, which are used by an application to implement record locking are as follows:

- **Lock Octet Block.** Locks a region of octets within a file.
- **Unlock Octet Block.** Unlocks a region of octets within a file.

Print Server Support SMBs

The print server SMBs can be used to queue files to a print queue, check the status of a print queue, and change queue status. The print server SMBs are as follows:

- **Create Spool File.** Marks a new print spool data stream.
- **Spool Octet Block.** Transfers a block of data to be spooled.
- **Close Spool File.** Marks the end of a print spool data stream.
- **Return Print Queue.** Gets the contents of the server print queue.

Message Delivery SMBs

The message delivery SMBs can be used to send and receive a message as a single transmission, send and receive a message with several transmissions, broadcast a message to all stations, and forward messages to another station. The message delivery SMBs are as follows:

- **Send Single Block Message.** Sends a message that is a single block.
- **Send Broadcast Message.** Sends a single block message to all user names on the network.
- **Send Start of Multiblock Message.** Signals the start of a message that consists of multiple blocks.
- **Send Text of Multiblock Message.** Sends text of message that is multiple blocks.
- **Send End of Multiblock Message.** Signals the end of a multiple block message.
- **Forward User Name.** Requests that the server receives messages for the given user name.
- **Cancel Forward.** Requests that the server no longer receives messages for the given forwarded user name.
- **Get Machine Name.** Obtains the machine name for a user name.

subsequently been developed by IBM and Microsoft. The *Named Pipes* facility is one such system for interprocess communication that was codeveloped by IBM and Microsoft for their LAN Server and LAN Manager network operating system products. The Named Pipes mechanism has been implemented in a variety of networking software subsystems.

The Named Pipes interface allows a program to send data to or receive data from another program in a way similar to issuing ordinary file management commands. The data is sent and received in the same way as it would be if it were being read to or written from a file. The two programs communicating over a named pipe can be local (located on the same system) or remote (on different systems in a network). The programs are unaware of whether communication is local or remote.

Duplex Communication

A named pipe provides two-way communication that operates in a similar manner as a full-duplex channel. The program at each end of the named pipe has a read buffer and a write buffer and can both read and write concurrently. If desired, access to a named pipe can be restricted so that communication takes place in one direction at a time.

Client-Server Relationship

When two programs communicate using a named pipe, one program operates in the role of the *server* and the other in the role of the *client*. The server process creates the named pipe and then waits for the client process to open it. Once the client process opens the named pipe, either process can write to or read from the named pipe. Either of the processes can then close the pipe. After a named pipe is closed by a client, it can be opened again by the same or another client.

Named Pipe Instances

A server can establish multiple *instances* of a named pipe. Each instance can be used to communicate with a different client. This allows a server to communicate with multiple clients using a single named pipe.

Types of Named Pipes

A named pipe can be a *message* pipe or an *octet* pipe (called a *byte* pipe in IBM and Microsoft documentation). When an application writes data to a message pipe, it creates a header that defines the length of the message being written. When an application writes data to an octet pipe, no header is necessary. When an application reads data from a message pipe, it can be read either as a message stream or an octet stream. If it is read as a message stream, an entire message is read as a unit based on the message length in the header. If it is read as an octet stream, headers are skipped over, and data is read up to the size requested in the read function call.

Named Pipe Function Calls

The Named Pipes facility defines a set of function calls. These function calls are used to create, open, and close named pipes, read and write data over them, and determine their status. The most commonly used named pipe function calls are described in Box 21.3.

BOX 21.3 Named pipe function calls.

Server Function Calls

The following function calls are used by a server process to communicate over a named pipe:

- **DosMkNmPipe.** Creates a named pipe.
- **DosConnectNmPipe.** Causes the server to wait for a client to open a pipe.
- **DosRead/DosReadAsync.** Reads data written to a named pipe by the client process.
- **DosWrite/DosWriteAsync.** Writes data to a named pipe.
- **DosDisConnectNmPipe.** Prepares the pipe to be opened by the next client.
- **DosClose.** Deallocates a pipe.

Client Function Calls

The following function calls are used by the client process to communicate over a named pipe:

- **DosOpen.** Opens a named pipe for communication between the client and the server.
- **DosWaitNmPipe.** Causes the client to wait for an available instance of a pipe.
- **DosRead/DosReadAsync.** Reads data written to the named pipe by the server process.
- **DosWrite/DosWriteAsync.** Writes data to the named pipe.
- **DosClose.** Ends the client's access to the pipe.

Dialog Function Calls

The following function calls are used to coordinate client-server dialogs over a named pipe:

- **DosBufReset.** Allows communicating processes to synchronize their dialogs by blocking a process from using a named pipe until all the data it has written has been read by the other process.
- **DosTransactNmPipe.** Performs a transaction, or a write followed by a read, on a message pipe. It writes data to the named pipe and does not return until it reads a response from the pipe.
- **DosCallNmPipe.** Has the combined effect of a DosOpen, DosTransactNmPipe, and a DosClose.

Information Function Calls

The following function calls are used to set and obtain information about a named pipe:

- **DosPeekNmPipe.** Reads the contents of a named pipe without removing the data read from the pipe and returns information about the state of the pipe.
- **DosQNmPipeInfo.** Determines buffer sizes and pipe instance counts.
- **DosQNmPHandState.** Determines the state of the pipe handle.
- **DosSetNmPHandState.** Sets information such as the read mode and pipe mode of the pipe.

Additional LAN APIs

In addition to the Named Pipes facility, a number of additional APIs have been developed that provide services specifically related to local area network operation. These APIs, referred to as LAN APIs, were originally codeveloped by IBM and Microsoft Corporation as part of the LAN Manager and LAN Server network operating system. Many of these APIs have been implemented in other networking software subsystems.

These LAN APIs provide services for interprocess communication, workstation operation, printer and serial device control, and various administrative and management functions. The general functions provided by the APIs are described in Box 21.4.

BOX 21.4   Additional LAN APIs.

Interprocess Communication APIs

These APIs are used for interprocess communication in both local and remote environments. The following API categories are provided:

- **Mailslots.** Mailslot APIs provide one-way interprocess communication.
  - DosMakeMailSlot
  - DosDeleteMailSlot
  - DosMailSlotInfo
  - DosReadMailSlot
  - DosPeekMailSlot
  - DosWriteMailSlot

- **Alert.** Alert APIs provide notification of network events.
  - NetAlertStart
  - NetAlertStop
  - NetAlertRaise

- **NetBIOS.** NetBIOS APIs are used to provide communication by using the NetBIOS Transport protocol directly.
  - NetBiosEnum
  - NetBiosGetInfo
  - NetBiosOpen
  - NetBiosClose
  - NetBiosSubmit

Workstation APIs

The following API categories allow programs to use basic workstation services such as logging on, adding or deleting connections to remote resources, messaging, remote program execution, remote copying, and remote time-of-day:

- **Workstations.** Workstation APIs control the operation of clients.
  - NetWkstaSetUID
  - NetWkstaGetInfo
  - NetWkstaSetInfo

BOX 21.4 *(Continued)*

- **Use.** Use APIs are used to examine or control connections between clients and servers.

  — NetUseEnum
  — NetUseGetInfo
  — NetUseAdd
  — NetUseDel

- **Messages.** Message APIs are used to send, receive, read, log, and forward messages.

  — NetMessageNameEnum
  — NetMessageNameGetInfo
  — NetMessageNameAdd
  — NetMessageNameDel
  — NetMessageNameFwd
  — NetMessageNameunFwd
  — NetMessageBufferSend
  — NetMessageFileSend
  — NetMessageLogFileSet
  — NetMessageLogFileGet

- **Profile.** Profile APIs are used for saving and loading user profiles.

  — NetProfileSave
  — NetProfileLoad

- **Configuration.** Configuration APIs are used for getting information from the configuration file.

  — NetConfigGet
  — NetConfigGetAll

- **Remote.** Remote APIs are used to copy and move remote files, execute a program at the server, and get time-of-day information at a server.

  — NetRemoteTOD
  — NetRemoteCopy
  — NetRemoteMove
  — NetServerAdmin
  — NetRemoteExec

- **Service.** Service APIs start and control network service programs.

  — NetServiceEnum
  — NetServiceInstall
  — NetServiceControl
  — NetServiceStatus
  — DosPrintDestStatus

Administration APIs

The following API categories enable programs to work with basic server functions, such as sharing resources and administering sessions and connections:

(Continued)

BOX 21.4 *(Continued)*

- **Server.** Server APIs enable administration tasks to be performed on a local or remote server.
  - NetServerEnum
  - NetServerGetInfo
  - NetServerSetInfo
  - NetServerDiskEnum
- **Shares.** Share APIs control shared resources.
  - NetShareEnum
  - NetShareGetInfo
  - NetShareSetInfo
  - NetShareAdd
  - NetShareDel
  - NetShareCheck
- **Sessions.** Session APIs control network sessions established between clients and servers.
  - NetSessionEnum
  - NetSessionGetInfo
  - NetSessionDel
- **Connections.** The connections API lists all connections made to a server by a specific client or all the connections to the server's shared resources.
  - NetConnectionEnum
- **Files.** File APIs monitor which file, device, and pipe resources are opened on a server, and they close one if necessary.
  - NetFileEnum
  - NetFileGetInfo
  - NetFileClose

Access Control APIs

The following API categories allow programs to work with user accounts and resource access control permissions:

- **Access Permissions.** Access permission APIs are used to add, delete, and change access control records.
  - NetAccessEnum
  - NetAccessGetInfo
  - NetAccessSetInfo
  - NetAccessAdd
  - NetAccessDel
- **Users.** User APIs are used to add, delete, and change user accounts.
  - NetUserEnum
  - NetUserGetInfo
  - NetUserSetInfo
  - NetUserAdd
  - NetUserDel
  - NetUserPasswordSet

BOX 21.4 *(Continued)*

— NetUserGetGroups
— NetUserValidate

- **Group.** Group APIs are used to add, delete, and change user groups.

— NetGroupEnum
— NetGroupAdd
— NetGroupDel
— NetGroupAddUser
— NetGroupDelUser
— NetGroupGetUser

Printing and Character APIs

The following API categories allow the manipulation of print and serial devices, of their queues, and of jobs in queues:

- **Character Devices.** Character device APIs control shared, remote serial devices.

— NetCharDevEnum
— NetCharDevGetInfo
— NetCharDevControl
— NetCharDevQEnum
— NetCharDevQGetInfo
— NetCharDevQSetInfo
— NetCharDevQPurge

- **Print Queues.** Print queue APIs are used to manipulate spooled printer queues.

— DosPrintQEnum
— DosPrintQGetInfo
— DosPrintQSetInfo
— DosPrintQAdd
— DosPrintQDel
— DosPrintQPause
— DosPrintQContinue

- **Print Jobs.** Print job APIs are used to manipulate print jobs within a queue.

— DosPrintJobEnum
— DosPrintJobGetInfo
— DosPrintJobSetInfo
— DosPrintJobSchedule
— DosPrintJobDel
— DosPrintJobPause
— DosPrintJobContinue
— DosPrintJobGetID

- **Print Destinations.** Print destination APIs are used to manipulate print devices associated with one or more print queues.

— DosPrintDestEnum
— DosPrintDestGetInfo
— DosPrintDestControl

(Continued)

BOX 21.4   *(Continued)*

Auditing APIs

The following API categories enable programs to create and manipulate server audit records and error logs and to retrieve server statistics:

- **Audit.** Audit APIs are used to read and write audit log records and clear the audit log.
  — NetAuditOpen
  — NetAuditClear
  — NetAuditWrite
- **Error Log.** Error log APIs are used to read and write error log records and clear the error log.
  — NetErrorLogOpen
  — NetErrorLogClear
  — NetErrorLogWrite
- **Statistics.** Statistics APIs are used to get workstation or server operation and performance statistics.
  — NetStatisticsGet
  — NetStatisticsClear

NETBIOS TRANSPORT SERVICE AND PROTOCOL

The name NetBIOS refers to networking extensions of the facilities that have historically been provided by the basic input/output system (BIOS) included in read-only memory (ROM) in every IBM compatible computer. NetBIOS effectively extends the local I/O capabilities of a personal computer operating system to a networking environment.

NetBIOS defines an API for requesting Transport layer communication services and a protocol that describes how those services are provided. NetBIOS has become a de facto Transport layer standard for personal computer LAN communication, and NetBIOS services are provided by a wide variety of different networking software subsystems.

The name *NETBEUI* is sometimes used to refer to the protocol used to supply NetBIOS services and/or the software components used to implement NetBIOS. NETBEUI was the name of one of the software components originally developed by IBM and Microsoft to supply NetBIOS services for early personal computers.

NetBIOS Services

NetBIOS defines two types of Transport layer data delivery services—a connectionless, or datagram service and a reliable, connection-oriented service, often called a session service. Other types of support services are provided as well.

The following sections describe the major types of services that NetBIOS provides to software operating in the layers above the Transport layer.

NetBIOS Name Service

With NetBIOS, names are the basis for communication between application programs. NetBIOS maintains a table of names for each system identifying the name or names associated with application programs in that system. NetBIOS services are invoked based on the use of these names. NetBIOS allows a given application program to have multiple names and allows a given system to support multiple named users. Names can be added and deleted dynamically, and the same name can be assigned to different systems at different times. A name is either a unique name or a group name. Group names allow several users, on the same or different systems, to be addressed using a single name.

NetBIOS associates names directly with station addresses, and NetBIOS defines no separate Network layer addressing mechanism. For this reason, the NetBIOS Transport protocol is not well suited to use in an internet that consists of multiple LAN subnetworks interconnected using routers.

NetBIOS Session Service

Session service provides reliable data transfer by establishing a session between two names over which data can be transmitted. A given network user can be involved in multiple sessions. When a session is established, the session is assigned a one-octet session identifier to differentiate the different sessions a user might have active. Messages that are sent are acknowledged by the receiving station. If an expected acknowledgment is not received, the sender retransmits the message.

NetBIOS Datagram Service

Datagram service allows a user to send messages without first establishing a session. Messages can be sent to other network users by specifying individual names or group names or by broadcasting messages to all users. The datagram service does not use acknowledgments and thus should not be considered a reliable service.

NetBIOS Status and Control Services

The NetBIOS status and control services can be used to request and return status information for a particular network name and to terminate a trace that originated at a local or remote system.

Network Control Block API

The NetBIOS API is based on a control block called a *Network Control Block* (NCB). A program using the NetBIOS interface constructs an NCB that contains the required information and invokes a NetBIOS function using a mechanism that is dependent on the operating system environment. A command code in the NCB identifies the particular function to be performed. The program must also provide buffer areas that are used to hold messages being sent or received. Addresses contained in the NCB refer to these buffers.

Box 21.5 shows the format of the Network Control Block and describes its fields. Box 21.6 lists the major services that are provided by the NCB API in each of the four service categories.

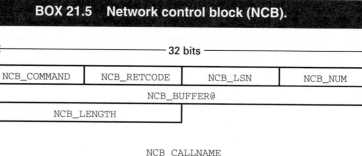

BOX 21.5 Network control block (NCB).

- **NCB_COMMAND.** Identifies the command to be performed by NetBIOS.
- **NCB_RETCODE.** A completion code returned by NetBIOS indicating whether the command was successfully completed.
- **NCB_LSN.** Indicates the local session number that was assigned to the session.
- **NCB_NUM.** A number provided by NetBIOS that represents a network name.
- **NCB_BUFFER@.** The address of the buffer area assigned by the application program.
- **NCB_LENGTH.** Indicates the length of the buffer area.
- **NCB_CALLNAME.** The network name of the entity that the application program wishes to communicate with.
- **NCB_NAME.** The name by which the system is known on the network.
- **NCB_RTO.** Specifies a timeout period for all receives associated with the session.
- **NCB_STO.** Specifies a timeout period for all sends associated with the session.
- **NCB_POST@.** Indicates the location of the routine to be executed when a command has been completed.
- **NCB_ADPTR_NUM.** Defines the adapter to be used.
- **NCB_CMD_CMPL.** The same value as NCB_RETCODE.
- **NCB_RESERVE.** Used for parameters associated with specific commands.

BOX 21.6 Network control block (NCB) API commands.

NetBIOS Name Service Commands

The NetBIOS NCB commands that users can issue to work with network names are as follows:

- **NCB.ADD.NAME.** Adds a unique name to the station's table of names.
- **NCB.ADD.GROUP.NAME.** Adds a group name to the station's table of names.
- **NCB.DELETE.NAME.** Removes a name from the station's table of names.
- **NCB.FIND.NAME.** Determines the location or locations associated with a specified name and returns station addresses and routing information in response.

NetBIOS Session Service Commands

The NetBIOS NCB commands that are associated with the session service are as follows:

- **NCB.CALL.** Opens a session with another name.
- **NCB.LISTEN.** Enables a session to be opened with the name specified in the command.
- **NCB.HANG.UP.** Closes a session with another name.
- **NCB.SEND.** Sends data to the session partner.
- **NCB.SEND.NO.ACK.** Sends data to the session partner but does not require an acknowledgment.
- **NCB.CHAIN.SEND.** Sends data to the session partner using two buffers that are chained together.
- **NCB.CHAIN.SEND.NO.ACK.** Sends data to the session partner using buffers that are chained together but does not require an acknowledgment.
- **NCB.RECEIVE.** Receives data from a specified session partner.
- **NCB.RECEIVE.ANY.** Receives data from any session partner.
- **NCB.SESSION.STATUS.** Obtains status information about one or all sessions for a given name.

NetBIOS Datagram Service Commands

The NetBIOS NCB commands used to send and receive datagrams are as follows:

- **NCB.SEND.DATAGRAM.** Sends a message to a specific user or users. The name can identify an individual user or it can be a group name.
- **NCB.SEND.BROADCAST.DATAGRAM.** Sends a message to all users on the network.
- **NCB.RECEIVE.DATAGRAM.** Receives a datagram.
- **NCB.RECEIVE.BROADCAST.DATAGRAM.** Receives a broadcast datagram.

NetBIOS Status and Control Commands

The NetBIOS NCB commands associated with status and control functions are as follows:

(Continued)

> **BOX 21.6**   *(Continued)*
>
> - **NCB.RESET.** Resets the NetBIOS interface.
> - **NCB.CANCEL.** Cancels a command.
> - **NCB.LAN.STATUS.ALERT.** Causes the application program to be notified of certain temporary error conditions.
> - **NCB.STATUS.** Determines the status of the NetBIOS interface.
> - **NCB.UNLINK.** Provides for NetBIOS compatibility with early versions.
> - **NCB.TRACE.** Activates a trace of all commands issued to the NetBIOS interface and all NetBIOS transmits and receives.

NetBIOS Frame

NetBIOS uses the services of the underlying LAN Adapter layer for physical communication across a LAN data link. When a NetBIOS frame is transmitted across a LAN data link, the entire frame, including all its fields, is treated as data. The content of the NetBIOS frame is meaningful only to NetBIOS in the sending and receiving stations and is not manipulated by the underlying LLC or MAC sublayers.

Box 21.7 shows the frame format defined for NetBIOS and describes the fields in the NetBIOS frame. Box 21.8 describes some of the different types of frames that are used by the NetBIOS protocol in implementing the services in each of the four NetBIOS service categories.

SUMMARY

IBM and Microsoft together provide a wide variety of networking software subsystems for personal computers that run the MS-DOS, Windows, Windows/NT, and OS/2 operating systems. The IBM and Microsoft approach to networking can be divided into an Application layer that provides application-oriented services, a Transport layer that provides end-to-end connectivity between networked systems, and a LAN Adapter layer that supports the major LAN data link technologies.

The Application layer defines Server Message Blocks (SMBs), named pipes, and additional LAN APIs for requesting high-level networking services. SMBs are data structures that make up an API for requesting communication services and a protocol defining the formats of SMBs and describes the procedures governing how they are exchanged between systems. SMBs and the services they provide can be divided into four categories—session control, file access management, print server support, and message delivery. A named pipe is a mechanism for interprocess communication that provides a two-way communication channel for implementing a client-server relationship between two communicating processes. The named pipes API provides server function calls,

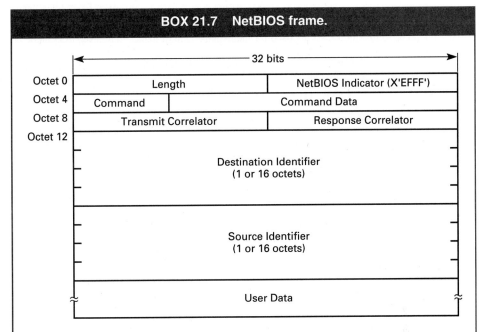

BOX 21.7   NetBIOS frame.

- **Length.** The length of the NetBIOS header.
- **NetBIOS Indicator.** Indicates that subsequent data is destined for NetBIOS.
- **Command.** Identifies the function of the frame and its format.
- **Command Data.** Data specific to a particular type of frame.
- **Transmit Correlator.** Correlates a value returned in a response with a previous message.
- **Response Correlator.** Correlates a value to be returned in a response (in the transmit correlator field) with this message.
- **Destination ID.** Identifies the message destination. This can be either a name or a session number assigned when a NetBIOS session is established.
- **Source ID.** Identifies the message source. This can be either a name or a session number assigned when the NetBIOS session was established.
- **User Data.** The information passed to NetBIOS by the user.

client function calls, dialog function calls, and information function calls. The Application layer also provides additional sets of LAN APIs for interprocess communication, workstation communication, administration functions, access control facilities, printing and character functions, and auditing facilities.

The Transport layer defines the NetBIOS API and transport protocol. NetBIOS has become a de facto standard for Transport-layer communication and is implemented in a wide variety of network software subsystems. The NetBIOS API is based on data struc-

BOX 21.8   NetBIOS frame types.

NetBIOS Name Service Frames

The following frames are used for the management of names in the NetBIOS name table:

- **ADD_GROUP_NAME_QUERY.** Checks for duplicate names before adding a group name to the table.
- **ADD_NAME_QUERY.** Checks for duplicate names before adding a unique name to the table.
- **ADD_NAME_RESPONSE.** Indicates that a name is in use at another system.
- **NAME_IN_CONFLICT.** Indicates that duplicate names have been detected.

NetBIOS Datagram Service Frames

The following frames are used to transmit data using the datagram service:

- **DATAGRAM.** Sends a datagram to a specific name.
- **DATAGRAM_BROADCAST.** Sends a datagram to all names.

NetBIOS Session Service Frames

The following frames are used to establish and terminate sessions and to transfer data over a session.

- **NAME_QUERY.** Requests the location on the network that is associated with a name.
- **NAME_RECOGNIZED.** Returns the address associated with a name.
- **SESSION_INITIALIZE.** Requests that a session be established.
- **SESSION_CONFIRM.** Acknowledges a request to establish a session.
- **SESSION_END.** Terminates a session.
- **SESSION_ALIVE.** Verifies that a session is active.
- **DATA_FIRST_MIDDLE.** Sends the first or middle frame of a multiframe message.
- **RECEIVE_CONTINUE.** Acknowledges a DATA_FIRST_MIDDLE frame.
- **DATA_ONLY_LAST.** Sends the last frame of a multiframe message or the only frame of a single-frame message.
- **DATA_ACK.** Acknowledges a DATA_ONLY_LAST frame.
- **NO_RECEIVE.** Indicates that some or all of a message was not able to be accepted by the receiving user.
- **RECEIVE_OUTSTANDING.** Indicates that a user is able to resume receiving data.

NetBIOS Status and Control Frames

The following frames are used for status and control purposes:

- **STATUS_QUERY.** Requests status information.
- **STATUS_RESPONSE.** Returns requested status information.
- **TERMINATE_TRACE.** Terminates a trace at a local or remote station.

tures called Network Control Blocks (NCBs) that define commands programs issue to request communication services. Services provided by NetBIOS include name services, session services, datagram services, and status and control services.

Chapter 22 introduces the Novell NetWare family of networking software that is also used in the personal computer networking environment.

Novell NetWare

Novell, Inc. markets the NetWare family of local area network operating system products that are widely used in the personal computer environment. As we introduced in Chapter 17, the protocol family implemented by NetWare products is often called the *IPX* protocol family after the name of the main Network layer protocol in the NetWare family.

Most of the products in the NetWare family are used to implement a server-based computing environment in which user systems functioning as clients request networking services of dedicated servers. One or more computing systems are ordinarily designated as NetWare servers that typically provide file server, print server, and electronic mail services. Client and server systems communicate with one another over a single LAN data link or over an internet. NetWare software is also available for creating peer-to-peer networks in which a dedicated server is not necessary.

NetWare servers run specialized software that provides operating system services as well as networking software facilities. NetWare server software is typically priced according to the number of client systems that can be concurrently logged on to the server. Individual user systems run NetWare client software that runs in conjunction with the user system's operating system and allows the user to access the networking services that are provided by NetWare servers. NetWare client software is available from Novell as well as from a number of third-party software vendors. NetWare client support is also built into some operating system software.

NETWARE ARCHITECTURE

Figure 22.1 illustrates the basic architecture that underlies the NetWare product family and shows its relationship to the OSI model. The following are descriptions of each of the NetWare architectural layers.

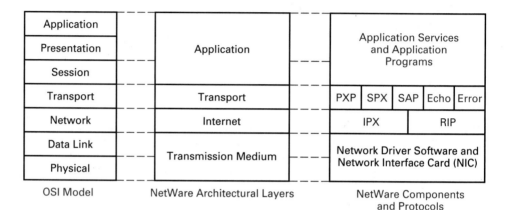

Figure 22.1   NetWare architecture.

Transmission Medium Layer

The NetWare Transmission Medium layer is associated with the Data Link and Physical layers of the OSI model. NetWare products support a wide variety of LAN technologies in the Transmission Medium layer, including Ethernet, Token Ring, LocalTalk, and ARCnet.

Internet Layer

The Internet layer is closely analogous to the Network layer of the OSI model. The following two protocols operate in the NetWare Internet layer:

- **Internet Packet Exchange Protocol.** The *Internetwork Packet Exchange* (IPX) protocol provides a connectionless, or datagram, transmission service and also provides routing services when NetWare is part of an internetwork.

- **Routing Information Protocol.** The *Routing Information Protocol* (RIP) is used for communication between end systems and routers and between routers for the purposes of determining routes to be used for relaying user traffic through an internet.

Transport Layer

The NetWare Transport layer is analogous to the Transport layer of the OSI model and supports end-to-end communication between a client and a server system. The following are the five major protocols that operate in the NetWare Transport layer:

- **Packet Exchange Protocol.** The *Packet Exchange Protocol* (PXP) provides an unreliable end-to-end connectionless data transport service.

- **Sequenced Packet Exchange Protocol.** The *Sequenced Packet Exchange* (SPX) protocol provides a connection-oriented transport service. A connection is established between the communicating users, and acknowledgments are used for error detection and recovery.

- **Service Advertising Protocol.** The *Service Advertising Protocol* (SAP) is a broadcast protocol that NetWare servers employ to inform NetWare clients of the services that are available.

- **Echo Protocol.** The *Echo Protocol* allows an end system to verify the existence of a route to another end system in the internet.

- **Error Protocol.** The *Error Protocol* provides for detecting and reporting on errors between an end system and a router to which it is directly attached.

Application Layer

The NetWare Application layer is associated with the Session, Presentation, and Application layers of the OSI model. NetWare provides a wide variety of application services, including printer sharing, file sharing, application sharing, directory processing, and network administration. User application programs also operate in the NetWare Application layer.

NETWARE ADDRESSING

A NetWare network can consist of a single LAN or an internet consisting of two or more interconnected LAN subnetworks. To accommodate complex internets, NetWare defines a Network layer addressing mechanism that can be used to uniquely identify systems in an internet.

Internet Addresses

Each system in a NetWare network has an *internet address* having two parts, as shown in Fig. 22.2. Each individual subnetwork in the internet is assigned a 4-octet *network number* value. The network administrator typically assigns a unique network number to each subnetwork in the internet. Each individual point of attachment to a subnetwork (each NIC installed in a system) is then identified by a 6-octet *node address* value. On local area networks that conform to the IEEE/ISO/ANSI LAN architecture, the NIC's globally-administered MAC address is typically used as that NIC's node address. Thus, the network administrator does not ordinarily have to assign node address values to systems.

Although NetWare network administrators are free to assign network numbers in any desired manner, Novell Corporation provides the service of assigning unique ranges of network numbers to any organization that applies for them. Novell provides this ser-

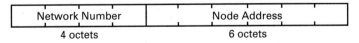

Figure 22.2   NetWare internet address format.

vice to make it easy for different organizations to interconnect their individual NetWare internets without creating addressing conflicts.

Socket Addresses

Processes communicate with one another using data structures called *sockets*. A socket number identifies a particular process within a system. A socket address consists of an internet address plus a 16-bit socket number. Certain socket number values are reserved for standard NetWare services and protocols; others can be used by application processes. The format of a socket address is shown in Fig. 22.3.

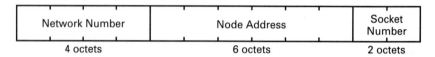

Figure 22.3   NetWare socket address format.

The remainder of this chapter describes the services and protocols that operate in each of the NetWare architectural layers, beginning with the Application layer.

NETWARE APPLICATION SERVICES

NetWare software provides a number of application services, including file sharing, printer sharing, electronic mail, and network management. The following sections describe the most commonly used NetWare application services.

File Sharing

NetWare provides its own file management system, called the *NetWare File System* (NFS), that a NetWare server uses to manage access to the files maintained on the server. NFS is designed to provide high levels of performance and integrity in a file sharing environment. The NetWare File System hierarchically organizes disk storage into volumes, directories, subdirectories, and files. Users are granted access to specific directories on a file server. To use a directory, the user employs operating system facilities on the client system to assign a drive letter to a particular file server directory. All references to that drive letter are then processed using the file server directory.

When a user requests access to a directory, the user typically specifies the type of access that is required, and the server grants access rights accordingly. Access rights can be granted for an entire directory or for individual files. Files and directories can also be assigned attributes related to sharing that override user rights. For example, if a file is assigned the Delete Inhibit attribute, a user will not be able to delete the file even though the user may have the Erase access right. Possible access rights and attributes for files and directories are listed in Box 22.1.

Directory Access Rights

- **Supervisory.** All rights to directory/subdirectories/files.
- **Read.** Open files in a directory, read contents, and execute.
- **Write.** Open and write (modify) contents of files.
- **Create.** Create files and subdirectories in a directory.
- **Erase.** Delete a directory, its files, and its subdirectories.
- **Modify.** Change directory and file attributes and rename.
- **File Scan.** View names of subdirectories and files.
- **Access Control.** Give rights to other users, modify rights.

Directory Attributes

- **Delete Inhibit.** Prevent directory from being erased.
- **Hidden.** Hide a directory from a DOS DIR command.
- **Purge.** Purge all files in directory when deleted.
- **Rename Inhibit.** Prevent a directory from being renamed.
- **System.** Hide a system directory from a DOS DIR command.

File Access Rights

- **Supervisory.** All rights to the file.
- **Read.** Open a file, read contents, and execute the program.
- **Write.** Open and write (modify) contents of a file.
- **Create.** Salvage a file after it has been deleted.
- **Erase.** Delete a file.
- **Modify.** Change a file's attributes and rename.
- **File Scan.** View name of a file and its full path name.
- **Access Control.** Modify rights to file.

File Attributes

- **Archive Needed.** Assigned to files modified after backups.
- **Copy Inhibit.** Restrict copy rights for Macintosh users.
- **Delete Inhibit.** Prevent file from being erased.
- **Execute Only.** Prevent files from being copied permanently.

(Continued)

BOX 22.1 *(Continued)*

- **Hidden.** Hide a file from a DOS DIR scan.
- **Indexed.** Speed access to large files.
- **Purge.** Purge a file when deleted.
- **Read Audit.** Audit reads to a file.
- **Read Only.** Cannot write to, erase, or rename file.
- **Read Write.** Default setting for a file.
- **Rename Inhibit.** Prevent a file from being renamed.
- **Sharable.** File can be used by more than one user.
- **System.** Hide a system file from a DOS DIR scan.
- **Transactional.** Protect against incomplete operations on the file.
- **Write Audit.** Audit writes to a file.

In addition to attributes and access rights, NetWare provides data integrity facilities that can be used to perform record and field locking and to back out changes related to a transaction if the transaction fails before being completely processed.

Printer Sharing

Printer sharing services support the shared use of printers attached either to a server or some other system on the network. When printing is performed using a shared printer, print queues are used to store print jobs until a printer becomes available. Multiple print queues can be assigned to one printer, and multiple printers can share the same print queue. Queue management facilities include queuing jobs and printing jobs from the queue, canceling print jobs, reordering queues, holding and releasing jobs, redirecting a queue to a different printer, and using preprinted forms for printing.

Messaging

NetWare includes a basic messaging facility that allows a user to send a message to an individual user, a group of users, or all users. The message appears on the bottom line of the recipient's screen.

Network Administration

NetWare administration facilities can be used as follows:

- Define individual users and groups of users, along with their access rights to network resources and security restrictions to be observed.
- Define login scripts that create an appropriate network environment when a user logs on to the network.
- Manage resource accounting so that services used by different users are accounted for and reported appropriately.

- Define and manage security facilities, including passwords, disk usage constraints, encryption, audit trails, and login time constraints.
- Monitor network activity levels and capacity status.

NetWare Core Protocol (NCP)

The NetWare Core Protocol (NCP) handles all client requests for services from a server. NCP uses IPX for transmission across the network and provides its own mechanisms for connection control and sequence numbering to provide a reliable data transfer service. Unlike most of the other protocols in the NetWare protocol family, Novell does not make the specifications for NCP publicly available. Novell considers the protocol proprietary and makes it available to developers only under license agreements.

NETWARE LOADABLE MODULES

The NetWare architecture allows both Novell and third-party software vendors to easily extend the capabilities of the NetWare environment. Extensions that are added to the base NetWare software that runs in a NetWare server are called *NetWare Loadable Modules* (NLMs). In early releases of the NetWare software NLMs were called *Value Added Processes* (VAPs), and the VAP acronym is still used in some of the NetWare documentation. A number of NLMs have been developed, both by NetWare and by third-party software vendors. Some facilities that have been added to NetWare through NLMs include the following:

- Electronic mail facilities.
- Relational database management systems.
- Support for file systems other than the NetWare File System, including Macintosh and UNIX file systems, the Network File System (NFS) developed by Sun Microsystems, and the OSI File Transfer and Access Management (FTAM) protocols.
- Support for additional network management tools and facilities, including SNMP and NetView.
- Support for protocols and APIs other than those that are part of the standard NetWare architecture, including NetBIOS, AppleTalk, and TCP/IP.

NETWARE APPLICATION PROGRAM INTERFACES

NetWare includes an extensive set of APIs that can be used by an application program to access NetWare services. Each NetWare API consists of a set of function calls. The function calls use various registers and sometimes Request and Reply packets for sending and receiving data. The data passed and returned varies widely from one call to another.

In addition to the NetWare APIs, NetWare also supports the use of the Named Pipes interface described in Chapter 21. This allows applications that have been developed using Named Pipes for interprocess communication to operate across a NetWare network.

IPX/SPX Services API

One way that an application program can access NetWare services is by directly invoking IPX or SPX transport services. To send data using IPX or SPX, the application must provide a properly formatted IPX or SPX Data packet. IPX/SPX calls use a data structure called an *Event Control Block* (ECB) to control data transmission. Box 22.2 shows the structure of an ECB and describes its fields.

The calls available for IPX and SPX services are shown in Box 22.3.

Application Services APIs

In addition to the IPX/SPX APIs, NetWare also makes available a number of APIs for requesting NetWare application services. The following are brief descriptions of a number of different application services for which APIs are defined:

- **Print Services.** *Print services* are used to capture data and direct it to a server for printing. Captured data is stored in a queue until it is printed.

- **Queue Management Services.** *Queue management services* can be invoked directly and can be used for queuing and servicing any type of job.

- **File Services.** *File services* can be used to copy files, change file attributes and other file information, erase files, purge files, and restore erased files.

- **Locking Services.** *Locking services* can be used to lock files or records using physical or logical locks or semaphores.

- **Directory Services.** *Directory services* allow an application to request information about volumes, work with directory handles, map drives, create, delete, and rename directories, and administer directory-level security.

- **Transaction Tracking System Services.** *Transaction tracking system services* allow an application to invoke data integrity services. A sequence of file changes can be defined as a transaction. If a failure occurs before a transaction has completed processing, any changes made as part of the transaction are backed out and data is restored to its original state before processing of the transaction began.

- **Directory Services.** NetWare servers maintain databases of information about network users, queues, and other servers. The directory provides the basis for translating names into internet addresses. Earlier releases of NetWare server software used a local directory service called the *bindery* for name translations. More recent NetWare server software implements a global directory service that accesses a naming database that can be distributed throughout a NetWare network.

- **Connection and Workstation Services.** These services support the general client-server computing paradigm. *Connection services* are used to establish, manage, and terminate connections between workstations and servers. *Workstation services* provide and manage information about the workstation shell. File server services allow an application to monitor and manage file servers.

- **Value-Added Process Services.** *Value-added process (VAP) services* can be used to create processes that run on a server.

- **Service Advertising Protocol Services.** *Service advertising protocol services* are used by servers to provide information about their existence and location on the network. SAP

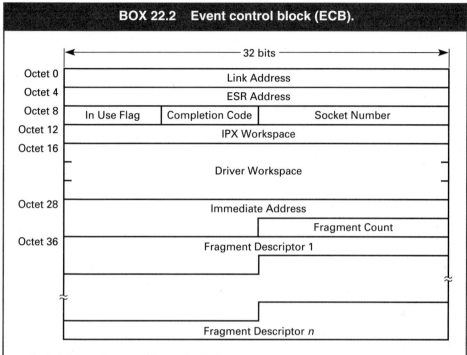

BOX 22.2   Event control block (ECB).

- **Link Address.** Reserved for use by IPX.

- **ESR Address.** The address of an application-defined event service routine that IPX/SPX can invoke when processing of the call is completed.

- **In Use Flag.** Indicates whether IPX/SPX is currently using or holding the ECB, and if so, for what purpose.

- **Completion Code.** Indicates the final status of call.

- **Socket Number.** Identifies the socket used by the process associated with the call. For a send call, it is the socket number from which the packet is sent. For a receive call, it is the socket number on which the packet is received.

- **IPX Workspace.** Reserved for use by IPX.

- **Driver Workspace.** Reserved for use by the network driver.

- **Immediate Address.** The node address of the system to which the packet is being sent or from which it was received.

- **Fragment Count.** The number of buffers containing the packet to be sent or to use for the packet being received.

- **Fragment Descriptor.** The size and address of a buffer used in sending or receiving the packet. The Fragment Count indicates the number of Fragment Descriptors in the ECB.

BOX 22.3   IPX/SPX Services API calls.

IPX Calls

- IPX Open Socket
- IPX Close Socket
- IPX Get Local Target
- IPX Send Packet
- IPX Listen For Packet
- IPX Schedule IPX Event
- IPX Cancel Event
- IPX Get Interval Marker
- IPX Get Internet Address
- IPX Relinquish Control
- IPX Disconnect From Target

SPX Calls

- SPX Initialize
- SPX Establish Connection
- SPX Listen For Connection
- SPX Terminate Connection
- SPX Abort Connection
- SPX Get Connection Status
- SPX Send Sequenced Packet
- SPX Listen For Sequenced Packet

---

information is sent by creating SAP packets and then transmitting them via IPX. There are no specific API calls associated with SAP services.

- **Accounting Services.** There are also NetWare services available to help with network management and administration. *Accounting service* calls provide an application with information about usage of network resources, such as time logged in, disk space used, number of pages printed, and so on.

- **Diagnostic Services.** *Diagnostic services* let an application perform tests, gather statistics, display tables of network information, and access information concerning the configuration of systems and the structure of the internet.

Many of the API calls that are defined for requesting the foregoing application services are listed in Box 22.4. The specific calls that are available in an actual NetWare network depend on the specific version of the NetWare server software that is used. The NetWare documentation should be consulted for information about all the API calls that can be issued.

BOX 22.4   NetWare API calls.

Print Services API Calls

- Start LPT Capture
- Flush LPT Capture
- Cancel LPT Capture
- End LPT Capture

- Spool Data to a Capture File
- Close and Queue Capture File
- Get Default Capture Flags
- Set Default Capture Flags
- Set Spool Flags

BOX 22.4 *(Continued)*

- Start Specific LPT Capture
- Flush Specific LPT Capture
- Cancel Specific LPT Capture
- End Specific LPT Capture
- Get Specific LPT Capture Flags
- Set Specific LPT Capture Flags
- Get Default Local Printer
- Set Default Local Printer
- Get Printer Status
- Get Banner User Name
- Set Banner User Name
- Set Capture Print Job
- Set Capture Print Queue
- Specify Capture File
- Spool Existing File
- Get Spool Queue Entry
- Remove Entry from Spool Queue

Queue Management Services API Calls

- Create Queue
- Destroy Queue
- Read Queue Current Status
- Set Queue Current Status
- Create Queue Job and File
- Close File and Start Queue Job
- Remove Job from Queue
- Get Queue Job List
- Read Queue Job Entry
- Change Queue Job Entry
- Change Queue Job Position
- Attach Queue Server To Queue
- Detach Queue Server From Queue

- Service Queue Job and Open File
- Finish Servicing Queue Job and File
- Abort Servicing Queue Job and File
- Change to Client Rights
- Restore Queue Server Rights
- Read Queue Server Current Status
- Set Queue Server Current Status
- Get Queue Job's File Size

File Services API Calls

- File Server File Copy
- Get File Attributes
- Set File Attributes
- Get Extended File Attributes
- Set Extended File Attributes
- Get File Information
- Set File Information
- Erase Files
- Restore Erased Files
- Purge Erased Files
- Purge All Erased Files
- Update File Size

Locking Services API Calls

- Get Lock Mode
- Set Lock Mode
- Log File
- Lock File Set
- Release File
- Release File Set
- Clear File
- Clear File Set
- Begin Logical File Locking
- End Logical File Locking

(Continued)

BOX 22.4 *(Continued)*

- Log Physical Record
- Lock Physical Record Set
- Release Physical Record
- Release Physical Record Set
- Clear Physical Record
- Clear Physical Record Set
- Log Logical Record
- Lock Logical Record Set
- Release Logical Record
- Release Logical Record Set
- Clear Logical Record
- Clear Logical Record Set
- Open Semaphore
- Examine Semaphore
- Wait On Semaphore
- Signal Semaphore
- Close Semaphore

Directory Services API Calls

- Get Volume Name
- Get Volume Number
- Get Volume Info With Handle
- Get Volume Info With Number
- Get Volume Information

Transaction Tracking System Services API Calls

- TTS Is Available
- TTS Begin Transaction
- TTS End Transaction
- TTS Transaction Status
- TTS Abort Transaction
- TTS Get Transaction Thresholds
- TTS Set Transaction Thresholds
- TTS Get Workstation Thresholds
- TTS Set Workstation Thresholds

Bindery Services API Calls

- Open Bindery
- Close Bindery
- Create Bindery Object
- Delete Bindery Object
- Scan Bindery Object
- Rename Bindery Object
- Is Bindery Object In Set
- Add Bindery Object To Set
- Delete Bindery Object From Set
- Get Bindery Object ID
- Get Bindery Object Name
- Verify Bindery Object Password
- Change Bindery Object Security
- Change Bindery Object Password
- Create Property
- Delete Property
- Scan Property
- Read Property Value
- Write Property Value
- Change Property Security
- Get Bindery Access Level

Connection/Workstation Services API Calls

- End Of Job
- Attach To File Server
- Detach From File Server
- Enter Login Area
- Login To File Server
- Logout
- Logout From File Server
- Get Connection Information
- Get Connection Number
- Get Object Connection Numbers

BOX 22.4   *(Continued)*

- Get Internet Address
- Get Station Address
- Get Connection ID
- Get Default Connection ID
- Get Preferred Connection ID
- Set Preferred Connection ID
- Get Drive Handle Table
- Get Drive Flag Table
- Get Drive Connection ID
- Get File Server Name Table
- Get Shell Version Information
- Set NetWare Error Mode
- Set End Of Job Status
- Get Number Of Local Drives
- Change Password
- Map User To Station Set
- Map Object To Number
- Get Station's Logged Information
- Map Number To Group Name
- Get Member Set M Of Group G

VAP Process Control Services API Calls

- Allocate Segment
- Calculate Absolute Address
- Change Process
- Change Segment To Code
- Change Segment To Data
- Create Process
- Declare Extended Segment
- Declare Segment As Data
- Delay Process
- Do Console Error
- Get Interrupt Vector

- Get Process ID
- Get VAP Header
- Initialization Complete
- Kill Process
- Set External Process Error
- Set Hardware Interrupt Vector
- Set Interrupt Vector
- Shell Pass Through Enable
- Sleep Process
- Spawn Process
- VAP Attach To File Server
- VAP Get Connection ID
- VAP Get File Server Name
- Wake Up Process

VAP Console Control Services API Calls

- Clear Screen
- Console Display
- Console Error
- Console Message
- Console Query
- Console Read
- Get Screen Mode
- Set Screen Mode
- In String
- Out String
- Print String
- Read Keyboard

Accounting Services API Calls

- Get Account Status
- Submit Account Hold
- Submit Account Change
- Submit Account Note

(Continued)

BOX 22.4 *(Continued)*

Diagnostic Services API Calls—IPX/SPX Component

- Return IPX/SPX Version
- Return IPX Statistics
- Return SPX Statistics
- Start Sending Packets
- Abort Sending Packets
- Start Counting Packets
- Return Received Packet Count

Diagnostic Services API Calls—Driver Component

- Return Shell Driver Configuration
- Return Shell Driver Diagnostic Statistics
- Return Bridge Driver Status
- Return Bridge Driver Configuration
- Return Bridge Driver Diagnostic Statistics

Diagnostic Services API Calls—Shell Component

- Return OS Version
- Return Shell Address

- Return Shell Statistics
- Return Connection ID Table
- Return Server Name Table
- Return Primary Server Number
- Return Shell Version

Diagnostic Services API Calls—Shell VAP Component

- Return VAP Shell Address
- Return VAP Shell Statistics
- Return VAP Shell Version

Diagnostic Services API Calls—Bridge Component

- Return Bridge Statistics
- Return Local Tables
- Return All Known Networks
- Return Specific Network Information
- Return All Known Servers
- Return Specific Server Information

TRANSPORT LAYER PROTOCOLS

The NetWare Transport layer provides for end-to-end communication between a client system and a server system. The two major protocols that operate in the NetWare Transport layer are the Sequenced Packet Exchange (SPX) protocol and the Service Advertising Protocol (SAP).

Sequenced Packet Exchange (SPX) Protocol

The *Sequenced Packet Exchange* (SPX) protocol provides a connection-oriented transport service. SPX uses the datagram delivery service provided by IPX, and an SPX packet is carried within an IPX datagram.

A connection is established between two communicating SPX users before they are able to exchange data. Packets sent are sequence numbered, and the receiving side uses the sequence numbers to check for missing, duplicate, or out-of-sequence packets. Successfully received packets are acknowledged by returning the next expected sequence number in the Acknowledgment Number field of a packet being sent back to the sender. Flow control is provided by the number of listen buffers that are available. SPX may send packets in a given direction only until the number of unacknowledged packets is equal to the number of listen buffers available on the receiving side. As the number of buffers varies, SPX is able to send more or fewer packets before receiving an acknowledgment.

SPX Protocol Packet

Box 22.5 shows the format of the packet used with the SPX protocol and describes its fields.

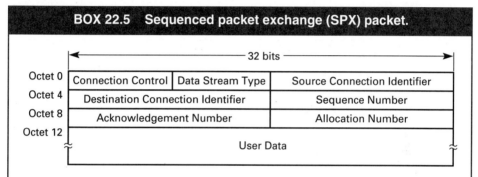

BOX 22.5   Sequenced packet exchange (SPX) packet.

- **Connection Control.** Used to request an acknowledgment or to identify a system packet that is processed by SPX and not passed up to a higher layer.
- **Data Stream Type.** Used to request or acknowledge the termination of a connection.
- **Source Connection Identifier.** Identifies the number assigned to the connection on the source socket end when the connection was established. A particular socket can be used concurrently for multiple connections.
- **Destination Connection Identifier.** Identifies the number assigned to the connection on the destination socket end.
- **Sequence Number.** A sequence number assigned to the packet being sent.
- **Acknowledgment Number.** The sequence number of the next packet expected to be received by this user. This acknowledges the successful receipt of all packets with a sequence number less than this value.
- **Allocation Number.** Specifies the number of listen buffers available for receiving packets on this end of the connection.

Service Advertising Protocol (SAP)

The Service Advertising Protocol (SAP) allows servers to make their services known throughout the network. When a server is first activated, it broadcasts on its own subnetwork a SAP packet containing its name, routing information, and the type of service it offers. The server then periodically broadcasts this information on its local subnetwork. Routers, which are used to interconnect networks, maintain a table of the information contained in the SAP packets they receive. Routers also exchange the information contained in SAP packets among themselves, so that the tables eventually contain information about all the servers in the internet. The procedures used by the routers to gather and update this information are the same as are used on the Routing Information Protocol (RIP), described later in this chapter.

If a client workstation needs to access a particular type of server, it sends out a SAP Request packet to any server or router on its local subnetwork. The server or router will then send a Response packet containing the name and address of one or more servers of the specified type.

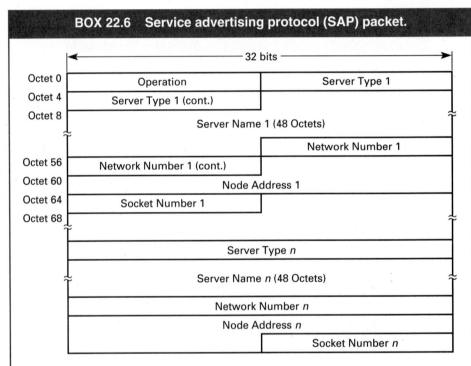

BOX 22.6   Service advertising protocol (SAP) packet.

- **Operation.** Identifies the packet as one of the following types:
  - — Request by a workstation for the name and address of the nearest server of a certain type.
  - — Response to the nearest server request.
  - — Request for the names and addresses of all servers of a certain type.
  - — Response to an all servers request.
- **Service Type.** Identifies the type of server described in the following fields.
- **Server Name.** The network name by which the server is known.
- **Network Number.** Identifies the subnetwork to which the server is attached.
- **Node Address.** Identifies the server.
- **Socket Number.** Identifies the process in the server to which packets should be passed.

SAP Packet

Box 22.6 shows the format of the packet used with SAP and describes its fields.

INTERNET LAYER PROTOCOLS

The NetWare Internet layer provides the services that are required to move packets from one system to another through an internet. The two major protocols operating in the Internet layer are the Internetwork Packet Exchange (IPX) protocol and the Routing Information Protocol (RIP).

Internetwork Packet Exchange (IPX) Protocol

The Internetwork Packet Exchange (IPX) protocol provides a best efforts data delivery service for datagrams passed down by higher-level protocols. IPX also plays a role in the routing function in an internet.

IPX Protocol Packet

Box 22.7 shows the packet format for IPX and describes the fields in the IPX packet header.

NETWARE ROUTING

A source system can determine by examining the internet address in a packet whether the destination system is on the same LAN data link as the source system. If the Destination Network Number field in a packet contains a value that is equal to the source system's own network number, then the destination system is on the source system's own LAN, and the source system uses the services of the Transmission Medium layer to deliver the packet directly to the destination system.

If the Destination Network Number field in a packet contains a value that is different from the source system's own network number, then the destination system is on some other LAN data link in the internet. In order to send a packet to a destination system on some other LAN, the source system delivers the packet to a router on the source system's own LAN. The router then uses its routing table to determine the next destination for the packet.

Routing Information Protocol (RIP)

The Routing Information Protocol (RIP) is a distance-vector routing protocol that defines how routers and end systems exchange routing information and how a router acquires, accesses, and maintains routing information. Various facilities of RIP can be used by both end systems and routers to perform the following functions:

- An end system can request route information from a router.
- A router can request route information from other routers.
- A router can respond to a request from an end system or a router.
- A router can send out unsolicited route information to other routers.

BOX 22.7 Internet packet exchange (IPX) protocol packet.

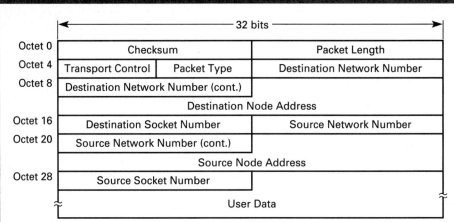

- **Checksum.** Included for compatibility with XNS specifications. This field is not used by IPX.
- **Packet Length.** The length of the IPX packet, including both header and data.
- **Transport Control.** Used during routing across an internetwork to count the number of networks crossed.
- **Packet Type.** Identifies the type of data in the Data field. Possible types include RIP, NCP, or SPX data.
- **Destination Network Number.** Identifies the subnetwork to which the destination system is attached.
- **Destination Node Address.** Identifies the destination system.
- **Destination Socket Number.** Identifies the particular process within the destination system to which the packet should be passed for processing.
- **Source Network Number.** Identifies the subnetwork in which the source system is located.
- **Source Node Address.** Identifies the source system.
- **Source Socket Number.** Identifies the particular process in the source station that created this packet.

Routing Information Table

Each router maintains a routing information table that it uses to determine where to send each packet it receives from systems on its own LAN. There is an entry in the routing table for each subnetwork in the internet. Each entry contains the following information:

- **Network Number.** Identifies the subnetwork associated with this routing table entry.
- **Hop Count.** Measures the number of additional routers that must be used to reach the destination subnetwork from this router. No route is allowed to have more than 16 hops.

- **Ticks.** Provides a measure of the time it takes to reach the destination subnetwork. The value of this field depends on the number of links that must be crossed and also the characteristics of those links. The purpose of this field is to allow a router to select the fastest route, which may not necessarily be the shortest.

- **NIC.** Identifies which NIC the router should use to transmit the packet to the destination subnetwork.

- **Forwarding Router Address.** Provides the internet address of the next system to which a packet should be sent to reach the destination subnetwork.

- **Time-Out.** This field maintains a timer for the router table entry. If the router receives no information for a given entry over a certain period of time, it assumes the route to that subnetwork is down and deletes the associated table entry.

RIP Packet

End systems and routers exchange routing information using RIP packets. Box 22.8 shows the format of the RIP packet and describes its fields. Note that a packet contains a single Operation field and one or more sets of Destination Network, Number of Hops, and Number of Ticks fields, thus allowing a packet to be sent to multiple destination networks.

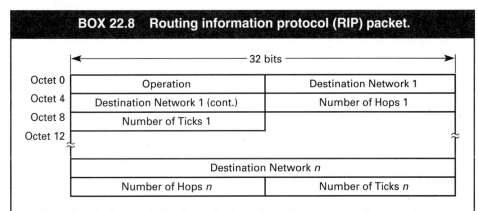

BOX 22.8   Routing information protocol (RIP) packet.

- **Operation.** Indicates whether the packet is used as a Request (1) or a Response (2).
- **Destination Network.** Contains the destination network number.
- **Number of Hops.** Contains a count of the number of routers through which the packet has passed. Each router increases the count, and if the count reaches 16 the packet is discarded.
- **Number of Ticks.** Contains an estimate of the time it has taken the packet to travel to the most recent router through which the packet has passed. Each router adds an amount to the value depending on the characteristics of the link over which the router forwards the packet.

Locating a Router

An end system can use a function of RIP to locate a router on the end system's own LAN. In order to locate a router, the source system broadcasts on its own LAN a RIP Request packet containing the destination network number. All routers on that LAN receive the Request packet. The router with the shortest path to the destination subnetwork sends back a RIP Response packet, which gives the source system the address of the router to use. The source system then sends the packet to the indicated router.

Initializing the Routing Information Table

Routers use RIP packets to exchange routing information so that each router always has a complete and current routing information table. Certain exchanges take place when a router is first brought up on the network and others occur on a continuing basis.

When a router is first activated, it initializes its table with information about the networks to which it is directly attached using information that was built into the router when NetWare was installed. Next, the router broadcasts this information in a RIP Response packet on its local subnetworks. In order to limit the traffic generated by routing information exchange, all broadcasts of RIP Request and Response packets are limited to directly-connected subnetworks. They are not passed on by routers to other networks. The router then broadcasts a RIP Request packet, asking other routers to provide any routing information they have. Routers that receive the Request packet send back a RIP Response packet with information from their routing information tables.

Best Information Algorithm

When sending out routing information, routers use a *best information algorithm* that works to limit the amount of information sent out and to prevent misrepresentation of alternate routes. According to the best information algorithm, a router does not send out any routing information for the subnetwork on which the Response packet is being sent, nor does it send any routing information that the router originally received over that subnetwork.

Maintaining the Routing Information Table

Each router periodically broadcasts a RIP Response packet containing information from its routing information table. The best information algorithm determines the networks for which information is included. Routers that receive this packet use it to update their routing information tables. If a router receives information that causes it to change a table entry, it immediately passes that information on so that changes spread quickly through the internet.

If a router knows that it is being brought down, it sends out a RIP packet indicating the routes that will no longer be available. Nonavailability is indicated by setting the hop count to 16.

SUMMARY

Most of the products in the Novell NetWare family are used to implement a client-server environment in which dedicated server systems provide networking services to user client systems. The NetWare approach to networking identifies a Transmission Medium layer that provides access to widely used LAN data link technologies, an Internet layer that handles the transmission of datagrams through the network, a Transport layer that handles end-to-end communication functions, and an Application layer that provides application-oriented communication services.

The communication facilities that NetWare software provides in the Application layer include services for file sharing, printer sharing, messaging, and network administration. The NetWare Core Protocol (NCP) handles client requests for services provided by servers. The NetWare architecture defines network loadable modules (NLMs) that Novell and third-party software vendors use to extend the range of application services that the NetWare software provides.

The protocols implemented in the Transport layer include PXP, SPX, SAP, Echo, and Error. The Packet Exchange Protocol (PXP) provides a connectionless data transport service. The Sequenced Packet Exchange (SPX) protocol provides a connection-oriented data delivery service. A connection is established between the communicating users, and acknowledgments are used for error detection and recovery. The Service Advertising Protocol (SAP) is a broadcast protocol that NetWare servers employ to inform NetWare clients of the services that are available. The Echo Protocol allows an end system to verify the existence of a route to another end system in the internet. The Error Protocol provides for detecting and reporting on errors between an end system and a router.

The protocols implemented in the Internet layer include IPX and RIP. The Internetwork Packet Exchange (IPX) protocol provides a connectionless data delivery service and also provides routing services in an internetwork. The Routing Information Protocol (RIP) is used for communication between end systems and routers and between routers for the purposes of determining routes to be used for relaying user traffic through an internet.

Chapter 23 describes the TCP/IP approach to computer networking that is used in a wide variety of computing environments.

Chapter **23**

TCP/IP

As we introduced in Chapter 17, *TCP/IP* is a widely used suite of computing networking transmission and routing protocols. TCP/IP, short for *Transmission Control Protocol/Internet Protocol*, is named after the two major protocols included in the protocol suite that grew out of a research project that began in 1969 and was funded by the U.S. Department of Defense. The TCP/IP protocols are based on the packet-switching ideas developed for the *ARPANET*, whose acronym was based on the name of the *Advanced Research Projects Agency* (ARPA) that funded its development. ARPA is now called the *Defense Advanced Projects Agency* (DARPA). The early ARPANET tied together a number of research computers using conventional leased telecommunications lines.

The original idea behind the TCP/IP protocol suite was to define a standard set of procedures to allow individual computer networks—such as the local area networks run by individual organizations—to be connected to the ARPANET. The TCP/IP protocols allow the interconnected individual networks to give the appearance of a single, unified network—called an *internet*—in which all computers can freely exchange data with each other as if they were all directly connected.*

Both the ARPANET and the TCP/IP protocol suite were extremely successful, and the TCP/IP protocols are used throughout the world in a great number of computer networks. The original ARPANET has changed and evolved into what is now often called the *Worldwide Internet*, or simply the *Internet*. Today's Worldwide Internet interconnects thousands of networks containing millions of computers in universities, national laboratories, and commercial organizations.

Networking software that implements the major TCP/IP protocols is available on a wide range of computing systems, from the largest mainframes to the smallest personal computers. It is included as an integral part of many variants of the UNIX operating sys-

---

*The individual networks that are interconnected to form a TCP/IP internet are equivalent to the subnetworks we have been referring to in earlier chapters. However, the term *subnetwork,* or *subnet,* has a different connotation in the TCP/IP environment, and we use the term *network* in this chapter to refer to an individual LAN or WAN data link.

tem. It can be used in conjunction with IBM's MVS, VM, OS/400, OS/2, and AIX operating systems and with Microsoft's MS-DOS, Windows, and Windows NT system software. Digital Equipment Corporation's VMS and Ultrix operating systems provide TCP/IP communication support, and TCP/IP communication software is also available for use on Apple Macintosh equipment. Many network operating systems for personal computers, such as NetWare, LAN Manager, LAN Server, and PATHWORKS incorporate support for the TCP/IP protocols as well as support for their own native communication protocols.

TCP/IP ARCHITECTURE

Figure 23.1 illustrates the architecture that underlies TCP/IP and shows its relationship to the OSI model. The following sections describe the functions of each of the layers in the TCP/IP architecture and introduces the functions of each of the major protocols making up the TCP/IP protocol suite.

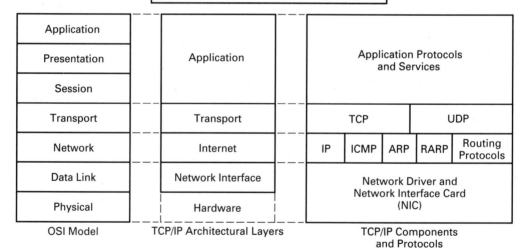

Figure 23.1 TCP/IP architecture.

Network Interface Layer

The main function of the Network Interface layer is to handle hardware-dependent functions and to present a standardized interface to the Internet layer of TCP/IP.

The TCP/IP suite of protocols does not specify details concerning the protocols to be used in the Network Interface layer and below. The Network Interface layer of TCP/IP is responsible for accepting messages from the Internet layer and preparing them for transmission across any desired type of data link technology.

An individual TCP/IP network may be a local area network, using LAN data link protocols such as Ethernet, Token Ring, or FDDI. An individual TCP/IP network may also be implemented using a wide area network data link technology, such as a point-to-point leased or dial-up line, satellite link, or specialized digital circuit. One of the reasons TCP/IP has become widely used is that it can be used in conjunction with almost any type of underlying physical circuit and data link technology.

One important function of the Network Interface layer is to examine each frame that the network interface card (NIC) receives and to determine, from the way in which control bits in the frame are set, for which of the Internet layer protocols the frame is intended. This is called a *demultiplexing* function and is illustrated in Fig. 23.2.

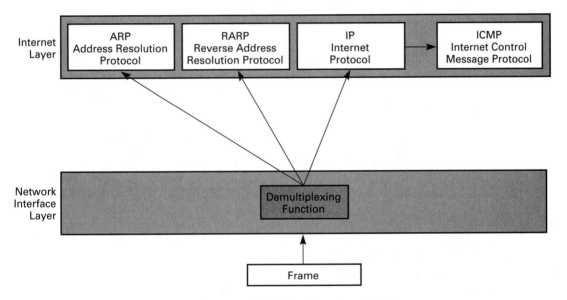

Figure 23.2   Network Interface layer demultiplexing.

Internet Layer

The TCP/IP Internet layer provides routing and relaying functions for carrying packets of data from a source system to a destination system through an internet. This is the layer at which routing decisions are made that determine the path over which each packet travels.

The following TCP/IP protocols operate in the Internet layer:

- **Internet Protocol.** The *Internet Protocol* (IP) is the core protocol of the TCP/IP protocol suite. It provides a connectionless, best-efforts data delivery service that is used in moving packets from one system to another through the internet.
- **Internet Control Message Protocol.** The *Internet Control Message Protocol* (ICMP) employs the services of IP to allow systems to report on error conditions and to provide information about unexpected circumstances.

- **Address Resolution Protocol.** The *Address Resolution Protocol* (ARP) helps a source system deliver data directly to a destination system when the two systems are on the same physical network. It allows the source system to determine the destination system's physical hardware address given the destination system's internet address. TCP/IP internet addresses are discussed later in this chapter.

- **Reverse Address Resolution Protocol.** The *Reverse Address Resolution Protocol* (RARP) allows a system that does not yet have its internet address to obtain it. RARP is typically used to support workstations and intelligent terminals that do not have their own disk storage.

Transport Layer

The Transport layer provides an end-to-end data delivery service that application processes use to exchange messages over the internet. Protocols operating in the Transport layer use the services of IP to deliver messages.

The following are descriptions of the two major TCP/IP Transport layer protocols:

- **User Datagram Protocol.** The *User Datagram Protocol* (UDP) is the simpler of the two transport protocols. It is a best-effort, connectionless Transport layer protocol that adds little to the underlying IP datagram delivery service.

- **Transmission Control Protocol.** The *Transmission Control Protocol* (TCP) is a connection-oriented Transport layer protocol that provides for reliable, sequenced stream data delivery.

An application process can use either UDP or TCP to request data transfer services. The protocol that an application developer chooses to use depends on whether the application requires only a best-efforts, datagram data delivery service or whether it requires the reliability controls provided by a connection-oriented data transfer service.

Application Layer

TCP/IP defines a wide range of application layer protocols that provide services to network users, including remote login, file copying and sharing, electronic mail, directory services, and network management facilities. Some application protocols are widely used, others are employed only for specialized purposes.

The following are brief descriptions of the most commonly used TCP/IP Application layer protocols:

- **PING Connectivity Testing.** *PING,* which is short for *Packet InterNet Groper,* can be used to test for connectivity between any two systems in the internet. In using PING, a user typically executes a program named **ping** that sends an ICMP Echo Request message to another system. When a system receives an ICMP Echo Request message, it sends an ICMP Echo Reply message back to the original sender. For each Echo Reply message that it receives, PING calculates the amount of time elapsed since it sent the original Echo Request message. This provides the PING user with an estimate of the round-trip delay that is being experienced in exchanging data with the specified system.

- **Telnet Remote Login.** Telnet allows a user to log in to some other system in the internet. The Telnet protocol establishes a client-server relationship between the local user (the client) and the remote Telnet application (the server). Telnet handles the data transfers that are required between the system implementing the client and the system implementing the server. These data transfers make it appear as if the user is logged into the remote system directly, even though the user is actually communicating with the local system.

- **Rlogin Remote Login.** The Rlogin service is related to Telnet but is typically provided only by variations of the UNIX operating systems. Telnet allows a user at any type of TCP/IP system to log into any other type of TCP/IP system. The local system and remote system may be running entirely different operating systems. The Rlogin service is normally used when a user at a local UNIX system wants to login to a remote UNIX system. For the UNIX user, Rlogin is somewhat easier to use than Telnet and provides a few additional services.

- **Rsh Remote Execution.** The *Rsh* remote execution service allows the user to issue, at the local system, a command to request an operating system function or to request the execution of an application program on some other system in the internet. When using the Rsh service, the user enters a command at the local system, and the command is then sent to and executed on the remote system. The results of the command or the results of the application program execution are then returned to the user at the local system. A similar service to Rsh called *Rexec* is available on some TCP/IP systems as well.

- **FTP File Transfer.** The *File Transfer Protocol* (FTP) implements a file transfer service that is typically employed by TCP/IP end users. FTP allows the user to transfer data in both directions between the local system and a remote system. FTP can be used to transfer files that contain either binary data or ASCII text. Certain versions of FTP also allow for the transfer of files containing EBCDIC data. Files can be transferred one at a time, or a single request can cause multiple files to be transferred. FTP also provides ancillary functions, such as listing the contents of remote directories, changing the current remote directory, and creating and removing remote directories. FTP uses TCP to transfer data. It uses the reliability controls that are automatically provided by a TCP connection to ensure that data is transferred reliably and that a transferred file is an exact copy of the original. FTP is described further later in this chapter.

- **TFTP File Transfer.** The *Trivial File Transfer Protocol* (TFTP) is a simple file transfer facility that also provides the ability to transfer data in both directions between the local system and a remote system. TFTP implements its own reliability controls and can run on top of any type of transport service. UDP is used by most TFTP implementations. The end-to-end reliability controls that TFTP implements take the form of a message sequencing system, timeouts, and retransmissions to ensure that files are transferred intact. TFTP is generally used only by system software that performs such functions as downline loading of program code; it is not intended to be employed directly by end users.

- **SMTP Electronic Mail.** The *Simple Mail Transfer Protocol* (SMTP) is used for the transfer of electronic mail messages. SMTP is designed to be used by electronic mail software that provides the user with access to messaging facilities. Mail facilities allow the user to send messages and files to a user connected to the local network, to a user connected to some other network in the internet, or to a user connected to a non-TCP/IP network that has a connection to the TCP/IP internet. Many types of electronic mail systems have been implemented for the TCP/IP environment, some of which can be interconnected with the electronic messaging systems of other types of networks such as PROFS and DISOSS in the IBM environment, and with public electronic mail services, such as MCI Mail and CompuServe. SMTP is described further later in this chapter.

- **Kerberos Authentication and Authorization.** Kerberos is an encryption-based security system that provides mutual authentication between a client component and a server component in a distributed computing environment. It also provides services that can be used to control which clients are authorized to access which servers. In the Kerberos system, each client component and each server component is called a *principal* and has a unique *principal identifier* assigned to it. These principal identifiers allow clients and servers to identify themselves to each other to prevent fraudulent exchanges of information. Authorization of a client to access a particular server can be implemented independently from the authentication service.

- **X Windows Presentation Facilities.** X Windows is a set of distributed graphical presentation services that implement a windowing system on a graphics display. It implements a client-server relationship between an application program (the client) and the windowing software in a workstation or terminal that controls a window on the graphical display (the server). The client and server can be running in different computing systems or in the same computing system. The X Window system allows a user at a graphics workstation to have multiple windows open on the screen, each of which might be controlled by a separate client application program. The X Window system defines a protocol that is used to transmit information between the client application program and the server windowing software.

- **DNS Name Resolution.** Each system attached to a TCP/IP internet has at least one 32-bit internet address assigned to it. Each system also typically has a unique name to make it possible for users to easily refer to the system without knowing its internet address. Since the underlying TCP/IP protocols, such as IP, TCP, and UDP all refer to individual systems using their internet addresses, each system must implement a *name resolution* function that translates between system names and internet addresses. In small TCP/IP internets, the function of translating between a system name and the internet address associated with that system can be performed by the system itself through a configuration file typically named **hosts.** In a large internet, it is unwieldy to try to maintain name-to-address mappings for each individual system in local **hosts** files. The *Domain Name System* (DNS) is a directory service that can be used to maintain the mappings between names and internet addresses in a limited number of places in the internet rather than at the location of each system. DNS is described further later in this chapter.

- **NFS Remote File Service.** The *Network File System* (NFS) implements a number of high-level services that provide authorized users with access to files located on remote systems. System administrators generally designate one or more systems in the internet to play the role of file servers. These systems run NFS server software that make certain designated directories on their disk storage devices available to other systems. A user accesses an NFS-mounted directory in the same manner as accessing a directory on a local disk. The fact that a directory is an NFS-mounted directory on a remote system is typically transparent to the user of the local system.

- **SNMP Network Management.** Network management services are typically provided in a TCP/IP internet through software that implements the *Simple Network Management Protocol* (SNMP). SNMP defines a Management Information Base (MIB), which is a database that defines all the objects that can be managed in the internet. SNMP also defines the formats of a set of network management messages and the rules by which the messages are exchanged. The network management messages are used to make requests for performing network management functions and to report on events that occur in the network. SNMP is introduced in Appendix D.

REQUESTS FOR COMMENTS (RFCs)

The authoritative sources for information about the current status of TCP/IP protocols are called *Requests for Comments* (RFCs). RFCs are available in machine-readable form on the Worldwide Internet or in hard-copy form from the Internet Network Information Center (NIC). The NIC is operated by Government Systems, Inc. (GSI), 14200 Park Meadow Drive, Suite 200, Chantilly, VA 22021. The NIC, from time to time, publishes a new RFC entitled *Official Internet Protocols*. The most recently published version of this document contains a list of the RFCs describing TCP/IP protocols.

A set of two RFCs provides important reference sources concerning the protocols that are typically implemented in TCP/IP systems:

- **RFC 1122—Requirements for Internet Hosts—Communication Layers.** This RFC concentrates on protocols that operate in the Internet and Transport layers.

- **RFC 1123—Requirements for Internet Hosts—Application and Support.** This RFC concentrates on protocols that operate in the Application layer.

These two RFCs identify the specific RFC that is the original source that defines each TCP/IP protocol, corrects errors that were detected in the original protocol description since its publication, and supplements the original protocol specifications in various ways.

INTERNET ADDRESSING

Each system that is attached to a TCP/IP internet is assigned a unique, 32-bit *internet address* value. The general format of an internet address is shown in Fig. 23.3. The initial bits of the internet address identify the internet address type and describe how the 32-bit address is divided between a *Network Identifier* field and a *Host Identifier* field. (Systems attached to a TCP/IP internet are often called *hosts*.) The Network Identifier field identifies the individual network on which the source or destination is located; the Host Identifier field identifies a particular system on that network.

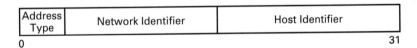

Figure 23.3   Internet address structure.

Internet addresses are distinct from the physical hardware addresses of the NICs installed in systems. Each type of data link technology that is used to implement a particular network in a TCP/IP internet may define its own physical hardware addressing scheme. For example, a network implemented using a local area network technology may employ IEEE/ISO/ANSI 48-bit MAC addresses as physical hardware addresses. TCP/IP protocols provide methods of converting between 32-bit internet addresses and the physical hardware addresses used on a particular data link.

Internet Address Formats

In TCP/IP, internet addresses are 32 bits in length and contain two parts—a *network identifier* and a *host identifier*. The initial bits of the network identifier identify what *class* the address belongs to. The formats of the internet addresses for four commonly used address classes are shown in Fig. 23.4.

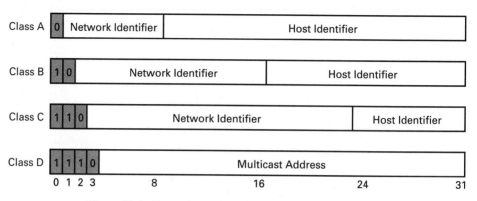

Figure 23.4 Four primary forms of TCP/IP internet addresses.

The following are descriptions of each of these four classes of internet addresses:

- **Class A Addresses.** An address whose first bit is set to 0 is a class A address. A class A address provides 7 bits to identify the physical network and 24 bits to identify systems on that network. In any internet there can be up to 126 networks that use class A addresses. Since a class A address provides 24 bits for uniquely identifying systems, a class A network can, for practical purposes, contain an almost unlimited number of systems.

- **Class B Addresses.** An address whose first two bits are set to 10 is a class B address. A class B address provides 14 bits to identify the network and 16 bits to identify systems. A class B address allows for up to $2^{14}-2$ different physical networks and up to $2^{16}-2$ different systems on each network.

- **Class C Addresses.** An address whose first three bits are set to 110 is a class C address. A class C address provides 21 bits to identify the network and 8 bits to identify systems. A class C address allows for up to $2^{21}-2$ different physical networks but only up to 254 different systems on each network.

- **Class D Addresses.** An address whose first four bits are set to 1110 is a class D address. A class D address is used to implement a form of multicasting in which an address refers to some collection of systems in an internet, all of which receive the data units having the specified multicast address.

The internet addressing scheme allows for relatively few class A networks. For example, in the Worldwide Internet, only very few class A addresses still remain unallocated, and it is no longer possible for an individual organization to get a class A address assignment. Class B and class C addresses are the only types of addresses available for assignment to individual organizations.

In order to ensure that network identifiers are unique across the entire Worldwide Internet, a central authority assigns the address classes and the address values or ranges of address values to be used by individual organizations when their networks connect to the Worldwide Internet.

Subnets

TCP/IP network administrators can use a single network identifier in multiple networks by defining *subnetworks*, or *subnets*. When using subnetting, some of the high-order bits in the host identifier portion of the address are used to identify individual subnets. A value called a *subnet mask* must be used by each system to identify how the internet address bits should be interpreted in a particular network.

Dotted-Decimal Notation

When writing down internet addresses, or when software displays them to human users, a form of notation called *dotted-decimal notation* is typically used to represent 32-bit TCP/IP internet addresses. For example, assume a system has the following internet address:

10000010 00001111 00000100 00000001

The above internet address would be written down or displayed in dotted-decimal notation as follows: 130.15.4.1.

A separate decimal number is used to represent the value of each individual octet of the address.

Ports

A system can typically support multiple independent processes, each of which can be communicating with processes running in other systems in the internet. An individual process within a system is represented by a data structure called a *port*. Each application process running in a TCP/IP system must be assigned a 16-bit *port number* to uniquely identify it within that system. Each application process that is using TCP/IP communication services is assigned one or more ports on its system.

When a source application process sends data to a destination application process, it must provide three pieces of information:

- The data to be sent.
- The internet address of the host on which the destination application process is running.
- The number of the port on the destination host that is assigned to the destination application process.

The remainder of this chapter examines the operation of the primary protocols that operate in each layer of the TCP/IP architecture, beginning with three representative Application layer protocols.

REPRESENTATIVE APPLICATION PROTOCOLS AND SERVICES

The following sections further describe three widely used TCP/IP application protocols and services: the File Transfer Protocol (FTP), the Simple Mail Transfer Protocol (SMTP), and the Domain Name System (DNS).

File Transfer Protocol (FTP)

The *File Transfer Protocol* (FTP) supports the transfer of files from one system to another. FTP is designed to operate across systems of different types and accommodates a variety of differences in how files are stored, accessed, and protected. The way in which FTP accommodates these differences is by allowing file attributes to be specified as part of the file transfer request. These attributes include *data type*, *file type*, and *transmission mode*.

Data Types

FTP defines four possible data types:

- **ASCII.** The ASCII data type denotes data represented using the 7-bit ASCII coding system with each ASCII character stored in an 8-bit octet. This is referred to as NVT-ASCII.
- **EBCDIC.** The EBCDIC data type denotes data represented using the IBM EBCDIC 8-bit encoding system.
- **Image.** The Image data type denotes data treated as a continuous bit stream.
- **Logical Octet Size.** With the Logical Octet Size data type, the number of bits in each octet is explicitly specified. This logical grouping of bits into octets is preserved across the file transfer operation.

The ASCII and EBCDIC data types are most often used with text files. Image and Logical Octet Size data types are typically used for binary program images and for encoded and tabular data that cannot be handled in the form of text.

File Types

The file types defined by FTP are as follows:

- **File Structure.** A file having the *file structure* file type consists of a string of octets terminated by an End of File marker.
- **Record Structure.** A file having the *record structure* file type consists of a set of records. When a record structured file is transferred, the end of each record is indicated by an End of Record marker.
- **Page Structure.** The *page structure* file type was defined for a file structure used with DEC's TOPS-20 systems, used extensively in the early days of the ARPANET. This file type is no longer commonly used.

Although the number of file types defined is limited, they have proven sufficient to accommodate the majority of file transfer operations typically required in the TCP/IP environment.

Transmission Modes

The data type and file type attributes address the way a file is stored in the source and destination systems. The *transmission mode* attribute is concerned with the way in which a file is transferred across the internet. Transmission mode options are designed to deal with restarting an interrupted data transfer operation and with enhancing file transfer efficiency. Possible transmission modes include the following:

- **Stream.** With the *stream* transmission mode, data is sent over the network with no specialized processing. The stream transmission mode can be used with all file types.

- **Block.** With the *block* transmission mode, data is encapsulated into records. Each record contains a count field, the data, and an End of Record marker. With the block transmission mode, the source and destination systems keep track of the progress of the transfer, and if the transfer is interrupted, the transfer can be restarted from the last correctly received record.

- **Compressed.** With the *compressed* transmission mode, data is compressed before transmission by replacing contiguous sequences of the same character with a single occurrence of the character and a count of the number of times the character occurs. The destination FTP process expands the data back to its original form.

FTP Operation

FTP employs two separate TCP connections to accomplish a file transfer. A *control connection* is used to pass control information, in the form of commands and replies, back and forth between the FTP processes running in each system. A *data transfer connection* is used for the actual transmission of file data and acknowledgments.

The FTP process in the system that is making the file transfer request is called the *FTP client*. The FTP process in the system receiving the request is the *FTP server*. The process involved in executing a file request is as follows:

1. A user (person or application program) invokes FTP services and passes the FTP client the name of the system to receive the request. The FTP client opens a TCP connection with the FTP server on the designated system using the standard destination port number associated with FTP. This connection is the control connection.

2. The FTP client sends commands to the FTP server with the account name and password of the user. The FTP server allows the receiving system to perform any necessary authentication of the user's access rights and sends replies back to the FTP client indicating whether authentication was successful.

3. The FTP client sends commands indicating the file name, data type, file type, and transmission mode to be used for the transfer and whether the FTP client will send a file to the FTP server or receive a copy of a file from the FTP server. The FTP server sends replies indicating whether or not the transfer options are acceptable.

4. The FTP server opens another TCP connection with the FTP client to use for data transfer, using a destination port number previously sent to it by the FTP client.

5. The sending FTP process packages data as agreed upon in the options and sends it to the receiving FTP process using the data transfer connection. Standard TCP flow control, error checking, and retransmission procedures are used to ensure that the file is transferred correctly and completely.

6. When the entire file has been transferred, the sending FTP process closes the data transfer connection. The control connection can then be used to begin another data transfer operation, or it also can be closed.

Data Formats

FTP defines the formats to be used for the commands and replies sent across the control connection. A command consists of a 4-octet NVT-ASCII character string. A reply consists of a 3-digit numeric code followed by an optional text string. The first digit of the numeric code indicates the general status of the reply, as follows:

1. Positive preliminary reply
2. Positive completion reply
3. Positive intermediate reply
4. Transient negative reply
5. Permanent negative reply

A complete list of the defined commands and replies is included in the FTP specification.

Simple Mail Transfer Protocol (SMTP)

The Simple Mail Transfer Protocol (SMTP) defines how mail messages are transferred between SMTP processes on different systems. The protocol does not define how mail to be sent is passed from a user to SMTP, nor does it specify how SMTP delivers mail to a receiving user. SMTP also does not define the internal format of mail messages. SMTP deals only with the exchanges that occur between the two SMTP processes.

The SMTP process with mail to send is called the *SMTP client*, and the SMTP process that receives mail is the *SMTP server*.

An SMTP operation consists of three steps:

1. A connection between the SMTP client and the SMTP server is established.
2. Mail is transferred across the connection.
3. The connection is closed.

We will look at each of these three steps next.

Connection Setup

When there is mail to send, the SMTP client opens a TCP connection with the SMTP server at the destination system using a destination port number that is associated with SMTP. The client then sends a Hello command containing the name of the sending user. The SMTP server returns a reply indicating its ability to receive mail.

Mail Transfer

Mail transfer begins with a Mail command containing the name of the user sending the message. This is followed by one or more Rcpt commands that identify the intended recipients of the message. A Data command begins the transfer of the actual message text. The Data command is followed by a series of data units that contain the message text. The SMTP server responds to each command with an appropriate reply.

TCP mechanisms for error detection and retransmission are used to ensure successful transfer of mail messages. When the SMTP server has successfully received the message for a given destination user, the client SMTP process removes that user from the list of destinations for the message. When all destinations have been sent copies of the message, the message and its list of destinations are removed from the sending message queue. SMTP can be considered a reliable delivery service in that it ensures that a message reaches the destination *system*. However, SMTP defines no procedures to guarantee that the message is successfully delivered to the destination *user* at that system.

When message transfer for a given message has been completed, the TCP connection can be used to transfer another message, the direction of transfer can be changed to allow the destination system to send messages back, or the connection can be closed.

Connection Closing

The SMTP client closes the connection by issuing a Quit command. Both sides then execute a TCP Close operation to release the TCP connection.

Data Formats

The commands used with SMTP begin with a 4-octet command code, encoded in NVT-ASCII, which can be followed by an argument. Box 23.1 lists the basic SMTP commands. SMTP replies use the same format as FTP—a 3-digit numeric value followed by a text string.

BOX 23.1 SMTP commands.		
• HELO	• SEND FROM:	• HELP (string)
• MAIL FROM:	• SOML FROM:	• NOOP
• RCPT TO:	• SAML FROM:	• QUIT
• DATA	• VRFY (string)	• TURN
• RSET	• EXPN (string)	

Domain Name System (DNS)

As we introduced earlier, in a TCP/IP internet, each system has both a name and an internet address. Most TCP/IP user commands allow systems to be referred to by either their names or their internet addresses. Since system names are easier to remember than their internet addresses, most users prefer to use names in TCP/IP commands. A *resolver* process running on each system in the internet performs the processing that is required to translate system names into their associated internet addresses.

Name Resolution Using hosts Files

In a small internet, simple 1-8 character names are used to name systems, and the mappings between names and addresses are maintained in a local file, often called **hosts**, that is maintained by each system. The resolver process in each system translates a system name into its corresponding internet address by looking up the name in the local **hosts** file.

When local **hosts** files are used for name resolution, the network administrator must ensure that the **hosts** files in all the systems in the internet are updated each time a system is added to or deleted from the internet. In a large internet that changes frequently, keeping **hosts** files up-to-date becomes a cumbersome process.

Name Resolution Using the Domain Name System

The *Domain Name System* (DNS) provides a networkwide directory service that maps between system names and internet addresses. When DNS is used for name resolution, each system still runs a resolver process. However, instead of consulting a local **hosts** file, the DNS resolver contacts another system somewhere in the internet that is running a *nameserver* process. The nameserver uses a directory database to perform the name translation operation and sends the results back to the resolver on the local system.

A DNS nameserver maintains a tree-structured directory database that contains sets of names called *domain names*. A domain name refers to a *domain*, defined by a system administrator, that consists of a collection of systems in the internet or to an individual system. A domain name consists of a sequence of simple names separated by periods.

Domain names can be assigned in any desired way, but most installations follow the conventions for domain names that have been established by the Worldwide Internet. A typical domain name in the Worldwide Internet looks like the following:

myhost.sra.com.

A domain name reads from left to right from the most local name to the most global name. A domain name that refers to an individual system is called a *fully-qualified domain name*. The name **myhost.sra.com** is an example of a fully-qualified domain name that refers to a particular system. The name **sra.com** refers to the domain of all the systems attached to networks administered by an organization named SRA, and the name **com** refers to the domain of all the systems in all the networks in the Worldwide Internet that are administered by commercial organizations.

The hierarchical naming scheme implemented by DNS allows the simple name **myhost** to be used to refer to systems in different domains without conflict as long as a different higher-level qualifier is used in a fully-qualified domain name to differentiate one system from the other. If a user enters a command using a simple name to refer to a resource in the user's own domain, the resolver automatically appends the high-level qualifiers of the user's own domain before sending the name to a nameserver for translation.

DNS Message Format

The resolver process in a system sends requests for name resolution to a nameserver process using DNS messages. The nameserver also sends responses back to the resolver using DNS messages. Box 23.2 shows the format of a DNS message and describes its fields.

A naming database maintains different types of information, and each query specifies the particular type of information that is requested. Some of the different types are shown in Box 23.3. The naming database can also contain different sets of information for use with protocol suites other than TCP/IP. The query identifies the protocol suite for which the query is being made.

BOX 23.2 Domain Name Service (DNS) message.

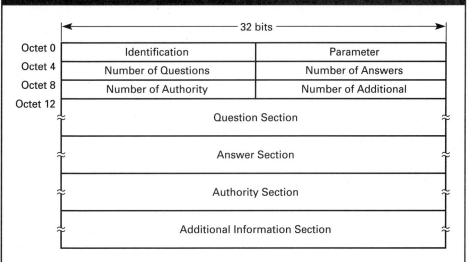

- **Identification.** A value used to correlate a response with its associated request.
- **Parameter.** Identifies the type of query and certain processing options to be applied.
- **Number of Questions.** Specifies the number of queries in this request. The Question Section of a request can contain information about multiple queries.
- **Number of Answers.** Specifies the number of answers in the response. The Answer Section of a response can contain information about multiple answers.
- **Number of Authority.** Specifies the number of authority resource records in the response. The Authority Section of a response can contain multiple resource records.
- **Number of Additional.** Specifies the number of additional information resource records in the response. The Additional Information Section of a response can contain multiple resource records.
- **Question Section.** Contains queries in the format shown below. A query consists of a Query Domain Name field containing the fully-qualified domain name about which information is required, a Query Type field specifying the type of information required, and a Query Class field identifying the protocol suite with which the name is associated.

- **Answer Section.** Contains information returned in response to a query in the format shown below. The Resource Domain Name, Type, and Class fields are from the original query. The Time To Live field specifies how long this information can be used if it is

(Continued)

447

BOX 23.2 *(Continued)*

cached at the local system. The format of the Resource Data field depends on the type of information requested.

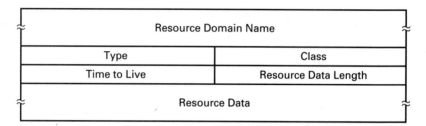

Resource Domain Name	
Type	Class
Time to Live	Resource Data Length
Resource Data	

- **Authority Section.** Identifies the server that actually provided the information if a name-server has to contact another nameserver to provide a response. The format for this field is the same as for the Answer Section.

- **Additional Information Section.** Contains additional information related to the name in a query. For example, for a type MX query, the name of a system that is a mail exchanger is returned as the answer. The Additional Information Section contains the internet address associated with that name.

BOX 23.3 DNS types.

Type	Contents
A	32-bit IP host address.
CNAME	Canonical Domain Name for an alias.
HINFO	Name of CPU and operating system.
MINFO	Information about a mailbox or mail list.
MX	Name of a host that acts as mail exchanger for a domain.
NS	Name of the authoritative server for a domain.
PTR	Domain name.
SOA	Multiple fields that specify which parts of the naming hierarchy a server implements.
TXT	Uninterpreted string of ASCII text.

DNS Operation

When DNS is invoked, the resolver process in the local system may be able to provide the requested information from information it has cached from previous requests. DNS does not define specific rules of operation for saving and using cached information but allows an implementation to use caching. The Time To Live value controls how long the information can be used.

If the resolver process cannot provide the requested information locally, it formats a request message and sends it to a nameserver. The DNS protocol requires each resolver to know how to reach at least one nameserver. The resolver sends the request to the nameserver using standard TCP transmission facilities.

Nameservers are linked hierarchically, reflecting the hierarchical structure of domain names. Root servers are able to recognize top-level domain names and know which server resolves each top-level name. The server for a top-level domain name knows the servers that can resolve subdomains under that domain name and so on proceeding down. Figure 23.5 shows an example of a possible hierarchy of nameservers. Given a request to resolve the name **myhost.sra.com**, the root server would know the nameserver for **.com**, and the nameserver for **.com** would know the server for **sra.com**, which would be able to resolve all full names with the **sra.com** high-level qualifier.

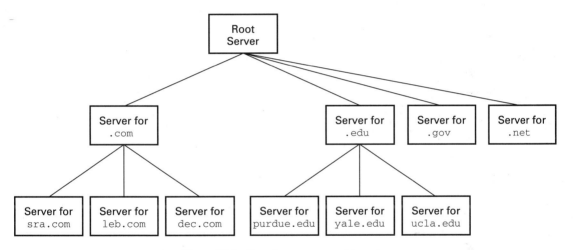

Figure 23.5   Sample name server hierarchy.

If a nameserver receives a request for a name resolution operation and is able to fully resolve the name using its own directory database, it returns the requested information to the resolver. If the nameserver is unable to fully resolve the name, the processing the nameserver performs next depends on whether the Parameter field in the request specified that the request is iterative or recursive:

- **Iterative Requests.** If the request is an *iterative* request, the nameserver returns to the resolver the address of the nameserver that should be contacted next to resolve the name. It is then the responsibility of the resolver to contact the new nameserver.

- **Recursive Requests.** If the request is a *recursive* request, the nameserver itself contacts the nameserver that can provide the requested information, obtains the name resolution information from that nameserver, and then returns the information to the resolver in a response.

Each nameserver must know how to contact at least one root server, so every nameserver has the capability of being able to determine which nameserver in the internet can resolve any valid fully-qualified domain name that it receives.

The DNS protocol includes features that can increase the efficiency of name resolution operations. In addition to implementing caching functions in the resolver process, caching can also be performed by a nameserver so that names that are referenced frequently can be resolved more quickly. A compressed name format can be used when there are multiple answers to a request and the domain names have parts of the name in common. Rather than including a particular simple name multiple times, only one copy of the name needs to be included in the response, and pointers to that copy are used where it occurs in other domain names.

DNS also supports inverse queries, where an internet address is specified in the query and its associated domain name is returned in the response.

APPLICATION PROGRAMMING INTERFACES

TCP/IP application programming interfaces (APIs) define communication services that can be invoked by user-written application programs. The two most commonly used TCP/IP APIs are the *Sockets* and the *Transport Layer Interface* (TLI) APIs. Application programs can also access the services of a *remote procedure call* (RPC) facility in invoking communication services.

Other types of application programming interfaces are also available in some TCP/IP environments, but they are used less often than Sockets, TLI, and RPC and are not discussed in this book.

Sockets Interface

The *Sockets* interface was initially developed for the variation of the UNIX operating system developed by the University of California at Berkeley. This variation of UNIX is called *BSD UNIX*. (The BSD acronym stands for *Berkeley Software Distribution*.) By using the Sockets interface, two application programs, one running in the local system and another running in the remote system, can communicate with one another in a standardized manner. The Sockets API is the most widely used TCP/IP API at the time of writing.

The Sockets API is typically used to implement a client-server relationship between two application programs running in different computing systems. The client and the server programs each invoke functions that set up an association between them. The client and the server application then invoke functions to send and receive information between them over the internet in a similar manner to calling functions that are used to perform ordinary file I/O.

The association between the two programs is based on the use of data structures called *sockets*, which allow access to TCP/IP services. A particular socket identifies a port number and an internet address. Multiple application programs can share the same socket.

The Sockets API can be used to provide access to protocols other than TCP/IP, such as the Xerox XNS and the OSI protocols. When used with TCP/IP, the Sockets API supports a connectionless data transfer service using UDP, a connection-oriented data transfer service using TCP and a direct interface to IP services.

The Sockets API provides a series of system calls that application programs invoke to request communication services. The system calls included in the Sockets interface were originally developed for use with the C programming language. Corresponding functions have also been implemented for various other programming languages. The most commonly used C-language Sockets system calls are listed in Box 23.4.

BOX 23.4   Sockets C-language system calls.

System Call	Function
socket	Specifies the communication protocol to be used.
bind	Assigns a name to a socket.
connect	Establishes a connection with a server.
listen	Indicates that a server is willing to receive connections.
accept	Waits for a connection request to arrive from a client.
send	Sends data.
sendto	Sends data to a specified socket.
recv	Receives data.
recvfrom	Receives data from a specified socket.
close	Closes a socket.
readv	Reads data from noncontiguous buffers.
writev	Writes data from noncontiguous buffers.
sendmsg	Sends a message.
recvmsg	Receives a message.
getpeername	Gets the name of the process connected to a given socket.
getsockname	Gets the name of a socket.
getsockopt	Gets the options associated with a socket.
setsockopt	Sets the options associated with a socket.
select	Allows a process to wait for the occurrence of any one of multiple events.

Connectionless Data Transfer

Figure 23.6 shows the sequence of Sockets system calls that might be invoked in a program to implement connectionless data transfer. No error detection and retransmission is provided by the underlying UDP data delivery service.

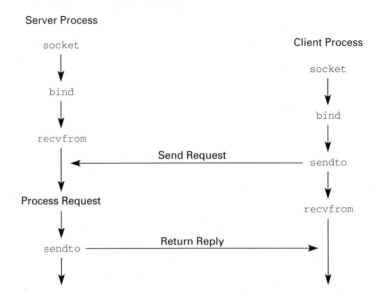

Figure 23.6 Typical Sockets API functions for connectionless UDP transport.

Connection-Oriented Data Transfer

Figure 23.7 shows the sequence of Sockets system calls that might be invoked to implement connection-oriented data transfer. With connection-oriented data transfer operations, the server first initializes itself and then waits for a client to request a connection. The client then eventually requests a connection and transmits data across the connection. The underlying TCP data delivery service provides error detection, retransmission, and flow control mechanisms.

Transport Layer Interface (TLI)

The *Transport Layer Interface* (TLI) API was originally defined for use with AT&T System V UNIX and is now available with a number of different TCP/IP implementations. The TLI API is similar to Sockets in that it provides an interface between an application program and a communication protocol such as TCP/IP. The TLI API is not as widely used at the time of writing as the Sockets API.

For TCP/IP, the TLI API provides access to connectionless data transfer services using UDP and connection-oriented data transfer services using TCP. Rather than consisting of system calls, the TLI API is implemented through a library of functions.

Box 23.5 lists the C-Language function calls that are defined by the TLI API.

Connectionless Data Transfer

Figure 23.8 shows the sequence of TLI functions that might be used to implement connectionless data transfer.

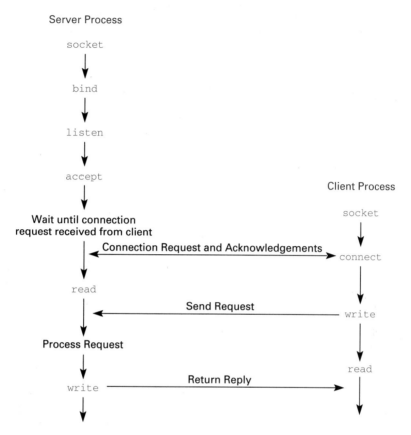

Figure 23.7 Typical Sockets API functions for connection-oriented TCP transport.

Connection-Oriented Data Transfer

Figure 23.9 shows the sequence of TLI functions that might be used to implement connection-oriented data transfer.

Streams Facility

TLI uses a facility called *Streams* as its interface to a communications protocol, such as TCP/IP. Streams provides a full duplex connection between a user process and a device driver using stream I/O functions. Streams allows the insertion of processes between the Streams interface and the device driver. When used for network communication, the communication protocol lies between the Streams interface and a network device driver. This is illustrated in Fig. 23.10. Box 23.6 lists the system calls that are part of the Streams facility. A TLI implementation invokes these system calls and hides the Streams interface from ordinary application programs.

BOX 23.5 TLI C-Language function calls.

Function Call	Function
t_error	Sets an error return code.
t_open	Identifies the transport provider.
t_alloc	Allocates a structure.
t_bind	Assigns an address to a transport endpoint.
t_connect	Initiates a connection with a server.
t_listen	Waits for a connection request from a client.
t_accept	Accepts a connection request from a client.
t_snd	Sends data.
t_rcv	Receives data.
t_sndudata	Sends a datagram (connectionless transfer).
t_rcvudata	Receives a datagram (connectionless transfer).
t_rcvuderr	Receives error information for a datagram.
t_look	Obtains the current event associated with a transport endpoint.
t_sndrel	Requests an orderly release of a connection.
t_rcvrel	Acknowledges a request for orderly release of a connection.
t_snddis	Disconnects a connection.
t_rcvdis	Receives data with a disconnect request.
t_close	Closes a transport endpoint without terminating the connection.
t_getinfo	Gets the information returned by t_open.
t_getstate	Gets the current state of a transport endpoint.
t_optmgmt	Gets or sets protocol-dependent options.
t_rcvconnect	Accepts a connection request from a client asynchronously.
t_sync	Synchronizes data structures with the current state of a transport endpoint.
t_unbind	Disables a transport endpoint.

Remote Procedure Call (RPC) Facilities

A *remote procedure call* (RPC) facility provides an easy-to-use method that application developers can use to implement communication applications. An RPC facility allows application components to communicate with one another in a transparent fashion over the internet using an ordinary procedure call mechanism.

Figure 23.11 illustrates a typical RPC functional model. A module called a *stub* in the local system mimics the presence of the actual procedure to which the client calling

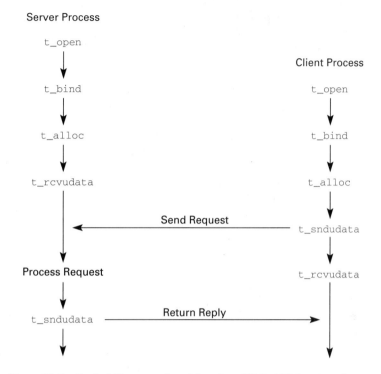

Figure 23.8 Typical Transport Level Interface (TLI) API functions for connectionless UDP transport.

procedure is attempting to pass control. There is a unique stub in the client process for each set of procedures that use the RPC facility. The client stub, in turn, requests the services of the RPC facility on behalf of the client. The RPC facility uses TCP/IP communication services to transmit parameter information to and from the RPC facility in the remote system.

When the RPC facility in the server system receives the parameter information generated as a result of the procedure call, it loads the server module containing the requested procedure and passes control to it, using a stub unique to that procedure. The called server procedure then passes results information back to its stub. The RPC facility then transmits the results back to the client.

The client and server procedures exchange parameter information and results as if they both resided in the same system, and the fact that an internet is being used to communicate parameter information is hidden from them.

There are two major software subsystems that are typically used to provide remote procedure call facilities in the TCP/IP environment—the RPC facility developed by Sun Microsystems and the RPC facility developed by Hewlett-Packard, Inc.

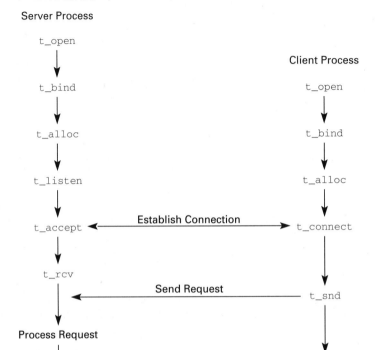

Figure 23.9   Typical TLI API functions for connection-oriented TCP transport.

Sun RPC

An implementation of the *Sun RPC* facility is provided in most operating systems that are based on BSD UNIX. The Sun RPC facility is also provided on a number of other UNIX and non-UNIX operating systems and is available with any implementation of Sun's Network File System (NFS). The source code for the Sun RPC facility is available from Sun Microsystems for a minimal charge.

The Sun RPC facility consists of the following components:

- **RPCGEN Compiler.** This is a compiler that accepts remote procedure call interface definitions and generates the stubs that are needed in the client and server programs.

- **External Data Representation (XDR) Facility.** The XDR facility provides a standard method for encoding parameter data so it can be used in a portable fashion in a heterogeneous system environment.

- **Runtime Library.** This library includes all the routines that are required to allow client and server programs to invoke the Sun RPC facilities.

- **Portmapper.** The Portmapper process is used to provide programs with information about the location of callable services.

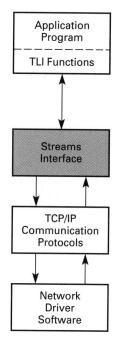

Figure 23.10 TLI uses the Streams facility as an interface to TCP/IP communication protocols.

BOX 23.6   Streams system calls.

Call	Function
open	Opens a streams device.
close	Closes a streams device.
read	Reads data from a streams device.
write	Writes data to a streams device.
ioctl	Performs control functions on a streams device.
putmsg	Writes a message consisting of a control part and a data part.
getmsg	Reads a message consisting of a control part and a data part.
poll	Determines the status of streams devices.

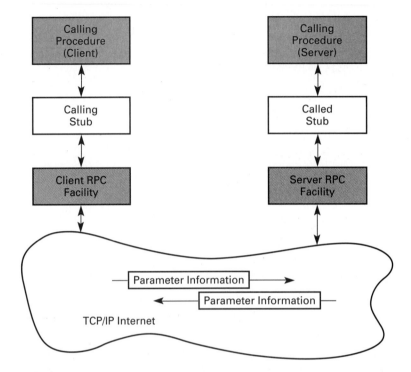

Figure 23.11 RPC facility functional model.

Hewlett-Packard RPC

The *Hewlett-Packard (HP) RPC* facility was originally developed by Apollo Computer Inc., which was subsequently acquired by Hewlett-Packard. It is provided as part of a software subsystem called the Network Computing System (NCS). The HP NCS is a programmer toolkit that allows programmers to access the HP RPC facilities in a similar manner to Sun RPC. Like Sun RPC, the NCS software subsystem is implemented on a wide variety of UNIX and non-UNIX operating systems. The NCS subsystem consists of the following components:

- **NIDL Compiler.** The Network Interface Definition Language (NIDL) compiler allows users to specify the interface between a client application component and a server application component. The NIDL compiler generates client and server stubs in a similar manner to the Sun RPCGEN compiler.

- **Network Data Representation (NDR) Facility.** This is a facility that allows the user to define how structured data values used in a procedure call are encoded for transmission through the internet.

- **Runtime Library.** The runtime library contains the executable code that can be included with user programs to implement remote procedure call facilities.

- **Location Broker.** The location broker maintains a database of information about the location of callable services.

TRANSPORT LAYER PROTOCOLS

Transport protocols provide application processes with end-to-end data transfer services. The following sections describe the operation of the major TCP/IP protocols that operate in the Transport layer of the TCP/IP architecture. The two protocols described here are the User Datagram Protocol (UDP) and the Transmission Control Protocol (TCP).

User Datagram Protocol (UDP)

The User Datagram Protocol (UDP) permits packets to be sent with a minimum of protocol overhead. With UDP, delivery is not guaranteed. There is no checking for missing, out-of-sequence, or duplicate packets, and no acknowledgments are sent.

Box 23.7 shows the format of a UDP datagram and describes the fields in the UDP header. UDP datagrams are often called *user datagrams* to distinguish them from IP datagrams. UDP datagrams are carried through the internet encapsulated within IP datagrams.

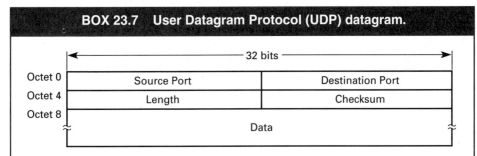

BOX 23.7 User Datagram Protocol (UDP) datagram.

- **Source Port.** The number of the port used by the process in the source system that originated the user datagram.

- **Destination Port.** The number of the port used by the process in the destination system that is to receive the user datagram.

- **Length.** The total length, in octets, of the user datagram, including the header and the Data field.

- **Checksum.** A checksum value used in validating the fields in the user datagram.

The only error checking provided by UDP is via the Checksum field. If the checksum value calculated by the receiving station does not agree with the checksum contained in the user datagram, the receiving system discards the user datagram. It is possible for UDP to lose user datagrams, to deliver them in a sequence different from that in which they were sent, or to duplicate them. Because it is possible for these errors to occur, UDP cannot be considered a reliable data delivery service. The application itself must implement any required reliability controls when it uses the UDP Transport layer protocol.

Transmission Control Protocol (TCP)

The *Transmission Control Protocol* (TCP) also operates in the TCP/IP Transport layer. TCP provides a connection-oriented, reliable data transfer service that is used to transmit an unstructured stream of octets from a port in the source system to a port in the destination system. Before data delivery can begin, the TCP user at one end requests a connection, both the TCP itself and the TCP user at the other end agree, and TCP establishes the connection.

TCP provides a full-duplex data delivery service. The source and destination TCP processes use the services of the underlying IP protocol to exchange messages called *segments*. Segments are encapsulated in IP datagrams for transmission using the services of IP. TCP itself does not impose any structure on the data being transmitted, and segments are transparent to the two TCP users, who can view the transmitted data as a continuous stream.

Box 23.8 shows the format of a TCP segment and describes its fields. Segments can be of any desired size. Octets that are transferred from one TCP user to another appear at the destination system in the same sequence in which they were sent. With TCP, either an identical copy of the data stream appears at the destination, or the connection is released and the two TCP users are informed that a failure has occurred.

The following sections describe some of the mechanisms that TCP uses in providing a reliable, sequenced data delivery service.

Connection Control and Data Transfer

When a TCP user in the source system requests a connection with a TCP user in the destination system, TCP sends a message to the destination system requesting the establishment of a TCP connection. The source user must specify the internet address of the destination system and the port number associated with the destination TCP user. Assuming the TCP process in the destination system can accept the connection, it sends back an acknowledgment message. The source system then sends its own acknowledgment message to confirm that the connection has been established. As part of the connection establishment procedure, the two systems agree on initial sequence numbers to use, based on sequence numbers included in the connection request and acknowledgment messages.

Once a TCP connection has been established, TCP implements a full-duplex path between the two users of the TCP and transfers data over a TCP connection from transmit buffers in the sending system to receive buffers in the destination system.

A TCP connection can be released at any time by the TCP service itself or by either of the TCP users. To release the connection, a system sends a message indicating that it has no more data to send. The other system returns an acknowledgment message, and no further data can be sent in that direction. When the other TCP user is finished sending data, it closes its end of the connection in a similar manner.

Error Detection and Retransmission

TCP uses a system of positive acknowledgments and segment retransmission. Each segment sent contains a Sequence Number field that indicates the octet position in the overall data stream of the data contained in that segment. The TCP process in the receiv-

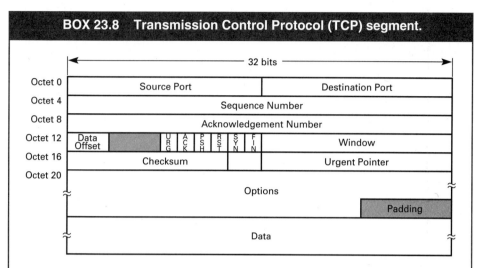

BOX 23.8　Transmission Control Protocol (TCP) segment.

- **Source Port.** The number of the port assigned to the process in the source system that originated the segment.

- **Destination Port.** The number of the port assigned to the process in the destination system that is to receive the segment.

- **Sequence Number.** Indicates the octet sequence number of the first octet of data contained in the Data field.

- **Acknowledgment Number.** Indicates the octet sequence number of the data octet that is expected to be received from the partner system.

- **Data Offset.** The length of the TCP header measured in 32-bit words. Padding is used between the TCP header and the Data field to ensure that the Data field begins on a 32-bit word boundary.

- **Flags.** Bits used to control the operation of the protocol.

- **Window.** A receive window size value used to implement flow control procedures.

- **Checksum.** A checksum value used in validating the fields in the segment.

- **Urgent Pointer.** Indicates the location of urgent data within the data stream being transmitted.

- **Options.** Fields used to implement protocol options. The only option field defined at the time of writing is a 32-bit maximum segment size field. This field is encoded in the form of a 16-bit introducer followed by a 16-bit maximum segment size value, thus allowing for a segment size up to 65,535 octets.

ing system checks the Sequence Number value in each received segment to ensure that there are no missing, duplicated, or out-of-sequence segments. As the recipient sends data back, it includes an Acknowledgment Number field value that indicates the sequence number of the octet position of the next octet it expects to receive. This acknowledges successful receipt of all octets in the data stream prior to the octet identified in the Acknowledgment Number field.

When each segment is sent, the TCP process in the sending system starts a timer. If the timer expires before that segment is acknowledged, the sender retransmits the segment. Since TCP transmission is full duplex, each TCP user keeps track of sequence numbers for data it is sending and for data it has received.

TCP also uses checksums for error detection. A checksum value is calculated and included in each segment that is sent. When a segment is received, the recipient calculates a checksum value. If the calculated value does not agree with the value contained in the segment, the segment is discarded. Since the erroneous segment is not acknowledged, the sender eventually times out and retransmits the segment.

Flow Control

TCP also uses acknowledgments to implement flow control procedures to balance the relative speeds of the sender and the receiver. When a connection is established, a window size is agreed upon for transmission in each direction. The window size specifies the number of octets that the sender is allowed to transmit before receiving an acknowledgment. Each acknowledgment that is returned also contains a new window size value that determines the number of octets that can be sent before the next acknowledgment. The window values in acknowledgments can be adjusted upward or downward to respond to changing conditions in the network.

Congestion occurs when the internet, or part of the internet, is overloaded and has insufficient communication resources for the volume of traffic it is experiencing. TCP does not contain explicit mechanisms for controlling congestion at intermediate points in the internet. However, a properly chosen retransmission scheme can help avoid congestion.

INTERNET LAYER PROTOCOLS

The protocols that operate in the TCP/IP Internet layer provide services to the Transport layer protocols. The protocols that operate in the Internet layer are the Internet Protocol (IP), the Internet Control Message Protocol (ICMP), the Address Resolution Protocol (ARP), and the Reverse Address Resolution Protocol (RARP).

Internet Protocol (IP)

The *Internet Protocol*, generally referred to by its acronym IP, operates in the TCP/IP Internet layer. IP routes packets across interconnected networks and performs packet segmentation and reassembly functions. Other protocols operating in the TCP/IP Internet layer provide support to the basic IP routing function.

The Internet Protocol (IP) performs two primary functions:

- Determining a route and relaying packets across the internet.
- Segmenting a packet, if necessary, to accommodate a network that has a small maximum packet size and then reassembling the packet when it reaches its destination.

Box 23.9 shows the packet format defined by IP and describes the fields in the IP header. IP packets are often called *IP datagrams*.

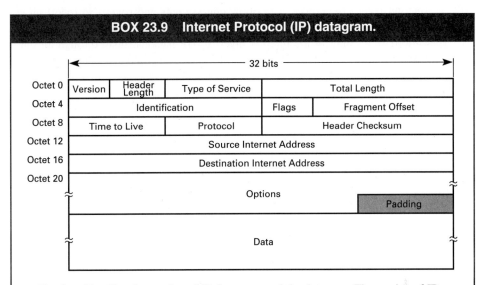

BOX 23.9   Internet Protocol (IP) datagram.

- **Version.** Identifies the version of IP that generated the datagram. The version of IP current at the time of writing is 4. A datagram having a version number different from 4 is discarded.

- **Header Length.** The length, in octets, of the IP header.

- **Type of Service.** An 8-bit code that indicates the quality of service that is desired for the datagram.

- **Total Length.** The length, in octets, of the entire datagram, including the header and the Data field.

- **Identification, Flags, and Fragment Offset.** Fields used to handle segmentation and reassembly if it is required.

- **Time to Live.** A value that indicates how long the datagram can remain in the internet before being discarded. This value is decremented by each router that processes the datagram. If the value reaches 0 before the datagram reaches the destination system, the datagram is discarded.

- **Protocol.** Identifies the Transport Layer Protocol with which the datagram is associated. The value for TCP is 6, and the value for UDP is 17.

- **Header Checksum.** Used to check the data in the IP header itself in a received packet to ensure that the header was not damaged during transmission.

- **Source and Destination Internet Addresses.** Identify the source and destination systems. The source and destination internet addresses are passed to IP along with the packet to be transmitted and are used by IP for routing.

- **Options.** Up to 40 octets of additional information to control functions such as routing and security.

Internet Control Message Protocol (ICMP)

The *Internet Control Message Protocol* (ICMP) is another protocol that operates in the Internet layer. Its purpose is to allow end systems and routers to report on error conditions and to provide information about unexpected circumstances. Although ICMP is viewed as residing in the Internet layer, ICMP packets travel through an internet in the form of IP datagrams. ICMP uses the IP best-efforts delivery service in a similar manner to a Transport layer protocol in moving ICMP packets through an internet. Fields in the header information of an IP datagram identify a packet as being an ICMP packet.

The following are some of the most common purposes for which ICMP is used:

- A system can determine whether a destination system is currently reachable.
- A router can inform a system that there is a better route that it can use in sending subsequent IP datagrams to a particular destination network.
- A system can tell a router that IP datagrams are arriving too fast for the system to process them.
- A system can tell a router that it has received a bad IP datagram, such as one that has exceeded the amount of time it is allowed to exist in an internet or one that has incorrect parameter information in its header.
- Systems can exchange packets that are used to synchronize their clocks.
- Systems can exchange packets that contain subnet mask values that inform each other of the specific formats of their internet addresses, indicating how many bits are used to identify a subnetwork and how many are used to identify individual systems.

Address Resolution Protocol (ARP)

The *Address Resolution Protocol* (ARP) is used by IP in helping it to route IP datagrams to the correct destination system. It can be used by IP in a source system to help it deliver an IP datagram to a system or router on the same physical network as the source system.

Internet Addresses

A portion of a system's internet address uniquely identifies the physical network to which it is attached. Therefore, the IP process running in a system can examine the destination internet address in an IP datagram and can easily determine the identity of the individual physical network to which the packet should be sent. However, a system's internet address may have no direct relationship to the system's physical hardware address. When the IP process running in one system wishes to deliver data to another system on its own network, it may know the internet address of the destination system, but it may not yet know the system's physical hardware address, which is needed by the Data Link layer for transmission over a data link.

Mapping Internet Addresses to Physical Hardware Addresses

In some cases, it is possible to provide each system on a network with a table that maps the internet addresses of all the systems and routers on that network to physical hardware addresses. However, most LANs use a 48-bit MAC address as a physical hardware address and permit a great many devices to be attached to an individual LAN. Such a LAN may be constantly changing as some users turn their machines off or remove them from the LAN and as other users attach new systems to the LAN. For such a situation, a dynamic scheme is required that allows systems to automatically maintain tables that are used to convert internet addresses into their associated physical hardware addresses. This is the function of ARP.

ARP Operation

ARP in each system maintains an *ARP cache* containing the mappings of internet addresses to physical hardware addresses for the systems on its own network that it currently knows about. When the IP process running in a system needs to deliver an IP datagram to a system on its own LAN, it looks up the system's internet address in its ARP cache. If the cache has an entry for that internet address, IP retrieves the associated physical hardware address in that ARP cache entry and delivers the IP datagram to the NIC having that address.

When a system is first powered up, its ARP cache is empty. Assume that the IP process in system A is attempting to deliver an IP datagram to system B but that system B's internet address is not yet in system A's ARP cache. IP then uses ARP to determine system B's physical hardware address.

The following steps are performed to determine system B's physical hardware address:

1. The ARP process running in system A broadcasts an ARP packet on the LAN containing system B's internet address.

2. The ARP processes running in all the systems on the LAN receive this broadcast packet.

3. System B recognizes its own internet address in the broadcast packet and replies to the system that sent the broadcast packet with a packet containing system B's physical hardware address.

4. When system A receives the reply from system B, system A stores system B's internet address to physical hardware address mapping in its ARP cache.

5. The IP process running in system A can now use the information in the new ARP cache entry to determine system B's physical hardware address and can directly deliver the IP datagram that is destined for system B.

There is an additional refinement to ARP that reduces the network traffic associated with running the protocol. This refinement is based on the assumption that it is likely that when system A has data to send to system B, that system B will later need to send data back to system A. In anticipation of this likelihood, when the ARP process running in system A sends an ARP broadcast packet asking for system B's physical hardware address, system A also places into that ARP packet its own internet address to physical hardware address mapping. When system B receives system A's ARP broadcast packet, system B adds system A's internet address to physical hardware address mapping to its own ARP cache. This eliminates the necessity of the IP process in system B to run ARP should it later have to send data back to system A.

Reverse Address Resolution Protocol (RARP)

A protocol related to ARP, but used for the opposite purpose, is the *Reverse Address Resolution Protocol* (RARP). RARP allows a system that knows only its physical hardware address to obtain the internet address that it should use in communicating with other systems. RARP is typically of use only to systems on a LAN data link that do not implement disk storage, often called *diskless workstations*. Terminals that implement the X Windows protocols—sometimes called *X Terminals*—may also use RARP to obtain their internet addresses.

In order for RARP to operate, at least one system on the LAN must be designated as a *RARP server*. A diskless workstation obtains an internet address by broadcasting on the LAN a RARP packet giving the workstation's physical hardware address. The RARP packet asks any RARP server on the LAN to reply with the internet address that is associated with that physical hardware address.

A RARP server maintains a table that maps the physical hardware addresses of the diskless workstations it serves to the internet addresses that those diskless workstations should use. When a RARP server receives a broadcast packet from a diskless workstation asking for an internet address, it looks up the physical hardware address in its table, obtains the internet address corresponding to that physical hardware address, and replies with the internet address that the diskless workstation should use.

TCP/IP ROUTING

The routing function in a TCP/IP internet has the responsibility of determining the path over which each IP datagram should travel from a source system to a destination system. Each end system and router maintains a routing table that it uses to determine the best next destination for each datagram it processes that must be sent to some other physical network. An end system's routing table must have at least one entry—an entry containing the address of a *default router*. An end system's default router is typically assigned when the TCP/IP communication software is configured for that system.

When a source system has an IP datagram to deliver to a destination system in another network, it consults its routing table to see if has an entry matching the address of the destination network. If the routing table has no entry corresponding to the destination network, the source system sends the datagram to the default router. If the default router is not the most direct route for a particular destination, the router returns an ICMP Redirect packet to the source system, giving it the address of the router it should use for subsequent datagrams destined for that destination network. The source system updates its routing table and directs future datagrams for that destination to the specified router.

Routing Protocols

The basic routing function is handled in a TCP/IP network by IP, and many small TCP/IP internets operate using only basic IP routing facilities. In larger internets, additional routing protocols are used by routers to exchange routing information with each other. There are many different routing protocols that routers can employ. The choice of the routing protocols that are used in any given TCP/IP internet is generally based on the size and the structure of the internet.

Autonomous Systems and Gateways

A TCP/IP internet is made up of one or more *autonomous systems*. An autonomous system consists of a set of computer systems and data links, making up one or more physical networks, that is administered by a single authority. An authority might be, for example, a university, a corporation, or a government agency.

Routers are often referred to as *gateways* in TCP/IP literature. The TCP/IP usage of the term gateway should not be confused with the term gateway as we defined it in Chapter 16. Routers that are used only within a single autonomous system are called *interior gateways*. Routers that connect one autonomous system to another are called *exterior gateways*.

Interior Gateway Protocols (IGPs)

The routers within an autonomous system are free to use any desired interior gateway protocol in communicating among themselves. A number of interior gateway protocols are in common use in TCP/IP internets. The following are brief descriptions of the more common of these:

- **RIP.** The *Routing Information Protocol* (RIP) is run by a routing program called [C] routed. The program was developed and distributed as part of 4.3BSD UNIX and became quite widely used without actually being defined in a formal specification. RIP uses a distance-vector routing algorithm that employs hop counts as distance measurements. With RIP, routers periodically broadcast routing information, and both routers and end systems use the routing information to update their routing tables.

- **Hello.** The *Hello* protocol is similar to RIP except that it makes routing decisions based on estimated delays rather than hop counts. Hello includes a mechanism for synchronizing clocks in different systems and uses timestamps on packets sent between systems to estimate routing delays.

- **OSPF.** The *Open Shortest Path First Protocol* (OSPF) uses a link-state routing algorithm that is similar to the OSI routing algorithm defined in ISO 10589. Routers exchange information about their own data links and then use that information to develop a map of the network topology. Routes are calculated based on the topology. Periodically, routers test neighbor availability, and broadcast status information about links. A router can also request information about specific links. OSPF allows for multiple routes to a destination based on different types of service, such as low delay or high throughput. OSPF is better suited than RIP or Hello to larger autonomous systems. The OSPF specification is available in the published literature and is an open standard that many router vendors have implemented.

Exterior Gateway Protocol (EGP)

In order for data to flow between two autonomous systems in a large TCP/IP internet, a router in one autonomous system must be able to communicate with a router in the other autonomous system. A commonly used routing protocol that allows routers in different autonomous systems to communicate is the *Exterior Gateway Protocol* (EGP). EGP is defined by a TCP/IP RFC and is implemented by many different router vendors.

Box 23.10 shows the format of the Exterior Gateway Protocol (EGP) packet that routers exchange and describes its fields. Box 23.11 lists the different EGP packet types that EGP defines.

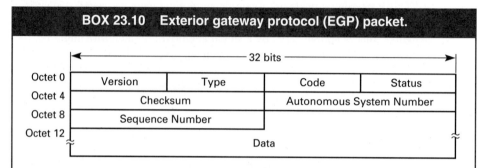

BOX 23.10   Exterior gateway protocol (EGP) packet.

- **Version.** Identifies the version of EGP being used.
- **Type.** Identifies the type of packet.
- **Code.** Further identifies a packet type.
- **Status.** Provides type-dependent status information.
- **Checksum.** Used to verify that the packet was not damaged during transmission.
- **Autonomous system number.** Identifies the autonomous system sending the packet.
- **Sequence number.** Used to match responses to requests.
- **Data.** Contains additional information specific to a particular packet type.

BOX 23.11   EGP packet types.

Packet Type	Type	Code	Description
Routing Update	1		Information on reachable networks
Poll Request	2		Requests a routing update
Acquisition Request	3	0	Requests a gateway to become a neighbor
Acquisition Confirm	3	1	Agrees to become a neighbor
Acquisition Refuse	3	2	Declines to become a neighbor
Cease Request	3	3	Requests termination of being neighbor
Cease Confirm	3	4	Acknowledges termination as neighbor
Hello	5	0	Tests that neighbor is alive
I Heard You	5	1	Response to Hello packet

Exterior Gateway Protocol Functions

EGP packets are used to perform three functions:

- Agreeing to exchange routing information with another autonomous system.
- Checking that a router in another autonomous system is still responding.
- Obtaining routing information from another autonomous system.

Each of the foregoing functions is described in the following sections.

Neighbor Acquisition

The process of agreeing to exchange information with another autonomous system is called *neighbor acquisition*. When a router functioning in the role of an exterior gateway wishes to exchange information with a router in another autonomous system, it sends an EGP Acquisition Request packet to that router. The other router responds with either an Acquisition Confirm or Acquisition Refuse packet. Assuming the response is positive, the two routers are then able to exchange routing information and the two gateways are then known as *exterior neighbors*.

As part of the acquisition packet exchange, the two routers agree on how frequently each router will be tested to see if it is still responding and how frequently requests for routing information can be sent.

If, at a later time, a router no longer wishes to be available to its neighbor, it sends an EGP Cease request. The neighbor responds with an EGP Cease Confirm.

Neighbor Reachability

Periodically, each router that is operating in the role of an exterior gateway checks its exterior neighbors by sending them EGP Hello packets. The neighbors respond with EGP I Heard You packets. If a neighbor does not respond after a certain number of tries, it is considered to be down and is no longer available for routing.

Routing Information Updating

When a router functioning as an exterior gateway wants to receive routing information from an exterior neighbor, it sends an EGP Poll Request packet. This packet identifies a *source network* that is common to the two exterior neighbor routers. The exterior neighbor router returns routing information in an EGP Poll Response. Only destinations that are part of the autonomous system that is providing the information are included in the information in the Poll Response. The distances shown for reaching the different destination networks are based on entering the autonomous system via the specified source network.

EGP implements a distance-vector form of routing protocol. However, the measure used for distance is not defined as part of the EGP specification. Each autonomous system defines its own distance measure. This means that distance values included in a Poll Response are comparable from route to route with an autonomous system, but they may not be comparable from one autonomous system to another.

SUMMARY

The Transmission Control Protocol/Internet Protocol (TCP/IP) protocol suite defines procedures for interconnecting individual networks to form an internet in which computers can freely exchange data. The TCP/IP approach to networking identifies a Network Interface layer that provides access to widely used LAN and WAN data link technologies, an Internet layer that handles the transmission of datagrams through the network, a Transport layer that handles end-to-end communication functions, and an Application layer that provides application-oriented communication services.

The TCP/IP Application layer includes a wide variety of application-oriented services and protocols including PING for connectivity testing, Telnet and Rlogin for remote login, Rsh for remote execution, FTP and TFTP for file transfer, SMTP for electronic mail, Kerberos for authentication and authorization, X Windows for windowing presentation services, DNS for name resolution, NFS for remote file services, and SNMP for network management.

The Transport layer protocols include UDP and TCP. The User Datagram Protocol (UDP) is a best-effort, connectionless transport protocol that adds little to the underlying IP datagram delivery service. The Transmission Control Protocol (TCP) is a connection-oriented transport protocol that provides for reliable, sequenced stream data delivery.

The Internet layer includes IP, ICMP, ARP, RARP, and various routing protocols. The Internet Protocol (IP) provides a connectionless, best-efforts data delivery service that is used in moving packets from one system to another through the internet. The Internet Control Message Protocol (ICMP) allows systems to report on error conditions and to provide information about unexpected circumstances. The Address Resolution Protocol (ARP) allows a source system to determine a destination system's physical hardware address given the destination system's internet address. The Reverse Address Resolution Protocol (RARP) allows a system that does not yet have its internet address to obtain it. The basic routing function in a TCP/IP internet is performed by IP; however, in internets that employ routers, the routers often run additional routing protocols that allow them to exchange routing information with each other.

Chapter 24 describes AppleTalk, Apple's approach to computer networking.

AppleTalk

The popularity of Apple computers in the business environment has led to increased use of AppleTalk, Apple's networking protocol family, for computer networking. One reason for AppleTalk's popularity is its ease of use. Support for the AppleTalk protocols have been included as a standard part of most Apple hardware and system software so that basic networking capability is included in every machine. The protocols are also built into other devices, such as many laser printers, so that AppleTalk networks with shared printer capability can be built simply by plugging the devices together with the appropriate cables and connectors. Software is also available from Apple that allows an Apple computer system to function as a file server on an AppleTalk network.

A typical AppleTalk network provides simple device-to-device communication, printer sharing, print spooling, and file sharing services. Network installation and reconfiguration is both easy to do and inexpensive. No special software or hardware is required, and no special network administration is required to operate small AppleTalk networks. Large networks can be constructed and interconnected using routers and wide area networking data links, allowing for the implementation of geographically dispersed internets involving large numbers of networked systems.

Many third party developers have used AppleTalk as a development platform and provide products that extend the capabilities of AppleTalk-based networks. For example, it is possible to construct AppleTalk networks that include non-Apple computing systems from a variety of vendors. Third party products also extend the range of functions that an AppleTalk network can provide, implementing such facilities as electronic mail and dial-up access to AppleTalk networks.

APPLETALK ARCHITECTURE

AppleTalk protocols reflect the general layered architecture defined by the OSI Model. Figure 24.1 lists the various protocols in the AppleTalk protocol family and shows their relationships to the layers of the OSI Model.

AFP – AppleTalk Filing Protocol	RTMP – Routing Table Maintenance Protocol
ADSP– AppleTalk Data Stream Protocol	NBP – Name Binding Protocol
PAP – Printer Access Protocol	DDP – Datagram Delivery Protocol
ASP – AppleTalk Session Protocol	AARP – AppleTalk Address Resolution Protocol
ZIP – Zone Information Protocol	LLAP – LocalTalk Link Access Protocol
ATP – AppleTalk Transaction Protocol	ELAP – EtherTalk Link Access Protocol
AEP – AppleTalk Echo Protocol	TLAP – TokenTalk Link Access Protocol

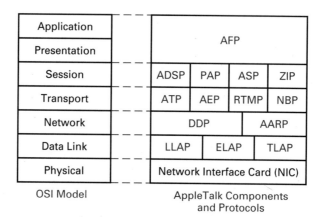

Figure 24.1   AppleTalk architecture.

Data Link Layer

Protocols operating in the Data Link layer provide for connectivity between systems that are attached to the same AppleTalk LAN data link. The Data Link and Physical layers implement three types of LAN data links over which the higher-level AppleTalk protocols can operate.

The AppleTalk specification itself includes the *LocalTalk Link Access Protocol* (LLAP). LocalTalk provides for the transmission and reception of frames by devices on the network. LLAP includes specifications for medium access management, data link addressing, data encapsulation/decapsulation, and frame transmission.

AppleTalk also supports the use of Ethernet and Token Ring LAN data link technology through the *EtherTalk Link Access Protocol* (ELAP) and the *TokenTalk Link Access Protocol* (TLAP).

LLAP, ELAP, and TLAP are described in Chapter 15.

Network Layer

Protocols operating in the Network layer provide for connectivity between any two end systems in the network. Two AppleTalk protocols operate in the OSI model Network layer. These protocols provide services that are used by the protocols associated with the layers above the Network layer:

- **Datagram Delivery Protocol.** The *Datagram Delivery Protocol* (DDP) delivers packets, called *datagrams,* on a best-efforts basis. DDP also plays a role in performing the routing functions needed to deliver datagrams across interconnected data links in a larger AppleTalk network.

- **AppleTalk Address Resolution Protocol.** The *AppleTalk Address Resolution Protocol* (AARP) plays a role in the process that is used to determine a node's network address. AARP is also used to provide a translation service that converts an AppleTalk network address into an EtherTalk or TokenTalk station address.

Session and Transport Layers

Protocols operating in the Session and Transport layers provide a number of services useful to application programs, including reliable, end-to-end data transfer services. AppleTalk includes eight protocols that are associated with the OSI model Session and Transport layers.

Data Transfer Protocols

Three of the Session and Transport layer protocols are designed to provide reliable data transfer services:

- **AppleTalk Transaction Protocol.** The *AppleTalk Transaction Protocol* (ATP) provides a form of reliable data transfer that does not require a logical connection between the source and destination systems. ATP is based on the use of units of data called *transactions*.

- **AppleTalk Data Stream Protocol.** The *AppleTalk Data Stream Protocol* (ADSP) provides a connection-oriented service that is reliable and full-duplex. ADSP clients at both ends of the connection can send streams of data that will arrive in sequence and without missing or duplicated data.

- **Printer Access Protocol.** The *Printer Access Protocol* (PAP) provides a connection-oriented data transfer service that allows connections to be established and released and permits messages to be reliably sent over a connection. The word printer in the protocol's name is historical, and PAP can be used for any type of reliable data transfer between a client and a server system.

Support Protocols

Five additional protocols in the Session and Transport layer provide various types of support services:

- **AppleTalk Echo Protocol.** The *AppleTalk Echo Protocol* (AEP) is used to test the accessibility of a system and to make an estimate of the round-trip transmission time required to reach that system.

- **AppleTalk Session Protocol.** The *AppleTalk Session Protocol* (ASP) is used to establish a session relationship between two programs running in AppleTalk systems. ASP provides services that can be used to ensure that a series of messages are delivered without duplication and in the same sequence in which they were sent.

- **Name Binding Protocol.** AppleTalk allows users to refer to network objects by name rather than by network address. The *Name Binding Protocol* (NBP) performs a name translation service that converts the name of an object to its AppleTalk network address.

- **Zone Information Protocol.** Large AppleTalk networks that interconnect multiple data links can be divided into *zones*. The *Zone Information Protocol* (ZIP) supports the Name

Binding Protocol in large networks consisting of multiple zones by mapping between zone names and LAN data links.

- **Routing Table Maintenance Protocol.** In a large AppleTalk network, routers are used to interconnect individual LAN data links. Routers use the *Routing Table Maintenance Protocol* (RTMP) to communicate with one another for the purpose of exchanging routing information. RTMP provides for establishing and maintaining routing tables that DDP uses for performing routing functions.

Application and Presentation Layers

The functions of user application programs operate in the OSI model Application and Presentation layers. AppleTalk defines a single application-oriented protocol:

- **AppleTalk Filing Protocol.** The *AppleTalk Filing Protocol* (AFP) is used to implement remote file access services that allow AppleTalk users to access the files stored on remote systems.

APPLETALK ADDRESSING

As we described in Chapter 15, each system attached to an AppleTalk LAN data link has a *node ID* associated with it. An AppleTalk network consisting of a single AppleTalk LAN data link, in which each system has a unique node ID, is called a *nonextended network*. It is possible to interconnect individual LAN data links to form an *extended network*, or internet.

Extended Networks

In an extended AppleTalk network, individual LAN data links are interconnected using routers. An internet connection can be implemented in a variety of ways, some of which are shown in Fig. 24.2 and described below:

- A connection between two AppleTalk LAN data links can be implemented by a router that belongs to the two AppleTalk LANs.
- A point-to-point communication link can connect two routers.
- An intermediary backbone LAN can connect two or more AppleTalk LANs.

To distinguish between systems on an extended network, each individual AppleTalk LAN data link is identified by a 16-bit *network number* value. An extended AppleTalk network has a range of network numbers associated with it within which all the network numbers of individual LAN data links must fall.

An extended AppleTalk network is organized into *zones*. A zone contains a subset of the systems in an AppleTalk network. Zones can be assigned in any desired manner. The systems in a zone can be on different LAN data links, or different groups of systems on the same LAN data link can be placed into different zones. Each system must belong to one, and only one, zone. A system chooses its zone at the time it is activated.

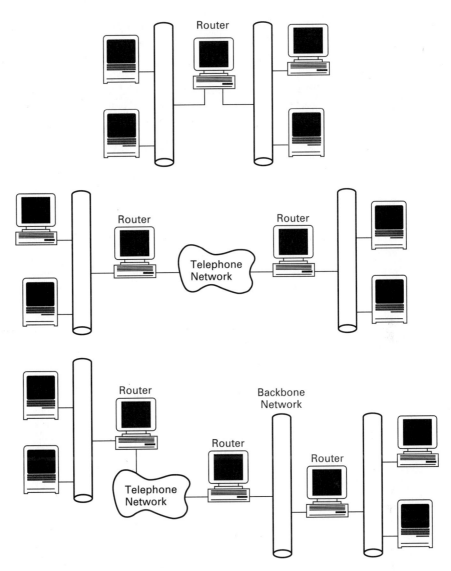

Figure 24.2   AppleTalk router configurations.

AppleTalk Node Addresses

Each system on an AppleTalk network is identified by a network address called a *node address*. The node address of an AppleTalk system consists of a combination of the network number value of the LAN data link to which the system is attached and the system's node ID value. The format of an AppleTalk node address is shown in Fig. 24.3.

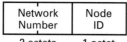

Network Number	Node ID
2 octets	1 octet

Figure 24.3   AppleTalk node address format.

AppleTalk Internet Socket Addresses

Communication in an AppleTalk network is based on the use of data structures called *sockets*. AppleTalk allows multiple processes within a single system to communicate over the network using the Datagram Delivery Protocol (DDP) that operates in the Network layer. Each process uses a socket data structure to send and receive data. Each communicating process is called a *socket client*. Each socket is identified by an 8-bit socket number. Certain socket numbers are permanently assigned. For example, protocols like RTMP, ZIP and NBP have fixed socket numbers through which they interface with DDP. Other socket numbers are assigned dynamically as a process needs one.

Each socket client in an AppleTalk network is uniquely identified by a complete *internet socket address*. An internet socket address identifies both the system and the socket client within the system that is communicating. An internet socket address consists of a socket number, a network number, and a node ID, as shown in Fig. 24.4.

Socket ID	Network Number	Node ID
1 octet	2 octets	1 octet

Figure 24.4   AppleTalk internet socket address format.

APPLICATION AND PRESENTATION LAYER PROTOCOLS

The AppleTalk architecture defines a single protocol, the AppleTalk Filing Protocol (AFP), that operates in the OSI model Application and Presentation layers. The following section describes the operation of AFP.

AppleTalk Filing Protocol (AFP)

The AppleTalk Filing Protocol (AFP) provides file sharing services that can be used with Apple computers as well as other types of systems. AFP is based on the sending of request and reply messages between a client system and a server system. AFP uses the AppleTalk Session Protocol (ASP), which we describe later, to establish a session between the client system and the server system, and to provide reliable, sequenced transport of the request and reply messages.

AFP Software

Support for AFP client and server functions are built into Apple system software. Apple's systems software provides peer-to-peer file sharing capabilities that allow ordinary user systems to publish selected volumes or directories that they wish to make available to other users. A user system operating in the role of an AFP server makes files available to other user systems that operate in the role of AFP clients. AFP client and server support can also be provided on other types of systems using software available from third-party software vendors.

In an AppleTalk network, one or more systems can also operate in the role of dedicated file servers that provide AFP services to other systems. Special-purpose file server software, such as Apple's *AppleShare* software, can be used to implement dedicated AFP servers.

File System Structure

AFP assumes a file system structure made up of resources that are addressable through the network. These resources include AFP servers, volumes, directories, files, file forks, and the Apple desktop database.

An *AFP server* is a system that allows other systems on the network to access and share files stored on the disk in the same way as if the files were stored locally. An AFP server manages one or more file storage units called *volumes*.

Each disk attached to an AFP server consists of one or more volumes. Data is stored on a volume in the form of *files*, with sets of files grouped together in *directories*. A volume can be one of three types:

- **Root.** A root volume has a flat structure where all the files on the volume are contained in a single directory.
- **Fixed Directory ID.** A fixed directory ID volume has a hierarchical structure. There can be levels of directories, where one directory contains lower-level directories within it. Each directory has a Directory ID, and a Directory ID value is never reused, even if the directory it belongs to is deleted.
- **Variable Directory ID.** A variable directory ID volume has hierarchical directories. The Directory ID used to identify a particular directory is assigned to that directory only for the duration of an AFP session that is processing it.

Each file can have two *file forks* associated with it. A *data fork* contains the actual data that makes up the file. A *resource fork* holds system resources used in conjunction with the file, such as icons and drivers. Not all files have resource forks.

The *Apple desktop database* is used by an AFP server to hold information that the Finder normally obtains from the desktop file. The Finder uses the information to build its user interface to the objects on a disk volume.

Security

AFP includes three features that can be used to implement protection from unauthorized access to shared resources. They are as follows:

- User authentication
- Volume passwords
- Directory access control

When a user system operating as an AFP client logs in to a system operating as an AFP server, a user authentication method can be specified. If user authentication is performed, it can be done by submitting a password, either as clear text or in encrypted form. Clear text should be used only if the network is physically secure from eavesdropping.

Individual volumes can be assigned passwords. When a client system first attempts to access a password-protected volume, the password must be supplied.

Directory rights can be used to allow different users different types of access to directories and the files they contain. Possible directory rights are as follows:

- **Search.** Allows the user to list the parameters of directories contained within this directory.

- **Read.** Allows the user to list the parameters and read the contents of files contained in this directory.

- **Write.** Allows the user to modify the contents of the directory, including parameters and contents of files and directories in this directory. The user can also add and delete files and directories to this directory.

Each directory can have a group affiliation, whereby a group of users are assigned a certain set of access rights to the directory. A given user can belong to more than one group and have different rights to different directories.

File Integrity

AFP uses *file sharing modes* and *synchronization rules* to protect the data integrity of shared files. File sharing modes and synchronization rules determine whether a user is able to access a particular file while it is being used by some other user.

When a user application opens a file, it can specify file sharing modes in the form of an *access mode* and a *deny mode*. The access mode indicates the way in which the user application will be using the file. Possible access modes are read, write, read-write, and none. A deny mode specifies which rights should be denied to other users that try to open the file while the first user is still accessing the file. Possible deny modes are also read, write, read-write, and none.

Synchronization rules indicate which combinations of access modes and deny modes will allow a second file open to be successful. For example, if a file is opened with access mode read-write and deny mode write, a second open with access mode read and deny mode none will be successful, while a second open with access mode read-write and deny mode none will not be successful.

AFP Services

The services provided by AFP can be categorized by the resource they affect. The calls that are used to request AFP services are listed in Box 24.1.

SESSION AND TRANSPORT LAYER PROTOCOLS

AppleTalk includes eight protocols that are associated with the OSI model Session and Transport layers. AppleTalk documentation uses the term *packet* to refer to the data units exchanged by many of the AppleTalk protocols, so the term packet is not used only to refer to data units exchanged by Network layer protocols.

BOX 24.1   AFP calls.

AFP Server Calls

- **FPGetSrvrInfo.** Obtains server information needed to open a session.
- **FPGetSrvrParms.** Obtains information on server volumes.
- **FPLogin.** Initiates the dialog to open a session.
- **FPLoginCont.** Sends an encrypted value to the server as part of password processing.
- **FPLogout.** Terminates a session.
- **FPMapID.** Obtains the user or group name corresponding to a user or group ID.
- **FPMapName.** Obtains the user or group ID corresponding to a user or group name.
- **FPChangePassword.** Changes a user's password.
- **FPGetUserInfo.** Obtains information about a user.

AFP Volume Calls

- **FPOpenVol.** Gives a user access to a volume.
- **FPCloseVol.** Terminates a user's access to a volume.
- **FPGetVolParms.** Obtains a volume's parameters.
- **FPSetVolParms.** Updates a volume's parameters.
- **FPFlush.** Causes the server to write to disk any data that has been modified.

AFP Directory Calls

- **FPSetDirParms.** Modifies a directory's parameters.
- **FPOpenDir.** Opens a directory and retrieves the directory ID.
- **FPCloseDir.** Closes a directory.
- **FPEnumerate.** Lists the files and directories contained within a specified directory.
- **FPCreateDir.** Creates a directory.

AFP File Calls

- **FPSetFileParms.** Modifies a file's parameters.
- **FPCreateFile.** Creates a file.
- **FPCopyFile.** Copies a file to another volume.

AFP File or Directory Calls

- **FPGetFileDirParms.** Retrieves parameters associated with the specified file or directory.
- **FPSetFileDirParms.** Sets parameters associated with the specified file or directory.
- **FPRename.** Renames a specified file or directory.

(Continued)

BOX 24.1 *(Continued)*

- **FPDelete.** Deletes a specified file or directory.
- **FPMoveandRename.** Moves a file or directory to some other parent directory and renames it.

AFP Fork Calls

- **FPGetForkParms.** Reads a fork's parameters.
- **FPSetForkParms.** Modifies a fork's parameters.
- **FPOpenFork.** Opens a fork.
- **FPRead.** Reads the contents of a fork.
- **FPWrite.** Writes to a fork.
- **FPFlushFork.** Requests the server to write to disk any data in the server's buffers.
- **FPOctetRangeLock.** Locks a range of octets in a fork.
- **FPCloseFork.** Closes a fork.

AFP Desktop Database Calls

- **FPOpenDT.** Gives a client system access to the Desktop database on a specified volume.
- **FPCloseDT.** Terminates a client's access to the Desktop database.
- **FPAddIcon.** Adds a new icon bitmap to the Desktop database.
- **FPGetIcon.** Retrieves the bitmap for a specified icon.
- **FPGetIconInfo.** Retrieves a description of an icon.
- **FPAddAPPL.** Adds an application's APPL mapping to the Desktop database.
- **FPRemoveAPPL.** Removes an application's APPL mapping from the Desktop database.
- **FPGetAPPL.** Obtains the APPL mapping for the next application in the list of applications for a given file creator.
- **FPAddComment.** Stores a comment associated with a particular file or directory.
- **FPRemoveComment.** Removes a comment associated with a particular file or directory.
- **FPGetComment.** Obtains a comment associated with a particular file or directory.

Three of the Session and Transport layer protocols provide reliable, end-to-end data transfer services. The AppleTalk Transaction Protocol (ATP) provides a connectionless, transaction-oriented data transfer service, the AppleTalk Data Stream Protocol (ADSP) uses connections to provide a stream-oriented data transfer service, and the Printer Access Protocol (PAP) uses connections to provide a message-oriented data transfer service useful in implementing client-server relationships.

The other five of the Session and Transport protocols provide various types of support services. The AppleTalk Echo Protocol (AEP) is used to test the accessibility of a system, the AppleTalk Session Protocol (ASP) is used to establish a session relationship between two AppleTalk systems, the Name Binding Protocol (NBP) converts the name of an object to its AppleTalk network address, the Zone Information Protocol (ZIP) maps between zone names and LAN data links, and the Routing Table Maintenance Protocol (RTMP) is used to establish and maintain routing tables.

The following sections describe the operation of the first seven of the AppleTalk Session and Transport layer protocols. The operation of RTMP is described later in this chapter when we discuss AppleTalk routing.

AppleTalk Transaction Protocol (ATP)

The *AppleTalk Transaction Protocol* (ATP) provides for the reliable, loss-free delivery of packets from a program associated with a source socket to a program associated with a destination socket. ATP is based on the notion of a *transaction*, which consists of a request and its corresponding response. The request must consist of a single packet and the response can consist of from one to eight packets. Each request is assigned a 16-bit transaction ID. The transaction ID is also included in a response packet, allowing a response to be correlated with its corresponding request. If a response is not received within a specified time limit, the request is retransmitted. This mechanism is used to ensure the request is received and processed.

Before a client can receive transaction requests, it must open a listening, or responding, socket. The client requests ATP to open a responding socket and then waits to receive a request. When a request arrives, the client processes the request and sends back a transaction response.

Each request contains a bit map that indicates how many packets are expected in the response. If a partial response is received, the request is retransmitted with an altered bit map, so that only the missing response packets need to be sent again. This process is illustrated in Fig. 24.5. If a responder does not have enough data to make up the requested number of packets, the responder is able to send an end-of-message signal to indicate the last response packet.

Two types of transactions are defined—*at-least-once transactions* and *exactly-once transactions*. With at-least-once transactions, if the request is retransmitted, the responder reprocesses the request and sends another response. With an exactly-once transaction, the first time the request is processed, the results are saved. If the same request is retransmitted, the saved results are sent again as the response, and the request is not reprocessed. Once the requester has received the entire response, it sends a release packet, so the responder can discard the saved results. Saved results are also time stamped. After a certain period of time, the saved results are discarded.

ATP Packet

Box 24.2 shows the packet format used with ATP and describes the fields in the ATP packet header.

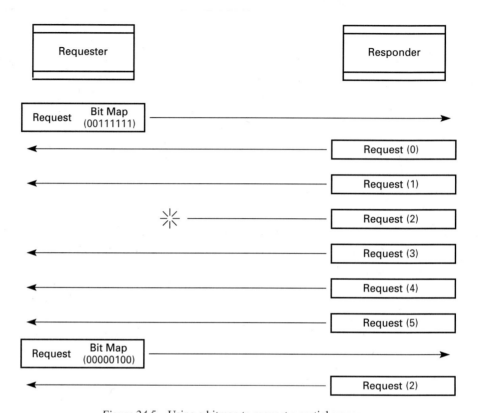

Figure 24.5   Using a bitmap to request a partial response.

ATP Services

The services that are provided by ATP are invoked using the calls listed in Box 24.3.

AppleTalk Data Stream Protocol (ADSP)

The *AppleTalk Data Stream Protocol* (ADSP) establishes a logical association, called a *connection*, between two users of the ADSP service before data transfer can take place. A connection consists of an association between two sockets. In performing data transfer operations across a connection, ADSP uses sequence numbers and acknowledgments to implement error detection and retransmission functions. ADSP also includes a flow control mechanism.

Each end of an ADSP connection is identified by its internet socket address and has a connection ID associated with it. ADSP assigns a connection ID to each of a pair of sockets when it establishes a connection between them. A socket can take part in multiple connections at one time, but there can be only one connection established between any given pair of sockets. Thus a pair of connection IDs identifies a particular connection.

Once the connection has been established at both ends, the connection is considered open and data can be transferred across it. If a connection has been closed at

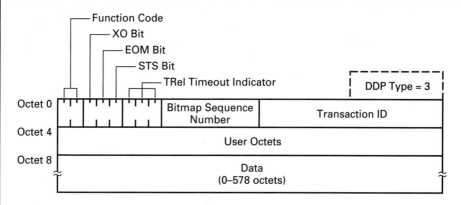

BOX 24.2 AppleTalk Transaction Protocol (ATP) packet.

- **Control—Function Code.** Identifies the type of packet being sent as a transaction request, a transaction response, or a release packet. A release packet is used with an exactly-once transaction to indicate that the results no longer need to be stored.

- **Control—XO.** An *Exactly-Once* bit used to identify an exactly-once transaction.

- **Control—EOM.** An *End Of Message* bit used to indicate the end of the data being sent by the responder.

- **Control—STS.** A *Send Transaction Status* bit used with an exactly-once transaction when the responder has limited buffer space and needs to know which response packets no longer need to be stored.

- **Control—TRel Timeout Indicator.** A *TRel timeout indicator* used to indicate how long results should be saved for an exactly-once transaction.

- **Bitmap/Sequence Number.** In a transaction request, the *Bitmap* indicating the number of packets expected in the response; in a transaction response, the *Sequence Number,* used to sequence the packets in the response.

- **Transaction ID.** A *Transaction ID* identifying a particular transaction and used to correlate a response with its request.

- **User Octets.** A field that is not defined by the ATP protocol and is left for use by higher level protocols.

BOX 24.3 ATP calls.

- **Send a Request.** Causes an ATP request packet to be sent to a specified destination socket address.

- **Open a Responding Socket.** Opens a listening socket for receiving ATP requests.

- **Close a Socket.** Closes a responding socket.

- **Receive a Request.** Receives an ATP request over an open responding socket.

- **Send a Response.** Sends ATP response packets to the source of an ATP request.

both ends, the connection is a closed connection. A connection that is established at one end but closed at the other is considered to be half-open. ADSP implements a timer-based mechanism that causes a half-open connection to eventually be automatically closed.

ADSP Data Packet

Box 24.4 shows the format of the packet used with ADSP and describes the ADSP packet header fields.

There are a number of mechanisms that ADSP uses in providing a reliable, sequenced data transfer service between two socket clients. Key ADSP control mechanisms are described in the sections that follow.

BOX 24.4   AppleTalk Data Stream Protocol (ADSP) packet.

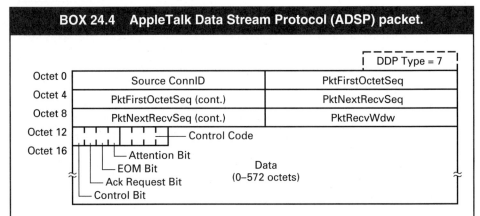

- **Source ConnID.** The connection ID assigned to the system sending the packet.

- **PktFirstOctetSeq.** The sequence number of the first octet in the packet's data. Sequence numbering is based on the position of each octet in the data stream being sent.

- **PktNextRecvSeq.** The sequence number of the next octet this system expects to receive. It acknowledges receipt of all octets preceding this octet.

- **PktRecvWdw.** Specifies the amount of buffer space, in octets, that is available for receiving data from the other system.

- **ADSP Descriptor—Control Bit.** Identifies the packet as a control packet or data packet.

- **ADSP Descriptor—Ack Response Bit.** Requests an immediate acknowledgment.

- **ADSP Descriptor—EOM Bit.** Indicates that the data in this packet is the end of a message. The data in the data stream being transmitted can be logically divided into multiple messages.

- **ADSP Descriptor—Attention Bit.** Identifies the packet as an Attention packet. Attention packets are used to send messages between the two ADSP users outside the normal flow of data. Attention packets are sequence-numbered separately from packets making up the normal data flow.

- **ADSP Descriptor—Control Code.** Identifies the type of an ADSP control packet.

Error Detection and Retransmission

ADSP uses a system of positive acknowledgments with retransmission. Each packet sent contains a sequence number that indicates the octet position in the overall data stream of the data in the packet. The recipient checks the sequence numbers to make sure there are no missing, duplicate, or out-of-sequence octets. As the recipient sends data back, it includes a number that indicates the sequence number of the octet position of the next octet it expects to receive. This acknowledges successful receipt of all octets in the data stream prior to the one identified by this number.

When a sender transmits a packet it starts a timer. If the timer expires before that packet is acknowledged, the sender retransmits the packet. Since ADSP transmission is full duplex, each ADSP socket client keeps track of sequence numbers for data it is sending and for data it has received.

In addition to sequence numbers in data packets, ADSP uses control packets that can be used in the acknowledgment and retransmission process. An Acknowledgment control packet is used when an ADSP socket client wishes to send an acknowledgment or a request for an acknowledgment and has no data to send in a data packet. A Retransmit Advice control packet is used to request retransmission of data beginning with the sequence number specified in the packet. It can be sent if a number of errors have been detected to speed the start of retransmission.

A Forward Reset control packet is used to abort delivery of all unacknowledged data that has been sent by a client. When this control packet is received, the receiving client removes all undelivered octets from its buffers and returns a Forward Reset Acknowledgment control packet. The Forward Reset control packet specifies the sequence number where transmission will resume. The two clients use this to resynchronize their sending and receiving.

Flow Control

ADSP also uses acknowledgments to implement flow control procedures to balance the relative speeds of the sender and the receiver. When a connection is established, a buffer size is specified for receiving data in each direction. This buffer size specifies the number of octets that the sender is allowed to transmit before receiving an acknowledgment. Each acknowledgment that is returned also contains a buffer size value that determines the number of octets that can be sent before the next acknowledgment. The buffer size value in the acknowledgments can be adjusted upward or downward to respond to changing conditions in the system.

Connection Control

Control packets are also used for connection control. When a client wishes to open a connection, it sends an Open Connection Request packet to the client at the other end. This packet contains the internet socket address, connection ID, and buffer size of the sending socket client, and the sequence number that should be given to the first octet of data sent by the other end. The receiving socket client uses this information to establish the connection on its end. It then returns an Open Connection Request and Acknowledgment control packet containing the same information for its end. The original socket client establishes the connection on its end and sends an Acknowledgment control packet, so that both socket clients know the connection is open. If a client is unable to accept a connection opening request, it sends back an Open Connection Denial control packet.

Since a connection is not yet open, the delivery of these control packets is not reliable. If a socket client does not receive a response within a certain time period, it retransmits the request. A connection can also be established using an internet socket address for a socket client other than the one to which the original request was sent. In this case, the internet socket address to be used for the connection is returned in the Open Connection Request and Acknowledgment control packet.

A connection can be closed by either client by sending a Close Connection Advise control packet to the other end. If one end becomes unreachable for some reason, the connection becomes half-open. This is detected when no packets are received from the other end for a period of time. When this happens, a Probe control packet is sent repeatedly to the other end. If no response is received after a specified number of tries, the connection is closed.

Printer Access Protocol (PAP)

The Printer Access Protocol (PAP) is based on a connection between a pair of systems, one of which is a client system and the other a server system. Both the client and the server can have multiple connections operating at one time. Each connection is uniquely identified by a connection ID. Historically, PAP was developed to allow user systems to send print jobs to a print server, and each connection was associated with a print job to be processed. However, PAP is a general-purpose protocol and can be used with any type of client-server communication.

PAP Packets

PAP uses the same packet format as ATP and employs the user octets defined in the ATP packet header. The first octet of the user data is used to identify the PAP packet type. The rest of the information contained in a PAP packet varies with the packet type. Box 24.5 lists the contents of various types of PAP packets.

PAP Services

The calls that are used to request PAP services are listed in Box 24.6.
The following sections describe some of the services that are provided by PAP.

Connection Establishment

Before a connection can be established, the server must be initialized. PAP opens an ATP listening socket for it. PAP also uses NBP services to register the name of its services in the name directory, with the listening socket as the internet socket address. The server begins operation in a blocked state. When the server is prepared to accept jobs, it indicates to PAP the number of connections, or jobs, it is prepared to accept. This puts the server in the waiting state.

BOX 24.5 Printer Access Protocol (PAP) packets .

OpenConn

ATP User Octets

Octet 1   ConnID
Octet 2   Function code (1)

ATP Data

Octet 1   ATP responding
                  socket number
Octet 2   Flow quantum
Octets 3,4   Wait time

SendData

ATP User Octets

Octet 1   ConnID
Octet 2   Function code (3)
Octets 3,4   Sequence number

Tickle

ATP User Octets

Octet 1   ConnID
Octet 2   Function code (5)

CloseConn

ATP User Octets

Octet 1   ConnID
Octet 2   Function code (6)

SendStatus

ATP User Octets

Octet 2   Function code (8)

OpenConnReply

ATP User Octets

Octet 1   ConnID
Octet 2   Function code (2)

ATP Data

Octet 1   ATP responding
                  socket number
Octet 2   Flow quantum
Octets 3,4   Result
Octets 5-n Status information

Data

ATP User Octets

Octet 1   ConnID
Octet 2   Function code (4)
Octet 3   EOF

ATP Data

Data

CloseConnReply

ATP User Octets

Octet 1   ConnID
Octet 2   Function code (7)

Status

ATP User Octets

Octet 2   Function code (9)

ATP Data

Octets 5-n Status information

BOX 24.6   PAP calls.

- **PAPOpen.** Initiates a connection-opening dialog with the server.
- **PAPClose.** Closes a connection.
- **PAPRead.** Reads data from the other end of the connection.
- **PAPWrite.** Writes data to the other end of the connection.
- **PAPStatus.** Obtains status information for the server.
- **SLInit.** Opens a server listening socket.
- **GetNextJob.** Indicates the server is ready to accept one more connection.
- **SLClose.** Closes a server process.
- **PAPRegName.** Registers a service name.
- **PAPRemName.** Removes the name of a service.
- **HeresStatus.** Updates server status information.

When a client system has a job to send and wants to establish a connection, it requests a connection by specifying a service name. PAP opens a socket for the connection, generates a connection ID, and uses NBP services to determine the address associated with the name of the service. PAP sends an OpenConn packet to the server containing the client system's socket address, connection ID, and the flow quantum. The flow quantum indicates the amount of buffer space the client system has available for reading data.

If the server is still in the blocked state, PAP returns an OpenConnReply that indicates "server busy." If the server is in the waiting state, it begins an arbitration process. During the arbitration process, PAP waits a fixed length of time to see if other connection requests are received.

A connection request indicates how long a client has been waiting for the connection. At the end of the waiting period, PAP establishes connections based on which clients have been waiting the longest. An ATP listening socket at the server is opened for each connection, and an OpenConnReply is sent back with this socket address and the flow quantum for the server. This establishes the connection.

If, after this process, the server can accept no more connections, it returns to the blocked state. If the server still can accept additional connections, it enters the unblocked state. If a connection request arrives while the server is in the unblocked state, the connection is established without going through the arbitration process.

Data Transfer

Once a connection is established, either the client or the server can read or write data over it. Data transfer in PAP is read-driven. A PAP SendData packet is sent as a request for data when a system is ready to accept data. When a system has data to write, if a SendData packet has been received, the data is sent in PAP Data packets, using ATP transaction response packets. If a SendData packet has not been received, PAP queues the request until a SendData packet does arrive. The amount of data sent cannot exceed the flow quantum of the receiving end. When all the data for a particular job has been sent, an end-of-file indicator (EOF) is included in the last Data packet. All SendData packets contain a sequence number. PAP uses this sequence number to ensure that a read request is not processed more than once.

Connection Maintenance

Both the client system and the server system keep a timer that is reset whenever a packet is received over the connection. If the timer expires, the connection is assumed to have gone down and is closed. Either side can send a Tickle packet to keep the connection open if it has no other packets to send.

Connection Termination

Either side can close a connection. Typically, after sending all the data for a particular job, the client system closes the connection. PAP sends a CloseConn packet to the other system, which returns a CloseConnReply packet. This exchange terminates the connection.

AppleTalk Echo Protocol (AEP)

The *AppleTalk Echo Protocol* (AEP) allows a system to send an Echo Request packet to some other system. A system that receives an Echo Request packet returns an Echo Reply packet, which contains a copy of the Data field contained in the Echo Request packet. AEP allows a system to determine whether some other system, called the *echoer*, is accessible on the network. AEP also provides an estimate of the time it takes to transmit a packet back and forth between the two systems (round trip time).

AEP Packet

Box 24.7 shows the format of the AEP packet and describes its fields. Notice that AEP packets are sent using socket number 4 in Type 4 DDP datagrams.

AppleTalk Session Protocol (ASP)

The AppleTalk Session Protocol (ASP) allows a client to send a sequence of commands, or transaction requests, with reliable delivery of the commands in the sequence sent. It is based on the use of a session, which is a logical connection between two ASP users. A session has a session identifier that uniquely identifies it. ASP uses the reliable transaction delivery services of ATP in performing its services. ASP sessions are asymmetrical, with one system being considered the client and the other the server. Only the client is allowed to establish a session and send commands. The server processes commands and returns results. A server can have multiple sessions in operation at the same time.

ASP Packets

ASP uses the same packet format as ATP. The ASP packet uses the four user octets defined in the ATP packet header. The first octet of the user octets is used to identify the ASP packet type. The rest of the information contained in an ASP packet varies with the packet type. Box 24.8 lists the contents of various ASP packets.

BOX 24.7 AppleTalk Echo Protocol (AEP) packet.

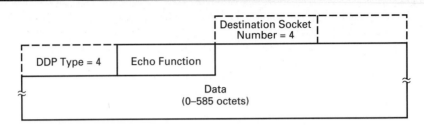

- **Echo Function.** Identifies the packet's function. A value of 1 indicates that the packet is an Echo Request packet; a value of 2 indicates that the packet is an Echo Reply packet.
- **Data.** The user of AEP can use the Data field to distinguish between different Echo Request packets the user may send.

BOX 24.8 AppleTalk Session Protocol (ASP) packets.

CloseSess

ATP User Octets

Octet 1 Function code (1)
Octet 2 Session ID

Command

ATP User Octets

Octet 1 Function code(2)
Octet 2 Session ID
Octets 3,4 Sequence number

ATP Data

Command data

GetStatus

ATP User Octets

Octet 1 Function code (3)

OpenSess

ATP User Octets

Octet 1 Function code (4)
Octet 2 Client socket number
Octets 3,4 ASP version number

CommandReply

ATP User Octets

Octets 1-4 Command results

ATP Data

Command reply data

GetStatusReply

ATP Data

Status information

OpenSessReply

ATP User Octets

Octet 1 Server socket number
Octet 2 Session ID
Octets 3,4 Error code

BOX 24.8 *(Continued)*

Tickle

ATP User Octets

Octet 1   Function code (5)
Octet 2   Session ID

Write

ATP User Octets

Octet 1   Function code (6)
Octet 2   Session ID
Octets 3,4   Sequence number

ATP Data

Command data

WriteContinue

ATP User Octets

Octet 1   Function code (7)
Octet 2   Session ID
Octets 3,4   Sequence number

ATP Data

Available buffer size

Attention

ATP User Octets

Octet 1   Function code (8)
Octet 2   Session ID
Octets 3,4   Attention code

WriteReply

ATP User Octets

Octets 1-4   Command results

ATP Data

Command reply data

ATP Data

Data to write

ASP Services

In performing its services, a client system sends command and control packets, which are transported as ATP transaction requests, and the server returns command and control replies, transported as ATP transaction responses. The calls that are used to request ASP services are listed in Box 24.9.

The following sections describe some of the services that ASP performs.

Opening a Session

Before a session can be opened, the server must establish an ATP listening socket. The client sends an OpenSess packet to the listening socket, containing the client's socket

---

BOX 24.9   ASP calls.

Server Calls

- **SPInit.** Passes information needed for initialization between the server and ASP.
- **SPGetSession.** Accepts an SPOpenSession command from the client.
- **SPGetRequest.** Provides buffer space for the receipt of client commands.
- **SPCmdReply.** Returns command results and reply data.
- **SPWrtContinue.** Notifies the client that a requested write operation can be performed.
- **SPWrtReply.** Indicates the end, either successful or unsuccessful, of a write operation.
- **SPNewStatus.** Updates server status information.
- **SPAttention.** Sends an attention code to the client.

Client Calls

- **SPGetStatus.** Obtains server status information.
- **SPOpenSession.** Opens a session.
- **SPCommand.** Sends a command to the server.
- **SPWrite.** Requests the server to perform a write operation.

Server and Client Calls

- **SPGetParms.** Retrieves maximum size for command data and the flow quantum.
- **SPCloseSession.** Terminates a session.

---

number. The server returns an OpenSessReply, with the server socket number to use for the session and the session ID. If there is a problem with opening the session, an error code is sent back.

Closing a Session

Either session partner can close a session, by sending a CloseSess packet. The packet contains the session ID. The other partner returns a CloseSessReply, to acknowledge that the session is terminated.

Sending Commands

A client sends commands in an SPCommand packet. A sequence number in the packet is used to ensure that the commands are delivered in sequence. The server sends results back in CmdResult packets.

Sending Write Data

A client can also send blocks of data to be written at the server. The client first sends an SPWrite packet, notifying the server that there is data to be sent. The server returns a WriteContinue packet, specifying a buffer size. The client sends the data to be written in WriteContinueReply packets. When the server has completed the write operation, it sends a WriteReply packet.

Maintaining a Session

There are two mechanisms that can be used to help keep a session operational. Both the client and the server keep a timer that is reset whenever a packet is received on the session. If the timer expires, the session is assumed to have gone down and is closed. Either side can keep the session open by sending Tickle packets if it has no other packets to send. A server can send an Attention packet to the client if there is a condition that requires the client's attention. The Attention packet contains an attention code identifying the condition. The code is not meaningful to ASP. It is passed to the user of ASP and is interpreted at a higher level.

Getting Server Status

A client can get status information about a server before a session is opened. This is done by sending a GetStatus packet to the server's listening socket. The status information is returned in a GetStatusReply packet.

Name Binding Protocol (NBP)

AppleTalk includes a name service that users employ to access network resources by name rather than by node address. The *Name Binding Protocol* (NBP) provides a way of mapping from a name to an internet socket address. With AppleTalk, the services available on the network are called *network visible entities*. Each network visible entity is assigned a unique name, consisting of three fields—object, type, and zone. The *object* field identifies the entity, the *type* field provides information about its attributes, and the *zone* field identifies a subset of the AppleTalk network on which the entity resides. A particular entity is allowed to have multiple names, known as *aliases*.

The name binding process associates a name with an internet socket address. Since addresses are assigned dynamically, name binding must also be done dynamically. Name binding can be done when the entity is first activated in a process called *early binding*. Name binding can also be done the first time the entity is accessed in a process called *late binding*.

Each system maintains a *names table* that contains the mappings between names and internet socket addresses for all entities in that system. The *names directory* consists of all the names tables in the internet.

NBP Packet

Box 24.10 shows the packet format used with NBP and describes the fields contained in the NBP packet.

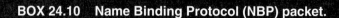

BOX 24.10   Name Binding Protocol (NBP) packet.

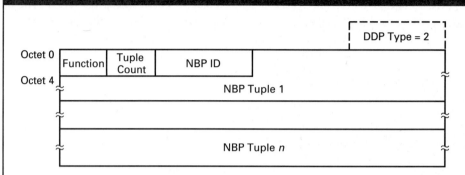

- **Function.** Identifies the type of packet as one of the following:
  — 1 Broadcast Request
  — 2 LkUp
  — 3 LkUp-Reply
  — 4 Forward Request
- **Tuple Count.** A count of the number of NBP tuples in the packet.
- **NBD ID.** Identifies a particular Broadcast Request or LkUp request, so that a reply can be correlated with the original request.
- **Entity Address.** The internet socket address—consisting of a network number, node ID, and socket number—corresponding to the name being looked up.
- **Entity Name.** The object, type, and zone fields making up the name being looked up. Each field has an associated length field.

NBP Services

Box 24.11 lists the calls that are used to request NBP services.

The following are descriptions of some of the major services that NBP performs.

BOX 24.11   NBP calls.

- **Register a Name.** Causes a name to be added to the system's names table.
- **Remove a Name.** Removes the specified name from the system's names table.
- **Look Up a Name.** Finds a name in the names directory and returns its associated internet socket address. A partial name can be specified, leading to the return of multiple fully specified names and their addresses.
- **Confirm a Name.** Confirms whether or not the specified address corresponds to the specified name.

Name Registration

Name registration is used to add a name to the names table and the names directory. Before adding a name, NBP verifies that the name is not in use on another system. It does this using the name lookup operation described next. If the name lookup finds the name, NBP notifies the service requester that the name is in use—otherwise the name is added to the names table.

Name Lookup

The name lookup operation determines if a name is registered in the names directory. The service may be requested to obtain the address associated with the name or to determine whether or not the name is in use. The name lookup operation works differently on nonextended and extended networks.

With a nonextended network, the following steps are used:

- NBP first looks in the names table on the system where the lookup service was requested. If the name is found in the table, NBP returns the requested information to the service requester. For name registration, NBP returns an indication that the name is in use. For an address mapping request, NBP returns the address associated with the name.

- If the name is not found in the table, NBP broadcasts a LkUp packet containing the name. Each system on the network with an NBP process receives the packet and checks its table. If a match is found, the system returns the address in a LkUp-Reply packet. NBP then passes an appropriate reply to the service requester.

- NBP uses DDP for packet transmission, and delivery is on a best-efforts basis. If no reply is received in a specified time period, the packet is retransmitted. If no reply is received after a maximum number of retries, NBP assumes the name is not in use. For a name registration request, the name is then added to the names table. For an address mapping request, the service requester is informed that the name does not exist on the network.

With an extended network, name lookup is based on the use of zones. When name lookup is requested, the name must include the zone field. The name lookup process for an extended network is as follows:

- NBP first looks in the names table on the system where the lookup service was requested. If the name is found in the table, the corresponding address or a name-in-use indication is returned.

- If the name is not found in the table, NBP sends a Broadcast Request packet to a router on the local network.

- The NBP process on the router prepares and sends Forward Request packets to each network that contains systems in the zone that the name belongs to. When the Forward Request packet reaches a router on the specified network, the router broadcasts a LkUp packet on that network.

- The system that finds the name in its names table sends back a LkUp-Reply packet, which is routed back to the original requesting system. NBP then returns the address or a name-in-use indication to the service requester.

- If no reply is returned after repeated tries, NBP adds the name to the names table or returns a name-does-not-exist indication.

Name Confirmation

A name confirmation request specifies both a name and the address that is assumed to correspond to that name. NBP then does a name lookup involving only the system where the name is assumed to exist.

Name Deletion

When name deletion is requested, NBP removes the specified name from the names table.

Zone Information Protocol (ZIP)

As we have already described, an extended network is divided into multiple zones. Each zone contains a subset of the networks in the internet, and each system belongs to only one zone. Each router maintains a *Zone Information Table* (ZIT) that contains a mapping between network numbers and zone names for all networks in the internet. The *Zone Information Protocol* (ZIP) defines how the Zone Information Table is maintained and how zone information is provided. ZIP services can be used to obtain the following zone information:

- A list of all zone names in the internet.
- A list of zone names used on the requestor's network.
- The zone name used for the requestor's system.
- The zone name, multicast address, and network number range to use for a newly activated system.

The list of all zone names in the internet is obtained using GetZoneList request and reply packets. A list of zone names for the requestor's network is obtained using GetLocalZone request and reply packets. The zone name for the requestor's system is obtained using GetMyZone request and reply packets. The packet formats used for ZIP requests and replies are shown in Fig. 24.6. ZIP uses ATP services to send these packets, and the ATP user octets are used to contain ZIP information.

When a system is activated, it obtains its zone name using GetNetInfo request and reply packets. These packets are sent using DDP services, with the formats shown in Fig. 24.7. The request may contain a saved zone name, which is checked for validity. If the name is invalid or if there is no zone name in the request, the reply contains the default zone name from the zones list for the network. The reply also contains a multicast address that is used to send packets only to the systems that belong to that zone. The system must register the multicast address as an address it receives. The network number range start and end values are used as part of the dynamic address acquisition process that determines the node address for the system.

Zone Information Table

In order to provide zone information, each router maintains a Zone Information Table (ZIT). Routers use ZIP Query and Reply packets to maintain their Zone Informa-

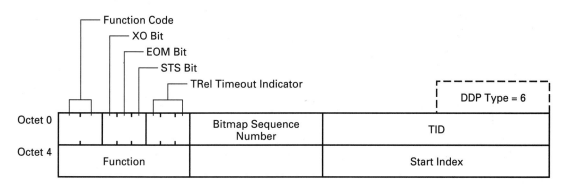

Request Packet

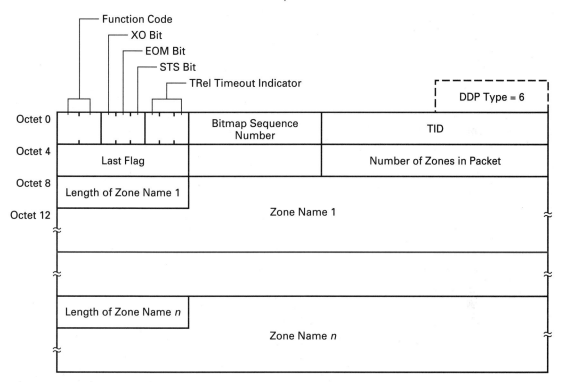

Reply Packet

Figure 24.6 Zone Information Protocol (ZIP) request and reply packet formats.

tion Tables. A router receiving a ZIP Query responds with a ZIP Reply returning any zone names that it knows. The ZIP process periodically checks the routing table to discover new network numbers for the ZIT. The ZIP process also identifies network num-

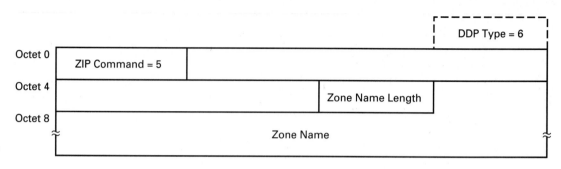

GetNetInfo Request Packet

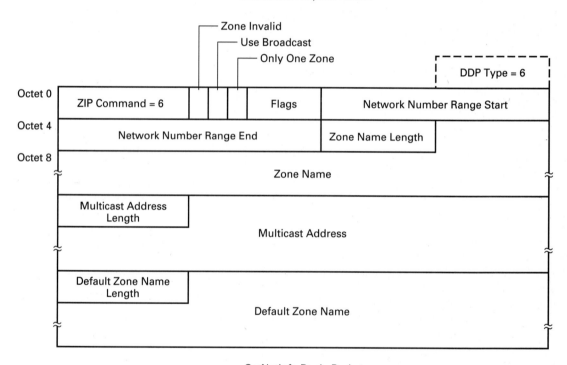

GetNetInfo Reply Packet

Figure 24.7 GetNetInfo packet formats.

bers that no longer appear in the routing table and should be removed from the Zone Information Table.

ZIP Query and Reply Packets

Box 24.12 shows the format of the ZIP Query and Reply packets and describes their fields. ZIP Query and Reply packets are sent using DDP services, so the basic for-

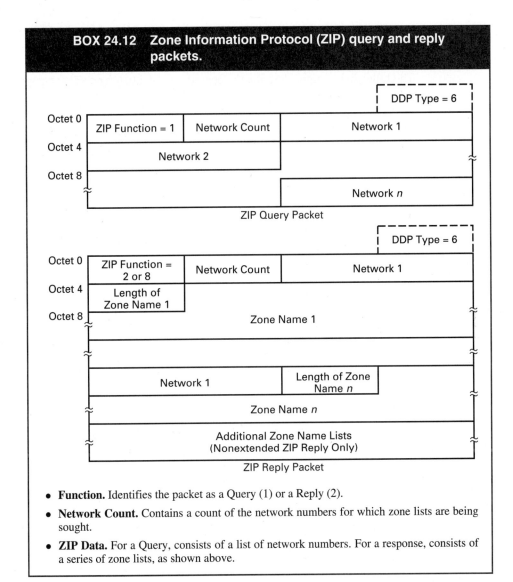

BOX 24.12 Zone Information Protocol (ZIP) query and reply packets.

- **Function.** Identifies the packet as a Query (1) or a Reply (2).
- **Network Count.** Contains a count of the network numbers for which zone lists are being sought.
- **ZIP Data.** For a Query, consists of a list of network numbers. For a response, consists of a series of zone lists, as shown above.

mat is that used for DDP packets. If there are more zone names than will fit in one Reply packet, a series of replies, known as *Extended ZIP Replies*, are used.

NETWORK LAYER PROTOCOLS

The Network layer is used to handle the basic functions that are needed to establish communication between two end systems. Two AppleTalk protocols operate in the OSI model Network layer. The Datagram Delivery Protocol (DDP) provides a best-efforts datagram packet delivery service and the AppleTalk Address Resolution Protocol (AARP) plays a role in the dynamic address assignment process that is used to determine a system's node ID value.

The following sections describe the operation of the two AppleTalk Network layer protocols.

Datagram Delivery Protocol (DDP)

The *Datagram Delivery Protocol* (DDP) provides the following services:

- Delivery of datagrams from a source system to one or more destination systems on a best-efforts basis.

- Routing of datagrams when multiple AppleTalk LAN data links are interconnected to form an extended network.

- Dynamic address acquisition for new systems joining the network.

DDP Packet Header Formats

Box 24.13 shows the formats of the headers used with DDP packets and describes their fields. DDP uses either a short header format or an extended header format:

- **DDP Short Header Format.** The *short* header format is used on a nonextended network. The short header contains only the source and destination Socket Number fields and not Network Number or Node ID fields. The data link header contains the node IDs of the source and destination systems, so it is not necessary to repeat them in the DDP header. Since both systems are on the same LAN data link, source and destination network numbers are also not required.

- **DDP Extended Header Format.** The extended header format is used on an extended network. The extended header contains the full internet socket address of both the source system and the destination system, including socket number, network number, and node ID values.

Dynamic Address Acquisition

DDP plays a role in the process of dynamically determining the node address of a new system that joins the network. When a system is powered on and attached to the network, it must acquire a node address. The process used depends on whether the system is part of an extended or nonextended network:

- **Nonextended Network Address Acquisition.** For a nonextended network, DDP uses the services of the LocalTalk Link Access Protocol (LLAP) to generate a unique node ID value, as described in Chapter 15. The DDP process on the system then attempts to use a facility of RTMP to obtain a network number value from a router on the data link. If there is no router on the data link (generally the case on a nonextended network) there will be no reply to the request for a network number, and the system sets its network number to 0.

- **Extended Network Address Acquisition.** For an extended network, DDP uses data link services to obtain a provisional node address that the system can use to contact a router. The mechanism used to generate the provisional node address uses AARP services.

BOX 24.13 Datagram Delivery Protocol (DDP) packets.

Short Header Format

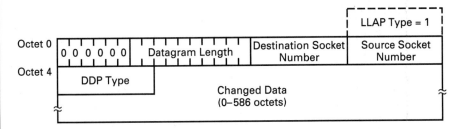

- **Datagram Length.** The length, in octets, of the datagram.
- **Destination and Source Socket Numbers.** Identify the socket numbers used by the source and destination processes.
- **DDP Type.** Identifies the specific higher-level protocol that is the user of the DDP data transfer service.

Extended Header Format

Octet 0	0 0	Hop Count	Datagram Length	DDP Checksum	
Octet 4	Destination Network Number			Source Network Number	
Octet 8	Destination Node ID	Source Node ID	Destination Socket Number	Source Socket Number
Octet 12	DDP Type		Data (0–586 octets)		

LLAP Type = 2

- **Hop Count.** Used to limit to 15 the number of data links a packet traverses in reaching its destination. The hop count field starts with a value of 0 in a new packet and is incremented by each router that processes the packet. If a router receives a packet containing a hop count of 15, it discards the packet.
- **Datagram Length.** The length, in octets, of the datagram.
- **DDP Checksum.** Optionally used to detect packets that have been corrupted during transmission.
- **Source and Destination Network Addresses.** Contains the network numbers and node IDs of the destination and source systems and the socket numbers assigned to the source and destination processes.
- **DDP Type.** Identifies the higher-level protocol that is the user of the DDP data transfer service.

The provisional node address is used to send out a GetNetInfo request. The response to the GetInfo request includes the range of network numbers assigned to the system's own local network. If the network number in the provisional node address falls within this range, the system keeps the provisional node address as its final node address. If the network number in the provisional node address is not in the range, the system passes the range of network numbers received in the GetInfo request to the data link service, which uses AARP to obtain an address that falls within the range. If the system receives no response to the GetNetInfo request, it continues to use the original provisional node address as its final node address.

DDP Services

The DDP interface is an abstract interface that defines the boundary at which a socket client issues calls to access DDP services. Box 24.14 lists the semantics of the calls that are used to request DDP services. The actual API that is used to request DDP functions is determined by an implementation of DDP and is not described by the AppleTalk specification.

BOX 24.14   DDP call semantics.

- **Open a Statically Assigned Socket.** Opens a socket for the specified socket number.
- **Open a Dynamically Assigned Socket.** Opens a socket and returns the socket number of the socket opened.
- **Close a socket.** Closes a specified socket.
- **Send a Datagram.** Sends a packet from a specified source socket to a specified destination internet socket address.

AppleTalk Address Resolution Protocol (AARP)

The AppleTalk Address Resolution Protocol (AARP) plays a role in the dynamic address acquisition process used to assign a node address when a node is first activated. It is also used to translate between AppleTalk node addresses and MAC station addresses when EtherTalk or TokenTalk is used on a particular LAN data link.

Dynamic Address Acquisition

When AARP is asked to generate a provisional node address, it uses the following process:

1. AARP selects a tentative node address. If the last-used address for this node has been saved in nonvolatile storage, this value is used. If there is no stored address, a network number is chosen from the range hex 'FF00' to hex 'FFEE', and the node ID is chosen at random.

2. AARP checks the tentative address against its Address Mapping Table. If the address is already in the table, AARP modifies the node ID and repeats the check.

3. When an address is found that is not in the table, AARP broadcasts Probe packets on the local network. If a node receiving the Probe packet has that address, it sends an AARP Response back. AARP then modifies the address and repeats steps 2 and 3. The AARP Probe packet format is shown in Fig. 24.8.

4. If no response is received after sending repeated Probe packets, the tentative address is returned as the provisional address.

Address Mapping Table Maintenance

AARP uses an address mapping table to map between node addresses and MAC station addresses for Ethernet and Token Ring LAN data links. AARP maintains the address mapping table by monitoring all packets received by a node on an Ethernet or token-ring data link. It uses the node addresses and MAC addresses contained in the packets and the frames that contain them to maintain the address mapping table.

When AARP receives a request from EtherTalk or TokenTalk for address translation, it checks its table. If the table contains an entry for the specified node address, AARP returns the corresponding station address. If the table does not contain the needed entry, AARP broadcasts an AARP Request packet querying other nodes for the appropriate station address. The node with the specified node address returns an AARP Response packet with the requested station address. AARP then adds this information to its table and returns the station address to the service requester.

AARP ages entries in the Address Mapping Table and eventually removes them. There are two methods defined, and an AARP implementation must use at least one of them. In the first method, there is a timer for each entry. The timer is started whenever

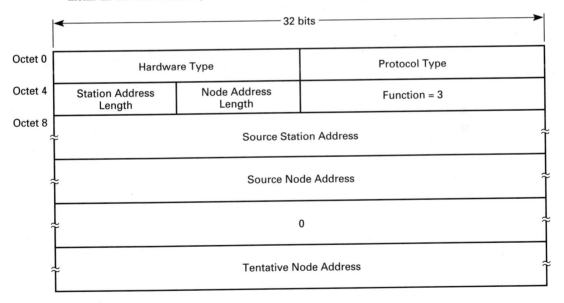

Figure 24.8 AppleTalk Address Resolution Protocol (AARP) Probe packet format.

the entry is added to the table, modified, or confirmed. If the timer expires, it means the entry has not been modified or confirmed within the specified time period and the entry is removed from the table. The second method removes the entry if a packet is received that is trying to dynamically assign the node address to a newly activated node.

AARP is a general protocol and can be used to map other types of network addresses into data link addresses. If a node supports multiple protocols, for example, AppleTalk and TCP/IP, AARP could also be used to map TCP/IP internet addresses into an Ethernet or Token Ring MAC address. AARP maintains a separate Address Mapping Table for each type of address translation to be performed.

AARP Packet

Box 24.15 shows the formats of AARP Request and Response packets and describes their fields.

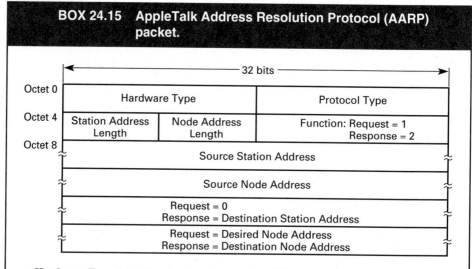

BOX 24.15   AppleTalk Address Resolution Protocol (AARP) packet.

- **Hardware Type.** Identifies the type of network as Ethernet (1) or Token Ring (2).
- **Protocol Type.** Identifies the protocol family being used as AppleTalk ('809B').
- **Station Address Length.** Gives the length of station addresses.
- **Node Address Length.** Gives the length of node addresses.
- **Function.** Identifies the packet as a Request (1) or a Response (2).
- **Source Station Address.** Station address of the node sending the Request.
- **Source Node Address.** Node address of the node sending the Request.
- **Destination Station Address.** Station address of the intended destination node. This address is present only in responses.
- **Destination Node Address.** Node address of the intended destination node.

APPLETALK ROUTING

A key function of the Datagram Delivery Protocol (DDP) is to determine the route over which each datagram should travel through the internet in traveling from a source system to a destination system. If a datagram is being sent to a destination system on the same LAN data link as the source system, it is transmitted directly using data link services. If the destination system is on some other data link in the internet, the source system sends the datagram to a router on the local data link. The router then uses its routing table to determine the next destination for the datagram and sends the datagram there. For each hop through the internet, the next destination can be either another router or, if the destination network has been reached, the final destination system.

When a router is first activated, it uses stored information to initialize its routing table. In AppleTalk terminology, a router attaches to a network through a *port*. Each port has associated with it stored information, called its *port descriptor*. For certain routers, the port descriptor includes the network number range for the network to which the port is attached and the node address of the router on that network.

At least one router on each network, known as the *seed router*, must have the network number range for the network defined in its port descriptor. It is the responsibility of the network administrator to see that this information is entered, that the network number ranges of different networks do not overlap, and that if the range is entered for more than one router on a network, that all routers have the same range. A router uses the stored network number ranges and node addresses from its different ports to initialize its routing table.

Routing Table Maintenance Protocol (RTMP)

The Routing Table Maintenance Protocol (RTMP) defines how a router acquires, accesses, and maintains the information it uses to make routing decisions. AppleTalk's routing algorithm is a distance-vector routing algorithm.

RTMP Data Packet

Each router periodically sends out an RTMP Data packet containing information from its routing table. Figure 24.9 shows the formats of the RTMP Data packet. There are two variations in the packet format depending on whether the packet is used on a nonextended or an extended network.

The RTMP Data packet is broadcast on the router's directly connected networks. A split horizon algorithm is used to limit the amount of routing information exchanged. The split horizon algorithm specifies that no information is sent for a route where the next node is a router on the network over which the RTMP Data packet is being broadcast. When a router receives an RTMP Data packet, it compares it to its routing table and makes any required changes.

Routers maintain a time for each table entry. If no information is received for a given entry for a period of time, the route in question is considered to be no longer avail-

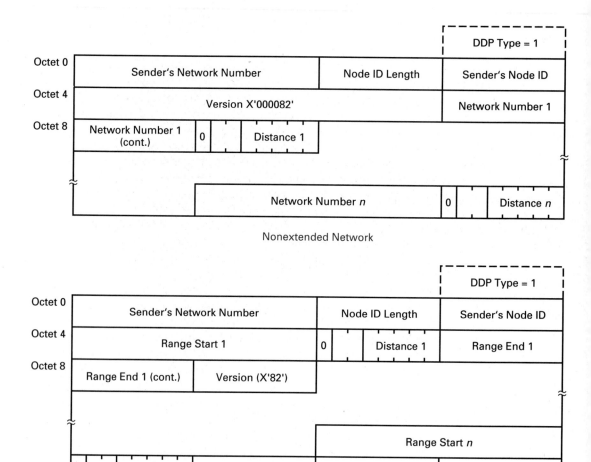

Figure 24.9　Routing Table Maintenance Protocol (RTMP) Data packets.

able, and the hop count is set to 31. This hop count value is included in the next RTMP Data packet the router sends out, notifying other routers that the route is down.

End Node Routing Information

To play its role in routing, each end node must know its network number range and the address of one router on its own LAN data link. The way in which this information is obtained depends on whether the end node is part of an extended or nonextended network.

For an end node on an extended network, this information is usually obtained when the node is first activated using a ZIP GetNetInfo request. On an ongoing basis, the node monitors all RTMP Data packets that are broadcast on its LAN. If the network number

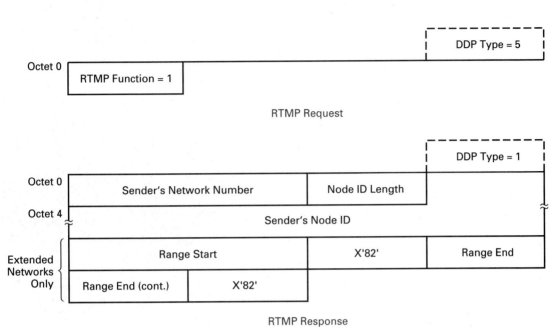

Figure 24.10   RTMP Request and Response packets.

range in the packet matches that of the node, the node stores the address of the router that sent the Data packet as its router address.

For a nonextended node, the node monitors RTMP Data packets received and stores the network number and sending router node ID values from each packet. A node can also broadcast an RTMP Request packet. Routers on the network reply with an RTMP Response packet, which provides the network number and router node ID. Figure 24.10 shows the formats of the RTMP Request and Response packets.

A node, either end node or router, can specifically request routing information by sending out an RTMP Route Data Request packet. A Route Data Request packet has the same format as an RTMP Request packet but has an RTMP function code of 2 or 3. A router that receives this packet responds by sending back an RTMP Data packet. If the function code in the Route Data Request packet is 2, the split horizon algorithm is applied to the data returned. If the function code is 3, the split horizon algorithm is not applied. The Data packet returned is addressed specifically to the node that sent the Route Data Request.

SUMMARY

The AppleTalk network architecture defines Apple's approach to computer networking. Support for AppleTalk networking is built into most Apple hardware and system software and is also implemented by a variety of third-party vendors. The AppleTalk architecture does not define its own layering structure but uses the layers of the OSI model to show relationships among protocols.

User application programs perform their functions in the Application and Presentation layers. An AppleTalk application-oriented protocol is the AppleTalk Filing Protocol (AFP), used to implement remote file access services.

The protocols operating in the Session and Transport layers perform data transfer functions and provide support services. The three data transfer protocols are ATP, ADSP, and PAP. The AppleTalk Transaction Protocol (ATP) provides a form of reliable data transfer that does not require a logical connection between the source and destination systems. The AppleTalk Data Stream Protocol (ADSP) provides a connection-oriented stream data delivery service that is reliable and full-duplex. The Printer Access Protocol (PAP) provides a connection-oriented message data transfer service that permits messages to be reliably sent over a connection. The five Session and Transport layer support protocols are AEP, ASP, NBP, ZIP, and RTMP. The AppleTalk Echo Protocol (AEP) is used to test the accessibility of a system and to make an estimate of the round-trip transmission time required to reach that system. The AppleTalk Session Protocol (ASP) is used to establish a session relationship between two programs. The Name Binding Protocol (NBP) performs a name translation service that converts the name of an object to its AppleTalk network address. The Zone Information Protocol (ZIP) maps between zone names and LAN data links. The Routing Table Maintenance Protocol (RTMP) is used by routers for the purpose of exchanging routing information with end systems and other routers.

Protocols operating in the Network layer are DDP and AARP. The Datagram Delivery Protocol (DDP) delivers datagrams on a best-efforts basis and plays a role in routing. The AppleTalk Address Resolution Protocol (AARP) helps a system to determine its network address.

The AppleTalk Data link layer includes support for Apple's own proprietary LocalTalk Link Access Protocol (LLAP). Support is provided for Ethernet LANs through the EtherTalk Link Access Protocol (ELAP) and for Token Ring LANs through the TokenTalk Link Access Protocol (TLAP).

PART VI

APPENDICES

Appendix **A**

Zero-Slot LANs

The term *zero-slot LAN* is used in the personal computer networking environment, in which networking is generally accomplished by installing a network interface card (NIC) in an expansion slot in the personal computer. With a zero-slot LAN, networking is accomplished using software that does not require a special adapter card, generally using one of the computer's serial or parallel ports to support communication between systems.

ZERO-SLOT LAN NETWORKING SOFTWARE

Most software for zero-slot LANs consists of simple file transfer software that allows files to be sent back and forth between two computers connected with a point-to-point cable via their serial or parallel ports. However, some zero-slot LAN software provides full networking support in the same manner as conventional network operating system software. For example, Artisoft markets a version of the LANtastic network operating system software that allows a small peer-to-peer LAN to be created using serial or parallel ports.

Zero-slot LANs had more appeal in years past when NICs typically cost hundreds of dollars. In today's environment, conventional LAN NICs, especially for ARCnet and Ethernet LAN technology, make zero-slot LAN software technology less appealing because of the relatively slow communication that it supports.

NOTEBOOK COMPUTER NETWORK CONNECTION

One environment in which connecting to a LAN using no peripheral slot will remain appealing is in the notebook PC market. There are a variety of methods in which LAN communication can be accomplished with personal computers that provide no conventional expansion slots.

Parallel Port NICs

In the notebook PC environment, it is common to employ an external NIC that attaches to the notebook computer via the system's parallel port. Such a NIC allows a notebook PC that has limited expansion capability to be connected to a conventional LAN data link in the same manner as a desktop computer. The only drawback with the parallel port technique for connecting a NIC concerns data transfer speed. The data transfer speed between a parallel-port NIC and the computer is generally slower than the speed supported with a conventional NIC installed in a conventional expansion slot.

PCMCIA NICs

At the time of writing, notebook PCs are becoming widely available that have standard Personal Computer Memory Card International Association (PCMCIA) expansion slots. A PCMCIA slot allows credit-card sized peripherals to be attached to the notebook PC. A number of NICs specially designed for installation in a notebook PC's PCMCIA slot are becoming available. The PCMCIA method of attaching a NIC to a notebook PC supports essentially the same data transfer speeds as conventional NICs.

DIAL-IN NETWORK ACCESS

Another technique for connecting a personal computer to a LAN without requiring a NIC is through the use of networking software that supports dial-in access to LAN capabilities. For example, Apple's system software and Microsoft's Windows for Workgroups, as well as many other PC network operating system software, allow local area networks to be established that allow dial-in access. One or more of the systems on the LAN is designated as a host for dial-in access, and some other computer can connect to that system's serial port, either directly by dedicated cable or via a modem and telecommunications facility.

The computer making the connection to the host computer's serial port becomes a full-fledged node on the network and is able to request any communication services that the LAN provides. The only disadvantage to this method is that data transfers take place at the limited speed of the serial port.

Wide Area Networking Technology

In computer networks, wide area network (WAN) data link technology is generally used to implement point-to-point connections between devices. WAN data links can be used in an enterprise internetwork to interconnect individual computers. However, it is more common for wide area networking data links to be connected to bridges or routers that interconnect the various LAN data links that make up the enterprise internetwork. Individual computers are then typically connected to the LANs.

A number of different types of wide area networking data links can be used to interconnect LANs in an enterprise internetwork. Although the focus of this book is on the technology behind local area network data links, this appendix briefly describes the characteristics of the various types of wide area networking data links that are used in enterprise internetworks. The emphasis in this appendix is on the station identification and Network layer protocol identification mechanisms that WAN data link technology implements.

CONVENTIONAL COMMON CARRIER LINKS

Conventional common carrier data links take the form of various types of analog telecommunications circuits. These range from ordinary telephone circuits that are provided via the switched telephone network to specialized high-speed telecommunications circuits that can be leased on a month-to-month basis from a common carrier.

Of particular importance, where high-speed telecommunications circuits are required, are the T1 and T3 transmission facilities that most telecommunications common carriers provide. A T1 circuit provides a 1.544 megabit per second (Mbps) digital transmission facility, and a T3 circuit provides a 45 Mbps digital transmission facility. Also available from most common carriers are fractional T1 facilities that provide a variety of transmission speeds by multiplexing a T1 facility and sharing its capacity among multiple users.

Point-to-point telecommunications data links typically use a data link protocol that is based on an international standard called *High-Level Data Link Control* (HDLC). The physical protocols used in conjunction with the various types of LAN technology described in this book are also based on the HDLC standard.

The HDLC protocol has its roots in the *Synchronous Data Link Control* (SDLC) protocol developed by IBM in the early 1970s for use in SNA. IBM's SDLC protocol is now considered to be a functional subset of the HDLC protocol and is in conformance with the international standard.

Frame Format

Box B.1 shows the format of the HDLC frame and describes its fields.

BOX B.1   HDLC frame.

Beginning Flag	Address	Control	Information		Frame Check Sequence	Ending Flag
1 octet	1 octet	1 or 2 octets	0 – *n* octets		2 or 4 octets	1 octet

- **Beginning Flag.** A single octet containing the unique bit configuration 0111 1110 used to identify the beginning of the frame.

- **Address.** The Address field is used on an unbalanced data link to assign a unique station identification value to each station.

- **Control Field.** Identifies the type of frame being transmitted, conveys information necessary for the proper sequencing of frames, and carries control information.

- **Information.** Carries the user data portion of the frame. It consists of either control information or data passed down from a user. Some control frames do not include an Information field.

- **Frame Check Sequence.** Contains either a 16-bit or a 32-bit cyclic redundancy check (CRC) value used for error detection.

- **Ending Flag.** Contains the same bit configuration as the beginning flag (0111 1110) and identifies the end of the frame.

Frame Types

There are three types of HDLC frames that all share the same general format. The following are brief descriptions of each frame type:

- **Information Frames.** The primary function of Information frames (I-frames) is to carry user data.

- **Supervisory Frames.** Supervisory frames (S-frames) carry information necessary for supervisory functions that control the transmission of I-frames.

- **Unnumbered Frames.** Unnumbered frames (U-frames) are used to carry data and to perform various types of control functions.

Station Identification

On a point-to-point HDLC data link, no station identification function is necessary. While each HDLC frame has a station address field for compatibility with the standard, the value it contains is unimportant. Each frame sent has only one possible destination—the communications adapter at the other end of the data link.

Network Layer Protocol Identification

The HDLC standard makes no provision for a Network layer protocol identification function. This is a disadvantage of HDLC that makes it not well suited for use over WAN data links in an enterprise internetworking environment.

With HDLC, user data can be carried in Information frames (I-frames) by only one Network layer protocol at a time. However, some schemes have been devised for carrying information conforming to multiple protocols over an HDLC link. With these schemes, data for one Network layer protocol is carried in I-frames. Data conforming to other Network layer protocols is then carried using U-frames by including a protocol identifier in the Information field of each U-frame. Such a system of network layer protocol identification is typically suitable only for use in a situation where the amount of traffic carried in U-frames is small compared to the traffic carried in I-frames.

Because of HDLC's lack of an explicit protocol identification facility, other protocols, such as the Point-to-Point protocol and the Frame Relay protocol have been developed that are based on the HDLC standard.

POINT-TO-POINT PROTOCOL

The Point-to-Point protocol is an adaptation of HDLC that grew out of work done by the Internet Engineering Task Force. The Point-to-Point protocol improves on HDLC by adding the Network layer protocol identification mechanism that is required for enterprise internetworking. The Point-to-Point protocol allows a point-to-point connection to be established between two network devices that allows frames associated with multiple Network layer protocols to flow over the data link without interfering with one another.

Frame Format

The Point-to-Point protocol frame format is based on the generic HDLC transmission frame and is generally conformant with it. Box B.2 shows the format of the Point-to-Point protocol transmission frame and describes its fields.

Station Identification

On a data link that uses the Point-to-Point protocol, no station identification function is necessary. Each Point-to-Point protocol frame contains an Address field for compatibility with the HDLC standard, but the Address field's value is always hex 'FF'. Each frame

BOX B.2   Point-to-point protocol frame.

Beginning Flag	Address (X'FF')	Control (X'03')	Protocol	Information	))	Frame Check Sequence	Ending Flag
1 octet	1 octet	1 octet	2 octets	0 – *n* octets		2 octets	1 octet

- **Beginning Flag.** Consists of a single octet containing the unique bit configuration 0111 1110 and identifies the beginning of the field.
- **Address.** Contains the value hex 'FF'.
- **Control Field.** Contains the value hex '03'.
- **Protocol Field.** Identifies the Network layer protocol with which the packet in the Information field is associated.
- **Information.** Used to carry the user data portion of the frame.
- **Frame Check Sequence.** Contains a 16-bit cyclic redundancy check (CRC) value used for error detection.
- **Ending Flag.** Contains the same bit configuration as the Beginning Flag field (0111 1110) and identifies the end of the frame.

sent has only one possible destination—the communications adapter at the other end of the data link.

Network Layer Protocol Identification

The Network layer protocol identification function is provided by the Protocol field that has been added to the HDLC frame between the Control field and the Information field. The documentation of the Point-to-Point protocol lists the identifier values to be used for each Network layer protocol supported by the standard. Although the Point-to-Point protocol was designed primarily for use in TCP/IP internets, protocol identifiers have been assigned to the Network layer protocols to support all the protocol families described in Chapter 17.

X.25

One alternative to using conventional common carrier telecommunications circuits in a computer network is to use the virtual circuits provided by a public packet-switched data network (PSDN). Many of today's public data networks, especially outside of the United States, use packet-switching techniques and conform to CCITT *Recommendation X.25*. Recommendation X.25 defines a standard way for attaching a computer or other intelligent device to a PSDN.

X.25 PSDNs are generally operated by either a common carrier or a private telecommunications service provider. An organization generally contracts with a PSDN service provider to implement point-to-point connections between pairs of user computers. Each user machine has a single point of connection into the PSDN but can make logical point-to-point connections with any number of other user machines.

Virtual Circuits

A PSDN conforming to X.25 typically offers to its users two major types of point-to-point transmission facilities:

- **Permanent Virtual Circuits.** A user of a PSDN may wish to be permanently connected with another network user in much the same way as two users are connected using a leased telephone connection. A *permanent virtual circuit* (PVC) provides this facility.

- **Switched Virtual Circuits.** When an X.25 user requests the establishment of a *switched virtual circuit* (SVC), the network establishes a virtual circuit with another user, the two users exchange messages for a time over the virtual circuit, and then one of the two users requests disconnection of the virtual circuit. A switched virtual circuit is often referred to as a *virtual call* (VC).

Frame Format

The X.25 frame format conforms to the HDLC specification. Box B.3 shows the format of the X.25 frame and describes its fields.

Station Identification

Each computer that is attached to an X.25 PSDN is assigned a network address that is used to identify the computer in the network. The network addressing scheme and func-

---

BOX B.3   X.25 frame.

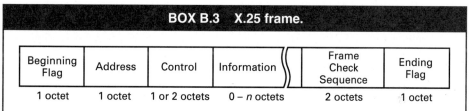

Beginning Flag	Address	Control	Information	Frame Check Sequence	Ending Flag
1 octet	1 octet	1 or 2 octets	0 – *n* octets	2 octets	1 octet

- **Beginning Flag.** Consists of a single octet containing the unique bit configuration 0111 1110 and identifies the beginning of the frame.

- **Address.** Contains hex '01' for commands flowing from the computer into the PSDN, and hex '03' for responses flowing from the PSDN to the computer.

- **Control Field.** Determines the type of frame being transmitted, conveys information necessary for the proper sequencing of frames, and carries control information.

- **Information.** Carries the user data portion of the frame.

- **Frame Check Sequence.** Contains a 16-bit cyclic redundancy check (CRC) value used for error detection.

- **Ending Flag.** Contains the same bit configuration as the Beginning Flag field (0111 1110) and identifies the end of the frame.

tions for establishing virtual circuits are defined by X.25. However, these functions operate at the level of the Network layer of the OSI model and, thus, the X.25 network addressing scheme is not equivalent to the station addressing schemes implemented for other forms of data links.

Once an X.25 virtual circuit has been established for use to connect a pair of devices in an enterprise internetwork, no station identification function is necessary at the level of the Data Link Layer. The X.25 virtual circuit appears to the upper layers exactly as any other type of point-to-point communication facility. From the viewpoint of using an X.25 virtual circuit as a point-to-point data link, each packet sent has only one possible destination—the communications adapter at the other end of the virtual circuit.

Network Layer Protocol Identification

A given computer attached to a given PSDN is allowed to concurrently establish up to 4095 different *logical channels* over the same virtual circuit. Each logical channel is assigned a different 12-bit *logical channel number*. Logical channels can be used to distinguish one Network layer protocol from another by using a different logical channel number in the packet header for each packet sent. Again, however, this protocol identification scheme is different from the ones used with other forms of WAN data links because it depends on information carried in the X.25 packet header rather than in the frame header. Therefore, Network layer functions are involved in handling the protocol identification mechanism when X.25 virtual circuits are used in enterprise internetworks.

X.25 facilities provide a wider range of functions for implementing multiple-protocol enterprise internetworks than do conventional telecommunication data links. However, since these facilities operate at the level of the Network layer of the OSI model, devices and software that use X.25 virtual circuits to carry data through a computer network must be aware of the protocols that they are carrying. Additional overhead is generally associated with these functions. Also, because of the complex routing decisions that must be made in moving data through an X.25 network, throughput is generally limited to relatively low levels.

Frame Relay data links, described next, provide a higher-performance alternative to X.25 virtual circuits.

FRAME RELAY

Frame Relay networks supply services that are similar to those provided by X.25 packet-switching networks. However, routing decisions in a Frame Relay network are relatively simple and are made in the Data Link layer rather than in the Network layer. Frame Relay networks support a variety of transmission speeds, but the target speed is generally in the neighborhood of the speeds supported by T1 facilities.

A major difference between Frame Relay networks and X.25 networks is that Frame Relay networks do not provide the error correction facilities that are provided by X.25 networks. If the Information field of a frame is corrupted as it moves through a Frame Relay network, the frame is discarded and does not appear at its destination. Error correction procedures must be implemented at a higher layer in the user equipment. However, this is ordinarily not a serious limitation, since error correction procedures are generally implemented in the higher layers even when X.25 virtual circuits are used.

Like X.25 networks, Frame Relay networks are generally operated by either a common carrier or by a private telecommunications service provider. An organization generally contracts with a Frame Relay service provider to implement point-to-point connections between pairs of user computers. Each user machine has a single point of connection into the Frame Relay network but can make logical point-to-point connections with any number of other user machines.

Frame Format

The Frame Relay frame is conformant with the HDLC standard. Box B.4 shows the format of the Frame Relay frame and describes its fields.

BOX B.4   Frame Relay frame

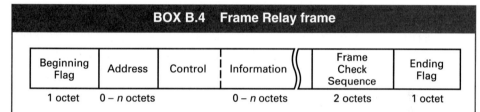

- **Beginning Flag.** Containing the unique bit configuration 0111 1110.
- **Address.** The Address field is at least 2 octets in length and is sometimes longer. It contains a *data link connection identifier* (DLCI) that identifies the specific virtual circuit the frame is associated with. The Address field also contains bits that can be used to implement congestion control functions.
- **Control Field.** The HDLC Control Field is treated as part of the Information field by the Frame Relay protocol.
- **Information.** Carries the user data portion of the frame.
- **Frame Check Sequence.** Contains a 16-bit cyclic redundancy check (CRC) value used for error detection.
- **Ending Flag.** Contains the same bit configuration as the Beginning Flag field (0111 1110) and identifies the end of the frame.

Station Identification

The *data link connection identifier* that identifies a particular virtual circuit provides the station identification mechanism that identifies the station at the other end of the virtual circuit. A computer that is connected to a Frame Relay network can communicate with any number of other computers by placing an appropriate data link connection identifier value in each frame that it transmits. Note that this station identification mechanism operates in the Data Link layer rather than in the Network layer as with X.25 virtual circuits.

Network Layer Protocol Identification

The data link connection identifier can also be used to provide the protocol identification function. One computer can establish any number of virtual circuits with another computer attached to the Frame Relay network. Each virtual circuit connecting the two computers is assigned a different data link connection identifier and can be used to carry packets associated with a different Network layer protocol.

OTHER WIDE AREA NETWORKING TECHNOLOGIES

The previous sections have introduced the most important of the wide area networking technologies that are being used today to implement wide area networking connections in enterprise internetworks. There are a number of other technologies that are in various stages of development and standardization that will become more important in the future. The following are brief descriptions of these technologies.

ISDN

An *Integrated Services Digital Network* (ISDN) is a public telecommunications network—typically administered by a common carrier or another telecommunications provider—that supplies end-to-end digital telecommunications services that can be used for both voice and nonvoice purposes. Two levels of service have been defined for ISDN:

- **Basic Rate Interface (BRI).** This level of service defines a bit rate of 144 Kbps, which is divided into two 64-Kbps channels for the user and one 16-Kbps channel for signaling.
- **Primary Rate Interface (PRI).** The primary rate interface level of service consists of 23 64-Kbps channels and one 64-Kbps channel for signaling, providing a bit rate to the user of 1.544 Mbps.

The main data link protocol employed with ISDN circuits is called *ISDN Data Link Control* (IDLC), which is technically aligned with HDLC. Procedures for establishing ISDN connections between two computers are defined by protocols that operate at the level of the Network layer of the OSI model, and so Network layer software is typically involved in establishing an ISDN connection.

ISDN services include both packet-mode services and circuit-mode services. Packet-mode ISDN services offer services that are similar to those provided by an X.25 PSDN. Circuit-mode services can be used as replacements for conventional telecommunications circuits.

Broadband ISDN

Broadband ISDN (B-ISDN) represents a probable future direction of the telephone industry and will require that the conventional copper-wire local loops that now go into subscriber premises be replaced by optical fiber cables. B-ISDN services are built on top of a Physical layer specification called SONET. A number of bit rates have been specified for SONET signal transmission, including the following:

- SONET OC-1 — 51 Mbps
- SONET OC-3 — 155 Mbps
- SONET OC-12 — 622 Mbps
- SONET OC-48 — 2.4 Gbps

B-ISDN has the potential of providing extremely high-bandwidth wide area networking connections. For example, the OC-3 and higher levels of service provides higher bit rates than an FDDI LAN and could be used in creating enterprise internetworks that operate at higher than LAN speeds over large geographic areas.

Distributed Queue Dual Bus

The Distributed Queue Dual Bus (DQDB) protocol defines a technology that can be used to provide LAN-like services over a wider geographic area. The type of network that the DQDB protocol operates over is generally referred to as a *Metropolitan Area Network* (MAN). The DQDB protocol is relatively independent of the underlying physical transmission medium and can operate at speeds as low as 44 Mbps and as high as the SONET STS-3 speed of 155.52 Mbps. DQDB provides a service that is similar to that defined by IEEE 802.2 Logical Link Control.

Switched Multimegabit Data Service

The Switched Multimegabit Data Service (SMDS) is a wide area packet-switching service that is likely to be built on top of B-ISDN services to provide packet-switching services similar to an X.25 network. However, SMDS provides services at speeds up to 44 Mbps rather than the relatively slow speeds provided by a typical X.25 PSDN.

Asynchronous Transfer Mode

Asynchronous Transfer Mode (ATM) is a form of networking technology that has the potential for better integrating the different types of communication technologies that are now used over local area networks and wide area networks. ATM is introduced in Appendix C.

Appendix **C**

Asynchronous Transfer Mode

Asynchronous transfer mode (ATM) is the name of a new telecommunications technology that is currently undergoing standardization. Although the ATM standardization effort is being driven by the telephone industry, ATM has the potential for unifying many of the different forms of electronic communication that are currently in use today.

THREE INFORMATION INFRASTRUCTURES

The world of electronic communication currently has three fundamentally different information infrastructures: the telephone network for voice communication, the cable television and broadcasting system for video, and packet switching technologies for computer networking. There is some overlap among these infrastructures. For example, transmission facilities intended to support voice communication are used to implement computer networks and are also used to transmit video signals. And the cable television industry has made some inroads in allowing computer communication to coexist on the same cable used to transmit television signals. But, the three infrastructures have evolved in parallel for fundamentally different purposes.

The three separate information infrastructures are all moving from analog technology to digital technology for transmission multiplexing and switching. At some point in the future, it will be desirable for these separate information infrastructures to merge so that the same network can be used to carry any type of information. This merging is currently underway, but it will be some time before it can be completely accomplished. There are many hurdles, not all of which are technical, that will need to be overcome. ATM technology is a step in the direction of allowing our three information infrastructures to merge.

EVOLUTION OF COMPUTER COMMUNICATION

To understand the technology behind ATM, it is helpful to see the way computer networking technology is evolving.

Circuit Switching

The earliest forms of electronic communication used *circuit-switching* techniques. The telephone network is essentially a circuit-switching network in which a dedicated circuit is established between two users for the duration of a telephone call. Circuit switching is ideal for ordinary telephone circuits because the required bandwidth is relatively low, the full bandwidth is ordinarily required during the entire duration of a call, and calls are relatively long (measured in minutes rather than microseconds).

Early forms of computer communication used circuit-switching techniques to interconnect computer equipment simply because the only communication facilities available that spanned long distances were ordinary telephone circuits.

Packet Switching

Computer communication does not lend itself well to the type of circuit switching used in the telephone system. In a typical computer application, we would like to transmit short bursts of data very rapidly between two communicating machines, but there may be relatively long periods of time between bursts. In a typical application where a person at a user-interface device communicates with a server system, we would like a communication channel having a very high transmission speed, but we typically send information over the channel for only a very small percentage of the time.

The *packet-switching* techniques that are used today in computer networks allow a number of users to share a high-capacity transmission channel. Packet switching works well for computer data at low to moderate transmission speeds. But packet switching is not well suited for voice or video communication. The delays introduced by the packet switches are too long and too unpredictable for voice or video applications.

It turns out that packet-switching techniques do not work well for computer data at very high transmission speeds. On a network that supports very high transmission speeds, say billions of bits per second, the overhead introduced by conventional routers that handle the routing function in software is too high. Traditional packet-switching mechanisms are especially ill suited for a network that must handle a mix of traffic of different types, such as voice, video, and computer data.

Conventional circuit switching is also ill suited for very-high-speed networking because no single user needs more than a small percentage of the total capacity of the transmission channel. A fundamentally different type of switching technology is needed to meet the needs of very-high-speed communication.

ATM CELL SWITCHING TECHNOLOGY

ATM technology is designed to meet the needs of heterogeneous, high-speed networking. ATM implements a form of very fast packet switching in which data is carried in fixed-length units called *cells*. Each cell is 53 octets in length, with only 5 octets used as a header in each cell.

ATM employs mechanisms that can be used to set up virtual circuits between users, in which a pair of communicating users appear to have a dedicated circuit between them. Very fast cell-switching techniques, implemented entirely in hardware, are used to implement the virtual circuits.

The result of ATM technology is to provide users with the advantages of circuit switching in that the network can guarantee a certain transmission capacity and level of service between two users. Each user can request the network bandwidth that is required for a particular application, and the ATM network can provide the user with that bandwidth. The very-high-speed transmission facilities can be shared among all users, as with packet switching, with each user using only the bandwidth required by that user.

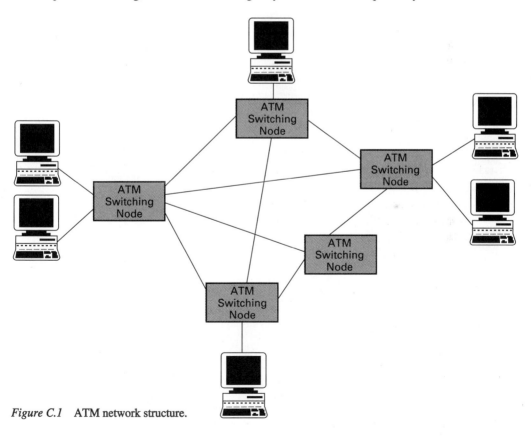

Figure C.1   ATM network structure.

ATM LANs

ATM technology can be used to create networks that have many of the characteristics of today's local area networks. With ATM, devices will be attached to interface units called *ATM switching nodes,* as shown in Fig. C.1. Switching nodes can be interconnected using dedicated cabling, as in today's LAN.

The interconnections between ATM switching nodes can be configured so that any desired amount of transmission capacity can be provided to the networked systems, giving communicating users the appearance of a very-high-speed dedicated connection between them.

ATM WANs

ATM technology can also be used to create wide area networks. When telecommunications providers make public ATM facilities available, it will be possible to interconnect ATM switching nodes using public, long-distance telecommunications facilities that use the same switching techniques as are used in a local ATM network. Such a configuration is shown in Fig. C.2.

ATM Cell Format

ATM defines two types of cells, having slightly different cell formats:

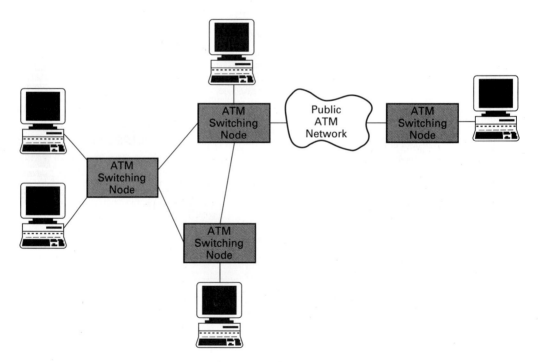

Figure C.2   ATM wide area network.

- **User-Network Interface Cells.** A *user-network interface* (UNI) cell is used to transmit data between a user device and an ATM switching node.

- **Network-Network Interface Cells.** A *network-network interface* (NNI) cell is used to transmit data between ATM switching nodes.

Box C.1 shows the format of an ATM UNI cell and describes the fields in the cell header. An ATM NNI cell is identical to the UNI cell except that there is no Generic Flow Control field, and those bits are used as part of the Virtual Path Identifier field.

Transmission Facilities

ATM technology is designed for use over a wide range of physical transmission technologies, ranging from private cabling to various forms of long-distance telecommunications transmission. Box C.2 lists some of the transmission technologies that public ATM networks may support.

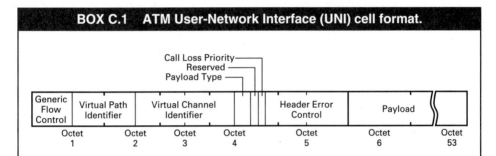

BOX C.1 ATM User-Network Interface (UNI) cell format.

- **Generic Flow Control.** Used to ensure that users are given fair access to the transmission facilities when a single ATM access point is serving more than one user.

- **Virtual Path Identifier.** Used, together with the Virtual Channel Identifier field, to identify a *virtual path* (VP) between two nodes. A virtual path is a collection of one or more virtual channels associated with the same user end point.

- **Virtual Channel Identifier.** Used, together with the Virtual Path Identifier field, to identify a *virtual channel* (VC) between two nodes. A virtual channel is a unidirectional virtual circuit associated with a particular user.

- **Payload Type.** Used to differentiate between cells carrying user data and cells carrying ATM control information.

- **Reserved.** Reserved for future use.

- **Call Loss Priority.** Used to determine the eligibility of a cell for being discarded during a period of network congestion.

- **Header Error Control.** Used to detect corruption of the information contained in the cell header.

- **Payload.** Contains the data portion of the cell.

BOX C.2   Representative ATM transmission technologies.

OC-1 SONET. 51 Mbps transmission over optical fiber.

OC-3 SONET. 155 Mbps transmission over optical fiber.

OC-12 SONET. 622 Mbps transmission over optical fiber.

OC-48 SONET. 2.4 Gbps transmission over optical fiber

T1 Carrier. 1.544 Mbps using conventional telephone transmission.

T3 Carrier. 44.736 Mbps using conventional telephone transmission.

Classes of ATM Service

The ATM architecture defines four classes of service that a user connected to an ATM switching node can request, depending on the needs of the application:

- Class A. Circuit emulation with a constant bit rate.
- Class B. Audio and/or video transmission with a variable bit rate.
- Class C. Connection-oriented service for data transmission.
- Class D. Connectionless service for data transmission.

Hybrid Networks

Although ATM technology can ultimately replace the technology used in today's LANs and WANs, it is likely that ATM switching technology will initially be used in conjunction with conventional LAN and WAN technology. For example, conventional LAN data links are likely to be connected to ATM switching nodes. This provides LAN users with another, higher-performance method of interconnecting LANs. It is also likely that conventional WAN data links will be used to connect distant ATM switching nodes in places where native ATM transmission facilities may not yet be available. A possible hybrid configuration is shown in Fig. C.3.

THE FUTURE OF ATM

The proponents of ATM claim that ATM technology will be the grand unifier of voice, video, and data transmission. ATM represents the closest approximation to a true bandwidth-on-demand transmission service that has yet been devised.

For the data user, ATM has the potential of removing today's distinction between local area networking and wide area networking. As we make clear in this book, the technologies used in local area networking and wide area networking are today fundamentally different. We require specialized devices, such as bridges and routers, to interconnect LAN and WAN data links. ATM technology will allow the same technology to be used

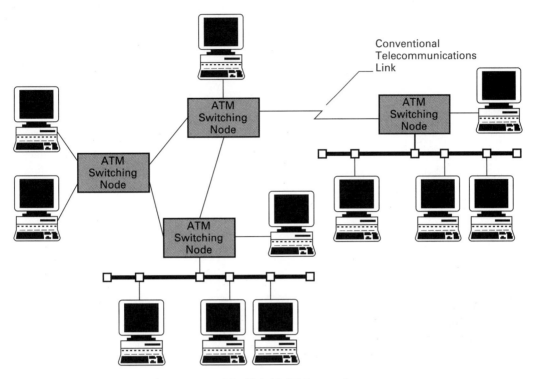

Figure C.3   Hybrid ATM network.

over short-distance, dedicated cabling as is used over long-distance common carrier circuits.

    With the high transmission speeds ATM technology is designed to support, it will be possible to make the distance between two communicating devices transparent to application programs. With such technology, it will be possible to build applications that work in an identical manner whether the two communicating systems are in the same room or across the globe.

Appendix **D**

Network Management

A requirement of many organizations is the ability to manage local area networks—and large enterprise internetworks as well—that consist of equipment purchased from many different vendors. This appendix describes some of the approaches that are used in managing local area networks and enterprise internetworks.

ISO CMIP APPROACH TO NETWORK MANAGEMENT

Most of today's approaches to network management are based on the emerging international standards for network management that are being developed by ISO. ISO's approach to network management is called *Common Management Information Protocol* (CMIP). The CMIP international standards divide management functions into the following five *specific management functional areas* (SMFAs):

- Configuration management
- Fault management
- Performance management
- Security management
- Accounting management

Structure and Identification of Management Information

The ISO CMIP approach to network management defines the notion of *objects*, which are elements that need to be managed. An object might contain a value that a system administrator may need to either inspect or set. An object might alternatively contain a value that a system administrator may only need to inspect.

The documentation of the *Structure and Identification of Management Information* (SMI) developed by ISO defines a set of rules for how managed objects are described and how management protocols can be used by network management applications to access the value of an object and to set an object's value.

Management Information Base

The ISO approach to network management defines a *Management Information Base* (MIB), which is a repository, or database, that defines all the objects that can be managed in a network. Portions of the MIB are distributed among all the devices in the network— such as end systems, routers, terminal servers, and so on—that need to be managed. Managed objects are grouped according to the layering structure of the particular type of network being managed. For example, in an OSI network, the objects would be organized according to the layering structure defined by the OSI model. In a TCP/IP network, the objects would be organized according to the layering structure of the TCP/IP architecture, and so on.

Abstract Syntax Notation One

Managed objects are named and described using an international standard notation called *Abstract Syntax Notation One* (ASN.1). ASN.1 is a data description notation that allows the format and meaning of data structures to be defined without specifying how those data structures are represented in a computer or how they are encoded for transmission through a network. For example, ASN.1 allows a numeric data element to be defined as an INTEGER but does not specify anything about how that integer should be represented or encoded (one's complement, two's complement, packed-decimal, etc.). The advantage to using a notation like ASN.1 to define management information is that it can be described in a way that is completely independent of any particular form of information processing technology.

Object Identification and Description

Each object that can be managed in a network is given a unique identifier and is precisely described using ASN.1 notation. These object descriptions are then stored and maintained in the MIB for access by network management agents. Communication between a network management application and a managed object takes place via a network management protocol.

There are a variety of specific approaches that vendors have taken with respect to network management, many of which are aligned with the overall ISO approach. We describe three of these approaches in this appendix:

- IBM's approach to network management, which is based on Systems Network Architecture (SNA).

- Digital Equipment Corporation's approach, which is part of its Network Application Support architecture for open distributed computing.

- The *Simple Network Management Protocol* (SNMP) approach. SNMP has been defined for the TCP/IP environment but is being employed in conjunction with a number of the protocol families described in Chapter 17 and is part of both IBM's and DEC's own overall architectures for distributed computing.

IBM'S NETVIEW NETWORK MANAGEMENT

IBM's direction in network management is toward enterprisewide management of all of an organization's communication networks. In IBM's view, network management should include management of networks that handle voice, data, image, graphics, and text—anything that can be sent over a network. Network management facilities should also allow for the monitoring and control of networks conforming to any network architecture.

The major functions that are part of IBM's SNA approach to network management can be divided into four categories, which are closely aligned with the ISO approach:

- Problem management
- Configuration management
- Change management
- Performance and accounting management

Problem Management

Problem management deals with a problem from its detection through its resolution. It is concerned with problems that occur to the hardware, software, and communication links that make up the network. The process of problem management consists of the following steps:

- **Problem Determination.** Detecting the loss or potential loss of the availability of a network resource and isolating the problem to the component—hardware, software, or microcode—that is failing.
- **Problem Diagnosis.** Determining the specific cause of a problem and the action required to resolve it.
- **Problem Bypass and Recovery.** Implementing procedures that allow the problem to be partially or completely circumvented.
- **Problem Resolution.** Taking action to correct the problem and to restore the failing component to service.
- **Problem Tracking and Control.** Tracking problems from detection to resolution. This may involve storing problem resolution, status monitoring, and problem status data in a problem database.

In the SNA environment, network nodes generate problem notification messages called *alerts*. An SNA device, such as an SNA terminal controller, generates alerts in response to problem situations and sends them to a centralized point for processing.

Configuration Management

Configuration management is concerned with the generation and maintenance of a configuration database containing information necessary to identify the physical and logical components of the network and their relationships to each other. As resources are added to or removed from the network, or the status of a network resource changes, configuration information is updated. The information maintained by configuration management can be used as part of problem determination and diagnosis and may also be used by change management.

Change Management

Changes to network resources, involving additions, deletions, or modifications to hardware, software, or microcode network components, occur frequently. These changes may be the result of problem bypass or correction procedures, or they may reflect changes to user requirements that necessitate changes to the network. Change management is involved with planning, tracking, and controlling these changes. Change management relates to configuration management, since the results of any changes must be reflected in the information maintained by configuration management. Change management also relates to problem management, since problem bypass and resolution procedures may generate a need for a change, which is then controlled by change management.

Performance and Accounting Management

Performance and accounting management is responsible for monitoring and evaluating the operating performance of the network and for recording and tracking usage charges at the network resource level. Performance and accounting management includes the following:

- **Response-Time Monitoring.** Monitoring end-user response times and invoking problem determination if specified levels are exceeded.
- **Availability Monitoring.** Monitoring the availability of network resources.
- **Utilization Monitoring.** Monitoring the level of usage of network resources and invoking problem determination if specified levels are exceeded.
- **Component Delay Monitoring.** Monitoring the delay incurred in accessing critical components and invoking problem determination if specified levels are exceeded.
- **Performance Tracking and Control.** Recording and reporting data on network performance. This data is used to identify areas where performance tuning is needed.
- **Performance Tuning.** Taking actions that will improve the performance of the network.
- **Accounting.** Recording and tracking usage charges so network costs can be distributed to users based on their usage of the network.

Points of Management Control

In the SNA NetView network management environment, there are three points of control for the network management process, as shown in Fig. D.1.

- **Focal Point.** A *focal point* provides a centralized view of network management. The focal point is the point at which the network management data that is generated throughout the network is consolidated. The focal point is also the point at which network management commands are issued to make something happen in the network. A focal point is typically implemented in a large-system processor. IBM's NetView product is an example of an implementation of a management focal point.
- **Entry Point.** An *entry point* is a distributed point of control for SNA resources. This is a point at which information concerning an SNA device, or a collection of SNA

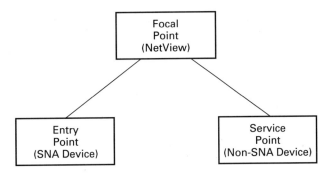

Figure D.1   Points of management control.

devices, is gathered for transmission to the focal point. Each collection of devices and associated software that implements an SNA node contains an implementation of an entry point.

- **Service Point.** A *service point* is a distributed point of network management control for any hardware and/or software product that does not conform to SNA formats and protocols. This is a point at which information concerning a non-SNA resource, or collection of resources, is gathered for transmission to a focal point. The software products in IBM's NetView product family are examples of implementations of service points.

DEC'S ENTERPRISE MANAGEMENT ARCHITECTURE

Digital Equipment Corporation's approach to network management is based on its *Enterprise Management Architecture* (EMA). EMA is made up of a number of subarchitectures that define how all types of components making up a distributed system can be monitored and controlled. For example, the network management architecture that defines the management aspects of DEC's DECnet/OSI networking products, which is technically aligned with ISO CMIP, is a subarchitecture that falls under the EMA umbrella. EMA is designed to provide a complete solution to managing large-scale, heterogeneous networks and systems of application programs and databases that operate in a multivendor environment.

Entity Model

At the heart of DEC's EMA is the *entity model*. The entity model uses the term *entity* to refer to any type of object in a distributed system that must be managed. The concept of an *entity* closely corresponds to the concept of an *object* in object-oriented computing. Management can be described as a feedback loop between a person, such as a system or network manager, and a set of entities consisting of the things that are managed, as shown in Fig. D.2.

The entity model defines two major classes of software components:

- **Management Directors.** A *management director* is a software system that managers use to manage the various components of a distributed system.

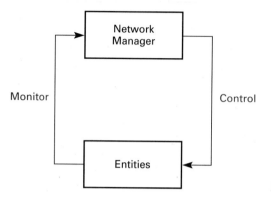

Figure D.2 Monitor/control feedback loop.

- **Agents.** An *agent* consists of a software component associated with the entity being managed.

Management directors communicate with agents by means of a *management protocol* that handles the flow of information between the two. The relationship between a management director, an agent, an entity, and a management protocol is shown in Fig. D.3.

The management information and operations that pass between management directors and agents are as follows:

- **Directives.** *Directives* flow from a management director to an agent, and responses to directives flow back from an agent to a management director. Directives consist of commands a management director issues to an entity, possibly as a result of a manager issuing an explicit command to the management director. Most management needs are satisfied by two directives—*Show* to read a value of interest to management and *Set* to change a value. The directives *Add* and *Remove* are also defined for management information consisting of a set of values. Directives for certain types of entities also include *actions*. Examples of actions applying to many types of entities are *Enable* and *Disable,* which allow an entity to be turned on and off. Many other actions are specific to a particular type of entity. The detailed definitions of actions are entity specific.

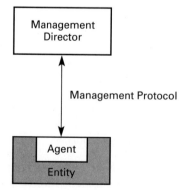

Figure D.3 Management director, agent, and management protocol.

- **Events.** *Events* flow from an agent to a management director. An event is generated when some specific normal or abnormal condition occurs that is of interest to management.

Entity Hierarchy

A distributed system is constructed from manageable components, and the more computing systems there are in the distributed system, the more manageable components there are. To allow effective management of distributed systems that implement very large networks, the components must be organized into a logical structure, and they must be named so managers can deal with the complexity. EMA uses an object-oriented hierarchical system for naming entities in which parent entities can have child entities subordinate to them.

Entity Classes

While all entities, from a management perspective, share a common architecture, they are far from similar in function. For example, in networking software, a Transport layer entity performs functions very different from those performed by a Network layer entity. However, entities can be grouped into *classes*, where all entity instances that are members of the same class are similar. In general, the architectural specification for a particular component—such as OSI Transport—defines a specific entity class.

    We are using network management here for examples of entities, but these notions apply equally to any types of entities that can be managed in a distributed computing environment, such as application programs, computing systems, printers, databases, storage devices, and so on.

    Within a particular class of entity, there may be a number of child entities. For example, within the OSI transport entity class, there is a child entity class called OSI Transport Port. A *port* defines an end point of an OSI Transport connection. There is an instance of the Port entity class within the OSI Transport entity instance for every OSI Transport connection currently in operation, as shown in Fig. D.4.

Entity Attributes

An entity has a set of internal variables defined for it. The variables that can be inspected or set by a management action are called *attributes*. The values of an entity's attributes represent all the information about the entity that are of concern to management. Box D.1 describes the four types of attributes that can be associated with an entity instance.

Entity Architectural Model

Although a distributed system employs many different types of entities that have very different characteristics, from a management perspective all entities have a common architecture. All entities are made up of the following:

- **Name.** Each entity has a *name* associated with it that uniquely identifies it in the distributed system.

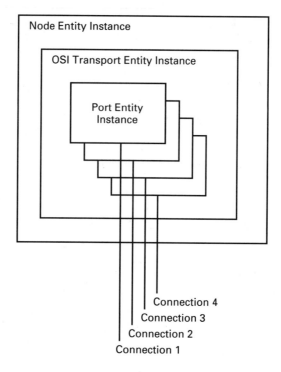

Figure D.4 Entity hierarchical structure.

BOX D.1   Entity attribute types.

- **Identification.** An *identification* attribute uniquely identifies an entity instance to management.

- **Characteristic.** A *characteristic* attribute allows a manager to control the operating parameters of an entity. In general, characteristic attributes take default values when the entity is created, and their values can be changed only through a network management action. The values of characteristic attributes are not changed during normal distributed system operation.

- **Status.** A *status* attribute allows a manager to inspect the current state of an entity. Unlike characteristic attributes, status attributes can change without management intervention. For example, the values of status attributes can change as a result of normal distributed system operation.

- **Counter.** A *counter* attribute indicates the number of times an operation has been performed by an entity or the number of times a particular condition has been detected. As with status attributes, counter attributes change in value as a result of normal distributed system operation.

- **State Machine Definition.** An entity's *state machine definition* defines a set of state variables whose values define the entity's state at any given instant.

- **Interfaces.** *Interfaces* to the entity define the operations that provide input to and output from the state machine.

Management Directors

Managers use *management director* software to control and monitor a collection of entities. For example, to control and manage a communication network, a network manager might use management director software specifically designed to manage the various components that make up a communication network.

An example of NAS software products that implement the management director architecture are members of DEC's DECmcc *Management Control Center* product family. System and network managers use DECmcc products to monitor and control manageable objects in the distributed computing environment.

To control the operation of a distributed system, a distributed system manager might use management director software designed to handle all aspects of the distributed system, with management of the communication network being only part of the management function. The management director framework has been specifically designed to be extensible to allow for the management function to be expanded in a consistent manner over time.

The management director provides an interface between a manager and a collection of manageable objects, each represented by an entity. Management directors are themselves manageable objects conforming to the entity model.

Figure D.5 shows the architecture of the management director framework. It includes the following components:

- **Kernel.** The *kernel* provides a set of services that support and integrate the other functions of the management director.

- **Management Information Repository.** The *management information repository* is a database of management information about the entities being managed.

- **Application Programming Interfaces.** A set of *application programming interfaces* (APIs) define how the other three types of management director components can be plugged into the management director. The management director APIs allow the other three components to be implemented in a manner independent of the particular hardware or operating system on which the kernel and the management information repository are run.

- **Presentation Modules.** A *presentation module* consists of software that handles a particular style of user interface between a manager and a management director. Any number of presentation modules can be plugged into the management director to handle different user interface styles. Presentation modules are independent of the entities being managed and of the functions that can be applied to them.

- **Function Modules.** A *function module* consists of software that handles a set of specific management applications. It implements a set of specific management actions that can be applied to a collection of entities. Function modules are independent of the entities being managed and of the user interface style a manager employs.

- **Access Modules.** An *access module* consists of software that handles communication with one or more of the entities being managed. Access modules are independent of the

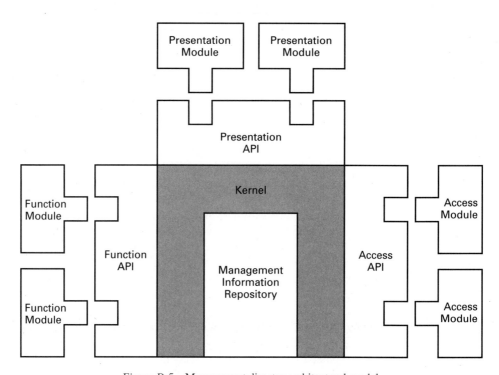

Figure D.5   Management director architectural model.

functions that can be applied to the entities and of the user interface style a manager employs. An access module operates as a *sink* that receives information about events the managed entities generate.

SIMPLE NETWORK MANAGEMENT PROTOCOL

The *Simple Network Management Protocol* (SNMP) was originally designed to provide a comprehensive approach to network management in the TCP/IP environment. However, as pointed out earlier, SNMP is now being applied in networks that conform to many of the protocol families described in Chapter 17.

The SNMP approach to network management was developed at a time when considerable work had already been done by ISO concerning the international standard approach to network management. This allowed the developers of SNMP to use the same basic concepts regarding how management information should be described and defined as those being developed by ISO.

SNMP Architecture

Figure D.6 shows the overall architectural structure of the network management components that work with SNMP. The following are brief descriptions of each of the SNMP architectural components:

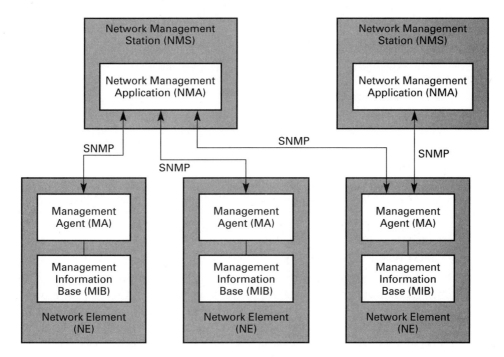

Figure D.6 Components associated with SNMP.

- **Network Management Station.** A *network management station* (NMS) is an end system in the network that executes a Network Management Application. A system administrator typically uses an NMS to monitor and control the network or a portion of it.

- **Network Management Application.** A *network management application* (NMA) is the program running in a network management station that monitors and controls one or more network elements.

- **Network Element.** A *network element* (NE) is a component in the network that maintains a management agent and a portion of the MIB that contains manageable objects. Examples of network elements are end systems and routers.

- **Management Agent.** A *management agent* (MA) is a program running in a network element that is responsible for performing the network management functions requested by a network management application. A management agent operates on the objects stored in the portion of the MIB that is maintained in that network element.

SNMP defines the formats of a set of network management messages and the rules by which those messages are exchanged. SNMP describes how network management applications in network management stations communicate over the network with management agents in network elements.

Network Management Application Functions

There are only two functions that a network management application can request of a management agent using SNMP:

- **Get.** A network management application can request that a management agent return the value (or values) associated with a manageable object.

- **Set.** A network management application can request that a management agent set the value (or values) associated with a manageable object.

SNMP Messages

In addition to information going back and forth that is associated with requests that a network management application makes of a management agent, SNMP defines a limited number of messages that a management agent can send in an unsolicited manner to a network management application. These messages typically describe the occurrence of asynchronous events.

Every defined SNMP message is capable of being carried through the network in a single message and is independent of any other message. Therefore, the SNMP protocol can operate over any form of unreliable datagram service.

CMOT (CMIP over TCP/IP)

As described earlier, the ISO Common Management Information Protocol (CMIP) defines an international standard approach to management. CMOT (CMIP over TCP/IP) is a specification that describes how CMIP can be used to manage a TCP/IP internet. CMOT works with the same Management Information Base (MIB) and Structure and Identification of Management Information (SMI) that has been defined for SNMP.

CMOT architectural components can be divided into two collections:

- **Agents.** An agent collects management information, executes network management commands, and performs tests on the values of managed objects.

- **Managers.** A manager receives network management information, issues network management commands, and sends instructions to agents.

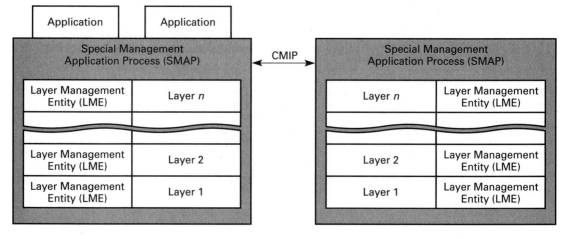

Figure D.7   Components associated with CMOT.

Figure D.7 shows the overall architectural structure associated with CMOT.

Managers and agents contain management information that is categorized according to the various TCP/IP architectural layers. With the management information associated with each layer is a *Layer Management Entity* (LME). A *System Management Application Process* (SMAP) in each manager and agent coordinates the information associated with all the LMEs in that component. The SMAP in a manager communicates with the SMAP in an agent over a TCP/IP internet using the CMOT protocol.

Glossary

AARP. AppleTalk Address Resolution Protocol.

ABSTRACT INTERFACE. An interface describing the interactions that can occur between two layers of an architecture. An abstract interface does not specify implementation details, nor does it describe any coding syntax that must be used to implement the interface.

ABSTRACT SYNTAX NOTATION ONE (ASN.1). An international standard data description notation that allows the format and meaning of data structures to be defined without specifying how those data structures are represented in a computer or how they are encoded for transmission through a network.

ACCESS CONTROL METHOD. Mechanism by which communicating systems manage their access to a physical transmission medium.

ACCESS UNIT. See *Hub.*

ACCREDITED STANDARDS COMMITTEE (ASC). A committee of the American National Standards Institute (ANSI) that develops standards that are later adopted and published by ANSI. Members of subcommittee X3T9.5 of the Accredited Standards Committee for Information Processing Systems developed the Fiber Distributed Data Interface (FDDI) local area network standard. See *American National Standards Institute.*

ACKNOWLEDGED CONNECTIONLESS LLC SERVICE. A service of the Logical Link Control sublayer in the IEEE/ISO/ANSI LAN architecture in which LLC-SDUs are acknowledged but no connection is established between LLC entities.

ADDRESS RESOLUTION PROTOCOL (ARP). In TCP/IP, a Network layer protocol that helps a source end system deliver data to a destination system on the same LAN data link. ARP can also be used by an end system to determine the physical hardware address of a router.

AEP. AppleTalk Echo Protocol.

AMERICAN NATIONAL STANDARDS INSTITUTE (ANSI). The national standards organization for the United States. ANSI is a nonprofit organization that writes the rules for standards bodies to follow and publishes standards produced under its rules of consensus. ANSI accredits standards committees to write standards in areas of their expertise.

ANSI. American National Standards Institute.

API. Application Programming Interface.

APPLETALK. Apple Computer's networking scheme, integrated into most Apple system software, that allows Apple computing systems to participate in peer-to-peer computer networks and to also access the services of AppleTalk servers. AppleTalk hardware and software is available for non-Apple equipment from third-party vendors.

APPLETALK ADDRESS RESOLUTION PROTOCOL (AARP). In AppleTalk, a Network layer protocol that helps a source end system to deliver data to a destination system on the same subnetwork. AARP can also be used by an end system to determine the physical hardware address of a router.

APPLETALK ECHO PROTOCOL (AEP). In AppleTalk, a Transport layer protocol that provides a system reachability test function.

APPLETALK TRANSACTION PROTOCOL (ATP). In AppleTalk, a Transport layer protocol that provides a reliable, connection-oriented, sequenced data transfer service.

APPLICATION LAYER. Layer seven and the topmost layer of the OSI model. The Application layer provides a means for application programs to access the system interconnection facilities to exchange information. Communication services provided by the Application layer hide the complexity of the layers below from the communicating programs.

APPLICATION PROGRAMMING INTERFACE (API). A specification defining how an application program invokes a defined set of services.

APPLICATION SERVER. A network system that implements software that allows other systems to request the services of application programs running on the application server.

APPN. Advanced Peer-to-Peer Networking. See *Systems Network Architecture.*

ARCNET. A relatively low-speed form of LAN data link technology (2.5 megabits per second), developed by Datapoint, in which all systems are attached to a common coaxial cable. ARCnet uses a token-bus form of medium access control in which a system transmits only when it has the token.

ARP. Address Resolution Protocol.

ARPA. See *Defense Advanced Research Projects Agency.*

ARPANET. An early packet switching network, funded by the Defense Advanced Research Projects Agency (DARPA) that lead to the development of the Worldwide Internet. See *Internet.*

ASC. Accredited Standards Committee.

ASN.1. Abstract Syntax Notation One.

ASYNCHRONOUS TRANSFER MODE (ATM). A form of very fast packet switching in which data is carried in fixed-length units called *cells.* Each cell is 53 octets in length, with 5 octets used as a header in each cell. ATM employs mechanisms that can be used to set up virtual circuits between users, in which a pair of communicating users appear to have a dedicated circuit between them.

ASYNCHRONOUS TRANSMISSION. A form of transmission using start and stop bits to control transmission in which a single character is transmitted in each data unit.

ATM. Asynchronous Transfer Mode.

ATP. AppleTalk Transaction Protocol.

AUTONOMOUS SYSTEM. In TCP/IP, a collection of end systems (hosts) and routers that are administered by a single authority.

BACKBONE LOCAL AREA NETWORK. A central local area network used to interconnect two or more other local area networks. Connection to the backbone LAN can be made using a repeater, bridge, router, or gateway, depending on the types of networks being interconnected.

BACKOFF DELAY. The length of time that a station on a network that employs the CSMA/CD (Ethernet) form of medium access control must wait before attempting to retransmit a frame after detecting a collision. See also *Deference process.*

BANDWIDTH. Term used to specify the capacity of a communication channel that refers to the difference between the highest and the lowest frequencies that are carried over the channel. The higher the bandwidth, the more information that can be carried.

BASEBAND TRANSMISSION. A form of transmission in which data signals are carried over the physical communication medium in the form of discrete pulses of electricity or light.

BAUD. A measurement of the signaling speed of a channel that refers to the number of times in each second the line condition changes. Bauds are equal to bits per second only if each change in line condition represents a single bit.

BELLMAN-FORD ROUTING ALGORITHM. See *Distance-vector routing algorithm.*

BGP. Border Gateway Protocol.

BINARY EXPONENTIAL BACKOFF. Technique used with the CSMA/CD (Ethernet) form of medium access control in which the backoff delay becomes longer each time the station detects a successive collision. See also *Backoff delay.*

B-ISDN. Broadband ISDN.

BLOCKING FUNCTION. In the OSI model, a function performed by a layer or sublayer entity that transmits two or more service-data-units (SDUs) in the form of a single protocol-data-unit (PDU).

BORDER GATEWAY PROTOCOL (BGP). In TCP/IP, a Network layer routing protocol that allows routers to communicate between autonomous systems. See also *Exterior Gateway Protocol.*

BRIDGE. A device operating at the level of the Medium Access Control sublayer that is used to interconnect two or more LAN data links that use either the same or different forms of medium access control. Sometimes called a *Filtering bridge.*

BROADBAND ISDN. A high-speed form of integrated services digital network, representing a probable future direction of the telephone industry, that uses optical fiber transmission. See *Integrated Services Digital Network* and *SONET.*

BROADBAND TRANSMISSION. A form of transmission in which the signals employed are continuous and nondiscrete and in which data is carried in the form of modulated electromagnetic waves.

BROADCAST ADDRESS. A station address containing all 1 bits that addresses all the stations attached to a LAN data link.

BROUTER. A network interconnection device that combines the functions of a router and a bridge. A brouter routes the data traffic associated with certain protocols and bridges all other data traffic. See *Bridge* and *Router.*

BUS TOPOLOGY. A network structure in which each system is directly attached to a common communication channel.

CABLING SYSTEM. A system of cable segments, cable connectors, and attachment units used to physically interconnect the stations on a LAN data link. In some cases, cable segments in a LAN are replaced with some form of wireless communication, such as radio, microwave, or infrared signaling.

CARRIER SENSE MULTIPLE ACCESS WITH COLLISION AVOIDANCE (CSMA/CA). A form of medium access control in which each system "listens" to the carrier while each transmission is in progress. After the transmission ends, each system waits for a specified period of time that is different for each system. If no other system has started transmitting by the time a particular system's waiting time has elapsed, it may begin sending.

CARRIER SENSE MULTIPLE ACCESS WITH COLLISION DETECTION (CSMA/CD). The Ethernet form of LAN data link technology, defined by ISO 802.3 and ISO 8802-3. Also refers to a generic means of medium access control in which stations transmit on a bus- or tree-structured transmission medium whenever the transmission medium is available and retransmit when collisions occur.

CCB. Command control block.

CCITT. International Telegraph and Telephone Consultative Committee.

CCITT RECOMMENDATION X.25. See *X.25.*

CDDI. Copper Distributed Data Interface.

CLASS I LLC. A Logical Link Control sublayer implementation that provides only the connectionless LLC service (type 1 LLC operation). See *Connectionless LLC service.*

CLASS II LLC. A Logical Link Control sublayer implementation that provides the connectionless LLC service (type 1 LLC operation) and the connection-oriented LLC service (type 2 LLC operation). See *Connectionless LLC service* and *Connection-oriented LLC service.*

CLASS III LLC. A Logical Link Control sublayer implementation that provides the connectionless LLC service (type 1 LLC operation) and the acknowledged connectionless LLC service (type 3 LLC operation). See *Connectionless LLC service* and *Acknowledged connectionless LLC service.*

CLASS IV LLC. A Logical Link Control sublayer implementation that provides the connectionless LLC service (type 1 LLC operation), the connection-oriented LLC service (type 2 LLC operation), and the acknowledged connectionless LLC service (type 3 LLC operation). See *Connectionless LLC service, Connection-oriented LLC service,* and *Acknowledged connectionless LLC service.*

CLIENT. In client-server computing, an application component that makes a request for a service of some other application component operating in the role of a server. See *Client-server computing.*

CLIENT-SERVER COMPUTING. A form of distributed computing in which application components operating in the role of clients request the services of other application components operating in the role of servers. Client and server components can run on the same computing system or on different computing systems connected by a network.

CMIP. Common Management Information Protocol.

CMIP OVER TCP/IP (CMOT). A specification that describes how the international standard Common Management Information Protocol (CMIP) can be used to manage a TCP/IP internet. See *Common Management Information Protocol*; see also *Simple Network Management Protocol.*

CMOT. See *CMIP over TCP/IP.*

COAX CABLE SEGMENT. A transmission medium segment in a local area network that conforms to the IEEE/ISO CSMA/CD (Ethernet) standard to which stations are attached.

COAXIAL CABLE. An electrical cable that contains a central copper conductor, surrounded by insulating material, and then surrounded by an outer tubular conductor that consists of braided wire mesh or a solid sleeve. A protective, nonconducting sheath ordinarily protects the outer conductor.

COLLISION. A condition on the transmission medium that occurs with the CSMA/CD (Ethernet) form of medium access control when two or more stations transmit signals concurrently.

COMMAND. A logical-link-control-protocol-data-unit (LLC-PDU) that is sent by an LLC sublayer entity that is initiating a data transfer operation. See also *Response*.

COMMAND CONTROL BLOCK (CCB). A control block used to request the functions defined by the Direct Interface for IBM local area networking products. See *Direct Interface*.

COMMON CARRIER. A company in the United States that furnishes communication services to the general public.

COMMON MANAGEMENT INFORMATION PROTOCOL (CMIP). A protocol used for network management being standardized by the International Organization for Standardization (ISO).

COMMUNICATION CHANNEL. A logical medium in a communication system over which data is transmitted.

CONCENTRATOR. Local area network equipment that allows multiple network devices to be connected to the LAN cabling system through a central point. Sometimes called a *Hub*.

CONCRETE INTERFACE. A specification that defines an application programming interface (API) or electrical and mechanical specifications for cables and connectors.

CONFIRMED SERVICE. A service provided by a layer or sublayer entity in which the service requester is informed by the distant peer layer or sublayer entity of the success or failure of the service request.

CONFIRM SERVICE PRIMITIVE. A service primitive that is issued by a service provider to notify the higher-level layer service requester of the results of one or more *request* service primitives that the service requester previously issued. See also *Indication service primitive*, *Request service primitive*, and *Response service primitive*.

CONNECTIONLESS LLC SERVICE. An unreliable data transfer service provided by the IEEE 802.2/ISO 8802-2 Logical Link Control sublayer in which there is no need to establish a prior association between the source and destination system before data transmission can take place. Each LLC-PDU sent using the connectionless LLC service is processed independently of any other LLC-PDU. No sequence checking is done to ensure that LLC-PDUs are received in the same sequence in which they were sent, and the receiving system sends no acknowledgment that it has received an LLC-PDU.

CONNECTIONLESS SERVICE. In the OSI model, a service provided by any layer or sublayer entity in which each data unit sent is sent and processed independently of any other data units. No sequence checking is done to ensure that data units are received in the same sequence in which they were sent, and the receiving station sends no acknowledgment that it has received a data unit. No flow control or error recovery is provided. A connectionless service is often called a *Datagram* service.

CONNECTION-ORIENTED LLC SERVICE. A reliable data transfer service provided by the IEEE 802.2/ISO 8802-2 Logical Link Control sublayer in which delivery of LLC-PDUs is guaranteed as long as an LLC connection is maintained between a source LLC service-access-point and a destination LLC service-access-point. With the connection-oriented LLC service, a connection between the source and the destination LLC sublayer entities must be established before data transfer can begin, the connection must be maintained while data transfer proceeds, and the connection can be terminated when data transfer is no longer required.

CONNECTION-ORIENTED SERVICE. In the OSI model, a service provided by any layer or sublayer entity in which the delivery of data units is guaranteed as long as the connection is maintained between a source service-access-point and a destination service-access-point.

CONNECTION-ORIENTED TRANSPORT PROTOCOL (ISO 8073). In the OSI architecture and in DECnet/OSI, a Transport layer protocol that provides a reliable, sequenced data transport service.

COPPER DISTRIBUTED DATA INTERFACE (CDDI). A variation of the Fiber Distributed Data Interface (FDDI) standard adapted for twisted-pair cable. See *Fiber Distributed Data Interface*.

CSMA/CA. Carrier sense multiple access with collision avoidance.

DAC. Dual-attachment concentrator.

DARPA. Defense Advanced Research Projects Agency.

DATAGRAM. An informal name for the data unit exchanged during the operation of a connectionless data delivery protocol.

DATAGRAM DELIVERY PROTOCOL (DDP). In AppleTalk, a Network layer protocol that provides an unreliable, connectionless datagram delivery service.

DATAGRAM SERVICE. See *Connectionless service*.

DATA LINK LAYER. Layer two of the OSI model. The Data Link layer is responsible for providing data transmission over a single link from one system to another. Control mechanisms in the Data Link layer handle the transmission of data units, often called frames, over a physical circuit. Functions operating in the Data Link layer allow data to be transmitted, in a relatively error-free fashion, over a sometimes error-prone physical circuit. This layer is concerned with how bits are grouped into frames and implements error-detection mechanisms that identify transmission errors. With some types of data links, the Data Link layer may also perform procedures for flow control, frame sequencing, and recovering from transmission errors.

DCE. Distributed Computing Environment.

DDP. Datagram Delivery Protocol.

DECNET. A term used by Digital Equipment Corporation to refer to its own line of networking products that conform to the Digital Network Architecture (DNA).

DECNET/OSI. A term used to refer to DECnet products that conform to Phase V, the most recent phase of the Digital Network Architecture (DNA). A major characteristic of DECnet/OSI products is that they implement the major protocols that are published by ISO to support the OSI model.

DECNET PHASE IV. A term used to refer to DECnet products that conform to Phase IV of the Digital Network Architecture (DNA). The most current phase of DNA is Phase V. See also *DECnet/OSI*.

DECNET PHASE V. See *DECnet/OSI*.

DEFENSE ADVANCED RESEARCH PROJECTS AGENCY (DARPA). Agency of the U. S. government that funded the development of the ARPANET, the network that lead to the development of the Internet. See *Internet*.

DEFERENCE PROCESS. On a CSMA/CD (Ethernet) LAN data link, the process of monitoring the status of the transmission medium and determining when to begin retransmission. See also *Back-off delay*.

DESTINATION MAC ADDRESS. Address identifying the station or stations on a LAN data link to which a MAC frame is being sent. See also *MAC address* and *Station*.

DESTINATION-SERVICE-ACCESS-POINT ADDRESS. See *DSAP address*.

DIFFERENTIAL MANCHESTER ENCODING. A form of Manchester encoding in which a transition occurs during each bit time, as with conventional Manchester encoding, but in which the interpretation of the transition from positive to negative or from negative to positive depends on whether the previous bit time represented a 0 or a 1.

DIGITAL NETWORK ARCHITECTURE (DNA). Digital Equipment Corporation's proprietary network architecture, which has passed through a series of phases. The most current phase of DNA is DNA Phase V. See also *DECnet, DECnet Phase IV,* and *DECnet/OSI*.

DIGITAL ROUTING PROTOCOL (DRP). In DECnet Phase IV, a Network layer protocol that uses a distributed adaptive routing algorithm that implements hierarchical routing in which a large network can be divided into areas.

DIRECT INTERFACE. An IBM application programming interface (API), based on a control block called a Command Control Block (CCB), that allows a program to directly request Medium Access Control sublayer services.

DISK SERVER. A network system that implements software that allows other network systems to share the disk server's disk units.

DISTANCE-VECTOR ROUTING ALGORITHM. A form of routing algorithm, sometimes called a *Bellman-Ford* algorithm, in which each router learns about the network topology by exchanging routing information packets with its neighbor routers. See also *Link-state routing algorithm*.

DISTRIBUTED COMPUTING ENVIRONMENT (DCE). A specification for distributed computing, developed by the Open Software Foundation (OSF). The DCE includes interfaces for a Remote Procedure Call Service for program-to-program communication, a Threads Service for controlling multitasking activities, a Directory Service for handling naming functions, a Distributed File Service for managing remote file access facilities, a Distributed Time Service for handling date and time-of-day requests, and a Security Service for performing authorization and authentication functions.

DISTRIBUTED QUEUE DUAL BUS (DQDB). A protocol used in a form of Metropolitan Area Network (MAN) technology that can be used to provide LAN-like services over a wider geographic area. DQDB provides a service that is similar to that defined by IEEE 802.2/ISO 8802-2 Logical Link Control.

DLC INTERFACE. An application programming interface (API) defined for IBM local area network products, through which an application program can directly invoke the services of the Logical Link Control sublayer.

DNA. Digital Network Architecture.

DNS. Domain Name System.

DOMAIN NAME SYSTEM (DNS). In TCP/IP, a directory service that can be used to maintain the mappings between names and internet addresses in a limited number of places in the internet rather than at the location of each system.

DOTTED-DECIMAL NOTATION. A form of notation typically used in the TCP/IP environment to represent 32-bit internet addresses in the form of four decimal numbers, separated by periods, with each number representing the decimal value of one octet of the address.

DQDB. Distributed Queue Dual Bus.

DROP CABLE. Used with some forms of LAN data link technology to attach the network interface card (NIC) to the transmission medium.

DRP. Digital Routing Protocol.

DSAP ADDRESS. In the IEEE/ISO/ANSI LAN architecture, an address that identifies the LLC sublayer user, or users, that are to receive the LLC-PDU. The destination service-access-point address can be either an *individual* address, which identifies a single SAP; or it can be a *group* address, which identifies a set of SAPs. See also *SSAP address*.

DUAL-ATTACHMENT CONCENTRATOR (DAC). On a Fiber Distributed Data Interface (FDDI) LAN data link, a device having three or more medium interface connectors (MICs). One of the MICs is of type A, one is of type B, and one or more are of type M. The type A and B MICs are used to connect the concentrator to the dual ring and the type M MICs are used to connect other single-attachment stations having MICs of type S to the concentrator. See *Medium interface connector*, *MIC type A*, *MIC type B*, *MIC type M*, *MIC type S*, and *Single-attachment station*.

DUAL-ATTACHMENT STATION (DAS). On a Fiber Distributed Data Interface (FDDI) LAN data link, a station having two medium interface connectors (MICs) that allow the station to be attached to two separate full-duplex transmission medium segments used to implement a dual ring structure. See *Medium interface connector*.

DUAL-CABLE BROADBAND. A broadband network configuration in which each device is attached to two cables. One cable is used to send and the other to receive. See also *Broadband transmission*.

ECHO PROTOCOL. In NetWare and in the Xerox Network System, a Transport layer protocol that allows an end system to verify the existence of a route between one end system and another end system in the network.

EGP. Exterior Gateway Protocol.

ELAP. EtherTalk Link Access Protocol.

ENCAPSULATION FACILITY. A network interconnection facility that allows two systems that conform to a given network architecture to communicate using a network that conforms to some other network architecture. See also *Tunnel* and *Portal*.

ENDING DELIMITER. A field in a MAC frame that identifies the end of the information field and the beginning of the first octet of the frame check sequence (FCS) field.

END SYSTEM. A device in a communication system that serves as the source or final destination of data. See also *Intermediate system*.

END SYSTEM TO INTERMEDIATE SYSTEM ROUTING EXCHANGE PROTOCOL (ISO 9542). In the OSI architecture and in DECnet/OSI, a Network layer protocol that allows an end system to exchange messages with a router for the purpose of automatically configuring an end system into an OSI internet. ISO 9542 allows an end system to be connected to an OSI internet without requiring manual network management intervention.

ENTERPRISE INTERNETWORK. A computer network, often called an *internet*, designed to serve the needs of an entire enterprise. An internet is typically constructed of individual local area network data links interconnected using network interconnection devices and wide area network data links.

ENTITY. In the OSI model, an active element within a layer. A particular layer provides services to entities running in the layer above.

EQUIPMENT ROOM. In the EIA cable plant architecture, those physical places at which cables are physically terminated.

ERROR PROTOCOL. In NetWare and in the Xerox Network System, a Transport layer protocol that provides for detecting and reporting on errors between an end system and a router to which the end system is directly attached.

ES-IS PROTOCOL. End System to Intermediate System Routing Exchange Protocol (ISO 9542).

ETHERNET. A form of LAN data link that implements the IEEE 802.3/ISO 8802-3 CSMA/CD standard. On an Ethernet LAN data link, stations are attached to a common transmission facility, such as a coaxial cable or twisted-pair cable, and a station typically attempts to transmit whenever it has data to send. See *CSMA/CD*.

ETHERNET CABLE. Informal name for the 50-ohm, 10 mm coaxial cable specified in the IEEE/ISO CSMA/CD (Ethernet) 10BASE5 medium specification. Often called *thick Ethernet* cable to distinguish it from the 5 mm coaxial cable specified by the 10BASE2 medium specification.

ETHERNET VERSION 2. A form of LAN data link technology, developed by Digital Equipment Corporation, Xerox, and Intel, that served as the basis for the IEEE/ISO CSMA/CD (Ethernet) standard.

ETHERTALK LINK ACCESS PROTOCOL (ELAP). In AppleTalk, the data link protocol that provides Ethernet LAN support. Standard IEEE/ISO Logical Link Control (LLC) interfaces and data formats are used to provide the connectionless Type 1 LLC service.

EXTENDED LAN. A network that consists of two or more separate LAN data links, using either the same or different forms of medium access control, that are interconnected using bridges. See also *Bridge*.

EXTERIOR GATEWAY PROTOCOL (EGP). In TCP/IP, a Network layer routing protocol that is used by routers that must communicate with routers in other autonomous systems. See also *Border Gateway Protocol*.

FAST ETHERNET. Term used to describe the standards being developed to define a 100 Mbps version of the CSMA/CD (Ethernet) standard.

FCS. Frame check sequence.

FDDI. Fiber Distributed Data Interface.

FIBER DISTRIBUTED DATA INTERFACE (FDDI). A form of local area network, developed by members of subcommittee X3T9.5 of ANSI, in which systems are connected to one another using point-to-point fiber-optic cable segments to form a ring topology. An FDDI data link supports a data rate of 100 Mbps.

FIBER-OPTIC CABLE. A cable that contains one or more thin cylinders of glass, each of which is called a *core*. Each core is surrounded by a concentric cylinder of glass called the *cladding*, which has a different refractive index than the core. The core of a fiber-optic cable carries signals in the form of a modulated light beam.

FIBER-OPTIC INTERREPEATER LINK. See *FOIRL*.

FILE SERVER. A network system that implements software allowing other network systems to share the data files stored on the file server's disk units.

FILE TRANSFER PROTOCOL (FTP). In TCP/IP, a user-oriented Application service that allows the user to transfer files in both directions between the local system and a remote system. FTP uses the reliability controls that are provided by the TCP transport protocol to ensure that data is transferred reliably and that a transferred file is an exact copy of the original.

FILTERING BRIDGE. See *Bridge*.

FOIRL. A CSMA/CD (Ethernet) medium specification for a fiber-optic interrepeater link cable segment. An FOIRL cable segment is used to implement a relatively long-distance, point-to-point connection between two repeaters. FOIRL cable segments can be up to 1000 meters in length, thus allowing longer distances to be spanned between repeaters than can be spanned using a coaxial cable segment.

4b/5b Code. In the Fiber Distributed Data Interface (FDDI) specification, the scheme used to encode data for transmission in which 5-bit symbols correspond to 4-bit binary data values.

Frame. An informal name for the protocol-data-unit (PDU) exchanged between peer Data Link layer entities or between peer Medium Access Control sublayer entities.

Frame Check Sequence (FCS). The field in a MAC frame that is used to implement an error detection mechanism and contains the results of a cyclical redundancy check (CRC) calculation performed on the bits contained in the frame.

Frame Relay. A data network that provides services that are similar to those provided by X.25 packet-switching networks. In a Frame Relay network, routing decisions are made in the Data Link layer rather than in the Network layer. Frame Relay networks support a variety of transmission speeds, but the target speed is generally in the neighborhood of the speeds supported by T1 facilities.

Frame Status Field. A field in a MAC frame, used with some forms of medium access control, that contains information such as whether an error was detected, the address was recognized, or the frame was copied.

FTP. File Transfer Protocol.

Gateway. A device that operates at the level of the OSI model Application layer, used to interconnect networks that may have entirely different architectures. Different protocols can be used at any of the functional layers, with the gateway converting from one set of protocols to another. In some TCP/IP literature, the term gateway is sometimes used to refer to a device that performs the function of a router in a TCP/IP internet. See *Router*.

Globally-Administered MAC Addressing. A form of LAN station addressing in which MAC addresses are 48 bits in length and whose values are globally unique. Address values are set by the organization that manufactures the network interface card (NIC). A manufacturer applies to the IEEE for a unique block of addresses and assigns to each NIC that it manufactures a unique MAC address from its assigned block. Sometimes called *Universal addressing*.

Group Address. A MAC address, whose first bit has the value 1, that identifies a particular group of stations.

Guaranteed Delivery Service. In the OSI model, a service provided by a layer or sublayer in which delivery is not explicitly confirmed but is guaranteed by the service provider.

HDLC. High-level Data Link Control.

High-Level Data Link Control (HDLC). An international standard, bit-oriented, wide area network protocol that operates at the level of the OSI model Data Link layer.

Host. In TCP/IP, a term used to refer to any end system attached to a TCP/IP internet.

Hub. See *Concentrator*.

ICMP. Internet Control Message Protocol.

IDP. Internetwork Datagram Protocol.

IEEE. Institute of Electrical and Electronics Engineers.

I-Format LLC-PDU. See *Information LLC-PDU*.

Indication Service Primitive. In the OSI model, a service primitive that is issued by the lower-level service provider to notify a higher-level service requester that a significant event has occurred. See also *Confirm service primitive*, *Request service primitive*, and *Response service primitive*.

INDIVIDUAL ADDRESS. A MAC address, whose first bit has the value 0, that identifies a single station.

INFORMATION LLC-PDUs. The primary function of an *Information LLC-PDU* (I-format LLC-PDU) is to carry user data. However, I-format LLC-PDUs sometimes also perform control functions. See *Logical-link-control-protocol-data-unit*.

INSTITUTE OF ELECTRICAL AND ELECTRONIC ENGINEERS (IEEE). A professional society whose members are individual engineers. The IEEE operates under ANSI guidelines when it develops standards. The IEEE Computer Society Local Area Network Committee (Project 802) has focused on standards related to local area networks and has produced a set of LAN standards that have been accepted by ISO as international standards.

INTEGRATED SERVICES DIGITAL NETWORK (ISDN). A public telecommunications network—typically administered by a common carrier or another telecommunications provider—that supplies end-to-end digital telecommunications services that can be used for both voice and nonvoice purposes.

INTERMEDIATE SYSTEM. A device in a communication system that may lie between two end systems and is concerned with performing routing and relaying functions. See also *End system*.

INTERMEDIATE SYSTEM TO INTERMEDIATE SYSTEM INTRA-DOMAIN ROUTING EXCHANGE PROTOCOL (ISO 10589). In the OSI architecture and in DECnet/OSI, a Network layer routing protocol that implements a link-state routing algorithm for automatically calculating optimum routes for relaying traffic from one router to another through an OSI internet.

INTERNATIONAL ORGANIZATION FOR STANDARDIZATION (ISO). The dominant information technology standardization organization whose individual members consist of individual national standards organizations. The ISO member organization from the United States is the American National Standards Institute (ANSI). See also *American National Standards Institute*.

INTERNATIONAL TELEGRAPH AND TELEPHONE CONSULTATIVE COMMITTEE (CCITT). The leading organization involved in the development of standards relating to telephone and other telecommunications services. CCITT is a part of the International Telecommunications Union (ITU), which in turn is a body of the United Nations. The delegation to the ITU from the United States is the Department of State.

INTERNET. Term used to refer to an enterprise internetwork typically constructed using individual LAN data links that are interconnected using network interconnection devices and wide area network data links. In TCP/IP, a collection of individual hosts and data links interconnected using routers.

INTERNET. The world's largest TCP/IP internet, which interconnects thousands of networks containing millions of computers in universities, national laboratories, and commercial organizations. Sometimes called the Worldwide Internet.

INTERNET CONTROL MESSAGE PROTOCOL (ICMP). In TCP/IP, a Network layer protocol that allows end systems to report on error conditions and to provide information about unexpected circumstances.

INTERNET PACKET EXCHANGE (IPX) PROTOCOL. In NetWare, a Network layer protocol that provides an unreliable, connectionless, datagram delivery service.

INTERNET PROTOCOL (IP). In TCP/IP, a connectionless Network layer protocol that provides a best-efforts datagram delivery service.

INTERNETWORK. See *Internet*.

INTERNETWORK DATAGRAM PROTOCOL (IDP). In the Xerox Network System, a Network layer protocol that provides an unreliable, connectionless, datagram delivery service.

IP. Internet Protocol.

IPX. Internet Packet Exchange protocol.

ISDN. Integrated Services Digital Network.

IS-IS PROTOCOL. Intermediate System to Intermediate System Intra-Domain Routing Exchange Protocol (ISO 10589).

ISO. International Organization for Standardization.

ISO 8073. See *Connection-Oriented Transport Protocol*.

ISO 8473. See *Protocol for Providing the Connectionless-Mode Network Service*.

ISO 8878. See *Use of X.25 to Provide the OSI Connection-Mode Network Service*.

ISO 9542. See *End System to Intermediate System Routing Exchange Protocol*.

ISO 10589. See *Intermediate System to Intermediate System Intra-Domain Routing Exchange Protocol*.

JAMMING SIGNAL. In the CSMA/CD (Ethernet) form of LAN data link technology, the signal that a station transmits when it detects a collision condition on the transmission medium. The jamming signal is sent to ensure that all stations know that a collision has occurred.

KERBEROS. An encryption-based security system that provides mutual authentication between a client component and a server component in a distributed computing environment. Kerberos also provides authorization services that can be used to control which clients are authorized to access which servers.

LAN. Local area network.

LAN ADAPTER. IBM term for a network interface card (NIC) used to allow a device to be attached to a local area network data link. See *Network interface card*.

LAN DATA LINK. A multiaccess communication facility that consists of two or more devices connected using local area network technology.

LAN MANAGER. A family of network operating system software for personal computers codeveloped by Microsoft and IBM and marketed by Microsoft.

LAN SERVER. A family of network operating system software for personal computers codeveloped by Microsoft and IBM and marketed by IBM.

LAN STATION. See *Station*.

LAN SWITCH. A network interconnection device used to allow the network interface card in a computing device to be connected to one of multiple LAN transmission medium segments.

LANTASTIC. A family of network operating system software for personal computers marketed by Artisoft.

LINK-STATE ROUTING ALGORITHM. A form of distributed adaptive routing algorithm in which each router knows the complete topology of the network in terms of the existence of all other routers and the links between them. Each router broadcasts information about the routers to which it is directly attached and the status of the data links between them. A router constructs a map of the internet from this information, consisting of a graph with routers as systems and links as edges. Routers are then able to calculate routes from this graph using the Dijkstra shortest path algorithm. See also *Distance-vector routing algorithm*.

LLAP. LocalTalk Link Access Protocol.

LLC. Logical Link Control.

LLC-PDU. Logical-link-control-protocol-data-unit.

LLC-SDU. Logical-link-control-service-data-unit.

LOCAL AREA NETWORK (LAN). A term used to refer to a form of data link technology that is used to implement a high-speed, relatively short-distance form of computer communication. The term is also used to refer to a computer network constructed using LAN data link technology.

LOCALLY-ADMINISTERED MAC ADDRESSING. A form of LAN station addressing, in which MAC addresses are either 16 bits or 48 bits in length. With locally-administered addressing, the organization installing the network is responsible for assigning a unique MAC address to each network station. This is often done with DIP switches on the NIC or it might be done using a software function. See also *MAC address* and *Globally-administered MAC addressing*.

LOCALTALK. A low-speed form of LAN data link technology—part of Apple Computer's AppleTalk networking scheme—that uses a carrier sense multiple access with collision avoidance (CSMA/CA) form of medium access control. See also *AppleTalk* and *Carrier sense multiple access with collision avoidance*.

LOCALTALK CONNECTOR. A device used to connect a LocalTalk NIC to the original form of transmission medium defined by Apple for use with LocalTalk data links. See also *LocalTalk* and *PhoneNet connector*.

LOCALTALK LINK ACCESS PROTOCOL (LLAP). The AppleTalk protocol that defines operations associated with LocalTalk LAN data links. See also *LocalTalk* and *AppleTalk*.

LOGICAL LINK CONTROL (LLC) SUBLAYER. A sublayer of the Data Link layer, defined by IEEE 802.2 and ISO 8802-2, that is responsible for medium-independent data link functions. It allows the layer entity above to access the services of a LAN data link without regard to what form of physical transmission medium is used. In the context of the OSI model, the LLC sublayer provides services to the Network layer.

LOGICAL-LINK-CONTROL-PROTOCOL-DATA-UNIT (LLC-PDU). The data unit exchanged between peer Logical Link Control sublayer entities.

LOGICAL-LINK-CONTROL-SERVICE-DATA-UNIT (LLC-SDU). The data unit that a LAN data link user passes to the Logical Link Control sublayer when requesting a data transfer service.

MAC. Medium Access Control.

MAC ADDRESS. In the Medium Access Control sublayer of the IEEE/ISO/ANSI LAN architecture, a value that uniquely identifies an individual station that implements a single point of physical attachment to a LAN data link. Each station attached to a LAN data link must have a unique MAC address on that LAN data link. Sometimes called the *Station address*.

MAC FRAME. Informal name for the medium-access-control-protocol-data-unit (MAC-PDU). See also *Frame*.

MAC-PDU. Medium-access-control-protocol-data-unit.

MAC-SDU. Medium-access-control-service-data-unit.

MAIL APPLICATION PROGRAMMING INTERFACE (MAPI). An application programming interface (API) for electronic messaging developed by Microsoft.

MAN. Metropolitan Area Network.

MANAGEMENT INFORMATION BASE (MIB). In the ISO Common Management Information Protocol (CMIP), a repository, or database, that defines all the objects that can be managed in a network. Portions of the MIB are distributed among all the devices in the network—such as end systems, routers, terminal servers, and so on—that need to be managed.

MANCHESTER ENCODING. A form of data encoding in which each bit time that represents a data bit has a transition in the middle of the bit time.

MANUFACTURING AUTOMATION PROTOCOL (MAP). A group formed under the leadership of General Motors to address the networking needs of factory automation applications. See also *Technical and Office Protocols (TOP)*.

MAP. Manufacturing Automation Protocol.

MAPI. Mail Application Programming Interface.

MBPS. Megabits per second.

MEDIUM ACCESS CONTROL ADDRESS. See MAC address.

MEDIUM-ACCESS-CONTROL-PROTOCOL-DATA-UNIT (MAC-PDU). The data unit exchanged between peer Medium Access Control (MAC) sublayer entities. Sometimes referred to by the informal name *MAC frame*.

MEDIUM-ACCESS-CONTROL-SERVICE-DATA-UNIT. The data unit that a user of the Medium Access Control (MAC) sublayer service passes to the MAC sublayer when requesting a data transfer service.

MEDIUM ACCESS CONTROL (MAC) SUBLAYER. A sublayer of the Data Link layer, defined by the IEEE/ISO/ANSI LAN architecture, that is concerned with how access to the physical transmission medium is managed. The MAC sublayer provides services to the Logical Link Control (LLC) sublayer.

MEDIUM ATTACHMENT UNIT. Optional component defined in the IEEE/ISO CSMA/CD (Ethernet) standard that handles all functions that are dependent on the transmission medium being used. When used, it is often implemented in a device called a *transceiver*.

MEDIUM INTERFACE CABLE. Used with some forms of LAN data link technology to attach the network interface card (NIC) to the transmission medium.

MEDIUM INTERFACE CONNECTOR (MIC). On a Fiber Distributed Data Interface (FDDI) LAN data link, the physical connector that allows a port on a station to be connected to a full duplex transmission medium segment. See *MIC type A*, *MIC type B*, *MIC type M*, and *MIC type S*.

MEDIUM SPECIFICATION. The part of a local area network standard that defines for a particular type of transmission medium the physical and electrical characteristics of the transmission medium and the method by which a station is attached to the transmission medium.

METROPOLITAN AREA NETWORK (MAN). A form of networking technology, related to LAN technology, that span distances up to about 20 or 30 miles. Metropolitan area networks are sometimes used to bridge the gap between wide area networks and local area networks.

MIB. Management Information Base.

MIC. Medium interface connector. See *MIC type A*, *MIC type B*, *MIC type M*, and *MIC type S*.

MIC TYPE A. In a Fiber Distributed Data Interface (FDDI) station or concentrator, a medium interface connector that is the *input* of the path for the primary ring. See *Medium interface connector*.

MIC TYPE B. In a Fiber Distributed Data Interface (FDDI) station or concentrator, a medium interface connector that is the *output* of the path for the primary ring. See *Medium interface connector.*

MIC TYPE M. In a Fiber Distributed Data Interface (FDDI) concentrator, a medium interface connector that is used to connect the concentrator to a cable segment that leads to a MIC of type S, which is generally in a lower-level single-attachment station or concentrator. See *Medium interface connector, MIC type S, Single-attachment concentrator, Single-attachment station.*

MIC TYPE S. In a Fiber Distributed Data Interface (FDDI) single-attachment station or concentrator, a medium interface connector that is used to connect the station or concentrator to a cable segment that leads to a MIC of type M, which is generally in a higher-level concentrator. See *Medium interface connector, MIC type M, Single-attachment concentrator, Single-attachment station.*

MIDSPLIT BROADBAND. A broadband network configuration in which the cable bandwidth is divided into two channels, each using a different range of frequencies. One channel is used to transmit signals and the other is used to receive.

MODEM. A device that implements *Modulator-demodulator* functions to convert between digital data and analog signals.

MODULATION TECHNIQUE. Signaling technique in which a data signal is superimposed on a carrier signal by varying the carrier signal's amplitude, frequency, or phase.

MULTILEVEL DUOBINARY SIGNALING. A signaling system used in networks that conform to the IEEE/ISO Token Bus standard that allows for three distinct amplitude levels symbolically represented as {0}, {2}, and {4}. Nondata bits are represented by the signal value {2}, 0 bits by {0}, and 1 bits by {4}.

MULTIPORT REPEATER. A repeater in a network that conforms to the IEEE/ISO CSMA/CD (Ethernet) standard to which individual local area network stations are attached, each with its own cable segment.

NAC. Null-attachment concentrator.

NAME BINDING PROTOCOL (NBP). In AppleTalk, a Transport layer protocol that provides a directory service in which names can be assigned to objects, such as application programs and services available over the network. The service translates between names and the network addresses of the systems associated with those names.

NAMED PIPES. An application programming interface for interprocess communication, jointly developed by IBM and Microsoft, in which a data structure called a *named pipe* is referenced by function calls to send data between a pair of communicating processes.

NBP. Name Binding Protocol.

NCB. Network Control Block.

NCP. NetWare Core Protocol.

NETBEUI. A name sometimes used to refer to the Transport layer protocol used in conjunction with NetBIOS. See also *NetBIOS.*

NETBIOS. An application programming interface (API) and Transport layer protocol, developed by IBM and Microsoft for use in the personal computer networking environment. The NetBIOS protocol operates in the OSI model Transport layer and provides data delivery services to application programs and higher-level protocols. The NetBIOS Transport protocol is sometimes called NetBEUI after the program module that first implemented it. NetBIOS has become a de facto Transport layer standard for personal computer LAN communication, and NetBIOS services are provided by a wide variety of different networking software subsystems.

NETWARE. A family of network operating system software for personal computers that is marketed by Novell.

NETWARE CORE PROTOCOL (NCP). In NetWare, a Transport layer protocol that handles all client requests for services from a server and allows users to access NetWare application-level services.

NETWARE LOADABLE MODULE (NLM). In NetWare, an extension that is added to the base NetWare software that runs in a NetWare server.

NETWORK ARCHITECTURE. A comprehensive plan and a set of rules that govern the design and operation of the hardware and software components used to create computer networks. Network architectures define sets of communication protocols that govern how communication takes place.

NETWORK-AWARE APPLICATION. An application program that explicitly invokes network communication services.

NETWORK CONTROL BLOCK (NCB). The control block used to implement the NetBIOS application programming interface. See also *NetBIOS*.

NETWORK FILE SYSTEM (NFS). In TCP/IP, an application service that provides authorized users with access to files located on remote systems. System administrators generally designate one or more systems in the internet as NFS servers that make certain designated directories on their disk storage devices available to other systems. A user accesses an NFS-mounted directory in the same manner as accessing a directory on a local disk.

NETWORK INFORMATION CENTER (NIC). Organization, operated by Government Systems, Inc. (GSI), 14200 Park Meadow Drive, Suite 200, Chantilly, VA 22021, that is responsible for the administration of the Internet. See also *Internet*.

NETWORKING SOFTWARE. Software that implements high-level networking functions that end users employ for doing useful work. In the personal computer environment, networking software is often implemented in subsystems called network operating systems.

NETWORK INTERFACE CARD (NIC). A circuit board installed in a computing device used to attach the device to a network. A NIC performs the hardware functions that are required to provide a computing device with physical communication capabilities.

NETWORK LAYER. Layer three of the OSI model. The Network layer is concerned with making routing decisions and relaying data from one system to another through the network. The facilities provided by the Network layer supply a service that higher layers employ for moving data units, often called *packets*, from one end system to another, where the packets may flow through any number of intermediate systems.

NETWORK OPERATING SYSTEM. A software product, typically used in the personal computer environment, that provides high-level networking functions to users and application programs.

NETWORK-PROTOCOL-DATA-UNIT (NPDU). The data unit exchanged by peer Network layer entities.

NETWORK SERVICES PROTOCOL (NSP). In DECnet Phase IV, a Transport layer protocol that provides a reliable, sequenced, connection-oriented, end-to-end data delivery service.

NETWORK-TRANSPARENT APPLICATION. An application program not specifically designed to take advantage of networking facilities.

NFS. Network File System.

NIC. Network interface card or, in the Worldwide Internet, the Network Information Center.

NLM. NetWare Loadable Module.

NONCONFIRMED SERVICE. In the OSI model, a service provided by a layer or sublayer entity in which the service requester is not informed of the success or failure of the service request. With such a service, any required error handling must be provided by higher-level layers.

NOVELL NETWARE. See *NetWare*.

NPDU. Network-protocol-data-unit.

NSP. Network Services Protocol.

NULL-ATTACHMENT CONCENTRATOR (NAC). On a Fiber Distributed Data Interface (FDDI) LAN data link, a concentrator that contains only medium interface connectors (MICs) of type S for connection to single-attachment stations. See *Medium interface connector*, *MIC type S*, and *Single-attachment station*.

100BASE-X. See *Fast Ethernet*.

OPEN SHORTEST PATH FIRST (OSPF) PROTOCOL. In TCP/IP, a Network layer routing protocol that operates within a single autonomous system and implements a link-state routing algorithm.

OPEN SOFTWARE FOUNDATION (OSF). A nonprofit organization established by a number of computer manufacturers to develop a common foundation for open systems computing.

OSF. Open Software Foundation.

OSF DCE. See *Distributed Computing Environment*.

OSI. Open systems interconnection.

OSI MODEL. The seven-layer *Reference Model for Open Systems Interconnection*, developed by members of the International Organization for Standardization (ISO) and documented in ISO 7498, that provides a common basis for the coordination of standards development for the purpose of systems interconnection.

OSPF. Open Shortest Path First.

PACKET. Informal name for the network protocol-data-unit (NPDU).

PACKET EXCHANGE PROTOCOL (PEP; PXP). In the Xerox Network System (PEP) and the Novell NetWare family (PXP), a Transport layer protocol that provides application programs with an unreliable, connectionless, end-to-end data transport service.

PACKET SWITCHING. A Network layer mechanism in which data is routed and relayed through the network in units called *packets*. Each packet carries its own addressing information and is typically handled by the network independently of other packets.

PARALLEL PORT. A communication device in a computer system that allows data to be transmitted and received an octet at a time with a separate circuit used for each bit.

PARALLEL PORT NETWORK INTERFACE CARD (NIC). An external NIC that attaches to a computing system's parallel port. Such a NIC allows a notebook PC that has limited expansion capability to be connected to a conventional LAN data link in the same manner as a desktop computer.

PATHWORKS. A family of network operating system software for personal computers marketed by Digital Equipment Corporation.

PCI. Protocol-control-information.

PCMCIA. Personal Computer Memory Card International Association.

PCMCIA NETWORK INTERFACE CARD (NIC). An external NIC that attaches to a computing system's Personal Computer Memory Card International Association (PCMCIA) expansion slot. PCMCIA slots are often used on notebook personal computers to allow credit-card sized peripherals to be attached to the personal computer.

PC NETWORK—BASEBAND. An IBM LAN data link hardware product line that implements a CSMA/CD form of medium access control using baseband transmission.

PC NETWORK—BROADBAND. An IBM LAN data link hardware product line that implements a CSMA/CD form of medium access control method using broadband transmission.

PDU. Protocol-data-unit.

PEER-TO-PEER PROTOCOLS. See *Protocol*.

PEP. Packet Exchange Protocol.

PHONENET CONNECTOR. A connector used to connect a LocalTalk network interface card (NIC) to a LocalTalk LAN data link implemented using twisted-pair telephone wiring. Sometimes called a *PhoneTalk connector*. See also *LocalTalk connector*.

PHYSICAL LAYER. Layer one of the OSI model. The *Physical* layer is responsible for the transmission of signals, such as electrical signals, optical signals, or radio signals, between communicating machines. Physical layer mechanisms in each of the communicating machines typically control the generation and detection of signals that are interpreted as 0 bits and 1 bits.

PING. In TCP/IP, an Application service that can be used to test for connectivity between any two systems in the internet.

POINT-TO-POINT LINK CABLE SEGMENT. A transmission medium segment in a local area network that conforms to the IEEE/ISO CSMA/CD (Ethernet) standard that serves only to link two repeaters and to which no stations are attached.

POINT-TO-POINT PROTOCOL (PPP). An adaptation of HDLC that grew out of work done by the Internet Engineering Task Force and that improves on HDLC by adding the Network layer protocol identification mechanism that is required for enterprise internetworking. The Point-to-Point protocol allows a point-to-point connection to be established between two network devices that allows frames associated with multiple Network layer protocols to flow over data links without interfering with one another.

PORT. A communication device in a computer system that can be used to transmit and receive data. A data structure in a network software subsystem used to control data transmission activities.

PORTAL. Term used to refer to each end of an encapsulation facility. Two portals can be viewed as implementing a tunnel that transports messages through a network conforming to a foreign network architecture. See *encapsulation facility*.

POSTAL, TELEGRAPH, AND TELEPHONE ADMINISTRATION (PTT). A public organization in many countries that provides communications services to the general public in a similar manner to a common carrier in the United States.

PPP. Point-to-Point Protocol.

PREAMBLE. A field used with some forms of medium access control that precedes the start frame delimiter field of the MAC frame and is used for synchronization purposes.

PREDECESSOR STATION. In a network that conforms to the IEEE/ISO Token Bus standard, the station on the network having the next higher MAC address from which a station receives frames.

PRESENTATION LAYER. Layer six of the OSI model. The Presentation layer is the lowest layer interested in the *meaning* of the streams of bits that are exchanged between communicating programs and deals with preserving the *information content* of data transmitted over the network. The Presentation layer in the two communicating systems negotiates a common syntax for transferring the messages exchanged by two communicating programs and ensures that one system does not need to care what form of internal data representation the other system is using.

PRIMITIVE. See *Service primitive*.

PRINT SERVER. A network system that implements software allowing other network systems to share the print server's printers.

PROJECT 802. A committee of the IEEE responsible for the development of an architecture and standards for local area networking. IEEE Project 802 LAN standards have been accepted as international standards by ISO.

PROPAGATION TIME. The length of time it takes a MAC frame to travel between two stations.

PROTOCOL. A set of rules or conventions that define the formats of data units handled by a particular layer or sublayer entity and the data flows that take place in exchanging data units between peer layer or sublayer entities.

PROTOCOL-CONTROL-INFORMATION (PCI). Control information, taking the form of a header and sometimes also a trailer, that a layer or sublayer entity attaches to the data in a service-data-unit to create one or more protocol-data-units.

PROTOCOL-DATA-UNIT (PDU). The data unit that a layer or sublayer entity transmits across the network to a peer layer or sublayer entity.

PROTOCOL FOR PROVIDING THE CONNECTIONLESS-MODE NETWORK SERVICE (ISO 8473). In the OSI architecture and in DECnet/OSI, a Network layer protocol, often called the ISO Internet protocol, that provides an unreliable, datagram data delivery service.

PTT. Postal, Telegraph, and Telephone Administration.

RARP. Reverse Address Resolution Protocol.

REDIRECTOR. A software function in networking software that intercepts all I/O function calls and checks to see if the call applies to a resource under the control of a server rather than to a local resource. The redirector handles the network communication that is required to handle I/O requests for access to remote resources.

REMOTE PROCEDURE CALL (RPC) FACILITY. A facility for interprocess communication in which an application program issues function and procedure calls by name to program modules that may reside in other network systems. Arguments and results are automatically transmitted through the network transparently to the application program.

REPEATER. A device that operates at the level of the Physical layer and is used to relay signals between two or more cable segments that implement a bus- or tree-structured LAN data link.

REQUEST FOR COMMENTS (RFC). Documentation of the operation of the protocols making up the TCP/IP protocol suite. RFCs are available in machine-readable form on the Internet or in hardcopy form from the Internet Network Information Center (NIC).

REQUEST SERVICE PRIMITIVE. In the OSI model, a service primitive that is issued by a service requester to request that a particular service be performed by a lower-level layer and to pass parameters needed to fully specify the requested service. See also *Confirm service primitive*, *Indication service primitive*, and *Response service primitive*.

RESPONSE. A logical-link-control-protocol-data-unit (LLC-SDU) that is sent by an LLC sublayer entity in reply to a command. See also *Command*.

RESPONSE SERVICE PRIMITIVE. In the OSI model, a service primitive that is issued by the higher-level service requester to acknowledge or complete some procedure previously invoked by the lower-level service provider through an *indication* service primitive. See also *Confirm service primitive*, *Indication service primitive*, and *Request service primitive*.

REVERSE ADDRESS RESOLUTION PROTOCOL (RARP). In TCP/IP, a Network layer protocol that allows an end system that does not yet have its network address to obtain it. RARP is typically used to support workstations and intelligent terminals that do not have their own disk storage.

RFC. Request for Comments.

RING TOPOLOGY. A network configuration in which the cabling forms a loop, with a simple, point-to-point connection attaching each system to the next around the ring. Each system acts as a repeater for all signals it receives and retransmits them to the next system in the ring at their original signal strength.

RIP. Routing Information Protocol.

RLOGIN. In TCP/IP, an Application service that allows a user at a UNIX system to log into some other UNIX system. See also *Telnet*.

ROUTER. A network device that sends and receives Network protocol-data-units (packets) and relays packets from one device to another through the network. Sometimes called an *Intermediate system*. In TCP/IP literature, a router is sometimes called a *Gateway*.

ROUTING INFORMATION PROTOCOL (RIP). In TCP/IP, in NetWare, and in the Xerox Network system, a Network layer routing protocol that allows routers to communicate with one another for the purposes of determining routes and for relaying user traffic from one router to another through the network.

ROUTING TABLE MAINTENANCE PROTOCOL (RTMP). In AppleTalk, a Transport layer routing protocol that allows routers to communicate with one another for the purposes of determining routes and for relaying user traffic from one router to another through the internet.

RPC. Remote procedure call.

RS-232-D. An EIA standard for asynchronous data communication. See also *Asynchronous transmission*.

RSH. In TCP/IP, an Application service that allows the user to issue, at the local system, a command to request an operating system function or to request the execution of an application program on some other system in the internet.

RTMP. Routing Table Maintenance Protocol.

SAC. Single-attachment concentrator.

SAP. Service-access-point and Service Advertising Protocol.

SAP ADDRESS. In the OSI model, a value representing a point of access into a layer. In the Logical Link Control sublayer of the IEEE/ISO/ANSI LAN architecture, a value that represents a particular mechanism, process, or protocol that is requesting LLC sublayer services. Each mechanism, process, or protocol that is concurrently using the services of the LLC sublayer in a given station must use a different SAP address.

SAS. Single-attachment station.

SDU. Service-data-unit.

SEGMENTATION FUNCTION. In the OSI model, a function performed by a layer or sublayer entity that creates two or more protocol-data-units from a single service-data-unit.

SEQUENCED PACKET EXCHANGE (SPX) PROTOCOL. In NetWare, a Transport layer protocol that provides application programs with a reliable, sequenced, connection-oriented data transport service.

SEQUENCED PACKET PROTOCOL (SPP). In the Xerox Network System, a Transport layer protocol that provides application programs with a reliable, sequenced, connection-oriented data transport service.

SERIAL PORT. A communication device in a computer system that allows data to be transmitted and received a single bit at a time.

SERVER. A computing system in a network that runs software that provides services to other computing systems. In client-server computing, an application component that provides a service for one or more other application components operating in the role of clients. See *Client* and *Client-server computing*.

SERVER MESSAGE BLOCK (SMB). A term that refers to an API that application programs use to request high-level application services and also to a protocol for providing those services. The SMB services and protocol were originally developed for networking software that operated in the MS-DOS environment. Many newer networking software subsystems for the OS/2, Windows, and Windows/NT environments continue to support the SMB interface and protocol.

SERVICE-ACCESS-POINT (SAP). In the OSI model, the point at which the services of a layer are provided. Each service-access-point has a SAP address, by which the particular entity that is employing a layer service can be differentiated from all other entities that might also be able to use that layer service. In the IEEE/ISO/ANSI LAN architecture, the Logical Link Control sublayer implements service-access-points that identify each user of the LAN data link in a particular station.

SERVICE-ACCESS-POINT ADDRESS. See *Service-access-point* and *SAP address*.

SERVICE ADVERTISING PROTOCOL (SAP). In NetWare, a Transport layer broadcast protocol that NetWare servers employ to inform NetWare clients of the services that are available.

SERVICE-DATA-UNIT (SDU). In the OSI model, the data unit that a layer or sublayer entity passes down to the adjacent layer or sublayer below it in requesting a data transmission service.

SERVICE PRIMITIVE. In the OSI model, a description of the semantics (not coding syntax) of one element of a layer or sublayer service. A particular service primitive can be issued by a service requester to a service provider or by a service provider to a service requester.

SERVICE PROVIDER. In the OSI model, a layer or sublayer entity that provides a service to an adjacent layer or sublayer entity above it.

SERVICE REQUESTER. In the OSI model, a layer or sublayer entity that requests a service of an adjacent layer or sublayer entity below it.

SESSION LAYER. Layer five of the OSI model. The Session layer is responsible for organizing the dialog between two communicating programs and for managing the data exchanges between them. It imposes a structure on the interaction between two communicating programs and defines three types of dialogs: two-way simultaneous interaction, where both programs can send and receive concurrently; two-way alternate interaction, where the programs take turns sending and receiving; and one-way interaction, where one program sends and the other only receives. In addition to organizing the dialog, Session layer services include establishing synchronization points within the dialog, allowing a dialog to be interrupted, and resuming a dialog from a synchronization point.

S-FORMAT LLC-PDU. See *Supervisory LLC-PDU.*

SIMPLE MAIL TRANSFER PROTOCOL (SMTP). In TCP/IP, an Application protocol used for the transfer of electronic mail messages. SMTP is designed to be used by electronic mail software that provides the user with access to messaging facilities.

SIMPLE NETWORK MANAGEMENT PROTOCOL (SNMP). In TCP/IP, an application protocol that defines the formats of network management messages and the rules by which the messages are exchanged.

SINGLE-ATTACHMENT CONCENTRATOR (SAC). On a Fiber Distributed Data Interface (FDDI) LAN data link, a device having two or more medium interface connectors (MICs). One of the MICs is of type S for connection to a concentrator and one or more MICs are of type M for connection to single-attachment stations. See *Medium interface connector, MIC type S, MIC type M,* and *Single-attachment station.*

SINGLE-ATTACHMENT STATION (SAS). On a Fiber Distributed Data Interface (FDDI) LAN data link, a station having a single medium interface connector (MIC) of type S. A single-attachment station is typically connected, via a single transmission medium segment, to a concentrator implementing a MIC of type M. See *Medium interface connector, MIC type M,* and *MIC type S.*

SLOT TIME. The length of time it takes for a signal to travel the maximum allowable distance from one end of the network to the other and back again.

SMB. Server Message Block.

SMDS. Switched Multimegabit Data Service.

SMTP. Simple Mail Transfer Protocol.

SNA. Systems Network Architecture.

SNAP. Subnetwork Access Protocol.

SNAP LLC-PDU. Data unit, sometimes called a SNAP PDU, exchanged by peer entities implementing the IEEE Subnetwork Access Protocol. SNAP LLC-PDUs carry SSAP and DSAP address values of hexadecimal 'AA'. See *Subnetwork Access Protocol.*

SNAP PDU. See *SNAP LLC-PDU.*

SNMP. Simple Network Management Protocol.

SOCKETS INTERFACE. A networking application programming interface initially developed for the variation of the UNIX operating system developed by the University of California at Berkeley (BSD UNIX). By using the Sockets interface, two application programs, one running in the local system and another running in the remote system, can communicate with one another in a standardized manner.

SONET. Physical layer communication facilities, using fiber optics, on which broadband ISDN services are based. OC-1 SONET provides a 51 Mbps data rate, OC-3 SONET provides a 155 Mbps data rate, OC-12 SONET provides a 622 Mbps data rate, and OC-48 SONET provides a 2.4 Gbps data rate.

Source MAC Address. Address identifying the station that originated a MAC frame. See also *MAC address* and *Station*.

Source Routing Bridge. A bridge used to form an extended LAN consisting of a structure in which there can be more than one path between any two LAN stations. With source routing bridges, each station is expected to know the route over which to send each data unit. If a station does not know the route, or if a previously known route is no longer active, the station sends out route discovery data units over the bridges and then determines from the responses that come back the appropriate route to use. Source routing bridges are typically used only with Token Ring LAN data links. See *Extended LAN* and see also *Transparent bridge*.

Source-Service-Access-Point (SSAP). A service-access-point that identifies the originator of a data unit. See *Service-access-point*.

Spanning Tree. A graph structure that includes all the bridges and stations on an extended LAN but in which there is never more than one active path connecting any two stations. See *Bridge*, *Transparent bridge*, and *Extended LAN*.

Spanning Tree Bridge. See *Transparent bridge*.

SPP. Sequenced Packet Protocol.

SPX. Sequenced Packet Exchange protocol.

SSAP Address. In the IEEE/ISO/ANSI LAN architecture, an address that identifies the service-access-point (SAP) that is responsible for originating the LLC-PDU.

Start Frame Delimiter. A MAC frame field that contains a particular bit pattern and indicates the beginning of a frame.

Star Topology. A network configuration in which there is a central point to which a group of systems are directly connected. With the star topology, all transmissions from one system to another pass through the central point, which may consist of a device that plays a role in managing and controlling communication.

Start-Stop Transmission. See *Asynchronous transmission*.

Station. A collection of hardware, firmware, and software that appears to other stations as a single functional and addressable unit on a LAN data link. A station implements a single physical point of connection to the transmission medium. A station is a collection of one or more hardware and/or software components that performs the functions of the LLC sublayer, the MAC sublayer, and the Physical layer.

Station Address. See *MAC address*.

Station Management. A function defined by some forms of medium access control that is responsible for control functions, such as resetting a MAC sublayer entity and specifying values for constants used in the network.

Subnet. In TCP/IP, the use of a single network identifier in multiple networks. When using subnetting, some of the high-order bits in the host identifier portion of the address are used to identify individual subnets. A value called a *subnet mask* is used by each system to identify how the internet address bits should be interpreted in a particular network.

Subnetwork. A collection of systems that are attached to a single virtual transmission medium so that each system in the subnetwork is one hop from any other system on that subnetwork. A *hop* is defined as a traversal from one system to another across a single data link, as viewed from the perspective of software operating in the OSI Network layer.

SUBNETWORK ACCESS PROTOCOL (SNAP). A protocol defined by IEEE, that implements a mechanism for distinguishing LLC-PDUs that are carrying packets associated with one Network layer protocol from LLC-PDUs that are carrying packets associated with some other Network layer protocol.

SUBNETWORK-ACCESS-PROTOCOL-LOGICAL-LINK-CONTROL-PROTOCOL-DATA-UNIT. See *SNAP LLC-PDU.*

SUBVECTOR. In IBM Token-Ring Network MAC control frames, a field, formatted with a 1 or 3 octet length field followed by data, that is carried within a vector in the frame Information field. See *Vector.*

SUCCESSOR STATION. In a network that conforms to the IEEE/ISO Token Bus standard, the station having the next lower MAC address to which a station transmits data units.

SUPERVISORY LLC-PDUs. *Supervisory* LLC-PDUs (S-format LLC-PDUs) are used to carry information necessary to control the operation of the LLC sublayer protocol. See *Logical-link-control-protocol-data-unit.*

SWITCH. See LAN switch.

SWITCHED MULTIMEGABIT DATA SERVICE (SMDS). A high-speed wide area network packet switching service that is built on top of broadband ISDN services to provide services similar to an X.25 network.

SYSTEM. Any computing device attached to a network that implements one or more stations for communicating with other systems. In the OSI model, a set of one or more computers, the associated software, peripherals, terminals, human operators, physical processes, transfer means, and so on, that forms an autonomous whole capable of performing information processing and/or information transfer.

SYSTEMS NETWORK ARCHITECTURE (SNA). IBM's own proprietary network architecture, widely used in the IBM large-system environment. Many networks built using IBM equipment and software conform to SNA specifications. SNA defines specifications for constructing the hardware and software components that make up an SNA network and include definitions of the formats of data units and the protocols that govern how data units flow over the network. SNA defines two forms of networking: *SNA subarea networking* and *Advanced Peer-to-Peer Networking* (APPN).

T1. A digital telecommunication facility, available from telecommunications providers, that supports a bit rate of 1.544 Mbps.

T3. A digital telecommunication facility, available from telecommunications providers, that supports a bit rate of 45 Mbps.

TCP. Transmission Control Protocol.

TCP/IP. Transmission Control Protocol/Internet Protocol.

TECHNICAL AND OFFICE PROTOCOLS (TOP). A group, sponsored by The Boeing Company, whose purpose is to address the networking needs of engineering and general office applications. See also *Manufacturing Automation Protocol.*

TELNET. In TCP/IP, an Application service that allows a user at the local system to log into any type of remote TCP/IP system. See also *Rlogin.*

10BASE2. Shorthand notation for an IEEE/ISO CSMA/CD (Ethernet) medium specification in which the data rate is 10 Mbps, the transmission technique is baseband, and the maximum cable segment length is 185 meters. 10BASE2 is the CSMA/CD medium specification that specifies the use of 50 ohm, 5 mm coaxial cable, sometimes called *ThinWire* or *ThinNet* cable.

10BASE5. Shorthand notation for an IEEE/ISO CSMA/CD (Ethernet) medium specification in which the data rate is 10 Mbps, the transmission technique is baseband, and the maximum cable segment length is 500 meters. 10BASE5 is the CSMA/CD medium specification that is based on the original Ethernet Version 2 Specification and specifies the use of 50 ohm, 10 mm coaxial cable often called *Ethernet cable* or *thick Ethernet cable*.

10BASE-T. Shorthand notation for an IEEE/ISO CSMA/CD (Ethernet) medium specification in which the data rate is 10 Mbps, the transmission technique is baseband, and the maximum cable segment length is 100 meters. 10BASE-T is the CSMA/CD medium specification that specifies the use of twisted-pair cable.

10BROAD36. Shorthand notation for an IEEE/ISO CSMA/CD (Ethernet) medium specification in which the data rate is 10 Mbps, the transmission technique is broadband, and the maximum cable segment length is 3600 meters. 10BROAD36 is the CSMA/CD medium specification that specifies the use of 75 ohm coaxial cable typically used to carry cable television signals.

TFTP. Trivial File Transfer Protocol.

THICK ETHERNET CABLE. See *Ethernet cable*.

THINWIRE CABLE. Informal name for the 50-ohm, 5 mm coaxial cable specified in the IEEE/ISO CSMA/CD (Ethernet) 10BASE2 medium specification.

TIME-SEQUENCE DIAGRAM. A graphical form of documentation used in ISO standard service definitions that describes the sequence in which service primitives are issued.

TLAP. TokenTalk Link Access Protocol.

TLI. Transport Layer Interface.

TOKEN. A special data unit, used with token bus, token ring, and FDDI LAN data links, that is passed from station to station to control access to the transmission medium. Only a station that possesses the token is allowed to transmit MAC frames.

TOKEN BUS. A LAN data link technology, defined by IEEE 802.4 and ISO 8802-4, in which systems are connected to a common transmission medium in a similar manner to an Ethernet LAN. A system is allowed to transmit only when it has a special data unit, called the *token*, that is passed from one system to another.

TOKEN RING. A LAN data link technology, defined by IEEE 802.5 and ISO 8802-5, in which systems are connected to one another using point-to-point twisted-pair cable segments to form a ring structure. A system is allowed to transmit only when it has the token, which is passed from one system to another around the ring.

TOKEN-RING NETWORK. The name of IBM's implementation of the IEEE/ISO Token Ring standard.

TOKENTALK LINK ACCESS PROTOCOL (TLAP). In AppleTalk, the data link protocol that provides Token Ring LAN support. Standard IEEE/ISO Logical Link Control (LLC) interfaces and data formats are used to provide the connectionless Type 1 LLC service.

TOP. Technical and Office Protocols.

TOPOLOGY. Characteristic of a communication network that concerns both the *physical* configuration of the cabling that is used to interconnect communicating systems and the *logical* way in which systems view the structure of the network. See *Bus topology*, *Ring topology*, and *Star topology*.

TRANSCEIVER. Device that implements the medium attachment unit component defined by the IEEE/ISO CSMA/CD (Ethernet) standard that is used to attach a station to the transmission medium.

TRANSMISSION CONTROL PROTOCOL (TCP). In TCP/IP, a connection-oriented Transport layer protocol that provides for reliable, sequenced, stream data delivery.

TRANSMISSION CONTROL PROTOCOL/INTERNET PROTOCOL (TCP/IP). A set of communication protocols that grew out of a research project that was funded by the U. S. Department of Defense. The TCP/IP networking scheme implements a peer-to-peer client-server architecture. Any computing system in the network can run TCP/IP server software and can provide services to any other computing system that runs complementary TCP/IP client software.

TRANSMISSION MEDIUM. The cable or other physical circuit that is used to interconnect systems in a network.

TRANSMISSION TECHNIQUE. The type of signaling that is used to exchange information over a physical transmission medium. See also *Baseband transmission* and *Broadband transmission*.

TRANSPARENT BRIDGE. A bridge that is used to form an extended LAN consisting of a tree structure in which only one active path connects any two stations in the extended LAN. Stations on the interconnected LANs are not aware of the presence of transparent bridges. Transparent bridges learn appropriate routes for messages by observing transmissions that take place on the LANs to which they are connected and forward messages that they receive to the opposite network when required. See also *Extended LAN* and *Source routing bridge*.

TRANSPORT LAYER. Layer four of the OSI model. The Transport layer is the lowest layer required only in two end systems that are communicating. The Transport layer forms the uppermost layer of a reliable end-to-end data transport service and hides from the higher layers all the details concerning the actual moving of streams of bits from one computer to another. The functions performed in the Transport layer include end-to-end integrity controls that are used to recover from lost, out-of-sequence, or duplicate messages.

TRANSPORT LAYER INTERFACE (TLI). A networking application programming interface (API) that was originally defined for use with AT&T System V UNIX and is now implemented by a variety of networking software subsystems, especially in the TCP/IP environment.

TRIVIAL FILE TRANSFER PROTOCOL (TFTP). In TCP/IP, a simple file transfer service that implements its own reliability controls and can run on top of any type of transport service. UDP is used by most TFTP implementations. The end-to-end reliability controls that TFTP implements take the form of a message sequencing system, timeouts, and retransmissions to ensure that files are transferred intact. TFTP is generally used only by system software that performs such functions as downline loading of program code; it is not intended to be employed directly by end users.

TRUNK CABLE. Used in some forms of medium access control to refer to a transmission medium cable segment.

TRUNK COUPLING UNIT. Used with some forms of medium access control to connect a station to the transmission medium.

TUNNEL. Term used in reference to an encapsulation facility. An encapsulation facility can be viewed as two portals that implement a tunnel that transports messages through a network conforming to a foreign network architecture. See also *Encapsulation facility*.

TWISTED-PAIR CABLE. A cable that contains one or more pairs of insulated copper conductors that are twisted around one another to provide a degree of protection from electrical interference.

Type 1 LLC Operation. Form of Logical Link Control sublayer protocol operation that provides the connectionless LLC service. See also *Connectionless LLC service.*

Type 2 LLC Operation. Form of Logical Link Control sublayer protocol operation that provides the connection-oriented LLC service. See also *Connection-oriented LLC service.*

Type 3 LLC Operation. Form of Logical Link Control sublayer protocol operation that provides the acknowledged connectionless LLC service. See also *Acknowledged connectionless LLC service.*

UDP. User Datagram Protocol.

U-Format LLC-PDU. See *Unnumbered LLC-PDU.*

Universal Addressing. See *Globally-administered MAC addressing.*

Unnumbered LLC-PDU. Logical-link-control-protocol-data-units that are sometimes used to carry data and are sometimes used for special functions, such as performing initialization procedures and invoking diagnostic sequences. See *Logical-link-control-protocol-data-unit.*

Use of X.25 to Provide the OSI Connection-Mode Network Service (ISO 8878). In the OSI architecture and in DECnet/OSI, a Network layer protocol that provides the OSI connection-oriented Network service.

User Datagram Protocol (UDP). In TCP/IP, a Transport layer protocol that provides a best-efforts, connectionless datagram delivery service.

Value-Added Process (VAP). See *NetWare Loadable Module.*

VAP. Value-Added Process. See *NetWare Loadable Module.*

Vector. In IBM Token-Ring Network MAC control frames, a frame Information field formatted with a 2-octet length field followed by data. See also *Subvector.*

Vendor Independent Messaging (VIM). An application programming interface (API) for electronic messaging jointly developed by Lotus, Novell, Apple, and Borland.

VIM. Vendor Independent Messaging.

VINES. A family of network operating system software marketed by Banyan Systems.

VistaLAN/1. A family of LAN products, available from Allen-Bradley, that uses a token-bus form of medium access control. VistaLAN/1 products use broadband transmission over a bus- or tree-structured network.

WAN. Wide area network.

Wide Area Network (WAN). Networks that tie together computing devices that are widely separated geographically.

Wireless Transmission. Form of data communication in which infrared or radio signals are used to exchange information without requiring devices to be physically interconnected using cabling.

Wiring Closet. A room or cabinet that serves as a central point from which cables lead to individual local area network stations. See also *Equipment room.*

Worldwide Internet. See *Internet.*

X.25. An international standard, documented in CCITT Recommendation X.25, that defines the interface between a computing device and a packet-switched data network (PSDN).

Xerox Network System (XNS). A network architecture for internetworking, defined by Xerox, that allows for the interconnection of individual Ethernet LAN data links and for connecting

Ethernet LANs with packet-switched public data networks. The XNS architecture has been published by Xerox and has been made generally available to the public. The XNS architecture is one of the earliest of the published architectures for internetworking, and a number of local area network vendors have adopted forms of the XNS protocols for use in their own products.

XNS. Xerox Network System.

X WINDOW SYSTEM. A set of distributed graphical presentation services that implement a windowing system on a graphics display. The X Window System implements a client-server relationship between an application program (the client) and the windowing software in a workstation or terminal that controls a window on the graphical display (the server). The client and server can be running in different computing systems or in the same computing system.

ZERO-SLOT LAN. A form of computer networking in which communication is generally accomplished using software that accesses a computer system's serial or parallel ports. Zero-slot LAN software often provides facilities similar to those provided in a conventional local area network.

Index

The Conceptual Prism of
Information Technology:

THE JAMES MARTIN BOOKS

Information Technology Management and Strategy	Methodologies for Building Systems	Analysis and Design	CASE
AN INFORMATION SYSTEMS MANIFESTO	STRATEGIC INFORMATION PLANNING METHODOLOGIES (second edition)	STRUCTURED TECHNIQUES: THE BASIS FOR CASE (revised edition)	STRUCTURED TECHNIQUES: THE BASIS FOR CASE (revised edition)
INFORMATION ENGINEERING (Book I: Introduction)	INFORMATION ENGINEERING (Book I: Introduction)	DATABASE ANALYSIS AND DESIGN	INFORMATION ENGINEERING (Book I: Introduction)
INFORMATION ENGINEERING (Book II: Planning and Analysis)	INFORMATION ENGINEERING (Book II: Planning and Analysis)	DESIGN OF MAN-COMPUTER DIALOGUES	**Languages and Programming**
STRATEGIC INFORMATION PLANNING METHODOLOGIES (second edition)	INFORMATION ENGINEERING (Book III: Design and Construction)	DESIGN OF REAL-TIME COMPUTER SYSTEMS	APPLICATION DEVELOPMENT WITHOUT PROGRAMMERS
SOFTWARE MAINTENANCE: THE PROBLEM AND ITS SOLUTIONS	STRUCTURED TECHNIQUES: THE BASIS FOR CASE (revised edition)	DATA COMMUNICATIONS DESIGN TECHNIQUES	FOURTH-GENERATION LANGUAGES (Volume I: Principles)
DESIGN AND STRATEGY FOR DISTRIBUTED DATA PROCESSING	**Object-Oriented Programming**	DESIGN AND STRATEGY FOR DISTRIBUTED DATA PROCESSING	FOURTH-GENERATION LANGUAGES (Volume II: Representative 4GLs)
Expert Systems	OBJECT-ORIENTED ANALYSIS AND DESIGN	SOFTWARE MAINTENANCE: THE PROBLEM AND ITS SOLUTIONS	FOURTH-GENERATION LANGUAGES (Volume III: 4GLs from IBM)
BUILDING EXPERT SYSTEMS: A TUTORIAL	PRINCIPLES OF OBJECT-ORIENTED ANALYSIS AND DESIGN	SYSTEM DESIGN FROM PROVABLY CORRECT CONSTRUCTS	**Diagramming Techniques**
	OBJECT-ORIENTED METHODS: A FOUNDATION	INFORMATION ENGINEERING (Book II: Planning and Analysis)	DIAGRAMMING TECHNIQUES FOR ANALYSTS AND PROGRAMMERS
	OBJECT-ORIENTED METHODS: PRAGMATIC CONSIDERATIONS	INFORMATION ENGINEERING (Book III: Design and Construction)	RECOMMENDED DIAGRAMMING STANDARDS FOR ANALYSTS AND PROGRAMMERS
	OBJECT-ORIENTED TOOLS		ACTION DIAGRAMS: CLEARLY STRUCTURED SPECIFICATIONS PROGRAMS, AND PROCEDURES (second edition)